D0212801

A Passion for Birds

A Passion for Birds

AMERICAN ORNITHOLOGY

AFTER AUDUBON

MARK V. BARROW, JR.

PRINCETON UNIVERSITY PRESS

PRINCETON, NEW JERSEY

Library of Congress Cataloging-in-Publication Data

Barrow, Mark V., 1960–

A passion for birds : American ornithology after Audubon / Mark V. Barrow, Jr.

p. cm.

Includes bibliographical references (p.   ) and index.

ISBN 0-691-04402-3 (alk. paper)

1. Ornithology—United States—History.   I. Title.

QL672.73.U6B37   1997

598′.0973—dc21   97-18600

This book has been composed in Times Roman

http://pup.princeton.edu

Printed in the United States of America

1   2   3   4   5   6   7   8   9   10

CONTENTS

ILLUSTRATIONS

ACKNOWLEDGMENTS

DURING THE long process of researching and writing this book, I have incurred countless debts. I am grateful to the staffs at each of the many archives I consulted (a full list is in the bibliography) for permission to use, quote manuscripts, and reproduce images from the material under their care. Several staff members repeatedly went far beyond the call of duty and deserve special mention: Mary LeCroy, at the American Museum of Natural History; Libby Glenn, Bill Cox, Bill Deiss, and Pamela Henson, at the Smithsonian Institution Archives; and Janet Hinshaw, at the Museum of Zoology, University of Michigan. Special thanks also to Barbara Stein of the Museum of Vertebrate Zoology at Berkeley, Clark Elliott of the Harvard University Archives, Dana Fisher of the Museum of Comparative Zoology Archives, Llyn Sharp of the Virginia Museum of Natural History, and Holly Prees of the Massachusetts Audubon Society. I was able to visit many of these and other repositories with generous financial support in the form of a National Science Foundation Graduate Fellowship, a Smithsonian Institution Ten-Week Graduate Fellowship, a Travel Grant from the College of Arts and Science at Virginia Tech, and two Research Grants from the Department of History at Virginia Tech.

Mentors, colleagues, friends, and even several complete strangers provided invaluable aid at various stages along the way. Keir Sterling and Marianne Ainley not only answered several queries during the formative stages of the project, but also generously granted me access to their unpublished history of the American Ornithologists' Union. Everett Mendelsohn and Barbara G. Rosenkrantz provided me with continuous encouragement and sage counsel throughout my six years at Harvard. Alexi Assmus, Bob and Emily Morrison, and Liz Watkins offered warm hospitality during my travels to archives and meetings. Others who provided favors large and small include Ken Alder, Gar Allen, Dean Amadon, Tobey Appel, Allan Brandt, Rick Bonney, Hughes Evans, Deborah Fitzgerald, Donald Fleming, Pat Gossel, Kathleen Jones, Liz Keeney, Amy Nelson, Lynn K. Nyhart, Raymond A. Paynter, Jr., Barbara Reeves, John Reiger, Sam Schweber, David Spanagel, and Polly Winsor. Thank you all for everything and apologies to anyone I may have inadvertently left out.

Many people have taken time from their own busy schedules to read parts of the manuscript and provide helpful comments. Among those who did so during the later stages of the project are Marcia Barrow, Walter J. Bock, Richard W. Burkhardt, Jr., Joseph Cain (who also shared his helpful notes on the Ernst Mayr Papers), William E. Davis, Jr., Mike Fortun, Jürgen Haffer, Liz Keeney, Sally G. Kohlstedt, Ralph H. Lutts, Ernst Mayr, Gregg Mitman, Bob Morrison, Philip Pauly, Ron Rainger, Marc Rothenberg, Keir Sterling, Peter Stevens, and two anonymous referees. They provided badly needed encouragement, pointed the way to new sources and interpretations, forced me to clarify ideas, and rescued me from many infelicities. However, I have not always followed their advice, so I must accept responsibility for any errors that remain.

The folks at Princeton University Press have been a real delight to work with on this project. My editor, Emily Wilkinson, and her assistants, Kevin Downing and Sam Elworthy, were incredibly supportive of, and patient with, this anxious first-time author. Anita O'Brien skillfully copyedited the manuscript, while Jan Lilly did a wonderful job with the book design. And Jane Low guided the whole thing through the production process with a rare combination of efficiency, expertise, and compassion. The concern, professionalism, and humanity of everyone at the press set a very high standard for others to follow.

Most importantly, I want to thank my family. For too many years now they have been forced to live with this project, and they have always believed in me even when my own faith faltered. Mom and Dad have provided unstinting love, encouragement, and support that I have come to appreciate even more as my own children have begun to grow up. I will be forever grateful for all they have done. Aunt Marge hand-colored the original engraving used for the book jacket. My younger siblings—Will, John, Angela, and Amy Barrow—put up with me as a child and put me up as an adult during several research trips to New York. My four children—Mark, Alexander, Hannah, and Lizzie—have been an unceasing source of pride, joy, and inspiration without a word of complaint about my many hours of enforced absence. And especially I want to thank my wife, Marcia, who has been there for longer than I can remember. She has nurtured me in body and spirit, borne the brunt of raising our four wonderful children, and quietly endured the many hardships of graduate school and a beginning career in academia. Mere words fail to express the depth of my gratitude and love. As a small token of appreciation, I dedicate this book to her.

A Passion for Birds

IN 1887 a worried mother from Alameda, California, wrote to seek advice from Robert Ridgway, curator of birds at the U.S. National Museum. It seems that her twenty-year-old son, Henry Reed Taylor, was intent on pursuing a career in ornithology. Was there any future in this vocation? she wondered. Unfortunately, Ridgway, one of only a few paid ornithologists in America at the time, could offer little encouragement for this anxious mother and her determined young son:

> I would say that if one is without the means of living independently of the study of natural history (in any of its branches), he stands a very poor chance indeed of deriving the greatest benefit from its study. It is very necessary, in fact, to have some regular business, profession, or other occupation which shall supply the means of defraying one's expenses. The study of natural history affords those whose tastes run in that direction a very agreeable and instructive *recreation*, and the means of employing pleasantly and profitably hours of enforced idleness which might otherwise be passed in far more harmful ways. As a *means of livelihood*, however, it must, in at least ninety-nine cases out of a hundred, prove a complete failure, success being . . . a question not only of exceptional ability, but also of exceptional circumstance.[1]

A voracious collector of birds' eggs and nests, Taylor was one of the thousands of Americans who began pursuing some form of natural history in the second half of the nineteenth century.[2] As industrialization, urbanization, and economic expansion increasingly reshaped the nation's landscape, growing numbers of enthusiasts began collecting natural objects and observing animals in their natural surroundings. For these middle- and upper-class Americans, regular forays into fields and forests fulfilled a vague but real longing to regain contact with a natural world that modern civilization seemed bent on destroying.

As Ridgway's reply to Taylor hinted, advocates of collecting promised numerous other benefits for those who embraced the activity: recreation, exercise, adventure, and a sense of accomplishment as collectors filled their homes with a bewildering array of beautiful objects, ranging from fossils and ferns to butterflies and birds. Local natural history societies, popular periodicals, and expansive correspondence networks offered encouragement and advice for aspiring collectors, while providing regular avenues for specimen exchange. Heightened public interest in natural history also spawned local and national businesses that sought to capitalize on collectors' apparently insatiable appetite for information, supplies, and specimens.

By the century's end, observation of wildlife—especially in the form of bird-watching—had also come into vogue. Soon tens of thousands of Americans were joining Audubon societies, purchasing new, easy-to-use field guides, and keeping systematic records of the species they encountered in the wild. By the early twentieth century, interest in wildlife had become so widespread that even mass-circulation periodicals provided regular coverage of seemingly esoteric scientific controversies—like the question of whether animals could reason and the debate over whether their coloration was adaptive.[3]

In the midst of this explosion of popular interest in natural history, scientific ornithologists in the United States and Canada struggled to forge a discipline and profession.[4] Initially the common goal around which this small, dedicated group of experts sought to focus was the production of an exhaustive inventory of North American bird forms. The founding of the American Ornithologists' Union (AOU) in 1883 marked one in a series of milestones in the ongoing campaign to gain legitimacy for their emerging discipline. As Ridgway's letter suggested, however, expanding occupational opportunity in ornithology proved more elusive.

Of course, ornithologists were not the only scientists striving to consolidate their discipline into a profession. Although the process of professionalization in science occurred at varying rates across different specialties and nations, the general trend was unmistakable. Throughout the nineteenth century, gentlemanly amateurs—men of wealth, leisure, and social standing who had long dominated the practice of science—slowly but steadily lost ground to full-time paid specialists.[5] As historian of science Everett Mendelsohn observed more than three decades ago, professionalization represented a "second scientific revolution," a profound change in the structure and practice of science every bit as fundamental as its more widely appreciated sixteenth- and seventeenth-century predecessor.[6]

Historians and sociologists have long struggled to understand how certain occupations have achieved the prestige, authority, and autonomy associated with modern professions and even to define the term "profession" itself. Until recently, two basic approaches have dominated this "thankless task."[7] In the first—the so-called trait approach—researchers have constructed checklists of attributes common to fields conventionally recognized as professions, with medicine, law, and the ministry usually taken as paradigmatic examples.[8] A profession, according to this school of thought, is a full-time occupation defined by some combination of the following characteristics: possession of an abstract and systematic body of knowledge that commands authority; formal educational requirements; routine (often state-sanctioned) procedures for certifying and licensing practitioners; associations to enforce standards, honor achievement, and exert control within the field; and a general orientation toward public service.[9]

Since the 1960s many historians and sociologists have criticized the trait approach as static, ahistorical, and naive. According to proponents of the alternative "power" approach, previous scholars had generally failed to grasp the crucial difference between the image of competency, altruism, and service that professionals projected before the public and the (less flattering) reality of their ongoing quest to maintain status, privilege, and monopolistic domination in their field.[10] Although proponents of the trait and power approaches disagree on many points, both have stressed the establishment of institutionally sanctioned boundaries between experts and their potential rivals as central to the process of professionalization.

While many scholars examining the development of scientific professions have adopted one of these two basic frameworks, others have begun to highlight their shortcomings.[11] For example, in a seminal article published in the mid-1970s, historian of science Nathan Reingold offered a serious challenge to the rigid amateur-professional dichotomy that had long plagued the literature on professionalization.[12] He was also among the first to appreciate that definitions derived from professions as currently construed fail to map neatly onto past circumstances. Reingold questioned whether advanced degrees, formal certification procedures, and employment opportunities were appropriate criteria for delineating the social dynamics of nineteenth-century scientific communities at a time when, in the words of Howard Miller, there was "no well-defined recognized niche in the occupational structure for a man who devoted his life to scientific research."[13] Accomplishment and motivation, Reingold argued, are much more useful for reconstructing relationships within those earlier communities.[14]

In a long series of publications that began appearing at about the same time as Reingold's article, the sociologist Robert A. Stebbins further blurred the traditional professional-amateur distinction.[15] As a participant-observer of several contemporary communities in science, art, sport, and entertainment, Stebbins discovered numerous well-established professions that continued to interact with avocational practitioners, often in significant ways. Stebbins argued that the diverse practitioners within a given field are best understood as interconnected and interdependent components of what he called a "professional-amateur-public system."

In the last twenty years scholars have explored many scientific fields—astronomy, botany, archaeology, meteorology, entomology, and others—that seem to support Reingold and Stebbins's insights.[16] Some scientific specialties—those demanding a particularly challenging level of technical expertise or access to expensive and sophisticated equipment—effectively kept amateurs at bay. But others, especially where crucial data was relatively easy to record yet dispersed across vast geographic (or, in the case of astronomy, celestial) expanses, remained open to continued amateur participation.

Ornithology provides a classic example of an inclusive scientific field.[17] By the end of the nineteenth century, it shared many attributes that scholars have identified as key to the process of professionalization. It was based on a systematized body of abstract knowledge and—through the AOU—quickly established institutionalized mechanisms for certifying its practitioners. There were even a handful of jobs available to ornithologists, primarily as curators in the large urban natural history museums established during this period. Yet scientific ornithologists continued to depend on a variety of collectors, taxidermists, sport hunters, and others to supply the specimens and observations needed to conduct their research. By 1905 Frank Chapman, a curator of birds at the American Museum of Natural History, noted that "in no other branch [of science] are the professionals so outnumbered by the amateurs; and this fact it seems to us, should be constantly held in mind in any consideration of ornithological interests."[18] Even after graduate training became the norm and employment prospects began to brighten in the 1920s and 1930s, scientific ornithologists remained firmly tied to a larger community of variously motivated bird enthusiasts who provided research data, funding, and a supply of future scientists.

Some scientists tolerated a continuing amateur presence because of the useful data that carefully monitored avocational ornithologists might contribute. The Smithsonian ornithologist and herpetologist Leonhard Stejneger seemed to have this strongly hierarchical model of scientific cooperation in mind when he declared in 1905 that "The amateur's proper field is in the gathering of facts, the professional's is to apply them."[19] But others appreciated the more fundamental contributions that dedicated amateurs were capable of making. By the 1970s the renowned ornithologist and evolutionary biologist Ernst Mayr was still celebrating the "splendid work" that amateurs were doing in his field.[20]

The case of ornithology confirms other recent studies showing that a preoccupation with the process of professionalization has obscured a crucial social reality in the development of many scientific fields: namely, that even as scientists sought to establish disciplines and professions, they often remained firmly bound to a variety of amateur enthusiasts. Professional scientists, amateur practitioners—even technicians, patrons, specimen suppliers, administrators, and others—were (and are) important parts of what historians and sociologists have recently begun to conceptualize as "communities," "social worlds," "networks," and "professional-amateur-public systems."[21] Each of these characterizations has slightly different connotations, but they all point to essentially the same thing: a recognition of the fundamental diversity of the scientific enterprise.

That is not to suggest that scientific communities were egalitarian or free from friction. In the case of ornithology, scientists struggled long and hard to establish standards, expand career opportunities, control research, and achieve other goals consistent with traditional notions of professionalization. The account that follows makes clear, however, that their success at implementing their professional agenda remained partial at best. Certainly the well-documented resistance mounted by those who resented scientists' attempts to control the field played a role in that failure. However, I suspect that the scientists themselves also contributed. Throughout the period covered by this study, scientific ornithologists remained ambivalent about continued public interest in their field. On the one hand, they clearly worried about issues like status and prestige, autonomy and authority. On the other, they seemed reluctant to cut themselves off entirely from the Henry Taylors of the world. Ridgway's letter and countless others like it in archives across North America are testimony to scientific ornithologists' continuing connection with bird enthusiasts of all kinds.

This social history of American ornithology focuses on the relationship between scientific ornithologists committed to the production of technical knowledge and the broader community of variously motivated enthusiasts that developed alongside them. Based on an extensive examination of archival material, popular and scientific periodicals, and a variety of other primary and secondary sources, I have sought to reconstruct the layered interactions between expert ornithologists seeking to forge a discipline and profession and the collectors, taxidermists, natural history dealers, birdwatchers, conservationists, and others with whom they were affiliated. My study begins in the middle of the nineteenth century, with the first stirring of a disciplinary consciousness in American ornithology, and ends on the eve of World War II, when the field finally achieved the hallmarks of a full-blown profession.[22]

Chapter 1 explores the sources and consequences of America's growing fascination with natural history in the years following the Civil War and the emergence of what I call the culture of collecting. The next chapter narrows its gaze to one segment of that larger culture, the ornithological community, and traces the rise of expansive collecting networks that had scientific ornithologists at their center and a variety of collectors on their periphery. With encouragement from scientists, the appearance of reliable collecting manuals, and the increasing popularity of game hunting, bird collecting became an important (though male-dominated) pastime in the United States by the end of the nineteenth century.

The ornithological community, once firmly united by a shared interest in collecting specimens, became more fragmented in the years following the creation of the AOU in 1883. Chapter 3 shows how a small group of scientific ornithologists founded the AOU and how they used the new organization to further their disciplinary and professional aspirations. It also documents the resistance offered by those who resented scientists' attempts to control the association. Chapter 4 focuses on the issue of nomenclatural reform, a concern that, more than any other, had prompted the creation of the AOU. Proponents of the self-proclaimed "American school" of ornithology not only sought to produce a single, authoritative list of North American bird forms, they also wanted that list to incorporate an innovation they (falsely) claimed as their own: trinomial nomenclature. The campaign for formal recognition of subspecies became yet another source of tension between scientific ornithologists and other bird enthusiasts. Many of the latter challenged not only the need to recognize the minute distinctions upon which subspecific differences were based, but even the need for any kind of specialized scientific nomenclature.

Chapters 5 and 6 document the AOU's extensive involvement in turn-of-the-century wildlife conservation initiatives. Although central to the mobilization of the first Audubon movement that began in the 1880s (chapter 5) and the second, more enduring version that began in the 1890s (chapter 6), the AOU never resolved the fundamental tension between its commitment to bird protection and its repeated assertions of the right to collect even obviously threatened species. At the same time, the bird protection movement caused friction within the larger ornithological community when scientific ornithologists moved to narrow the definition of "legitimate" collecting in the hope of maintaining the privilege for themselves. Because of this and other conflicts, the AOU's commitment to bird protection was marked by periods of intense activism punctuated by periods of retrenchment.

Closely related to the bird protection movement was the remarkable growth of popular interest in birdwatching, a development explored in chapter 7. Scientific ornithologists hoping to cultivate allies for the bird protection movement, generate income from the sale of field guides, and recruit volunteers to monitor bird movements and population trends were among the strongest promoters of birdwatching in the United States. After the turn of the century, the activity gained a popularity beyond the wildest dreams of its supporters. In the process, however, it also provoked additional dissension within the ornithological community as birdwatchers rushed to publish increasing numbers of unverifiable "sight records"—observations of species and subspecies beyond their established ranges.

The final chapter examines the campaign to reform the AOU and American ornithology more generally in the years surrounding the Great Depression. Leading the call for change were the first generation of scientific ornithologists with graduate training. With aid from Ernst Mayr, an émigré ornithologist from Germany who came to the United States in the early 1930s, reformers sought to broaden the focus of ornithology, raise the standards of research, and instill the AOU with a stronger professional consciousness. Yet, even as they sought to reform American ornithology, the new university-trained scientists continued to recognize a role for amateur ornithologists.

In 1978, nearly a century after the creation of the AOU, the noted ornithologist Harold Mayfield argued that the relationship between professional and amateur ornithologists might best be characterized as "symbiotic."[23] Even in the modern era of increasing specialization, advanced biological degrees, and ornithological careers, Mayfield claimed, amateur ornithologists still had much to offer the science of ornithology. I would argue that bird enthusiasts of various sorts have been an important part of the ornithological community from the beginning and that the development of the science of ornithology can only be properly understood through a study of the interactions within that community.

CHAPTER ONE

The Culture of Collecting

One winter day early in 1867 a frail eight-year-old boy named Theodore Roosevelt discovered a dead seal placed on exhibit outside his neighborhood market. The creature so fascinated him that he decided to start a natural history collection and convinced the storekeeper to give him the seal's skull as his first acquisition.[1] By the end of the year the "Roosevelt Museum of Natural History" contained more than a hundred additional specimens, including the nests and eggs of birds, seashells, minerals, pressed plants, and other natural objects. Through regular efforts in the field, contributions from sympathetic relatives, exchanges with other collectors, and purchases from dealers, Roosevelt continued to add to his collection over the next decade. He even convinced his parents to let him take lessons in mounting animals from the famed New York taxidermist John G. Bell. Roosevelt's boyhood museum marked the first manifestation of a lifelong interest in natural history for this future president of the United States.

Though Roosevelt was more earnest than some of his contemporaries, his experience was hardly unique. In the second half of the nineteenth century thousands of Americans began filling their homes with an array of "choice extracts from nature."[2] Then as now, these collectors were motivated by a variety of considerations.[3] The aesthetic appeal of the objects they gathered, a competitive spirit, and a curiosity about the natural world lured many Americans out into the nation's fields and forests in search of new acquisitions. So too did a desire to cultivate self-improvement, to gain exercise, to display gentility, to increase wealth, and to escape temporarily from the confines of a modern urban existence.[4] Some collectors believed that the specimens they amassed provided a way to gaze at the mind of God.[5] A few even hoped to make a contribution to science.

The nineteenth-century collecting phenomenon was not something entirely new. For over three centuries a "cabinet of curiosities," appointed with a hodgepodge of natural and fabricated objects, had served as a sign of culture and learning among the European upper classes.[6] Anxious to emulate their counterparts abroad, wealthy Americans began amassing similar collections in the early eighteenth century.[7] It was not until the burgeoning middle class adopted the practice in the mid-nineteenth century, however, that natural history collecting really flourished in this country.[8] What began with an interest in gathering botanical specimens in the 1830s expanded dramatically in scope and scale over the next several decades, particularly in the years after the Civil War.

This unprecedented flurry of activity led to the creation of what might be described as a culture of collecting. Beginning in the middle of the nineteenth century, American collectors forged a community united not only by a shared interest in amassing natural history objects, but also through vast correspondence networks, membership in scientific societies, subscriptions to natural history periodicals, and patronage of commercial firms that catered to the natural history trade. Young and old, male and female, beginner and expert alike were all a part of this extensive and heterogeneous community in which specimens were bought, sold, traded, and admired.[9]

The Culture of Collecting

The post–Civil War growth of popular interest in natural history was firmly rooted in several fundamental social, economic, and technological changes.[10] Between 1860 and 1900 the total population of the United States more than doubled, the gross national product quadrupled, and the total number of people living in urban areas increased more than five times. By 1900 more than sixteen metropolitan areas had populations in excess of a quarter million, and, excluding the South, for the first time most Americans lived in cities. During this period the nation also pushed relentlessly westward, adding twelve new states and several territories. Within the span of only two generations, America was transformed from a largely rural, agrarian nation to an urban, industrial giant.

The construction of an extensive transportation and communication infrastructure linked the expanding nation together as never before. Two key technological systems first brought into limited production in the 1840s, the railroad and the telegraph, soon provided for the rapid and reliable interchange of information, products, and people across the vast expanses of the North American continent.[11] Railroads spanned a total of thirty thousand miles by 1860, and the rate of growth accelerated in the decades that followed. By 1890 mileage had increased more than fivefold, while extensive bridge construction and interindustry standardization joined the separate lines into a truly national system. The railroads not only brought the nation closer together by decreasing the time, expense, and discomfort usually associated with earlier forms of long-distance travel, they also created a model for the large-scale, vertically integrated corporations that proliferated in the years after the war.[12]

Other developments eased the dissemination of knowledge. In the years surrounding the war, improvements in presses, plates, paper, and typesetting machines revolutionized the publishing industry by greatly increasing printing speed while decreasing the unit cost for newspapers, periodicals, and books.[13] Postal rates for printed matter, which had slowly but steadily decreased throughout the nineteenth century, dropped dramatically between 1874 and 1885, when officials introduced new second- and third-class rate schedules.[14] At the same time better access to education and a boost in literacy rates resulted in a greater demand for reading material of all types.[15] One consequence of these developments was what one historian has called "a mania of magazine-starting." Within the two decades after the Civil War the total number of American periodicals jumped from seven hundred to thirty-three hundred.[16]

It took equally fundamental changes in attitude for these social, economic, and technological transformations to translate into a broad popular interest in natural history. Among the most important of these new sensibilities was a fresh appreciation for nature and leisure. The Europeans who first settled the New World tended to view the vast North American continent as either an evil, chaotic wasteland or a storehouse of economically valuable resources.[17] In either case the reigning assumption was that God had issued a divine mandate to carve out an ordered civilization from the wilderness and to exploit nature to its fullest. But by the nineteenth century, as the process of conquering nature had reached increasingly higher levels of perfection, a backlash began to coalesce.

One early and lasting counterpoint to the predominant ethos of development and domination was a series of aesthetic, philosophical, and literary movements known collectively as Romanticism.[18] These various strands began to emerge in the late eighteenth century among European intellectuals rebelling against the austere neoclassicism, mechanistic spirit, and arch-rationalism of the Enlightenment. Romantics tended to find inspiration in the imagination, the emotional, the mysterious, the primitive, and the sublime. Perhaps most importantly in this context, they also attached a new aesthetic and spiritual value to the natural world. By the early nineteenth century the naturalistic landscapes of the Hudson River School, the anthropocentric wildlife portraits of John James Audubon, and the effusive poetry of William Cullen Bryant provided evidence that Romantic currents had found their way to the New World. Although Romanticism failed to supplant the dominant utilitarian vision of nature, by the middle of the nineteenth century it had become a permanent fixture on the American cultural scene.

Transcendentalism, a peculiarly American version of Romanticism that originated in the 1830s, proved equally influential and tenacious.[19] Two of Transcendentalism's major prophets, Ralph Waldo Emerson and Henry David Thoreau, argued that the means to self-renewal and self-realization was self-surrender before the altar of nature.[20] For the increasing number of late-nineteenth-century Americans sympathetic to Thoreau's dictum—"In wildness is the preservation of the world"—Transcendentalism provided a potent argument for the preservation of nature.[21] Even in its more pervasive dilute forms, the new doctrine suggested regular contact with nature as an antidote for the many ills that plagued an increasingly urban and industrial America.

As the century wore on, more and more Americans embraced the Transcendentalist diagnosis and prescription.[22] For some, periodic retreats into the relative wilderness of the many state and national parks established after the Civil War acted as a balm to soothe the irritations brought on by an increasingly bustling and artificial way of life.[23] Others sought relief in the more secure and accessible middle grounds crafted between the extremes of nature and civilization: the landscaped urban park, the borderland suburb, and the local country club.[24] Many were content to enjoy the nature experience vicariously, through a growing number of essays and books that interpreted the natural world for their readers.[25] Although they pursued a variety of approaches in their quest to get "back to nature," one thing was certain: as civilization loomed ever larger in their daily lives, many Americans experienced an almost primordial yearning to reestablish some form of contact with nature.[26]

Closely related to the newfound respect for nature was an increasing appreciation for leisure.[27] The pious pioneers who settled the continent had elevated the toil associated with taming the American wilderness to the level of divine pursuit. Increasing secularization during the ensuing centuries may have minimized the explicitly religious connotations of this deeply ingrained work ethic, but it did little to diminish its hold on the growing middle class; early nineteenth-century European visitors, accustomed to a much more measured pace of life, constantly marveled at the "franticness and busyness" of Americans.[28] Not until the middle decades of the century did the gospel of work finally began to relinquish its stern grip as Americans at last "learned to play." A slow but steady decline in the average workweek was paralleled by a robust expansion in the number of leisure opportunities, including bicycling, picnicking, camping, amusement parks, and a host of new participant and spectator sports, to name just a few.[29] Yet as historian Daniel Rodgers has pointed out, most middle-class Americans continued to reject outright idleness or repose. Throughout the second half of the nineteenth century, the leisure activities pursued were frequently as "energetic as work itself" and usually imbued with a higher purpose.[30]

Collecting was an appropriately purposeful pastime that the American and British middle class increasingly pursued with zeal.[31] With unprecedented enthusiasm, Victorians on both sides of the Atlantic rushed to fill their homes with a bewildering array of objects, ranging from coins, stamps, and curios to ferns, figurines, and photographs.[32] The middle-class collecting craze was already so prevalent by 1868 that Charles Eastlake's *Hints on Household Taste* entered a futile protest against the trend of displaying "too many knick-knacks" on "too many 'what-nots.' "[33]

Few, if any, heeded Eastlake's advice. Rather, most commentators emphasized the benefits of collecting and strongly encouraged the practice. Among the most vigorous proponents of the collecting urge was John Edward Gray, keeper of the zoological cabinet at the British Museum and author of one of the first manuals for stamp collectors, published in 1862. According to Gray: "The use and charm of collecting any kind of object is to educate the mind and the eye to careful observation, accurate comparison, and just reasoning on the differences and likenesses which they present, and to interest the collector in the design or art shown in the creation and manufacture, and the history of the country which produces or uses the objects collected."[34]

Many argued that amassing natural history specimens—minerals, pressed plants, insects, shells, stuffed birds, and eggs—was even more edifying than collecting artificial objects like stamps and coins. The American pastor and educator E. C. Mitchell urged parents to encourage their children to take up the practice at a tender age. The experience thereby gained would lead to an appreciation of "the works of God in nature," stimulate the mind, and arouse an "active enthusiasm" for the process of learning. To those who dared complain about the space taken up by collections, Mitchell replied: "almost any house can afford to spare the child a few shelves, or a home-made box or cabinet. And it will help to train and systemize the child's mind, to feel that he has a place of his own, where he can keep his treasures, and for the good order of which he is responsible."[35] Others echoed Mitchell's enthusiasm for natural history, arguing that the collector was afforded "not only pleasure, but study, a love of the great and glorious things, recreation, exercise and the promoter of all things which tend to make nobler manhood and womanhood."[36] One devotee even claimed that collecting natural objects cultivated the powers of discernment and careful observation necessary for a successful business career.[37] Whether they accepted all the arguments of its advocates, Americans with a vague longing for nature and a new appreciation for leisure turned to natural history collecting with increasing frequency in the second half of the nineteenth century.

QUANTITATIVE DIMENSIONS

What began as a limited expansion of popular interest in natural history before the Civil War exploded in the decades following the truce at Appomattox. While it is impossible to measure the precise dimensions of this pervasive activity, some appreciation for the conspicuous postwar growth of the culture of collecting can be gained by examining changes in some of its individual components.

The closest thing we have to a direct measure of the surge in the number of collectors is the various editions of *The Naturalists' Directory*, first published in 1865.[38] The initial edition, compiled by former Agassiz student Frederic Ward Putnam, contained the names, addresses, and fields of specialty for more than four hundred naturalists, most of whom were collectors.[39] The appearance of a published listing of American naturalists suggests that the collecting community had reached an important milestone. More striking still is the growth in the number of entries in subsequent editions of the work. The number of naturalists recorded in the edition Putnam published only one year later increased almost four times, to nearly sixteen hundred.[40] By 1879 the number of entries more than doubled again, to nearly thirty-three hundred, before peaking at nearly six thousand in the early 1890s.[41] While yearly variations in the size of the *Directory* might reflect the editor's earnestness in soliciting names, the general trend was one of vigorous growth. Yet the listing can hardly be taken as comprehensive, for only the most committed collectors would have bothered submitting their names.

The creation of scientific societies devoted to natural history provides another indication of its increasing appeal. As historian Ralph Bates's study demonstrates, by 1865 there were only 36 active scientific societies in the United States.[42] For many of these institutions the collection, preservation, and description of natural objects provided a major focus. However, after the war the numbers quickly mounted. According to lists published in *The Naturalists' Directory*, by 1878 there were 141 local and state societies that concentrated on some form of natural history, and by 1884 that number had grown to more than 200.[43]

Even more impressive is the rise of a new kind of natural history society aimed primarily at youth. Named after the charismatic naturalist and popular icon Louis Agassiz, the Agassiz Association began modestly.[44] Harlan H. Ballard, a school administrator from Lenox, Massachusetts, organized the first chapter in 1875 to encourage his students to "collect, study, and preserve natural objects."[45] Five years later Ballard began calling for other interested parties across America to create local chapters. The response was overwhelming, and by 1884 collecting enthusiasts had established more than six hundred local chapters of the Agassiz Association with a total of over seven thousand members.[46] Thirteen years later Ballard claimed a cumulative total of twelve hundred chapters and twenty thousand members, which, according to one observer, were united with the single purpose of "exchanging specimens and corresponding with one another on matters of common interest."[47]

In 1882 Ballard issued the first of four editions of his Agassiz Association handbook. Ballard designed his brief introduction to the world of natural history collecting to supplement a regular Agassiz Association department in *St. Nicholas Magazine* and a short-lived attempt to initiate an independent publication for the organization, *The Swiss Cross* (1887–1889).[48] Though compact, Ballard's handbooks were brimming with practical advice on organizing association chapters; building proper storage cabinets; procuring natural history books; and (most importantly) collecting, preserving, buying, and exchanging a variety of specimens, ranging from pressed plants, seaweed, minerals, and insects, to bird skins and eggs.

Around the turn of the century a broader initiative aimed specifically at children began to eclipse Ballard's activities. Nature study was a pedagogical reform movement dedicated to the proposition that children needed regular, firsthand exposure to the natural world.[49] Some advocates, like the biologist Clifton F. Hodge, believed that nature study might shield urban youth against "idleness and waste of time, evil and temptation of every sort"; others, like the horticulturalist Liberty Hyde Bailey, hoped the reform might help stem the population drain from rural areas.[50] Whatever their concerns, in 1905 proponents of the idea began publishing *Nature Study Review* to promote the initiative, and three years later they organized the American Nature Study Society.[51] In 1911 Anna Botsford Comstock, one of the founders of the movement, published her seminal *Handbook of Nature Study*, a widely adopted textbook that went through twenty-four editions and remains in print today.[52]

An examination of trends in periodical publication provides additional evidence of the groundswell of popular interest in natural history during the second half of the nineteenth century.[53] A count based on three extensive bibliographies of "minor" natural history periodicals published during this period reveals modest beginnings in the mid-1870s, when only a handful were issued in any given year.[54] Improved printing technologies, reduced postal rates, and mounting public interest promoted a tremendous growth in natural history journals in the early

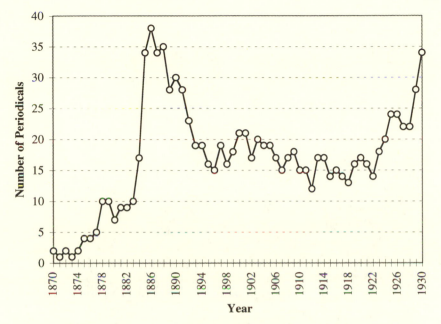

Figure 1. Minor natural history periodicals published in the United States and
Canada, 1870-1930. Compiled from Burns, "Bibliography of Scarce or Out of Print
North American Amateur and Trade Periodicals"; Fox, "American Journals Omitted
from Bolton's 'Catalog'"; and Underwood, *Bibliography of North American
Minor Natural History Periodicals.*

1880s (fig. 1). By 1886 nearly forty such periodicals were available. This was
followed by a precipitous decline due to market saturation, the depression of
1893, and more rigid enforcement of postal regulations. For the next three decades the number of natural history periodicals remained relatively constant, before increasing again in the late 1920s and early 1930s.

Until the end of the nineteenth century, dealers issued many of these periodicals, which were often little more than thinly veiled advertisements for their wares
(fig. 2). Local postmasters occasionally followed the letter of postal regulations
and refused to grant second-class rates to publications that failed to be issued at
some regular stated interval, lacked a legitimate subscription list, or were not
"devoted to literature, the sciences, arts, or some special industry."[55] For example,
in 1890 Charles H. Prince was denied second-class rates for his newly created *The
Oologist's Advertiser*. But like many other publishers in the same predicament,
Prince simply changed the name of his periodical to *The Collectors' Monthly* and
successfully reapplied for preferential rates.[56] Increasingly impatient with flagrant
abuses of the system, in 1901 the postmaster general began systematically revok-
ing the second-class privilege from suspect publications.[57] Among the casualties
of this enforcement campaign were *American Ornithology for the Home and
School* and *The Atlantic Slope Naturalist.*[58]

Figure 2. Cover of *Random Notes on Natural History* (1884).
This short-lived trade journal, published by the natural history firm
Southwick and Jencks, had a beautifully illustrated cover and an
unusually frank title.

Many of the dozens of natural history periodicals established in the second half
of the nineteenth century enjoyed healthy circulations, if not long lives.[59] For
example, the *American Magazine of Natural Science* (1892–1894) and *The Owl*
(1886–1888) each claimed a circulation of two thousand.[60] The *Hoosier Naturalist* (1885–1888), *The Spy Glass: A Magazine for Collectors* (1888), and *The
Young Oologist* (1885) boasted a regular readership of five thousand. And the
Naturalists' Leisure Hour and Monthly Bulletin (1887–1893) reported seven
thousand subscribers.

More striking are the figures for special issues, which were distributed widely in an attempt to gain new subscribers and to publicize the businesses that sponsored them. For example, in 1883 Henry A. Ward distributed sixteen thousand copies of his *Natural Science Bulletin*.[61] During the next two years the owner of the *Ornithologist and Oologist*, Frank Blake Webster, issued nearly forty thousand copies of his periodical.[62] And at the height of his business in 1893, Frank H. Lattin passed out over twenty thousand copies of a single issue of the *Oologist*.[63]

The publishers responsible for these last three periodicals were all natural history dealers, who provide a final indicator of the growth of popular interest in collecting. Local taxidermy shops, which had long served as gathering places for area naturalists and frequently offered natural history specimens for sale, were early manifestations of these enterprises. With the growth of popular interest in natural history and the increasing ease of transacting business across the nation, many commercial establishments began cultivating a more national clientele for their specimens, supplies, and publications. During the last several decades of the nineteenth century, more than one hundred enterprising naturalists established American businesses to promote and profit from the broad popular enthusiasm for amassing natural history specimens.[64]

Collecting Conflicts

Although members of the diverse community of collectors existed together amicably for much of the second half of the nineteenth century, the potential for conflict was always present. One of several unresolved tensions was between the entrepreneurial and Romantic impulses that informed the desire to amass and display natural objects.[65] The establishment of numerous businesses devoted to the sale of natural history specimens (fig. 3) tended to reinforce the idea that nature was a resource or commodity, existing solely for human ends. For example, the wide distribution of natural history dealers' catalogs undoubtedly influenced the ornithologist Elliott Coues to declare in his best-selling collecting manual of 1874: "How many examples of the same bird do you want?—*All you can get. . . .* Bird skins are *capital*."[66] Support for the idea of human domination of nature even found expression in the very act of collecting itself. After all, those tidy cabinets of specimens were composed of the lifeless remnants of once autonomous beings that were removed from their natural context and reordered according to the whims of collectors.[67]

Romanticism confounded the economic calculus that undergirded the commodification of nature and even challenged the legitimacy of the idea of human domination of the natural world. Certainly the Romantic sensibility alerted collectors to discover beauty in the natural objects around them and was one of the major factors leading to the large-scale growth of natural history collecting. But Romanticism also suggested that our interactions with nature were imbued with a spiritual dimension that defied economic valuation. For some followers the

Figure 3. Cover of specimen price list, Goodale and Frazer, Boston, Massachusetts, 1890.

doctrine even implied that humans ought to be kinder and gentler in their dealings with the natural world. The fundamental tension between these opposing conceptions of nature remained largely unarticulated until rise of the Audubon movement and the growth of popular interest in birdwatching at the turn of the century.

A second cleavage point within the culture of collecting existed between expert naturalists whose central commitment was to the production of scientific knowledge and the much larger number of collectors for whom the collection itself was often an end. As the century progressed, scientific naturalists became increasingly impatient with dealers and collectors who failed to record the proper data with the

specimens they gathered, who eschewed scientific nomenclature, or who stub-
bornly refused to acknowledge the authority of experts. These and other tensions
would later provoke a schism in the culture of collecting. For much of the second
half of the nineteenth century, however, members of the collecting community
managed to gloss over their differences in motivation, ability, and level of commitment. Exactly how this was negotiated within one subset of the culture of
collecting, the ornithological community, is the subject of the next chapter.

CHAPTER TWO

Desiderata: Bird Collecting
and Community

RECRUITING RIDGWAY

While sorting through his mail in the spring of 1864, Smithsonian Assistant Secretary Spencer Fullerton Baird found a letter that caught his eye. It was from Robert Ridgway, a fourteen-year-old boy from Mt. Carmel, Illinois, who wanted to know the name of a bird he and two of his friends had discovered on one of their recent forays into the woods.[1] Accompanying the letter was a carefully rendered color portrait of the bird in question. Always eager to recruit young naturalists to join his extensive collecting network, Baird identified the bird as a purple finch, complimented Ridgway on his "unusual degree of ability as an artist," forwarded a copy of the Smithsonian circular on collecting specimens, and suggested he use scientific rather than local names of birds in future correspondence. Like he had done many times before, Baird closed his reply with an offer to help the young lad in any way he could.[2] As Ridgway revealed in a moving letter the next year, Baird was the first person to encourage his interest in birds:

> I am a poor boy; the oldest of a family of seven children; my father is the junior partner in a drug-store, the slim proceeds of which are scarcely enough to supply us with the necessaries [sic] of life. In all my labors and studies I have had to support myself—or supply myself with material for drawing &c, which I can just barely do by result of a small capital invested in the drug-store and which at first amounted to only 20 cts. My parents do not fully understand my views and motives and consequently I do not expect to receive that encouragement which I would expect to receive from them. My mother is willing to do a good part for me, but my father says that my study and drawing is more expensive than beneficial and calls it mere child's play. To you therefore,—as my only friend except my parents, do I go for *counsel*.[3]

The connection with Baird proved to be a turning point in Ridgway's life. At Baird's constant urging, over the next few years he mailed a regular supply of descriptions, drawings, eggs, and crudely prepared skins to the Smithsonian.[4] When Ridgway turned seventeen, Baird invited him to Washington, taught him how to make proper bird skins, and arranged for him to serve as a collector on Clarence King's United States Geographical Exploration of the Fortieth Parallel. After two successful seasons exploring the Great Basin region in the West, Baird hired his young protégé to complete the technical descriptions and drawings for his three-volume *History of North American Birds: Land Birds* (1874).[5] He also convinced the book's publisher to pay Ridgway a regular salary until he could secure the funds to retain him as a curator of ornithology at the Smithsonian in 1874.[6] Under Baird's tutelage, Ridgway soon became proficient in the finer points of technical ornithology and, like his mentor, became an accomplished "collector of collectors."[7]

The Baird-Ridgway relationship was unique only in the prominence of the individuals involved. During the second half of the nineteenth century experienced ornithologists routinely nurtured the efforts of other collectors. They did so by publishing detailed guides on how to collect, preserve, and identify birds as well as by recruiting neophytes for their expansive collecting networks. Those networks typically included not only beginning bird enthusiasts, but also a variety of more advanced collectors, dealers, taxidermists, sport hunters, and scientists. Until the end of the century these diverse elements formed an extended ornithological community united by a common interest in amassing North American birds and their eggs.

Middle-class Americans with more leisure time on their hands turned to bird collecting for many of the same reasons they began to amass other natural history objects: a desire to escape, however fleetingly, from an increasingly urban and industrial America, to test one's mettle against the elements, and to return with the aesthetically pleasing specimens that found a prominent place in many Victorian homes (fig. 4). Of course, collectors could simply purchase desirable specimens from the dozens of taxidermy and natural history establishments that proliferated in the second half of the nineteenth century. But for many the experience of collecting itself provided much of the activity's allure. As Spencer Trotter, a prominent Philadelphia ornithologist, asked: "What branch of science comes nearer to satisfying the primitive instinct that takes him into the woods to hunt and fish or for the mere sake of steeping the senses in the fresh, rank life of things, and at the same time abundantly satisfying the acquisitive and classifying habit of mind?"[8] And as Trotter hinted, the tools, methods, motivations, and sometimes even the intended object of bird collecting also bore a striking resemblance to another increasingly popular middle-class activity: game hunting.

The individuals who comprised the extended ornithological community were firmly united by a common desire to possess specimens of North American birds and eggs. For some, these specimens were little more than objects to be carefully amassed and proudly displayed; for others, they were primarily commodities to be bought, sold, and traded; and for a relative few, they were the raw material for research into the taxonomic relationships and geographical distribution of North American avifauna. Despite the diverse and often mixed motivations of most individual collectors, for much of the second half of the nineteenth century the specimen itself provided the glue that held together the extended ornithological community.

Figure 4. Collectors gathering "rare birds and eggs" in
Florida, 1888.

EARLY AMERICAN COLLECTIONS

Although naturalists had amassed bird collections for ages, not until the middle
decades of the eighteenth century did they finally devise effective procedures to
protect specimens from the ravages of decay and insects. As historian Paul Farber
has shown, these techniques remained controversial or shrouded in secrecy for
decades following their initial discovery, but by the early nineteenth century, the
use of various arsenic preparations became a standard method to preserve bird
skins.[9] Simpler procedures for preserving eggs—by blowing out the contents
through small holes made at each end—appear to have been developed at about
the same time.[10] These preservation techniques did not entirely solve the problem

of decay and insect infestation—curators still had to remain vigilant—but they nonetheless became a major factor in the establishment of extensive, stable ornithological collections at the end of the eighteenth and the beginning of the nineteenth centuries.[11]

Charles Willson Peale pioneered preservation and taxidermy techniques in this country at the end of the eighteenth century, and Peale's Philadelphia Museum, established in 1786, contained the largest and most important American ornithological collection of its day.[12] Stocked with specimens gathered by himself, his sons, and other naturalists, Peale's private establishment included most North American bird species known during this period. An 1805 catalog claimed that the bird collection exceeded 760 specimens.[13] Among the most prominent of the many contributors to and users of the Peale collection were Alexander Wilson, author of the nine-volume *American Ornithology* (1808–1814), and Charles Lucien Bonaparte, the nephew of Napoleon, who completed a four-volume supplement to Wilson's work (1825–1834).[14]

Following the standard museum practice of his day, Peale invariably mounted his specimens for exhibit. But unlike his colleagues here and abroad, Peale not only succeeded in placing his birds in lifelike attitudes, he also displayed them in cases with painted landscape backgrounds intended to represent the native environment of the species. Peale's bird displays thus became early, primitive examples of the habitat exhibits perfected in the second half of the nineteenth century.[15] Although Peale's Philadelphia Museum was disbursed in 1850, examples of his taxidermic technique survive to this day in the Museum of Comparative Zoology at Harvard.[16]

Another Philadelphia institution, the Academy of Natural Sciences, also established an early and important ornithological collection in the United States. Immediately after its founding in 1812 the organization began amassing specimens for its museum.[17] Following the election of William Maclure as president in 1817, the academy started a periodical and a more active accession program. Through purchase, exchange, and donation, the academy's collection greatly increased under Maclure's twenty-three-year reign. By 1840 the ornithological collection alone numbered around thirteen hundred specimens.[18]

Even more impressive growth came just a few years later when Thomas B. Wilson placed his extensive private bird collection on permanent deposit at the academy.[19] Although trained as a physician, Wilson never practiced medicine. Instead he devoted himself to amassing natural history specimens, especially insects, birds, and rocks. Besides mounting expeditions throughout much of the eastern United States and portions of Canada, Wilson traveled to Europe to purchase the extensive collection of Prince Massena d'Essling, Duc de Rivoli (which alone contained at least ten thousand mounted specimens and five thousand species), the John Gould type collection of Australian birds, the Captain Boys Indian collection, and others. Following Wilson's acquisitions, Philip Lutley Sclater, secretary of the Zoological Society of London, pronounced the academy's collection "probably superior to every Museum in Europe and therefore the most perfect in existence."[20]

With Wilson's contributions, the academy's ornithological collection was not only the largest in North America, it was also one of the few with an extensive series of non–North American birds. Its curator, the Philadelphia merchant and publisher John Cassin, became one of only a handful of U.S. ornithologists from this period to become an authority on foreign birds.[21] Cassin attracted no protégé, and when he died in 1869 the collection languished for nearly two decades.[22]

After an aborted attempt at establishing a society devoted to natural history a few years after the founding of the Academy of Natural Sciences, in 1830 New England naturalists organized a more enduring organization, the Boston Society of Natural History.[23] With miscellaneous donations from explorers, naturalists, missionaries, and sea captains, the society's collection quickly grew in size and diversity. By 1840 the ornithological collection alone numbered 475 specimens, and by ten years later it had surpassed the 1,200 mark.[24] In 1849 the organization established a separate department of oology, which was placed under the direction of the Boston physician and publisher Thomas M. Brewer. The Boston Society ornithological collection continued to grow slowly until 1865, when curator Henry Bryant donated the collection of Count Lafresnaye de Falaise. This important acquisition contained 8,656 mounted specimens representing some 4,000 species and many types. Like the Rivoli collection, it consisted largely of non–North American species.[25]

Other institutions and individuals in the United States initiated important ornithological collections in the first half of the nineteenth century. Several colleges, scientific societies, state natural history surveys, and entrepreneurs gathered birds and eggs for exhibit and (less often) study.[26] In addition, a handful of individual naturalists—like John James Audubon, Spencer Fullerton Baird, George N. Lawrence, John Cassin, and John Kirk Townsend—amassed extensive private collections during this period to conduct research and provide material for others.[27] But compared to what came in the second half of the nineteenth century, the scale of this collecting activity remained limited and the ornithological community remained relatively small and undifferentiated from the larger natural history community.

COLLECTING NETWORKS

The establishment of extensive collecting networks was one of a series of developments that signaled a fundamental turning point in the scope and scale of American natural history collecting more generally and bird collecting in particular. Louis Agassiz began one of the first and largest of these networks shortly after his arrival on American shores in 1846. One year later he decided to accept a professorship of natural history and geology at Harvard, a position created for him when the Lawrence Scientific School was organized.[28] From the start the flamboyant Swiss naturalist captivated the American public while cultivating a broad popular interest in natural history. Agassiz's devotion to popularization was at least partially self-interested; he quickly discovered that an enlightened public was the best means to insure a steady supply of specimens and funds for his ambitious publication, research, and museum-building agenda.

Agassiz regularly solicited specimen donations through printed circulars broadcast to a wide segment of the American natural history community.[29] The response was overwhelming. The regular stream of specimens sent in by Agassiz's extensive network of collectors, gathered by his growing staff of student assistants, and purchased from European sources quickly overwhelmed the series of temporary structures housing the burgeoning museum. With a job offer for the prestigious National Museum of Natural History in France in hand as a bargaining chip, Agassiz finally raised the funds needed to build a large, permanent structure, the Museum of Comparative Zoology, which he hoped would soon rival the great European natural history institutions. In 1860 alone, when the first of what were eventually to become several wings of the new building was occupied, donations and purchases added ninety-one thousand specimens to the MCZ collection.[30] To answer critics of his seemingly insatiable appetite for specimens and funds, Agassiz resorted to a biological analogy: "it is with museums as with all living things; what has vitality must grow. When museums cease to grow, and consequently to demand ever-increasing means, their usefulness is on the decline."[31]

Although Agassiz's ostensible policy was to avoid collecting in areas already well represented in existing American museums, several of his student assistants began amassing extensive bird skin, skeleton, and alcoholic collections for the MCZ.[32] For example, Addison E. Verrill came to Harvard in 1859 with a keen interest in birds and, at Agassiz's suggestion, began gathering a collection of sea-bird embryos before turning to the study of marine invertebrates. Three years later, J. A. Allen, whose curiosity about birds was more enduring, arrived in Cambridge to study under Agassiz.

Allen had begun collecting natural history specimens while a young teenager on his family's farm in Springfield, Massachusetts.[33] In the winter of 1862 he enrolled as a special student under Agassiz with the proceeds from the sale of his prized collection of mounted birds.[34] After his first term, Allen began cataloging the small MCZ bird collection, which at the time consisted of "several hundred skins (possibly a thousand or two, all North America), and several thousand alcoholics."[35] When Verrill left to join the faculty at Yale in 1864, Allen became principle curator of the MCZ's bird and mammal collections. Taking his cue from his mentor, over the next two decades Allen issued regular pleas for specimen donations, purchased birds from natural history dealers, and exchanged duplicates with a network of collectors. He also collected extensively himself in Massachusetts (1862–63), New York (1864), Brazil (1865), the Midwest (1867), Florida (1868–69), the Great Plains and Rocky Mountains (1871–72), and Yellowstone (1873).[36] Because of his efforts, by 1869 the MCZ bird collection numbered twenty thousand, including six thousand specimens preserved in alcohol.[37] When Allen finally left for the American Museum of Natural History in 1885, the MCZ catalog contained entries for over thirty-three thousand birds.[38]

While Agassiz and his student assistants were building the MCZ into an internationally renowned research museum, Agassiz's principal rival, Spencer Fullerton Baird, was assembling his own impressive collection in Washington, D.C. Smithsonian Secretary Joseph Henry hired the Dickinson College professor to be his assistant in 1850.[39] Although he had numerous official duties, including administering the Smithsonian's publication and international exchange programs, Baird's overriding interest was building a world-class natural history collection. His own personal natural history cabinet, one of the largest in the nation at the time, required two boxcars to transport to Washington and became the nucleus for what eventually became known as the United States National Museum. Upon his arrival Baird immediately set to work to expand the collection. With little available money to purchase specimens outright, Baird worked feverishly to construct one of the most extensive collecting networks ever created.

Through widely broadcast printed directions for gathering, preserving, and transporting specimens, persuasive letters to would-be collectors, encouraging follow-up letters to those who sent in material, and carefully cultivated connections with high-ranking government and military officials, Baird charmed, cajoled, and otherwise coaxed an impressive number of Americans into providing the national collection with material. Soldiers stationed at distant military outposts and individuals attached to the trans-Mississippi exploring expeditions proved a particularly fruitful source of new specimens.[40] Baird in turn provided his collectors, who were often lonely and far removed from civilization, with encouragement, published acknowledgments, advice, Smithsonian publications, collecting supplies, specimen identifications, money, social contact, and the potential to have new species named in their honor.[41] The product of this fruitful collaboration was a national collection that was constantly pushing at the seams. What had been six thousand specimens when Baird arrived in 1850 numbered several hundred thousand when he became secretary of the Smithsonian twenty-eight years later.[42]

The growth of the national ornithological collection mirrored that of the Smithsonian as a whole. The bird collection began in 1850 with Baird's private cabinet, containing 3,696 specimens, the vast majority of which were North American birds.[43] During the 1850s important acquisitions came from the series of government-sponsored western explorations and boundary surveys as well as the specimens previously gathered by the U.S. Exploring Expedition (1838–1842).[44] By the end of 1860 the number of entries in the bird department's catalog reached 20,785; by the end of 1870, 61,145; and by the end of 1880, 81,434.[45]

Although larger than most, Baird's collecting network was only one of hundreds of similar, interlocking networks established in the middle decades of the century. To maintain a continued supply of new specimens for their cabinets, most serious bird collectors during this period remained in regular contact with an array of collectors, hunters, taxidermists, dealers, and scientists. George A. Boardman, a frequent Baird correspondent, provides a typical example. Boardman was a lumber-mill owner from Calais, Maine, who began collecting birds around 1840, following a business trip to South America and the West Indies.[46]

Impressed by the striking flora and fauna he encountered during his trip, Boardman started gathering examples of local birds and mammals to learn more about the creatures inhabiting his native Maine. Boardman's collection grew slowly until he abandoned active management of his lumber operation in the late 1850s and early 1860s.

During the next few years Boardman devoted increasing time to his collection, which he augmented by field work in places as far away as Florida and Minnesota; extensive exchanges with naturalists across the nation; and purchases from taxidermists, dealers, game markets, and local gunners who knew he was always on the lookout for unusual specimens.[47] One of his many regular correspondents, Dr. William Wood of East Winsor Hill, Connecticut, opened the first of a series of letters to Boardman with a statement exemplifying the expectation that a fellow collector would be eager to trade specimens: "My object is to open an exchange with you of skins and eggs and I trust I need make no apology for addressing one engaged in the same pursuit as myself."[48] In 1863, when Boardman's growing collection of mounted birds became so large that it no longer fit into the glass cases installed in his house, he built a sixteen-by-twenty-foot museum for it. At the time of his death in 1901, the Boardman collection numbered some twenty-five hundred specimens.

SERIAL COLLECTING

Other private collections reached much more ambitious proportions. Access to extensive networks of collectors and dealers helped drive the trend toward larger and larger collections. Also important were new research concerns: an interest in geographical distribution that began at the time Baird and Agassiz were establishing their museums, and the new appreciation of variation initiated by the publication of Darwin's *Origin of Species* (1859).[49] Before these developments, collectors generally aimed to acquire a mounted pair of each species or, in the case of eggs, a single clutch. But beginning in the middle of the century, bird and egg collectors sought out increasingly larger series of each species to document its distribution and variation. The advice of Coues's best-selling guide to ornithology (first published in 1874) strikingly reflects this new emphasis on serial collecting:

> *How many Birds of the Same Kind do you want?—All you can get*—with some reasonable limitations; say fifty or a hundred of any but the most abundant and widely diffused species. You may often be provoked with your friend for speaking of some bird he shot, but did not bring you, because, he says, "Why you've got one like that!" This is just as reasonable as to suppose that because you have got one dollar you would not like to have another. Birdskins are capital; capital unemployed may be useless but can never be worthless. Birdskins are a medium of exchange among ornithologists the world over; they represent value—money value and scientific value. If you have more of one kind than you can use[,] exchange with some one for species you lack; both parties to the

transaction are equally benefited. . . . Your own "series" of skins of any species is incomplete until it contains at least one example of each sex, of every normal state of plumage, and every normal transition state of plumage, and further illustrates at least the principal abnormal variations in size, form and color to which the species may be subject; I will even add that every different faunal area the bird is known to inhabit should be represented by a specimen, particularly if there be anything unusual in the geographical distribution of the species.[50]

Under the mandate to amass series, North American bird collections expanded rapidly in the second half of the nineteenth century. Private collections of several thousand birds became increasingly common. Particularly ambitious collectors—like James Fleming of Ontario, Max Peet of Ann Arbor, Michigan, Outram Bangs of Cambridge, Massachusetts, and John Thayer of Lancaster, Massachusetts—gathered as many as twenty-five thousand or more specimens through purchase from dealers, sponsored expeditions, exchanges with individuals and institutions, and their own field work.[51]

Several active collectors broke the forty thousand mark. William Brewster (fig. 5), a founder of the Nuttall Ornithological Club (1873) and the American Ornithologists' Union (1883), began collecting birds and eggs in the area around Cambridge, Massachusetts, at the age of ten. The product of a wealthy banking family, Brewster arranged to devote his entire time to ornithology by his twentieth birthday. Five years later, in a survey of Smithsonian correspondents undertaken by Baird, Brewster listed his occupation as "amateur ornithologist" and indicated that his collection numbered some five hundred mounted specimens, three thousand skins, and approximately a thousand eggs of North American birds.[52] At the time of his death in 1919, Brewster bequeathed well over forty thousand specimens to the MCZ, where he had served as honorary curator since Allen's departure in 1885.[53] The large body of surviving correspondence generated while Brewster was amassing his collection reveals how much he relied on an extended community of amateur and professional collectors, dealers, taxidermists, scientists, and others to bring together one of the three or four largest private collections of North American birds ever assembled.[54]

Louis B. Bishop of New Haven, Connecticut, also began collecting birds at a young age.[55] His early casual interest in birds became more serious by the age of twelve, when he and his schoolmate, Leonard C. Sanford, met an older Yale student who taught them how to skin and mount the birds they killed with their slingshots.[56] Two years later Bishop received his first gun. After graduating from Yale College (1886) and Medical School (1888), he continued medical studies in the United States and abroad before returning to New Haven to practice medicine. Bishop was able to pursue his lasting enthusiasm for ornithology only during his spare moments until he retired from medicine in 1908. By the time he sold his collection to the Field Museum in 1939, he had amassed over fifty-three thousand bird skins.

In the 1890s Bishop met another physician-collector, Jonathan Dwight of New York City. The two soon developed an intense but friendly rivalry. Dwight had

Figure 5. William Brewster, reclining with his collecting pistol, ca. 1890. Brewster was a leading light in the development of American ornithology but never held a professional position.

begun amassing eggs at age fourteen. When he enrolled in Harvard in 1876, he came under the influence of the young men who had recently organized the Nuttall Ornithological Club and soon began collecting skins. After earning his bachelor's degree, he spent several years working for his father's engineering firm before entering Columbia University Medical School, where he graduated in 1893. During his spare hours Dwight continued to build up his collection while publishing a series of important papers on the sequence of plumage molts in birds.[57] At the time of his death in 1929, Dwight's collection of sixty-five thousand "carefully labelled and catalogued" skins went to the American Museum of Natural History in New York, where it had long been on deposit.

Under the mandate to amass series, egg collections could reach equally prodigious proportions. In 1883, at the time of his appointment as an honorary curator of ornithology at the Smithsonian Institution, Charles E. Bendire's collection contained 8,000 North American birds' eggs.[58] In 1894 J. Parker Norris, Sr., and J. Parker Norris, Jr., a father and son collecting team from Philadelphia, claimed to have gathered an extensive oological collection consisting of 573 North American species, more than 5,000 sets, and 20,000 eggs.[59] In 1901 John Lewis Childs, a wealthy egg collector and nursery owner in Floral Park, New York (on Long Island), purchased a *single* collection of over 30,000 eggs.[60] He continued to add to his collection until his death in 1921. And in 1925 Richard M. Barnes, a Chicago lawyer and long-time editor of *The Oologist*, donated 38,721 North American birds' eggs to the Field Museum, where he had long served as assistant curator of oology.[61]

SPORTING NATURALISTS

In addition to its connection with scientists and scientific institutions, bird collecting was also intimately related to the age-old practice of game hunting. Well into the second half of the nineteenth century, the two activities remained so closely related that the scientist Charles Batchelder declared that there was not "much of a dividing line between ornithologists and sportsmen."[62] John Cassin, who had made the same comparison much earlier, considered bird collecting to represent the pinnacle of field sports, an opinion that was widely shared:

> Bird collecting is the ultimate refinement—the *ne plus ultra* of all the sports of the field. It is attended with all the excitement, and requires all the skill of other shooting, with a much higher degree of theoretical information and consequent gratification in its exercises. . . . Personal activity, coolness, steadiness of hand, quickness of eye and ear will be of service, and some of them indispensable, to successful collecting. . . . Great is the life of the woods, say we, and the greatest of all sports is bird collecting.[63]

Beyond supplying an important source of food for American settlers, from the beginning hunting also had more ritualistic and recreational dimensions.[64] The activity provided an opportunity to join with friends in the outdoors, to leave behind cares and worries in single-minded pursuit of game. By the first half of the nineteenth century, the sporting side of hunting was increasingly emphasized, and certain attributes became expected of every gentleman hunter: intimate knowledge of the life and habitat of his quarry, skill with a gun, the ability to train and use dogs, and a well-developed sense of fair play.[65]

As early as 1783, the anonymously published *Sportsman's Companion* had begun to codify the body of knowledge and values associated with sport hunting.[66] By the mid-nineteenth century, a steady stream of publications, like Elisha J. Lewis's *Hints to Sportsmen* (1851) and Frank Forester's *The Complete Manual for Young Sportsmen* (1856), counseled the growing number of American recreational hunters on the techniques and social graces associated with the pursuit of game.[67]

By the 1870s sport hunting really took off in the United States. During the first few years of that decade the number of North American organizations devoted to sport hunting tripled to just over three hundred.[68] In addition, several nationally circulated periodicals, like *American Sportsman* (1871), *Forest and Stream* (1873), and *Field and Stream* (1874), began publication. These periodicals not only provided recreational hunters with a greater sense of identity and community, they also furnished naturalists with publication outlets.[69] The most important and long-lived of these new sporting periodicals was *Forest and Stream*, started by the sportsman, author, and editor, Charles Hallock.[70] In announcing the new periodical to George Boardman in 1873, Hallock indicated that he aimed to "make it the standard authority and work of reference on sporting matters and topics of natural history."[71]

Taxidermy provided another point of intersection between the closely related activities of game hunting and bird collecting. Sport hunters often wanted their prized takes shaped into permanent trophies to decorate their homes and offices with proof of their prowess. Sometimes they tried to mount skins themselves, with the aid of published guides like William Bullock's handbook (1st American ed., 1839) and Lewis's *Hints to Sportsmen*.[72] But more often than not they relied on professional taxidermists, whose establishments became more commonplace with the increase in sport hunting.

John G. Bell, who had accompanied Audubon during his expedition to the upper Missouri in 1843, owned one of the most famous taxidermy establishments in New York City during the mid-nineteenth century. According to one prominent ornithologist, Bell was a "friend and associate" of Audubon, Baird, Cassin, and other prominent naturalists, who named several species in his honor as a sign of their esteem.[73] Like most of his fellow taxidermists, Bell not only catered to sport hunters, but also did a brisk business in mounted specimens and skins purchased by collectors and others who desired to decorate their homes and businesses.[74] His shop on the northwest corner of Broadway and Worth Street became a regular haunt for hunters, collectors, and naturalists. One of those who frequented the shop as a teenager, Theodore Roosevelt, later recalled that "Mr. Bell was a very interesting man, an American before-the-war type. He was tall, straight as an Indian, with white hair and a smooth-shaven, clear-cut face; a dignified figure, always in a black frock coat. He had no scientific knowledge of birds or mammals; his interest lay merely in collecting and preparing them."[75]

In addition to specimens brought in by gunners and market hunters, Bell often located prized finds at Fulton Market, one of several New York City game and produce markets.[76] At a time when the line between game and nongame species remained indistinct, these markets offered an enticing assortment of birds for sale to collectors.[77]

New York recreational hunters and naturalists also regularly gathered at the establishment of another well-known taxidermist from this period, John Wallace, "a stout, dark-haired, . . . forceful looking man, rather short in stature with a decided cockney accent."[78] Eugene P. Bicknell, a founding member of the AOU, recalled with fondness his frequent youthful visits to Wallace's shop on upper William Street in the 1860s and 1870s:

> Thither as a youth I used often to go, hesitant of troubling this always busy man, yet
> impelled by expectation! Almost always there would be news of unusual local birds, for
> many were the specimens that came to that work-shop, and it even might befall, on good

days, that I should be allowed to take into my hands some rarity not yet dispossessed of the fresh beauty of its natural form and plumage.[79]

For several months in 1871, fifteen-year-old C. Hart Merriam, another AOU founding member, spent his weekends away from school learning taxidermy at Wallace's.[80]

One reason so many birds passed through Wallace's hands was that his firm processed them for the millinery trade, a practice that was to become a source of tension between scientists and taxidermists with the rise of the bird protection movement a few years later.[81] Working on Wallace's eight-man assembly line provided temporary employment for the ornithologist W. E. D. Scott following graduation from the Lawrence Scientific School in 1873. Before securing a position at Princeton, Scott spent three months helping to skin, poison, and stuff the four hundred or so birds brought in daily by local gunners.[82]

Philadelphia was also home to several taxidermy establishments frequented by naturalists and hunters alike. Spencer Trotter's compelling description of Chris Wood, "a typical old-time bird collector and taxidermist," is one of the most detailed accounts of the taxidermist-naturalist that has survived and is well worth quoting at length:

> "Chris" lived in a small house on the north side of Market Street west of Thirty-fourth. His taxidermic shop, on the ground floor front, I can still see perfectly, and it had a smell peculiarly its own. I can see it again whenever I get a whiff of raw bird-flesh and arsenic. Back of a counter, littered with the materials of his craft, stood "Chris," in a cardigan jacket, skinning birds. I can see him clearly as I write this—always cheerful and friendly to the boy who must have bothered him many times. I am somewhat hazy as to a row of glass-door cases, containing mounted specimens back of where he stood, but there were drawers under the cases—deep drawers filled with bird-skins thrown in helter-skelter without labels. Mrs. "Chris," a short darkish woman, used to urge "Chris" to "laybil" his specimens, but "Chris" knew where each one had been taken, so he said, and I believe that he was fairly accurate, though there were several hundred bird-skins in those drawers. I used to spend afternoons rummaging among these specimens and bought a good many, some very interesting ones. Twenty-five cents was the price for fairly common species of small bird, though I paid him ten dollars for the hybrid swallow which I had described. "Chris" did a fairly good business, I think, mounting birds that were brought to him by sportsmen, and he was always quite reasonable in his charges. . . . He was a fast and skilful worker and would strip the skin off a small bird, dose it with arsenic and push in the cotton while he talked away—one bird after another in quick succession— and the skins remarkably good, quite free from blemishes of any sort.[83]

More widely known was John Krider, whose shop on Second and Walnut Streets in Philadelphia "was long the popular resort of the local sporting fraternity."[84] A taxidermist, gunsmith, and professional collector, Krider traveled extensively up and down the Eastern Seaboard and as far west as Denver in search of specimens for his own collection and to sell. In the early 1870s he made several trips to Lake Mills, Iowa. There he secured specimens of a new hawk, which was later named in his honor. Unlike most taxidermists, Krider actually placed some of his field observations into print. His first book on the habits of American game birds, published in 1853, was followed by a series of notes in *Forest and Stream* and a second book, *Forty Years Notes of a Field Ornithologist*, published in 1879.[85]

For as long as ornithology remained focused on collecting, it remained closely affiliated with the sporting community. Even scientifically oriented ornithologists often began their interest in birds as recreational hunters, and many scientists, such as Frank Chapman, William Brewster, and Charles B. Cory, continued to enjoy hunting throughout their lives.[86]

Collecting and Identification Guides

Naturalists constructing networks and the rise in sport hunting each contributed to the growth of bird skin and egg collecting in the United States. A third related factor, the appearance of published bird identification guides and collecting manuals, also promoted the activity of bird collecting. A steady stream of books and articles published during second half of the nineteenth century provided detailed, practical advice on how to procure, preserve, and identify birds and their eggs (fig. 6). These publications not only introduced budding naturalists to collection and identification techniques, they also served as a source of inspiration and legitimation for the activity of collecting itself. Older ornithologists from this period frequently reminisced how discovery of a particular how-to book or article had stimulated a youthful zeal in amassing specimens.

Baird, Agassiz, and other institutionally affiliated naturalists issued some of the first brief collecting manuals available in the United States.[87] Their concise and widely distributed pamphlets provided rudimentary instructions on how to locate, preserve, and transport natural history specimens of all kinds. Those who sent in material, however, invariably required further guidance to refine their techniques. Information on collecting and mounting animals, particularly birds and mammals, was also available from a number of books on taxidermy aimed at recreational hunters and travelers.[88] But these sources tended to be sketchy and unreliable. Not until well into the second half of the nineteenth century were more trustworthy and complete manuals readily available.

C. J. Maynard's *The Naturalists' Guide* (1870) was the first American publication to provide detailed, reliable advice on collecting and preserving zoological specimens, especially birds.[89] Born in Newton, Massachusetts, in 1845, Maynard left school at age sixteen.[90] After attempts at farming and watchmaking, he opened a small watch repair and taxidermy shop in his hometown.[91] In 1866 Maynard went into business with the taxidermist William H. Floyd of Weston, Massachusetts. One of their first jobs was to unpack and remount the large Lafresnaye collection for the Boston Society of Natural History, a task that took a full year to complete. Soon after that experience Maynard opened his own taxidermy and natural history establishment and began making sales to local collectors.[92]

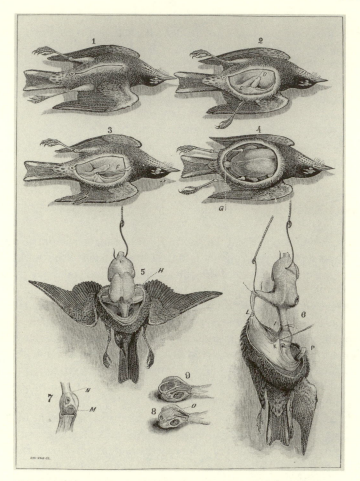

Figure 6. Illustration of how to skin a bird. From Davie, *Methods
in the Art of Taxidermy* (1894), one of the many late-nineteenth-
century manuals that introduced beginning collectors to
the rudiments of securing and preserving birds and their eggs.

Besides useful advice on when and where to find birds, Maynard's illustrated
guide included recommendations on the most basic equipment—guns, shoes,
clothes, and dogs—required to obtain them. Upon locating a bird, the collector
needed to get it back home with minimum damage to its plumage. According to
Maynard, this was achieved by using a gun of the proper bore, loaded with shot
of the right size, and with just the precise amount of gunpowder to pierce and kill
the bird, but not to make a second exit hole.

The most important part of Maynard's guide was his instructions for preparing
and preserving bird skins. After a brief list of the required tools and materials, he
devoted several pages to the safe use of arsenic.[93] Next came instructions for
recording the age, sex, measurements, stomach contents, date of collection, local-

ity of collection, and colors of the eyes, feet, and bill of the collected bird. Maynard's up-to-date suggestions on registering specimen data were no doubt a
reflection of his extensive contact with Allen at the MCZ. After detailed instructions on how to prepare bird skins, Maynard concluded the section on bird collecting with a discussion of how to mount freshly skinned and dried birds.[94] Appended to Maynard's widely read book was a catalog of nearly three hundred
birds found in eastern Massachusetts.[95]

Elliott Coues's *Key to North American Birds* (1872) was even more influential
in developing American collectors.[96] Ever self-assured, articulate, and controversial, Coues (pronounced "Cows") was among the most important American ornithologists in the second half of the nineteenth century.[97] Born in Portsmouth, New
Hampshire, in 1842, he moved with his family to Washington, D.C., at age
eleven. After obtaining his A.B. (1861) and M.D. (1863) from Columbian College, he enlisted as an assistant surgeon in the army. For the next ten years he was
stationed at a variety of remote posts, including a number of western locations.

Coues first met Baird shortly after arriving in Washington as a youth. According to his biographers, for the next three decades Baird served as Coues's "mentor, friend, and confidant, and in those years, far more than any other individual,
influenced and shaped his career."[98] Baird not only helped forge the young Coues
into a first-rate scientific ornithologist, he also used his extensive Washington
contacts to arrange transfers to favorable collecting localities on the United States
Northern Boundary Survey (1873–1876) and the United States Geological Survey (1876–1880). But because of Coues's difficult personality, Baird never hired
him on a permanent basis at the Smithsonian.

As early as 1868 Coues contemplated publishing a multiauthor "manual of
American taxidermy."[99] When that project failed to come to fruition, Coues began
work on "an infallible artificial Key to N.A. birds, enabling anyone, without the
slightest knowledge of ornithology, to identify any specimen in a few seconds."
Coues claimed to have tested a manuscript version of the new key on his wife.
Though barely able to distinguish a "tarsus from a tail," she correctly identified all
the specimens presented her.[100] After providing the text, many of the woodcuts,
and $1,000 for the project, Coues was greatly relieved when the Naturalists'
Agency of Salem, Massachusetts, finally published two thousand copies of the
book in October 1872. According to one reviewer, soon Coues's *Key* became a
"familiar and useful companion alike to the amateur and professional ornithologist."[101] Coues's reliable *Key* contributed more than any other single work to the
tremendous growth in bird collecting that followed its publication.

The commercial and critical success of Coues's *Key* encouraged him to publish
again a year later. His next venture, *A Check List of North American Birds* (1873),
was largely based on his earlier *Key* and, like that publication, included a number
of forms designated by the trinomial nomenclature that Coues and other scientific
ornithologists were beginning to promote.[102] Coues hoped his new *Check List*,
which he had printed on only one side of the paper to allow it to be used as
specimen labels, would supplant a similar list issued by Baird in 1859 as the
accepted standard for naming North American birds.[103]

Here you Have It!

BEAN'S BREECH-LOADING GUN CANE.

SCENE 1.   As it looks when walking out with your Best Girl.

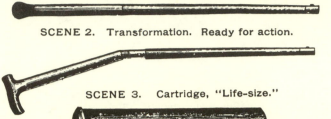

SCENE 2.   Transformation.   Ready for action.

SCENE 3.   Cartridge, "Life-size."

Unlike other cane guns the stock, which is 14 inches long, drops when in position for firing, giving a bend of 3¼ inches, being the same as a shot-gun.   They have a rebounding hammer, a trigger, firing pan, and extractor.
  PRICES: Cane Gun, $15.   Shot Shells, per 100, $2.50.   Cleaning Rod, $1.50.   Fishing Rod Attachment, 2 joints, $1.50.
  No one need, after reading this, ever exclaim, "What funny things we see when we do not have a Gun!"   This Gun is a strong shooter, and nothing has yet been offered that is so completely concealed.   No person would notice it from an ordinary heavy cane.   It is just what collectors want.   For full particulars, address

E. L. GAY,   -   -   21 Neponset Ave., Hyde Park, Mass.

Figure 7. Advertisement for Bean's breech-loading gun cane, 1889.

A year later Coues appended the *Check List* to his *Field Ornithology* (1874), a "manual of instructions for procuring, preparing and preserving birds."[104] Written in Coues's inimitable style, the book contained even more exhaustive instructions for the bird collector than Maynard's earlier guide. For example, where Maynard had merely suggested the twelve-gauge shotgun as the best for birds, Coues included a lengthy discussion of other weapons as well. Like Maynard, Coues recommended the breech-loading, double-barrel shotgun as the best all-around collecting weapon, but he also discussed the pros and cons of single-barrel guns, muzzle loaders, special breech-loading pistols ("the best 'second choice'"), and cane guns. The latter were single-barrel guns disguised to look like walking sticks (fig. 7). Although some collectors praised the unusual weapons, Coues claimed his own experience with the cane gun had been "limited and unsatisfactory": "[T]he handle always hits me in the face, and I generally missed my bird." Despite its shortcomings, however, there were two circumstances under which he recommended the subterfuge: "If you approve of shooting on Sunday and yet scruple to shock popular prejudice, you can slip out of town unsuspected. If you are shooting where the law forbids destruction of small birds,—a wise and good law that you may sometimes be inclined to defy,—artfully handling of the deceitful implement may prevent arrest and fine."[105]

In his advice on how many and what kind of birds to seek, Coues tried to dispel widely held misconceptions about the special value of "rare" birds. Like other kinds of collectors, those amassing birds invariably went to great pains to obtain species that seemed scarce, elusive, or otherwise difficult to get. For example, in 1885, Walter Hoxie, of Frogmore, South Carolina, reported to Brewster of his repeated attempts to secure specimens of the Bachman's warbler, which had not been collected since its original description in 1833:

> This summer and fall I shot away nearly twenty five pounds of dust shot in the vain attempt to secure a specimen [of Bachman's warbler]. I spent days and days at it. Shot every small bird that excited my least suspicion. Also a dozen or more *butterflies* & I even descended to lizards and grasshoppers. Everything that I couldn't make out clearly had to suffer for I had B[achman]'s W[arbler] "on the brain." Result—about a hundred good skins of various small birds & two hundred & sixteen "millinery's" for which I realized 6 cents apiece. . . . I shall open a spring campaign with unabated zeal & un-dampened hopes.[106]

Coues believed that with the exception of those few species truly on the verge of extinction—and Bachman's warbler may have one of these—birds did not tend to be rare in nature. Rather, species that seemed rare in a particular geographic area were simply on the margins of their normal ranges. When collecting in a new or little-known locality, Coues recommended going after the most characteristic and abundant birds first, which he believed were the ones most likely missing from existing collections.[107]

In 1884 Coues published a second, revised edition of his *Key*, which incorporated his *Field Ornithology* and an extensive section on the classification and structure of birds.[108] This edition, which he dedicated to Baird, contained twice as many pages and nearly four times the text as the first. Combining a collecting and identification guide in a single volume, Coues's second edition was an even greater commercial success than the first. In his *Autobiography*, Frank Chapman, curator of ornithology at the American Museum of Natural History, reflected how momentous his discovery of the book in a New York City bookstore window was to his development as an ornithologist:

> That was a memorable day. I acquired that book and for the first time learned that there were living students of birds, worthy successors of Wilson and Audubon. From that moment I was no longer handicapped for lack of tools. Here was a work which from the preface to index offered an inexhaustible store of information, its technicalities so humanized by the genius of its author that they were made attractive and intelligible even to the novice. In my opinion there never has been a bird manual comparable to Coues' *Key*, the work of a great ornithologist and a master of the art of exposition.[109]

The book was so popular that Coues reported that the first printing of the second edition had been nearly exhausted only one year after it was printed.[110] As a result, third (1887) and fourth (1890) editions, with only minor revisions, soon followed. A further enlarged and revised fifth edition (1903) was published several years after Coues's death in December 1899.

In the same year as the third edition of Coues's *Key*, Ridgway published a rival bird identification manual.[111] In a letter to Baird requesting financial aid to complete the book in January 1886, Ridgway indicated that he had designed his manual so "the *merest tyro* could not fail to determine without question any species of North American bird, in any state of plumage."[112] The main difference between the Ridgway and Coues keys was that the former was based largely on the diagnostic characters of the species and genera—the particular attributes scientists used to construct their formal classifications—while Coues's volume was avowedly artificial, arranged solely for the convenience of its users. First published in 1887, Ridgway's *Manual* for the "sportsman and traveller as well at the naturalist" went into several subsequent editions.[113]

In 1891 two more influential collecting guides appeared. First was Ridgway's twenty-seven-page pamphlet, "Directions for Collecting Birds," distributed widely and without charge to Smithsonian correspondents.[114] Despite its compact size, the pamphlet was a serviceable alternative for those who were unwilling or unable to purchase Coues's more expensive *Key*. The same year, William T. Hornaday, former Ward's Natural Science Establishment employee and later chief taxidermist at the Smithsonian Institution, published *Taxidermy and Zoological Collecting*, a lengthy book that included an extensive section on bird preparation.[115] Hornaday's advice reflected the sense of urgency many collectors brought to the pursuit of specimens as the century came to a close:

> The rapid and alarming destruction of all forms of wild animal life which is now going on furiously throughout the entire world, renders it imperatively necessary for those who would build up great zoological collections to be up and doing before any more of the leading species are exterminated. It is already too late to collect wild specimens of the American bison, the California elephant seal, the West Indian seal, great auk, and Labrador duck. . . . Now is the time to collect. . . . [I]t is my firm belief that the time will come when the majority of vertebrate species now inhabiting the earth in a wild state will be either totally exterminated, or exist only under protection.[116]

For some individuals, like Hornaday, anxiety about extinction eventually led to a conversion from specimen collector to wildlife protector. However, most collectors seemed more intent on gathering the last examples of threatened species than on saving them.[117]

Most bird-collecting guides also made at least passing reference to eggs. Not until 1885, however, with the simultaneous appearance of the first editions of Oliver Davie's *Nests and Eggs of North American Birds* and Frank Lattin's *Oologists' Handbook*, were inexpensive books devoted entirely to American nests and eggs widely available.[118] Davie was a taxidermist and natural history dealer from Columbus, Ohio, whose identification and collecting guides enjoyed extensive sales.[119] In 1889, within months after the publication of the third edition of his nest and egg handbook, he reported that twenty-four hundred of three thousand copies originally printed had already been shipped.[120] Lattin's book was a small checklist of North American birds that included exchange values assigned to most species and a set of instructions for collecting, displaying, and exchanging eggs. Lattin, a dealer from Albion, New York, offered his book as a premium for those who subscribed to his periodical, *The Young Oologist* (later renamed simply *The Oologist*).[121] He also sold copies of compact checklists designed to be used by collectors to designate duplicates and desiderata for parties hoping to strike up an exchange.[122]

Advice on how to collect birds and eggs was also a prominent feature of the many natural history periodicals issued during the second half of the nineteenth century.[123] For example, Lattin's inaugural issue of *The Young Oologist* (published in 1884) included an article by the well-known egg collector, J. Parker Norris: "Instructions for Collecting Birds' Eggs."[124] Other authors in this and similar periodicals offered recommendations on the variety of subjects suggested by their titles: "Methods of Climbing for Nests," "Courtesy and Business in Exchanging," "Auxiliary Gun Barrels for Collecting Bird Specimens," "Arrangement of an Oological Collection," "Instructions for Collecting and Preserving Birds and Eggs," "About Collecting Chests," and "A Convenient Collecting Gun."[125] One well-known collector recommended hiding a disassembled gun in a newspaper to escape possible prosecution whenever collecting birds out of season or in areas where other protective laws were enforced.[126] Another suggested that egg collectors could obtain free use of climbing irons—tools used to scale trees—by inquiring at their local telegraph office.[127]

Many writers agreed that a collector received much more gratification from a "well arranged, labelled and reliable collection . . . procured entirely by the student and owner, than in a whole case . . . collected by unknown or remote persons."[128] Hard, honest work in the field resulted in not only a beautiful collection, a source of lasting pride for its owner, but also information and experience that could be gained in no other way: intimate knowledge of the habits and habitats of birds, relaxing recreation, healthy exercise, a fulfilling sense of accomplishment, and even the thrill of discovery.[129] Later in life Henry Henshaw fondly recalled the excitement of his early collecting experiences while tramping with Brewster in the Fresh Pond area of Cambridge, Massachusetts: "We were constantly spurred on by the feeling that we were treading the unknown, and that at any moment we might make a new discovery."[130]

Despite the widely touted benefits of personal collecting, few could resist the urge to expand their collections through purchase and exchange. In an 1888 article for the *Ornithologist and Oologist*, Walter Hoxie described how he gradually overcame his initial aversion to exchange as he quickly filled the gaps in his personal collection of North American birds.[131] The pervasiveness of printed checklists, guides that placed an exchange value on particular species, directories of collectors, exchange notices in periodicals, and published advice on the practice is testimony to the fundamental role that specimen exchange played in the culture of collecting.[132]

At the same time, exchange and purchase created a new set of problems for the collector interested in ascertaining the authenticity of specimens. Fraud was an ever-present possibility, and deception might take many forms. Extralimitals, birds found outside their usual range, were especially prized by collectors, and to raise the value of relatively common species, dealers and exchangers sometimes lied about the true geographic origin of a particular specimen.[133] Another common ploy was to falsely identify specimens and pawn them off on unsuspecting collectors.[134] It was difficult for all but the most knowledgeable ornithologist to recognize indistinct species and all the variations in plumage due to age, season, sex, and location. The practice of intentionally misidentifying specimens to increase their value became easier when scientists began to delineate subspecies, which were typically based on minute distinctions not discernible to the casual collector.[135]

For egg collectors, fraud was especially problematic and difficult to detect. Unlike skins, which carried their own identification with them, eggs could not be definitively identified without reference to the parent birds. Egg collecting manuals invariably recommended taking the parents whenever there was the slightest doubt about their identity, advice that was frequently ignored.[136] As a result, collectors receiving eggs were almost entirely at the mercy of the honesty and knowledge of the other party. Beyond lying about the identity or geographic origin of birds, which were problems even for skins, some unscrupulous individuals even tried painting their eggs to resemble rarer species.[137] Notices warning collectors of these and other fraudulent practices regularly appeared in natural history periodicals.[138]

In the last three decades of the nineteenth century, the wide availability of bird-collecting manuals, identification guides, and how-to articles in periodicals opened the world of ornithology to a growing number of collectors. By providing readily available information on procuring, preserving, and identifying birds, these publications helped decentralize the collecting networks that had previously been focused on the small number of expert naturalists. One result of this increasing independence was that collectors became more willing to challenge the authority of expert naturalists on whom they had once depended for even the most basic information on their favorite avocation. At the same time, the large natural history periodical press provided a public forum for airing the aspirations and concerns of collectors. The broader community of collectors soon came to criticize scientists on a variety of issues.

PERILOUS PURSUITS

Bird and egg collecting were not just strenuous activities; they presented real dangers to their practitioners. Injuries were common, and occasionally even deaths occurred. Many of these hazards were not specific to the activity of collecting. Bruises, broken bones, and insect bites were the occasional consequence of any form of outdoor activity. But the experience of wandering around the countryside with loaded weapons and climbing cliffs and trees exposed bird and egg collectors to unique perils.

Some of these dangers resulted from the unusual circumstances in which collectors sometimes found themselves. Throughout most of the middle decades of the nineteenth century, when the federal government was engaged in a brutal campaign to conquer Native Americans, frontier collectors often felt threatened just being alone in the wilderness. One particularly productive collector from this era, Charles E. Bendire, amassed an immense number of eggs while stationed at western outposts in the 1850s through the 1870s.[139] More than once Bendire found himself in tight situations out in the field. His closest call probably came in Arizona in the early 1870s.[140] After climbing a cottonwood tree in pursuit of zone-tailed hawk eggs, Bendire noticed several Apache Indians lingering on the horizon. Shaken at the possibility of being spotted in such a visible and vulnerable position, Bendire nonetheless maintained his composure. He carefully placed the prized egg in his mouth, shimmied down the tree, and quickly rode back to the fort. After prying apart his jaws to remove the large egg from his mouth, Bendire summoned the troops, who took off in pursuit of the Apaches.

Firearms presented dangers no matter where the collector ventured, and collecting guides invariably contained warnings about the need for extreme caution when carrying loaded guns.[141] Yet despite these warnings, injury from accidental discharge did occasionally occur. In 1895 John S. Cairns, a young collector from Weaverville, North Carolina, was killed when his gun went off unexpectedly while collecting in the Black Mountain area of the state.[142] More celebrated was the accidental death of Joseph H. Batty, a taxidermist and millinery dealer turned professional collector for the American Museum of Natural History.[143] During his three and one-half years in Latin America collecting for the AMNH, Batty had experienced a great deal of hardship, including drought, plague, and political revolution.[144] Despite these and other obstacles, however, he managed to send back over three thousand mammals and twice that many birds before his gun accidently fired, killing him instantly in 1906. In a revealing obituary Allen portrayed Batty as a martyr to science and endowed him with the attributes of the ideal collector: "a man of great physical endurance, courage, persistency, and enthusiasm."[145]

As a group, egg collectors seemed to fare worse than their skin-collecting colleagues. Nests built in the heights of trees and cliffs to thwart potential predators were also strong deterrents to all but the most hardy collectors. For example, in 1921 Richard C. Harlow, a prominent oologist and coach of the Penn State boxing team, narrowly escaped death while trying to collect highly desirable raven eggs in the Seven Mountains region of Pennsylvania.[146] Midway down a ninety-foot cliff, a rock dislodged and struck Harlow in the head. The blow stunned him, forcing him to loosen his grip on the rope. Somehow he managed to retain a partial hold while sliding rapidly down to the ground. After lying unconscious for a half hour, he stumbled to the nearest town with relatively minor injuries: one hand cut to the bone, the other badly seared, and a severely bruised head.

Other egg collectors were less fortunate. In 1913 thirty-three-year-old William B. Crispin of Salem, New Jersey, fell more than two hundred feet to his death while trying to collect the contents of a duck hawk's nest from the Nocka-minon Cliffs, a few miles up the Delaware River from Philadelphia.[147] He was not discovered until a day after the accident, when several young women collecting wildflowers stumbled across his body.

Francis J. Birtwell, a former student of the Bussey Institute and the Lawrence Scientific Schools at Harvard, was forced to leave for the drier environs of New Mexico after being diagnosed with tuberculosis.[148] Enrolling in the Territorial University, Birtwell began a study of New Mexico birds for his graduation thesis. One day in 1901, while collecting eggs from near the top of a sixty-five-foot pine in Willis, New Mexico, Birtwell panicked when gusting winds suddenly began to sway the tree. He called to his recent bride for help, and she quickly secured a rope and several young men to aid the shaken collector. But while he was being lowered by a rope thrown from below, a knot somehow became lodged in a fork of the tree, leaving Birtwell dangling thirty feet from the ground. In the process of trying to free himself, the rope slipped from under one of his arms and fastened firmly about his throat. Despite repeated attempts to save him, Birtwell soon ceased his desperate struggles. It was not until an hour later that his body was finally lowered to the ground.

The tragic death of John C. Cahoon, a well-known collector and dealer from Taunton, Massachusetts, elicited an unprecedented outpouring from the collecting community. At an early age "he became interested in birds and animals, guns, pistols, hunting and fishing."[149] In 1878 the fifteen-year-old Cahoon began collecting and mounting birds while serving as an apprentice in a local pharmacy. Over the next few years he devoted increasing time to his favorite pursuit, and by the early 1880s he had opened a small natural history business. For six months in 1887 he collected in Southern Arizona and Mexico for William Brewster.

After collecting in St. John's, Newfoundland, in 1889, Cahoon became the subject of a newspaper article that began with the headline "Daring Act of American Ornithologist at Birds Island. He Scales a Perpendicular Cliff Three Hundred Feet High. Shuddering Fishermen Lean on Their Oars and Witness the Dangerous Ascent." The article went on to describe Cahoon's exploits, stressing the calm demeanor of the brave young collector even when his life was clearly endangered: "With death staring him in the face, he was quite cool and collected, talking with the men below. He is a man of splendid nerve power."[150]

When collecting from nearby cliffs two years later, Cahoon was not so calm and composed. After lowering himself from the top of a two-hundred-foot cliff and gathering four eggs from the nest of a raven, Cahoon was in the process of making his ascent when he reached a point where the cliff was overhanging. With the weight of his body holding the rope tightly against the rocks, Cahoon struggled for twenty minutes in an attempt to continue upward. Exhausted, he then tried to lower himself to the shelf where the raven's nest rested. But with his strength sapped, Cahoon's descent became increasingly uncontrolled. Not until the following day were authorities able to retrieve his body from the blood-soaked waters at the base of the cliff. In the notice of his tragic death, the editor of the *Ornithologist and Oologist* lionized Cahoon as "A good boatman, a determined collector, a dead shot, of a kind and joyous disposition, honest brave and accommodating,—*a typical American collector.*"[151]

Women Ornithologists

One of the most striking features of the ornithological community in the second half of the nineteenth century is that it was almost entirely male. During this period, women occasionally became accepted, if marginal, members of the botanical and entomological collecting networks in the United States.[152] However, only one woman, Martha Maxwell of Colorado, is known to have done *any* bird collecting on her own during the entire nineteenth century.[153]

Tramping through the countryside in search of specimens ran against the grain of the prevailing ideology that bound middle-class women tightly to the domestic sphere.[154] As Nell Harrison, a female schoolteacher from York, Nebraska, complained in 1902, "Men can go freely into the fields and follow the birds everywhere, while fashion and conventionality debar women from the same privilege."[155] But bird and egg collecting also posed their own, more unique difficulties for women. First, ornithological collecting demanded proficiency with a gun, a skill that few women cultivated.[156] Second, collectors were required to take the lives of creatures that were often portrayed in anthropomorphic terms. Birds sang, performed courtship rituals, cared for their young, and exhibited other behaviors that were easy to characterize in humanlike terms. In particular, the nurturing qualities often associated with birds seems to have elicited special sympathy from women, who were expected to serve a similar role in the home. And finally, climbing trees and scaling cliffs were physically demanding and dangerous activities even for male collectors.

Beyond Maxwell, there were a few other women who made a limited entry into the nineteenth-century ornithological community predominantly focused on collecting. Graceanna Lewis was John Cassin's "one and only student" at the Academy of Natural Sciences in Philadelphia from 1862 until his death in 1869.[157] Both were Quakers with egalitarian leanings: Lewis once remarked of Cassin, "[H]e never seemed to think it strange that a woman should wish to study."[158] Although never known to have collected, with Cassin's careful guidance and access to the unrivaled academy collection, Lewis became an accomplished and widely recognized systematist: she discovered a new species among the birds at the academy, published several articles, offered public lectures on ornithology, and had her papers presented before scientific societies. In addition, she issued the first installment of a projected ten-part *Natural History of Birds* in 1868. Whether due to the failure to obtain the necessary subscribers or the death of her supportive mentor and close friend Cassin in 1869, Lewis failed to complete the work.

The women responsible for the publication of *Illustrations of the Nests and Eggs of Birds of Ohio* had better luck bringing their ambitious project to fruition. In July 1879 Genevieve Estelle Jones and Eliza J. Schultze issued their first three hand-colored, life-size plates to immediate critical acclaim (fig. 8). In his reviews of this and subsequent installments, Elliott Coues frequently compared the exquisitely executed lithographs to the work of Audubon.[159] But after completing a few additional plates, the thirty-two-year-old Genevieve succumbed to typhoid

Figure 8. Plate of the field sparrow's nest and eggs, from Jones and Jones, *Illustrations of the Nest and Eggs of the Birds of Ohio* (1886). Although highly praised at the time of publication, the work soon fell into obscurity.

fever.[160] Eliza Schultze continued to draw the plates, while Genevieve's mother, Virginia (Smith) Jones, stepped in to color them. In 1880 Schultze withdrew from the project entirely. Virginia Jones completed the remaining plates, and two local women were hired to do most of the coloring. All of those involved with the project were proud that the drawings were based on freshly collected material, but it was Genevieve's brother, the physician Howard Jones, not the women, who gathered the specimens upon which the illustrations were based. He also wrote the text for the book.[161]

When women were involved with bird collecting, it was usually behind the scenes, as (often unacknowledged) helpmates for their husband collectors. For example, in the spring of 1898, Frank Chapman spent his honeymoon in familiar collecting grounds in the Indian River region of Florida. Following a successful search for the then-rare (and now extinct) dusky seaside sparrow, Chapman's recent bride, Fannie Bates Embury, decided to try her hand at bird-skinning. Much to Chapman's "astonishment, joy, and chagrin," she almost immediately mastered the art.[162] Fannie Chapman then suggested that her husband mount an expedition to a nearby island containing a breeding colony of pelicans. Aware of the special difficulty of preparing the oily skinned, oddly shaped birds, Chapman reluctantly agreed. Fannie Chapman handled the difficult task admirably, and the specimens eventually became part of a large habitat group at the American Museum of Natural History. From that point on, she regularly served as Chapman's assistant on expeditions.

Except for the case of women, the ornithological community remained relatively open throughout much of the second half of the nineteenth century. A shared interest in specimens united the scientists, sport hunters, collectors, dealers, and others who comprised that extended and diverse community. As the nineteenth century came to a close, however, many factors converged to divide that community. The next several chapters show how a series of institutional, intellectual and social transformations created a wedge between the more technically oriented ornithologists and other bird enthusiasts.

CHAPTER THREE

Forging Boundaries, Creating
Occupational Space

THE GATHERING

On the morning of 26 September 1883 nearly two dozen of the nation's leading ornithologists gathered in the library of the American Museum of Natural History. They ventured to New York from as far away as Oregon, Louisiana, and Canada in response to an urgent call that J. A. Allen, Elliott Coues, and William Brewster had issued two months previously. A sense of anticipation filled the room as Brewster stepped up to the podium and called to order the inaugural meeting of the American Ornithologists' Union.[1] Over the next three days members of the fledgling organization adopted a constitution and set of bylaws, elected officers, appointed committees, voted in new members, and resolved to initiate a periodical. The official report of the proceedings commented favorably on the "utmost harmony" that had prevailed throughout the deliberations and predicted that the founding of the AOU would "mark an important era in the progress of ornithology in America."[2]

Though with a different cast of characters, during this period a similar scene was repeatedly played out in meeting halls across the United States. As American science matured and diversified in the decades surrounding the turn of the century, its practitioners increasingly sought to organize themselves into specialized national societies. A desire to promote research, acknowledge scientific achievement, and define the boundaries of emerging disciplines and professions played an important role in the creation of many of these new societies.[3] For some organizations, like the American Society of Zoologists created in 1889, the attempt to further that set of agendas translated into a restrictive membership policy effectively excluding not only most amateur practitioners, but even those with paid positions in museums, governmental agencies, and other nonacademic institutions.[4] Other national disciplinary societies, like the American Chemical Society established in 1876, adopted a more inclusive strategy that united a broad spectrum of enthusiasts.[5]

The founders of the AOU decided to pursue a middle course between these extremes. Even the most ardent scientific ornithologists recognized the crucial role that collectors, hunters, dealers, taxidermists, and others continued to play in their field. Perhaps more importantly, most scientific ornithologists also conceded that a large membership base was essential to support the ambitious periodical the AOU hoped to publish. While anxious to maintain their authority, control the direction of research, and fulfill their disciplinary and professional aspirations, they were not yet ready to bar the larger ornithological community entirely from their doors. The founders of the AOU attempted to resolve their dilemma by establishing a two-tiered membership structure—composed of a few "active members," predominantly scientific ornithologists who effectively controlled the organization, and a much larger number of "associate members," who provided much of the income upon which it depended to survive. Through this hierarchical membership strategy AOU leaders sought to achieve the best of both worlds.

Despite reports of accord at the founding meeting, the AOU soon found itself embroiled in a series of controversies and struggles. In the face of opposition both in the United States and abroad, the union fought to maintain the taxonomic focus of American ornithology and to establish a single, authoritative system of scientific nomenclature for North American birds.[6] At the same time the organization strove to brighten the dismal employment prospects within the field of ornithology. And when one of its most prominent members became involved in a public scandal involving the granddaughter of John James Audubon, the AOU was also forced to grapple with the issue of how to deal with the extra-scientific activities of the ornithologists affiliated with it. The most recurrent controversy in the new organization, however, involved the two-tiered membership structure adopted at the founding meeting.

Not surprisingly, many of those excluded from active membership—the seat of power and authority in the AOU—resented it. Critics repeatedly charged that the society was elitist and that associate members were being asked to support an organization in which they were denied a real voice. Eventually, as the volume of complaint continued to mount, AOU leaders responded with a series of reforms. However, they managed to keep the basic hierarchical structure of the organization intact.

For much of the second half of the nineteenth century the ornithological community remained heterogeneous and inclusive. These once permeable boundaries began to solidify with the creation of the AOU. At a time when there were few professional positions and no advanced degrees in the field, active membership in the AOU provided an important means of certifying an individual's scientific accomplishment. It was what one AOU leader later called the "equivalent to the granting of a degree in ornithology."[7] But even as they successfully defended their right to differentiate themselves from the larger ornithological community, AOU leaders sought to strike a balance between the need to establish their authority and autonomy and their desire to maintain the goodwill, specimens, observations, and funds provided by that larger community.

THE NUTTALL CLUB

The first ornithological society in the United States was created in the early 1870s when several young bird enthusiasts from Cambridge, Massachusetts—William Brewster, Ruthven Deane, and Henry W. Henshaw—began gathering regularly to share their collecting exploits and pore over Audubon's *Birds of America*.[8]

Gradually others with a similar interest joined the weekly climb up the steep steps to Brewster's attic, including Henry A. Purdie, a Boston businessman in his early thirties who was ten years older, but no less enthusiastic, than his fellow collectors, and W. E. D. Scott, who had recently enrolled in the Lawrence Scientific School at Harvard.

After two years of informal meetings, in November 1873 the group decided to found the Nuttall Ornithological Club and invited four additional members to join. Named after Thomas Nuttall, the well-known British naturalist who was a lecturer in natural history at Harvard in the early nineteenth century and author of a popular *Manual of the Ornithology of the U.S. and Canada* (1832, 1834), the new organization elected a slate of officers, adopted a constitution, and drew up a set of bylaws.[9] The formal requirements for membership were straightforward and minimal. Resident members were to be elected from "persons living in the vicinity of Cambridge" who were "specially interested in ornithology," while corresponding members were to be elected from "persons residing at a distance."[10] From the beginning the organization attracted individuals with varying levels of expertise and from differing social, occupational, and educational backgrounds. The one prominent exception to the generally inclusive membership policy was women, who were barred from resident membership in the Nuttall Club for the next century.[11] A common interest in collecting and studying North American birds united the youthful but otherwise diverse group of wealthy gentlemen, businessmen, taxidermists, natural history dealers, and students at Harvard College and the Lawrence Scientific School who joined the organization.

Nuttall Club leaders soon encountered difficulty maintaining interest in the new venture, and by the autumn of 1875 they were debating whether "the N.O.C. should live or die."[12] They eventually decided to rejuvenate the lethargic society through a vigorous membership drive and the publication of a quarterly journal. C. J. Maynard, a taxidermist and natural history dealer with extensive publishing experience, and founding member Henry Purdie were elected joint editors of the new enterprise.[13] The two proudly placed the twenty-eight-page inaugural issue of the *Bulletin of the Nuttall Ornithological Club* before the membership early in May 1876.

Problems with the publication arose immediately. Sorting out the details from surviving records is difficult.[14] What is clear is that in late May 1876, J. A. Allen, who had become a resident member only one month earlier, gained election as an associate editor and then editor-in-chief of the *Bulletin*. Allen then arranged for several prominent ornithologists and Nuttall Club corresponding members—Elliott Coues, George N. Lawrence, and Spencer F. Baird—to be named associate editors.[15] Maynard was furious at what he viewed as a coup and soon severed all connections with the organization.[16] For the next seven years, reviewing potential papers, editing proofs, procuring subscribers, addressing labels, and other activities associated with keeping the periodical afloat provided a central focus for the Nuttall Club.[17]

Another incident two years after Allen began editing the *Bulletin* also engendered controversy and threatened the authority of the young organization. The episode began at an unusually well-attended meeting on 28 January 1878, which was devoted to the "sparrow question," an issue then raging in the local and national press. Beginning in the early 1850s, urban residents in the United States had imported and released thousands of English sparrows (*Passer domesticus*) in an attempt to establish the common European species on their side of the Atlantic. Importers valued the bird not only as a tangible reminder of the Old World fauna for which many immigrants yearned, but also as a likely predator of noxious insect larvae.[18] Unlike most native birds, English sparrows seemed to thrive in the bustling, burgeoning cities. The species quickly expanded beyond the initial points of introduction as a stowaway on grain shipments carried on the extensive railroad network that connected American cities.[19]

By the 1870s the initial optimism surrounding sparrow introduction was clearly on the wane. Some observers began to express concern that the "pugnacious, irascible, irritable creatures" were devouring more grain than insects, while driving out native species.[20] As these negative reports came to light, critics spoke against new sparrow introductions and promoted eradication programs to reduce existing populations.

The two major protagonists in the "sparrow wars" were both prominent ornithologists. Army surgeon Elliott Coues, the most vocal and persistent critic of the bird, represented the views of most ornithologists. His primary opponent was Thomas M. Brewer, the physician, publisher, and author who had been an early advocate of sparrow introduction in Boston and one of the few ornithologists to remain a staunch supporter of the much maligned bird. Coues and Brewer skirmished over the issue in print several times before meeting together in Washington early in January 1878. According to Coues, during that meeting he suggested that the Nuttall Club, to which both men belonged, debate the question and issue an official ruling.[21]

The club's sparrow meeting itself turned out to be uneventful. Seventeen of the twenty-three resident members attended, and all uniformly condemned the feathered intruder. Among those who joined the chorus of criticism were not only more experienced members, like Brewster, Purdie, Allen, and Deane, but also several new additions, including Theodore Roosevelt, a Harvard sophomore who had joined only a few months earlier, and Henry D. Minot, a Harvard freshman and close friend of Roosevelt.[22] Noticeably absent was the sparrow's most vocal champion, Brewer, who turned down an invitation to attend.[23] Abstracts of the proceedings were widely reprinted in local newspapers and at least one national periodical.[24]

The Nuttall Club's condemnation of the sparrow provoked a strong reaction in the local press. Several anonymous editorials ridiculed the organization as a body of "Cambridge juveniles" and "precocious boys" entirely unqualified to speak with authority on the issue in question.[25] Allen and other Nuttall leaders initially decided not to respond and thereby draw further attention to the embarrassing attacks. Although Brewer repeatedly denied the charge, most members suspected that he was responsible for the traitorous outbursts.[26] The final straw came in yet another anonymous editorial in the Boston *Journal* that referred to the Nuttall

Club as an "association of overmodest young gentlemen, comprising lads fitting for college and undergraduates, with a sprinkling of others a few years their seniors" who boldly "undertook to settle 'the sparrow question' for the entire nation."[27] As Allen wrote to Nuttall President Brewster, the abusive editorial was "too much for me & I could keep silent no longer."[28]

Allen fired off letters to several Boston papers in an attempt to repair the Nuttall Club's tarnished reputation. He pointed out that the organization was an "association of persons interested in the study of ornithology," whose membership was really "national in character, every publishing ornithologist in the United States being identified with it." Even sparrow proponent Thomas M. Brewer was a resident member. While it was true that there were many young undergraduate members, there were also several Harvard graduates and "officers connected with scientific departments" at that distinguished institution. Allen concluded by claiming that the recent reports of the sparrow meeting in Boston papers were "unfair," "misleading," and riddled with "gross misstatements."[29] Brewster also publicly defended the group before the issue gradually faded from the Boston papers.[30]

A series of events during the next five years proved an even greater threat to the organization. Failure to attract a quorum (five members) at several meetings in 1879 led to the abandonment of the ambitious weekly meeting schedule. In the hope of achieving greater participation at each meeting, members voted to amend the bylaws to make the regular meeting times on the first and third Monday evenings of each month between 1 October and 15 June. Counteracting this change, though, was a drop in resident membership from a high of twenty-five in 1878 to seventeen by 1880.[31] The young men who comprised the bulk of the club's membership had graduated or gone off to make their way in the world without attracting replacements. The decrease in attendance at the meetings became precipitous by the fall of 1882. In October of that year and January of the next, scheduled meetings were canceled for "want of quorum." Following a single meeting in February 1883, no meetings were called until June, at which only five members were present. Clearly the organization was floundering.

CREATING THE AOU

The apathy that had gripped the Nuttall Ornithological Club was one of several factors that precipitated plans to organize American ornithologists on a national level. Brewster, a moving force behind the Nuttall Club, was especially discouraged at the continued inability to attract a quorum at meetings. In a letter of 10 February 1883, he voiced his growing frustration and hinted at a drastic solution he had recently been contemplating:

> The home [resident] members, with the exception of Purdie and Allen, don't seem to care a hang whether the Club and its organ live or die. We had our third blank meeting last Monday; only four members present. I often feel tempted to go to work on a plan I have had in mind for some time, one which includes the dissolution of the Club and the

organization of a new association which shall consist only of persons who care enough about ornithology to do their share of the work. . . . An American Ornithologists' Union, limited to, say, twelve members, could, I think, be made up in such a way as to be a very strong institution.[32]

Meanwhile, a second development suggested the need for a truly national ornithological society. The recent publication of two widely adopted and often contradictory lists of North American birds—by Robert Ridgway in 1880 and Elliott Coues in 1882—engendered increasing nomenclatural chaos that threatened to rend the American ornithological community into two opposing camps.[33] Since both lists commanded loyal followings and neither author was willing to concede to the other, some kind of compromise was needed to break the impasse.

A hint at one possible solution to the dilemma came in the January 1883 issue of the *Bulletin of the Nuttall Ornithological Club.* In a typically clever and whimsical piece, Coues indicated that several birds had recently visited him and offered their congratulations at the completion of seven volumes of the *Bulletin.* One of his feathered visitors, a sagacious hawk owl, then brought up the subject of "late catalogues and nomenclators of North American Birds" and suggested "calling a Congress of American Ornithologists to discuss, vote upon, and decide each case in which the doctors disagreed . . . the congressmen to bind themselves to the decision of the majority. The plan seemed to him . . . the only way to secure the greatly desired uniformity of nomenclature."[34]

Shortly after this publication appeared, Coues, Allen, and Brewster began preliminary discussions about organizing a national society of ornithologists. Those tentative talks quickly turned more serious when the editor of a western paper responded to Coues's hint in the January *Bulletin* with his own call for a national association. Coues feared that the idea was now "in the air," and that he, Brewster, and Allen should be prepared to act quickly to keep the organization under their control: "There is no knowing how soon we may need to move with silence, sagacity and celerity to shape it as we want it. It *must not* be taken away from Cambridge, nor out of our hands. . . . We have got to be alive, and shoot the thing on the wing, or it will fly by into some other game-bag."[35]

In a series of exchanges over the next several months, Coues, Brewster, and Allen hashed out the details for the inaugural meeting and basic structure of the AOU. The question of how best to announce the meeting was one of the first and most crucial. Initially Coues favored publication of an open invitation in the July issue of the *Bulletin of the Nuttall Ornithological Club.*[36] By early June, Allen and Brewster had convinced him that private invitations mailed to a select few were preferable to keep out "aspirants for unearned glory," to give the call "a social and personal weight which no promiscuous publication could," and "to make it something of an honor to be a member."[37] As a compromise, Coues suggested a published notice in the July *Bulletin* announcing that invitations had been (or would be soon) issued. This would provide "all the desirable publicity *to the movement,* and yet keep the call itself as privately in hand as we think proper."[38]

The next problem was deciding who to invite. Coues, Brewster, and Allen used several criteria to generate the final invitation list of forty-eight names. From early in the process, all three founders agreed on a policy of "keeping active membership small and select . . . to make it something of an honor and to keep it working smoothly." Coues suggested they formulate "some definite theory of who are eligible and who are not" to head off criticism of the final invitation list and to reduce the temptation to increase its size to maximize income for the young organization. He also proposed publication of "recognized works of good repute" as "theoretical gauge" for determining whether to issue an invitation to a particular individual.[39]

Although the AOU was ostensibly a scientific organization, scientific reputation was only one of several factors that had a bearing on whether an individual received an invitation to its founding meeting. Coues argued that to avoid the "slightest appearance of cliquism or sectionalism" the invitations should be "as catholic as possible, *geographically speaking.* The western names are well, for this if for no other reason." Besides, those at a great distance were unlikely to make the lengthy trip to New York anyway.[40] He also thought it appropriate to include the well-to-do who might lend prestige and funds to the organization. For example, Coues suggested invitations be sent to George B. Sennett, "a first rate fellow, moneyed, who would be pleased I am sure"; to Henry D. Minot, who had good "relations"; and to George Bird Grinnell, the wealthy editor of *Forest and Stream.*[41]

By early August plans were sufficiently advanced to justify issuing a formal call for the organizational meeting of the AOU. According to the printed invitation, the purpose of the society was the "promotion of social and scientific intercourse between American ornithologists" and "the advancement of Ornithology in North America."[42] Beyond these broad goals, a "special object" was the adoption of a "uniform system of classification and nomenclature, based on the views of the majority of the Union, and carrying the authority of the Union." Allen, Coues, and Brewster signed the invitation and appended their affiliation with the Nuttall Ornithological Club to each of their respective names.

Twenty-three ornithologists attended the three-day organizational meeting of the AOU convened at the American Museum of Natural History in New York on 26 September 1883.[43] Neither Baird, who had previously sent his regrets, nor Allen, who was ill, could make the trip. However, both gave their blessings to the fledgling organization, and, like all those in attendance at the inaugural meeting, both were declared founding members.[44] With a detailed agenda in hand, Brewster called the first session to order, only to be upstaged when his cofounder Coues was elected acting chair.[45] After that rocky start, things went pretty much as planned. Following a lengthy discussion the assembled ornithologists passed Allen, Coues, and Brewster's provisional constitution and bylaws. These documents created four classes of membership: active (limited to fifty), foreign (non-U.S. or Canadian, limited to twenty-five), corresponding (U.S., Canadian, and foreign, limited to one hundred), and associate (U.S. and Canadian, unlimited in number).[46] Of these four classes, only active members could vote, hold office, and nominate new members. But even they were not complete equals. The true seat of power of the union was its council, initially composed of the president, two vice-presidents, a secretary-treasurer, and five elected councilors.

On the second day of the meeting, acting chair Coues created six committees and appointed members for each.[47] At the time of the meeting, systematics formed the core activity of scientific ornithology, and discrepancies between the two competing lists of North American birds had been a major reason for founding the AOU. As a result, the Committee on the Classification and Nomenclature of North American Birds was the most active, influential, and enduring committee in the organization. As one indication of its importance, all three founders, along with Ridgway and Henshaw, served on the initial nomenclature committee.

Coues also appointed five other, shorter-lived committees at the first AOU meeting. Thirteen members joined the Committee on Migration of Birds, chaired by C. Hart Merriam. Several AOU members also agreed to serve on a committee charged with considering the subject of "Faunal Areas." Under Merriam's leadership these two committees were soon merged during a campaign to expand professional opportunity in and obtain government patronage for ornithology. Two minor committees, on Avian Anatomy and Oology, soon disbanded due to inactivity. The final committee, on the "eligibility or ineligibility of the European House Sparrow in America," met for two years before issuing a brief final report condemning efforts to introduce the bird in the United States.[48]

As Coues had urged from the earliest deliberations, the most important step in the formation of the AOU was securing a suitable publication.[49] The three founders decided to keep the issue under wraps at the organizational meeting, lest it slip from their control. Rather, as was to be typical of most important issues for the new society, the publication issue was raised in a council meeting on the evening of 28 September 1883. There Brewster claimed that as president of the Nuttall Ornithological Club "he was authorized to say, though he could not do so officially," that the club was willing to offer the "prestige and subscription list" of its publication to the union if the resulting publication was presented to the public as a second series of the *Bulletin*. The council accepted Brewster's curiously "authorized" but "unofficial" offer and voted to begin publication of the AOU journal under Allen's editorship in January 1884.[50] At a special meeting held in December, the council named the new periodical *The Auk*.[51] The name, like that of the union itself, was modeled on the British Ornithologists' Union, whose publication was entitled *The Ibis*.[52] The council also appointed four associate editors: Coues, Ridgway, Brewster, and Montague Chamberlain, a bookkeeper and later partner in a large wholesale grocery firm in St. John, New Brunswick.[53]

Thus within several months of its inaugural meeting, the AOU assumed the basic structure it would maintain for the next fifty years. Unlike its predecessor, the relatively heterogeneous and egalitarian Nuttall Ornithological Club, it was to be a strongly hierarchical organization controlled by a few "active" members. While the organization struggled to deal with this potentially divisive issue, it also sought to take other measures to consolidate the discipline of ornithology and expand professional space in the field. As AOU leaders grappled with these and other challenges, they tried to strike a balance between their desire to erect clear boundaries between themselves and the larger ornithological community and their need to maintain continued contact with the group upon which they depended for specimens, funds, legitimacy, and a supply of future ornithologists.

"AMATEURS" AND THE AOU

The public announcement that invitations to the founding meeting were in the mail led to widespread confusion and complaint.[54] When a furious Joseph M. Wade, the editor and owner of the *Ornithologist and Oologist* (fig. 9), protested to Merriam about not being invited to the AOU organizational meeting, Merriam fired off a letter to Brewster.[55] According to Merriam, Wade learned of the initiative through the notice in *Forest and Stream* and regarded his failure to receive a personal invitation as "a direct *snub*."[56] Most apparently assumed, as Merriam had, that "amateurs would make up the bulk of the members" in the new society.[57]

Unlike most of those who failed to receive an invitation or gain election to active membership in the new society, Wade possessed the means to respond publicly. In a sarcastic editorial written for the November 1883 issue of the *Ornithologist and Oologist*, Wade attacked the new organization and its predecessor, the Nuttall Ornithological Club. According to Wade, the Nuttall Club had been "too much of the Pharisee order" in ignoring the more humble collector, "'the bone and sinew' of our beautiful science." To add insult to injury, the organization had long claimed that its *Bulletin* was the "only" ornithological periodical in the country when it had not begun publication until a full year after the *Oologist*, the predecessor of Wade's *Ornithologist and Oologist*. But it was the invitation-only inaugural gathering of the AOU that was the main object of Wade's ire: "A meeting of the most exclusive kind has been recently held in New York. And this convention of scientists have named their new society 'The American Ornithological [*sic*] Union.' The mistake is, it is not American, and it is formed too much on the principle of our city social clubs where each member carries a Yale key. It won't work in science, gentlemen; all nature belongs to all men."[58]

Wade continued by ridiculing scientific ornithologists' preoccupation with nomenclatural issues: "You sadly mistake the importance of the mission. It matters little what you call him, the Blue Jay screams just as loud for rich and poor, for boy and man alike. It is a mystery to us why the names of our birds should be such a bone of contention. It always reminds us of a lawyer discovering during a trial a nice point of law and forgetting that he has a client to look after."[59] He then ran through a list of members of the new organization, providing commentary on who had and had not been invited to the founding meeting. Among those unjustly excluded were "the editor of this paper" and the taxidermist, dealer, and author C. J. Maynard, who was "studying bird life when many of the present members [of the AOU] were toddling around in petticoats."

For reasons that remain unclear, Wade's outburst never saw the light of day. John Hall Sage, who was elected an active AOU member at the first meeting and

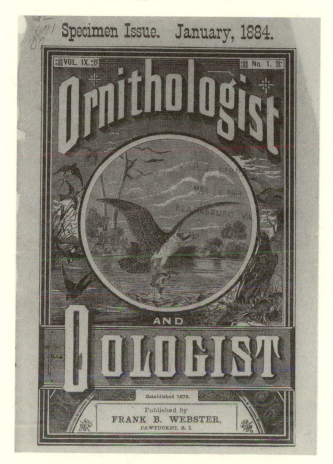

Figure 9. Cover of the *Ornithologist and Oologist*, 1884.
Until its demise in 1893, the collecting-oriented *O and O*
provided a forum for regular criticism of the AOU and
scientific ornithology more generally.

later served as secretary of the organization for nearly three decades, learned of
the attack before its actual publication. Somehow he convinced Wade to suppress
it. Wade delayed mailing the November issue of the *Ornithologist and Oologist*
to give him time to replace his editorial with a more benign article.[60]

Despite his decision not to publish his caustic editorial, Wade remained at
odds with the newly founded organization. In a letter written after the first meeting, Chamberlain informed Brewster of rumors that several of those excluded
from the original AOU were "preparing for the war path" against the new organization. According to Chamberlain, "Maynard or Minot, or perhaps the pair in a
team with Wade," intended to start a new periodical "in opposition to the
A.O.U.," a periodical that would likely be a "continuation of the O[rnithologist]
and O[ologist]."[61]

Brewster passed Chamberlain's letter on to J. A. Allen with the suggestion that its author be named an associate editor of the yet unnamed AOU publication. According to Brewster, Chamberlain was a "staunch, high minded gentleman of unusual ability and intelligence" who had the potential to develop into a "wise and effective sub-leader." He would surely prove a valuable ally in the event that the movement against the AOU continued to grow: "If there is going to be a fight we cannot be too strong."[62]

In his next letter, Chamberlain announced that he had been "harmonizing away at Wade and Maynard," trying to convince "the soreheads" that the AOU was only desirous of doing what was best for itself and "ornithology at large." Chamberlain also revealed he had "made Wade a straight offer for the O & O" and that he would "outbid the others to keep them from making it an anti-Union organ," but he was pessimistic regarding his chances for success.[63] Within three weeks Chamberlain was writing to Brewster that "I entirely concur in your opinion that it is both useless and unnecessary to make any further efforts at conciliating the 'soreheads'—we may have to fight. . . . They made no small effort at raising discord in the ranks of the A.O.U. & will keep on at it—and will not stop trying unless they are gagged."[64]

AOU founders attempted to incorporate the larger ornithological constituency of taxidermists, dealers, and collectors—which they had barred from active membership in the new society—into a second tier of associate members. The AOU Council presented its first nominating list of associate members on the third day of the inaugural meeting. According to Merriam, the secretary-treasurer of the union, the final list of eighty candidates had been selected "with great care" from among three hundred proposed names. Those singled out represented "a most important—indeed, vital—element, consisting as they do of the *amateur* working ornithologists of North America, the men from among whom future candidates for Active Membership must be selected."[65] Since only a handful of the active members of the AOU actually made a living through the practice of ornithology, clearly Merriam was using the term "amateur" to denote a level of commitment to and/or expertise in scientific ornithology, not as a statement about occupational status. Among the initial list of associate members was a broad spectrum of bird enthusiasts, including the nature writers John Burroughs and Bradford Torrey; the dealer-taxidermists Manly Hardy, Fred T. Jencks, and C. J. Maynard; and the magazine publisher Joseph M. Wade.[66]

The night after the election of the first slate of associate members, the AOU Council met to firm up plans for its proposed publication. The question of how to allow for the interests of the large number of "amateurs" again arose. During the proceedings, Merriam and Chamberlain consistently advocated the need to recognize

the existence, power and importance of the large amateur element in American Ornithological Science[,] for this element comprises the great bulk of working field collectors and observers throughout the land. These enthusiastic field naturalists are the men who gather the greater part of the material, in the way of specimens and facts, upon examination and exploration of which the progress of Ornithology in this country largely depends.[67]

Both ornithologists suggested that the "younger and less experienced portion of this class" required "an organ less technical in character than the Ibis, or even the Bulletin of the Nuttall Club." Council members then discussed whether the AOU could best serve this need by establishing a separate "amateur publication" or "an amateur department" in its regular serial publication. In the end the council left the decision to J. A. Allen, the newly elected editor of the *Auk*, in consultation with his panel of associate editors.

Their decision to aim the new periodical toward a more technically oriented audience remained one of several sources of tension between the smaller group of scientific ornithologists who created and controlled the AOU and the much larger group of associate members who provided the income needed to keep the organization and its periodical afloat. Although Allen included a more popular "Notes and News" section in the *Auk*, in part to cultivate a wider interest in the new journal, associate members repeatedly complained about being asked to support a periodical that was largely beyond their grasp.[68] Before the end of the first year of publication, Chamberlain was complaining to Merriam, "What are we to do with *The Auk*? It is not meeting the demand of the bulk of the students of ornithology—it is heavy with technicalities—devotes too much space to the science of bird skins and bird names and too little to bird[']s lives."[69]

Forging a Profession I

Through its two-tiered membership policy, the AOU sought to differentiate between the more dedicated, capable, and technically oriented scientific ornithologist and the much larger community of variously motivated bird enthusiasts. At the same time, the emerging organization sought to expand the limited employment opportunities in the field of ornithology. Historian Marianne G. Ainley has recently noted that when the AOU was founded in 1883, only five of the organization's twenty-five original members—Allen, Baird, Coues, Henshaw, and Ridgway—made a living from the practice of science. Only two of these five—Allen and Ridgway—were employed primarily as ornithologists.[70]

The first major campaign to carve out professional space in ornithology was an outgrowth of the Committee on Migration of Birds. The chair of the committee, C. Hart Merriam, was one of the few AOU founders with any formal training in natural history.[71] Raised on a farm in rural Locust Grove, New York, where his father had retired from a successful brokerage and banking career at a young age, Merriam had ample opportunity to pursue his interest in collecting birds and mammals. His parents encouraged his interest, and when Merriam's father was elected to Congress in 1871, he took his sixteen-year-old son to Washington to meet Spencer F. Baird at the Smithsonian Institution. Impressed by the promise exhibited in Merriam's bird and mammal skins, Baird suggested that the boy take taxidermy lessons to refine his techniques. Merriam spent the next several months at John Wallace's taxidermy establishment in New York City before Baird arranged for him to accompany Ferdinand Hayden's expedition into northwestern Wyoming in the spring of 1872.[72] In the fall of 1873 Merriam enrolled in Williston Seminary, Easthampton, Massachusetts, to prepare himself for the entrance examinations at Yale's Sheffield Scientific School. Following a year at Williston Seminary and three years at Yale, Merriam entered the College of Physicians and Surgeons in New York. While in medical school he roomed with two of his fellow students, A. K. Fisher and Edgar A. Mearns, who were also naturalists and later founding members of the AOU. After Merriam received his M.D. degree in 1879, he returned home to Locust Grove to begin a successful medical practice.[73]

Like many other physicians, Merriam found that his rural medical practice allowed him ample opportunity to pursue his interest in natural history.[74] During the next several years he managed to establish a reputation as one of the most accomplished ornithologists and mammalogists in the United States. One measure of his standing among his colleagues was his election as secretary-treasurer of the AOU at its founding meeting in 1883.[75]

Merriam also became the first chair of the AOU Committee on Migration, a duty he undertook with characteristic intensity. He immediately prepared a four-page circular that detailed the proposed work of the committee and provided instructions for potential "collaborators."[76] The goal of the ambitious study was not only to discover the average dates of arrival at and departure from various locations for several common and easily recognizable migratory species, but also to collect data to learn "the causes which influence the progress of migration from season to season."[77] Merriam sought the active "co-operation of every ornithologist, field-collector, sportsman, and observer of nature in North America" for the project. He made it clear that he considered a "large corps of observers" as "absolutely essential to the success of the undertaking."[78]

Merriam requested each of his volunteer observers to prepare a list of the birds found in their area, to indicate whether those species were permanent residents or migrants, to estimate their relative abundance, and to provide dates of the first appearance, arrival and departure of the bulk, and departure of last individual specimen seen for each migratory species. This information, along with observations of a series of meteorological and "correlative" phenomena (e.g., the date of flowering of various plants), was to be forwarded to one of thirteen district supervisors, who in turn was to pass it on to Merriam. The chair was then to "arrange, condense, and systematize" the data and present it to the union with his "comments, deductions or generalizations." In short, the basic structure of the committee was similar to the collecting networks that had long been characteristic of ornithological research in the United States.

To secure as many observers as possible, Merriam mailed his bird migration circular to eight hundred newspapers across the country. As a result of the publicity generated, some three thousand individuals requested additional information on the venture, and nearly seven hundred volunteers actually turned in observations to their district superintendents by the end of the first year. In addition, Merriam distributed twelve hundred sets of schedules and circulars to lighthouse keepers in the United States and Canada, from whom he received nearly three hundred additional returns. In his annual report to the AOU in 1884, Merriam indicated that the number of returns was so "exceedingly voluminous" that it was "utterly impossible to elaborate on them without considerable pecuniary aid."[79]

It is not clear exactly when Merriam first thought of approaching the federal government to provide that aid. The general idea of government support for scientific research certainly was not new to him: he had served as a naturalist on the federally funded Hayden Survey as a teenager and several years later had tried (unsuccessfully) to get state officials to sponsor an ornithological survey of New York.[80] But Merriam's decision to seek federal support for the AOU migration committee's work most likely was the immediate result of a recent meeting of the First International Ornithological Congress in Vienna, which he had attended the preceding April. At its inaugural meeting the International Congress had created a Committee on Migration of Birds, which requested delegates from each of the participating countries to appeal for governmental support to organize and maintain "migration stations" and to "publish annual reports of the observations made."[81]

At Merriam's urging, members attending the annual AOU meeting in 1884 passed a motion authorizing the council to petition the U.S. Congress and the Parliament of Canada "in behalf of the Committee on Migration."[82] N. S. Goss, an active member from Kansas, then convinced the AOU to merge the Committee on Bird Migration with the Committee on Geographical Distribution of Species (originally named the Committee on Faunal Areas).[83] At a special meeting later that evening, the AOU Council voted to ask Congress to create a Division of Economic Ornithology within the Department of Agriculture and appointed Merriam to draw up a suitable document relaying that request.[84]

In proposing a federal Division of Economic Ornithology, the AOU was hoping to gain federal support for a nearly three-decade-long research tradition in applied ornithology.[85] Beginning in the 1850s a number of American ornithologists had begun systematic investigation into the food habits of birds in an effort to delineate their relationship to agricultural production. Based on field observations and an analysis of the stomach contents of the species under investigation, economic ornithologists categorized birds as beneficial, and thereby deserving of special protection, or injurious, and thereby deserving of persecution. State natural history surveys and agricultural boards were major sponsors of these early economic studies, and in the eyes of Merriam and the AOU, federal support was the next logical step.

If the AOU funding request was to have any chance of success before a hard-nosed Democratic Congress, Merriam recognized it would have to stress the practical benefits of the committee's work. His funding proposal emphasized the large quantity and "great value" of the data thus far gathered through his large network of observers.[86] Only with government aid could this extensive data—which was not only of obvious "scientific interest," but also important for "practical agriculturalists"—be properly analyzed and publicized.[87] In Merriam's optimistic estimate, "the farmers of the United States would profit to the extent of many thousands of dollars per annum by availing themselves of the results of these inquiries."[88]

Merriam finished drafting the AOU petition, arranged for it to be signed by the AOU Council, and presented it to Congress in January 1885. Rep. William H. Hatch from Missouri, chair of the House Agricultural Committee, and Sen. Warner Miller of New York, an old Merriam family friend and chair of the Senate Agricultural Committee, placed copies of the document before their respective chambers for consideration.[89] Merriam and Baird testified for the proposal during House Agricultural Committee hearings held later that month, and the full House quickly approved the creation of a small Division of Economic Ornithology within the United States Department of Agriculture's larger Division of Entomology.[90] The House version of the Agricultural Appropriation Bill creating the new office failed to increase the funding for the Division of Entomology, which understandably alarmed C. V. Riley, the agency's chief. Riley wrote to Sen. Miller expressing support for the AOU proposal and concern at the lack of appropriations for the new agency.[91] Miller convinced the Senate to give $10,000 for the new division, but the appropriation was reduced to $5,000 during Conference Committee negotiations.[92] Although modest, the allocation was enough to hire two full-time naturalists to staff the agency.

After the Division of Economic Ornithology was authorized and funded, the next task was locating someone suitable to head it. In a curious letter to J. A. Allen, Merriam indicated that he had the "liveliest interest" in the work of the AOU migration committee but did not want the position if the request for government funds were successful.[93] Soon after Congress approved the $5,000 appropriation, Riley informed Allen that Coues was lobbying to get himself appointed. Riley said that he had cabled Merriam, who was abroad for several months, to find out his intentions and assured the AOU president that he would be guided by the wishes of the union.[94] At this point Merriam cabled back that he would accept the position if it was offered to him, but only if he could direct the agency's work as he saw fit.[95] At a special council meeting convened after Merriam's return in mid-April, Allen announced that the commissioner of agriculture wanted the AOU to nominate someone to take charge of the new division. Much to the chagrin of Coues, the council unanimously chose Merriam as its nominee.[96] He assumed the new post on 1 July 1885 and immediately hired his old friend and fellow ornithologist A. K. Fisher as his assistant.

Despite this small beginning, Merriam's agency soon grew in size and scope. After lobbying the appropriate members of Congress, in 1886 Merriam arranged to have his organization divorced from Riley's Division of Entomology, to double its appropriation to $10,000, and to expand its investigations to mammals and birds.[97] The new Division of Economic Ornithology and Mammalogy continued to undertake food habit, migration, and geographical distribution studies and also took over the large body of material gathered by the defunct AOU Committee on the English Sparrow.[98] Over the next decade the division gradually came to focus on investigations of the distributions of birds and mammals, a shift in orientation recognized by an official name change to the Division of the Biological Survey in 1896.[99] Congress continued to increase the young agency's budget until it soon became a major employer of ornithologists and mammalogists in the United States and the linchpin in the federal government's burgeoning wildlife program.

FORGING A PROFESSION II

In 1884, the same year that the AOU had first sought to increase employment opportunities in ornithology through federal patronage, it also contacted several large North American natural history museums in an effort to persuade them to hire qualified ornithological curators. The move was precipitated by a speech Philip Lutley Sclater delivered during the AOU's second annual meeting in 1884. Sclater, secretary of the Zoological Society of London and joint editor of British Ornithologists' Union's *Ibis*, had first visited the United States in 1856 and brought back glowing reports on the nation's ornithological collections.[100] He returned to the United States nearly two decades later, soon after Elliott Coues had visited England in the winter of 1883–1884.[101] No doubt it was Coues who invited Sclater, Howard Saunders, and several other British ornithologists to attend the second meeting of the AOU in 1884. While escorting the British contingent on a tour of several eastern cities, Coues probably suggested that Sclater speak to the union about the need for paid curators at American institutions.[102]

In October 1884, on the second day of the annual meeting, AOU President J. A. Allen called for Sclater to address the assembled members. After apologizing for any offense that might result from his remarks, the prominent British ornithologist voiced extreme concern about "three large & valuable collections of birds [in the United States]" that were "not under the care of paid working ornithologists." The extensive collections at the Boston Society of Natural History, the American Museum of Natural History in New York, and the Academy of Natural Sciences in Philadelphia each contained many type specimens upon which original published descriptions had been based, and yet in all three collections Sclater had seen firsthand evidence of neglect: insect damage, improperly labeled specimens, and poor arrangement.[103] Sclater argued that these institutions had an obligation to prevent "the loss or injury of such specimens" whose destruction would represent "a great & irreparable loss to science." He called on the union to urge these institutions to take "immediate action in this matter."[104]

Although William Brewster defended the Boston Society of Natural History's ornithological collection, for which he served as honorary curator, most AOU leaders welcomed Sclater's plea as a possible means to expand professional opportunity in their field. The AOU Council took up the issue at its meeting on the day following Sclater's address. After a motion by Merriam, the council voted to appoint Allen and Coues to a committee to "prepare memorials addressed to the Trustees" of the three institutions mentioned in Sclater's speech. In their letter the two were to call attention to the condition of these collections and "recommend immediate employment, by said institutions, of competent paid curators."[105]

At the time of the AOU's decision to approach the three institutions, the Museum of Comparative Zoology at Harvard was experiencing a bout of severe financial distress. Louis Agassiz's son, Alexander—a trained naturalist who had made a fortune as a mining engineer for the Calumet and Hecla Mining Company in Michigan—had personally bankrolled the institution since his father's death in 1873.[106] But recently Alexander Agassiz had laid off several assistants and hinted to J. A. Allen, his longtime curator of birds and mammals, that he was finding it harder to keep him on the payroll.[107]

Early in 1885 Allen received a job offer to become a curator of birds and mammals at the American Museum of Natural History, one of the three institutions singled out in Sclater's speech and the AOU's memorial campaign. Morris K. Jesup, a railroad broker who had been selected as museum president in 1881, was a capable administrator with a much more forceful vision of the museum's mission than his two predecessors.[108] During his twenty-seven-year presidency, Jesup not only improved exhibits and public outreach programs, he also committed himself to making the museum a locus of scientific research and to hiring qualified staff to curate the expanding collections. It is unclear exactly what role the AOU's efforts played in Jesup's decision to hire Allen, but it seems more than a coincidence that the decision came immediately following the AOU's campaign to expand professional opportunity in ornithology.

Upon his arrival in May 1885, Allen began building the AMNH bird and mammal department into a national center for scientific research.[109] His first task was to catalog the specimens under his charge, some thirteen hundred mammals and thirteen thousand birds, most of which were on exhibit. From the beginning Allen also pushed vigorously to expand the museum's study collection.[110] After two years of prodding, in 1887 museum officials finally authorized the purchase of the George N. Lawrence collection (twelve thousand bird skins), the Lawrence library (approximately a thousand volumes), and the Herbert H. Smith collection (four thousand skins). The same year Allen persuaded Edgar A. Mearns to donate his collection of Arizona birds (over two thousand specimens) and D. G. Elliot to present his collection of two thousand humming birds. Allen boasted that with these accessions, the AMNH bird collection "had suddenly been transformed from merely a show collection to one of impressive scientific importance."[111]

Over the next thirty-six years, Allen also recruited many able assistants, beginning with Frank M. Chapman in 1888, to help care for the bird collection. In 1908 Chapman was promoted to curator of birds, and in 1920 to chair of the newly created department of birds. At Allen's and Chapman's constant urging, museum officials hired many additional staff. By the 1930s the American Museum of Natural History had one of the strongest bird collections (nearly seven hundred thousand specimens) and largest and most-renowned curatorial staffs in the world.

The Shufeldt Affair

While the AOU provided the institutional means to further the disciplinary and professional aspirations of scientific ornithologists, it was also a social organization. Like the more general scientific and learned societies established in Great Britain and the United States since the end of the seventeenth century, the AOU functioned simultaneously as a scientific institution and an exclusive gentlemen's club (fig. 10).[112] These two aspects of the society were inseparable in the minds of most active members, for whom annual AOU conventions were as much an opportunity to establish and renew friendships as to transact the business of the organization or to keep up with current research in the field.

Except for occasional rumblings from those denied active membership in the organization, these scientific and social aspects of the AOU coexisted with relatively little tension throughout the organization's early years. But as the nineteenth century drew to a close, a major scandal rocked the organization and forced it to examine its dual nature. The scandal, which unfolded in the years 1896 and 1897, involved a founding member of the union, Robert W. Shufeldt, and his recent wife, Florence Audubon, a granddaughter of the revered artist and naturalist John James Audubon. Charges that Shufeldt had committed adultery and then blackmailed his new wife in an attempt to thwart her effort to divorce him led to calls to expel the former army surgeon from the union. Many AOU members argued that despite his obvious scientific achievement, Shufeldt's scandalous behavior was conduct unbecoming of a gentleman and hence disqualified him from further affiliation with the organization. The incident provoked such strong feelings among AOU members because it threatened to impugn not only the Audubon family name, but also that of the AOU itself. According to Coues, a close friend of the Audubons and leader of the campaign to oust Shufeldt, it was imperative to "purge the Union of such a pestilent member" who threatened the institution's "peace and dignity," if not its "actual existence." Coues argued vigorously that "Shufeldt must go for the honor, dignity, and even safety of the A.O.U."[113]

At the time of the scandal, Shufeldt was among the most accomplished scientific ornithologists in the country.[114] The son of a rear admiral in the U.S. Navy, he began collecting natural history specimens at a young age. A wealthy uncle presented him with the eight-volume octavo edition of Audubon, which further encouraged the youngster's nascent interest in ornithology. After attending Cornell for three years and graduating from Columbian Medical College (later renamed George Washington University) in 1876, Shufeldt secured a position as an assistant-surgeon in the U.S. Army. He served lengthy tours of duty in several locations, including frontier Wyoming and New Mexico, before obtaining an early retirement in 1891 due to a heart ailment. At various times before and after retiring from activity duty he also served as a curator at the Army Medical Museum in Washington and an honorary curator of comparative morphology at the Smithsonian Institution. His initial scientific publication, on the bone structure of the burrowing owl (1881), was the first in a long series of technical works on the

Figure 10. American Ornithologists' Union group photograph, 1895. This photograph, taken at the AOU's annual meeting in Washington, reveals the extent to which the organization was an almost exclusively male affair at the close of the nineteenth century.

osteology, morphology, and paleontology of birds. He also authored popular articles and books on a variety of subjects. By 1924 he had an impressive fifteen hundred publications to his credit.

Shufeldt first met the forty-two-year-old Florence Audubon in 1895, three years after his previous wife committed suicide in an insane asylum.[115] After publishing a short biographical article on John James Audubon, he had received several letters from another of the famed naturalist's granddaughters, Maria R. Audubon, who lived together with her sister, Florence, and their mother in Salem, New York.[116] In October 1894 Maria Audubon and Shufeldt coauthored a short article on the last known portrait of Audubon.[117] The collaboration soon led to a close friendship between Shufeldt and the two Audubon sisters. In September 1895, one month after they first met, Shufeldt and Florence Audubon were married.

Unfortunately, marital problems immediately befell the Shufeldt household in Takoma Park, Maryland. Versions of exactly what led to the couple's breakup vary, but within two months of the marriage, Florence Audubon Shufeldt had fled back to her mother's house in New York.[118] She claims that when she attempted to file for divorce, her husband blackmailed her by threatening to publish a particularly graphic account of impotency in women if she continued with the proceedings.[119] Although couched in terms of an objective scientific discussion, to anyone familiar with the couple it was clear that the main target of Shufeldt's generally misogynistic outburst was his second wife.[120] Shufeldt claimed that his previously unmarried wife—who had earlier been engaged for twelve years—came from an "extremely erotic family," exhibited many "decided signs of melancholia," was "fond of strong drink," and prone to "self-abuse."[121] Florence Shufeldt argued that she sought a divorce because her husband was carrying on an open affair with his Norwegian housekeeper, Alfhild Dagny Lowum, who was twenty years his junior. During the divorce proceedings, several witnesses swore to have seen Shufeldt and Lowum in compromising situations before and after his marriage to Audubon.[122]

News of the Shufeldt scandal shocked the American scientific community. When Smithsonian Secretary S. P. Langley discovered that Shufeldt had been circulating copies of his article on impotency in women stamped "Compliments of Dr. R. W. Shufeldt, Smithsonian Institution, Washington, D.C.," he immediately wrote a letter condemning "such use of the name of the Institution" as "against his wishes" and in violation of the rules of the Smithsonian.[123] Shufeldt defended his article, which he claimed was "of a strictly scientific nature" and printed in the official journal of the Medico-Legal Society of New York City, "the most distinguished organization of its kind." The two hundred reprints he had circulated elicited "the highest possible praise" from physicians and jurists across the nation.[124] Unconvinced, Smithsonian officials quietly dropped Shufeldt's name from their list of affiliates in the fall of 1897.[125]

Shufeldt's quiet departure from the Smithsonian was in stark contrast to the situation in the AOU. As early as January 1897, a day after he received a copy of Shufeldt's "libelous" article, Elliott Coues wrote William Brewster, the current president of the union, arguing that "we should be able to rid ourselves of a person who is a disgrace to humanity."[126] Brewster indicated that after obtaining the consent of the Audubon family to pursue the matter, the next step was for someone to formally charge "Dr. Shufeldt with conduct which shows him to be an improper person to be connected with the Union."[127] As Brewster pointed out, AOU bylaws permitted expulsion of any member "by a two-thirds vote of the Active Members present at a stated meeting, three months' previous notice of such proposed action having been given by the Secretary to all Active Members, and to the member accused."[128]

Coues then wrote Allen, Merriam, and other AOU leaders informing them of Shufeldt's misconduct and asking for their counsel on how to proceed.[129] All expressed indignation at Shufeldt's behavior.[130] However, several of those canvassed also expressed deep reservations about initiating formal expulsion proceedings. For example, D. G. Elliot recommended pushing for Shufeldt's resignation for fear that if the AOU tried to expel him, the society might be drawn into an embarrassing lawsuit with uncertain results. Elliot considered it "doubtful" that "a Court or Jury would regard this accusation as regards his fitness to be a member of a scientific society, the test of which is scientific ability by published works and not by social ethics."[131] After consulting with an attorney about the legality of the AOU expelling one of its members, in late June 1897 Coues and

Merriam mailed formal charges against Shufeldt to AOU Secretary John Sage.[132] At the suggestion of Judge Charles Almy, a personal friend of Brewster, the specific wording of the charge was changed from "conduct unbecoming of a gentlemen" to "he is an improper person to be connected with the A.O.U."[133]

With the support of key AOU leaders, Sage mailed a printed circular to all active members that specified the charges against Shufeldt and announced that expulsion proceedings were to take place at the next AOU meeting in early November.[134] Sage's circular prompted Shufeldt to file a set of countercharges in which he claimed that his two chief accusers—Coues and Merriam—had themselves engaged in "conduct unbecoming of a gentleman, in being party to a scheme to create a public scandal."[135] According to Shufeldt, the two were motivated solely by "personal animosity," and they had engaged in "making false statements of the grossest possible character" in their campaign to discredit him.[136]

In the months leading up to the annual meeting, several AOU leaders questioned the wisdom of trying to force Shufeldt from the organization, while others devised strategies for carrying the expulsion to completion. Coues continued to argue that the AOU should serve as a "court of honor" to decide whether Shufeldt was "an improper person to be connected with the Union."[137] Allen indicated that several members with whom he was in contact thought "it was a mistake to take up the matter at all, & that the best way out of the case would be to drop it by considering the charges as not properly subject to the action of the Union." For many there was a lingering doubt about the necessity of "washing of much foul linen" in public and even whether the AOU, as a scientific organization, had jurisdiction in the case. Those who doubted whether the society should take up the expulsion issue continued to argue that "the Union is not a *social* but a *scientific* body, & as such it is doubtful how far the moral character of its *members* is open to consideration."[138]

In the end those with misgivings about bringing the case before the union prevailed. At the meeting on 8 November 1897, the ten assembled council members considered the case for hours. According to Coues, they were of "one opinion of the wretch, but exactly opposite as to the expediency of expelling him." When it became impossible to reach a consensus on the issue of expulsion, the council and then the full membership passed a "hastily patched up resolution," which stated that the charges were fully sustained by the evidence, but that the AOU had "no jurisdiction" in the case.[139]

Had the matter ended there, the apparent message of the Shufeldt affair would have been that the AOU conceived itself primarily as a scientific organization only minimally concerned with the private lives of its members. But in a strange twist of events that betrayed the extent to which the notion of the AOU as a gentlemen's club still prevailed, two days after the council decided it had no jurisdiction in the case, it unanimously passed a motion instructing the editor of the *Auk* to decline any articles Shufeldt might submit to the AOU's official journal.[140] It is not clear that Allen, the editor during this period, ever enforced the resolution. In any case, it was not until 1909 that another article appeared in the

Auk under Shufeldt's name. But the fact that the council felt compelled to take punitive action against him itself was significant. The episode demonstrates that although the AOU was ostensibly a scientific organization, for some of its leaders, considerations of the moral conduct of its members remained important.

MEMBERSHIP REDUX

The AOU consciously pursued a different membership strategy from that adopted by many more exclusive, discipline-based scientific societies created in America during the closing decades of the nineteenth century. Unlike societies that limited their membership to a narrow group of technically proficient, professional practitioners, from the beginning AOU leaders believed that recruiting and maintaining a large associate membership was critical to the well-being of their new organization.[141]

Several factors account for this more inclusive approach to institutionalization in ornithology. One of these was the continued heterogeneity of the North American ornithological community. As I have tried to show thus far, during the period surrounding the formation of the AOU, scientific ornithologists in the United States relied heavily on an extensive network of variously motivated individuals to provide the large series of specimens upon which their taxonomic and faunistic studies were based. Although this dependence on a broad spectrum of collectors, sport hunters, taxidermists, and natural history dealers was already beginning to diminish at the time of the creation of the AOU, in the absence of formal educational opportunities in field of ornithology, active AOU members continued to feel an obligation to the group from which the next generation of scientific ornithologists would eventually emerge. For example, in 1903 the editors of the *Auk* argued that the AOU was primarily "an association of professional ornithologists, or advanced workers in ornithology," but that from the beginning its leaders had also sought to "secure the affiliation with all American bird students,—to bring amateurs into touch with the professionals, in the hope that their interest in bird study would thereby be fostered and their efforts be in a measure favorably guided by being brought into contact with the more experienced workers."[142] At the same time, a broad base of associate members provided legitimation and increased political support for ornithology and the AOU. And perhaps most importantly, associate members represented a crucial source of income for the organization: the $3.00 in dues they contributed each year provided the bulk of the funds needed to keep the *Auk* financially solvent.

Because of their previous experience with publishing the *Bulletin of the Nuttall Ornithological Club*, AOU founders had recognized the need to build a sufficiently large membership base to support the society's ambitious publication program. In the early years of the organization, before attracting enough dues-paying associate members, the AOU issued frequent appeals to expand the periodical's circulation to avoid increasing its price or decreasing its size and regularity.[143] As a printed letter that AOU Treasurer William Dutcher began circulating in 1898

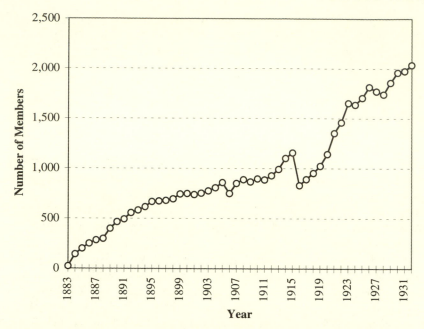

Figure 11. Membership in the American Ornithologists' Union, 1883-1932. Compiled from Chapman and Palmer, eds., *Fifty Years' Progress of American Ornithology, 1883–1933* (1933).

reveals, the union made no secret that its need for funds to keep its periodical afloat fueled the desire to increase associate-level membership:

> It is imperative that there shall be a very substantial increase in the membership of the Society to enable it to meet its current expenses; practically all of the income received from membership fees and sales of publications are at once reinvested in publishing the "Auk." . . . If the Society's membership list can be increased to a thousand names, its financial future can be assured.[144]

Figure 11 shows the extent to which periodic membership campaigns were successful in increasing the size of the union during its first fifty years. In 1900, two years after Dutcher issued his call for expanding the membership of the AOU, the number of active and associate members stood at 748. By 1910 the total AOU membership had grown modestly, to nearly 900. In 1920 over 1,142 ornithologists were affiliated with the organization. And by 1930, following aggressive campaigns that AOU Secretary T. S. Palmer and Treasurer W. L. McAtee spearheaded, nearly 2,000 individuals belonged to the AOU. This steady growth not only reflects the zeal with which AOU members worked to expand their organization, but also the role that the rise of birdwatching played in increasing public interest in ornithology throughout this period.[145]

Of course, the AOU was not the sole beneficiary of the growth of interest in North American ornithology. In his sketch of the history of North American ornithology, Ernst Mayr has counted nearly twenty ornithological societies created between the years 1873 and 1893.[146] These local, state, and regional organizations brought together bird enthusiasts with a variety of motivations and levels of expertise. Among the most important of the local and state societies were the Linnaean Society of New York, founded in 1878 by C. Hart Merriam and former Nuttall members Ernest Ingersoll and Henry Balch Bailey, and the Delaware Valley Ornithological Club, founded in 1890 by several Philadelphia bird collectors.[147] The largest and most important regional ornithological societies were the midwestern-oriented Wilson Ornithological Club (founded in 1888) and the West Coast–oriented Cooper Ornithological Club (founded in 1893).[148] Both the organizations and the periodicals they initiated—the *Wilson Bulletin* and the *Condor*—remain active up to the present.

The success of these and other alternative ornithological societies in attracting members served both to diffuse and to promote criticism of the AOU. Many in these associations simply disregarded the AOU as a society with a largely eastern membership that almost invariably met in one of four East Coast cities and pursued an agenda with little relevance to their own interests.[149] But the new ornithological societies and their publications also provided a platform for venting criticism of AOU policies. This was especially true of Audubon societies and bird clubs that began to be organized near the end of the century and soon grew impatient with the continued collecting demands of scientific ornithologists.[150]

At the same time, the growth of the AOU itself created pressure to modify its two-tiered membership structure. The AOU's hierarchical membership policy limited the number of active members—those who actually controlled the organization—to fifty. This arbitrary limit, which represented an increasingly smaller percentage of the total membership, came under increasing attack as the nineteenth century came to a close.

Some criticism came from sources outside the AOU that had long been suspicious of the organization. The most prominent example was the collecting-oriented *Ornithologist and Oologist*, which regularly decried the AOU's membership structure, nomenclatural practices, and bird protection activities until the periodical fell victim to the depression of 1893. For example, in 1891 the *O & O*, as it was often referred to by contemporaries, published a limerick revealing its attitude toward the AOU's exclusive membership policy: "He was an aesthetic young fellow/ Who laughed in a tone very mellow,/ He joined the A.O.U.,/ With a tremendous ado,/ And now he is swell, swelled and sweller."[151] Three months later the periodical publicized the organizational meeting of a short-lived competitor to the AOU—the Association of American Ornithologists—which met at the taxidermy studio of F. S. Webster.[152] That same year one of the periodical's contributors complained of the "widening . . . gulf between an innumerable multitude of intelligent field workers and the select, exclusive circle of the ornithological union."[153]

Regular criticism also came from western ornithologists, especially members of the Cooper Ornithological Club, who argued that the AOU had failed to recognize the high level of scientific achievement several its members had reached. In

May 1900 Frank S. Daggett of Pasadena, California, complained of the continued absence of western names among the roles of active membership in the AOU:

> Up to the present time the A.O.U. has maintained a policy of seclusion by adhering arbitrarily to a rule that limits its active list to fifty members, to the exclusion of many worthy workers, and I find a strong sentiment exists that this policy be changed. Right here it might be well to mention some of the many reasons why the West, (and by that I mean all that section of the country not under the direct inspection of the Eastern scientific centers) should be more fully recognized in that body. The one most often put forward is the fact that interest, instead of being confined to a little coterie in the East, has spread all over the country until every state has its workers; not mere dabblers and "bird skinners," but active, intelligent workers who are covering their respective fields with credit.[154]

Daggett called special attention to the life history studies of the Cooper Ornithological Club, which he claimed were just as important and rigorous as the taxonomic studies that "gave [a] reputation to the founders of the A.O.U." Moreover, Daggett noted the low turnover rate among so-called active members, many of whom were now aged and inactive, but still unwilling to give up their coveted positions to the next generation of ornithologists. To remedy the situation, he advocated expanding the number of active members to "60 or 75" and/or placing those who had ceased to make scientific contributions on a special honorary list to free up their space.

The more serious, technically oriented ornithologists in the West also resented being lumped together in a single membership category with the increasing number of associate members who joined the AOU largely to support its bird protection activities or because of their interest in recreational birdwatching. Cooper Club member Richard McGregor expressed his anger at being "placed in the same class with Audubonians and fad protectionists" who not only failed to appreciate the finer points of scientific ornithology, but also often opposed the collecting upon which much technical bird study was based.[155] In his editorial in the July–August 1900 edition of the *Condor*, McGregor suggested that the current list of associate members be divided into two categories to distinguish between "amateur ornithologists and the bird protectionists." McGregor's suggestion was quickly seconded and elaborated upon by AOU insider Frank Chapman, who proposed creating a class of more advanced "senior associates" limited to one hundred individuals.[156]

In response to these and other suggestions, the ornithologists assembled at the AOU meeting for 1900 gave preliminary approval to several changes in the organization's bylaws. These included: (1) an increase in the number of active members from fifty to seventy-five; (2) the creation of a new class of elective members, limited to seventy-five, which would be intermediate between associate members and active members; and (3) a change in the name of active members to fellows, and associate members to associates.[157] According to the notice in the *Auk*, there was "little doubt" that the amendments would be fully ratified at the next AOU meeting, in 1901. The proposed changes prompted a highly supportive editorial in the *Condor*, which noted that the move was met with "an indisputable feeling of satisfaction" by western ornithologists, who hoped to gain election to some of the new slots.[158]

Women also hoped to benefit from the change in bylaws. Not until two years after its founding did the AOU finally elect its first female associate member, Florence Merriam (whose name had been placed into nomination by her well-connected brother, C. Hart Merriam).[159] As was then the case with most other scientific societies in the United States, however, Merriam and subsequent female members remained restricted to a "visibly subordinate level" within the AOU.[160] Even so, they continued to join, particularly when the organization became active in the Audubon movement during the closing years of the nineteenth century. By 1900 AOU membership rolls included the names of eighty female associate members (approximately 11 percent of all its members), but none had ever gained nomination for election to active membership in the male-dominated society.[161] When the AOU gave its final approval to the new category of "elective members" in 1901, Florence Merriam Bailey, Mabel Osgood Wright, Olive Thorne Miller, and a few other women soon achieved the honor. However, the percentage of female elective members remained minimal before the 1960s (5 percent or below), and not until 1929 did the AOU elect Bailey as its first female "fellow." Long after women began to make significant contributions to ornithology, they remained marginalized within the AOU.

The new category of elective members, created by a final vote at the 1901 meeting, helped mollify critics of the AOU, but the failure of the bid to increase the limit on the number of fellows during that same meeting left the door open for continued complaint. In 1908 John Lewis Childs, the proprietor of a large seed and plant business in Floral Park, Long Island, questioned what he believed was an arbitrary limit on the total number of fellows and elective members of the AOU.[162] Childs was an avid collector who had amassed one of the largest private collections of North American eggs ever gathered. He also edited and published four volumes of his own periodical, *The Warbler*, between 1903 and 1913. There is little doubt that Childs would have been elected an active member at the time of the founding of the AOU. Yet, having joined the AOU as an associate in 1900, he had still failed to gain election to the new members class by 1906.

On the face of it, Childs's criticism of the AOU membership policy seemed to echo the complaint made twenty-five years previously by *Ornithologist and Oologist* editor Joseph Wade: "It seems to me that this [limit] is unjust, unreasonable and un-American from every point of view."[163] But Childs made it clear that he was not advocating an abolition of membership categories or standards. Rather, he believed that when an elective member reached a "certain standard" or level of competence (which he thought could be established by the "Board of Fellows"), they should automatically be granted fellowship in the AOU, no matter how many individuals were already occupying that category. As it now stood, there were several "'fellows' whose work, whose renown or whose service to ornithology is far inferior to that of several 'members' who cannot be advanced to 'fellows' because that class is full."[164] According to Childs, the same was true of associates hoping to become elective members, the position he had been in until resigning from the AOU in 1906.

In attempting to answer Childs's objections, *Auk* editor Witmer Stone first admitted that there were some currently in the "class of Fellow" whose "services to ornithology" were "far inferior to those rendered by many in the class of Members." But according to Stone, the situation was an artifact of history resulting from the "tremendous advancement" in ornithology since the AOU was organized twenty-five years previously. Stone rejected Childs's scheme for abolishing the limits for each membership category to correct this injustice. Rather, he argued that "experience" had "long shown that a standard can be established *and maintained* only by declaring that certain classes of membership shall not exceed a certain number." According to Stone, fifty was a "reasonable limit" for the number of fellows, "if this class is to have any significance."

Seven years after the Childs-Stone exchange, Harold H. Bailey, a naval architect from Newport News, Virginia, son of a founding member of the AOU, and close friend of Childs, offered his own criticism of the membership policies of the AOU in several ornithological periodicals.[165] Bailey argued that there was widespread dissatisfaction with the membership structure of the AOU, which concentrated power and prestige in the hands of a few fellows. He pointed out that elective members (which comprised approximately 8 percent of the total AOU membership) and associates (which comprised 90 percent) each were required to pay yearly dues and yet had no "vote or voice" in the business matters of the organization. Rather, important decisions were typically made by a small number of fellows in "star chamber" business meetings, which remained closed to the "main supporters of the Union."[166] Although he fell short of calling for complete abolition of the hierarchical membership structure, he seemed to have been moving firmly in that direction: "The current grades in the membership in the Union are unsatisfactory and undemocratic."

Stone began his latest defense of AOU membership policy with the obvious comment that "election to any limited society or membership is bound to be unsatisfactory to some." He reiterated his earlier point that it was impossible to establish a "definite standard" for each class of membership that would prevent the need for elections. Rather, he believed the only practical way to insure the high caliber of members was to make the difficult choice between candidates by election based on their relative merits. According to Stone, the enlargement of any particular class of membership would immediately debase the honor the election represented. As to allowing elective members and associates to become voting participants in the AOU, Stone argued that the organization had no desire to hide its actions and that there was "every probability of the adoption at the next meeting of a suggested plan whereby elective members will be allowed to share with the fellows the business management of the Union."[167] The only reason this action had not been taken earlier, he argued disingenuously, was that AOU leaders wanted "to relieve the general membership of a burden" and allow the open sessions to be "devoted entirely to ornithological matters."[168]

In 1915 the AOU held its first regular meeting outside the East.[169] The fellows assembled in San Francisco voted unanimously to adopt an amendment to the AOU bylaws that allowed elective members to "share with Fellows the business of the Union and the election of Officers, Members, and Associates."[170] However, this power sharing move did not go far enough for Bailey, who, as an associate member, was still denied voting rights in the AOU. He resigned in protest in December 1915.[171]

By the mid-1930s even Witmer Stone was beginning to express doubts about the continued wisdom of the restrictive membership policy. In a letter transmitting several proposed bylaw changes in 1935, Stone pointed out that he had "been very much impressed by the feeling, which is wide spread, that we should be organized more like the Mammal Society and get away from the ultra-conservative plan that seemed desirable at the time the A.O.U. was founded."[172] There was still a limit, however, to how far most AOU leaders were willing to go with their reform. At the 1936 meeting, elective members were finally granted the privilege of holding the offices of secretary, treasurer, and councilor.[173] But associates remained outside the circle of power. The boundaries that had been erected with the creation of the AOU remained in place fifty years later.

From its creation in 1883, the AOU provided an institutional focal point for the struggles between scientific ornithologists attempting to forge a discipline and a profession and the much broader ornithological community that was often unsympathetic to the aspirations of its more technically oriented colleagues. In an era when graduate degrees and professional opportunities were scarce, scientists supported a multitiered membership structure in their national disciplinary society as a means to encourage and reward scientific achievement. However, many of those excluded from the upper echelons of the AOU resented being asked to support an organization that seemed increasingly unresponsive to their own needs. As it turned out, the issue of AOU membership was only one of several concerns that came between scientists seeking to remake ornithology into a rigorous scientific discipline and the broader ornithological community upon which the scientists continued to depend.

Nomenclatural Reform and the Quest for Standards and Stability

DISCIPLINING ORNITHOLOGY

Systematics—the naming, classification, and description of organisms—represented the core activity of scientific ornithology in the United States throughout the second half of the nineteenth century.[1] Nowhere is this more boldly asserted than in the introduction to Robert Ridgway's magnum opus, *The Birds of North and Middle America*, a multivolume technical manual that represented the fruit of more than three decades of intensive labor.[2] According to Ridgway, there were "two essentially different kinds of ornithology: *systematic* or *scientific*, and *popular*." The first dealt with "the structure and classification of birds, their synonymies, and technical descriptions," while the latter touched on birds' "habits, songs, nesting, and other facts pertaining to their life-histories." Although Ridgway admitted that scientific and popular ornithology were "closely related and to a degree interdependent," as a primary architect of late nineteenth-century American ornithology, he left no doubt about where his allegiance ultimately lay:

> Popular ornithology is the more entertaining, with its savor of the wildwood, green fields, the riverside and seashore, bird songs, and the many fascinating things connected with out-of-door Nature. But systematic ornithology, being a component part of biology—the science of life—is the more instructive and therefore more important. Each advance in this serious study reveals just so much more of the hidden mysteries of creation, and adds proportionately to the sum of human knowledge.[3]

By the time he penned these words in 1901, a number of scientific ornithologists and many more in the broader American ornithological community took strong exception to Ridgway's rigid characterization of their endeavor.[4] But in terms of identifying what had been at the heart of serious ornithological research for the preceding half-century and what remained its central defining activity, Ridgway was essentially correct.

One need only compare typical publications from the first and second half of the nineteenth century to see striking evidence of a remarkable transformation, a narrowing of a much broader ornithological gaze. Volumes once considered the acme of North American ornithology—like Alexander Wilson's *American Ornithology* (1808–1814) and John James Audubon's *Birds of America* (1827–1838)—contained not only a complete enumeration of all the birds known to inhabit the continent, but also exquisite hand-colored drawings and detailed accounts of the behavior and life histories of each individual species.[5] However, the appearance of Baird, Cassin, and Lawrence's Pacific Railroad Survey Report in 1858 marked the beginning of a new era. While this landmark study still contained colored plates of the new species discovered in the West, it entirely ignored descriptions of the life history and behavior of birds that had been central to the earlier compilations of Audubon and Wilson. The text of the publication that provided the inspiration for the next generation of scientific ornithologists contained only exhaustive synonymies, technical descriptions of plumage variations, and reports of geographical distribution.

This profound change in the content of ornithological publications reflected an equally profound shift in their intended audience. Where Wilson and Audubon sought to make their work accessible to a broad audience that included scientists and novices alike, the dreary tomes that characterized scientific ornithology in the second half of the nineteenth century were increasingly aimed at the small number of technically oriented specialists. A complete inventory of North American species remained an overarching goal throughout the century—it was what one ornithologist called the "alphabet of ornithology"—but following the death of Audubon in 1851, scientists increasingly narrowed the focus of their investigations.[6] Research into the external morphology and geographical distribution of North American birds, largely based on the vast skin collections amassed during the second half of the century, increasingly dominated American ornithological science.

In limiting themselves to taxonomic and faunistic studies, American ornithologists were clearly taking their cue from abroad. According to historian Paul Farber, between the years 1820 and 1850 European ornithologists succeeded in firmly establishing their field as a scientific discipline characterized by "an international group of recognized experts, working on a set of fruitful questions, using an accepted rigorous method, and holding a common goal."[7] That goal was the production of an exhaustive catalog of the birds of the world, organized to reflect their natural relationships.[8] But as Farber points out, substantial progress in this ambitious endeavor exacted a heavy toll. In their rush to construct a complete inventory of the world's birds, scientists increasingly ignored the lives of the individual species comprising that inventory.

American ornithologists worked both with an awareness of and in curious opposition to this European tradition. They wholeheartedly embraced the challenge to create a complete inventory of bird forms, but, unlike their counterparts abroad, who had access to cosmopolitan collections gathered from the far corners of expanding empires, Americans limited their vision almost entirely to their own continent. Americans also accepted the need for uniform standards to govern the process of naming and describing birds, but they sought to reform the widely accepted Strickland Code, the code of nomenclature adopted by the British Association for the Advancement of Science in 1842.[9]

By the second half of the nineteenth century, achieving the goal of a single, authoritative list of North American birds remained elusive. The very factors that would seem necessary to construct a definitive list—an increase in the number of ornithologists and the systematic exploration and gradual settlement of the continental United States—had instead resulted in a proliferation of claims for inclusion in the catalog of North American birds. By the early 1880s two divergent lists, each of which gained many devoted followers, had been created in separate attempts to sort out these competing claims. But because neither list was able to supplant the other, and neither author was willing to back down, nomenclatural chaos continued to threaten the integrity of ornithological research in this country.

The ostensibly scientific goal of nomenclatural reform also had a strongly political dimension. The American nomenclatural reform movement was informed by personal ambition, individual rivalries, nationalistic pride, and the promotion of a particular research agenda: what I call the subspecies research program. The backbone of this program was the call for formal recognition of distinct geographical races (or subspecies) by the addition of a subspecific designation to the more traditional binomial name. Although the idea of using trinomial nomenclature was clearly not without precedent in Europe, its promoters almost invariably presented it as a distinctly American innovation.[10] One ornithologist's boast is typical: "Trinomialism is known as the 'American School' of ornithology, and the central idea is the 'American idea.'"[11]

The subspecies program not only set American ornithologists apart from many (though not all) of their European colleagues, it also became a source of tension in the United States. Many members of the extended ornithological community not only rejected the need to recognize the minute distinctions upon which subspecific differences were characterized, but even the need for a specialized scientific nomenclature. The issue was one of several that divided the relatively small group of technically oriented specialists from the larger ornithological community. For those primarily oriented toward collecting and displaying birds—and not toward the production of scientific knowledge—the pages of ink spilled over nomenclatural quibbles seemed entirely wasted.

A primary reason for the creation of the AOU in 1883 was to sort out the competing lists of North American birds and provide institutional sanction to the subspecies research program. Within three years of the organization's founding, AOU leaders published an official Code and Checklist that embodied their distinct nomenclatural vision. Despite significant opposition both in the United States and abroad, this document soon gained the authority its creators desired. In 1901, the same year that Ridgway declared systematic ornithology superior to popular ornithology, the delegates gathered at the Fifth International Congress of Zoology in Berlin ratified an International Code of Nomenclature that embodied many principles first enunciated in the AOU Code, including the provision for trinomial nomenclature.

The larger goal of nomenclatural stability remained elusive, however, as North American ornithologists continued to create new subspecies based on smaller and smaller distinctions and to discover prior names for previously accepted forms. By the turn of the century, even several original proponents of trinomialism began to question whether its practitioners had gone too far.

THE GEOGRAPHY OF SPECIES

Theory and practice were inextricably linked in the development of the American version of the subspecies concept. The particular form of the concept embodied in the AOU Code and Checklist first became the subject of sustained discussion in the United States in the early 1870s, but the idea had its roots in the pervasive interest in geographical distribution in the years surrounding the publication of Darwin's *Origin of Species*.[12] As early as the 1840s MCZ founder Louis Agassiz began to sketch his theory of "biological provinces."[13] In broad strokes, Agassiz delineated the boundaries for what he believed to be the unique, large-scale associations of animals inhabiting different portions of the world.[14] The only way to gain accurate knowledge of the extent of these associations was by gathering as much information as possible concerning the distribution of their component species.

Agassiz also believed that geographical distribution data was crucial in determining the natural boundaries of species within a genus. His classic *Essay on Classification* (1857) characterized the higher taxonomic categories—basic types, classes, orders, families, and genera—using strictly morphological differentia.[15] But Agassiz rejected using morphology alone to delineate the boundaries of species, which he believed were to be defined based on the fact that they "belong to a given period in our globe" and "hold definite relations to the physical conditions then prevailing and to the animals and plants then existing." First among his lengthy list of examples of "definite relations" exhibited by species was geographical range.[16] Agassiz considered this data to be so important that he once claimed "every new fact relating to the geographic distribution of well known species is as important to science as the discovery of new species."[17]

Agassiz's interest in geographical distribution also found expression in the printed circulars he regularly issued to collectors, sport hunters, and naturalists in an effort to maintain a steady stream of specimens flowing into his museum. Among the advice on collecting, preserving, and shipping natural history objects contained in these circulars was the reminder that all specimens, even of the most common species, were welcomed if their geographic origin was properly indicated: "A great mistake, constantly made by those who desire to contribute to the increase of the Museum, consists in the supposition that only rare specimens are desirable. It should be understood that beyond a 150 miles from Cambridge, every specimen, which may be sent in with a label indicating its origin, will be greatly received and acknowledged."[18]

Agassiz's rival museum builder, Spencer Fullerton Baird, was also vitally interested both in determining the geographical distribution of individual species and in reconstructing the broader associations of organisms inhabiting larger geographic areas. Like Agassiz's circulars, Baird's printed instructions for collectors highlighted his desire to achieve wide geographical representation for the species in the Smithsonian collections: "As the object of the Institution in making its collections is not merely to possess the different species, but also to determine

Figure 12. Smithsonian Institution Bird Gallery, 1885. This photograph shows birds preserved as old-fashioned taxidermic mounts and as more modern study skins.

their geographical distribution, it becomes important to have as full series as practicable from each locality."[19]

Baird's statement hints at one result of the increasing theoretical emphasis on geographical distribution: changing collecting practices. Until the middle decades of the nineteenth century, private collectors and museums generally aimed to acquire a single pair, male and female, of each desired species.[20] Additional examples of the same species were usually considered duplicates to be traded, sold, or discarded. An increased interest in geographical distribution and a separate but related growth in the study of variation within species led naturalists to amass increasingly large series of specimens. Although serial collecting had begun in the United States prior to the appearance of the *Origin of Species*, Darwin's book, and the subsequent interest in evolutionary studies it engendered, greatly accelerated this trend.

As I have already noted, serial collecting resulted in a tremendous increase in the size of individual and institutional collections. This growth, in turn, forced changes in exhibition practices. While museums had previously tended to display all of the specimens contained in their collections, the large amount of material amassed through serial collecting resulted in pressure to create separate research collections removed from the public eye. In ornithology, serial collecting also resulted in a movement away from the practice of mounting birds (fig. 12) and toward the production of "study skins," which were much more convenient to store and less prone to damage from dust, light, and insects.[21]

Accompanying the growth of serial collecting was a move toward increased precision in specimen description. In this respect, Baird's ornithological volume of the Pacific Railroad Survey Reports was clearly an epoch-making work.[22] Baird's contribution was one of a series of reports presenting the scientific findings of the survey teams sent out in the mid-1850s to evaluate possible routes for the transcontinental railway.[23] But rather than limiting his report simply to a description of the avian species collected by the naturalists attached to the survey teams, Baird used the opportunity to produce a complete survey of North American avifauna, providing exact diagnoses of all known species and genera, with copious synonymy and critical commentary.

Of course, the idea of publishing a complete enumeration of the North American bird forms was hardly new. Alexander Wilson, Charles Lucien Bonaparte, John James Audubon, and others had attempted exhaustive surveys in the first half of the nineteenth century.[24] But Baird presented much more precise and detailed information than his predecessors. Not only did he give exact descriptions of each species, he also provided a complete list of all the specimens on which his descriptions were based. These tabular lists contained data on each of up to fifty individual specimens, including museum catalog number; sex; information on when, where, and by whom the specimen was originally collected; and a standard series of up to ten different measurements of each bird, taken as closely as the nearest hundredth of an inch (fig. 13). Because of his innovations, Baird's Pacific Railroad Survey Report became a model for American naturalists struggling to bring more precision to natural history description.[25]

Thus in the middle decades of the nineteenth century, American naturalists showed a keen interest in geographical distribution and the practices necessary to support that interest—large series collections of species taken over widely ranging geographic areas and increasingly precise techniques of measurement and description capable of distinguishing even the most minute individual differences. It was only a small step to recognize that species might exhibit regular variations that correlated with the changing environmental conditions across their range.

THE "AMERICAN" SUBSPECIES CONCEPT

After carefully examining an extensive series of box turtles (*Cistudo carolina*) obtained through his collecting network in the 1850s, Agassiz recognized four separate and apparently constant North American forms of the species. Each of these four forms seemed to coincide roughly with a unique geographic area.[26] The forms were so distinct that Agassiz was unsure whether they represented several species or a single species with different well-marked geographic forms. Although he was soon to deny the existence of any kind of constant variation from

List of specimens.

Catal. No.	Sex.	Locality.	When collected.	Whence obtained.	Orig. No.	Collected by—	Length.	Stretch of wings.	Wing.	Remarks.
1367	♂	Carlisle, Pa..............	April 17,1844	S. F. Baird.......	......	....	8.91	14.66	4.66	....
1386	♂	.....do	April 21,1841	..... do.........			9.50	15.50	5.00	
816	♀	.....do	Oct. 19,1842	.... do.........			7.50	12.50	3.75	
10138	♂	Washington, D. C.		J. C. McGuire ...						
6941	......	Red river, H. B. T......		D. Gunn						
6942	....	.....do		..... do.........						
8589	......	Sauk Ford, Min	1853..........	Gov. Stevens....		Dr. Suckley.				
8590	......	.....do	1853.............	.....do.........		... .do				
	....	Union county, Ill............	April 23,——	N. W. University		R. Kennicott				
7002	♀	St. Louis, Mo.............	May 8,1857	Lt. Bryan	40	W. S. Wood..				
8338	♂	Independence, Mo.........	June 6,1857	Wm. M. Magraw.		Dr. Cooper...	9.25	14.75	5.12	
4644	♂	Ft. Pierre..............	April 27,1855	Col. Vaughan ...		Dr. Hayden..				
5325	... .	Medicine creek...........	....	Lt. Warren......		....do ...	9.25	15.75	5.00	
5326	♀	Medicine Hill...........	June 25,1856	.....do.........		...do	7.25	12.50	4.00	
4757	♂	B g Nemaha, K. T.......	April 23,1856	.....do.........		....do	9.25	15.00	4.75	
9332	♂	Frémont, on Platte........	July 1,——	.....do.........		....do	8.37	15.12	5.00	Iris dark brown....
9331	♂	Sand Hills of Platte........	Aug. 1,——	.....do.........		....do	8.75	15.00	4 75	
9329	♂	.....do	Aug. 10,——	.....do.........		....do	9.25	15.25	4.87	
9330	♂	Loup Fork of Platte......	July 3,——	.....do.........		....do	9.50	15.25	5.00	
9333	♂	..... do	July 1,——	.....do.........		....do	8.50	15.75	5.00	
5670	♂	Platte river.............	July 14,1856	Lt. Bryan	104	Lt. Bryan				
8944	♂	100 miles E. of Ft Kearney	Oct. 25,1857	Wm. M. Magraw.	226	Dr. Cooper .	9.62	15.75	5.25	
7092	♂	Republican river, K. T...	June 12,1857	Lt. Bryan... ...	34	W. Hammond				
5000	♀	Indianola.	Mar. 29,1855	Capt. Pope......	40	....	9.50	13.50	4.50	
4048	♀	Brownsville, Tex	Feb. 11,1853	Lt. Couch	20	....	7.00	11.75	4.00	
4049	♂	New Leon, Mex........	Mar. —,1851	.....do.........	170	....	8.50	13.50	4.75	
4047	♀?	.....do........	April —,1853	.....do.........	182	....	6.50	11.50	3.75	
4050	......	Saltillo, Mex........	May —,1853	.....do.........	17	....	8.00	13.00	4.75	
8591	......	San Elizario.............	Dec. —,1854	Maj. Emory......	7	Dr. Kennerly.				
5001	♂	Doña Ana, N. Mex.........	Nov. 11,1855	Capt. Pope......	155	....	9.00	15.50	5.00	
5003	♂	.. ..do	Nov. 3,1855	.....do.........	153	....	9.25	16.00	5.25	
8579	....	Fort Thorn, N. M........	....	Dr. Henry		....				
8574	♂	Fort Conrad, N. M.......	Oct. —,1853	Lt. Whipple.....		Dr. Kennerly.				
8576	......	Cold Spring, N. M........	Nov. 17,—	.....do.........	93	.....do				
8578	....	C'p 150, Cocomongo ranch, Cal.	Mar. 19,1854	. ...do.........	187	.....do	8.50	15.00	5.50	
8573	....	Espia, Mex.............	....	Maj. Emory	45	....do				
4952?	....	San José, Cal..........		A. J. Grayson....	14	....				
8582	♀	Ft. Vancouver, O. T.	Jan. 20,1854	Gov. Stevens....	19	Dr. Cooper...	8.25	12.75		
8583	♀	Ft. Steilacoom, W. T......	April	Dr. Suckley	342	.....do.........	8.00	12.60		
8581	♂	.....do	April 25,1856	.....do.........	341	.....do.........	10.00	14.00		
8585	♂	.....do	.... do	.....do.........	339	.....do.........	9 50	14.00		
8586	♂	.....do	.... do......	.....do.........	340	.....do.........	9.50	13.00		

Figure 13. Baird's list of red-winged blackbird specimens, 1858. An example of Baird's efforts to introduce more rigor into the practice of American natural history.

the species type, in 1857 Agassiz hinted at a research agenda that was to occupy many American naturalists for the next several decades: "The differences noticed may indicate different species; but they may also mark only varieties. There is, however, a remarkable circumstance connected with the specimens that come under my observations: their variations are limited to particular regions of the country."[27]

As early as 1868 Joel A. Allen accepted his mentor's challenge to investigate the possibility of regular patterns of geographic variation within certain species. Following an unsuccessful bid to obtain bird specimens through a widely circulated appeal, in the winter of 1868–1869 Allen mounted an expedition to Florida.[28] He hoped that by comparing a large series of birds of the same species obtained in Florida with enough examples collected in Massachusetts, more than one thousand miles to the north, he could shed light on the vexing problem of whether geographical varieties actually existed in nature.

Allen's research came in the wake of Agassiz's recent denial of the existence of constant variation from the species type. Where Agassiz once entertained the possibility that certain well-marked varieties might correspond with a given geographical location, more recently he had rejected the possibility because of his strong opposition to Darwin's *Origin of Species*.[29] Apparently Agassiz had come to recognize the evolutionary implications of his earlier position.[30]

Allen was also responding to several of Baird's recent publications that had touched on the subject of geographical variation. Beginning as early as his Pacific Railroad Survey Report of 1858, Baird had hinted that changes in size, form, and coloration of a species might correspond with the climatic differences of particular geographic regions.[31] One year later he again called attention to these climatic differences and announced his first general law of geographic variation: a gradual decrease in size of individuals of the same species with decrease in latitude or altitude of their birthplaces.[32] By 1866 Baird published a series of "laws" and "tendencies" of geographic variation. In addition to his previous correlation of size with latitude and altitude, he also noted a tendency toward absolute increase in the size of the bill in birds born farther south (even though they were subject to a general diminution of bulk across this same range) and that change in longitude from east to west led to increase in the length of tail and a general darkening of the color of birds.[33]

Apparently Baird did not consider his generalizations concerning geographical variation to be terribly monumental or original. They occur as passing references within much longer books and articles largely devoted to other subjects. Moreover, he provided only limited data to back up his assertions. And he was careful to cite a German predecessor, Constantin Gloger, who had noted regular geographical variation in European birds nearly three decades previously.[34]

While Baird's references to changes in birds across their geographic ranges remained brief, largely undocumented assertions, Allen's 1871 paper presenting the results of his Florida expedition contained a lengthy discussion of the phenomenon of geographical variation. Allen first showed that the level of individual variation in the size and color of species was much larger than had been previously appreciated; in some cases different specimens of the same species were found to vary as much as 20 percent in size. Because taxonomists had frequently relied on size to differentiate species and even genera, the failure to recognize the high level of individual variation had led to the introduction of "numerous strictly nominal species."[35]

Allen then differentiated between this background level of individual variation and larger trends in that variation reflected in population-wide averages. Because he believed the characteristics responsible for these trends were directly induced by temperature and humidity, Allen frequently referred to this latter type of variation as "climatic variation," a term he used interchangeably with geographical variation.[36] Allen demonstrated that morphological variation in populations could be roughly correlated with the location of the population by employing the same tabular presentation of data that Baird had first used in his Pacific Railroad Survey Report. However, Allen introduced a crucial innovation into his lists of specimens: tables with summaries showing the minimum, maximum, and average sizes of the specimens originating from various geographic locations (fig. 14).

Measurements of Southern Specimens of AGELÆUS PHŒNICEUS.

M. C. Z. No.	Coll. No.	Sex	Locality.	Date.	Collector.	Length.	Al. Ext.	Wing.	Tail.	Head.	Bill. Cul.	Bill. Hgt.	Bill. Wid.
4126	—	♂	Charleston, S. C.	———	L. Agassiz	9.55	14.75	4.75	3.65	1.90	1.00	.45	.37
4127	—	♂	" "	———	"	8.80	14.30	4.50	3.55	1.74	.87	.47	.40
4128	—	♂	" "	———	"	9.45	14.50	4.60	3 72	1.80	.90	.50	.40
4129	—	♂	" "	———	"	9.05	13.50	4.87	3.45	1.73	.85	.43	.42
4125	—	♂	" "	———	"	9.05	14.12	4.42	3.35	1.94	.95	.46	.35
—	—	♂	Hawkinsville, Fla.	Mar. 15,'69	J. A. Allen	8.25	13.60	4.34	—	—	—	—	—
—	1928		Jacksonville, "	Dec. 31,'69	C. J. Maynard	9 10	14 90	4 75	3.58	—	—	—	—
10565	1929	♂	" "	Dec. 31,'69	"	9.20	14.90	4.80	3.90	—	—	—	—
10561	2013	♂	" "	Dec. 31,'69	"	8.80	14 15	4.55	3 58	—	—	—	—
10574	2552	♂	Dummitt's, "	Mar. 8,'69	"	9 50	14.20	4.75	3.90	—	—	—	—
10573	2450	♂	" "	Feb. 24,'69	"	8.50	14.00	4.75	3.45	—	—	—	—
5153	—	♀	Hibernia, "	Jan. 30,'69	J. A. Allen	7 65	12.60	3.85	3.05	—	—	—	—
5154	—	♀	" "	Jan. 30,'69	"	7.85	12.50	3.90	3 07	—	—	—	—
5155	—	♀	" "	Jan. 30,'69	"	7.80	12.85	—	3 20	—	—	—	—
4141	—	♀	" "	Jan. 30,'69	"	8.00	12.25	3 80	3 05	—	—	—	—
5209	—	♀	Welaka, "	Feb. 8,'69	"	7.65	12.50	3 75	2 90	—	—	—	—
5208	—	♀	" "	Feb. 8,'69	"	7.50	11 85	3 63	2 75	—	—	—	—
5210	—	♀	" "	Feb. 8,'69	"	7.65	12.55	3.95	—	—	—	—	—

Measurements of California Specimens of AGELÆUS PHŒNICEUS.

M. C. Z. No.	Sex	Locality.	Date.	Collector.	Length.	Al. Ext.	Wing.	Tail.	Tarsus.
5885	♂	San Francisco, Cal.	Winter '59 – '60	A. Agassiz	8.50	14.98	4.83	3.50	1.63
5884	♂	" "	Winter '59 – '60	"	8.75	15 05	4 95	3.35	1.74
566	♂	" "	Winter '59 – '60	"	8 60	14 55	4.47	3 09	1.90
2188	♂	Gulf of Georgia, W.T.	Sept. —, '60	"	8.71	13.50	4.45	3.26	1.75
5889	♂	San Francisco, Cal.	Winter '59 – '60	"	7.58	12 80	4.03	2.73	1.63
5893	♀	" "	Winter '59 – '60	"	7.55	12.35	3.95	2.47	1.46
5887	♀	" "	Winter '59 – '60	"	7.81	12.80	4.25	3.96	1.54
5890	♀	" "	Winter '59 – '60	"	7 50	12.75	3 94	2.47	1.56
5886	♀	" "	Winter '59 – '60	T. G. Cary	7.82	12.77	4.04	2.62	1.56
2075	♀	" "	Winter '59 – '60	"	8.29	13.27	4 32	3.00	1.62
2074	♀	" "	Winter '59 – '60	"	8.18	13.25	3.85	2.95	1 67
2078	♀	" "	Winter '59 – '60	"	8.50	13.00	4.15	3 10	1 65
5888	♀	" "	Winter '59 – '60	A. Agassiz	7.25	12.25	3 90	3.71	1.50

Summary of the above Measurements of Specimens of AGELÆUS PHŒNIÇEUS.

Locality.	Sex	No. of Specimens		Length.	Al. Ext	Wing.	Tail.	Head.	Culmen	Height.	Width.
Massachusetts	♂	40	Aver.	9.16	14.71	4 69	3.63	1.79*	.88*	.46*	.39*
	♀	28	Aver.	7.53	12.24	3.86	2 93	1.57†	.75†	.395†	.357†
South Carolina and Florida	♂	11	Aver.	9.02	14.41	4.62	3.61	1.83	.91‡	.46‡	.39‡
	♀	7	Aver.	7.73	12.44	3.83	2.99	—	—	—	—
California	♂	7	Aver.	8.64	14.52	4.67	3.30	1.75	—	—	—
	♀	9	Aver.	7.83	12.70	4.00	2.99	1 57	—	—	—
Massachusetts	♂	40	Max.	9.85	15.35	5.00	3.90	1.94*	.97*	.50*	.45*
	♂	40	Min.	8.40	13.95	4.43	3.12	1.60*	.75*	.43*	.33*
	♀	28	Max.	8 55	13.55	4.26	3.15	1.68†	.82†	.44†	.43†
	♀	28	Min.	7.35	11.25	3.63	2 65	1.48†	.70†	.37†	.30†
South Carolina and Florida	♂	11	Max.	9.55	14.90	4.80	3.90	1.94‡	1.00‡	.50‡	.40‡
	♂	11	Min.	8.25	13.60	4 34	3.35	1.74‡	.86‡	.43‡	.35‡
	♀	7	Max.	8.00	12.85	3.90	3 20	—	—	—	—
	♀	7	Min.	7.50	11.85	3.63	2.75	—	—	—	—
California	♂	7	Max.	8.75	15.05	4.95	3.50	1 90	—	—	—
	♂	7	Min.	8.50	13 50	4.45	3.09	1.63	—	—	—
	♀	9	Max.	8.50	13.27	4 32	3.86	1.67	—	—	—
	♀	9	Min.	7.25	12 25	3.85	2 47	1 46	—	—	—

* 29 specimens.   † 19 specimens.   ‡ 5 specimens.

Figure 14. Allen's list of red-winged blackbird specimens, 1871.

Allen thus provided a wealth of empirical data to substantiate his generalizations about the level of regular geographical variation in several bird species.

Allen ended his discussion with a consideration of some of its implications. The original description of most American birds had been made by European ornithologists, often based on a single specimen. However, with access to a large series of specimens collected across their continent, American ornithologists had begun to show that many of these apparently distinct forms intergraded through specimens from intermediate localities. They were not distinct species, but only different "varieties, races, or simply forms" of a single species. Nomenclaturally, the appropriate way to handle these variant forms was to use the first name applied to any of them and to include with its specific description a statement of its tendency to vary with locality and the degree to which that tendency was developed.[37]

Ironically, although Allen failed to advocate the use of trinomials in the designation of geographical forms in 1871, his "Mammals and Winter Birds" paper did more to promote the wide-scale adoption of the practice in America than any other single work. It did so by providing evidence for a clear and simple distinction between species and subspecies (or what he then usually called geographical forms or varieties): subspecies are forms that intergrade across their range, while species do not. It was this distinction that provided the "guidance to a methodical and consistent trinomialism" promoted by the "American school."[38] Trinomial nomenclature had occasionally been used in both American and European ornithological works, but before Allen had formulated his "test of intergradation," its use was sporadic and often unsystematic.[39]

In a June 1871 review of "Mammals and Winter Birds of Florida," Elliott Coues challenged Allen's claim that geographical variants should all be referred to a single species. Instead he recommended that trinomial nomenclature ought to be used to designate such forms.[40] Coues also suggested that the distinct geographic forms Allen had described probably represented an initial stage in the formation of species.[41] In doing so he linked the geographic variation studies of Baird and Allen with the wider stream of American evolutionary speculation initiated by Darwin's *Origin of Species*.[42]

A year later Coues published his *Key to North American Birds*, the first comprehensive listing of American birds that systematically applied trinomials using Allen's newly formulated test of intergradation.[43] Coues recognized distinct geographic forms (or subspecies) of a species by giving them all the same specific name and providing each with a different third name, with the abbreviation "var." inserted between the specific and subspecific epithets.[44] One of the first artificial keys in zoology designed for both novice and advanced naturalists, Coues's *Key* was an immediate commercial and critical success.[45] As a result, both the idea of using trinomial nomenclature to recognize subspecies and the particular names contained in the *Key* gained a large following.

Between the time he published his 1871 paper and the time he assumed editorship of the Nuttall Club *Bulletin* in 1876, Allen had also become a proponent of recognizing geographical variation with trinomial nomenclature. His first use of that nomenclature, with the abbreviation "var." inserted between the specific and subspecific epithet, came less than one year after his "Mammals and Winter Birds" paper.[46] Five years later, Allen endorsed the use of pure trinomial nomenclature without intervening abbreviations. He noted that the discovery that "certain strains of deviation of pronounced types (i.e., geographic variation) occurred in a large number of species in different families" led to the recognition of "the subspecific relationship of many forms which when first made known seemed unquestionably of specific rank."[47] Now, he argued, ornithologists ought to provide nomenclatural recognition of such forms:

> The next step, and apparently a wholly logical one in the revolution, will doubtless be the general adoption of a trinomial system of nomenclature for the more convenient expression of relationship of what are conveniently termed "sub-species," so that we may write, for instance, *Falco communis anatum* in place of the more cumbersome *Falco communis* subsp. *anatum*. This system is already, in fact, to some extent in use here, though looked upon with strong disfavor by our transatlantic fellow-workers, who seem not fully to understand the nature of the recent rapid advance ornithology has been made in this country, or to appreciate the thoroughly substantial nature of the evidence on which it is based.[48]

Allen then pointed out that recognition of geographical variation and the subspecies was made possible by the successive waves of exploration undertaken by American collectors, which resulted in the acquisition of "hundreds and often thousands of specimens of a single species, representing the gradually varying phases presented at hundreds of localities."[49]

As editor of the *Bulletin of the Nuttall Ornithological Club*, Allen promoted the use of trinomial nomenclature in two ways. First, beginning with the initial volume in 1876, he regularly published papers with trinomial subspecies designations. Second, the *Bulletin* became a forum for frequent outcries for nomenclatural reform. In one extensive paper discussing the issue, Robert Ridgway argued that the binomial system created by Linnaeus was no longer adequate now that most naturalists recognized that species were not stable and fixed. Ridgway then issued what was becoming an increasingly familiar call for the recognition of subspecies "by a suitable amendment of the rules of nomenclature."[50] Under Allen's guidance, the subject of trinomial nomenclature failed to receive criticism in the *Bulletin*, even though there was significant opposition to the innovation both in the United States and abroad.[51]

Meanwhile, in 1880 Robert Ridgway published a catalog of North American birds that adopted trinomial nomenclature, but differed greatly from the checklist issued by Coues six years previously.[52] Throughout their lives, the two naturalists clashed on a variety of issues, but the animus between them was ultimately related to differences in temperament and the fact that in 1874 Ridgway secured a permanent appointment on the staff at the Smithsonian Institution, something that Coues had long desired but never achieved.[53] Ridgway revised the list and arranged for its separate publication a year later under the title of *Nomenclature of North American Birds* (1881).[54] Following the publication of Ridgway's list, one prominent ornithologist complained:

> I see by Ridgway's new catalogue that he has made a great change in our nomenclature, if it is accepted by ornithologists in general. It never will be in Europe and will cause much confusion to ornithologists who do not confine themselves to the study of a comparatively small tract of country. We shall also be finding varieties of varieties a few years from now and will see something like the following[:] Passer domesticus domesticus americanus longerostris nigricaudatus &tc &tc with a string of authorities following.[55]

But with the imprimatur of one of the nation's most prestigious scientific institutions behind it, Ridgway's list quickly won converts from Coues's earlier checklist.[56]

Never one to back down from controversy, Coues answered Ridgway's challenge by issuing his own revised checklist a year later.[57] The move prompted C. Hart Merriam to comment impatiently: "It seems very peculiar that our leading ornithologists can not agree upon the names by which we shall know our common birds. The contrary is, to say the least, extremely unfortunate."[58] Scientific ornithologists were not the only ones disturbed by the prospect of two contradictory lists. In a short notice appearing in the collecting-oriented *Ornithologist and Oologist*, the author complimented Coues's workmanship but decried the chaos it might introduce into specimen exchanges: "It will have extensive circulation, but it will be unfortunate if a portion of our collectors should recognize its numbers, as it will create confusion in every transfer, unless specimens are doubly numbered."[59] Within the next year, the controversy led to the call for the formation of the AOU to settle the issue.

THE AOU AND NOMENCLATURAL REFORM

Nomenclatural reform and the subspecies research program were foremost on the minds of the three AOU founders from the time they first began to contemplate the organization. As early as January 1883, Coues's thinly veiled call for a national association of ornithologists hinted at the pressing need to achieve nomenclatural uniformity as a primary reason to institutionalize ornithologists.[60] And the formal invitation to the inaugural AOU meeting issued by Coues, Brewster, and Allen in early August 1883 announced that a special object of the new organization would be the "revision of the current lists of North American Birds, to the end of adopting a uniform system of classification . . . carrying the authority of the Union."[61]

In responding to the invitation to attend the founding meeting of the AOU, Robert Ridgway announced his strong support for the proposed organization, and especially "the prospect of gaining unanimity in the matter of nomenclature."[62] In a letter to Allen a week later, Ridgway stressed the importance of keeping the matter of nomenclatural reform firmly in the hands of a few carefully selected scientific ornithologists:

> The great difficulty which I see in the way of having the question of nomenclature discussed by the "convention as a whole," is that this would involve the value of the views of a considerable number of amateurs, some of them with the crudest possible information on the subject, as opposed to the intelligent discussion of the subject by a few well informed specialists. The only way, in my opinion, would be to have the matter put into the hands of a committee composed exclusively of working ornithologists, and have this committee hold a special session for the purpose of coming to an agreement. . . . I cannot too strongly urge, however, the *necessity* of limiting such a committee to a very carefully selected number of working ornithologists who are known to possess intelligent views on the subject.[63]

But on this point Ridgway was preaching to the choir. The three AOU founders never intended to open up the nomenclatural issue for consideration by the larger ornithological community, which had not even been invited to the first AOU meeting. Rather, they worked to keep the issue under the control of a few of the most technically proficient ornithologists who held views similar to their own.

The Committee on Classification and Nomenclature was the first of several committees created on the second day of the AOU's inaugural meeting in September 1883.[64] As had been arranged before the meeting, temporary AOU Chairman Coues appointed himself, Allen, Brewster, Henry W. Henshaw, and Ridgway to the committee, which held its first series of seven sessions in Washington on 11–19 December 1883.[65] After reaching a consensus on the scope of its work, the basic nomenclatural rules to be incorporated into its proposed code, and several species to be included in its official list of North American birds, the committee divided itself into two subcommittees to hammer together a final report. Allen and Coues placed themselves on the subcommittee to compose the AOU's code of nomenclature, while Ridgway, Henshaw, and Brewster were charged with formulating the official checklist based on the new code. During these and subsequent deliberations in March and September 1884 and April 1885, the committee sought the aid of several other prominent American naturalists, including Theodore Gill, Leonhard Stejneger, C. Hart Merriam, Charles B. Cory, and, of course, Spencer F. Baird.

The committee presented its proposed code and checklist to the AOU Council for formal approval in April 1885, and the work was finally published nearly a year later, in March 1886.[66] Although largely based on the Strickland Code, which had first been adopted by the British Association for the Advancement of Science in 1842, the new AOU Code also contained several novel provisions that distinguished it from its predecessors. Among the major innovations claimed by the framers of the AOU Code were the adoption of the tenth edition of Linnaeus's *Systema Naturae* (1758) as the starting point of the law of priority (instead of the twelfth edition [1766]) and allowing names previously employed in botany to be available for zoology.[67] But the most important innovation was

Canon XI, which advocated the use of pure trinomial nomenclature to designate intergrading subspecific forms.[68] Allen used the lengthy "Remarks" section that followed Canon XI to clarify the committee's intent regarding the application of trinomial nomenclature:

> Trinomials are not necessarily to be used for those slightly distinct and scarcely stable forms which zoologists are in the habit of calling "varieties"; still less for sports, hybrids, artificial breeds, and the like; nor indeed to signalize some grade or degree of difference which it may be desired to note by name, but which is not deemed worthy of scientific designation. The system proceeds upon a sound scientific principle, underlying one of the most important zoological problems of the day,—no less a problem than that of the variation of animals under physical conditions of the environment, and thus of the origin of species itself. The system is also intimately connected with the whole subject of geographical distribution of animals; it being found, as a matter of experience, that the trinomial system is particularly pertinent and applicable to those geographical "subspecies," "races," or "varieties" which have become recognizable as such through their modification according to latitude, longitude, elevation, temperature, humidity and other climatic conditions.[69]

Allen continued by pointing out that it was not the "kind or quality, nor the degree or quantity, of difference" of one organism in relation to another that determined whether it should be labeled with a binomial or trinomial designation. Differences that were "constant," no matter how small, might be considered as distinct species and hence named using strictly binomial nomenclature. However, any difference "no matter how extreme in its manifestation, that is found to lessen and disappear when specimens from a large geographical area, or from contiguous faunal regions . . . is to be provided for by some other method than that which formally recognizes 'species' as the ultimate factors in zoological classification." Allen then succinctly summarized the American basis for the application of trinomial nomenclature: "*Intergradation* is the touchstone of trinomialism."[70]

In the concluding section of his commentary on Canon XI, Allen again revealed that the American promotion of trinomial nomenclature for intergrading forms was a source of nationalistic pride: "It is gratifying evidence, therefore, of the progress of Ornithology, and of the position attained by that branch of science in America, that the members of an American Ornithological Association have it in their power first formally to enunciate the principles of the new method, the practicality of which they have already demonstrated to their fellow workers in Zoology."[71]

As the editor of the *Auk*, Allen consistently promoted the adoption of the new AOU Code and Checklist. For example, he arranged for David Starr Jordan, a prominent ichthyologist and president of Indiana University, to write a sympathetic review of the publication for the *Auk*.[72] Although Jordan had some minor quibbles with two of the code's many canons, he was generally laudatory and hopeful that the AOU's handiwork would soon become the standard nomenclatural authority not only for American ornithology, but for "zoology and botany" as well.[73] In the early years of his editorship, Allen also routinely edited manuscripts submitted to the *Auk* to make them conform to new AOU Code and Checklist.[74]

AOU leaders initiated a series of related reforms to promote the subspecies research program and consolidate their discipline. One of these reforms involved the push to introduce uniform standards into the practice of scientific ornithology. In 1888 the council of the union appointed a special committee to devise "some uniform method of measuring birds."[75] Because scientists often created new subspecies based on small average differences in the lengths of birds and their appendages, consistency in the way those measurements were taken was crucial to the subspecies research program. Not surprisingly, the committee found that "systems employed by different authors varied widely" and two years later issued a report recommending standard methods of taking measurements of the bill and tail.[76] But for reasons that remain unclear, shortly after submitting what was supposed to be the first of several reports, the committee disbanded. It was over forty years later before there was another serious attempt to address the problem of inconsistency in bird measurement.[77]

In a separate call for reform in measurement practices during this same period, several Americans advocated abandoning "the confusing and irrational system of inches and hundredths in the measurement of birds and eggs" for the more "rational" and widely adopted metric system. For example, Merriam argued that the founding of the AOU marked the "commencement of a new era in American ornithology." Now that the union was about "to establish a stable nomenclature," it ought to give up "the barbarous scale of our forefathers and join the men of science of all nations in adhering to a system of weights and measures that is uniform throughout the world."[78] Again, this reform achieved only modest success. Although the AOU Council decided not to require the use of the metric system in the *Auk*, a number of authors began to use it routinely.[79]

In 1886, the same year as the appearance of the AOU Code and Checklist, Robert Ridgway published a nomenclature of colors in an effort to standardize this notoriously subjective attribute.[80] Containing named examples of some two hundred colors, the first edition of Ridgway's *Nomenclature of Colors for Naturalists* came to be used widely by scientific ornithologists both in the field and in museums. Ridgway, an accomplished artist, remained interested in the subject of color nomenclature throughout his lifetime, and in 1912 he published an expanded version of his reference work. The second edition of Ridgway's nomenclature contained over a thousand named colors.[81]

PLAIN ENGLISH

By the time the AOU issued its official checklist in 1886, collectors had begun to speak out against the introduction of trinomial nomenclature. The issue was part of a larger discussion about the amateur's inability to keep abreast of developments in an increasingly technical scientific ornithology. I have already mentioned the resentment that many AOU associate members felt at being asked to support the *Auk*, which was often unintelligible to all save a few knowledgeable specialists. Associates were especially critical of articles that failed to include the common names of birds, which collectors generally preferred over scientific names.[82] For the most part, they and the larger collecting community also rejected scientists' claims about the need to designate by formal names the increasingly minute morphological differences upon which most subspecific distinctions were based. Rallying under the banner of "Plain English," collectors sought to maintain ornithology's wide accessibility.

Underlying the controversy were fundamentally conflicting visions of the scientific endeavor. One was a more inclusive model that sought to reconcile the needs of scientists with those of the larger community of amateur practitioners. The other model presented the construction of boundaries between the technically oriented specialist and the novice as a necessary step in the continued development of science. Unlike many scientific disciplines that tended to move firmly in the direction of exclusivity and increasingly rigid boundaries as the nineteenth century came to a close, most scientific ornithologists continued to be guided by a combination of both visions. It was a tension that plagued ornithology well into the twentieth century.

As it did with several other divisive issues, the *Ornithologist and Oologist* provided a regular forum for opposition to the AOU. Recall that in November 1883 the periodical's editor and owner, Joseph M. Wade, had ridiculed scientific ornithologists' preoccupation with nomenclature in a suppressed editorial protesting the exclusive membership policy of the new AOU.[83] A few months earlier, Wade had published a short letter entitled "Plain English," which praised his editorial policy of rendering articles in a more accessible "popular style." According to the letter's author, Montague Chamberlain, too much scientific writing was rendered in overly jargon-ridden prose, which made it inaccessible not only to the public, but even to informed amateurs like himself, who studied "a branch of science for the pleasure to be derived from it or for a relaxation from more engrossing labor." Wading through the morass of obscure, polysyllabic appellations contained in most scientific treatises tried the patience of even the most dedicated amateur ornithologists:

> These [amateurs] are obliged, in order to keep informed of the latest discoveries, to read the determinations of the leading observers in their chosen departments, but it is in much the same spirit as that with which they submit to the manipulations of a dentist, that they worry through the tedious pages filled with unattractive and often obscure sentences, with Latin and Greek terms and names which are hard to spell, hard to pronounce, hard to remember, and harder still to understand.[84]

Scientific publications "could be written quite as easily and with as exact precision without the constant use of these technicalities." But authors purposefully used obscure prose to make their writing unintelligible to all but a select few, and thereby "to throw over science that veil of mystery which is so dear to the *savant*, and beneath which he delights to pose as the custodian of knowledge too profound for ordinary mortals to comprehend."

In a letter appearing a month later, Chamberlain also questioned the right of the self-styled "American School" to ignore the British Association's authority in nomenclatural matters. According to Chamberlain, the trinomialism promoted by the "American School" was not only contrary to the letter of the British Association's Strickland Code, but also uniformly condemned by European naturalists.[85]

For several years after 1886, much of the discussion of nomenclatural matters in the *Ornithologist and Oologist* centered on the new AOU Code and Checklist. For example, in May 1886 an anonymous editorial noted impatiently that with the recent appearance of the AOU's official inventory, there were now five disparate catalogs of North American birds.[86] The author hoped that this latest list would finally bring stability to nomenclature, but he doubted that the AOU list would immediately come into wide use since its $3.00 price tag placed it "beyond the reach of many who desire several lists for use in labelling and exchange."[87] After a brief editorial again decrying the steep price of the AOU list in 1888, a year later the periodical called the continued use of several contradictory systems "embarrassing" and suggested that collectors and dealers label their specimens, catalogs, and exchange lists using a fraction composed of the AOU number in the denominator and the Ridgway number in the numerator until all could agree on a single uniform system.[88]

During the next few years, the *Ornithologist and Oologist* pursued a different tack in its criticism of the AOU and its system of trinomial nomenclature: satiric verse. The first venture in this genre was a twenty-five stanza gem that openly ridiculed the practice of creating subspecies based on barely discernible differences in size or plumage color.[89] The poem described an amateur ornithologist's excitement upon receiving a common English sparrow mailed to him in jest by two close friends. After carefully inspecting his new specimen and comparing it to others of the same species already in his collection, the ornithologist was delighted to discover that his new sparrow was "just one shade darker, on the edge of the breast" and therefore could be designated as a new subspecies. The poem then described how the act of bestowing a subspecific epithet transformed the previously humble collector into a vainglorious ornithologist, whose dubious achievement was certain to result in his election as an honorary member of the AOU:

> When next we did meet him, three weeks to a day,
> You scarcely would know him, so changed was his way;
> A sense of his GREATNESS, his wisdom and skill,
> His manner, his action, his life seemed to fill.
>
> Now that his name is known wide and far,
> He'll hereafter smoke naught but a ten-cent cigar;
> And at the next meeting (the hints are not few)
> There are prospects of election as an "H" A.O.U.[90]

For those readers unable to discern the author's critical tone from the body of the poem, the concluding stanza left no doubt as to his attitude toward the proliferation of subspecies:

> Kind reader, we call to your careful attention
> This wonderful growth of a modern invention.
> Lord knows where we'll end if this craze increases,
> Such a trotting out yearly of created SUB-SPECIES.

Several months later the magazine published a second poem, which again simultaneously ridiculed the needless creation of subspecies, scientific ornithology, and the AOU.[91] The protagonist in the story was the editor of an unnamed ornithological periodical who, while sorting through his correspondence late one evening, came upon two curious letters. Both were from collectors who had recently captured several shrikes and had carefully noted the stomach contents of their specimens. The first collector found that the diet of his birds had consisted entirely of "insects, bugs, and the like." The second collector, who had shot his shrikes only after witnessing them prey upon other birds, not surprisingly found only the remains of "sparrows, and other small birds" in the stomachs of his specimens. The remainder of the poem detailed how the clever editor resolved the dilemma presented by these contradictory accounts of the shrike's diet by splitting the species into two subspecies:

> Now the editor, he was ambitious too,
>   He wanted his share of the fame;
> He wanted to see at some future time
>   An alphabet tacked to his name.[92]

> So he said to himself, I will settle this thing,
>   I'll make two sub-species of these;
> I'll take Mr. A's, which feed upon bugs
>   Which they glean from the ice-covered trees,

> And call it the *L. b. insec-ti-vorous*[93]
>   And the other will then follow on,
> In shall be the *L. b. ornitho-vorous*
>   And the thing shall be regarded as done.

> Now all ye august and mighty A.B.'s
>   Who hold our fates in your hands,
> Assemble your conclaves, and get out your "Keys"
>   And loosen the tightly drawn bands.

> Regard this poor mortal thus thirsting for fame,
>   He's anxiously waiting the Tail
> Which a letter will bring, to affix to his name
>   By the next "U.S.S.D." mail.

When the *Ornithologist and Oologist* fell victim to the depression of 1893, the AOU lost one of its most constant critics. Most other collecting-oriented periodicals tended to use common nomenclature in their pages and to ignore the issue of scientific nomenclature entirely. Typical of this strategy was the *O & O*'s chief rival for the patronage of collectors, the natural history dealer Frank H. Lattin's

Oologist. In the first year of publication, 1884, Lattin announced that since "ninety-nine one-hundredths, if not all collectors" abhorred Latin names, he would use "plain English" whenever possible.[94] When the AOU published its code, the review appearing in the *Oologist* was generally sympathetic, but it discussed only the changes in common names, not the scientific names it sanctioned.[95]

Where Lattin had tended to ignore the constant name changes in scientific nomenclature, Richard M. Barnes, the lawyer and egg collector who purchased the magazine in 1909, repeatedly raised the issue. Barnes attacked the tendency to create subspecies based on increasingly fine distinctions discernible only to specialists with access to extensive research collections. In one typical editorial, Barnes also decried the widening gap between "professional Ornithologists and amateurs." According to the editor of the *Oologist*, most of the "so-called 'professional' ornithologists" made a living from taxes assessed on the public, which included a great many amateur bird students. Yet these same "professionals" completely ignored the potentially valuable contributions of amateurs, while seeking to bolster their reputation by "discovering alleged geographic races of birds [i.e., subspecies], the delineation of which to the tax-paying public off of whom they live is, and always will be an unfathomable mystery."[96] Often Barnes condemned the "scientific snobbery" exhibited by those who insisted on using only Latin names when common names were much more accessible and often more stable.[97] Writing in the early decades of the twentieth century, Barnes had a vision for ornithology that was more in keeping with the heterogeneous community in the pre-AOU days than with the increasingly differentiated community of his time.

Discussion of amateur discontent with trinomialism was not confined to collecting journals. From the time of the first issue in January 1884, the *Auk* contained regular references to the popular outcry against nomenclatural recognition of subspecies. Again it was Montague Chamberlain, an earlier champion of the use of "plain English" in scientific treatises, who asked "Are trinomials necessary?" By this point, Chamberlain, who had recently been elected to the AOU Council and appointed associate editor of the *Auk*, was clearly acting with the knowledge and encouragement of AOU leaders.[98] They hoped that by airing the issue under carefully controlled circumstances, they might win converts to the subspecies program. As someone who had recently spoken out against excessive use of jargon and scientific nomenclature in ornithological writing, Chamberlain could credibly present himself as the champion of the amateur.

Chamberlain began by pointing out that in asking if trinomials were necessary, he was not trying to persuade advocates of the practice to repudiate it. Rather his goal was to "have the whole matter plainly set forth, and, if possible, an end put to the opposition to this system" among amateur ornithologists: "Let me state here, that I do not wish to assert that this opposition occurs in the ranks of the more advanced of American students—the 'scientists' . . . indeed so far as I am aware, it is found only among a portion of my brethren of the 'amateur element.' "[99] Montague also noted that opposition to trinomialism came from a number of "*savants* of Europe," who, with the sole exception of Henry Seebohm, had uniformly denounced the system.[100]

In his reply to Chamberlain's query, Allen detailed the logic behind trinomial nomenclature as it was promoted by the "American school" and then attempted to document support for the system abroad. In an effort to boost the authority of the practice he had helped create, Allen claimed that the trinomial system did not do "violence" to the earlier Strickland Code, but that it was a means "to meet simply and completely, a condition of things unknown and unsuspected when that . . . admirable system was conceived [i.e., evolution]." He also cited important European precedents for trinomialism, including Hermann Schlegel of the Leyden Museum, who had begun using trinomials as early as 1844. A few years earlier, American ornithologists, anxious to make a name for themselves, had ignored Schlegel's earlier use of trinomials. Now Allen attempted to use the name of the Dutch ornithologist to boost the authority of the AOU's actions. But in doing so Allen was careful to point out that ornithologists in the United States had begun advocating trinomials independent of their knowledge of Schlegel's earlier use: "While he antedates Americans in the systematic use of trinomials for intergrading forms, we are in position to know that the 'American school' was the spontaneous outcome of our studies of American birds, and that the use of trinomials was forced upon us by conviction of their utility and necessity."[101]

Apparently unconvinced by Allen's reply, three months later Chamberlain called for further clarification on several points. According to Chamberlain, "American amateur ornithologists" had no particular opposition to the use of three terms to distinguish varieties from species. Rather, they denied the "necessity of recognizing varieties by *any* distinctive appellation":

> We harbor no "Dr. Dry-as-dust" "craze" for a purely binomial nomenclature, but we do protest against the propagation of any system which unnecessarily creates obstacles to the study of science, instead of simplifying it; we do ask that our leaders shall not take a step backward and force upon us something which is . . . not only no improvement, but a palpable injury; that we not be dragged into a "craze" for trinomialism by following the lead of an "American school."[102]

According to Chamberlain, the "amateur element" had several complaints with trinomialism. First was the belief that "recognition of varieties" tended "to create confusion, in classification and nomenclature," and increased "the difficulty of identifying specimens." Moreover, if the argument for designating subspecies was carried to its logical conclusion, "*every* variation from a given type must receive a distinctive name; necessitating not alone the recognition of varieties of species, but also of varieties of varieties almost without limit." And finally, Chamberlain argued that if forms were distinctive enough to deserve different names, they should be designated as separate species, instead of mere varieties.

Allen replied by admitting that if doubters could see a large series of specimens firsthand, they would soon be convinced of the necessity for trinomial nomenclature. Any difficulties associated with general questions of classification and nomenclature and with the creation of subspecies more particularly were not due to the adoption of trinomial nomenclature, but were "necessarily inherent in the subject." According to Allen, there was a "philosophic principle" that under-girded the practice of bestowing trinomial nomenclature, and even the "unbeliev-ers" of which Chamberlain spoke were "not to be presumed to be so skeptical as to ignore the modern doctrine of evolution." Varieties, Allen asserted, were "in-cipient species" which were "still in the process of evolution." This fact had to be taken into account by the system of classification and nomenclature advocated by most American ornithologists. Experts might occasionally err in their judgment on where to draw the line between species and subspecies, but on the whole they were the only "safe guides."[103]

Following this initial set of exchanges, *Auk* editors generally avoided entering into direct discussion on the issue of continued amateur discontent with trinomi-alism. But the problem was repeatedly mentioned in passing within the context of the more general nomenclatural controversy that raged in the pages of *Auk* for the next fifty years.

As I have already suggested, amateur opposition to trinomialism was but one small part of that community's larger discontent with a scientific ornithology that seemed increasingly unconcerned with its needs. Yet scientists continued to de-pend on this larger community for specimens, legitimation, and financial support. Nowhere is this tension between professional dependence and amateur frustration more apparent than in a letter from an amateur ornithologist from Milwaukee, Walter B. Hull, to *Auk* editor J. A. Allen in 1897:

> Have the Editors of the Auk ever considered the advantage to be gained in publishing the common names of the birds, particularly the more common, in connection with the Latin? The habit of writers using Latin entirely seems to be contagious. For a purely scientific journal, *supported by scientists alone*, I could take no exceptions to that course. But for the Secretary to send out a sheet every fall, urging members to interest their friends, or in plain English, *get their money to help run the Auk*, and as a reward, send them a quarterly with descriptions of they know not what, while these same sub-jects of discussion may be flitting about their lawns and they none the wiser, though perfectly familiar with all our common birds. If the manager cannot take the time to insert the [common] names in case authors neglect so to do, then do *not* ask the layman to help support the publication of scientists, as the management has done ever since I have been acquainted with their methods—1889.[104]

Hull went on to state that he and most amateurs would rather see "plain English" in the *Auk* than the expensive color plates that regularly adorned its pages. He also claimed that he had experienced little luck in getting participants in local bird study classes to join the AOU. Although initially interested, when provided a sample copy of the *Auk*, these enthusiasts replied "Why don't you have it all in Latin, it would mean just as much to us." Hull indicated that he would withdraw his AOU membership if the situation did not improve soon, and concluded with the suggestion that "for business reasons, if no other, would it not be advisable to accommodate the layman."

TRINOMIAL WOES

As the nineteenth century drew to a close, the three major innovations promoted by the framers of the AOU Code—the establishment of the tenth edition of Linnaeus's *Systema Naturae* (1758) as the beginning point for the law of priority, the separation of zoological and botanical nomenclature, and the use of trinomial nomenclature to designate subspecies—gained wide acceptance among technically oriented zoologists in the United States and abroad.[105] As one indication of increasing European support for the practice of trinomialism, in 1898 the delegates gathered at the Fourth International Congress of Zoology in Cambridge, England, appointed a fifteen-member committee charged with drafting a single international code of nomenclature to supersede the various competing national and specialist codes.[106] After careful review of the existing codes, the committee incorporated the most important American innovations—including the designation of subspecies by use of a third term added to the traditional Linnaean binomial—into their proposed International Code of Zoological Nomenclature.[107] Three years later, the zoologists attending the Fifth International Congress in Berlin ratified a modified form of this draft code, and it was finally published in French, English, and German text as *Règles internationales de la Nomenclature zoologique* in 1905.[108]

Despite widespread support for trinomial nomenclature, the larger goal of establishing a single, stable list of North American bird forms remained elusive. The AOU Checklist was increasingly accepted as the sole authority for the scientific names of North American birds, but the names contained in the various editions of the list (2d ed., 1895; 3d ed., 1910; 4th ed., 1931) and their numerous supplements were subject to constant revision.[109]

One major factor responsible for the regular shuffling of bird names was rigid enforcement of the law of priority. American promoters of the practice had hoped its consistent application would lead to nomenclatural permanence by fixing a particular bird form to its first properly published name after the 1758 starting point.[110] During the first half-century following the publication of the first AOU Code and Checklist, however, the law of priority had failed miserably to deliver on this promise. Ornithologists continued to dredge up obscure ornithological publications containing earlier names, and the decision about whether a given previous name applied in a particular case was often complex and subject to differing interpretations.

The constant stream of name changes necessitated by the strict adherence to the law of priority (and other similar guidelines established in an effort to promote nomenclatural stability) did not pass unnoticed. One of the most notorious cases of nomenclatural variability during this period was the ubiquitous American robin, the red-breasted portent of spring that one author has recently described as "the most familiar and best-loved songbird in North America."[111] Though known to every schoolchild as the robin, the bird appeared in the first and second editions of the AOU Checklist under the scientific name *Merula migratoria*, in the third edition as *Planesticus migratorius*, and in the fourth edition as *Turdus migratorius*![112] As scientific ornithologist and popularizer Frank Chapman pointed out, in this case and many others during the previous half-decade, the lowly common name, long eschewed by many technically oriented ornithologists, had proven more enduring than its scientific counterpart.[113] Not surprisingly, in the face of the continued variability of technical nomenclature, many amateur ornithologists and collectors who had long championed common over scientific nomenclature felt vindicated.

Continued instability in technical nomenclature also disturbed many scientific ornithologists who noted the relative fixity of common names. For example, in 1905 William Leon Dawson, the author of a series of state bird books, sent an open letter to the AOU Committee on Nomenclature decrying the constant jumbling of technical names demanded by strict adherence to the law of priority. Dawson predicted that if the current trend continued, "we shall need to issue daily bulletins or publish diagrams of the nomenclatural barometer, after the fashion of the morning papers."[114] Four years later William Brewster repeated this complaint:

> Just as eels are said to have become reconciled to being skinned alive, so most ornithologists are learning, I suspect, to regard with resignation or indifference, not unmingled with disgust, the ever-increasing and apparently quite hopeless instability of their technical nomenclature. Fortunately there are the English names of birds to which one may turn with blessed sense of relief because of their comparatively fixed and stable character. For they have changed but little since the days of Wilson and Audubon, although purists have not failed to suggest that they should be critically looked into and perhaps extensively emended. Heaven forbid that this ever come to pass! It would mean universal chaos in ornithological nomenclature. Surely we have enough of trial and tribulation to bear with this ceaseless tinkering of the scientific names.[115]

Even more than application of the law of priority, the creation of new subspecies—by combining ("lumping") or, more often, breaking up ("splitting") forms previously designated as full species—was responsible for the overwhelming number of changes in nomenclature during the forty-five years between the first and fourth editions of the AOU Checklist.[116] As figure 15 shows, the number of full species recognized by the AOU nomenclature committee grew at a very modest rate during this period, beginning just below and ending just above the eight hundred mark. But the number of subspecies increased over threefold in the first four editions, from 183 in 1886 to 609 in 1931! In a review of the 4th edition, Joseph Grinnell, a California ornithologist and well-known splitter, predicted that at the current rate of increase, by the year 2000 the total number of North American bird forms would exceed 2,050, and that most of these (1,160) would be subspecies.[117]

The continued splitting of North American species was precisely the kind of taxonomic practice against which critics of the trinomialism railed. I have already

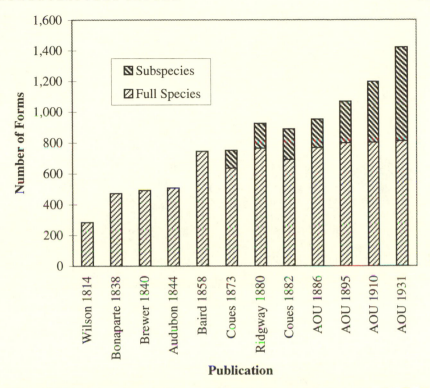

Figure 15. North American bird forms, 1814-1931. This graph indicates the total number of species and subspecies listed in various ornithological publications. Data from Coues, *The Coues Check List of North American Birds*, 2d ed. (1882), and Grinnell, "Some Inferences from the New Check-list" (1932).

noted the amateur community's discontent with the tendency to grant subspecific status to forms based on what they considered unnecessarily fine distinctions. "Feathersplitting," as this increasingly pervasive practice was often referred to by its critics, also disturbed many scientists. One response within the scientific community was humor. For example, a caricature that appeared in *Condor* in 1900 (fig. 16) depicted the "American Splitters' Union Headquarters," complete with a magnifying glass, microscope, color charts, and five prominent North American ornithologists known for their propensity to divide species into subspecies. During this period a joke began to circulate in ornithological circles concerning the creation of "north light subspecies," forms based on differences so slight that they seemed to be more the result of bird skins having been viewed through a window on the north, rather than the south, side of a building, than any appreciable difference in the specimens themselves.[118] And in 1910 William Brewster, who one year previously had decried the instability of technical nomenclature, wrote a biting letter to AOU President E. W. Nelson, in which he ridiculed the practice of designating subspecies based on increasingly minute distinctions:

Figure 16. The American Splitters' Union headquarters, 1900. This cartoon depicts several notorious creators of new subspecies, including (from *left to right*) Richard McGregor, Joseph Grinnell, Harry C. Oberholser, Edgar A. Mearns, and Wilfred Osgood.

> I have just read Grinnell's latest and it fills me with hope that the Yellow warbler that breeds in my garden may be a good and new subspecies. After I have determined this by slaying him and ascertaining that his left wing is one-thousandth of a millimeter shorter than his right (owing, no doubt, to the fact that as the garden is small he has to fly always in a circle when taking his daily exercise) I shall name him *Dendroria aestiva hortensis*.[119]

As the predictions of critics—who feared that the practice of designating subspecies using trinomial nomenclature was a Pandora's box certain to result in a confusing proliferation of new names—seemed increasingly to have been fulfilled, even some original American proponents of the subspecies program began to complain of the recent trends in its application. The first major call for a careful reassessment of the practice of designating subspecies based on increasingly minute distinctions came from J. A. Allen in 1890. In an article entitled "To What Extent Is It Profitable to Recognize Geographical Forms among North American Birds?," Allen provided a brief history of the splitting and lumping North American bird forms.[120] He argued that there had been "at least three well-defined oscillations of the ornithological pendulum."[121] In the period leading up to 1870, the tendency had been to create too many new species and genera from the multitude of forms sent back by the naturalists attached to the various western surveys active during the period. In the years immediately following 1871, however, there had been a swing in the opposite direction, and taxonomists had tended to reduce previously accepted species to the rank of geographical races or subspecies.[122]

This roughly five-year period of lumping was followed by a nearly a decade of relative "equilibrium" during which the AOU Code and Checklist had been constructed. But according to Allen, during the previous five years systematists had "started the pendulum again in the direction of finer discriminations and excessive splitting."[123] In an argument that explicitly challenged the legitimacy of a completely separate sphere for experts, Allen warned that recent taxonomic tendencies had led to an unnecessary and dangerous proliferation of subspecies:

[G]reat caution should be exercised in bestowing trinomials, in order to guard against drawing too fine distinctions. Very little is gained by naming races distinguishable only by experts, aided by a large amount of material, or where the differentiation is largely a matter of slight average difference between forms contiguous in habitat—forms which nine out of ten ornithologists of average acuteness and experience, and with only ordinary resources, will be more or less unable to satisfactorily distinguish. . . . Only the exercise of due discretion can prevent the reduction of "our beneficial system of trinomials" to an absurdity.[124]

In 1903, on the twentieth anniversary of the first AOU Committee on Nomenclature and Classification, Allen again sounded the alarm. In concluding a brief review of changes in nomenclature contained in the first two editions of the AOU Checklist and its numerous supplements, Allen referred to the "'hair-splitting' tendencies of the day, of which complaint is more or less prevalent." And again he expressed not only his anxiety about the practice of designating subspecies, but also his fear that scientific ornithology was becoming increasingly divorced from the needs of the larger ornithological community:

The degree of difference necessary for formal recognition in nomenclature is ever likely to be a bone of contention, its decision being, in the nature of the case, more or less a matter of temperament as well as of opinion. The danger of excessive splitting is greater now than ever before, since we have reached a point where comparatively few strongly marked local forms remain to be discovered and named, while the number of enthusiastic young workers is steadily increasing. Plainly, not every degree of differentiation that can be recognized by the trained expert needs recognition by name, and not every slightly differentiated form that can be distinguished readily on comparison of large series of specimens should be considered as entitled to a place in a list of North American birds. The trinomial system unfortunately lends itself readily to abuse, and can easily be made to bring the whole system of naming subspecies into disrepute.[125]

During this period an increasing number of other prominent American scientists spoke against the practice of splitting species based on minute distinctions. For example, in 1899 Theodore Gill, an internationally renowned ichthyologist and one of the scientists consulted during the construction of the first AOU Code and Checklist, complained of the "embarrassing" and "undue prominence" American ornithologists were giving to subspecific forms. Gill feared that continued "splitting" would lead to "an interminable number of subspecies." Like early critics of trinomialism, he argued that scientists should describe species in "generalized terms, that is, including all the variants, and the diversification into subspecies indicated in terse phraseology immediately after the diagnosis of common characteristics."[126] A few years later Leverett M. Loomis, curator of ornithology at the California Academy of Sciences in San Francisco, echoed Gill's sentiment when he maintained that the geographical variation that had led to subspecific designation should be treated the same as variation due to sex, age, season, and the like: the tendency should simply be noted in the specific description of the birds.[127]

In a steady stream of critical articles, with titles like "The Exaltation of the Subspecies," "The Fallacy of the Tendency towards Ultraminute Distinctions," and "The Tyranny of the Trinomial," other well-known scientists decried the abuse of the subspecies system and proposed various solutions to resolve the dilemma.[128] Besides the complete elimination of nomenclatural recognition or the toning down of the prominence of the subspecies, several ornithologists proposed a less radical solution to mitigate some of the confusion associated with the nearly constant change of names: issuing official checklists only once a decade without the almost yearly supplements.[129]

Despite the protests of their more conservative colleagues, technically oriented ornithologists continued to create new subspecies, while most amateurs continued to protest what they considered the unnecessary division of the species. The issue was one of several that reflected the increasing distance between the two groups. By the early twentieth century, scientists began to suggest that the split was a perfectly normal result of the continued development of science. Published in the same year that Ridgway declared the superiority of "systematic" over "popular" ornithology, the sentiments of the scientific ornithologist and mammalogist Wilfred H. Osgood were typical of those who began to argue for the legitimacy of a separate sphere for the scientist:

> The tendency to revolt among the "lay" class against the so-called splitting seems to be not so much because it is thought to be based on unsound principles, but more because it brings about a multiplication of names which are hard to remember and because it makes identification of individual specimens difficult. The popular ornithologist, following in the footsteps of other popular scientists, has reached the point where he cannot keep pace with the man who gives up his life to technical work. There was a time when country gentlemen of the Gilbert White type were able to keep fairly abreast of all branches of natural science, but now to be expert in any one branch requires almost a lifetime of study. The question arises—is this a deplorable condition or is it the outcome of a vast increase in the quantity and quality of material, a corresponding increase in facilities for work, and a convenient access to useful contributive results of investigation in other branches of science? Is it strange that the careful ornithologist should continually add named and labeled facts to the sum of knowledge as well as the astronomer with his telescopes discover new stars and the histologist with his new methods of preservation find unexpected conditions?[130]

Perhaps what is most significant about Osgood's statement is the tentativeness with which he proposed that the increasing distance between scientific and lay ornithologists was to be expected and welcomed. Osgood's arguments—which are posed as questions, not positive declarations—reflect the continuing ambivalence that many scientific ornithologists felt about their increasing divergence from other bird enthusiasts. Although desirous of increasing their autonomy, scientists were still unable, and often unwilling, to divorce themselves completely from the larger ornithological community from which they had emerged and upon which they continued to depend for legitimation and funds. The attempt to find a way to reconcile the needs of expert and novice bird enthusiasts became even more problematic with the development of the bird protection movement at the end of the nineteenth century.

CHAPTER FIVE

Embracing and Abandoning
Bird Protection

CHAPMAN'S PARAKEETS

On a damp March morning in 1889, gunfire pierced the calm near the headwaters of Florida's Sebastian River. By the time the ensuing confusion had quieted a few moments later, at least three Carolina parakeets (*Cornuropsis carolinensis*) lay dead within the lush, subtropical vegetation that bordered the meandering river. A fourth bird, only mildly wounded, was also captured by its assailants.

The four parakeets collected that day were remnants of a once vast North American population.[1] The only species of the parrot family (*Psittacidae*) endemic to the United States (fig. 17), the bird originally ranged widely across the southeastern portion of the country. But over two hundred years of settlement had taken its toll. Deforestation had destroyed much of the moist habitat—typically mature sycamores and cypress trees growing on riverbanks and in swamps—the species required to live and reproduce. The parakeet also suffered relentless persecution at the hands of farmers, who feared that voracious flocks would destroy their valuable crops. By the late 1880s the few surviving Carolina parakeets were largely confined to the uninhabited regions of Florida. Although some ornithologists claimed that extensive populations remained in the unexplored regions of the state, most agreed with Charles E. Bendire's gloomy assessment: "Civilization does not agree with these birds, and . . . nothing else than complete annihilation can be looked for. Like the Bison and the Passenger Pigeon, their days are numbered."[2]

As if habitat destruction and persecution by farmers were not enough, the parakeet also came under attack as a result of the post–Civil War rage for collecting birds. Natural history collecting has always had a strongly aesthetic dimension.[3] Not surprisingly, then, particularly showy species like the parakeet—with its brilliant plumage of green, yellow, red, and orange hues—were highly sought-after additions to the growing number of private and institutional bird collections begun in North America during the second half of the nineteenth century. And collectors of all kinds have always eagerly pursued rare or unusual examples of the objects they are amassing. Thus in a dangerous downward spiral repeated for a disturbing number of bird species, a decrease in the number of parakeets served to increase their value to collectors, whose predations further decreased the remaining population. Faced with the impending extinction of this and other species, the taxidermist William T. Hornaday's urgent advice reflected the dominant ethos of the culture of collecting: "*Now* is the time to collect."[4]

Figure 17. Audubon's engraving of the Carolina parakeet.
By the end of the nineteenth century bird collectors went to
great lengths to obtain specimens of this increasingly rare
(and now extinct) species. From the octavo edition of
Audubon, *Birds of America* (1840-1844).

As the final stronghold of the Carolina parakeet, Florida became a mecca for
naturalists seeking to capture the few surviving examples of this rapidly diminishing bird.[5] Among those anxious to collect the rare species was the young ornithologist Frank M. Chapman. After two years of searching he had finally found his
parakeets that March morning in 1889.[6]

The product of a wealthy family of bankers and lawyers, at age sixteen Chapman had graduated from Englewood Academy in New Jersey with little sense of

what he wanted to do with his life.[7] With no inclination to continue his education, he became a clerk at the American Exchange National Bank in New York City, an enterprise for which his father had once served as lawyer. A chance encounter with Fred J. Dixon, an ornithologist whom he met during his daily commute to the bank, sharply focused Chapman's previously inchoate interest in nature, hunting, and the outdoors.[8] Soon Chapman also met Clarence B. Riker, a young man his own age who had recently returned from a collecting expedition on the Amazon River.[9] Riker, who had discovered a new bird species during his travels, enchanted Chapman with exotic tales of ornithological adventure. It was as if a whole new world had opened up to him.

Inspired by contact with these and other ornithologists, Chapman entered into his newfound hobby with a heretofore uncharacteristic intensity.[10] In the spring of 1884 he volunteered to join the large network of observers gathering bird migration data for the AOU. Each of the six days per week he worked at the bank, Chapman rose before daybreak to observe and collect birds during the half-mile walk between his house and the West Englewood rail station. Whenever possible he spent additional hours in the field on his return trip in the evening. Although he had to be at the train station by 7:30 A.M. and he often remained at the bank until 6:00 P.M., Chapman averaged nearly two and a half hours in the field each workday that spring.

In the fall of 1886 the twenty-two-year-old Chapman stunned his "mystified colleagues" when he announced he was abandoning his promising banking career to pursue ornithology full-time.[11] Less than two years later he received an offer to become Allen's assistant at the American Museum of Natural History. The professionally conscious C. Hart Merriam chided Chapman for taking the position at the bargain rate of $50 per month: "Were it not that Mr. Allen needs you so very much, I should move to have you tarred and feathered for accepting at that price."[12] But as Chapman himself admitted, he came to the museum with "only a beginner's knowledge of local birds and had everything to learn concerning the more technical side of ornithology."[13] Under Allen's guiding hand, the American Museum proved to be the perfect environment to obtain that knowledge.

For several years Chapman arranged to continue his annual southern migration to collect specimens (fig. 18). In March 1889, while collecting birds and mammals in the Indian River region of Florida, he learned that Carolina parakeets had been spotted less than five miles from his base camp, a hunting lodge in Micco. Chapman and his guide, Jim, a nephew of the owners of the lodge, left early the next morning in hot pursuit of their quarry.

When they arrived near the headwaters of the Sebastian River later that afternoon, the two men immediately caught sight of the brilliant birds on the opposite bank. As he noted in his journal, this long-anticipated encounter with the parakeet thrilled Chapman: "You can imagine my excitement when he [Jim] called to me; I scampered for our guns and we immediately boarded the boat, pushed across and landed just in time to see seven Paroquets darting like lightening through the pines, twisting and turning in every direction. This was my first view of *Cornurus* in the state of nature, a sight I have long desired to feast my eyes on and which in imagination I have seen many times."[14]

Figure 18. Frank Chapman and William Brewster preparing bird specimens in Florida, 1890. Florida was one of Chapman's favorite collecting grounds.

A downpour the following morning temporarily extinguished hopes for finding the prized bird again but failed to dampen the two naturalists' enthusiasm. The very next day, Chapman proudly proclaimed that despite "cloudy threatening skies" he had finally met with success: "It is all the same to me now, rain, hail, sleet, snow, anything, sun or no sun. [M]y mind is illumined by a serene joy which casts a radiance over the darkest landscape, for I have met *Cornurus* and he is mine, three adults and a young one."[15]

Two days later Chapman and his guide encountered a second flock of parakeets. After securing five more specimens of the rare bird, Chapman was ecstatic. But his excitement soon turned to melancholy as the potentially grave consequences of his actions began to dawn on him. That night, after gathering the bodies of his cherished birds before him, Chapman noted in his journal:

> I admired them to my heart's content, counted them backwards and forwards[,] troubled over them generally, all the time almost doubting whether it was all true—for now we have nine specimens and I shall make no further attempt to secure others, for we have almost exterminated two of the three small flocks which occur here, and far be it from me to deal the final blows. Good luck to you poor doomed creatures, may you live to see many generations of your kind.[16]

Within two days Chapman's resolve was put to a decisive test when he located what he believed to be the last flock of parakeets in the vicinity. Despite his stated intention to refrain from further molesting the bird, the overwhelming urge to possess the coveted species again triumphed. Using religious imagery that was later to pervade the bird protection movement, Chapman revealed his guilt over having collected additional specimens of the threatened species: "Good resolutions like many other things are much easier to plan than to practice. [T]he parakeets tempted me and I fell; they also fell, six more of them making our total fifteen."[17]

Chapman's determination to amass as many specimens of the parakeet as possible was hardly unusual. During the second half of the nineteenth century, scientific ornithologists occasionally acknowledged the importance of gathering life-history and behavioral data on birds, but the ornithological community as a whole focused almost exclusively on collecting. The parakeet itself provides compelling evidence for this general orientation. Over eight hundred specimens of Carolina parakeet skins, skeletons, and eggs gather dust today in museums around the world, yet scientists learned little concerning the life and behavior of this tragic species before the last known individual died in the Cincinnati Zoo in 1918.[18]

As his journal entries suggest, however, Chapman was not oblivious to the plight of the parakeet and other endangered species. During the next half-century that Chapman devoted to enlarging the American Museum's ornithological collection, he was also a potent force in the bird protection movement. Long before the atomic age, the period most historians have identified as the beginning of an emerging social consciousness among scientists, Chapman and many other prominent ornithologists began acting on their own understanding of social responsibility.[19] Chapman and his fellow scientists sincerely believed that their knowledge of the desperate predicament of birds carried with it the obligation to act: to educate the public, to lobby for appropriate legislation, and to do everything in their power—that is, everything short of banning collecting—to protect American bird life from the forces that threatened it. As founding editor of *Bird-Lore* (the official publication of the second Audubon movement) and lifetime board member of state and national Audubon societies, Chapman stood on the front lines of a remarkably successful national campaign to awaken American sympathy for the living bird.

Chapman's life thus represents in a microcosm the larger tension that characterized scientific ornithology at the turn of the century. Chapman, like the ornithological community as a whole, sought to *protect* birds while asserting the absolute right to *collect* them for scientific purposes. It is this essential tension that I explore in the two chapters that follow. My focus is the bird protection committee of the AOU. The AOU served as a mouthpiece for the disciplinary and professional aspirations of scientific ornithologists, and its bird protection committee, created in 1884, provides a unique window onto that community's attitudes toward collecting and protecting birds.

The American bird protection movement, which began in last two decades of the nineteenth century, was a broadly based reform coalition composed of humanitarians, preservationists, recreational hunters, scientists, and others. It was extraordinarily successful in raising public consciousness about the plight of native American birds, especially song birds. The common enemy that united the otherwise diverse elements within the movement was large-scale commercial hunting of birds for plumes and meat. Through a series of state and federal laws, an aggressive educational campaign, and the establishment of protective refuges, the movement reversed the population decline of many species.

However, ornithologists' extensive involvement in bird protection efforts also had unanticipated consequences. The AOU bird protection committee played a central role in initiating and sustaining the American bird protection movement. But as that movement gained in size and independence, scientific ornithologists were forced to defend an increasingly yawning gap between the rhetoric of protection and the reality of current ornithological practice. In an effort to bridge this gap, scientific ornithologists attempted to redraw the traditional boundaries that had defined their practice. Commercial natural history and egg collecting—once considered integral parts of the edifice of ornithological science—were repudiated in an effort to silence criticism and thereby ensure the continued opportunity for "scientific" collecting.

DISCOVERING EXTINCTION

As historian Robert H. Welker has pointed out, the movement to protect birds in this country may have culminated in the actions of large, powerful groups at the end of the nineteenth century, but it began with "separate acts of protest by individuals."[20] While America marched westward under the banners of "progress," "inexhaustible resources," and "manifest destiny," a few lone voices began to cry out for the countless creatures destroyed in the process.[21] Naturalists, sport hunters, and explorers—men who had spent considerable time in the field and witnessed the effects of wildlife destruction firsthand—figured prominently among those early, isolated expressions of concern. As the nineteenth century wore on, these lone voices united into an anxious chorus echoing across the continent. For some Americans, progress had suddenly become a dual-edged sword.

By the middle decades of the nineteenth century, the rapid decline of two formerly abundant species, the buffalo (*Bison bison*) and the passenger pigeon (*Ectopistes migratorius*), forever shattered the myth of inexhaustiblity and helped ignite widespread discussion about the destruction of American wildlife.[22] Both species elicited superlative descriptions from explorers and settlers who had encountered the prodigious numbers that once ranged across the North American continent. But in the decades following the Civil War, both suffered almost simultaneous population collapses as their habitat was destroyed by development and their numbers thinned at the hands of market hunters. There had been human-induced extinctions before the fall of the buffalo and the passenger pigeon, but these earlier episodes failed to elicit much concern about either the fallen species or the more general processes responsible for their demise. The rapid collapse of these two species served as haunting reminder that humans possessed the ability to forever alter the natural world and seemed to jar some Americans from their smug complacency.

The total extent of the passenger pigeon population that once inhabited North America will never be known with certainty, but it is likely that no other bird on the continent has ever approached the species in number.[23] In one famous account from the early part of the nineteenth century, the ornithologist Alexander Wilson witnessed a continuous stream of migrating wild pigeons for over five and a half hours near Frankfort, Kentucky.[24] Wilson calculated that over two billion birds darkened the sky above him that afternoon, an estimate consistent with descriptions at other locations until the middle decades of the nineteenth century.

Deforestation increasingly destroyed the breeding habitat of the passenger pigeon—the hardwood forests of the Northeast—forcing the remaining population westward. Alerted to the presence of their intended victims by an extensive network of telegraph lines, market hunters invaded vast nesting congregations, capturing and murdering prodigious numbers with nets, fires, and guns. The birds, both living and dead, were then shipped by rail to urban markets. What had been a gradual decline became precipitous in the 1870s, and by 1900 there were no more reliable sightings in the wild.[25] The last passenger pigeon died at the Cincinnati Zoo in 1914.[26]

The buffalo barely escaped a similar fate, reaching a population size as low as one thousand or less before the initiation of successful efforts to bring the species back from the brink of extinction.[27] Indians and bison had long coexisted on the North American continent, but the coming of the white man marked the beginning of the end for both. The large, gregarious beast provided an easy target for the waves of settlers who pushed the frontier line ever westward. But it was the arrival of the railroad in the middle decades of the century that assured the rapid destruction of the still robust bison population.[28] The animal furnished nourishment for the hungry laborers who built the western railroad lines that knitted the nation together. More important for the future of the buffalo, the railroad provided a quick, inexpensive, and reliable means for bringing the hunters to their mobile quarry and for shipping hides and meat back to markets. At the same time, federal officials encouraged the brutal destruction, hoping to confine to reservations the resistant bands of Plains Indians who depended on the buffalo for food, clothing, and shelter.[29]

Although several commentators had suggested that the end of the buffalo was imminent, the young ornithologist and mammalogist J. A. Allen was among the first to do a detailed study of the decline.[30] To regain his failing health and acquire western specimens for the Museum of Comparative Zoology, in April 1871 he and two assistants set off on a nine-month expedition to the Great Plains and the Rocky Mountains. High on the list of specimens Allen hoped to secure was the buffalo. With the aid of railroads (which granted special rates for the party), professional hunters (who helped secure specimens), and U.S. Army officials (who provided a base of operations for the naturalists), the expedition proved a stunning success. Included among the thousands of specimens shipped back to Cambridge over the next nine months was an extensive series of buffalo skins, skeletons, and skulls procured near Fort Hays, Kansas.[31]

In 1876, almost five years after his return from the West, Allen published an exhaustive monograph, *The American Bison, Living and Extinct*. The first part of the study consisted of meticulous technical descriptions of the two extinct and one living species of North American buffalo. The second, longest, and final section of the monograph examined the former and present range of the sole surviving species of American bison. During the process of researching his monograph, Allen became convinced that this species was destined to endure the same fate as its long extinct cousins: "These facts are sufficient to show that the present decrease of the buffalo is extremely rapid, and indicates most clearly that the period of his *extinction* will soon be reached, unless some strong arm is interposed in his behalf."[32] In short, Allen became one of the first to recognize, document, and warn the public about the problem of anthropogenic extinction.

Not content to bury his alarming conclusions in an obscure academic tome, that same year Allen also published a series of five popular articles detailing the decline of the buffalo and other North American vertebrates. Allen's first paper, "The North American Bison and Its Extermination," summarized the results of his longer monograph and called the decline of the buffalo "one of the most remarkable instances of extermination recorded, or ever to be recorded, in the annals of zoology."[33] In a second article appearing six months later, Allen expanded his circle of concern to include other large indigenous mammals. While examining the literature on travel and exploration that had provided persuasive evidence of the decline of the bison, Allen also gleaned information on the former status of several other species. He soon discovered that a disturbing number of large mammals—like the moose, the gray wolf, the panther, the lynx, the black bear, the wolverine, the caribou, the elk, the Virginia deer, and others—had also suffered severe declines since the beginning of white settlement and that some might soon be facing the same fate that seemed to await the bison.

Although the specific story for each of these species varied, the broad outlines were similar. In their headlong rush westward, European settlers had transformed "hundreds of thousands of square miles of wilderness into 'fruited fields,' dotted with towns and cities, and intersected by a network of railways and telegraphs lines."[34] At every turn the "progress of the white race on this continent" had been marked by "reckless and wanton destruction of animal life."[35] During the nation's centennial, when most Americans celebrated the taming of the landscape, Allen offered a somber counterpoint to the apotheosis of progress.

In this same pioneering series of articles Allen also highlighted the problem of bird destruction. A short notice in the *American Naturalist* called attention to the extermination of the great auk (*Pinguinus impennis*) at one of its last great colonial nesting sites, Funk Island in Newfoundland.[36] According to one of Allen's correspondents, these large, flightless birds had been abundant on the islands until mercilessly hunted down for their feathers in the 1830s and 1840s. Now no more remained there or anywhere else in the world.

In two longer articles Allen discussed the decline of several avian species in his native Massachusetts and the eastern United States more broadly. Again, early descriptions of abundance provided a baseline against which to measure current population levels. According to Allen, at least four birds—the great auk, the wild

turkey, the sandhill crane, and the whooping crane—had become wholly exterminated within the boundaries of Massachusetts since the beginning of European
settlement.[37] A great many others, including the pileated woodpecker, the passenger pigeon, the heath hen, the American swan, most of the wading and swimming birds, and nearly all the rapacious species had also suffered marked declines. Allen's more general account of the decline of birds in the United States
suggested that at least one other bird, the Carolina parakeet, was also in grave
danger.[38]

These drastic changes in bird life had not passed entirely unnoticed. Allen
pointed out that several states and territories had enacted laws to protect "beneficial birds": game birds and those nongame species thought to prey on, and
thereby keep in check, the noxious insect populations that destroyed crops. But
these laws had thus far been generally ineffective and rarely enforced. Allen concluded the last of this prescient series with a variation on his now familiar theme:
"Unless something is done to awaken public opinion in this direction and to enlist
the sympathies of the people in behalf of our persecuted birds, the close of the
next half-century will witness a large increase in the list of wholly exterminated
species."[39]

Allen looked to two existing communities, sport hunters and humanitarians, as
possible advocates for the birds. As historians John Reiger and James B. Trefethen have emphasized, recreational hunters were among the first to decry the
large-scale, commercial exploitation of wildlife, and they have remained active in
conservation causes up to the present.[40] Beginning as early as the colonial period,
the local extermination of game species had occasionally led to the creation of
protective laws.[41] But it was not until the mid-nineteenth century that those who
hunted for sport began to demand more stringent regulations to protect their
would-be targets. Hunting clubs, game protective associations, and related organizations proliferated beginning in the 1840s. By the 1870s a series of national
weeklies—which included coverage of hunting, fishing, conservation, and natural history—helped foster a sense of shared national identity for the sporting
community.[42] Informed by an ethos of "fair chase" and anxious to maintain a
continued supply of game well into the future, recreational hunters provided a
politically powerful voice for wildlife protection. Allen recognized the effectiveness of sport hunting organizations in limiting "the destruction of game and fish
species," but he was skeptical about their willingness to fight vigorously for nongame species, especially small songbirds, which did not appeal "so strongly to
their self-interest."[43]

Besides sport hunters, Allen hoped that "associations for the 'Prevention of
Cruelty to Animals'" might also contribute to the cause of bird protection. Unlike
hunters, who were largely informed by self-interest and utilitarian motives, humanitarians were moved by a distaste for animal pain and suffering. The humane
movement was an extension of the Darwinian revolution, which helped bridge
the gap between humans and the beasts, and it came at the heels of the development of effective anesthetics, which first suggested the possibility of a world

without pain.[44] Henry Bergh, a wealthy young New Yorker with little previous sense of direction, discovered the cause in England during his grand tour in the 1860s. He returned home in 1866 to create the American Society for the Prevention of Cruelty to Animals, which, despite its name, largely confined its activities to the state of New York. Over the next two decades animal lovers organized dozens of state humane societies. Initially humanitarians focused on alleviating suffering in domestic animals, but they also regularly expressed concern about the plight of wildlife.

In his 1876 essay on bird destruction, Allen failed to mention a third strand of conservation that was also to be crucial in the fight to preserve wildlife from the continuing onslaught of civilization: the nature appreciation movement. Though this movement lacked the clear institutional manifestations of the sport hunting and humanitarian movements, it was nonetheless an increasingly potent force in defense of the American landscape. As mentioned earlier, nature appreciation in this country had its roots in the Romanticism and Transcendentalism of the early to mid-nineteenth century.[45] As the century wore on, it continued to reemerge under a variety of guises.[46] For some, periodic retreats into the relative wilderness of state and national parks offered a temporary antidote to the ills of an increasingly urban and industrial nation. But most Americans lacked the desire to retreat permanently from civilization. Rather, they sought a more secure middle ground between the extremes of nature and civilization: the urban park or cemetery, the borderland suburbs, and the country club. Whatever form nature appreciation took, one thing was clear: the more Americans removed themselves from nature, the more they came to value it.

Allen concluded his final article with a call for the formation of an entirely new organization, special "societies . . . whose express object should be the protection throughout the country of not only . . . innocent and pleasure-giving species, but also the totally innocuous herons, terns, and gulls, whose extermination is progressing with needless and fearful rapidity."[47] Although it would be over a decade before anyone would take up his suggestion, Allen's remarkable series of papers first alerted Americans to the specter of human-induced extinction.

EMBRACING BIRD PROTECTION

Bird protection was not among the principal items on the agenda of the technically oriented scientists who organized the AOU in 1883. However, it did come up as early as the second meeting of the union in October 1884, when William Brewster called attention to the "wholesale slaughter of birds, particularly Terns, along our coast for millinery purposes." Following Brewster's motion, the AOU voted to create a six-member "committee for the Protection of North American Birds and eggs against wanton and indiscriminate destruction."[48] At the request of J. A. Allen, president of the AOU, Brewster reluctantly agreed to serve as chair for the new committee, but he promptly resigned three months later, citing a lack of time, difficulties with his eyesight, and inability to attend the next AOU meeting as reasons for his withdrawal.[49] In the hope of finding someone willing to serve as chair, Allen then approached other members of the committee, including George Bird Grinnell, editor and part-owner of the sporting and natural history periodical *Forest and Stream*. Grinnell rejected Allen's offer but indicated that he strongly supported the work of the committee and had long contemplated a plan to use his magazine as a vehicle to promote bird protection.[50] A year later Grinnell launched the first Audubon Society through the pages of *Forest and Stream*.

When the issue of what to do with the bird protection committee again came up during the next meeting of the AOU in the fall of 1885, Brewster urged that the committee be continued with a chair who could "give the matter the attention and time its high importance demanded." C. Hart Merriam argued that work of the committee was "the most urgent before the Union."[51] Others in attendance agreed, but the issue of who would chair the committee remained unresolved when the annual meeting adjourned the next day.

The committee was finally roused into action two months later, at a meeting in New York on the afternoon of 12 December 1885.[52] Full of "new life and energy," the committee voted to increase its size from six to ten members and elected the oil-machinery manufacturer George B. Sennett as its chair.[53] Sennett's election marked the beginning of an intense period of activity for the bird protection committee. With seven members of the expanded committee residing in the vicinity of New York City, the ambitious new chair scheduled a series of over twenty regular Saturday afternoon meetings.[54] After discussing how it might carry out its charge most effectively, the committee decided to concentrate on educating the public regarding the scope and consequences of the bird destruction problem.[55]

Toward this end, the new committee began gathering information for the publication of a bird protection bulletin. As early as 1 December, almost two weeks before the first meeting of the reorganized committee, the editor of *Science* had offered his journal as a forum to "come to the aid of our native birds."[56] After gathering material for the next two months, the committee published a sixteen-page supplement to *Science*. With the aid of G. E. Gordon, president of the American Humane Association, the committee distributed over one hundred thousand additional copies of its manifesto.[57]

The first AOU bulletin introduced many arguments that were to become standards within the bird protection movement. The introductory, longest, and most important essay was authored by none other than J. A. Allen. Echoing his earlier warning, he insisted that without immediate action, "many species, and even genera" of North American birds appeared to be heading for the same fate as the rapidly diminishing American bison. What became a standard litany of specific threats followed this general cry of alarm. Commercial game hunting, egging for the restaurant trade, egg collecting by boys, and indiscriminate shooting by "sportsmen," immigrants, and "colored people" were each briefly discussed and uniformly condemned.[58] But the principle target of Allen's wrath was the millinery trade, a force that remained the nemesis of the bird protection movement for over three decades.

Although feathers had long been used to decorate hats, it was not until the end of the nineteenth century, when fashion-conscious middle-class women adopted the practice, that it represented a serious threat to bird populations.[59] Mass circulation magazines, like the *Delineator*, *Harper's Bazar*, *Argosy*, and *Vogue*, fueled the craze for the latest fashions coming out of New York, London, and Paris. Millinery designers turned to bird feathers for something eye-catching to decorate their wares. And feminine fashion mavens gobbled up the procession of ever-changing styles. As Allen admitted, determining the precise level of destruction was frustratingly difficult, but a stroll down any American street revealed that the habit of trimming hats with feathers was pervasive: "We see on every hand— in shop window, on the street, in the cars, and everywhere women are seen— evidence of its enormous extent."[60] According to Allen, the new feather fad represented a threat to North American birds "many times exceeding all the others together."[61]

Allen recognized that in condemning the "wholesale destruction of birds," he was potentially exposing ornithologists to criticism for engaging in what might seem like equally voracious collecting practices. The issue had first been raised three months earlier when the nature writer John Burroughs labeled ornithological collectors, the "men who plunder nests and murder their owners," as "among the worst enemies of our birds."[62] After recounting several examples of what he considered excessive collecting gleaned from the pages of natural history journals, Burroughs concluded with a clear indictment of scientific ornithology:

> Thus are the birds hunted and cut off, and all in the name of science; as if science had not long ago finished with these birds. She has weighed and measured and dissected and described them and their nests and eggs, and placed them in her cabinet, and the interest of science and humanity now is that the wholesale nest-robbing cease. I can pardon the man who wishes to make a collection for his own private use, though he will find it less satisfactory and valuable than he imagines; but he needs but one bird and one egg of a kind; but the professional nest robber and skin-collector should be put down, either by legislation or with dogs.[63]

Although Burroughs found large-scale commercial and "scientific" collecting deplorable, he did not oppose collecting under all circumstances. His first book, *Wake-Robin* (1871), urged novice bird students not to be squeamish about resorting to the collecting gun: "First you find your bird; observe its ways, its song, its call, its flights, its haunts; then shoot it (not ogle it with a glass), and compare with Audubon. In this way the feathered kingdom will soon be conquered."[64] But according to Burroughs, once having "mastered the birds" in this manner, the "true ornithologist leaves his gun at home."[65] He had little patience for the "closet" ornithologist, the museum worker who rarely ventured to the fields and forests and apparently lacked interest in the lives of the birds he was naming, describing, and classifying: "He is about the most wearisome and profitless creature in existence. With his piles of skins, his cases of eggs, his laborious feather-splitting, and his outlandish nomenclature, he is not only the enemy of birds, but the enemy of all who would know them rightly."[66]

Had Burroughs been unknown, his critique might have been safely ignored. But Burroughs was a widely read nature writer whose popular essays often centered on birds. In the eyes of the public, he was an authoritative ornithologist. Therefore, his harsh words demanded a response.[67] As was often the case, it was J. A. Allen who took up the cudgels for scientific ornithology. In a short, vituperative reply, Allen accused Burroughs's essay of being "grossly erroneous in statement" and "slanderous in spirit."[68] He continued on the offensive by pointing out that Burroughs had failed even to mention the most potent threat against birds: "wholesale slaughter of birds for millinery purposes." According to Allen, the total destruction of birds for "scientific or *quasi*-scientific purposes is 'but a drop in the bucket,'" when compared to that of the millinery trade.[69]

In the bird protection committee bulletin, Allen expanded upon his earlier defense of scientific collecting. His argument of scale soon became a standard within the community of scientific ornithologists.[70] After estimating the total number of specimens in museums and private collections in this country to be at most five hundred thousand and the number of birds annually slaughtered for millinery purposes to be at least five million, Allen concluded that the millinery trade offered a far graver threat to American bird life than did scientific collectors. When the large number of years it took to bring together existing ornithological collections was considered, Allen argued that plume hunters took a toll "a thousand times greater than the annual destruction of birds (including also eggs) for scientific purposes."[71]

Of course, there were difficulties with Allen's argument. First was the perennial problem of gathering accurate statistics both on the level of ornithological collecting and on the number of birds killed by the millinery trade. More importantly, even if the often repeated argument of scale was an accurate description of the relative impact of ornithologists and milliners on *overall* bird populations, it failed to recognize that ornithologists went to great lengths to take *rare* birds—as Chapman had done with the parakeet in Florida (fig. 19)—and hence could have a devastating effect on local populations of threatened species.[72]

A publication that appeared soon after the first bird protection bulletin shows why ardent protectionists might question the collecting practices of scientific ornithology. In a three-part article for *Auk*, former Agassiz student and Nuttall Club member W. E. D. Scott called attention to the severe population decline in several rookeries on Florida's west coast.[73] During a five-week reconnaissance trip in the spring of 1886, Scott had visited a number of nesting and roosting sites. Six years previously he had seen countless herons, egrets, pelicans, ibises, gulls, terns, and other water birds at these sites, but now they were virtually barren. The culprits, Scott argued, were commercial plume hunters, local men who made a handsome income selling bird skins and plumes for anywhere from ten cents to a dollar each to taxidermists and other northern buyers. Scott was unable to catch up with the most notorious plume buyer, Alfred Lechevalier, but he did interview the taxider-

Figure 19. William Brewster with an ivory-billed woodpecker, 1890. Frank
Chapman found this specimen during an expedition along the Suwannee River
in Florida.

mist Joseph H. Batty of New York City, who had "not less than sixty men . . .
working on the Gulf Coast" that season.[74]

Yet Scott saw no inconsistency in decrying commercial hunting as a "great and
growing evil" and on the same page noting glibly that he had collected "about two
hundred and fifty birds" during this single trip, including a series of sixty examples of a single subspecies of the sandwich tern, *Sterna sandvicensis acuflavida.*
What now seems even more remarkable is that less than two weeks after Scott
wrote Allen of his desire to publish his account of bird destruction in Florida so
he could "let the public get an idea of the magnitude of the slaughter and try to do
something to stop the cruelty," he was asking "How much can the museum afford
to spend in buying first plumages and series of the herons of this region? I have
a large lot that are very interesting."[75] Two years later Scott had nearly three
thousand Florida specimens he was trying to sell, including a series of *seventeen*
of the rare Bachman's warbler (*Vermivora bachmanii*)![76]

Continuing the series of apparent contradictions surrounding the episode, Joseph H. Batty, once vilified in the pages of the *Auk* as a despicable plume hunter,
was later lionized as a martyr of science.[77] It seems that in an era of increasing
state and federal legislation suppressing commercial hunting, Batty had "re-
formed his ways." He had abandoned plume hunting to become a collector for the
American Museum of Natural History, which paid him to send as many birds and
mammals as possible back to its expanding collections. Scott and Batty reveal the
ways in which the lines between scientists, professional collectors, and taxidermists remained fluid well into the latter decades of the nineteenth century. It is no
wonder, then, that some ardent protectionists began to claim that killing birds,
whether in the name of science or of fashion, was equally reprehensible.[78]

Following his brief survey of the threats that plagued North American birds, Allen turned to the crucial question of why the problem should concern the average citizen. After all, trade in decorative nongame birds provided income for numerous plume-hunters, taxidermists, manufacturers, and others involved in the millinery trade. Was not the obvious economic benefit derived from the sale of these otherwise valueless birds justification enough for the practice? Using aesthetic and utilitarian arguments that remained central to the bird protection movement for decades, Allen attempted to counter the still-dominant belief that nature was little more than a storehouse of potential resources waiting to be discovered, extracted, and sold.

Birds, Allen proclaimed, possess an "aesthetic value" which, though not readily renderable into the language of dollars and cents, was nonetheless real and important:

> Birds, considered aesthetically, are among the most graceful in movement and form, and the most beautiful and attractive in coloration, of nature's many gifts to man. Add to this their vivacity, their melodious voices and unceasing activity,—charms shared in only [a] small degree by any other forms of life,—and can we well say that we are prepared to see them exterminated in behalf of fashion, or to gratify a depraved taste?[79]

For Allen and others who advanced the aesthetic argument, a country without songbirds was like "a garden without flowers, childhood without laughter, an orchard without blossoms, a sky without color, [and] roses without perfume."[80]

For those who remained unmoved by Allen's appeal to the intrinsic beauty of the living bird, he offered a more practical defense of bird protection: "The great mass of our smaller birds, numbering hundreds of species, are the natural checks upon undue multiplication of insect pests."[81] Here Allen was resorting to essentially the same argument that economic ornithologists had been making for years. Working under the long-held assumption that nature remains in overall balance, they moved from a limited knowledge of the diets of birds to the conclusion that they were a primary agent in halting the potentially explosive growth of insect pest populations.[82] Although the field of economic ornithology was still in its infancy at the time he was writing, Allen was confident that investigations undertaken by the Department of Agriculture's recently created Division of Economic Ornithology and Mammalogy would merely provide finer detail for an outline that was already clearly in place.[83]

The bird protection committee conceived its primary mission to be one of alerting the public to the problem of bird destruction, but it also recognized the need for effective legislation to complement its educational efforts. The first bird protection bulletin contained a call for uniform state legislation to protect the songbirds and other nongame birds that had been largely ignored by sport hunters. The committee's suggested legislation became known as the AOU model law.[84] Prominent among the provisions of the proposed law—which made it illegal for anyone to kill, purchase, or sell any nongame bird, its nest, or eggs—was a section authorizing local natural history societies to grant permits for "scientific" collecting to anyone over the age of eighteen who could produce the required license fee ($1.00), a properly executed bond, and an affidavit signed by two recognized ornithologists.[85] From the time of its first publication, the permit clause—with its demand to differentiate legitimate scientific collecting from other forms of bird slaughter—became a source of tension between scientific ornithologists and the collectors, taxidermists, and natural history dealers who had once been closely allied with them.

GRINNELL'S AUDUBON SOCIETY

While the bird protection committee was preparing to publish its first bulletin, a second, closely related force for bird protection was established. The first Audubon Society was the brainchild of George Bird Grinnell, scientist, sportsman, patrician, and longtime publisher of *Forest and Stream*.[86] After receiving his A.B. from Yale in 1870, Grinnell became part of an army of students collecting western fossils for the paleontologist O. C. Marsh. Forced to abandon his family-owned New York investment business following the panic of 1873, Grinnell took a position as Marsh's assistant at the Peabody Museum in New Haven. The next summer he joined an expedition with General George Armstrong Custer, who had brought several scientists along with his troops in an attempt to disguise what was in reality a military mission in the Black Hills of the Dakota Territories. Custer invited Grinnell to join him again on his more famous and fateful campaign of 1876, but he declined in order to continue his studies in New Haven.

At almost the same time that J. A. Allen was writing his remarkable series of articles on the decline of North American mammals and birds, Grinnell was independently reaching a similar conclusion. As was often the case, witnessing the level of wildlife destruction in the West proved a revelation for Grinnell. In 1875 he accompanied William Ludlow on an exploration of Yellowstone National Park, which had been created only three years previously. As Grinnell announced in the letter that accompanied his report, the experience had convinced him that "the large game still so abundant in some localities will ere long be exterminated."[87]

By the time he received his doctorate from Yale in 1880, Grinnell and his father had gained a controlling interest in Charles Hallock's sporting and natural history periodical, *Forest and Stream*. Grinnell, who had served as natural history editor of the publication since 1876, became editor-in-chief, a position he was to hold for thirty-five years. Under Grinnell's guiding hand, the periodical consolidated its position as a leading voice in condemning the commercial exploitation of wildlife.

Soon after taking over *Forest and Stream*, Grinnell became involved with the AOU and its bird protection efforts. As a well-known naturalist and man of means, he was a logical choice to be invited to the organizational meeting of the AOU in 1883.[88] That same year he published the first in a series of letters and editorials condemning the destruction of songbirds at the hands of the millinery trade.[89] Convinced of the urgency of the problem, Grinnell agreed to serve as a member of the original AOU bird protection committee created in October 1884 but declined an offer to chair the committee when Brewster resigned three months later. As he indicated to Allen, he strongly supported the committee's mission but was too busy with his own bird protection initiative.[90]

On 11 February 1886, less than two weeks before the AOU bird protection committee issued its first bulletin, Grinnell published an editorial proposing the formation of an "Audubon Society" dedicated to the "protection of wild birds and their eggs."[91] The new organization was named after America's most famous artist-naturalist, John James Audubon, whose striking, anthropomorphic bird portraits had inspired many to see the creatures around them in a new, more sympathetic way. Although Audubon was capable of what now seems like excessive slaughter of wildlife, he was also among the first to notice and lament the decline of several species. Grinnell's decision was also influenced by his boyhood memories of Audubon Park, just north of Manhattan, where he had lived and attended a small school run by Audubon's widow, Lucy.

The basic plan of Grinnell's Audubon Society was straightforward. Membership was free and open to anyone who pledged to "prevent as far as possible, (1) the killing of any wild birds not used for food; (2) the destruction of nests or eggs of any wild birds, and (3) the wearing of feathers as ornaments or trimming for dress."[92] The national society was to be organized into local chapters, to which Grinnell promised to send "without charge, circulars and printed information for distribution." Grinnell was careful to stress that the work of the new society was not to replace, but to be "auxiliary to that undertaken by the Committee of the American Ornithologists' Union."[93] It was to be the popular arm of the bird protection movement. With backing from a number of prominent leaders and supporters of the humane movement—including Henry Ward Beecher, John G. Whittier, John Burroughs, George T. Angell, Henry Bergh, and G. E. Gordon—the first Audubon Society's membership rolls quickly mounted.

One of the first of the many local chapters of the Audubon Society was organized at the all-female Smith College in Massachusetts. Just over a month after Grinnell issued his call, Fannie Hardy and Florence Merriam, both members of families that included prominent naturalists, created the Smith College Audubon Society.[94] Shortly after launching their new society, Hardy wrote to Brewster informing him of their progress and asking him to address the "enthusiastic" but "lamentably ignorant" group. Hardy also detailed the members' efforts at self-education:

> One girl who has stripped all the feathers from her hats, is now trying to hire small boys to kill her birds to skin,—all in the interests of science of course, and I, remembering that I was a taxidermist before I was a bird defender, I am helping her on in it. Half a dozen more are only waiting until they can get some birds to work. But these are all of the biology class and don't mind about killing things. The rest are much more tenderhearted and think Nature is a goddess and Thoreau is the prophet of Nature.[95]

Early in May, Merriam arranged for Burroughs to lead the new society on a series of bird walks. As Merriam later noted, under his enchanting spell, "we all caught

Figure 20. Cover of *Audubon Magazine*, 1887. George Bird Grinnell began publishing this short-lived periodical in a failed attempt to generate revenue for his equally ephemeral Audubon Society.

the contagion of the woods." Following Burroughs's visit, a hundred young women, nearly a third of the student body, renounced the wearing of feathers and joined the new group.

The success of the movement as a whole mirrored that of the chapter at Smith College. By the end of 1886 the Audubon Society boasted over three hundred local chapters and nearly eighteen thousand members.[96] Early the next year Grinnell introduced *Audubon Magazine* (fig. 20) to "give stability to the Society, foster the zeal of the thousands now on its rolls, increase the membership, aid in carrying out the Society's special work, and broaden the sphere of effort."[97]

Beyond these lofty aims, he also hoped that income derived from the sale of the new magazine, which cost subscribers fifty cents per year, would alleviate the increasing financial burden posed by the growing society. The pages of *Audubon Magazine* featured news of the Audubon Society, popular articles on birds, children's stories, biographical sketches of Audubon and Wilson, and regular appeals like Celia Thaxter's call to the "tender and compassionate heart of the woman" to look upon the wearing of birds "as a sign of heartlessness and a mark of ignominy and reproach."[98]

CRITICS OF CONSERVATION

The appearance of the widely circulated AOU bird protection bulletin and the launching of Grinnell's Audubon Society awakened a nationwide discussion of the problem of bird destruction. American newspapers and periodicals were generally sympathetic to the protectionists' message, but from the start there was also opposition. Not surprisingly, the main targets of the bird protection movement—the milliners, who also had the most to lose by its success—were among the first to challenge protectionists' claims. Opposition also came from less likely sources: scientists, collectors, and taxidermists. During its brief period of activity in the mid-1880s, the AOU bird protection committee was repeatedly forced to defend its claims about the causes of and appropriate remedies for the problem of bird destruction.

Frank W. Langdon, a physician from Cincinnati, Ohio, who had been invited to help found the AOU three years earlier, was one of the few scientific ornithologists to challenge the bird protection committee publicly.[99] In a speech delivered before the Cincinatti Natural History Society in the spring of 1886, Langdon not only sought to discredit many of the statistics found in the committee's first bulletin, but also disputed the very premise of bird population decline upon which the bulletin had been based. Coming from a recognized expert on local birds, Langdon's widely publicized critique threatened not only to undermine the authority of the new committee, but also to stifle the organizing efforts of Grinnell's Audubon Society.[100]

Again it was J. A. Allen's acerbic pen that came to the rescue. After a short summary of the recent achievements of the bird protection movement, Allen claimed that "the only discordant notes heard from any quarters were the subdued mutterings of a few reprehensible taxidermists, caterers of the milliners, whose pockets were affected by the movement in favor of birds," and Langdon, an "ornithologist of some supposed standing as a man of sense and culture."[101] Unleashing all his stops, Allen called Langdon's arguments "palpably absurd," "perniciously misleading," and full of "false premises, misstatements, and misrepresentations." He refused to provide a detailed refutation—to do so might have granted his critique greater legitimacy—but he did point out that the Cincinnati Society of Natural History had nearly unanimously passed a resolution supporting the work of the AOU bird protection committee. The lone dissenting vote came from Langdon.

In the end what most divided Langdon and the bird protection committee was a divergent set of assumptions. Bird protectionists had begun, however tentatively, to question the right of humans to exploit nature without regard to the consequences. On the other hand, Langdon was a strong advocate of the more pervasive belief that it was "a well-established right of man to use all natural objects for the furtherance of his necessities, his convenience, or his pleasures."[102] For many in the generation of naturalists that came of age when the buffalo and the passenger pigeon teetered on the brink of extinction, this was no longer a tenable position.

A more serious and recurrent challenge to the work of the bird protection committee came at the next annual meeting of the AOU in November 1886. A letter from a disgruntled taxidermist who "complained bitterly" about the bird protection law that had recently passed in New York resulted in a lengthy discussion on the relationship between scientific ornithologists and taxidermists.[103] There to present the concerns of taxidermists was Frederic S. Webster, a former employee of Ward's Natural Science Establishment and a founder of the Society of American Taxidermists who maintained a private studio in Washington.[104]

At the 1886 AOU meeting, Webster expressed deep regret concerning "the attitude of ornithologists toward taxidermists, which seemed to be one of enmity rather than friendship." The source of his apprehension was the work of the bird protection committee, the newly launched Audubon movement, and more particularly the AOU model law, which, by allowing collecting of protected birds only "for strictly scientific purposes," threatened "to prevent work in legitimate taxidermy." Narrowly interpreted, the new law would remove an important source of income for private taxidermists, who had long offered stuffed bird specimens not only for museums and private cabinets, but also for decorating store windows and parlors.

William Brewster tried to reassure Webster, and all taxidermists, that scientific ornithologists were not out to destroy their business. Brewster had relied heavily on professional collectors and taxidermists to build up one of the largest private collections in the nation.[105] And he fought for their interests during the deliberations of the bird protection committee that led up to the first bulletin. At one point he warned that if the requirements for obtaining collecting permits were too strict, they would "sound the death knell for professional taxidermists and scientific collectors, who earn their living by selling birds. I consider such prohibition unjust, unwise, and uncalled for. Neither museums nor private collectors can dispense with professional taxidermists. Many of the latter are honorable men, and warmly interested in the protection of birds and the suppression of millinery collection."[106]

At the annual AOU meeting Brewster again came to the defense of taxidermists by pointing out that they "were respected by ornithologists, who looked upon them as efficient and indispensible allies." The bird protection committee supported granting permits to "honest taxidermists"; it only wanted to prevent the "abuse of the privilege of collecting" represented by "wholesale traffic in birds for commercial purposes by men who had no claim to be ranked as taxidermists."[107] Allen further clarified Brewster's sentiments by claiming that the AOU model law was not intended "to cripple legitimate taxidermy, but mainly and primarily to prevent destruction of birds for millinery purposes."[108] Despite these assurances, taxidermists justifiably remained skeptical. They were not the only ones who were concerned about the AOU's stand on collecting.

PERMIT PERTURBATIONS

The *Ornithologist and Oologist* had already been at odds with the AOU over its exclusive membership policy and its advocacy of trinomial nomenclature. Now, under the ownership of the natural history dealer Frank B. Webster (no relation to Frederic S. Webster), the magazine also became the central battleground between scientific ornithologists and the larger community of collectors, taxidermists, and dealers who felt excluded by the new AOU law.

The initial exchange was prompted by the numerous complaints of large-scale bird destruction at the hands of millinery interests that began appearing in *Forest and Stream* in 1883. An editorial in the June 1884 issue of the *Ornithologist and Oologist* responded with the claim that "the grievance is purely sentimental" and asserted that "birds of prey are far more destructive than either collectors or professional taxidermists."[109] AOU member Frederic A. Lucas, another former Ward employee now at the U. S. National Museum, responded with the standard economic argument: more than sentiment was at stake, for birds were responsible for keeping insect populations in check. He also flatly asserted that humans destroyed far more songbirds and insectivorous birds than birds of prey.[110]

At this point, the exchange became characterized by escalating levels of invective. In a response more sarcastic than sincere, the longtime Boston taxidermist W. W. Castle mocked Lucas for presuming that the public would accept his assertions about the level and causes of bird population declines simply because he was an employee of the U. S. National Museum. He also called for more specific statistics regarding the number and kinds of birds killed for millinery purposes.[111] Lucas temporarily bowed out of the argument at this point, but his friend L. M. McCormick continued to push the position that "only a small proportion of the birds sacrificed in the name of science and taxidermy are legitimately used."[112] In McCormick's view, millinery interests and overzealous collecting were playing havoc with the birds. After McCormick cited a series of examples in which systematic bird destruction had been followed by insect irruptions, Castle responded that his opponent had not provided "one scintilla of evidence" that songbirds and insectivorous birds were declining and that if they were, it was due to commercial hunting.[113] Following replies by Lucas and McCormick, the issue dropped from the pages of the *Ornithologists and Oologist*, only to return with a vengeance a year later.[114]

The publication of the AOU law and its quick passage in New York transformed the debate between scientific ornithologists and other bird collectors. The argument had previously turned on whether there was an actual decline in bird populations and to what extent commercial collectors, especially millinery collectors, were responsible. Now both sides accepted the premise of population decline and both pinned the primary blame on the milliners.[115] The point of contention shifted to the AOU model law, with its call for the elimination of nongame bird hunting except for "strictly scientific purposes" and especially the permit system. The recurring fear expressed in the pages of the *Ornithologist and Oologist* was that implementation of the permit system would necessarily result in the suppression of collecting by all amateurs, taxidermists, and dealers.

The opening volley came only a month after the appearance of the AOU model law, when C. H. Freeman urged that it would be "unwise to rigidly exclude all amateur students in ornithology from collecting specimens." Freeman appealed to the egalitarian sentiments of his audience to support his argument for a broad interpretation of who should be authorized to collect:

> It is rather harrowing . . . to the amateur who devotes only a portion of his leisure time to his favorite science, to be debarred from further investigations through the influence of men who in their association "organ" [the *Auk*] relate the comparison of specimens from their collection, with a cabinet of over ten thousand, with specimens from some equally overstocked cabinet of another "scientist." No. Such laws will not work, our Republic affords equal liberties to every one, provided the principles and intentions are alike, regardless of associations or pecuniary worth.[116]

A steady stream of editorials and letters challenging the AOU and its bird protection activities soon followed. Frederic H. Carpenter, whom Webster had recently hired as editor of the *Ornithologist and Oologist*, applauded attempts to eliminate bird destruction at the hands of milliners but decried the "tendency among associated [AOU] scientists to arrange themselves in opposition against the amateur and the taxidermists." Carpenter then attempted to show that taxidermists were "no more destructive" than ornithologists by comparing the number of birds collected by "eight prominent scientists" (48,340) with those handled over a roughly equal period by "ten taxidermists" (37,480). In the same editorial Carpenter also came to the defense of the "amateur student of bird-life": "When the love of nature draws one forth in pursuit of a congenial and profitable study of our birds, we are of the opinion that it should be as allowable by law as any exploration published in our scientific journals." In his experience, Carpenter argued, the "arrangement and records" of the bird collections amassed by "unknown workers in ornithology . . . compare most favorably with those of the *scientist*."[117] As revealed in a follow-up editorial the next month, Carpenter felt taxidermists had been betrayed by scientific ornithologists' refusal to defend their collecting prerogatives:

> In this dilemma they [taxidermists] are deserted by the class of men who should, from a sense of justice, have firmly stood by them. We refer to certain of the professional ornithologists, many of whom have employed these taxidermists to collect for them. If we interpret the law aright, the principal is held responsible with the agent; but these associated "scientists," when asked to give the reason for the "scarcity of birds" will with Pharisaical air, point the scornful finger at the taxidermist.[118]

The attack continued in the next issue of the *Ornithologist and Oologist*, with W. DeForrest Northrup decrying the way in which the issue of bird protection had split the previously cohesive ornithological community. In pushing for the permit clause, members of the AOU had ignored "the privileges of the young ornithologist." They had also refused to come to his defense when protectionists accused the amateur of excessive destruction of birds. Northrup hinted that if the facts were known, scientific ornithologists might soon have to answer similar charges: "What is the history of the Swainson's warbler in South Carolina and the prominent ornithologist [William Brewster] connected with their slaughter, who himself or by proxy secured all that could be found? But never mind, he is one of the committee for the *protection* of American birds."[119]

Scientific ornithologists could no longer stand to remain silent. Disturbed by Northrup's attack on his character, Brewster wrote to Allen to complain. Allen replied that the recent flurry of abuse directed at the bird protection committee was "an attempt to crystalize the antagonism of the taxidermist and unprincipled collector into an organized opposition to the movement in behalf of the birds" and "to foster ill-feeling on the part of 'amateurs' against 'high science' and scientific ornithologists."[120] Uncertain how to respond, he had written the longtime champion of the amateurs and AOU Councilor Montague Chamberlain to suggest that he reply.

Chamberlain accepted Allen's challenge. His initial rebuttal protested that in publishing the recent attacks on the AOU and its bird protection committee, the *Ornithologist and Oologist* had become a "vehicle for misrepresentation and injustice." Far from discouraging the work of young students, the AOU had sought to offer "all possible assistance in their studies." Scientific ornithologists recognized that "from the ranks of amateurs today must come the scientists of the future," and therefore the permit provisions of the AOU model law had placed amateurs "on the same footing as professional scientists."[121]

Chamberlain's letter generated two immediate responses. An anonymous correspondent asserted that whether the AOU bird protection committee originally had intended it, the permit system resulted in the suppression of amateur students in the East.[122] In a letter the next month Northrup again accused the AOU of trying to control who did and did not get permits by requiring that all applications be endorsed by "some scientific gentlemen" (i.e., "members of the A.O.U.").[123]

Again AOU representatives quickly came to the defense of their organization and the permit system. Chamberlain repeated his earlier claim that in his experience AOU scientists had freely given of their time and expertise to even the most rank beginner.[124] Unable to restrain himself, Allen also entered the fray. The AOU president admitted that he had been granted authority to issue collecting permits under New York's recently enacted bird protection law, but he vehemently denied giving favorable treatment to applications endorsed by AOU members. Thus far he had received fourteen applications, whose vouchers had been signed by twenty individuals. Most of these did not belong to the AOU. Allen claimed that none of the applicants had been denied permits because of unsatisfactory vouchers. According to Allen, the claims of discrimination lodged in recent numbers of the *Ornithologist and Oologist* were "not only unjust, but *entirely false.*"[125]

The level of tension between scientific ornithologists and other collectors gradually diminished as the bird protection committee withdrew from its active role in the bird protection movement and as the movement itself languished. But the rift that had opened up between scientific ornithologists and collectors was never fully repaired. Like the formation of the AOU and the institutionalization of the trinomial research program that came before it, the bird protection movement contributed to the breakup of what had been a congenial relationship during the heyday of the culture of collecting. Increasingly, cooperation gave way to mutual suspicion and even outright hostility.

Abandoning Bird Protection

In the mid-1880s, at the height of the first bird protection movement, it looked to many as if the movement might be here to stay. Afraid that the rising tide of protectionism might eventually prevent even the scientific ornithologist from collecting birds, Brewster spent the summer of 1886 "quietly" gathering examples of the commoner birds around his vacation home in Concord, Massachusetts. He feared it might be his last chance to "fill out his series."[126] Brewster was wrong.

After a short burst of activity, the first phase of the bird protection movement quickly faded. The AOU bird protection committee published a second bulletin promoting a version of the AOU model law passed by the New York legislature in May 1886.[127] AOU and Audubon members also lobbied successfully for the passage of a version of the law in Pennsylvania, Sennett's home state, in 1889.[128] But having secured what seemed to be adequate protective legislation in these two states, the committee seemed little inclined to expand its lobbying activities. By 1893 Sennett, who was preoccupied with the effects of the depression on his oil-machinery manufacturing business, asked the AOU to discharge his committee, arguing that the need for it was "no longer urgent, of late its function having been mainly advisory."[129]

Of course, nothing could have been farther from the truth. By 1893 amendment and repeal had emasculated or repealed existing protective legislation, and the practice of feather-wearing had continued to grow at an alarming rate. Notwithstanding the initial success of the Audubon Society, the committee had run up against a wall of indifference and apathy. At the same time, the activity of bird protection had created a division between scientific ornithologists and the larger collecting community. Since most AOU members remained reluctant to cut themselves off entirely from that larger community, they willingly accepted Sennett's request to dissolve the bird protection committee. Although AOU members reconsidered that action later in the meeting, the committee remained inactive for the next three years.

The Audubon Society suffered a similar fate. A period of robust membership growth in 1887, during which twenty thousand members joined, leveled off the next year. Even worse, few of the members were committed enough to subscribe to *Audubon Magazine*, which Grinnell hoped would provide the revenue to sustain the organization.[130] Frustrated, Grinnell stopped publication of the magazine with its January 1888 issue and abandoned the Audubon Society. With the demise of the AOU bird protection committee and Grinnell's Audubon Society, the bird protection movement seemed dead in its tracks.

CHAPTER SIX

Protecting Birds, Protecting Ornithologists

REVIVING THE MOVEMENT

On a chilly New England morning early in 1896, Harriet Lawrence Hemenway experienced an epiphany. While sitting in her home in one of Boston's most affluent neighborhoods, Hemenway stumbled upon a particularly vivid account of the destruction of herons by millinery hunters. Until that moment she had given little thought to the source of the beautiful feathers that adorned her hats and so many others at the turn of the century. Moved by the graphic descriptions of birds horribly mutilated in the name of fashion, she decided to take action to stop the cruelty.

With the aid of her cousin, Minna B. Hall, on 10 February 1896 Hemenway invited several of Boston's leading citizens to found the Massachusetts Audubon Society.[1] The purpose of the organization was "to discourage the buying and wearing, for ornamental purposes, of feathers of wild birds, and to otherwise further the protection of native birds."[2] The new society quickly elected William Brewster as president and began issuing a steady stream of pamphlets to bring its protectionist agenda before the public.[3] Soon anxious reformers in dozens of other states followed Hemenway's lead and founded similar societies.

There were other signs that after several years of slumber the Audubon movement might finally be stirring again. The most important of these occurred at the annual AOU meeting in November 1895, when AOU Treasurer William Dutcher gained appointment as chair of the bird protection committee. Fired with enthusiasm for the protectionist cause, Dutcher remobilized the lethargic committee and worked tirelessly to help establish state Audubon societies. In a highly successful educational, legislative, and enforcement campaign, the AOU's bird protection committee joined forces with a second, more enduring Audubon movement that continues to this day. This fruitful collaboration resulted in not only an American public alerted to the problem of bird destruction, but also an impressive series of state and federal legislative victories.

There were many reasons why the second bird protection movement succeeded where the previous one had faltered. First, it began with the creation of smaller, more manageable state societies, not a large national society, which had proven costly and unwieldy to administer during the short-lived Audubon crusade nearly a decade before.[4] Second, the new movement emerged in a cultural climate that not only was more conducive to reform, but also viewed regular contact with nature as an important means to ameliorate many of the problems plaguing modern America. Progressive-era activists regularly touted the benefits of getting "back to nature," and the bird protection cause both benefited from and promoted this new sensibility.[5] Third, the movement profited from close cooperation with the U.S. Department of Agriculture's Bureau of the Biological Survey, which provided crucial personnel and scientific data for the protectionists' armamentarium. But perhaps most important was the leadership of William Dutcher, the linchpin of both the AOU bird protection committee and the National Association of Audubon Societies. More than any other single individual, Dutcher was the engine that powered the bird protection movement through its crucial early years.

The educational and legislative successes of the bird protection movement also had important secondary consequences. Among these was a heightened tension between AOU scientists and other groups with whom they had once been closely affiliated: amateur bird and egg collectors, taxidermists, and natural history dealers. Tensions that had flared up briefly during the more ephemeral bird protection movement of the 1880s were now impossible to ignore or gloss over. As state officials began to restrict even scientific collecting of birds and eggs, many disgruntled ornithologists blamed the new Audubon societies for their woes. At the same time, restrictive permit policies forced ornithologists to attempt to narrow the definition of scientific practice to preserve the collecting privilege for themselves. In this process, scientists continued to distance themselves from entire groups—including natural history dealers, youthful collectors, and others—that had traditionally been associated with scientific ornithology.

But even this more restrictive definition failed to stem the continuing erosion of the collecting privilege. Consequently, when Dutcher engineered the creation of the National Association of Audubon Societies in 1905, the AOU repudiated its commitment to bird protection. In its stead the organization initiated a vigorous defense of scientific ornithology and its collecting practices. Not until nearly twenty-five years later, during a series of upheavals that rocked the conservation establishment—including an attack on scientific ornithologists from an AOU insider—did the union revive its protection activities.

Both contemporary participants and later historians have emphasized the remarkable successes of the second bird protection movement.[6] In this chapter I focus on the critical role that scientific ornithologists, and especially the AOU, played in initiating and sustaining this important movement. The AOU's entry into, withdrawal from, and subsequent reengagement with the issue of wildlife conservation provides an early and fascinating case study of a scientific community's attempt to define a social and political role for itself beyond the confines of the more traditional museum, laboratory, and classroom settings. The episode also demonstrates that entry into the political domain often exacts a cost. The bird protection movement became one of several factors that divided scientists and the larger ornithological community in the closing years of the nineteenth century and the beginning years of the twentieth.

DUTCHER'S PUSH FOR PROTECTION

During the thirteenth annual meeting of the AOU, held in November 1895, a representative from the Committee on the Protection of North American Birds rose to present his report. His message that evening was familiar to the small

Figure 21. William and Basil Dutcher skinning a loon, ca. late 1870s.

group assembled at C. Hart Merriam's home for the business session of the union. As had been the case for some time now, the bird protection committee had accomplished nothing during the preceding year.[7] In fact, the lethargic committee had been inactive since lobbying for passage of the AOU model law in Pennsylvania six years previously. Like many of the birds it ostensibly sought to protect, the committee was in serious danger of becoming extinct. That night, Elliott Coues moved to have the latest committee discharged, and newly elected AOU President William Brewster appointed a new bird protection committee. With the appointment of William Dutcher (fig. 21) as chair, prospects for the committee, and the birds, immediately began to brighten.

As had been the case with many of his fellow ornithologists, Dutcher's original interest in birds began as a sportsman.[8] In May 1879 he shot a bird that was new to him, in Shinnecock Bay, Long Island. He had the novel specimen identified and mounted by the well-known New York taxidermist John G. Bell. The bird, a female Wilson's plover, turned out to be a new record for the area, a fact that Dutcher eagerly recorded in the *Bulletin of the Nuttall Ornithological Club*.[9] The event marked a turning point in the life of the successful Manhattan insurance broker. The plover became specimen no. 1 of what soon grew to be an extensive collection of Long Island birds, and his published record became the first in a series of publications based on his collection. Dutcher's ornithological activities came to the attention of the AOU officials, who elected him an associate member in 1883 and treasurer three years later.

Within months after Dutcher's appointment as chair of the AOU bird protection committee, Harriet Hemenway organized the Massachusetts Audubon Society. Dutcher recognized that this kind of organization represented an invaluable ally in the fight to protect birds and began urging individuals in other states to establish similar societies.[10] By the end of 1896 two states—West Virginia and Pennsylvania—had followed Massachusetts's lead. With Dutcher's encouragement and support, during the next year scientists and reformers organized Audubon societies in Illinois, Minnesota, New Jersey, New York, Rhode Island, Wisconsin, and the District of Columbia.[11] The pace continued for the next six years, as interested individuals in twenty-six states joined to create additional Audubon societies.[12]

In its early years the second Audubon movement stressed education over legislation and enforcement activities. In an attempt to persuade women to relinquish their bird-wearing habits, protectionists distributed countless pamphlets, posters, and circulars containing graphic descriptions of the cruel methods used to obtain feathers.[13] Other accounts stressed the economic value of birds in checking the growth of noxious insect populations. Newspapers and lectures provided additional means to bring the protectionists' message before the public. In 1897 Frank M. Chapman, an assistant curator of ornithology at the American Museum of Natural History who was in particular demand on the lecture circuit, reported to William Brewster: "Protection and popular bird work are booming. I go to Washington the last of the month to address the teachers of the city in the afternoon and the Audubon Society in the evening and I have engagements also in Hartford, Bridgeport, Brooklyn, and Plainfield."[14]

Protectionists especially sought to reach impressionable young children (fig. 22). As Dutcher explained, "while legislation may be of vast benefit in protecting all bird life, yet we firmly believe that the true solution to the problem will be the education of children of our schools, both public and private. They should be taught in every grade, from kindergarten to the college, not only the aesthetic but the economical value of birds. . . . When we have educated our children, laws will be unnecessary."[15] Toward that end, Dutcher repeatedly urged AOU and state Audubon society members to push for the introduction of Bird Day, an idea first suggested in 1894 by C. A. Babcock, superintendent of schools in Oil City, Pennsylvania. Modeled on the successful Arbor Day celebrations introduced nearly twenty-five years earlier, Bird Day was devoted to "instructing the children in the value of our native birds and the best means of protecting them."[16] Ideally, the day—during which children would read original compositions, perform skits, listen to lectures, and recite poetry and prose about birds—would be the culmination of a year-long program of bird study.

Bird protection committee member Florence Merriam was sanguine that attempts to introduce bird study into schools would be aided by the recently initiated nature study movement, a turn-of-the-century educational reform initiative that sought to incorporate hands-on contact with nature into elementary and secondary school classrooms.[17] Several state Audubon societies offered training sessions to show teachers how to make bird study a regular part of their curriculum.[18]

Figure 22. Junior Audubon Society of Sutton, West Virginia, 1915. To reach children with their conservation message, Audubon Society leaders freely distributed bird-related literature, promoted nature study in schools, and (beginning in 1910) organized Junior Audubon Societies.

Although some protectionists worried that the success of nature study would lead to more carnage as teachers and students gathered birds and eggs to undertake their studies, most were heartened by the new opportunity.[19]

Under Dutcher's aggressive leadership, the AOU bird protection committee soon became, in all but name, a national Audubon society.[20] In addition to lobbying for the creation of new protective societies and the introduction of Bird Day, the committee served as a clearinghouse for individuals seeking information on the bird protection movement. To better meet the increasing workload and assure greater geographic representation of the committee, Dutcher expanded its membership to thirteen, including four women, who as a rule had previously been absent from the AOU.[21] The committee's lengthy annual reports detailed the activities of the Audubon movement and began to occupy more and more space in the *Auk*. Dutcher also arranged to have these reports separately printed for wider distribution.

By 1897 bird protection work was beginning to represent an increasing financial hardship for Dutcher. He wrote to Brewster that he "loved the work" and firmly believed that it was the "duty of every earnest man to do some good in the world," but he felt that his bird protection activities, to which he had devoted "fully one half" of his time, were threatening his ability to make a living in the insurance business.[22] By the end of 1897 a frustrated and overworked Dutcher resigned his chair, but he remained an active member of the bird protection committee.[23]

Dutcher's temporary replacement, Witmer Stone, proved to be just as committed to conservation as his predecessor. Stone was one of the few ornithologists in the nineteenth century lucky enough to parlay his boyhood interest in collecting natural history specimens into a professional position. In 1888, after graduating with an A.B. degree from the University of Pennsylvania, Stone became a Jesup Fund Student at the Academy of Natural Sciences of Philadelphia, where he remained for the next fifty years.[24] The ornithological collection at the academy had once ranked among the finest in the world. But at the time of Stone's arrival, it had suffered from nearly two decades of neglect. Besides reinvigorating the academy's bird collection, Stone helped to create two other ornithological institutions in the Philadelphia area. In 1890 he was a founder of the Delaware Valley Ornithological Club, one of the more vigorous of the numerous local ornithological societies created at the end of the nineteenth century. He was also an organizer and the first president of the Pennsylvania Audubon Society, created in 1897, a year before he was tapped to chair the AOU bird protection committee.

As committee chair, Stone continued the aggressive conservation policies initiated by Dutcher. Despite increasing calls for effective legislation, in his 1898 report Stone indicated that the committee had continued to stress education. Toward that end, the sixteen thousand members of fourteen state Audubon societies had issued over ninety thousand leaflets during the previous year.[25] Stone also called for a "cheap monthly magazine devoted to popular ornithology, to serve as an organ for the various Audubon societies." He hoped, as George B. Grinnell had over a decade previously, that a suitable periodical would relieve the committee of part of its growing workload.

For over a year Frank Chapman had also contemplated just such a magazine.[26] Although he had been an ornithologist at the American Museum for nearly a decade, he continued to make only a nominal salary. To supplement his meager income, Chapman had done what many entrepreneurial naturalists during his day were to do: he found a way to profit from the increasing popular interest in natural history, in his case through well-attended lectures and a series of best-selling field guides. With his marriage in March 1898, Chapman felt the need "to adopt some means of adding" further to his earnings.[27]

That means was *Bird-Lore*, a bimonthly magazine of popular ornithology that was also the official publication of the newly emerging Audubon societies. Before launching the first issue of the magazine in February 1899, Chapman had received the blessings of Stone and numerous state Audubon societies.[28] He also secured the services of Mabel Osgood Wright, a prominent nature writer and president of the Connecticut Audubon Society, to edit the Audubon department of the new periodical. *Bird-Lore* proved a successful venture from the outset. One year after Chapman began publishing the magazine, a relieved Witmer Stone reported that *Bird-Lore* had greatly reduced the bird protection committee's correspondence burden.[29]

Around 1900 the committee began to supplement its previous focus on education with increased legislative and enforcement activity. Several factors account for this reorientation. One of the most important was the passage of the Lacey

Act, named after its principal sponsor, Rep. John F. Lacey of Iowa, who was the author of a number of turn-of-the-century congressional conservation initiatives.[30] Signed into law on 25 May 1900, the Lacey Act authorized federal funds for the restoration of wild bird populations, established federal control on the importation of foreign birds and animals, and, most importantly for the bird protection movement, outlawed the interstate shipment of "wild animals and birds" taken in defiance of existing state laws.[31] The final form of the bill, which emerged after four years of congressional consideration, was written in close collaboration with T. S. Palmer, bird protection committee member and chief assistant of the USDA's Biological Survey. The Audubon coalition of scientists, humanitarians, and nature lovers fought vigorously for passage of the Lacey Act.[32] The most effective support, however, came from recreational hunters, especially G. O. Shields and his newly created League of American Sportsmen, who hoped the bill would further their campaign to eliminate the sale of game.[33] By providing individual state laws with the teeth of federal enforcement, the Lacey Act proved a powerful weapon in the protectionists' arsenal.

At about the time the passage of the Lacey Act seemed certain, the AOU bird protection committee, and more specifically William Dutcher, became increasingly active in enforcement work. As early as 1894, committee members had reported on the activities of individuals hired to protect the breeding colonies of seabirds on a limited number of East Coast islands.[34] But it was not until 1900, when the artist-naturalist and AOU member Abbott Thayer offered to raise the required funds, that enforcement became an integral part of the committee's work.[35] With the $1,400 collected the first year, Dutcher hired wardens to monitor breeding colonies along the northeastern coast, from the mouth of the Chesapeake Bay to Maine.[36]

Encouraged by the apparent success of recent enforcement activities and the passage of the Lacey Act, in 1901 Dutcher mounted an aggressive campaign to secure passage of the AOU model law. Prior to that year, only five states had enacted laws the committee considered "at all satisfactory" for the protection of nongame birds.[37] Working closely with other committee members, state Audubon societies, and sport hunting organizations, Dutcher and Palmer lobbied state legislatures up and down the eastern part of the country. As a direct result of this campaign, eleven states passed "a complete new law, or much needed amendments to existing laws" during the year.[38] Dutcher and Palmer continued to keep the pressure on, and by 1903 twenty-nine states had passed some version of the AOU model law.[39]

Dutcher and Palmer also played a key role in the creation of the first and many subsequent federal wildlife refuges. On 14 March 1903 President Theodore Roosevelt signed an unusual executive order establishing Pelican Island, a four-acre site on Florida's Indian River and home to a large nesting colony of brown pelicans, as a "preserve and breeding ground for native birds."[40] The action came after Chapman had visited the island in 1898 and 1900 and began urging the protection of its threatened inhabitants. In response to Chapman's plea, in 1902 Dutcher hired a warden to monitor the island during breeding season and filed paperwork to purchase it from the federal government on behalf of the AOU bird protection committee.[41] When the transaction became bogged down, a General Land Office employee suggested setting Pelican Island aside as a federal bird reservation.[42] The idea delighted Roosevelt, who was a strong supporter of conservation initiatives. It also thrilled Dutcher and Palmer, who with Frank Bond, an Audubon official and General Land Office agent, began pressing Roosevelt for the establishment of additional reservations.[43] The president seemed quite willing to accommodate their demands, and before leaving office in 1909 he used his executive authority to establish more than fifty additional reservations.[44]

Along with heightened legislative activity and the promotion of wildlife refuges came attempts to better organize the Audubon movement on a national level. Again, the major protagonist in the effort was Dutcher, who called the first meeting of state Audubon society representatives to coincide with the annual meeting of the AOU held in Cambridge, Massachusetts, in November 1900. The purpose of the proposed meeting was to establish "a closer relationship between the Societies and the Union, and to consider ways for the more systematic prosecution of the work of the Societies."[45] Nine representatives attended and created a committee to "formulate plans for the federation of the Audubon Societies."[46] They also planned a meeting to coincide with the next annual AOU conference to be held in New York in 1901.

During the next two years the work of the Audubon societies and the AOU bird protection committee were increasingly merged in the person of William Dutcher. At their 1901 meeting representatives from the state Audubon societies again rejected the idea of consolidation but did vote to create a loose confederation, the National Committee of the Audubon Societies of America, "to represent the societies whenever concerted action be deemed . . . expedient."[47] Dutcher was elected chair of this new national committee and chosen to replace Stone as the head of the AOU bird protection committee. The next year he issued a single lengthy report for both committees, which occupied fifty-eight pages in the *Auk*.[48]

In 1905 Dutcher orchestrated the creation of the National Association of Audubon Societies, a coalition of most of the state Audubon societies and forerunner to the National Audubon Society, which is still active today. That same year he also resigned from the AOU bird protection committee following complaints from members of the AOU Council about increasing restrictions on scientific bird collecting.[49] Although individual members of the AOU continued to play important roles in the bird protection movement, for the next twenty-five years after Dutcher's resignation the AOU relinquished its preeminent position in American wildlife conservation.

REDEFINING ORNITHOLOGY

The second bird protection movement brought to the surface again a central dilemma for a scientific ornithology that continued to depend heavily on collecting to provide it with the raw material for research. The problem was how to eliminate large-scale commercial hunting for plumes and meat, while maintaining the ability to collect birds for "scientific" purposes. Most scientific ornithologists supported the permit provision in the AOU model law as a way to resolve their difficulty. As mentioned earlier, that provision authorized granting a permit to collect birds to anyone who submitted the proper fee, an executed bond, and an affidavit from two recognized ornithologists.[50]

Although the permit system was serviceable in theory, several problems arose as it was put into wider practice in the closing decades of the nineteenth century. First, many in the broader community of collectors resented what they perceived as a high-handed attempt by scientists to limit their activities. A second, closely related difficulty was defining precisely what kind of collecting was "strictly scientific" and therefore allowable. In the culture of collecting that reigned throughout the second half of the nineteenth century, the boundaries between scientific ornithologists, amateur and professional collectors, taxidermists, and commercial dealers were fluid. Moreover, some individuals did what nearly everyone considered legitimate scientific collecting in conjunction with commercial collecting for the natural history trade or even more problematic millinery hunting. And if these difficulties were not enough, the decision concerning who would and would not be granted a permit was gradually removed from the hands of scientists and entrusted to state game commissions, which were increasingly suspicious of ornithologists' claims for the continued need for large-scale collecting. As the nineteenth century drew to a close, the bird protection movement in general, and the permit system in particular, again became a wedge between scientific ornithologists and the closely associated communities of collectors, taxidermists, and dealers.

The success of the second bird protection movement helped legitimize the views of the radical wing of the movement, the so-called ultra-protectionists, who were increasingly impatient with scientific ornithology's continued collecting demands. For example, the nature-writer Leander Keyser criticized the deplorable "record of bird-killing and nest robbing" contained in ornithological journals. For Keyser, bird collecting "even for scientific purposes" was by definition cruel.[51] If scientists were as interested in protecting birds as they claimed, they would "study birds in all the varied phases of their lives," not just "shoot them and despoil their nests as soon as found." Keyser admonished scientific ornithologists to practice what they preached: "If we really wish to spare the birds, I feel that professional ornithologists must set the example of mercy. As long as many of them continue to destroy with so ruthless a hand, our arguments against pot-hunters and fashion-mongers are robbed of all their moral force."[52]

A similar attack on scientific ornithology came from Reginald C. Robbins, a former Harvard philosophy graduate student with a Boston Brahmin background.[53] In 1901 Robbins published an obtuse, sixteen-page polemic entitled *Bird-Killing as a Method in Ornithology* and arranged to have it distributed with the January 1902 edition of the *Auk*.[54] Few ornithologists could follow Robbins's trying circumlocutions, but the central message of the pamphlet was discernible even to the casual reader: scientific ornithologists were responsible for an inordinate amount of unnecessary bird destruction.

Other attacks on scientific ornithology abounded. As the nineteenth century closed, William T. Hornaday, erstwhile employee of Ward's Natural Science Establishment and vigorous spokesperson for the culture of collecting, increasingly transferred his loyalty to the protectionists' camp.[55] For Hornaday the conversion from taxidermist and collector to conservationist and protector had come gradually, following a buffalo-collecting expedition mounted in 1886, while he was head taxidermist for the Smithsonian Institution. Outraged by the wanton and rapid destruction of this noble beast, Hornaday published a lengthy monograph, *The Extermination of the Bison* (1889), and other more popular articles to call wider attention to the problem.[56] He also persuaded Smithsonian authorities to establish a National Zoo, which he hoped would be used to preserve North American species, like the buffalo, which had reached critically low levels. Hornaday resigned from the Smithsonian when his design for the proposed zoo was rejected, but by 1896 he was hired as director of the Bronx Zoo, which the New York Zoological Society was then in the process of founding. During his twenty-six years with the organization, Hornaday remained deeply involved in wildlife conservation battles.

In an 1898 report for the New York Zoological Society, Hornaday charged scientific naturalists with ignoring the problem of bird and mammal destruction in North America. He admitted that a "few of the active members of the American Ornithologists' Union and the Audubon Society" had "taken a hand in the enactment of laws for the protection of birds generally," but he claimed that most had been too "wholly engrossed in their studies" even to notice the "carnage going on around them."[57] Hornaday's charges were exaggerated at best, but they reflected a widely shared perception not only among the more militant protectionists, but also among many in the general public.

Reeling under these and similar attacks and recognizing that much of the large-scale collecting done under the cover of science greatly stretched the bounds of legitimacy, the bird protection committee finally began to address the issue of excessive "scientific" collecting. As early as 1897 Committee Chair Dutcher recommended that "all permits issued by the proper authorities for collecting birds and their eggs should be absolutely confined to scientific purposes, and that in no sense shall they be construed to collect for commercial purposes."[58] Thorough discussion of the proposal failed to begin until after the publication of Hornaday's scathing indictment.

In his bird protection committee report for 1898, Witmer Stone proudly pointed to one result of the recent revival of the bird protection movement: the decrease in the number of birds brought to taxidermists' shops to be mounted. When asked about the state of his business, one disgruntled taxidermist is reported to have said: "It is simply dead. If it warn't [*sic*] for rugs and deer heads we couldn't live. Those —, —, — Audubon Societies and bird books and new-fangled laws are just crowding us out. The men are afraid to shoot or handle them in any shape. What's the birds for if they ain't to be used."[59] Though perhaps spurious, the report was nonetheless telling. Gone entirely were earlier claims about taxidermists and natural history dealers being "indispensable allies" to scientific ornithologists. Scientists increasingly sought to distance themselves from all forms of commercial natural history.[60]

In a more extensive discussion in the body of the report, Stone again raised the issue of the "sacrifice of birds to science," which he felt could no longer be "conscientiously ignored." He declared that the day had passed when everyone interested in bird study needed an extensive personal collection. Not only were large institutional collections available to serious students, but increasingly "many an ornithologist . . . well deserving of that title" pursued studies without a gun.[61]

Stone then singled out two particular groups he felt no longer deserved permits to collect birds for scientific purposes. First were those who received "scientific" permits to collect "for natural history dealers." "Far worse," though, in Stone's view was the "scourge of egg collecting."[62] In unambiguous terms, Stone denounced the widespread practice of large-scale egg-collecting as a "fad . . . encouraged and fostered by dealers until it became one of the most potent causes of the decrease of our birds."[63]

In considering whether to call for greater restrictions on egg collecting, Stone was walking a fine line. On the one hand, he wanted to maintain the credibility of the AOU by taking action against what many believed was an illegitimate extension of the collecting privilege. On the other hand, Stone and his colleagues recognized that egg collecting had often been the first manifestation of what eventually developed into a deeper, long-term, even scientific interest in birds. At the time Stone was writing, virtually every scientific ornithologist in America had first become attracted to bird study while amassing a youthful collection of birds or eggs (fig. 23).

The issue provoked strong feelings on both sides. As one prominent ornithologist was reported to have said: "I would rather see 1,000 birds killed through lack of laws, than have one promising Ornithologist discouraged through hardships imposed by arbitrary legislation."[64] Afraid that a call for a complete ban on youthful collecting would dry up the future supply of scientific ornithologists, Stone refused to condemn the activity outright. Instead, he called on "active ornithologists" to give would-be bird and egg collectors a few words of advice about the kinds and numbers of species whose collection might lead to a scientific contribution.[65]

The dilemma was one that the more thoughtful young collector also faced. In 1904 fifteen-year-old Frank T. Antes, one of the youngest associate members of the AOU, wrote to Brewster for advice on a subject that had "long been troubling" him:

> It is: ought I to collect birds in an age when so much is being done to protect them? I am
> now about at an age when I can take out a license and shoot birds for scientific purposes.
> I should like to do this for self-enlightenment on the plumages and structure, but on the
> other hand is it perfectly right to do this and also to talk to other people about how they

Figure 23. Alexander Wetmore, with *Bird-Lore*, opera glasses,
and bird collection, 1901. Fifteen-year-old Wetmore was the
kind of budding young naturalist that ornithologists worried
about discouraging through outright prohibitions on collecting.
Wetmore later worked for the Biological Survey, headed the
United States National Museum, and eventually became
secretary of the Smithsonian Institution.

must not kill birds or wear them on their hats? . . . If you will be kind enough to advise
me on this subject I shall be very obliged to you.[66]

In 1899 Stone had tried to answer Antes and all young would-be collectors with
a widely distributed pamphlet entitled *Hints to Young Bird Students.*[67] The pamphlet, which was signed by most professional ornithologists in America at the
time, amplified the comments found in the earlier bird protection committee report, including the attack on natural history dealers:

Do you know what scientific ornithology—real ornithology—is? Are you not influenced, to some extent at least, by "oological" magazines and dealers' price-lists of eggs,
from which you learn that it is important to secure *series of sets,*—which means hun-

dreds and thousands of eggs,—and wherein you also learn the market price of this or that egg, and value your specimens accordingly,—just as you do your postage stamps? This is not science, and the men who advocate this sort of collecting, and who have the largest collections of eggs, rarely contribute anything to our knowledge of birds, and are not advancing the science of ornithology. . . . There is nothing to be gained by the collecting of series, except the extermination of the birds, which is surely not your object.[68]

Stone still refused to condemn all youthful collecting, but he argued that would-be ornithologists would "learn more of value by a study of the living bird than by collecting skins."[69]

At the time Stone was writing, the business of natural history was already beginning to change. The reemergence of the vigorous bird protection movement in the mid-1890s had come on the heels of the panic of 1893. Many dealers were forced to sell out or abandon their businesses. Some, like Walter F. Webb and his one-time partner Frank Lattin, one of the largest egg and skin dealers in the country, moved into other, less contentious areas of natural history, like shells or books. Others, like Ward's Natural Science Establishment and Frank B. Webster's Naturalists' Supply Depot, began targeting less-problematic and higher-volume educational institutions rather than private collectors. Because of these changes, Stone's indictment seems to have generated little or no public reply from natural history dealers. But the army of egg collectors was another story.

For example, Stone's pamphlet provoked an angry reply from a prominent egg collector, J. Parker Norris, Jr., of Philadelphia, whose collection of over twenty thousand eggs ranked among the largest in the nation.[70] Norris began by admitting that he was responsible for the particular example of excessive egg collecting first raised by Hornaday and repeated by Stone (210 sets and 910 eggs of the Kentucky warbler). The eggs, he claimed, were scientifically legitimate; they had been gathered over a period of twelve years as preparation for an "elaborate monograph" on the warblers of North America.[71] Norris then went on the offensive, alleging that Stone was "neither sincere nor consistent" in his charges against egg collectors. He claimed to have found conclusive evidence that a recent collection Stone acquired for the Academy of Natural Sciences contained a "drawerful of skins of the Worm[-]eating Warbler, taken in Chester County in two seasons by Mr. H. Garrett (professional taxidermist). Before this was done the Worm-eating Warbler was a common summer resident in Chester County; now it is rare."[72] This accusation was particularly embarrassing for the current chair of the bird protection committee.

Norris continued by arguing that not just in this but in every instance skin collecting was more damaging to bird populations: "When you take a set of eggs the ♀ always lays another, but kill the parents and you destroy not only them but all the progeny they would have had and so on *ad infinitum*."[73] And finally he defended oologists' contributions to science by pointing proudly to the accomplishments of the patron saint of oology, Charles E. Bendire, an honorary curator at the U.S. National Museum, whose extensive egg collection provided the basis for the widely heralded two-volume *Life Histories of North American Birds*.

Figure 24. George W. Morse of Tulsa, Oklahoma, with his prized egg collection, 1929.
Many ornithologists gained their first introduction to bird study by collecting eggs.
With the growth of the Audubon movement and the increasing legal restrictions on
collecting, interest in the activity greatly diminished.

Norris also included a disparaging reference to the unceasing nomenclatural controversies that characterized the professional museum ornithologist:

> Quite as much interest and value had been contributed to the twin science of ornithology
> and oology by oologists as by ornithologists, particularly the closest [i.e., closet] type of
> ornithologists, who spend their time making and unmaking minute subspecific differ-
> ences. You will not find any oologist who knows nothing about ornithology, but it is
> most common to find ornithologists who know *nothing* about oology.[74]

As a defender of the rights of amateur and youthful collectors, Norris also
participated in a protracted series of exchanges on the issue of large-scale collecting, especially of eggs, which appeared in the *Osprey* and other periodicals aimed
at collectors.[75] The issue was one that divided scientists from the larger community of amateurs, who vigorously defended what they believed to be their own
legitimate collecting needs (fig. 24). It also threatened to divide the scientists
themselves. While most scientific ornithologists supported Stone's campaign to
suppress large-scale collecting by amateurs, commercial dealers, and others, several also continued to assert the rights of all collectors. As Coues maintained: "We
are the friend and helper of every boy who wishes to make a cabinet of eggs or
skins; we stand by every collector who takes birds or their eggs for proper purposes of ownership, study, exchange, or sale."[76]

CONSERVE THE COLLECTOR

In 1902 Charles B. Cory, president-elect of the AOU, replied with apparent irritation to an invitation to attend a meeting of the District of Columbia Audubon Society: "I do not protect birds. I kill them."[77] Though at least partially tongue-in-cheek, Cory's answer nonetheless hinted at what many scientists viewed as an increasingly problematic relationship between the AOU and the broader bird protection movement.

The reasons for the scientists' apprehensions were many. First, the AOU bird protection committee's earlier attempts to head off criticism had failed. Although the committee had gone on record against large-scale collecting by dealers, taxidermists, and youth, scientists continued to be accused of condoning and even participating in excessive collecting. In a particularly striking example of this disturbing trend, in 1902 Garrett Newkirk of Pasadena, California, wrote to *Condor* to protest the "cruel indifference to and lack of genuine sympathy with bird life, on the part of some of the scientific ornithologists." Newkirk admitted that "certain students . . . of nomenclature and classification" might be entitled to "collections . . . of dead and stuffed birdskins." "But," he continued, "the unflinching, destructive disposition of some, even of the better class of collectors, seems to me without excuse and abhorrent to the lover of life and Nature."[78]

Newkirk continued with a remarkable statement that betrayed the increasing radicalization of the bird protection movement. Where earlier bird protectionists tended to speak of the obligation to prevent needless suffering in animals (especially for millinery purposes), Newkirk asserted that birds had positive *rights* that were on a par with those of humans:

> They [scientists] would not think of killing, even in the Philippines, varying specimens of the genus Homo, merely for the purposes of anatomical study, to embellish some museum or to settle a disputed point of faunal geography. And yet they have no hesitation in taking the lives of other animals, who are in some respects *superior to themselves*, for just such purposes of curiosity, or, what is worse, for merely selfish ambition. Beings who love and mate, who build homes with infinite labor and pains, with marvelous wisdom and skill, these are hunted, robbed and killed, without any consideration of their rights.[79]

Exacerbating this and similar attacks from the radical wing of the bird protection movement was the perception that Dutcher was moving toward a stance of absolute protection.[80] One source of this belief was a letter published in 1903 in which Dutcher castigated P. M. Silloway, "an ornithologist of recognized ability," for collecting every egg he could locate in a colony of Holboell grebes in Montana:

> Twenty-eight eggs taken, some of them almost to the point of hatching, and for what,— that they might be measured to see if there was a fraction of an inch difference in the length or breadth of the empty shell, or to note if there was a slight variation in the shade

of the ground color. Could this not have been done without the sacrifice of twenty-eight young birds, and the consequent distress of the parents?[81]

Dutcher claimed that no one had a "higher appreciation of real scientific work" than he, but that "the taking of every egg, of a rare breeder, in a small colony, is in no sense scientific, but on the other hand, it is wasteful and reprehensible."[82] Even this apparently reasonable critique was disturbing to the many scientists who rejected any external limitation on their collecting activities. As A. K. Fisher wrote in reply, "a naturalist is better qualified to know his own needs than anyone else, and . . . it is unwise to condemn his methods of collecting even though they may seem extravagant from our point of view."[83]

Dutcher's rhetoric also began to reflect the increasingly religious tone of the more radical wing of the bird protection movement.[84] His annual report for 1903 often sounded more as though it had been penned by an evangelist than a scientist. For example, in the introduction he stressed the "spiritual" side of bird protection.[85] Dutcher then quoted a passage from Coleridge in which the romantic poet had admonished man to love the beasts just as God loved man.[86] And near the end of his report he called for the total elimination of all Sunday shooting in the states that still allowed it, to provide "absolute rest to bird life for the one day per week."[87]

Even more disquieting to the scientists were the increasing restrictions on collecting. The series of state laws that the bird protection committee had recently secured with the close cooperation of state Audubon and humane societies often limited what scientists considered entirely legitimate collecting. In some states the problem began when the authority to issue permits had been removed from scientific organizations and entrusted to state game commissions or wardens. Game officials tended to be more closely allied to the sporting community and less sympathetic to the collecting demands of scientists.

New York was a case in point. Under the terms of the original AOU model law passed in 1886, the state authorized the American Museum of Natural History to issue permits for scientific bird collecting. For nearly two decades J. A. Allen reviewed the applications and issued collecting licenses on behalf of the museum.[88] But in 1904 the state legislature amended the law to make the New York Forest, Fish, and Game Commission the sole permit-granting authority in the state. As State Game Protector J. Warren Pond soon reported, "much care has been taken to determine just who every applicant is and what his business is." In the face of this intense scrutiny, only five permits had been granted during the first five months in which the new law was in effect.[89]

Other states were even more restrictive. In a 1903 editorial complaining about the bond requirement in the AOU model law, Walter K. Fisher, editor of the *Condor*, asserted that "almost without exception it is a positive hardship to secure a permit to collect where the A.O.U. bill has been accepted, particularly in the case of non-residents." In Vermont only three permits to collect were in force at any given time. Even worse, Virginia's bird protection legislation lacked a provision for scientific collecting.[90] Fisher asked impatiently, "Where is *Ornithology* to come in?"[91]

At the same time, Walter's father, A. K. Fisher, orchestrated a successful campaign to eliminate the bonding clause from the AOU model law. Just before the annual AOU meeting in the fall of 1903, the elder Fisher wrote several prominent ornithologists to complain about the difficulty of obtaining collecting permits and the objectionable bond feature: "The present wave of hysteria rolling along & pervading bird protection is threatening to prevent collecting by ornithologists. I do not believe that the AOU should sanction unnecessary restrictions to legitimate collecting and consequently feel that the bonding feature in the AOU law should be cut out."[92] After securing support from several key AOU members, Fisher brought his reform proposal before the full council of the union, which decided to place the issue before the general membership at its business session. Despite strong opposition from Dutcher, AOU members voted to strike the offending clause from the AOU model law.[93]

Two years later, at the AOU annual meeting immediately following the creation of the National Association of Audubon Societies, Dutcher reported that his committee had been "inactive" the past year because "most of its members were connected with another society." Expanding upon his earlier theme, A. K. Fisher strongly urged that the bird protection committee be continued, but he argued that its mission should be reoriented to better represent "the interests of scientific ornithologists, the tendency being to prohibit all collecting." Chapman suggested that one way to begin this process of redefinition would be to have the committee composed only of scientists who were *not* active members of the National Association of Audubon Societies. An angry Dutcher replied that he felt the scientists had "misunderstood" the feeling of the Audubon societies toward scientific collecting and asked that his committee be discharged. AOU President Charles Batchelder then appointed Fisher to chair the new bird protection committee.[94]

Like his immediate predecessor, A. K. Fisher was a consummate AOU insider.[95] He had been a founding member of the union, a longtime member of its governing council, and an original district superintendent for the AOU migration committee. In the latter capacity he worked closely with the C. Hart Merriam, his friend and former classmate at the College of Physicians and Surgeons in New York. When Merriam became head of the Division of Economic Ornithology and Mammalogy (later the Bureau of the Biological Survey), he persuaded Fisher to abandon his medical practice and accompany him to Washington as an assistant. Fisher remained an important force within the agency for the next forty-six years. His most significant publication, a study of the diets of hawks and owls published in 1893, was typical of the reports regularly issued by the Biological Survey in its early years and long remained a standard in its field.[96]

As his comments of the last few years had suggested, Fisher's appointment marked a fundamental shift in the conservation policy of the AOU. Fearful of further erosion of the collecting privilege, the union entirely abandoned its leadership position in the nearly decade-long bird protection movement. Individual members, like Chapman, Allen, Dutcher, and others, continued to serve in key administrative positions within Audubon societies at both the state and national levels, but the AOU as an institution repudiated its earlier commitment to bird protection. Gone were the frequent appeals on behalf of the birds. Gone were the regular appearances before state and federal legislatures as representatives of the union. And gone too were the lengthy reports detailing the successes of the movement. For over twenty-five years the bird protection committee held no formal meetings and issued no printed reports. The issue of bird protection all but disappeared from the pages of the *Auk*.

Behind the scenes the situation was hardly better. Each year when called to give his annual report, Fisher responded that his committee had held no meetings and had no formal report to offer.[97] This was often followed by a brief account of his attempts to secure more liberal permit regulations in states that had restricted collecting. In 1908 Fisher even asserted that he did "not feel that the song-birds require the protection accorded them. Storms kill more than ornithologists. . . . We should oppose laws that do not give ornithologists a right to collect."[98]

A remarkable exchange during a 1909 council meeting revealed an older generation's frustration with the increasing restrictions on collecting and its failure to appreciate recent changes in the direction of ornithological research. The exchange began when Fisher indicated, as usual, that he had no formal report to offer on behalf of the bird protection committee but felt it was "more and more evident that the trouble in obtaining permits was affecting the study of ornithology." The state of Washington granted permits only to residents, thereby preventing even federal ornithologists from doing needed research there. In Texas "it was almost impossible to collect." And it continued to be difficult to get permits in New York. Fisher argued that even "boys should be allowed to collect if they can make bird skins," and that the AOU should "take steps to help young men fit themselves as ornithologists . . . so that ornithologists would not be annihilated."[99]

Several council members echoed Fisher's apprehensions. Calling the "moral effect" of the restrictions "tremendous," William Brewster argued that they would ultimately lead to "the extermination of practical ornithologists." Already it was "almost impossible" to get good records from the "opera glass observers," even though the latter published with complete confidence. Charles Batchelder argued that it was "time ornithologists should have protection," and that the committee should "formulate plans to bring about needed modifications of the methods of issuing permits for bird collecting." Merriam, D. G. Elliot, Stone, and Chapman each expressed sympathy with what had been said. The latter also admitted that "he had collected in his native state, New Jersey, without a permit" and recommended a bulletin to clarify how the union felt about collecting birds for scientific purposes.[100]

No bulletin emerged from the council's discussion, but three years later the bird protection committee's change in mission was publicly recognized by Witmer Stone, who had recently been appointed as editor of the *Auk*:

> It is certainly true that there are to-day, very few young men engaged in forming a collection of bird-skins, formerly regarded as a *sine qua non* to the development of an ornithologist. So serious has this matter appeared to some that it has been suggested that

the A.O.U. Committee for the Protection of North American Birds might well be changed to a Committee for the prevention of the extermination of North American ornithologists.[101]

Stone denied that Audubon societies had pressured states to restrict or eliminate permits for scientific collecting. Rather, he placed the blame for the recent difficulty in securing permits squarely on those few insensitive collectors who "displayed little or no sympathy with citizens who prefer live birds to dead ones, and armed with their permits have carried on collecting close to houses and grounds in a manner that has made them very obnoxious. These men are naturally regarded as examples of 'scientific ornithologists' and it is no wonder that they arouse opposition to the granting of any collecting licenses."[102]

Stone went on to argue that stringent laws were perhaps not even the main reason for the obvious decrease in the number of collectors. Long-term changes in the direction of ornithological research were as much or more to blame. Many former collectors had moved on to other organisms as the possibility of discovering new North American bird species or subspecies had reached a point of diminishing returns. Those who had remained in ornithology often rejected traditional taxonomic research for studies in "Anatomy, Animal Behavior, Development and Meaning of Coloration, and other broad problems of evolution" that did not necessarily involve skin collecting. Stone tried to reassure his anxious colleagues that despite the obvious decrease in the number of collectors, there was no "danger of ornithologists becoming extinct."[103]

Stone's decidedly upbeat assessment of the decrease in collectors was in sharp contrast to that published three years later by Joseph Grinnell (no relation to George Bird Grinnell), founding director of the Museum of Vertebrate Zoology (MVZ) at Berkeley, longtime editor of the *Condor*, and mentor for a generation of zoologists.[104] From the earliest days of the MVZ, he relied on a network of amateur and professional collectors to stock what he hoped would eventually become a world-class research institution. Continued frustration at his inability to locate and keep good collectors, as well as apprehension about the direction of an increasingly observation-based ornithology, prompted Grinnell to respond publicly.

Grinnell's polemical essay, "Conserve the Collector," marked the culmination of concern over the decline of collecting.[105] Deftly summarizing the attitudes of an earlier generation of scientific ornithologists, Grinnell mounted a full-scale defense of the collector. He began by asserting that "matters of precision and accuracy" in scientific ornithology were suffering as a direct result of the recent tendency to forsake the "shot-gun" method. The teeming hoards of field observers, or "opera-glass students" as they were often disparagingly referred to by their critics, were not dependable for "accuracy in identification of species and especially subspecies." Only the old-fashioned collector provided scientists with the actual specimens upon which an authoritative record of a region's avifauna and from which sound classificatory structures might be based. The rise of the opera-glass student and the concurrent demise of the collector meant that hard-won attempts to forge ornithology into a more rigorous scientific discipline might quickly erode: "Ornithology as a science is threatened, and it should not be allowed to lapse wholly into the status of a recreation or a hobby, to be indulged in only in a superficial way by amateurs or dilettantes."[106]

Collecting was also crucial to the proper training of ornithologists. Grinnell echoed a frequently expressed worry that "authoritative and expert systematic and field ornithologists" could not be developed except by personally collecting "adequate numbers of specimens in the field." During the process of stalking, capturing, and preparing birds, the collector gained a deep knowledge of the living and dead organism, knowledge that could be "secured in no other way."[107]

Grinnell argued that even if collecting permits were issued "freely to applicants upon avowed sincerity of purpose," it would pose no real threat to bird populations. He did not reject the idea of restricting the collection of "rare or disappearing species," like the Carolina parakeet or the ivory-billed woodpecker, but argued that daily overall "bag-limits" on collectors were unnecessary and undesirable. Because of the tremendous labor involved in preparing bird skins, even the most ambitious collectors rarely took more than twenty birds per day anyhow. Moreover, the total number of collectors was infinitesimally small compared to the large hunting community. In California, only a hundred permits to collect nongame birds were issued per year, as compared with some thirteen thousand game licenses.[108] He admitted that some collectors had "behaved indifferently toward people who were sensitive to bird killing," but he felt this could be prevented by establishing zones around more populated areas where collecting would be forbidden.[109] Finally, Grinnell argued that "all collecting adds sooner or later to scientific knowledge, either directly through printed contributions from the collectors themselves, or through the subsequent study of the material by others, often after it has been acquired by some public institution."[110] "Conserve the Collector" was an impassioned plea on behalf of a vanishing breed of ornithologist, the collector, from one of its most eloquent spokespersons.

In 1923, nearly two decades after Fisher began serving as chair, the AOU finally decided to appoint an entirely new bird protection committee. But the new committee, and its immediate successors during the next few years, continued to remain inactive and issued no printed reports.[111] Not until 1930, in the midst of a series of upheavals in conservation circles—including accusations of neglect leveled specifically at the AOU—was the committee finally roused back into action.

A Crisis in Conservation

It was the problem of extinction—the same issue that had first troubled J. A. Allen over a half-century previously—that finally roused the AOU bird protection committee from its twenty-five-year slumber. Beginning in the 1920s the issue had gained increasing saliency, with the gradual introduction of a more ecological perspective into conservation discourse. Where earlier concern surrounding animal extinction had been primarily rooted in moral, aesthetic, and utilitarian frameworks, the new perspective—informed by the emerging science of ecology—aimed to preserve the integrity of entire biological communities, whether for their own sake, or more often, for human appreciation and study.[112]

As environmental historian Thomas Dunlap has emphasized, it was the change in attitude toward predators—wolves, coyotes, hawks, owls, and eagles—that served as a bellwether for this revolutionary shift in perspectives.[113] Once almost universally portrayed as "vermin," fit only for systematic destruction, ecologically minded conservationists saw predators as crucial components in the reticulated nexus of relationships that knitted together all living organisms. According to this new perspective, predators contributed to the integrity and long-term stability of biological relationships that had been the products of millions of years of evolution.[114]

In the case of birds, hints of this newfound respect for predators had already begun to appear by 1920. That year several naturalists on the staff at the American Museum of Natural History sent a strongly worded letter to the AOU bird protection committee protesting a bounty law for bald eagles introduced in Alaska three years previously.[115] By 1919 territory officials had paid bounties on an alarming fifty-six hundred birds. If this deplorable destruction continued, the scientists feared that the bald eagle, "one of the largest and most magnificent birds, and the emblem of our nation," would soon be in "serious danger of extinction." The New York naturalists argued that the AOU, "the leading ornithological society of America," "should be taking the initiative on this," but to date the organization had remained "silent and indifferent."

A. K. Fisher's reply reflected the still-dominant utilitarian conservation perspective. Fisher, who was also in charge of the predator-control program for the Bureau of the Biological Survey, claimed that Alaskan bald eagles were highly destructive to young blue foxes (whose adult skins fetched anywhere from $100 to $400 each) and to salmon as they ascended streams to spawn. Hence, in purely economic terms the bounty was justified. In any case, Fisher continued, concerns about the danger of extinction were entirely unfounded, for most Alaskan territory remained uninhabited, and therefore safe habitat for the eagles.[116] Individually and collectively, the New York scientists continued to raise the issue throughout the year, but their concerns fell on deaf ears.[117]

The predator problem reemerged in 1926 when Henry R. Carey, a writer, associate member of the AOU, and active member of the Delaware Valley Ornithological Club, wrote to complain of a relative absence of hawks in recent United States bird census reports: "Judging from this record there can be no question but that many of our Hawks are doomed very soon to join the Passenger Pigeon and the Carolina Parakeet."[118] According to Carey, trappers and "sportsmen" were playing havoc with the hawks, which became easy marks during seasonal migrations, when they tended to concentrate in several well-known flyways. Not only would complete extermination of hawks lead to troublesome mouse and insect irruptions, it would forever impoverish the American landscape. Carey urged those concerned about hawk extinction to act before it was too late: "It is time that Nature Lovers claimed their share of rights from the Nature Wasters. It is time for us to protect for our children their rightful heritage."[119] Carey's letter generated a lengthy series of published replies during the next few years, but it too failed to stir the lethargic bird protection committee from its chronic state of inactivity.[120]

At the same time, the issue of predators was beginning to divide the AOU's sister scientific society, the American Society of Mammalogists. The society had been organized in 1919 by a group of Biological Survey scientists, but almost from the start the new organization became a battleground over the agency's recently instituted predator-control program. Beginning as early as 1915, survey scientists hired hunters, offered bounties, and (increasingly) broadcast poison bait to reduce populations of wolves, coyotes, mountain lions, bobcats, and other animals assumed to be destructive to livestock and game.[121] In the following decades western ranchers put increasing pressure on Congress to expand the limited program, and Congress, in turn, sought to appease its wealthy and influential constituents by allocating larger shares of the expanding survey budget to predator control. By the late 1920s the well-funded program came under mounting attack from naturalists who felt that the Biological Survey had moved from predator control to complete extermination as its primary goal. For example, in 1929 a committee of the American Society of Mammalogists issued the first of several critical reports that called the program "scientifically unjustified" and urged reform.[122]

It was against this backdrop that an explosive indictment of bird protection policy and practice appeared in June 1929. *A Crisis in Conservation: Serious Danger of Extinction of Many North American Birds* was the handiwork of W. DeWitt Miller, Willard G. Van Name, and Davis Quinn.[123] The pamphlet gained considerable attention within ornithological circles, in part because at least two of the three authors—Miller and Van Name—were already well-known to the scientists.

At the time *A Crisis in Conservation* appeared, Miller was an associate curator of ornithology at the American Museum of Natural History and an AOU insider. Hired as an assistant at the AMNH in 1903, the twenty-four-year-old insurance agent took full advantage of the museum environment to broaden his ornithological horizons.[124] Through extensive reading in the museum's well-stocked library, constant interaction with Chapman, Allen, J. D. Dwight, and other staff members, and careful examination of the burgeoning ornithological collection, Miller soon became an accomplished systematist. Formal recognition of Miller's progress followed in regular succession, with election to membership (1906) and fellowship (1914) in the AOU and promotion to assistant (1911) and associate curator (1917) at the AMNH. He was respected enough as a systematist that his colleagues appointed him to help Alexander Wetmore, of the U.S. National Museum, revise the classification of birds for the new edition of the AOU Checklist.[125]

Miller was also a fervent conservationist. Unlike most scientific ornithologists of the previous generation, Miller had never been much of a bird collector. He was, in the words of his eulogist and close friend James Chapin, "always respectful" of birds' "rights." Miller's respect for bird life extended to active involvement in the New Jersey Audubon Society, where he was a founding member and longtime vice president. Before helping author *A Crisis in Conservation,* he had been involved in several conservation crusades. For example, in 1923 he wrote to the *New York Times* to protest the destruction of mammals for purely ornamental summer furs, and a year later he exchanged several letters with the Du Pont Company over its sponsorship of a national crow-shooting contest.[126] In 1928 Miller made an extended survey of western forests with Willard G. Van Name, a colleague at the museum who was an associate curator of invertebrates. No doubt it was during this lengthy trip that the two scientists planned their attack.

Although he was an accomplished invertebrate zoologist with a Ph.D. degree from Yale (1898), Van Name was probably better known to ornithologists for his conservation activities. In 1915 his was the lone voice that tried to refute Grinnell's ardent plea to "conserve the collector."[127] Van Name was also a moving force behind the series of letters from American Museum naturalists protesting the Alaskan eagle bounty in 1920. Throughout the twenties he was increasingly involved with efforts to prevent commercial encroachment into, and to extend the boundaries of, national parks.[128] Now he had again turned his sights to the problem of wildlife destruction.

The primary target of *A Crisis in Conservation* was the National Association of Audubon Societies, which had been run by T. Gilbert Pearson since 1910, when Dutcher had suffered a debilitating stroke. On the surface the organization had flourished under Pearson's reign: it had steadily increased its membership, visibility, and endowment. But according to the critics, behind the rosy facade was an organization that had veered measurably from its original course. Under the domination of Pearson and other "professional conservationists . . . in the game for what there was in it for themselves," the NAAS had become complacent and too cozy with the government agencies, private organizations, and others it should have been policing.[129] While the NAAS stood by idly, innumerable bird species were rushing headlong toward extinction, with scarcely a voice raised in protest. The great auk, Labrador duck, passenger pigeon, Carolina parakeet, "also probably" the Eskimo curlew and heath hen, were already lost. A troubling number of additional species—the whooping crane, trumpeter swan, ivory-billed woodpecker, California condor, flamingo, golden plover, Hudsonian godwit, buff-breasted sandpiper, and upland plover—were now "beyond saving." And as many as twenty-six additional species were immediately threatened with a similar fate.[130]

Amid the series of scathing accusations, neglected opportunities, and alarmist predictions detailed in *A Crisis in Conservation,* one charge more than any other stung the scientists: the claim that they had remained entirely unmoved by the fate of birds faced with extinction:

> The subject of extinction of our birds has been all along and is in most cases still one that these people [professional ornithologists and writers] ignore, or if they allude to it at all it is commonly done in such a half-hearted, timid, apologetic and inconsequential way as to counteract any good effect that the allusion might possibly produce. How can the general public be expected to realize the danger of extinction that threatens many of our

birds while the distinguished ornithologists and authors of widely read books on birds to whom the public looks for guidance and warning of impending danger to our native species remain silent, indifferent or complaisantly satisfied with the situation and with the inefficiency of bird protection organizations of which they are in many cases officials?[131]

History was likely to stand in harsh judgment of the scientists who had abdicated their responsibility to inform the public that many species were in danger of being "wiped off the face of the earth."[132]

The product of two well-respected naturalists on the research staff of the AMNH, the serious accusations in A Crisis in Conservation provoked a series of replies. Unfortunately, Miller died less than two months after the pamphlet appeared, when his motorcycle ran head-on into a bus during one of his frequent New Jersey birding excursions. Following his death, Chapman, who was not only Miller's boss, but also editor of Bird-Lore and chair of the board of trustees of NAAS, tried to suppress the embarrassing pamphlet.[133] George H. Sherwood, director of the AMNH, declared that the entire staff of his museum was unanimous in condemning the claims in A Crisis in Conservation and ordered Van Name to refrain from publishing further except with prior approval of the museum.[134]

Rosalie Edge, a feisty conservation-minded New Yorker of independent means and mind, tried to raise the charges lodged against the NAAS at the society's annual meeting in 1929 but was rebuffed.[135] In private, the board of trustees of the organization, many of whom were also associated with the AMNH, decided that the best course of action was to ignore the troublesome pamphlet and hope the furor would blow over.[136] Never one to back down from a fight, Edge then contacted Van Name and Quinn, and together with Irving Brant, Roger Baldwin, Henry Carey, and others launched the Emergency Conservation Committee (ECC), a radical organization that served as a gadfly in conservation circles for the next two decades.[137] The ECC immediately began issuing a series of critical pamphlets aimed at the NAAS, the Bureau of the Biological Survey, and numerous other state, federal, and private wildlife organizations.[138] Within a few years, Edge and the ECC had forced the resignation of Pearson and the transfer of Bird-Lore from Chapman to the NAAS.

RENEWING THE CONSERVATION COMMITMENT

The AOU was not immune to the train of events set in motion by the publication of A Crisis in Conservation. The polemical pamphlet also pushed the bird protection committee back into action.[139] When the most recent chair of the committee offered no formal report at the annual meeting in 1929, the new president of the union, Joseph Grinnell, who was increasingly sympathetic to the conservationists' pleas, appointed a new committee.[140] In February 1930 he named one of his former graduate students, Henry Child Bryant, to head that committee.[141]

It became immediately clear that for the first time in twenty-five years things were going to be different for the bird protection committee. Soon after his appointment, Bryant wrote his fellow committee members urging them to support a recent congressional proposal to protect the bald eagle.[142] By May he had arranged for the new committee to meet. The ideas discussed during that initial meeting indicated that this committee's approach to scientific collecting was fundamentally different from that of its immediate predecessors. One member suggested that those who were issued permits for scientific collecting should be forced to publish within three years or face revocation of their license to collect, a proposal that would have been an anathema during Fisher's reign. Even more revolutionary was the proposal to create a "white list" of "rare and dangerous birds" that could not be collected even with a scientific permit.[143] By September Bryant was circulating drafts of a formal committee report.[144] The final version approved by the union included a platform that called for continued educational efforts in bird protection; special protection for birds of prey; opposition to the introduction of exotic birds into North America; reduction of dangers presented to birds by lighthouses, poison campaigns, discharge of oil in waters, and other "modern man-made developments"; and support for legislation and treaties that favored "real bird protection" while not hampering "sound scientific research."[145]

The new committee's unusual level of activity created something of a sensation at the 1930 AOU meeting in October. Grinnell called the committee's report "the event of the season," and Chapman voiced pleasure that the committee "had again come to life."[146] According to Bryant, "some of the old-timers were astounded that any report was to be submitted."[147] In the end, though, the committee was forced to compromise on its platform plank that, in the preliminary versions, had called for a "white list" of threatened birds to be immune from collection even by those possessing scientific permits. The final version called for increased protection for native birds that were "fast nearing extinction," but left it to the judgment of the individual ornithologist to determine which species required "better protection" and what the precise nature of that protection might be.[148]

Under Bryant's aggressive leadership, the AOU bird protection committee remained active for several years. Besides the recurrent problem of scientific collecting, the committee immediately had to deal with another potentially divisive issue: the Biological Survey's predator-control program. An April 1931 report on the ornithological work of the Biological Survey published in the *Auk* prompted several letters of protest when it failed to mention the agency's control program.[149] In response, the *Auk* published a highly critical editorial that placed the AOU firmly on the record with the American Society of Mammalogists in condemning the "nefarious work" of predator control, which threatened to bring the Biological Survey into "disrepute."[150]

A year later, the bird protection committee authored a resolution condemning systematic campaigns aimed at destroying birds "without regard to the status of the species and their ability to endure such destruction." The rationale given for the resolution revealed the extent to which ecological notions were beginning to enter conservation discourse. According to the resolution, which was passed by the entire membership of the union, the AOU "desires the preservation and maintenance of the avifauna of this continent, and of all continents, in the largest measure of *integrity*, and offers the spirit of that pronouncement as the proper one in which to approach all questions of law and practice which concern bird life."[151]

In spite of this more ecological perspective, which if pursued to its logical conclusion might have led to a formal call for reasonable restrictions on scientific collecting of endangered birds, the problem remained a thorn in the side of the AOU. At the annual meeting in 1935, S. Prentiss Baldwin, a retired businessman who had established an ornithological research station at his summer estate in Gates Mill, Ohio, presented a resolution calling on its members to refrain from "the collecting of skins and eggs of rare and apparently vanishing birds" and to "prevent traffic in fresh specimens for commercial purposes."[152] Through dubious behind-the-scenes machinations, a few well-placed opponents of the resolution managed to squelch it.[153] During a discussion of the proposed resolution in the AOU Council, Alexander Wetmore suggested a watered-down version based on the recommendations of the American Committee for International Wild Life Protection, which called on scientists to take specimens of "rare or disappearing species" only "with discretion."[154]

In separate responses to the resolution debacle, the ECC and the NAAS each put together their own recommendations on scientific collecting. Not surprisingly, the ECC's was the most far-reaching of the two proposals. It began with the claim that for a number of years the birds collected by "amateurs and private collectors" had not added to the knowledge of North American avifauna. Rather, such "superfluous" collecting presented "a very serious menace to the future of ornithology by hastening the extermination of many species." In no uncertain terms, the ECC recommended that *"no more permits for general and unlimited bird collecting be issued by either the federal or state governments"* and that *"no permits whatever* should be issued on any pretext for collecting certain species that are in great danger of extinction." According to the ECC, some twenty-five birds deserved complete and absolute protection.[155]

Even the NAAS, which was beginning to exhibit a measure of independence from scientific ornithologists, was unusually straightforward in condemning the collecting of endangered species. At a board of directors meeting in June 1936, the NAAS passed a resolution stating that in the United States the collecting of wild birds and eggs was "subject to abuses, opposed to sound conservation and EVEN THREATENING THE LOCAL OR GENERAL SURVIVAL OF VARIOUS SPECIES."[156] According to the NAAS, collecting specimens of wildlife was not an "inherent right" of the scientist; rather, it was a "privilege" to be granted only when carefully specified conditions had been met. Individual states and the federal government should carefully review the objects of proposed collecting to make sure they were worthy, and any permits granted should "COMPLETELY EXCLUDE CERTAIN THREATENED SPECIES FROM THE LIST OF THOSE WHICH MAY BE COLLECTED." The burden of proof concerning "need and desirability" of all proposed collecting should fall squarely with the applicant, and those approved to collect should be required to submit an annual report listing all species taken. Although falling short of the blanket condemnation of collecting contained in the ECC proposal, the NAAS resolution went far beyond a point with which most AOU scientists were comfortable.

The bird protection committee thus found itself under increasing pressure to draft its own collecting resolution. The initial attempt—which defended the continued need for specimens to conduct scientific research—also explicitly opposed the collecting of birds "as objects of curiosity or personal or household adornment," for commercial purposes, or taking "rare and vanishing birds where such collecting might affect adversely the status of the species."[157]

But even these apparently reasonable restrictions were problematic enough for a few influential council members to table the resolution during the AOU meeting in 1936.[158] Following this setback, NAAS President John Baker urged the bird protection committee to "publicize" both its proposed resolution and the fact that the AOU Council had ignored it.[159] A clearly frustrated Bryant wrote to AOU President A. C. Bent indicating that his committee was suffering from low morale following the council's action, which had been taken without any formal explanation.[160] Bent replied that he personally favored the proposed resolution and would see to it that it was presented at an open meeting of the union the next year.[161] During the 1937 annual meeting, AOU members passed a resolution that was almost identical to the one squashed by the council a year earlier. The major difference was that it specified in more detail the kinds of activities discouraged with threatened species: "The Union opposes . . . any scientific or other collecting or investigational activities which may in any way endanger of adversely affect the status of seriously depleted species by molestation, invasion of territory or otherwise."[162] Finally, over fifty years after the creation of its first bird protection committee, the AOU had come to realize that even scientific collecting had legitimate limits.

Why did the AOU finally cave in on the issue of collecting threatened species? For one thing, scientific ornithology looked very different from the days when Frank Chapman slogged through Florida swamps in search of the last Carolina parakeets. As ornithological research gradually broadened into new areas—like life histories, behavior, ecology, and physiology—the need to collect rare species no longer seemed so pressing. At the same time, the rise of birdwatching—a central aspect of the Audubon movement and the subject of the next chapter—resulted in a politically powerful interest group that was generally more aware of the threats facing native birds and often unsympathetic to the collecting demands of scientists. When Rosalie Edge and John Baker pressured the AOU to change its collecting policy, they spoke on behalf of a vast constituency that was difficult to ignore.

CHAPTER SEVEN

Birdwatchers, Scientists, and the Politics of Vision

COOPERATION AND CONFLICT

In 1916 the British zoologist Julian Huxley, then a young assistant professor of biology at the Rice Institute in Texas, lamented the increasing polarization between "amateur" field naturalists and "professional" biologists.[1] Huxley's "Bird-Watching and Biological Science," a lengthy two-part article published in the *Auk*, argued that the recent growth of popular interest in observing wild birds offered a unique opportunity to begin bridging this gap. With continued encouragement and proper guidance, the "vast army of bird-lovers and bird-watchers" could begin providing the data scientists needed to address what Huxley called the "fundamental problems of biology."[2]

To a large extent Huxley was preaching to the converted. Following the lead of their British counterparts, during the previous three decades American scientific ornithologists had repeatedly urged people to venture out to view their native birds. Although the specific term Huxley used—"bird-watching"—had yet to catch on in the United States, the activity it sought to describe clearly had.[3] By the end of the nineteenth century, thousands of middle- and upper-class birding enthusiasts were rushing to purchase field guides, erect bird feeders, and join Audubon societies.[4] For years bird collectors had provided the study skins necessary to construct a definitive inventory of North American bird forms, the central defining mission of scientific ornithology in the United States since the middle of the nineteenth century. Now some American ornithologists began arguing that networks of birdwatchers might provide the raw data on distribution, migration, and life-history to help forge a "new ornithology."

However, scientific ornithologists were far from uniformly enthusiastic about the growth of popular interest in birdwatching. Cooperative observational networks in which scientists dictated the terms of membership, monitored the contributions, and analyzed the results were one thing. But the proliferation of birdwatchers' "sight records"—published observations of species and subspecies beyond their established ranges—was something else entirely. Whether reliable or not, these records became a permanent part of the literature and the building blocks for the faunistic catalogs and taxonomic monographs that had long represented the core of ornithological research in the United States.

Nowhere is concern about the growth of sight records more evident than a letter to the editor that Jonathan Dwight published in the *Auk* in 1918, just two years after Huxley's article.[5] In many ways the letter's author was much more typical than Huxley of scientific ornithologists in the United States at the time.[6] Like most of his American colleagues, Dwight lacked either formal training or a paid position in ornithology, but he was active in the AOU, he published regular contributions to the scientific literature, and he eventually gathered the largest private collection of North American birds ever amassed.[7]

Dwight presented an anecdote to demonstrate the grounds for concern that he and many of his scientifically oriented colleagues shared about the recent increase in sight records. The incident involved a report he had received from two unnamed birdwatchers in Connecticut who claimed to have seen two male scarlet tanagers early in December of the previous year. If accurate, the record was potentially important because the scarlet tanager was a migratory species that had yet to be found so far north at such a late date. As Dwight pointed out, however, the record was clearly in error. Although his correspondents claimed to have been experienced and conscientious field students, they were apparently ignorant of a fact known to every serious ornithologist worthy of the name: in the autumn the male scarlet tanager sheds its characteristic red coat for one that is a less-descript dull yellow-green. The overzealous observers had apparently mistaken the ubiquitous cardinal for the more elusive scarlet tanager and then compounded their indiscretion by passing on their observation to Dwight. In this case the error was so obvious it was unlikely ever to have found its way into print. The incident was troubling nonetheless because it was symptomatic of the kind of mistakes that *did* appear in the literature with disturbing frequency as popular interest in birds had grown. As Dwight argued at the close of his letter, "truly a little knowledge is a dangerous thing."[8]

Huxley's invitation to cooperation and Dwight's rebuke represent extremes in the spectrum of responses to the emergence of birdwatching as an important middle-class leisure activity in the United States. Keenly aware of the central role that bird collectors had once played in the development of their field, many American ornithologists embraced Huxley's view that birdwatching enthusiasts represented potential allies in the production of knowledge. Scientists anxious to recruit members for observational networks and supporters for their conservation initiatives were among the most vigorous promoters of birdwatching. Yet these same scientists clearly experienced discomfort when birdwatchers began to independently publish their sight records in the dozens of turn-of-the-century ornithological periodicals. In the eyes of scientific ornithologists, the appearance of dubious, unverifiable records represented a threat to the authority of the scientific discipline they had struggled long and hard to construct.

A FIELD GUIDE TO BIRDWATCHING

The rise of public interest in birdwatching and the growth of the Audubon movement were so intimately related it is difficult to disentangle the lines of cause and effect between the two. What is clear is that both began in the last two decades of the nineteenth century and both were expressions of a larger Romantic backlash

against an increasingly urbanized, industrialized society that threatened to irrevo-
cably alter the American landscape.

From the beginning Audubon leaders recognized the crucial role birdwatching
might play in furthering their protectionist agenda. By reinforcing an emotional
and aesthetic bond between humans and birds, birdwatching helped convert ordinary citizens into ardent conservationists. Whether they ventured out into the field
or simply gazed at the birds attracted to their newly installed feeders, birdwatchers found profound delight in the animated, vocal, and often brightly colored
species they rushed to observe.[9] By the turn of the century Audubon societies
across the nation were promoting the activity through a variety of means, ranging
from organizing regular field trips, hawking field guides, and issuing checklists of
local species to promoting bird study in schools, sponsoring lecturers, and offering advice on how to build feeders, mix food, and locate bird baths.[10]

The appearance of a new kind of bird identification guide reflected as well as
promoted popular interest in birdwatching. Like those who engaged in other
forms of scientific and popular natural history, birdwatchers felt the urge not
merely to observe wild nature; they also wanted to pin names on the species they
located. The problem was that the standard identification manuals bird collectors
had long found indispensable, like Elliott Coues's *Key to North American Birds*
(1872) and Robert Ridgway's *Manual of North American Birds* (1887), were
large, cumbersome volumes that were difficult to carry in the field and designed
to be used only with the dead specimen in hand.[11] In the late 1880s and early
1890s, however, American authors began publishing the first compact identification guides designed for field use to help birdwatchers discover the names of the
living birds they encountered in the wild. Initially these field guides relied on
lengthy species descriptions and analytical keys, similar to those found in the
older collecting manuals. When it became clear that keys confused and intimidated many novice birdwatchers, authors increasingly turned to illustrations, especially color illustrations, to simplify field identification.

The first of this new generation of field guides came from the pen of Florence
Merriam.[12] From an early age Merriam developed a keen interest in natural history while tagging along on excursions with her older brother, the ornithologist
and mammalogist C. Hart Merriam. In 1886, while a student at Smith College,
she organized an early local Audubon chapter to discourage the practice of wearing feathers.[13] Using the experience gained in trying to teach her classmates the
names of the birds they encountered on their field trips, in 1887 Merriam began
publishing a series entitled "Hints to Audubon Workers: Fifty Birds and How to
Know Them" in Grinnell's *Audubon Magazine*.[14] The lengthy series, which included brief descriptions of the most common species found in the eastern United
States, continued until 1888. At the conclusion of the last installment, Merriam
appended a field key—arranged by habitat preference, color, song type, behavior,
bill shape, and nesting site—as an aid to identification. It was the first time anyone
had published a system of *field* identification for birds. In 1889 she expanded the
text of her lengthy series into her first book, *Birds through an Opera Glass*, which
included a total of seventy species.[15] Although sparsely illustrated by the stan-

dards of subsequent field guides, Merriam's book inspired thousands to take up the practice of birdwatching.

Merriam's best-selling guide also signaled the beginning of an avalanche of similar publications. Merriam herself subsequently issued numerous nature essays and field guides, including *A-Birding on a Bronco* (1896), *Birds in Village and Field* (1898), and *Handbook of Birds of the Western United States* (1902). Several other female authors—including Mabel Osgood Wright and Neltje Blanchan—also published best-selling identification guides before the turn of the century.[16] Although scientific ornithology had long been an overwhelming male-dominated enterprise, many of the authors of field guides, devotees of birdwatching, and supporters of the Audubon movement were female. While I have discovered little direct evidence that this fact alone contributed to the decidedly negative response that some (male) scientific ornithologists had to the rise of birdwatching, no doubt it did play a role.

By far the most influential figure in churning out new field guides and otherwise promoting the new birdwatching craze was Frank Michler Chapman, who joined the Department of Ornithology at American Museum of Natural History in 1888 and remained at the institution for over a half century.[17] Although he occupied one of the few professional positions in ornithology available in the United States at the time, Chapman was equally at home in the worlds of scientific ornithology, wildlife conservation, and birdwatching. He brought these sometimes conflicting interests together when he began issuing the periodical *Bird-Lore* in 1899, a little over a decade after Grinnell discontinued *Audubon Magazine*. The new periodical was a "popular journal of ornithology . . . addressed to observers rather than to collectors of birds," an orientation reflected in its motto—"A Bird in the Bush Is Worth Two in the Hand."[18] Not only was *Bird-Lore* brimming with useful information for bird enthusiasts of all ages, levels, and degrees of interest, it also served as the official organ of the various state Audubon societies and later the National Association of Audubon Societies.

Chapman's interest in bridging the gap between technical and popular ornithology had already manifested several years before the inaugural issue of *Bird-Lore*. His first major publication, *Handbook of Birds of Eastern North America*, originally issued in 1895 and reprinted in several editions, contained detailed advice on locating, collecting, and preserving birds "along approved scientific lines" together with a series of analytical identification keys designed to be used with specimens in the hand.[19] Almost as an afterthought, Chapman appended a series of helpful hints on naming the birds "without a gun" as well as an eight-page artificial field key—based on plumage colors and body size—to aid in identifying the more common eastern forms. Following a lengthy introduction to the study of birds, the bulk of the book consisted of somewhat technical descriptions of each of the more than five hundred species found in eastern North America.

Although Chapman's *Handbook* inspired a generation of scientifically oriented ornithologists, its general collecting orientation, tedious species descriptions, comprehensive scope, and relative lack of illustrations proved too daunting for many beginning birdwatchers. Inspired by the success of Merriam's and Wright's popular guides and hoping to reach a larger audience, soon Chapman tried his hand at a second book, *Bird-Life* (1897).[20] Like most identification guides on the market at the time, Chapman's latest venture limited its coverage (in this case to just upwards of a hundred of the most common species), offered brief, chatty descriptions, and included copious illustrations (in this case based on carefully rendered black-and-white drawings by the artist-naturalist Ernest Thompson Seton).[21] Chapman's book also included a modified version of the field key found in his *Handbook* to aid in identifying birds by sight alone. The scope and general tone of the book suggested that it was intended for the rank beginner.

Chapman's next field guide, *Color Key to North American Birds* (1903), represented a more decided break from tradition. According to the book's introduction, the author hoped to "make bird study possible for the thousands" who were intimidated by the idea of using analytical field keys.[22] The new volume was both easier to use and much more comprehensive than other turn-of-the-century bird guides. Each of the more than seven hundred species was illustrated with a crude but serviceable line drawing colored with "those markings which most quickly catch the eye."[23] Although Chapman continued the standard practice of organizing the birds into scientific Orders, an arrangement he considered both "natural" and "easily comprehended," within each Order he grouped birds according to their predominant colors or markings. To facilitate comparison of birds that were most similar in overall appearance (and to make the volume more economical to publish), Chapman placed the drawings and descriptions of several similarly colored species on a single page (fig. 25).

The illustrator for Chapman's *Color Key* was Chester A. Reed, the twenty-six-year-old son of the taxidermist, natural history dealer, and publisher Charles K. Reed of Worster, Massachusetts.[24] The Reeds had catered to the natural history specimen trade since the late 1880s, but with the emergence of the Audubon movement and the resulting legal restrictions on collecting, they reoriented their business toward birdwatching. In 1901 they began publishing *American Ornithology*, a copiously illustrated monthly designed to "present to the public a complete popular account of every bird found in North America."[25] Following the collaboration with Chapman, in 1906 the younger Reed issued a two-volume guide to birds east of the Rocky Mountains that became a standard for beginning birdwatchers until the 1930s.[26] The first volume included water birds, game birds, and birds of prey, while the second covered land birds. A third volume, posthumously published in 1913, treated birds west of the Rockies.[27]

Straightforward in design and use, Reed's guides contained a primitively rendered color portrait of each species along with a terse, no-nonsense description of its major characters, haunts, songs, nest, eggs, and range. The guides were compact—measuring approximately 3 ∞5 —andcontained only a single species on each page. By flipping through the illustrations, even children were supposed to be able to discover the name of most birds they were likely to encounter in the wild. Reed's immensely popular guides remained in print until the 1950s.[28]

Along with refinements in field guides, developments in optical technology also contributed to the growth in popularity of birdwatching. In 1853, when

607. Louisana Tanager (*Piranga ludoviciana*). L. 7.5. *Ad. ♂.* Yellow; back, wings, and tail black, head more or less red. *Ad. ♀.* Above olive-green, head rarely red-tinged; below dusky greenish yellow; wings and tail brownish edged with greenish, two yellowish white wing-bars. *Yng. ♂.* Like ♀, but head and rump greener, underparts yellower. *Notes.* Call, *clit-tuck*; song, resembles that of No. 608.

Range.—Western United States from the Plains to the Pacific; breeds from Arizona to British Columbia; winters in Mexico and Central America.

608. Scarlet Tanager (*Piranga erythromelas*). L. 7.4. *Ad. ♂.* Scarlet; wings and tail black. *Ad. ♀.* Olive-green, yellower below, wings and tail blackish brown, no wing-bars. *Yng. ♂.* Like ♀, but brighter, wing-coverts black. *Ad. ♂, Winter.* Like Yng. ♂, but wings and tail black. *Notes.* Call, *chip-churr*; song, a rather forced whistle, suggesting a Robin's song, but less musical, *Look-up, way-up, look-at-me, tree-top*; repeated with pauses.

Range.—Eastern United States, west to the Plains; breeds from Virginia and southern Illinois north to New Brunswick and Manitoba; winters in Central and South America.

609. Hepatic Tanager (*Piranga hepatica*). L. 7.8. Bill large. *Ad. ♂.* Vermilion, back grayish; tail dull red. *Ad. ♀.* No *wing-bars*; above *grayish* olive; crown and tail greener; below dusky yellow. *Yng. ♂.* Like ♀ and variously intermediate between it and ad. ♂. *Notes.* Call, *clut-tuck*; song, like that of No. 608, but somewhat more robin-like.

Range.—From Guatemala north in spring to New Mexico and Arizona; winters in Mexico and Central America.

610. Summer Tanager (*Piranga rubra*) L. 7.5; W. 3.8. *Ad. ♂.* Rosy red. *Ad. ♀.* Olive-yellow above, dusky saffron below. *Yng. ♂.* Variously intermediate between *Ad. ♂* and ♀. *Notes.* Call, *chicky-tucky-tuck*; song, resembles in form that of No. 608 but is more musical and less forced.

Range.—Eastern United States, west to the Plains; breeds from Florida and western Texas north to southern New Jersey, southern Illinois, and Kansas; winters in Central and South America.

610a. Cooper Tanager (*P. r. cooperi*). Similar to No. 610, but larger; W. 4; bill more swollen, colors paler.

Range.—"Breeds from southwestern Texas to the Colorado Valley, California, and from Arizona and New Mexico to northwestern Mexico; south in winter to western Mexico; casually to Colorado."

Figure 25. Illustration of tanagers from Chapman's *Color Key to North America Birds* (1903). Chapman's book provided one of the models for Roger Tory Peterson's now legendary field guide, which was first published in 1934.

Henry David Thoreau decided he wanted a closer look at the birds near his home in Concord, Massachusetts, he trekked into Boston to buy himself a spyglass, a simple Galilean telescope consisting of a concave eyepiece and a convex objective lens that had long been used for military and navigational purposes.[29] Three decades later, when thousands of Americans began to follow Thoreau's lead, opera and field glasses (fig. 26) were clearly the viewing instruments of choice. Consisting of two Galilean telescopes connected together, most often with a common focusing mechanism, binoculars had first been placed on the market in Europe in the early nineteenth century, though they apparently were not widely

Figure 26. Field glasses and binoculars, ca. 1920s. By the turn of the century,
birdwatchers had a variety of viewing instruments from which to choose.
Left to right: opera glasses, field glasses, a spyglass, prism binoculars, and
the Biascope, a particular brand of field glasses.

available in the United States until after the Civil War.[30] Field and opera glasses
provided only limited magnification (ca. 3∞ or 4∞), but they were compact and
had a relatively wide field of view, making them ideal for locating quickly moving objects like birds.

By the middle of the nineteenth century, several European instrument makers
began experimenting with prisms to increase the focal length of binoculars without unduly increasing their size or weight. But it was not until 1893, when the
famed German physicist and optical engineer Ernst Abbe began manufacturing
the first quality prism binoculars at the Zeiss Works in Jena, that the invention
was acceptable and widely available.[31] Prism binoculars provided greater magnification (ca. 7∞ to 10∞) and a larger field of view than field glasses, but they were
also quite expensive. Nonetheless, they provided unequaled viewing opportunities for those with deep enough pockets, and they quickly became standard equipment for serious birdwatchers.[32]

Photography also played an important role in promoting the growth of birdwatching. The fast lenses and dry plates necessary to capture images of wild
animals in their natural habitats first began to be developed in the late 1870s, but
it was not until two decades later that negative emulsions were sensitive and
reliable enough and camera lenses fast enough to achieve good results consistently.[33] Once these technological limitations had been broached, nature enthusiasts began producing a steady stream of wildlife photographs. By the 1890s photographs of birds began appearing regularly in scientific and popular periodicals
as well on lantern slides that frequently accompanied popular lectures on birds,

though often these early images were of captive animals or stuffed specimens placed in their natural habitat. In 1900 Frank Chapman published the first American book on the subject, *Bird Studies with a Camera*, which was quickly followed by a series of similar titles by Francis H. Herrick, A. Radclyffe Dugmore, William Finley, and Herbert K. Job.[34] Bird photography promoted birdwatching by providing the public with inspiring images of the bird in nature and the birdwatching photographer with a tangible reminder of his or her encounters in the wild.[35]

And finally, developments in transportation technologies carried an increasing number of birdwatching enthusiasts to the nation's fields and forest. The so-called safety bicycle, first placed on the market in the 1880s, was quiet and relatively easy to operate. It also allowed its riders to cover more territory in a given period than walking, while providing more flexibility than the railroad or the horse.[36] The strong endorsement of one bird student in 1890 is typical of the passion with which many naturalists extolled the virtues of the bicycle:

> I think the most healthful, instructive and pleasing exercise one may take, is to roam the country, through forest and meadow, and over brook and stream, in pursuit of the study of birds; and I think the second most healthful and pleasing exercise is bicycling; aside from walking, there is no exercise that puts every part of the body so in motion as does bicycling . . . and now combining these two pleasures, we have the sum total of health and happiness.[37]

After the turn of the century, birdwatchers increasingly turned to yet another new invention—the automobile—to transport them to their favorite haunts. Cars carried birders greater distances, allowed more total time in the field, and provided the opportunity to cover a greater diversity of habitats than other previous modes of transportation. What began as an expensive plaything for the rich became increasingly affordable by the 1910s and 1920s. And as the price plummeted, Americans rushed to adopt the new technology that was to change profoundly so many aspects of their lives.[38]

Easy-to-use field guides, more powerful binoculars, new photographic methods, and developments in transportation technologies clearly enhanced the experience of most birdwatchers, but alone they fail to explain the phenomenal turn-of-the-century popularity of the "rare and absorbing ritual" of birdwatching.[39] Rather, the explanation ultimately turns on the transformation of values that occurred during this period. By the end of the nineteenth century, some Americans were beginning to relinquish the pervasive view that birds and other forms of wildlife were merely *objects*; increasingly they came to be appreciated as *individuals* that were in some ways analogous to humans.[40] Or as Frank Chapman once commented in another context, birds "have not only a beauty which appeals to the eye, but often a voice whose message stirs emotions to be reached only through the ear. . . . [T]hey further possess humanlike attributes which go deeper still, arousing in us feelings which are akin to those we entertain toward our fellow-beings."[41]

While we lack direct measurements of precisely how many Americans answered the call of the wild bird at the turn of the century, there are indirect means

Figure 27. Trade card depicting a red-breasted grosbeak, 1898.
The first of the sixteen-card "American Singer Series" issued by the
Singer Manufacturing Co. The drawings for this series were by
John L. Ridgway, brother of Robert Ridgway, who also illustrated
scientific publications.

suggesting the number was quite significant. One such indicator comes the world
of advertising. Beginning in the 1880s, Church and Co., the manufacturer of Arm
and Hammer and Dwight Baking Sodas, began including small, chromolitho-
graphed bird cards with their product in an effort to encourage brand loyalty.[42]
The cards, which continued to be issued in numerous series over the next six
decades, were designed to be collected, traded, and pasted into albums. They
proved so effective in boosting sales that several other manufacturers copied the
practice (fig. 27). By 1912 Chapman proclaimed that the appearance of the latest
series of bird cards (this time from an American chewing gum maker) heralded
the dawn of an "ornithological millennium."[43]

The Clover. The Plover.

The Plover and the Clover can be told
apart with ease,
By paying close attention to the
habits of the Bees,
For ento-molo-gists aver, the Bee
can be in Clover,
While ety-molo-gists concur, there
is no B in Plover.

Figure 28. Woodcut from the physicist Robert Wood's delightful satire of field guides, *How to Tell the Birds from the Flowers* (1907).

Within the first several decades of the twentieth century, birdwatching had become so ingrained in American culture that it even became the object of humor. In 1907 the noted American physicist Robert Williams Wood published a satirical field guide entitled *How to Tell the Birds from the Flowers* (fig. 28).[44] The whimsical book, which had originally been composed to amuse his children, featured woodcuts juxtaposing pairs of common birds and plants together with descriptions written in an ingenious nonsense verse. Wood's delightful volume was so well received that it went through several editions and dozens of printings over the next forty years.[45] Another good-natured gibe at birdwatching appeared in 1935, when the *New Yorker* published a Gluyas Williams cartoon (fig. 29) depicting a group of "Audubon Bird Walkers" adding a scarlet tanager to their list.[46]

Williams's cartoon suggests a further indication of the growing popular interest in birdwatching: the proliferation of bird clubs.[47] As Chapman noted in 1915, these institutions were different from the more traditional ornithological clubs and societies that had been around in the United States since the 1870s. Where earlier ornithological organizations were composed mainly of "bird-students" who hoped to pursue "original scientific research," the members of new bird clubs were primarily "bird-lovers" interested in "the development of methods which will tend to increase our intimacy with the birds." Although a desire to pursue

CLUB LIFE IN AMERICA

The Audubon Bird Walkers Add a Scarlet Tanager to Their List

Figure 29. Cartoon depicting birdwatchers. By the 1930s hundreds of local
bird clubs and Audubon societies across the United States and Canada
promoted the activity of birdwatching. Drawing by Gluyas Williams;
  1935, The New Yorker Magazine.

scientific research might eventually develop in some members, bird clubs generally avoided technical discussions of "nomenclature, classification and avian psychology" to pursue an interest in "nesting-boxes, bird-baths and feeding
stands."[48] The first bird clubs began to be organized just after the turn of the
century, and within three decades there were hundreds in communities across the
United States.[49] In membership and function, bird clubs were often indistinguish-
able from local Audubon societies.[50]

Perhaps the most useful indicator of the scope of birdwatching at the turn of the century is the sale of field guides. When Frank Chapman launched *Bird-Lore* in 1899, he reported that during the previous six years New York and Boston publishers had sold more than seventy thousand popular books on birds.[51] By 1933, one year before the publication of the first edition of Roger Tory Peterson's now legendary field guide, Neltje Blanchan alone had sold more than 150,000 copies of *Bird Neighbors*, while Frank Chapman had sold more than 230,000 copies of his popular bird books, and Chester Reed, a phenomenal 633,523 copies of his compact bird guides.[52] And these three authors were just the tip of the iceberg.[53] All the evidence suggests that by the early twentieth century tens of thousands of middle-class Americans had adopted the practice of regularly venturing to the fields and forests in search of birds.

Constructing Observational Networks

The tremendous growth of popular interest in birdwatching presented both opportunities and dilemmas for the small community of scientific ornithologists in the United States. Those ornithologists who served as leaders in the Audubon movement—and a significant percentage did—clearly welcomed the political clout thousands of birdwatching enthusiasts provided. Scientists, birdwatchers, humanitarians, and others in the Audubon coalition were remarkably successful in shepherding protective legislation through state assemblies and the U.S. Congress.[54]

Some scientists, like Julian Huxley, clearly hoped that birdwatchers might also prove effective (though subordinate) allies in the production of scientific knowledge. Scientific ornithologists in the United States had long depended on networks of collectors to provide them with the specimens necessary to conduct their research. As the nineteenth century came to a close, many ornithologists began arguing that networks of *observers* could also provide useful scientific data. One of the earliest American examples of a large-scale cooperative venture of this kind has already been discussed: the expansive observational network C. Hart Merriam began in 1883 as chair of the AOU Committee on Migration of Birds.[55] The venture not only produced valuable information on the seasonal movement of North American birds, it also led to the funding of a federal agency that soon evolved into the Bureau of the Biological Survey.

Cooperative, observationally based bird study was also central to the mission of the Wilson Ornithological Club during its early years. The organization began in 1886 when an enthusiastic group of widely dispersed bird and egg collectors decided to form a correspondence society called the Young Ornithologists' Association.[56] Two years later the group changed its name to the Wilson Ornithological Chapter of the Agassiz Association after formally affiliating with Harlan Ballard's national network of natural history societies. Although its original membership was scattered, the organization gradually became centered in the Midwest. At the same time it increasingly focused on cooperative studies of the living bird.[57] In 1902 the group withdrew from the Agassiz Association and shortened its name to the more manageable Wilson Ornithological Club.[58]

Founding member Lynds Jones was central in guiding the club through its formative years.[59] Born in 1865 to a large midwestern farming family, Jones developed a fascination for birds' eggs by the age of seven. The discovery of Samuels's *Nests and Eggs of New England Birds* and Coues's *Key to North American Birds* coupled with encouragement from an older neighborhood boy and a schoolteacher fueled his youthful enthusiasm. By 1890 the burley, athletic Jones headed off to Oberlin College with an impressive egg collection (containing specimens from over 250 species) and a burning desire to turn his avocation into his life's work. After graduation he stayed on at Oberlin to work as laboratory assistant and instructor in zoology while earning his master's degree. In 1895 Oberlin officials gave Jones the opportunity to teach the first course in ornithology ever offered at an American institution of higher learning, a course he continued for more than three decades.[60] Ten years later Jones earned his Ph.D. degree from the University of Chicago as well as a promotion to associate professor at Oberlin. He remained at his alma mater until forced to retire in 1930.

Jones served in nearly all the major offices for the Wilson Club, but he probably exerted the most influence as editor, a position he held for thirty-five years. Although his own interest in ornithology began as a collector, early in his tenure as *Wilson Bulletin* editor he began actively promoting field observation and cooperative research.[61] For example, as early as 1897 Jones argued that real progress in solving fundamental questions about the geographic distribution, migration, and life history of North American birds could be achieved if the hundreds of young men who joined the Wilson Club faithfully submitted their observations to the various club committees established to compile and publish the information.[62]

That same year Jones's most enthusiastic student, close personal friend, and kindred spirit, William Leon Dawson, argued that keeping systematic lists of species observed, even of common birds, would be highly "profitable" both to birdwatchers and to science.[63] As chair of the Wilson Club's Committee on Geographic Distribution, Dawson urged his fellow members to maintain several kinds of systematic records: "daily horizons," lists of all the species found on a given day; "bird censuses" (sometimes called "censo-horizons"), lists of birds seen on a given day within a given area with numerical estimates of the abundance of each species; "annual horizons," lists of all species located during a given year; and "life horizons" or "life-lists," a cumulative record of all the species an individual had ever identified in the field. Although Dawson claimed it was "vulgar" to keep these lists merely for the sake of numerical comparison, both he and Jones continually stressed how their most recent counts stacked up against previous efforts in the field. They also repeatedly challenged their readers to better their records.[64]

Through their constant appeals in the pages of the *Wilson Bulletin*, Dawson and Jones not only recruited hundreds of observers, they also helped standardize the kinds of lists that birdwatchers kept. Soon birders across the nation were routinely competing to compile the longest lists of birds observed over the course of a day, year, and lifetime.[65] These lists served many of the same functions as the skins and eggs gathered by an earlier generation of collectors: they provided a tangible record of accomplishment that could provoke pleasant memories, serve as a source of pride, and even potentially represent a contribution to science, but without the destruction of life that skin collecting necessarily entailed. From the beginning, competition seems to have been a crucial stimulus to bird listing, even for those devotees with no scientific aspirations.

Dawson and Jones urged birdwatchers not merely to compile local lists, but also to submit them to the *Wilson Bulletin* for publication.[66] For example, in his early years as editor, Jones suggested numerous dates—New Year's Day, April 1, Fourth of July, and others—when his readers ought to undertake daily horizons and censuses for submission to the *Wilson Bulletin*.[67] He also published dozens of his own bird counts, including an extensive list he and Dawson compiled during a two-month, seven-thousand-mile whirlwind railroad tour through the West.[68]

Until the mid-1910s, local lists based on short-term observation formed a significant portion of the material printed in the *Wilson Bulletin*. It is hard for a modern reader not to get the impression that Jones's fascination with listing was at least partly based on the fact that he was routinely short of the copy needed to keep his periodical afloat.[69] But like many other ornithologists of his day, Jones also seemed convinced that birdwatchers' lists possessed genuine scientific value, as long as they were compiled by competent and conscientious observers. Not until 1924, on the eve of his retirement as editor of the *Wilson Bulletin*, did he admit that North American ornithology had finally reached a stage in which the "mere enumeration of the birds . . . found in some political division" no longer represented "a contribution to knowledge" and no longer warranted "the cost of publication."[70]

In 1900, three years after Dawson and Jones had first begun actively promoting horizons and censuses through the pages of the *Wilson Bulletin*, Frank Chapman proposed the first Christmas Bird Census in the pages of his newly launched *Bird-Lore*.[71] Historical accounts of the event have stressed Chapman's own version of the origin of the idea: the traditional Christmas Day hunt in which groups of hunters competed to kill the largest number of birds, with the results occasionally appearing in "leading sportsmen's journals."[72] Chapman hoped a similar competitive spirit would motivate birdwatchers to venture out into the December cold, and to heighten the sense of rivalry, he promised to publish their results in *Bird-Lore*. Less appreciated as an additional source of inspiration for the idea is the original AOU migration network, which had proved a formative influence on Chapman when he first became interested in ornithology.[73] Undoubtedly Chapman was also moved to action by one of Dawson's recent requests. Although winter had traditionally been the time of the year when bird enthusiasts were least active in the field, in November 1897 Dawson urged readers of the *Wilson Bulletin* to "put in a day or two, this coming holiday vacation, taking the census of all the birds found in their village, or on the farm, or, if in the city, in the neighboring park."[74] As Dawson pointed out, obtaining accurate counts in a given area would prove much easier when most birds had migrated to warmer surroundings.

Although Chapman's Christmas Bird Count began modestly, it soon developed into a major American ornithological tradition. Only twenty-seven birdwatchers responded to the original invitation to participate in the project, but with each subsequent year the number of observers, printed reports, species located,

Figure 30. Mrs. F. T. Bicknell in the field,
1918. Bicknell was president of the Los
Angeles Audubon Society, one of the many
organizations across North America that
regularly sponsored teams of birdwatchers for
the annual Christmas Bird Count.

and total birds counted continued to mount.[75] In 1909, less than a decade after the
first census, the more than two hundred birdwatchers who took part in the Christmas count located in excess of 150,000 birds.[76] Four years later the Canadian
artist-naturalist Allan Brooks teamed up with that inveterate lister William Leon
Dawson, then a resident of Santa Barbara, California, to produce the first Christmas count that surpassed a hundred species.[77] By 1935 the Los Angeles Audubon
Society (fig. 30) reported that a party of nineteen of its members located 170
species during its annual Christmas census.[78] Four years later the total number of
observers was rapidly approaching two thousand, the number of birds counted
exceeded two million, and the number of census parties with over one hundred
species numbered fifteen.[79]

The remarkable success of Chapman's idea was due in part to birdwatchers' efforts to become more systematic in the way they gathered their data. Lone census takers increasingly gave way to larger groups that could cover more territory and a greater variety of habitats. Relatively short forays gave way to longer surveys that could last as long as twelve hours or more. And haphazard wandering gave way to carefully orchestrated assaults in which rare birds were scouted out in advance and routes carefully chosen to maximize the number of species found on the day of the official census.[80] At the same time, the Audubon societies and bird clubs that regularly sponsored census teams elevated the Christmas count into a major annual social event that was keenly anticipated by its many participants. For many, if not most, of those who joined in the annual event, companionship and competition seem to have been more important than contributing to science.

In an attempt to standardize the reports that flooded his office each winter, Chapman and his assistants gradually instituted several changes in the ground rules for the Christmas census. The original instructions stated that counts should be made on Christmas Day, a request that was routinely ignored. By the fifteenth year, census organizers disqualified counts not made between 20 and 30 December.[81] Over the next three years the census was limited to a minimum of four hours and a maximum of twenty-four hours of observation, which was to be undertaken within an area of no more than fifteen miles diameter and within a specified seven-day period.[82] Later the minimum number of hours in the field was raised again to six and then seven hours. Chapman also began requiring that "unusual records" be accompanied by a brief statement indicating the circumstances surrounding the identification, and he freely used his editorial discretion to suppress any records he considered dubious.[83]

As a result of these and other efforts, by 1922 Chapman was boasting that the Christmas census was a "well-established institution" with an "obvious . . . scientific value" that increased with each subsequent year.[84] Other supporters were even more glowing in their evaluation of the undertaking, calling the annual event the "greatest cooperative ornithological project in North America" and proclaiming that "among all the activities of the amateurs, none is a greater contribution to science than the taking of the Christmas census."[85] However, given these and other claims about scientific utility, one of the remarkable things about the Christmas censuses was the paucity of publications they initially generated. By 1934, the year that the National Association of Audubon Societies purchased *Bird-Lore* from Chapman and took over the annual Christmas count, tens of thousands of hours in the field by thousands of volunteers had resulted in the publication of only two minor articles.[86]

BIRDWATCHING, BIRD BANDING, AND THE BIOLOGICAL SURVEY

While the Wilson Club and Frank Chapman were administering separate (though overlapping) birdwatching networks, the Biological Survey continued its cooperative migration studies. Like clockwork, in the spring and fall of each year officials sent out blank migration schedules to observers across the United States, and twice each year they received several hundred responses.[87] However, little had been done to process the increasingly unwieldy mound of records since 1888, when Wells W. Cooke published a pioneering bulletin on the migration of birds in the Mississippi Valley.[88] Prospects finally improved in 1901, when Cooke, "the father of cooperative study of bird migration in America," received an appointment at the agency and the opportunity to continue the studies he had helped initiate in the 1880s.[89]

The son of a Congregational minister, Cooke was born in Massachusetts in 1858 but moved with his family to Ripon, Wisconsin, at the age of six.[90] When he was twelve years old his parents bought him a shotgun, which he used to collect the heads and wings of local birds before learning the art of making proper skins. After graduating from Ripon College (A.B. 1879, A.M, 1882), he spent several years teaching native American children in Minnesota and Indian Territory. In the winter of 1881–1882 Cooke requested residents of the Mississippi Valley to send him lists of winter birds and dates of the first arrival of spring migrants in their local areas. The results of Cooke's cooperative venture, published in *Forest and Stream* and *Ornithologist and Oologist*, inspired AOU founders to create a migration committee at its inaugural meeting in 1883, and Cooke was recruited to serve as superintendent of the Mississippi Valley division. Before finally landing a position as a government biologist, he worked for nearly two decades as an agricultural researcher at various universities.

Cooke entered into his new Biological Survey position with characteristic enthusiasm. To impose order on the mounds of notes gathered from volunteers over the previous fifteen years, he began entering each migration record on a separate index card. Scanning ornithological periodicals provided additional data for the burgeoning migration and distribution file. When writer's cramp threatened to slow his progress, the right-handed Cooke simply taught himself to make entries with his left hand and then alternated between the two as needed. By 1910 the agency's bird migration file contained more than six hundred thousand entries, which Cooke regularly consulted while preparing a long series of publications on migration routes and dates.[91] The Biological Survey's file also became an authoritative source of information on migration and distribution for other important publications, such as Arthur C. Bent's *Life Histories* and the series of official AOU checklists of North American birds.

Beyond reinvigorating the Biological Survey's migration monitoring program, Cooke also expanded the agency's cooperative data collecting efforts. In 1911 he began conducting an annual spring census at his sister's farm on the Virginia side of the Potomac River, a few miles from Washington. After passage of the Weeks-McLean (Migratory Bird) Act (1913) highlighted the lack of hard data on avian population levels, Cooke received permission to expand his investigation. He composed a widely circulated letter requesting qualified observers from across the United States to undertake exact counts of all the breeding birds on forty- to eighty-acre tracts.[92] He was careful to point out that while anyone familiar with a handful of the most common birds could contribute to the survey's migration studies, accurate census work required that a volunteer "be able to identify all the birds nesting on the area he covers, or be able to give a recognizable description of those he is unable to name."[93]

The Biological Survey's census program briefly flourished before falling into long-term decline. Despite good-natured ribbing from his skeptical colleagues, Cooke received reports from nearly two hundred cooperators in 1914, a number that increased to just over three hundred the following year. Following Cooke's death from pneumonia in 1916, his daughter, May Thatcher Cooke, continued to administer the census network, but it languished. Finally, in 1937 the National Audubon Society started its own annual spring count, the "Breeding-Bird Census," an institution that continues to flourish today.[94]

A competing cooperative project—bird banding—soon overshadowed the Biological Survey's migration-monitoring network and its breeding bird census program. Although tagged birds had served as messengers since ancient times, it was not until 1899 that Christian Mortensen of Viborg, Denmark, began systematic banding of starlings as a method to study their migration patterns.[95] Leon J. Cole, a recent graduate of the University of Michigan, was the first American to suggest the practice at a meeting of the Michigan Academy of Science held in March 1901.[96] Apparently unaware of his European predecessors, Cole indicated that the idea had occurred to him after learning of the work of the United States Fish Commission, which had regularly tagged fish to track their movements.[97]

After several individual researchers began demonstrating the possibilities of bird banding, institutionalization quickly followed.[98] Cole led a three-person committee that organized a small-scale banding program under the auspices of the New Haven Bird Club in the winter of 1907–1908. The organization sponsored a more ambitious program the following year, distributing five thousand marked metal bands, of which approximately one thousand were actually placed on the legs of nestling birds.[99] The success of that effort encouraged Cole and other banding enthusiasts to organize a national society, the American Bird Banding Association (ABBA), at the annual AOU meeting in December 1909. Cole was elected president of the new organization by the thirty individuals attending the inaugural meeting of the ABBA. After he left the East Coast to accept a position at the University of Wisconsin in 1910, the society operated under the auspices of the Linnaean Society of New York from 1911 to 1919. At that point the Bureau of the Biological Survey accepted the ABBA's records and began administering bird banding activities on the national level. A series of regional organizations stepped in to fill the void left by the demise of the ABBA, including the New England Bird Banding Association (1922; changed to the Northeastern Bird Banding Association in 1924), the Inland Bird Banding Association (1922), the Eastern Bird Banding Association (1923), and the Western Bird Banding Association (1925).[100]

Early bird banders tagged nestling birds with the hope that someone would eventually find and return the tag when the bird died or was killed. The fact that there was only a limited window of time when the birds where big enough to be banded and small enough to remain in the nest and that banders were dependent on the chance recovery of dead birds greatly limited the usefulness of the new technique. In 1914 S. Prentiss Baldwin came up with the idea of using government sparrow traps to catch and band various species on his property.[101] During the next four years Baldwin banded over sixteen hundred birds at his summer estate in Gates Mills, Ohio, and his winter home in Thomasville, Georgia. In a paper published in 1919—which one of his admiring students called "one of the classic publications of all time" in ornithology—Baldwin publicized his revolutionary method of systematic trapping.[102] Individual birds could now be recaptured multiple times at various locations, thereby tracing their movements over time. They could also be marked with special colored bands that could be observed from afar.

With Baldwin's new method of trapping and sponsorship by the Biological Survey, bird banding began to take off in the United States in the 1920s. The agency hired the ornithologist Frederick C. Lincoln to administer the program, and by 1933 two thousand individuals across the nation had acquired the necessary federal license and tagged almost a million and one-half birds.[103] Seven years later the total number of banded birds had reached nearly five million, with over three hundred thousand later captured, shot, or found.[104] Bird banding gave a new meaning to the phrase "a bird in the hand," and the data gathered by this extensive network greatly increased the knowledge of bird migration patterns in North America.

COOPERATIVE LIFE-HISTORY STUDIES

Besides keeping lists of species observed in a given area, a few more earnest birdwatchers also routinely kept records on the life history and behavior of the birds they encountered in the field. Well before Huxley published his plea for cooperation between biologists and birdwatchers in 1916, a handful of scientific ornithologists in the United States began to rely on networks of observers who monitored nesting dates, feeding habits, and breeding behavior of birds rather than rushing around trying to log as many species seen as possible. But as long as ornithology remained focused on systematics, only a few scientists seemed interested in taking advantage of the data these observers collected.

In their rush to construct a complete inventory of North American avifauna, scientific ornithologists had largely ignored the *lives* of the creatures they so eagerly collected, measured, named, and described. This rather narrow approach to ornithological research did not pass unnoticed by several more introspective contemporaries, one of whom commented in 1891: "The present generation of Ornithologists have been too busy in hunting up new species and in variety-making to study the habits of birds with equal care and diligence, and it is to Wilson and Audubon and Nuttall that we are chiefly indebted even at this day for what we know of bird-life."[105]

Scientific ornithology's focus on collecting was reinforced by the Gilded Age tendency to view specimens as commodities and by the early pattern of professionalization within the discipline of ornithology. Until the expansion of employ-ment opportunities during the early twentieth century, museums provided the best hope for those who wished to pursue a vocation related to their interest in birds. However, museum administrators from this period generally expected their cura-tors and collectors to return from expeditions laden with specimens to fill their exhibit halls and study collections, not merely with less tangible (and, in the eyes of many, less valuable) observations. For example, in a series of letters in 1890, shortly after joining the staff at the American Museum of Natural History, Frank Chapman complained to William Brewster of the constant pressure to collect he felt whenever in the field on behalf of his employer:

> This miserable collecting. It is the curse of all higher feeling, it lowers a true love of nature through a desire for gain. I don't mean a specimen here and there, but this shoot-ing right and left, this boasting of how many skins have been made in a day or a season. We are becoming pot-hunters. We proclaim how little we know of the habits of birds and then kill them at sight. . . . Collecting, we have at the end of the day some tangible result to show for the day[']s work. . . . The American Museum desires specimens, not notes.[106]

Of course, research on living birds was not entirely ignored. Curiously, until the early twentieth century, oologists were the members of the larger ornitho-logical community with the strongest interest in life history studies. Though voracious collectors themselves, oologists tended to escape the preoccupation with nomenclature and classification that had gripped their skin-collecting col-leagues. Moreover, merely through the process of gathering eggs, they learned a great deal about the lives of birds, including many facts that remained unknown to the average skin collector (e.g., when and where a species bred and the average size of a brood). It was a relatively small step from being tangentially concerned with such basic information as an integral part of the process of securing eggs and nests to a more focused investigation of the lives of the birds that produced these objects.

The close connection between oology and the study of the life histories and "habits" of birds is best demonstrated through a series of ornithological publica-tions issued under the auspices of the Smithsonian Institution. In 1857 Thomas Mayo Brewer, the Boston physician, publisher, and oologist, completed the first of several projected volumes of *North American Oology*.[107] As the title suggested, Brewer's treatise contained detailed descriptions and beautiful lithographs of North American birds' eggs. However, it also included a great deal of information on the breeding ranges and habits of birds gathered from the earlier publications of Nuttall, Wilson, and Audubon, as well as observations based on his own and several "co-laborers'" experiences in the field.[108] Although Brewer continued to solicit donations of nests and eggs for ensuing volumes in the series, the work was abandoned, ostensibly due to the high cost of the illustrations.[109]

The Smithsonian series was begun anew in 1892, when Charles E. Bendire, an army surgeon who began collecting eggs in the late 1860s as a way to relieve boredom on frontier outposts, issued the first volume of his *Life Histories of*

North American Birds.[110] As with Brewer's earlier book, much of Bendire's data was culled from the standard ornithological texts, but he also relied heavily on his own investigation in the field as well as an extensive correspondence network.[111] Although Bendire's accounts tended to be much more detailed and original than Brewer's earlier work, the focal point of the work remained the illustrations, beautiful chromolithographs of eggs produced under Bendire's supervision from watercolors by John L. Ridgway.[112] Bendire completed a second volume for the series in 1895, before succumbing to nephritis two years later.[113] His successor, the wealthy egg collector William L. Ralph, continued to work on the project but died in 1907, before completing any additional volumes.[114]

Three years later, Arthur Cleveland Bent, a cotton machinery manufacturer, electrical utilities owner, and devoted oologist from Taunton, Massachusetts, approached Smithsonian Secretary Charles D. Walcott with a proposal to complete Bendire's series.[115] No doubt the success of several Wilson Club cooperative projects helped inspire the forty-four-year-old Bent. For example, in 1895 and 1900 Frank L. Burns had published lengthy life-history monographs on the crow and the flicker based largely upon data gathered by fellow Wilson Club members.[116] More recently Frank Chapman had initiated an even more ambitious cooperative life history venture. In 1904 Chapman requested readers of *Bird-Lore* to begin systematic observation of the various species of warblers for a book he was contemplating. In his call for aid Chapman had proclaimed that "cooperation" was "the watchword of bird study," the key to success of Bendire's *Life Histories*, and absolutely crucial to gain "anything approaching adequate biographies of even a single species."[117] Over three dozen observers, including several well-known ornithologists like William Brewster, W. W. Cooke, and Lynds Jones, contributed field notes for Chapman's *Warblers of North America*, published in 1907.[118]

Soon after he began negotiations with Smithsonian officials in 1910, Bent received authorization to resume work on Bendire's project. A businessperson with a strong work ethic and highly developed organizational skills, Bent was thorough and meticulous in his research. For example, he organized the life history data for each species in a uniform sequence: "spring migration, courtship, nesting habits, eggs, young, sequence of plumages to maturity, seasonal molts, feeding habits, flight, swimming and diving habits, vocal powers, behavior, enemies, fall migration, and winter habits." And in a move that signaled an increasing break from the strong oological orientation of earlier volumes, by the third installment of his series (published in 1922) Bent discontinued the practice of including color egg photographs in his work, illustrations that he had earlier considered as central to the project.[119] What Bent had originally believed would take six volumes to complete when he began work on his *Life Histories* in 1910 had mushroomed into twenty volumes by the time of his death in 1954.[120] Three additional volumes in the series were later completed under the supervision of the Harvard-trained ornithologist Oliver L. Austin, Jr.

Although Bent ranged far and wide and spent thousands of hours in the field gathering material for his life history series, from the start he recognized that the job was too big for any single individual to complete.[121] In his initial correspondence with Walcott, he indicated that he hoped to follow the same "general plan adopted by Maj. Bendire, making the work largely cooperative and adding such original material as I could furnish."[122] To recruit contributors, Bent mailed out countless circulars and issued repeated pleas in ornithological publications.[123] The favorable initial response encouraged Bent to continue the ambitious project. Over 150 individuals contributed eggs, notes, and/or photographs for the first volume, which was published to wide acclaim in 1919.[124] By the time the final volume was published over fifty years later, the total number of contributors reached more than eight hundred.[125]

Although long out of date, for decades the Bent series has remained a starting point for serious research on the life history of North American birds. It is also a project that was inconceivable without the eyes and ears of birdwatchers across the North American continent who shared their observations.

THE PROBLEM OF SIGHT RECORDS

While scientists generally welcomed birdwatchers into observational networks, they repeatedly expressed concern when these same individuals began to independently publish sight records of birds outside their well-established ranges. Scientists had long depended on networks of collectors to provide them with skins needed to document new species and their ranges. With the exception of those apparently rare cases of fraud, the bird skins that collectors submitted were considered valuable regardless of who actually gathered the specimen. However, by their very nature *observations* were subject to countless vagaries and a great deal of individual interpretation. Depending on a number of factors, ranging from the conditions under which a sighting had been made to the experience and reliability of the observer, a proposed record may or may not ultimately prove accurate and, hence, useful to science. The possibility of errors was further heightened since birdwatchers routinely competed to produce the longest list of species viewed in a given period of time.

The first instinct of most scientific ornithologists, then, was to reject records based on sight alone. Their concern was ultimately based on a decades-long struggle to forge ornithology into an autonomous scientific discipline and profession.[126] Consistent with that ongoing campaign, American ornithologists generally demanded that published claims about the existence or geographical distribution of any bird form be documented with a carefully collected, accurately labeled, and permanently preserved skin. This was particularly true when it came to the identification of subspecies, which were often based on differences in size or coloration that were so minute they could only be detected by careful examination of the specimen in hand, and then only when it was compared with an extensive series of similar forms. For an ornithological community that firmly believed in shooting first and answering questions later, sight identification of subspecies and most species seemed out of the question.[127]

The strong emphasis on specimen collecting and systematics was also reinforced by the pattern of professionalization in North American ornithology. As I have already suggested, until well into the twentieth century, only a few paid positions were available to research-oriented ornithologists, and most of these were curatorships at metropolitan natural history museums. Even if they were interested in pursuing behavioral and life history studies that did not require specimen collecting, the ornithologists who held these positions felt pressure to spend their time in the field amassing as many new specimens as possible, not collecting notes on their observations.

Their research agenda and their institutional location suggested that scientific ornithologists would be suspicious if not overtly hostile to sight records. In fact, scientists began to protest such records even before the first field identification guides had been published or the first Audubon societies organized. In 1883 the *Ornithologist and Oologist* published a brief article suggesting that field glasses might be used to identify birds without actually collecting them. An anonymous reviewer for the *Bulletin of the Nuttall Ornithological Club* fired back:

> It is to be hoped that this method will be reserved for those "who have no wish, strictly speaking, to become ornithologists or oologists," and that observations made by those who have "become acquainted" with birds in this way will never be put into print as a contribution to ornithology. . . . Watching birds through a field glass as a pleasant amusement we would not discourage, but as a method of identifying birds by novices, we do not know of a more excellent illustration of "how not to do it."[128]

The exchange set the tone for the protracted battle that followed. As members of the birdwatching community entered a growing number of sight records into the ornithological literature, scientific ornithologists grew increasingly vocal in their opposition to the practice. For example, in 1902 William Brewster cosigned a letter to the editor decrying the fact that too many careless sight records had been appearing in the *Auk*.[129] He concluded his protest with the suggestion that "no record of a bird merely observed, where there is any chance for error, be accepted, unless the observer be well known to the editor, or to some ornithologist of standing and judgment, who will vouch to the editor for the accuracy of the observer."[130] Over the next several decades, scientific ornithologists frequently repeated Brewster's suggestion that the so-called personal equation be considered when evaluating sight records, though as the size of the birdwatching community continued to increase, this criterion became increasingly unmanageable in actual practice.[131]

Four years after his *Auk* letter, Brewster published *Birds of the Cambridge Region* (1906), a long-awaited book that was immediately hailed as a "classic in the annals of faunistic ornithology."[132] In the preface to his book Brewster argued that, with few exceptions, records of birds in localities outside their known range ought to be ignored unless established by "actual specimens . . . determined by competent authorities."[133] For Brewster and most of his scientific colleagues, mere observation of a living bird established nothing "more than possible or probable occurrence of the species in question—according to the weight and character of the evidence." The only time Brewster was willing to suspend his deeply felt suspicion of sight records was with easy-to-recognize species—like the turkey vulture, swallow-tailed kite, and the cardinal—but only when they were reported by reliable ornithologists known to have had previous familiarity with these particular species in life.

That same year, 1906, Frank Chapman proposed another set of criteria by which to judge when sight records of birds observed outside their normal range might be considered worth publishing. Chapman argued that in some cases the standard that most "professional ornithologists" demanded—a captured specimen—resulted in unnecessary destruction of life as well as the loss of valuable information concerning the specimen in question. As an example of what might go wrong if collecting were pursued too exclusively, he pointed to the case of Brewster's warbler, which William Brewster had named, described, and published as a new species in 1876 based solely on morphological data obtained from study skins. It was not until decades later, when ornithologists began systematically observing the bird in the wild, that they finally discovered that Brewster's warbler was actually a hybrid between two distinct species: the gold-winged and blue-winged warblers.[134] Here was a clear case where the practice of shooting first and asking taxonomic questions later had kept scientific ornithologists in the dark for far too long. On the other hand, Chapman pointed out that even the most careful and experienced ornithologist had occasionally made errors in field identification that only became known when they subsequently collected the specimen in question.

Given these considerations, when should observations by the "opera-glass student" be accepted? Chapman offered a widely adopted set of criteria by which to judge the merit of sight records:

> (1) Experience in naming birds in nature, and familiarity, at least, with the local fauna. (2) A good field- or opera-glass. (3) Opportunity to observe the bird closely and repeatedly with the light at one's back. (4) A detailed description of the plumage, appearance, actions and notes (if any) of the bird, written while under observation. (5) Examination of a specimen of the supposed species to confirm one's identification.[135]

Even if all these requirements were fulfilled, Chapman argued, the validity of field identifications would "depend on the possibility of the occurrence of the species said to have been seen." Sight records of birds distant from their normally understood range should be rejected, even if all of the above conditions could be met.

Although long a promoter of birdwatching, over the next few years even Chapman grew increasingly impatient with the fantastic records that were constantly submitted to him as editor of *Bird-Lore*. By 1909 he had further hardened his position on the issue of sight records by summarily rejecting them whenever the bird in question was even slightly beyond the normal limits of its known range. So-called records of occurrence were a permanent part of the history of a given species and hence represented an important "contribution to the science of ornithology." The evidence upon which scientific records were based needed to be available for subsequent verification. The only way this could be accomplished, Chapman concluded, was to produce "the specimen on which the record was based."[136] While continuing to promote birdwatching as a valuable recreational activity, a means to recruit conservationists, and a method for gathering information on the seasonal movement of birds, Chapman had clearly moved into the camp of those who argued that scientific research in ornithology often demanded resort to the collecting gun.

Although the issue refused to disappear entirely, after the first two decades of the twentieth century several factors converged to diminish the controversy over sight records. First was the increasing difficulty in securing legal authorization to collect birds. Although the protective legislation the Audubon movement pushed through most state legislatures generally included a provision allowing for scientific collecting, many of the officials charged with enforcing those laws were reluctant to issue the necessary permits. A few officials refused to sanction *any* collecting at all. Some ornithologists simply ignored these legal restrictions and continued to collect just as they had always done in the past. However, the overall effect of this legislation was to make it much more difficult to meet the scientific ornithologists' demand that a specimen be taken to verify claims about the existence of a bird form beyond its previously established range.

At the same time that many state officials moved to restrict collecting, several scientists worked to improve techniques of field identification. The individual who did more than anyone else to make the practice more certain and acceptable was Ludlow Griscom.[137] From a young age he had developed an interest and proficiency in field identification as well as a strong resolve to become a professional ornithologist. After graduating from Columbia University in 1912, Griscom enrolled in the master's program at Cornell and became the first in an extensive line of graduate students who studied ornithology under Arthur A. Allen. His master's thesis was on the field identification of ducks, geese, and swans of the eastern United States.[138] Following graduation, he spent a decade working under Frank Chapman at the American Museum of Natural History before accepting a post as assistant curator at Harvard's Museum of Comparative Zoology. His scientific research centered on more traditional avian systematics, but throughout his life, Griscom continued to work on refining his field identification techniques, and he enjoyed regular birdwatching outings.

Griscom firmly believed that even though "amateur" bird students had generally relinquished the practice of collecting, they still had a great deal to offer scientific ornithology. His first major paper on the subject, "Problems of Field Identification," published in the *Auk* in 1922, claimed that the list of birds "practically impossible" or "very difficult" to identify in the field by a properly trained observer was very small and rapidly shrinking.[139] Barring physical defects that might impair an individual's ability to see or hear properly, Griscom continued, virtually anyone could become a trustworthy field observer, even if they pursued the activity "merely as a hobby."[140] In a characteristically flamboyant fashion, Griscom provided the strongest endorsement to date of the validity of sight identification.

Within the next year Griscom published his *Birds of New York City Region*, a guidebook that embodied his extensive knowledge of the avifauna of the region and his commitment to promoting rapid identification of birds based on characteristic, easy-to-recognize field marks.[141] One reviewer noted that the appearance of Griscom's book heralded the beginning of a new epoch: "In cutting away from many traditional requirements of the last generation" (i.e., the bird in hand as verification of records), Griscom had helped to forge a "new ornithology."[142] Griscom and his work also became the inspiration for the Bronx County Bird Club, a small but active group of young enthusiasts who regularly birded around the environs of New York City in the 1920s and 1930s and who later went on to distinguished careers in field ornithology.[143] One member of the group was Roger Tory Peterson, who has declared that "Griscom was our God and his 'Birds of the New York City Region' our Bible. Every one of us could quote him chapter and verse."[144] Peterson has also acknowledged the formative role that Griscom's field mark identification techniques played in the creation of his legendary *Field Guide to the Birds*, which was first published in 1934 and has since sold over three million copies.[145]

As the century wore on, scientific ornithologists grew more tolerant of Griscom's identification techniques and sight records more generally. An additional reason for this softening on the issue was the series of fundamental changes that the field of ornithology was experiencing.[146] One of the most far-reaching transformations was the emergence of graduate education in ornithology during the 1920s and 1930s. Newly established graduate programs produced a new generation of bird students who were more extensively and broadly trained than their predecessors, interested in a much wider variety of research problems, and qualified to begin careers in many newly emerging positions, ranging from wildlife managers to university professors.[147] Freed from the narrow methodological and institutional limitations of the previous generation, graduate-trained ornithologists broadened the boundaries of ornithological research into new areas—like ecology and behavioral studies. In pursuing these new research agendas they regularly practiced field identification, and they generally seemed more tolerant of the sight records of others.

Yet even with restrictions on collecting, improvements in field identification techniques, and the expansion of ornithological education and research, the controversy over sight records refused to disappear entirely. As late as 1928, Biological Survey ornithologist Frederick C. Lincoln was still arguing that the only valid evidence for adding a new species to the list of given region was the "preserved specimen with all the data attached."[148] Of course, Lincoln's claim was nothing new, but the response from two of the major technically oriented ornithological journals in the United States was. In their discussion of Lincoln's article, reviewers for the *Auk* and the *Wilson Bulletin* agreed that Lincoln's uncompromising rejection of all records not substantiated by a preserved specimen failed to take into account the profound changes that had occurred in the field of ornithology over the past few decades. While sight records still needed to be carefully evaluated to take into account "the record and ability of the observer," they certainly ought not be rejected out of hand.[149] Nearly two decades later, another Biological Survey ornithologist, W. L. McAtee, was still trying to make the case that scientific ornithology needed finally to relinquish its "specimen fetish."[150]

PALMER'S QUALMS

By the turn of the century, birdwatching had developed into an important leisure activity that tens of thousands of middle- and upper-class Americans regularly enjoyed. For most of those who ventured out to the nation's fields and forests in search of wild birds, birdwatching was primarily a form of recreation, a temporary escape from the hustle and bustle of an increasingly urban-industrial society and a chance to renew a deeply satisfying aesthetic and emotional bond with members of the feathered kingdom. For some, the lure of the list—the competition to produce the longest list of species viewed in a given day, during a particular season, or over a lifetime—provided additional incentive to pursue the popular activity.

A small subset of birdwatchers was also interested in contributing to the growth of the science of ornithology. With their eyes and ears spread across the vast North American continent, serious bird observers represented valuable potential allies in scientists' efforts to map out the precise distribution and migration patterns of North American birds. Scientists hoping to take advantage of this potential were among the strongest promoters of birdwatching and the most active organizers of observational networks. Yet, as I have shown, scientific ornithologists did not always welcome the contributions of birdwatchers, particularly when they claimed to have discovered species and subspecies beyond their well-established ranges. In this crucial respect the rise of birdwatching represented yet another point of tension between scientific ornithologists and the broader community of bird enthusiasts.

While the proliferation of sight records provoked frequent comment, rarely did scientific ornithologists complain publicly about the distribution and migration data that participants in birdwatching networks provided. One of only a handful of examples occurred when T. S. Palmer, Biological Survey staff member and long-time secretary of the AOU, criticized a single-day bird count from the Santa Barbara area that William L. Dawson published in the *Condor* in 1913: "It is questionable whether the best results are obtained by making a continuous wild rush between daylight and dark from one good bird locality to another, identifying and recording subspecifically, every note and every glimpse of feathers, in the sole effort to secure as large a list of species as possible." Yet even Palmer did not reject the idea of censuses made by "several persons in a definite area, where each could take time to cover his territory thoroughly and follow up and observe the various birds." In fact, he encouraged cooperative observational studies so long as contributors worked with foresight and care: "Let us have more bird horizons . . . made without recourse to automobiles and trolleys, omitting all doubtful species, with more attention given to the relative abundance of the common birds, and with less anxiety to record the largest number of species observed by one individual."[151] Like many ornithologists, Palmer was concerned that the race to compile the longest lists would inevitably lead to error.[152]

Yet while Palmer and other ornithologists were clearly concerned about minimizing the possibility of error, they recognized that the contribution of birdwatchers was crucial to large-scale migration and census studies. After all, North America is a vast continent, filled with more than seven hundred avian species, most of which move seasonally. No single individual, no matter how competent or earnest, could hope to begin adequately covering so many birds and so much territory in a single lifetime, and there were not yet enough scientific ornithologists able (or willing) to engage in the kind of large-scale cooperative projects that Chapman, Cooke, Bent, and others envisioned.

Necessity was not the only reason that Palmer and other scientists generally accepted the observations provided by birdwatchers with such a wide variety of motivations and abilities. Scientific ornithologists recognized that they were the ones who largely dictated the terms of interaction with the individuals who joined their observational networks. They not only established and enforced the ground rules for how acceptable observations were to be made, but also interpreted the data submitted. Under this arrangement, scientists could and did routinely reject any records that seemed suspect for whatever reason. Because of this ability to police volunteers and control data, scientists welcomed contributions to observational networks even as they railed against independently published sight records, which they perceived as a threat to their authority.

CHAPTER EIGHT

Reforming American Ornithology

THE STATE OF THE UNION

In May 1930 Joseph Grinnell, president of the American Ornithologists' Union, wrote to each of the other forty-seven fellows of the organization requesting "frank statements as to what . . . might be done to improve the effectiveness of the Union." Grinnell had taken this unusual step, he said, because of recurrent "rumors of criticism" suggesting that the AOU was not as active as it had once been "with respect to scientific accomplishment, or to practical bird protection, or to general spread of sound scientific knowledge." If replies to this informal survey revealed widespread discontent, he promised to use the powers of his office to "attempt to better the condition of the Union."[1]

Although Grinnell tried to be upbeat in his letter, the general tone contrasted sharply with the rosy statistics presented in the official annual reports of the AOU. If numbers alone could tell the story, the organization appeared thriving, even as the nation was on the cusp of its deepest and darkest depression. As a result of aggressive recruiting efforts, membership had grown steadily and by 1930 was rapidly approaching the two thousand mark.[2] The healthy increase in annual income provided by this influx of new members permitted an increase in the average number of pages printed in the *Auk*.[3] Participation in annual meetings also was robust: more than two hundred members had attended and sixty papers had appeared on the program at the most recent gathering in Philadelphia, where Grinnell was elected president.[4] While most ornithologists seemed to applaud this impressive growth, other more scientifically minded members were worried.

Twenty-seven fellows answered Grinnell's request for their assessment of the state of the union.[5] As might be expected, the general tenor of these responses ranged widely from "everything is fine" to "the Union is utterly failing in its mission."[6] One of the most critical replies came from Herbert Friedmann, a thirty-year-old curator of birds at the U.S. National Museum. Though more vocal than some of his colleagues, in many ways the letter's author was typical of the younger generation of ornithologists, the first to receive extensive biological training and the first to earn graduate degrees in their field. Like several of his cohort, Friedmann feared that most AOU members were utterly lacking in scientific aspirations and that the organization itself failed to uphold appropriate scientific standards in the papers delivered at its annual meetings or in the reviews and articles printed in the *Auk*. His frustration flowed in his reply to Grinnell:

> From the purely scientific point of view any body composed to a large extent of amateurish bird lovers (as against serious bird students) is more or less of a mixture of pleasure and annoyance to the minority whose interests are chiefly in research. Person-

ally, I have often wished that there were no sentimental bird lovers, as their contributions to the literature of ornithology have kept the subject in a condition of pseudo-science in the eyes of laboratory biologists.[7]

Since the AOU was "handicapped by a great host of rather uncritical, sentimental bird lovers," Friedmann continued, its leaders needed to work harder "to inculcate higher standards" in the articles and reviews they published. The model for scientific rigor that he (and other reformers) repeatedly evoked was Erwin Stresemann's *Journal für Ornithologie*, which Friedmann considered "far ahead" of the *Auk*.[8] Although there was obviously a danger that adopting "more strictly scientific standards would cause a drop in the subscription list to the Auk," he argued that in the end such a decline would be "worth while" and "no real loss."

As one of the early Ph.D-trained ornithologists in the United States and founder of a pioneering graduate program in ornithology, Grinnell was clearly sympathetic to Friedmann's complaints.[9] To insure that his and other concerns gained a hearing, at the next annual meeting of the AOU (held in October 1930), he presented a presidential address based on the results of his survey. Grinnell reported that several of his colleagues were clearly uncomfortable with the continued growth of "a large class of amateurs" within the AOU "who will never become real scientists."[10] These associate members now held an overwhelming majority in the AOU, and because the organization relied on the annual dues they contributed, some believed that they had even gained control of the union itself, "at least indirectly." One negative consequence of this large "amateur" presence was "too much genial tolerance of mediocrity" in the organization.

Grinnell then turned to a second issue that concerned him and several of his reform-minded colleagues. Over the years the AOU had allowed several important activities it had initiated to drift out of its control. As the wording of his initial query hinted, the specific example that Grinnell most had in mind was bird protection. Although the AOU had played a central role in creating the Audubon movement and nurturing it through its formative years, the organization had long since abandoned its leadership position in the movement. Grinnell was careful to quote a few AOU fellows who felt this break was entirely proper, but he also claimed that many others agreed with his assessment that the AOU bird protection committee ought to "become active" again and "do effective work independently of the Audubon Society."[11]

Near the end of his address Grinnell suggested a possible "means toward offsetting the necessity of catering to our amateur clientele" while simultaneously reinvigorating the lethargic bird protection committee. What the AOU needed was a sufficiently large endowment fund "to insure publication of sound ornithology irrespective of subscriptions to the Auk" and "to pay the expenses of our working committees, so that these can convene oftener and therefore more effectively."[12] If a sufficient endowment were raised, the AOU might even begin providing grants to support scientific research in ornithology.

After delivering his address, Grinnell approached longtime *Auk* editor Witmer Stone about publishing it for wider distribution. He must have done so with some trepidation for he knew Stone was a strong advocate of cultivating "the interest and support" of the AOU's large "amateur clientele."[13] In his reply to Grinnell's original request for feedback, Stone had argued that his forty-year involvement with the AOU made him competent to deny "any foundation for such criticism as you get rumors of." He admitted that because most of the financial support for the *Auk* came from associate members, it was important not to pitch "the journal entirely over their heads." However, Stone denied that his ongoing efforts to keep the *Auk* accessible had in any way "lessened its scientific standing."[14]

After speaking briefly with Stone, Grinnell provided him with a corrected copy of his speech and returned home to California with the clear expectation that it would appear in the next issue of the *Auk*.[15] Not until over five months later did he finally learn that Stone had decided not to publish it. In an apologetic letter Stone claimed that after reading the address "several times," he had developed "grave doubts about the advisability of publishing it." Not only would its appearance provide ammunition for those who considered the AOU too much of a "highbrow" organization, but it would also thwart efforts to raise the very endowment that Grinnell considered crucial for reviving the organization. No one would want to donate funds for a group "in which there was dissention."[16]

Although Stone attempted to suppress the embarrassing address, it nonetheless became the opening volley in a campaign to rejuvenate the hidebound AOU.[17] At a time when the nation experimented with various initiatives to deal with the crisis of the Great Depression, the first generation of university-trained ornithologists in the United States struggled to reform the practice and institutional structure of their discipline. With aid from Ernst Mayr, a young, outspoken émigré who had recently arrived from Germany, reformers sought to shift the focus of ornithological research, to raise the standards by which that research was conducted and judged, and to instill the AOU with a stronger professional consciousness. Yet, despite their concerns about establishing more rigorous standards for ornithological research, most reformers still did not seek to exclude amateurs entirely from their discipline, even as they sought to forge it into a full-blown profession. Rather, scientific ornithologists continued to encourage the efforts of *serious* amateurs, as long as that research conformed to the scientists' notions about what constituted legitimate ornithological practice.

GRADUATE TRAINING IN ORNITHOLOGY

Those who campaigned to overhaul the AOU in the 1930s shared a common educational background that fueled their enthusiasm for reform. Until the 1930s, scientific ornithologists in the United States had typically relied on self-education and apprenticeships to familiarize themselves with the set of practices and the body of knowledge associated with their field. Before then few avian researchers received formal training either in ornithology proper or biology more generally, and many of the most prominent ornithologists—like Robert Ridgway, Frank Chapman, and William Brewster—lacked college degrees of any sort, much less graduate degrees.

By the end of the nineteenth century formal advanced training was beginning to become available for most other scientific fields. Inspired by developments in Germany, American institutions of higher learning began experimenting with modern graduate programs in the early 1870s as part of a series of sweeping educational reforms.[18] The innovation was slow to take hold, though, and by the time the AOU was founded in 1883, the total number of doctoral dissertations completed per year in the United States was still averaging below fifty while the number of science-related dissertations was half that figure. Then came a period of rapid expansion in graduate education in the years surrounding the turn of the century. By 1910 the Ph.D. degree had been elevated into "the standard credential for entry into a diverse array of academic and professional careers," including careers in many (if not most) scientific disciplines.[19]

Initially ornithology proved a conspicuous exception to the general trend toward adopting higher education for training and certifying practitioners in scientific fields. Not until 1895 did Lynds Jones begin offering the first American undergraduate course in ornithology, and not until after the turn of the century was the first Ph.D. degree awarded in the field.[20] By the early 1930s more than a hundred American universities were regularly offering at least some coursework in ornithology (typically as part of a broader class in zoology), and at least thirteen institutions allowed graduate students to specialize in the discipline. Yet, in a survey of AOU members taken in 1933, only 12 percent of the fellows, 24 percent of the members, and 27 percent of the associates reported *any* college-level training in ornithology. By that same year a total of fewer than thirty individuals had completed doctoral dissertations on ornithological topics.[21]

Not coincidentally, while graduate education was becoming the norm for serious researchers in most scientific fields, biological practice in the United States experienced a series of profound transformations. In the words of historian Jane Maienschein, the turn of the century represented "a pivotal time for biology" as "the sorts of papers produced, the organisms used, the questions asked and the problems attacked, the methods and approaches adopted—all changed in . . . important ways."[22] At academic institutions across the nation, proponents of a new, laboratory-based, and often more experimental biology began to challenge the more established field- and museum-oriented descriptive natural history tradition. Fresh from graduate programs here and abroad, advocates of the new biology struggled to forge new biological disciplines—like genetics, cytology, and experimental embryology. They also sought to expand the boundaries of traditional natural history practice, which had long been characterized by the collection, description, naming, and classification of organisms based largely on their external characteristics. In newly established field-oriented disciplines—like ecology and animal behavior—study of the living organism and its relationship with its environment began to receive serious attention for the first time.[23]

At some colleges and universities, the attempt to incorporate the new biology with the older natural history was like trying to mix oil and water. For example, well into the twentieth century the Museum of Comparative Zoology (MCZ) remained a bastion for traditional natural history even as young, Ph.D.-trained, experimental scientists succeeded in creating a nationally recognized biology program at Harvard.[24] Under the leadership of longtime Harvard President Charles Eliot and the biologist E. L. Mark—who received his doctorate from the University of Leipzig in 1877—the Harvard biological curriculum was increasingly reoriented toward the new laboratory-based disciplines of histology, cytology, embryology, and genetics. Although the MCZ remained the actual site of biological training at Harvard until the early 1930s, the museum's curators and collections were increasingly divorced from that instruction, on both the undergraduate and graduate levels.

Ornithology was no exception to the intellectual and institutional inertia strongly in evidence at the MCZ.[25] Until World War II MCZ curators focused primarily on building up their world-class bird collection, which by the early 1930s had grown to over 250,000 specimens, the third largest in the United States.[26] They also continued to produce traditional taxonomic and faunistic publications based on those collections, including an ambitious, multivolume *Checklist of the Birds of the World* that James Peters began in the late 1920s.[27] Although Thomas Barbour attempted to reintegrate the MCZ into Harvard's thriving biological program soon after assuming directorship of the institution in 1927, his reform initiative achieved only limited success. Not until the 1950s did more than a handful of ornithologists receive graduate training at Harvard.[28]

Although it shared many connections with Harvard, the University of California at Berkeley, established in 1869, was more successful at integrating old and new approaches to biological research and training.[29] The individuals most responsible for expanding Berkeley's faculty and curriculum at the end of the nineteenth century and the beginning of the twentieth were the marine zoologist William E. Ritter and the protozoologist Charles A. Kofoid, both of whom were products of Harvard's Ph.D. program. Ritter initiated several new courses requiring laboratory work, founded the Scripps Institution of Biological Research, established postgraduate study in zoology at Berkeley, and headed the university's Department of Zoology, which included four senior teaching staff by the time of his retirement in 1909.[30] Three decades later, when Kofoid retired as chair of the department, the senior teaching staff had been expanded to eleven, and Berkeley had established a reputation as a premier center of academic biology in the United States.[31]

The individual most responsible for attracting ornithology students to Berkeley was Joseph Grinnell.[32] Born in Indian Territory to a restless Quaker physician and his wife, Grinnell began collecting birds and mammals as a boy growing up on the frontier. After moving several times, the Grinnell family finally put down roots in Pasadena, California, where young Joseph graduated from Throop Polytechnic Institute (which later became CalTech). There, on the outskirts of Los Angeles, he also became associated with the Cooper Ornithological Club, whose periodical (the *Condor*) he was to edit for more than three decades. After earning his master's degree at Stanford University in 1901, Grinnell began working toward his doctorate under David Starr Jordan before accepting a position as instructor in biology at his alma mater. That same year the twenty-four-year-old Grinnell was elected a fellow of the AOU, the youngest member ever to receive that honor. More than a decade later he finally completed his doctoral dissertation.[33]

Meanwhile Grinnell received the offer of a lifetime. In 1907 Annie M. Alexander—a dedicated, enthusiastic, and wealthy naturalist—recruited Grinnell to establish an ambitious new natural history museum she offered to fund. After negotiations to reconcile their differences, the two finally agreed that the new museum should be restricted primarily to the birds and mammals of California, oriented toward research, located on the Berkeley campus, and named the Museum of Vertebrate Zoology (MVZ).[34] Grinnell was delighted at the opportunity to head the new institution. The MVZ provided him with a permanent position, the specimens needed to conduct his research, as well as the opportunity to document the remnants of California's unique fauna before they were completely lost to development.[35] Concerned about raising the standards of natural history research, he immediately instituted a set of meticulous procedures for fieldwork, specimen documentation, and research presentation that became an MVZ hallmark.[36] The abundant supply of specimens that he, his staff, and his large network of collectors gathered proved crucial as Grinnell developed some of the fundamental concepts in ecology—like the "niche" and "competitive exclusion"—as well as made important contributions to other areas of evolutionary biology, particularly the relationship among geographical distribution, climate, and physical environment (fig. 31).[37] With Grinnell's leadership and Alexander's patronage, the MVZ quickly grew in size and stature.

After completing his Ph.D. degree in 1913, Grinnell also secured an appointment with the university's Department of Zoology. For nearly four decades he offered regular undergraduate courses and advised a steady stream of mammalogy and ornithology graduate students. The Berkeley ornithology program really began to flourish in the early 1930s, when Alden H. Miller joined the MVZ and the Department of Zoology after earning his Ph.D. degree under Grinnell.[38] By 1933 Grinnell and Miller were advising seven of the thirty-nine students who were writing dissertations on birds.[39]

During this period several other universities, such as Western Reserve and Michigan, also established active graduate programs in ornithology. Although both schools embraced the new biology just before the turn of the century, they also continued to promote more traditional approaches to natural history research. At Western Reserve the Ph.D.-trained zoologist Francis H. Herrick and the retired entrepreneur S. Prentiss Baldwin provided crucial leadership. Herrick, who gained appointment as the first head of the newly created Department of Biology in 1891, turned to bird study several years later, after long hours at the microscope began to take their toll on his eyesight.[40] Soon he became widely acclaimed for his use of photography to document avian behavior. Although lacking in formal biological training, Baldwin pioneered the use of live traps to band birds in the 1910s, developed several new devices to monitor bird movements and metabolic rates, and established the Baldwin Research Laboratory in 1924, where he hired Western Reserve students to serve as his assistants.[41] At Michigan, Alexander

Figure 31. Caricature of Joseph Grinnell, 1927. Part
of a series drawn by E. R. Kalmbach for the annual AOU
meeting, this cartoon lampoons Grinnell's tendency
to split off new subspecies of California birds and
mammals.

Ruthven—the herpetologist and longtime director of the Museum of Natural History—and (beginning in 1931) Josselyn Van Tyne—one of Ruthven's numerous doctoral students—attracted a slow but steady stream of graduate students with a special interest in birds.[42] By 1940 the Michigan program had produced eleven Ph.D.s who had written their dissertations on ornithological topics.[43]

By far the most productive site for graduate training in ornithology was Cornell University. From the time it opened its doors in 1868, the Department of Zoology was one of the institution's strongest academic programs.[44] The department began auspiciously when Louis Agassiz signed on as visiting professor of natural history and geology and secured permanent appointments for two of his most prized students. One of these, Burt G. Wilder, remained at Cornell for over four decades, where he became known as a tireless crusader and an important force in shaping the institution's biological curriculum.[45] Long before it became fashionable, Wilder insisted his students receive adequate laboratory instruction—even in large classes—and he was one of the first American educators to promote the idea of using the domestic cat as an introduction to vertebrate anatomy, much to the dismay of local humanitarians.[46] Among Wilder's many students were several renowned biologists recruited to join Cornell's faculty, including the entomologist John H. Comstock, the histologist Simon H. Gage, and the ichthyologist (and later college president) David S. Jordan.[47]

Not until after the turn of the century, when Arthur A. Allen arrived in Ithaca, did Cornell establish its reputation as America's most productive ornithological program. When Allen first came to Cornell as a freshman in 1904, he already had an extensive background in natural history.[48] His father was an attorney and avid naturalist who strongly encouraged his children's youthful interest in wildlife and the outdoors. After earning his bachelor's (1907) and master's (1908) degrees, Allen remained at Cornell to pursue his Ph.D. degree. He completed his dissertation, "The Red-winged Blackbird: A Study in the Ecology of the Cattail Marsh," in 1911 and published it three years later to an enthusiastic reception.[49] Based on stomach-content analyses and an extensive series of field observations, and illustrated with copious photographs, Allen's life history of this ubiquitous species was delineated with unprecedented thoroughness. In a review for the *Auk*, Witmer Stone praised Allen's monograph as "one of the best ecologic studies that has yet appeared," while Frank Chapman called it "the best, most significant biography which has thus far been prepared for any American bird."[50]

After completing his doctoral degree, Allen spent nearly a year in Colombia collecting birds for the American Museum of Natural History before returning to his alma mater to accept a position as instructor in zoology.[51] In 1915 he gained promotion to assistant professor in ornithology and began building a graduate program in ornithology at Cornell.[52] Both the specialized position and its associated program were the first of their kind in the nation.[53] Sixteen years and many graduate students later, Allen, an accomplished bird photographer and public speaker, was promoted to full professor of ornithology. By 1933 he had supervised sixteen of the thirty doctoral degrees in ornithology earned in the United States up to that point, and twenty-one of the thirty-nine graduate students currently focusing on the subject were enrolled at Cornell.[54] By the end of the decade Allen's "Grad Lab" was churning out an average of more than four master's and doctoral students per year.[55] Among the ornithologists who graduated from the program before World War II were such luminaries as Ludlow Griscom, Herbert Friedmann, John Emlen, Peter Paul Kellogg, Olin S. Pettingill, Jr., and George M. Sutton.[56]

Whether pursued at Cornell or at any of the handful of other institutions that offered similar training by the 1930s, graduate education had many far-reaching implications for the structure and practice of ornithology in the United States. In terms of the content of the field, scientists with advanced degrees accelerated the process toward diversification in ornithological research that had already begun by the early twentieth century. Through mandatory and elective coursework, required reading lists, participation in colloquia, and interaction with faculty and other students, ornithologists who earned graduate degrees typically gained exposure to a variety of theoretical and methodological approaches to biological research. No longer were specimen acquisition and microtaxonomy viewed as the only research agendas worth pursuing by serious avian researchers, as had generally been the case in the days when apprenticeships and self-education provided the most common paths to ornithological enlightenment. Gone too were many of the inhibitions about theorizing that most members of the earlier generation of American ornithologists shared.

At the same time that graduate education helped open avian research to new approaches, it also established a much clearer career trajectory for those who wanted to pursue ornithology as a vocation. For many years natural history museums and (to a lesser extent) state and federal agencies had provided the best employment prospects for the small number of ornithologists lucky enough to pursue ornithology as a vocation. While these institutions remained important employers, beginning in the 1930s and 1940s graduate-trained ornithologists gravitated toward positions in the rapidly expanding American university system.[57] By providing systematic and rigorous training, a reliable form of certification, and reasonable job prospects, graduate education helped transform scientific ornithology into a full-blown profession.

Enter Ernst Mayr

Although initially few in number, students fresh from newly established graduate programs represented an important force in the growing campaign to reform American ornithology. Compared with their predecessors, Ph.D.-trained ornithologists had a broader view of what constituted legitimate ornithological research, a stronger professional conciousness, and a greater concern with raising the standards of ornithological practice. Beginning in 1931 a leading voice among those demanding change was the German émigré naturalist Ernst Mayr. Mayr is best known as an accomplished evolutionary biologist and architect of the modern synthesis of the 1930s and 1940s.[58] Throughout his long career, however, he also played a key role in shaping the direction of American ornithology. Relying on his firsthand knowledge of European traditions, ample self-confidence, and determination, Mayr sought both to broaden ornithological practice and to increase the rigor with which it was pursued.

Born in 1904 to parents who enjoyed regular family excursions into the Bavarian countryside, Mayr developed a fascination with nature from a young age.[59] By the time he was a teenager he could name by sight and call all the birds in the area surrounding his home. Determined to continue a long family tradition, he enrolled as a medical student at the University of Greifswald, an institution chosen primarily because it was located in an ornithologically interesting area in the Baltic.[60] Although he excelled in his medical studies, his heart was clearly not in it. After spotting the first red-crested pochards seen in central Europe in over seventy-five years, he eagerly reported his find to Erwin Stresemann, the young curator of ornithology at the Berlin Zoological Museum.[61] Stresemann was so impressed with Mayr's enthusiasm that he recruited him to volunteer in the museum during university breaks. There, working in the shadow of one of Europe's finest ornithologist, Mayr realized that he wanted to fulfill his youthful dream of following "in the footsteps of Darwin and other great explorers of the tropics."[62] In 1925 he abandoned his medical training and enrolled at the University of Berlin. One year later he was awarded his Ph.D. degree summa cum laude for a dissertation on the range expansion of the serin finch written under Stresemann's guidance.[63]

Following graduation, Mayr worked as an assistant in the Berlin Museum while searching for a suitable opportunity to head off for the tropics. He finally received his wish in 1928 when he left on what turned out to be a series of three expeditions to Dutch New Guinea, Papua New Guinea, and the Solomon Islands. Working for the Berlin Museum, Walter Rothschild, and the American Museum of Natural History, Mayr spent more than two years traveling through an ornithologically rich part of the world, including several previously unexplored islands and mountain ranges.[64] Though his South Pacific expeditions were to be his last, they had a profound impact on his development as a biologist, and he spent the next several decades investigating their implications. The experience also led to his appointment as visiting research associate at the American Museum of Natural History, which was anxious to have someone process the mounds of specimens that had poured in from the Whitney South Seas Expedition during the previous decade.

Mayr arrived at the American Museum during what have been described as the "golden years" of the bird department.[65] Since 1920, when the department had been created by splitting the old Department of Mammalogy and Ornithology, it had enjoyed a period of unprecedented productivity, prosperity, and prominence. At the time Mayr joined, the staff already included four well-known research curators: Curator-in-Chief Frank Chapman, dean of American ornithology and author of pioneering monographs on the birds of Colombia and Ecuador; Robert C. Murphy, an authority on marine birds; James Chapin, a world expert on the birds of Africa, especially the Belgian Congo; and John T. Zimmer, a specialist on neotropical birds.[66] It was a remarkable concentration of talent that became even stronger with the addition of the young, ambitious, and capable Mayr. Although much of his workday was spent cataloging specimens and performing other routine curatorial duties, Mayr also made time to pursue his own research.[67] By the end of his first year at the American Museum he had described twelve new species and sixty-eight new subspecies of birds without making a serious dent in the material gathered by the more than decade-long Whitney South Sea Expedition.[68]

The department also benefited from strong financial backing. At the center of the patronage network supporting ornithology at the American Museum was the wealthy surgeon, sportsman, and bird collector Leonard C. Sanford.[69] Sanford, who was well known in New Haven and New York social circles, gave generously of his own fortune and cajoled others into supporting his goal of developing the American Museum bird collection into the finest in the world. His greatest achievement was convincing the Henry Payne Whitney family to donate the funds for several ambitious projects that Sanford had envisioned—often indepen-

Figure 32. Examining the Rothschild Bird Collection, ca. early 1930s. *Left to right*: Robert C. Murphy, Ernst Mayr, John T. Zimmer, and F. Trubee Davison.

dently of Chapman—including the Whitney South Sea Expedition, the Whitney Wing of the American Museum of Natural History, the Sanford Hall of the Biology of Birds, and the Whitney Hall of Oceanic Birds.[70]

Late in 1931 Sanford also convinced the Whitneys to purchase the world-renowned collection of birds that Walter Rothschild had been amassing at Tring, his estate in Hertfordshire, England, over the previous four decades.[71] When he needed money quickly to satisfy a former lover's demand for blackmail, Rothschild wrote to Sanford and asked if he might be interested in purchasing his 280,000-specimen bird collection. Sanford quickly jumped at the unique opportunity. After receiving promises of support from the Whitney family, he headed off to Tring with Robert Murphy and quietly negotiated a final deal. Murphy remained in England for several months to supervise the shipping of Rothschild's collection (fig. 32), which instantly filled many gaps in the American Museum's holdings and firmly secured its position as the leading bird collection in the world.[72] The purchase also convinced Mayr to remain at the institution as the newly established Whitney-Rothschild curator, yet another Sanford initative that the Whitneys agreed to fund.

Once Mayr received his permanent appointment, he initiated a series of attempts at reforming American ornithology. One of several ways he tried to influence the direction of ornithological research was by cultivating mentoring relationships with the promising young birdwatchers with whom he came in contact. Toward that end, in 1933 Mayr organized his own monthly seminar under the auspices of the Linnaean Society of New York.

The Linnaean Society began in 1878, when several naturalists from the New York City area decided to organize a local natural history society focused on birds.[73] Soon the new group was meeting twice monthly at the American Museum and issuing its own publications.[74] Under the influence of presidents J. A. Allen (1889–1897), Frank Chapman (1897–1899), and Jonathan Dwight (1899–1921), the Linnaean Society initially concentrated mainly on the technical aspects of ornithology, especially taxonomy. During the 1910s there were signs of a broadening perspective when the society began serving as a national clearinghouse for bird banding records. Later that decade, assembling local bird records, usually based on sight records, became a focal point for the organization.

Among the most active Linnaean Society members during this period were a group of eight young birders from the Bronx.[75] When they began attending meetings of the society, all were teenagers and all had been avid birdwatchers for years. Several had even established bird-feeding stations in city parks, published records of unusual sightings, and contributed reports for the annual Christmas census. After discovering each other at a meeting of the Linnaean Society in 1924, the teenagers decided to form a new association they dubbed the Bronx County Bird Club. With repeated practice and constant encouragement from Ludlow Griscom, who grilled them mercilessly when they reported unlikely finds at Linnaean Society meetings, the group quickly honed their field identification skills.

Under the influence of Griscom and others, the primary focus of the Linnaean Society and the Bronx County Bird Club had been on amassing records of local birds, with a special interest in rarities, accidentals, and early and late arrival dates for migrants. When Ernst Mayr began attending meetings of the Linnaean Society in the early 1930s, he was amazed at the differences between it and the German Ornithological Society, which he knew well from his years in Berlin. Although both were dominated by avocational ornithologists, he found the German Society to be "far more scientific, far more interested in life histories and breeding bird species, as well as in reports on recent literature."[76] In an attempt to bring the Linnaean Society more closely in line with his image of what a proper ornithological society should be, early in 1933 Mayr organized a regular monthly seminar in which participants took turns presenting abstracts of current avian literature, both foreign and domestic. After the first meeting, Irving Kassoy wrote Mayr declaring the seminar "a great success. Certainly we of the Bronx County Bird Club are very enthusiastic about it."[77] During the next several years, Bronx County Bird Club members were the most consistent of the dozen or so young men who regularly attended Mayr's seminar.

Mayr also encouraged seminar participants to take up a specific research project of their own. "Everyone should have a problem" was the way one Bronx County Bird Club member recalled Mayr's refrain.[78] Soon Irving Kassoy was staying up with the barn owls, Richard Herbert was pursuing peregrine falcons, Richard Kuerzi was trailing tree swallows, and William Vogt was watching willets and organizing the National Audubon Society's Breeding Bird Census.[79] Mayr helped shift the interest of these young birdwatchers from compiling local lists to the study of behavior and breeding birds, areas where he thought they could make a genuine contribution to science. Even Mayr himself was not immune to the interest in bird behavior he had helped to ignite. Writing to a British colleague in 1938, Mayr briefly recounted the history of his ongoing seminar and claimed that several times he had begun to undertake "behavior work" himself but could not carry through with it because of his "heavy schedule at the museum."[80]

One seminar participant, Joseph Hickey, later described the experience as the "turning point" in his life.[81] A native of the Bronx, Hickey first discovered birdwatching when the older brother of one of his close friends purchased a copy of Reed's *Bird Guide* to work on a Boy Scout merit badge. Soon Hickey and his friend John Matuszewski were wearing out the book's pages as they trekked through the Bronx in search of new finds. Several years and many outings later, the two became founding members of the Bronx County Bird Club. Despite his continuing fascination with birds, Hickey saw no possibility of a career in ornithology and instead took his B.S. degree in history at New York University in 1930, where he was a national champion in the mile run. Following graduation he became a track coach at NYU and then took a desk job at Consolidated Edison.

After Mayr encouraged him to become more scientific in his bird study, Hickey began taking night classes in biology at NYU and later pursued his master's degree under Aldo Leopold at the University of Wisconsin (1943) and his Ph.D. degree under Josselyn Van Tyne at the University of Michigan (1949). For his master's thesis he submitted a book, *A Guide to Bird Watching* (1943), which not only introduced beginners to the fundamentals of the sport but also provided more advanced information on migration watching, census techniques, distribution studies, bird banding, and life history research.[82] From cover to cover, Hickey's book echoed the message Mayr had been drumming into the heads of his young birding companions for over a decade: with proper guidance, serious birdwatchers could move beyond compiling local lists and make important contributions to science.[83] It was advice that many birdwatchers seemed eager to hear, if not always heed; within four and one-half months after its publication, Hickey's *Guide* had sold five thousand copies.[84] Mayr and Hickey remained good friends, and beginning in the 1940s Hickey became one of Mayr's staunchest allies in his ongoing attempts to reform the AOU.[85]

Mayr's relationship with local birdwatchers was not a one-way street. When he first arrived at the American Museum he knew no one, and while his colleagues in the bird department did their best to welcome him, they were all fifteen years or more his senior. However, after he began attending meetings of the Linnaean Society he "quickly made friends" with members of two groups with whom he regularly ventured out into the field: "Charlie Urner's New Jersey gang and the Bronx County Bird Club."[86] Mayr went out so often with the latter group that they even elected him a member in 1934.[87] As Joseph Hickey remembered it, "Mayr was our age and invited on all our (Griscom-type) field trips. The heckling of this German foreigner was tremendous, but he gave *tit* for *tat*, and any modern picture of Dr. E. Mayr as a very formal person does not square with my memory of the 1930's. He held his own."[88] One year after election to the Bronx Country Bird Club, Mayr participated in the group's first Christmas count to pass the one-hundred-species mark.[89] Mayr's extensive involvement with local birdwatchers not only furthered his reform agenda, but, as he later recalled, it also satisfied a deep-seated emotional need: "In those early years in New York when I was a stranger in a big city, it was the companionship and later friendship which I was offered in the Linnaean Society that was the most important thing of my life."[90]

MAKING SPACE FOR NICE

While working to expand the horizons of New York area birdwatchers, Mayr also actively promoted the career of Margaret Morse Nice. He was one of the first scientific ornithologists to appreciate and champion the work of this pioneer ethologist, who in his words "almost single-handedly initiated a new era in American ornithology."[91] Together the two played a crucial role in introducing the emerging field of ethology into the United States during the 1930s and 1940s.

Like Mayr, Morse was born into a family that immersed its children in nature from a young age.[92] Gardening, botanizing, and excursions into the countryside were all pursued with zeal. By the time she was nine years old, Nice began keeping notes on local birds around her home in Amherst, Massachusetts, and a family summer estate in Lyme, Connecticut. Three years later she received her "most cherished Christmas present," a copy of Mabel Osgood Wright's *Birdcraft*.[93] When she entered Mt. Holyoke College in 1901, she quickly found classmates who shared her enthusiasm for hiking, canoeing, and the outdoors, but nothing in her zoology classes to fire her imagination. As she later wrote in her autobiography: "I could see very little connection between the courses in college and the wild things I loved. I benefitted from the knowledge acquired of varied forms of life, but the approach to me seemed a dead one. I did not like to cut up animals. . . . I saw no future in laboratory zoology."[94] She graduated from Mt. Holyoke in 1906 and returned to her parents' home in Amherst with little sense of what she wanted to do with her life. Not until a year later, when she heard two lectures by Clark University professor Clifton F. Hodge, did she realize it was possible to study "*live* animals" seriously, perhaps even as a vocation.[95]

Despite protests from her parents, in 1907 Nice enrolled in Clark University to pursue her master's degree. One of only two women in the biology department, for two years she took courses and began thesis research on the food of the bobwhite.[96] She first attended the AOU's annual meeting in 1908, an experience that led her to conclude that "the role of ladies" in the organization "was largely ornamental."[97] Although she seemed to thrive at Clark, in 1909 she finally bowed to parental and societal pressure when she married physiology graduate student Leonard Blaine Nice and abandoned plans to expand her bobwhite study into a doctoral dissertation.[98] As historians Mitman and Burkhardt have pointed out, Nice is a classic case in which "gender-related cultural expectations provided major obstacles to . . . scientific talents and aspirations."[99]

In the face of those multiple obstacles, she did her best to carve out space for her beloved research. By keeping meals simple, sending out the wash, and "dispatch in the matter of cleaning," Nice managed to free up enough time to pursue a variety of scientific projects, even after the birth of her four daughters.[100] For the first decade after her marriage, her studies centered on the investigation of speech development in her children. It was a research program that she could tackle largely within the confines of her home and that resulted in several publications. Beginning in 1919 she recommitted herself to bird study after the purchase of a family car provided her with the mobility needed for extensive field trips. Nice became a regular presence at AOU and Wilson Society meetings, joined the Bureau of Biological Survey migration network, published a series of ornithological articles, and finished a book, *Birds of Oklahoma* (1924), with her husband.[101] She also initiated contact with Althea Sherman, the artist and self-trained ornithologist from Iowa whose innovative publications on the nesting behavior of the flicker, the house wren, and the chimney swift provided Nice with "inspiration and instruction."[102] In their letters the two shared their frustration at their failure to keep domestic duties from intruding on their scientific studies. Later in life, Nice bristled whenever anyone dismissed her work because she had failed to complete her Ph.D. degree and lacked a formal academic appointment. More than once she was heard to exclaim, "I'm *not* a housewife, I am a *trained zoologist*."[103]

Soon after the family moved to Columbus, Ohio, in 1927, Nice began banding song sparrows at Interpont, a large, heavily vegetated floodplain near her home that provided an ideal habitat for birds. By 1929 she was using colored celluloid bands to mark and follow the movements of individual birds, a technique that had been recently developed by one of Arthur Allen's doctoral students at Cornell.[104] For the next seven years, she continued to devote nearly all her spare time to the sparrow studies that were to make her famous.[105]

Nice first met Ernst Mayr in 1931, at an AOU meeting in Detroit.[106] The two seemed to hit it off immediately. According to Nice, Mayr was delighted to find an American "interested in more than faunistic records and pretty pictures."[107] He seemed particularly impressed with Nice's desire to learn more about the research being done abroad and her facility with foreign languages, a skill developed during her Mt. Holyoke days. At their first meeting Mayr suggested she request reprints from several Europeans pursuing life-history research, provided her with their addresses, and set her to reading the *Journal für Ornithologie* and other foreign periodicals American ornithologists typically ignored. Less than a month later Nice reported that she was disappointed to discover that the "Germans know all that we are doing, while we know almost nothing of what they are doing."[108]

In 1932 Nice traveled to Europe with her husband, who was attending an International Physiological Conference in Rome. Mayr helped her plan the itinerary and provided letters of introduction for several prominent ornithologists in Germany, Switzerland, France, Italy, and England, including the ethologist Oscar

Heinroth and Mayr's mentor in Berlin, Erwin Stresemann, with whom she spent ten days. When she mentioned her difficulty securing a publisher for her song sparrow studies because American journals refused to print lengthy articles, Stresemann offered to place her manuscript in the *Journal für Ornithologie*, one of the most prestigious ornithological journals in the world.[109] After Mayr declared the manuscript left him "speechless," she sent it on to Berlin, and her first major song sparrow publication—totaling nearly 150 printed pages—appeared in German in Stresemann's journal.[110]

With Mayr's cooperation and encouragement, Nice provided a vital link between the American and European ornithological communities. After returning to the United States, she thanked Mayr again for starting her "on the road to acquaintance with European bird literature" and said that she hoped to awaken a similar interest within her fellow citizens.[111] Toward that end she began writing several hundred critical abstracts per year of both foreign and domestic literature. Most of her abstracts dealt with life-history and behavioral studies, and the vast majority were published in *Bird-Banding*.[112] She and Mayr also lobbied to get abstracts, longer reviews, and articles from abroad published in other American ornithological periodicals. As she wrote Grinnell in 1932, trying to get reviews of foreign literature published in the *Condor*: "Too many American ornithologists have despised the study of the living bird; the magazine[s] and the books that deal with the subject abound in careless statements, anthropomorphic interpretations, repetition of ancient errors and sweeping conclusions from a pitiful array of facts." However, "in Europe the study of the living bird is taken seriously. We could learn a great deal from their writing."[113] Soon Nice was boasting to Mayr, "Aren't we having a fine success with our plans?"[114]

Mayr and Nice were particularly influential in disseminating European research on animal behavior, especially research from the emerging school of ethology that Konrad Lorenz and Niko Tinbergen were beginning to forge in the 1930s. After meeting Lorenz at the Eighth International Ornithological Conference in Oxford in 1934, Nice arranged for him to begin corresponding with American researchers Wallace Craig and Francis H. Herrick and abstracted his landmark "Kumpan" article.[115] During this period, she and Mayr wrote separate historical articles on the development of territory theory, both of which stressed European contributions.[116] In 1938 the two helped arrange for Niko Tinbergen's visit to the United States, and Nice spent a month with Lorenz at his home in Austria. There she learned how to raise baby birds and what to look for in their development for the next phase of her song sparrow research. One year later Mayr, who was then editor for the Linnaean Society of New York, published Tinbergen's *Behavior of the Snow Bunting in Spring*.[117] Not only were ethological ideas and techniques beginning to pervade Nice's research on song sparrows, but thanks to her and Mayr's continuing efforts, they gained a wide hearing throughout the English-speaking world.

One of the greatest favors that Mayr did for Nice was to push her into writing and arrange publication of her two-volume *Studies in the Life History of the Song Sparrow*, a work that firmly secured her place in the annals of American ornithology. After prodding from his regular birding companion, the publisher Charlie Urner, in 1934 Mayr agreed to serve as editor for the Linnaean Society.[118] Although he had no previous experience in the area, he knew the society needed to move beyond its typical fare of faunistic records if it hoped to gain more national and international visibility. Following the publication of Nice's lengthy song sparrow article in the *Journal für Ornithologie*, Mayr wrote her an encouraging letter in which he called her song sparrow work "the finest piece of life-history work ever done" and offered to publish the entire study in the *Transactions of the Linnaean Society of New York*, "even if it runs to three volumes."[119] According to Mayr, with the Depression reaching its height, he had a great deal of trouble convincing the society to publish an expensive "monograph by a bird watcher from Ohio," especially one that was "all statistical and most uninteresting." However, with support from Urner and several "young 'Turks'" in the organization, Mayr finally received the go-ahead. He even obtained authorization to print a thousand copies of the first volume, although the previous *Transactions* volume had only sold a hundred copies in three years.[120] Nice's first volume, *A Population Study of the Song Sparrow*, appeared in 1937 and was dedicated to "My Friend Ernst Mayr."[121] Besides providing personal satisfaction and the chance to further his reform agenda, editing this and other Linnaean Society publications supplied Mayr with valuable experience that he put to use again when he founded the Society for the Study of Evolution and began editing *Evolution* in the mid-1940s.[122]

Having gone out on a limb to publish Nice's work, Mayr did everything possible to make it a success. To secure as much notice as possible for the first volume, Mayr actively sought out appropriate reviewers. He sent a copy of the book to Aldo Leopold, who wrote a highly favorable review that he hoped Mayr could place in *Science*.[123] Mayr also convinced Joseph Grinnell to publish a short notice of the work in the *Condor* (even though the journal did not normally publish book reviews) and arranged for him to offer the volume for sale at the MVZ.[124] Another review copy went to the French ornithologist and aviculturist Jean Delacour, who praised Nice's study as "Perhaps the most important contribution yet published to our knowledge of the life of a species."[125] Following the book's publication in 1937, Nice was elected the first woman president of the Wilson Club and, after a campaign orchestrated by Mayr, to fellowship in the AOU, only the second woman to be so honored. Thanks in part to Mayr's promotional efforts, within several years the first printing of the volume one was sold out and the Linnaean Society had turned a profit. Clearly Mayr had been vindicated.

Reforming the AOU

While Mayr sought to expand ornithological practice in the United States, he also worked to revitalize the American Ornithologists' Union. He was not the only one worried about the direction of the organization. By the time the AOU was celebrating its fiftieth anniversary in 1933, many university-trained ornithologists were beginning to view it as an outmoded institution with less and less relevance to modern ornithological research. Besides Mayr, the most vocal critic in this reform campaign was Herbert Friedmann, a Ph.D.-trained ornithologist who was Mayr's contemporary in age. In one of their initial exchanges, Friedmann said he felt he had a "good deal in common" with Mayr in terms of general outlook and that the two of them would surely face stiff opposition as they tried "to educate the older school of ornithologists."[126]

Friedmann was born in 1900 in Brooklyn, New York, and became seriously interested in ornithology as a teenager, following regular visits to the bird exhibits at the American Museum of Natural History.[127] While attending City College in Manhattan, he began systematically observing the nesting behavior of the red-billed weaver bird at the New York Zoological Park. The study led to his first scientific publication and a decision to pursue a graduate degree at Cornell under Arthur A. Allen's direction.[128] In 1923, after completing his doctoral dissertation on cowbird parasitism, he began a three-year National Research Council–Rockefeller Foundation postdoctoral fellowship at Harvard, where he worked with the entomologist and animal behavior researcher William Morton Wheeler. Much of this fellowship period he spent chasing after parasitic birds in South America and Africa. When his fellowship ran out, Friedmann began teaching biology at Brown University and Amherst College. In 1929 he published his first book, *The Cowbirds: A Study in the Biology of Social Parasitism,* gained election to fellowship in the AOU, and accepted an offer to become curator of the bird collection at the U.S. National Museum in Washington, a position that had become vacant following the death of Robert Ridgway.[129]

Though the pay was much better than his former job at Amherst, Friedmann's new position frustrated him. His colleagues in the Division of Birds, Charles Richmond and Joseph H. Riley, were dedicated workers, but they were much older than he was, lacking in formal biological training, and content to pursue what he considered uninspired taxonomic studies.[130] As Friedmann later recalled, he felt they were "the old fashion type of ornithologist to whom a bird was not a living creature but a dead specimen" while his "interest in birds was in their biology and in their behavior and habits rather than straight taxonomy."[131] In addition, his supervisor, the Ph.D.-trained ornithologist and avian paleontologist Alexander Wetmore, was preoccupied with administering the U.S. National Museum and, in Friedmann's eyes, "failed to keep up with current thinking in biology."[132] Moreover, Friedmann had been hired with the expectation that he would finish Ridgway's multivolume *Birds of Middle and North America,* even though he believed the project was based on a hopelessly antiquated approach to ornithology.[133] The stock market crash that signaled the beginning of the Great Depression several months after he arrived in Washington thwarted plans to escape quickly to a university position but failed to dampen his enthusiasm for reform.

Soon after Mayr arrived in the United States, he and Friedmann began discussing a variety of proposals to revitalize the AOU, the *Auk,* and American ornithological practice more generally. For example, in a letter written in early 1932, Friedmann revealed that he had long ago reached the conclusion that "the A.O.U.

was hopeless as far as science was concerned, and that the 'Auk' was as incapable of progress as its equally dead name-sake": "If it were only possible to get A.O.U. people to study the change in the J[ournal] f[ür] Ornithologie since Stresemann took charge, it might be possible to talk to them, but it isn't. People like Chapin and others who have had enough *biological training* are satisfied, so what can you expect of individuals like Palmer, Stone, Peters, Murphy, etc."[134] Friedmann claimed that he had even contemplated starting a more scientific journal to compete with the *Auk* but was forced to abandon his plans with the beginning of the Great Depression, when finances were tight and he realized that there were "not enough real ornithologists to make a scientific journal self-supporting."[135] Friedmann may have been grandstanding for Mayr, but his sentiment accurately reflected the younger generation's growing impatience with the AOU.

One recurrent source of complaint was the process of selecting ornithologists to be honored with election to fellowship in the organization. Although the size of the ornithological community had grown steadily over the years, the AOU continued its original policy of strictly limiting the number of fellows to fifty. One result of this decision was that there were few openings for younger ornithologists, no matter how well-trained and accomplished they might be. Exacerbating this age imbalance was an ongoing geographical imbalance. Ornithologists outside the Washington-Philadelphia-Boston axis—the historical center of AOU membership—had long complained that they were routinely passed over when it came time to elect fellows into the organization.[136] Besides being unfair, critics feared that the failure to elect obviously qualified candidates to fellowship also led to a decline in the status of the honor "among zoologists in university circles."[137]

All these issues were on Joseph Grinnell's mind when he wrote Friedmann early in 1935 suggesting that his former student, Alden Miller, be nominated for fellowship in the AOU. According to Grinnell, "we badly need, on active status in the A.O.U., *young* workers—such as have proven their abiding interest in the field of ornithology and who have established favorable reputation on the basis of actual production." If the AOU did not begin electing qualified members of the younger generation into its two highest membership categories (fellowship and elective member), it would continue on the road toward "further senility," a trend that had already been "in evidence . . . for some years."[138] In his reply, Friedmann echoed Grinnell's concern about the declining position of the AOU:

> The tendency toward senility in the A.O.U. is a very noticeable one, and one that I think will take some time (and some deaths) to overcome completely. It is largely due to the fact that it is so much easier to do over and over again the obvious, superficial things that were the main problems in ornithology 50 years ago, and so many of our members are either set in their ways of thinking, or too impressed by the gray-beards of a past day, to do the harder but necessary deeper ornithology of the present.[139]

For several proponents of reform, the final straw came during the AOU's annual meeting held in Toronto later that year.[140] According to the critics, Washington-based ornithologists associated with the Smithsonian Institution and (especially) the Bureau of the Biological Survey had long controlled the election of officers, fellows, and members in the AOU. They could do this because of their large numbers—in 1930 they comprised more than 20 percent of the fellows and an even larger portion of those who typically attended the annual meetings—and because under the rules of the AOU, the first ballot was a nominating ballot. The Washington contingent tended to vote in unison on the first ballot, while the rest of the fellows usually spread their votes among several candidates. In 1935 there was a single opening for fellow, and the Washingtonians succeeded in electing the aging Edward A. Preble—a longtime veteran of the Bureau of the Biological Survey—over the up-and-coming Margaret Morse Nice. According to the critics, Preble was more a mammalogist than an ornithologist and in any case had failed to publish anything of note in over a dozen years, while the graduate-trained Nice had published a lengthy, innovative paper in the prestigious *Journal für Ornithologie* as well as a respectable number of more traditional reviews, articles, and books.[141] In the eyes of Mayr, Friedmann, and other Nice supporters, the 1935 election was yet another clear case in which the old-boy network had triumphed over scientific merit in the AOU.

Another issue needling reformers was the current editor of the *Auk*, the most visible and influential position in the organization. Witmer Stone had been a popular choice to take over management of the journal when founding editor J. A. Allen finally decided to step down in 1911. At the time Stone was a respected avian taxonomist with a decade of experience editing *Cassinia*. However, by the early 1930s he was in his mid-sixties, suffering from chronic heart disease, and (according to his critics) increasingly out of touch with modern ornithological trends. Concerns about Stone's editorial policy were one factor that prompted Joseph Grinnell to survey AOU fellows regarding the direction of the organization in 1930 and one of the things he highlighted in the presidential address based on that survey.[142]

The reservations about how Stone was editing *Auk* were varied. Several AOU members regretted his failure to exercise more editorial discretion. Stone had a reputation for writing lenient book reviews and accepting for publication nearly all the manuscripts that came across his desk. The result was a large backlog of submissions, long delays in publication, a decline in quality, and the imposition of a twenty-page limit for most articles.[143] In the face of these problems, many graduate-trained ornithologists—especially those pursuing more innovative life-history, behavioral, physiological, and ecological studies—sought other channels for their work, just as Nice had been forced to do with her first song sparrow paper.[144] Beyond these complaints was the concern that in an effort to maintain a healthy subscription list, Stone catered far too much to the large contingent of associate members who paid the bulk of the AOU's dues. According to the critics, the end of the "Stone Age" of the *Auk* was long overdue.[145]

Reform-minded ornithologists also worried about other AOU officers. In the early 1930s, the AOU's secretary—T. S. Palmer—and treasurer—W. L. McAtee—were both career employees of the Bureau of the Biological Survey, long-term holders of their respective offices, and paid what some considered an

Dr. P. and his work — an inspiration
and stimulus for young ornithologists

Figure 33. Caricature of T. S. Palmer, 1927. Part of
a series that E. R. Kalmbach produced for the annual
AOU meeting.

unreasonable portion of the AOU annual budget (ca. 20 percent) to carry out their
duties.[146] The largely self-trained Palmer particularly annoyed the younger ornithologists. Although he had once been an effective lobbyist for bird conservation,
he had never published much in the way of significant ornithological research.
Critics also charged that he demanded an unreasonable amount of time to transact
routine business at annual AOU meetings, he required too much space in the *Auk*
reporting on those meetings, and he sometimes failed to report nominations for
AOU fellows that were apparently not to his liking.[147] Moreover, he seemed ob-
sessed with gathering and publishing biographical data on deceased AOU members. It was a characteristic that may have endeared him to later historians, but it
irked his contemporary critics. Even his more sympathetic colleagues referred to
him as "Tomb Stone" Palmer (fig. 33).

After the 1935 election debacle, reformers moved into high gear. Early the
following year Stone's health began deteriorating rapidly. It was clear to all that
after twenty-five years as editor of the *Auk*, he would finally be forced to resign.
A search committee recommended that Glover M. Allen, a Harvard Ph.D. and
curator of mammalogy at the Museum of Comparative Zoology, be elected to
replace Stone, a nomination that AOU fellows approved at their annual meeting
in October 1936.[148] Although he too was better known as a mammalogist than as

an ornithologist, for the previous year Friedmann had been actively campaigning for Allen, whom he believed possessed the "scholarship and detached judgment" to move the publication forward again.[149] The reformers failed to replace Secretary Palmer when their candidate backed out at the last moment. When pressed, however, Palmer suggested that after twenty years in office, he would be willing to step down at the next annual meeting.[150]

Reformers also pushed through several changes in the AOU bylaws at the 1936 meeting. Following Friedmann's suggestion, AOU fellows voted to create a new category of membership, "emeritus fellow," though they failed to go along with the idea of making transfer to the new category automatic at a certain age or of allowing the AOU Council to mandate the process for those fellows who refused to volunteer.[151] At the same meeting, elective members gained the right to hold the offices of secretary, treasurer, and council member. The council, the principle governing body of the organization, was also increased from seven to nine members and divided into groups that would serve one-, two-, and three-year terms of office. The overall effect of these changes was to open the management of the AOU to a much broader segment of the organization, including many in the younger generation.

Emboldened by their success at the 1936 meeting, the reformers pushed for even deeper change the next year. Late in the summer of 1937, Mayr began circulating a draft of seven far-reaching amendments to the AOU constitution and bylaws along with a detailed explanation of why he thought each was needed.[152] In discussing his rationale for the proposals, Mayr repeatedly stressed how much the policies of the AOU varied from those of similar organizations in the United States and Europe.

Most of the reforms were designed to restore the scientific standing of the organization. In an effort to ensure that future AOU elections were based more on ornithological achievement than on politics, Mayr suggested that nominations for fellowship be accompanied by "a detailed statement of the qualifications of the nominee and by a bibliography of his principal scientific publications during the last five years." To improve the quality of the papers published in the *Auk* and delivered at the annual meetings, Mayr recommended the creation of two new committees: an editorial board that would assist the editor in soliciting, refereeing, and proofreading articles, and a program committee with the authority to accept and reject papers, invite speakers, and arrange special symposia.[153] In a variation of Friedmann's earlier suggestion, Mayr also advised that the AOU Council be authorized to transfer to the newly established category of emeritus fellow any fellow who had failed to attend the annual meeting or to publish any "scientific ornithological papers" in the preceding five years.

Two additional proposals were intended to shore up the financial position of the AOU, which had become increasingly precarious as the Depression dragged on. One sign of fiscal distress was a forced reduction in the size of the *Auk* after many financially strapped members stopped paying their annual dues. To free up funds for restoring the size and improving the appearance of the AOU's official publication, Mayr suggested eliminating the salary paid to the treasurer and secretary of the AOU.[154] Not only would making these two positions honorary be more consistent with practices at most other scientific societies throughout the world, but it would also weaken the resolve of officers like Palmer, who continued to seek reelection year after year. Mayr also felt it important that a summary of the income and expenses of the AOU be made public at annual meetings and printed in the *Auk*.

Mayr's most controversial proposal involved equalizing "duties and rights" of all classes of resident members (associates, members, fellows, and emeritus fellows).[155] Mayr felt that doing so would reinvigorate the lethargic organization by instilling a sense of enthusiasm and responsibility in all those connected with it. However, he decided to drop this proposal when several of his colleagues expressed fear that "some irresponsible group of conservationists might get hold of the Society" if associate members were granted too many rights.[156] Hoping to break the Washington monopoly on AOU elections, Mayr and his reform-minded colleagues also discussed appropriate candidates for fellowship as well as the offices of secretary and president, both of which were due to be vacated that year.

The 1937 annual meeting was a mixed bag for those hoping to rejuvenate the AOU. On the one hand, most of Mayr's reforms failed to gain immediate passage.[157] Apparently they were simply too much too soon for what remained an essentially conservative organization.[158] The fact that the proposals originated from a brash young outsider—Mayr was not yet even a fellow of the AOU when he began circulating them—also contributed to their downfall.[159] Even some of his strongest supporters considered Mayr too pushy for his own good. In a letter to Joseph Grinnell discussing possible successors to Stone, Herbert Friedmann claimed that Mayr wanted to be editor of the *Auk*, but that he would "be opposed by everyone—his insolent attitude and his groundless arrogance rule him out, although he has ability and energy."[160]

The news from the annual meeting was not all bad. Election results suggested that despite the general failure of Mayr's reform package, there was sentiment for change within the AOU. One hopeful sign was the election of both Mayr and Nice to fellowship in the AOU, the only members to be so honored at the 1937 meeting. Another was the election of the reformers' choice for secretary, Lawrence E. Hicks, a young ornithologist and botanist with a Ph.D. degree from Ohio State, a close friend of Nice, and secretary of the Wilson Ornithological Club.[161] For the previous year Friedmann had been promoting Hicks as a suitable replacement for Palmer, who reneged on his earlier promise to retire gracefully.[162] Even more heartening was the election of Friedmann himself to the presidency of the AOU.

Friedmann rode to office on a wave of optimism. As he wrote to Grinnell immediately following the meeting, he hoped to begin restoring the AOU to a position of "progressive active leadership in ornithological trends and tendencies in America." To begin achieving this ambition, he floated the idea of establishing a research committee "to determine the lines of work the Union should use its influence to advocate."[163] Friedmann felt that systematics was "already well taken care of," so the new committee should concentrate on promoting the "relatively untilled fields of avian physiology, genetics, [and] psychology." He also called for the AOU to cooperate more fully with other ornithological organizations in the United States, rather than continuing to ignore them as it had tended to do in the past. Once the AOU was showing signs of renewed vigor, then it would be time to begin an endowment campaign as a first step in making the *Auk* a "more comprehensive scientific journal," less dependent on "popular mass subscription."[164]

Like many reformers, Friedmann found it was much easier to damn than deliver. As one of his first acts of office, he did establish a research committee like the one discussed in his letter to Grinnell.[165] According to Mayr, however, the committee was never effective in promoting or coordinating ornithological research and was soon defunct.[166] At the first annual meeting over which he presided in 1938, Friedmann also received permission to appoint a committee to consider allowing major regional ornithological societies to elect representatives to the AOU Council.[167] The committee reported favorably on the idea, which was eventually approved at the 1940 annual meeting. Friedmann also successfully lobbied for the creation of a nominating committee to propose suitable candidates for election to the categories of fellows, members, honorary fellows, and corresponding fellows and to review the qualifications of those candidates.[168] However, Friedmann's dream of raising an endowment sufficient to liberate the AOU from its continued dependence on avocational ornithologists remained unfilled when he was voted out of office in 1939.[169]

Although the reformers were frustrated at the slow pace of change, they made significant progress during the 1930s and early 1940s. Through a series of amendments to the AOU's bylaws and constitution as well as several carefully orchestrated election campaigns, they largely succeeded in wresting control of the organization from the older generation of ornithologists. There were setbacks, of course. Not until 1950 was another Ph.D.-trained ornithologist, Josselyn Van Tyne, elected to the presidency of the organization, and the old guard continued to dominate the AOU Council for many years. From the late 1930s on, however, most other major officers of the AOU had at least some graduate training, and none served the excessive terms of office that had been common during the first fifty years of the AOU. There were still many battles for the reformers to fight, but clearly the AOU—and American ornithology more generally—had reached a crucial turning point.[170]

CONCLUSION

EARLY IN December 1923 nearly three dozen men—most of them serious avocational ornithologists—gathered in Cambridge, Massachusetts, to commemorate the fiftieth anniversary of the Nuttall Ornithological Club. The keynote speaker for the event was Witmer Stone, who was invited to share his reflections on what had been accomplished in American ornithology over the previous half-century. As a professional ornithologist for over thirty years, editor of the *Auk* for over a decade, and a recently retired president of the AOU, he possessed a unique insider's perspective on trends in his field.

Not surprisingly, Stone saw signs of progress all around him. Fifty years earlier, he noted, American ornithologists were much fewer in number and not nearly as differentiated as they were by the 1920s: "The technical ornithologists were not so technical, while the great host of present-day field students—the class of A.O.U. Associates—were largely conspicuous by their absence, and those between these extremes were more nearly on a common level."[1] In the early years of the Nuttall Club, American ornithology was also much more likely to have been practiced along the barrel of a shotgun. By Stone's reckoning, approximately 70 percent of the articles in the first two volumes of the *Bulletin of the Nuttall Ornithological Club* relied on collected specimens, a figure that had declined to only 20 percent in the most recent volume of the *Auk*.

Rather than continuing to construct faunal lists and create new subspecies of North American birds based on study skins, scientific ornithologists were now turning to "intensive study of the live bird."[2] For example, Stone himself had begun his career in the late 1880s as a traditional avian taxonomist, but by the time he delivered his address he was deeply immersed in the observational studies that were later incorporated into his award-winning book, *Bird Studies at Old Cape May* (1937).[3] As Stone confessed to the Nuttall Club that afternoon, he had discovered that "even an old collector" like himself could learn a great deal through patient observation with a good pair of binoculars.[4] Recent issues of the *Auk*, which contained papers on such diverse topics as "the origin of song, principles of migration, food analysis, methods of field identification, and bird-banding," provided additional evidence of a general shift in perspective toward the living bird.[5] And as ornithology had broadened its research agenda beyond "purely systematic study," Stone argued, it was finally "taking its proper place in relation to other sciences."[6]

Except for his optimistic claims about ornithology's status in the eyes of other scientists, few of Stone's contemporaries would quibble with his characterization of developments in their field. Indeed, there was ample evidence that over the previous half-century the American ornithological community had grown dramatically in size, become more differentiated in scope, and shifted its research orientation from collection- to observation-based studies. When S. L. Willard set out to publish a definitive *Directory of Ornithologists* in 1877, he compiled a modest list of 340 "collectors and students of ornithology" in the United States and Canada.[7] Less than four decades later, Frank Chapman was declaring that American ornithology was in the midst of an "Epoch of Popular Bird Study" as hundreds of thousands of birdwatchers purchased field guides, joined Audubon societies and bird clubs, and competed to record the most species.[8]

Stone's sense that the direction of ornithological research had changed over the previous fifty years was also sound. As late as 1901 Robert Ridgway had proclaimed that systematics was the only truly scientific form of bird study.[9] By 1933 an editorial in the *Wilson Bulletin* declared that

> Anatomy and classification have had their day. . . . Only here and there are morphological problems of importance found. . . . [M]ost of the systematists of today are driven to the work of making subspecies, the biological significance of which is doubtful. . . . The young man who looks forward to a professional career in ornithology would do well to consider the field of experimental laboratory work in development; or the field of economic ornithology and game management; or the field of animal behavior and psychology, including territory problems.[10]

Avian systematics was far from dead—Ernst Mayr's fundamental contributions to the evolutionary synthesis would soon prove that—but field-based ecological and behavioral studies were beginning to dominate ornithological science.[11]

While Stone may have accurately summarized recent changes in the scope and scale of American ornithology, he failed even to hint at two other closely related and equally crucial transformations looming on the horizon that afternoon: the emergence of graduate education and the growth of employment opportunities in ornithology. By the time Brewster and his contemporaries founded the Nuttall Club in 1873 and the AOU ten years later, American ornithologists were well on their way to forging a scientific discipline organized around the construction of a definitive inventory of North American bird forms. For the next several decades, however, they remained much less successful at finding a way to translate their ornithological expertise into definite career opportunities, even as they gradually expanded the definition of what counted as sound ornithology. With a few prominent exceptions, most ornithologists were forced to pursue their interest in birds solely as an avocation or as an adjunct to a related profession, no matter how dedicated and accomplished they might be.

The emergence of graduate training in ornithology in the 1910s and 1920s and the subsequent expansion of American higher education during the ensuing decades helped break the employment logjam for ornithologists. Gradually the field began to resemble a modern profession, complete with an extended period of formal training, codified procedures for certification, and reasonable employment prospects in colleges and universities, natural history museums, governmental wildlife agencies, and private conservation organizations. Graduate training also exposed students to a much wider variety of approaches to bird study than they had typically gained through apprenticeships or self-study. Thus it hastened the process of diversification in avian research that Stone had highlighted in his Nuttall Club address.

Yet even as ornithology finally began to resemble a modern profession in the 1930s and 1940s, it continued to depend on a variety of amateur practitioners. As we have seen, those lines of dependence were multiple. For example, avocational ornithologists continued to pay the bulk of the membership dues for the AOU, thereby making publication of the *Auk* possible even in the depths of the Great Depression. When critics—typically newly minted Ph.D.s—began calling for the *Auk* to raise its publication standards and to become more technically oriented in the 1930s, Stone repeatedly reminded them that the periodical could not possibly survive without the financial backing of a broad readership.

Expansive networks of serious amateur observers also remained the backbone of large-scale bird population monitoring projects that scientific ornithologists designed and administered. By 1939 nearly two thousand birdwatchers were contributing observations for the annual Christmas Bird Count, a number that would double again within the next decade.[12] That same year the Bureau of the Biological Survey's bird-banding network included nearly twenty-three hundred licensed volunteers, who had managed to band over three million birds since 1920.[13] While the unwieldy Christmas Bird Count records continued to defy systematic analysis for years, researchers quickly incorporated bird-banding returns into a series of publications.[14]

Amateur contributions to ornithology were not confined merely to gathering the data and providing the funds that professional scientists needed to conduct and publish their research. The most dedicated amateurs also continued to tackle their own research projects. Among the most prominent of the examples already mentioned was the Taunton, Massachusetts, businessman Arthur C. Bent, who lacked formal training in ornithology and never received a salary for his painstaking research. Yet from 1919 until his death in 1954, Bent managed to publish twenty-two volumes in his *Life Histories of North American Birds* series.[15] The monumental project won him accolades from the ornithological community and remained a standard reference work for decades.

Charles Broley, of Winnepeg, Manitoba, was another dedicated avocational ornithologist who made significant contributions to science.[16] After retiring from his position as a branch bank manager in 1938, Broley began banding Southern bald eagles near his winter home in west central Florida. Though he had to scale trees as high as a 150 feet or more to reach their nests, over the next twenty years Broley managed to place aluminum bands on as many as two thousand young bald eagles—more than had been banded across its entire range up to that point. He also monitored the breeding success of the nesting pairs on his banding circuit and in the process discovered a puzzling decline in eagle fertility. In the late 1950s Broley became the first to suggest a link between DDT—one of the new synthetic pesticides that became central to American agriculture in the post–World War II years—and the widespread reproductive failure of the eagle and other birds of prey. Subsequent research confirmed his hunch and eventually led to a ban on DDT use in the United States.[17]

The MIT-trained chemical engineer Crawford H. Greenewalt provides yet another example of an accomplished amateur ornithologist from this period.[18]

Greenewalt spent his entire career at the Du Pont Company, where he led the effort to scale up nylon production for commercial markets in the 1930s and later directed the construction of plutonium plants at Sanford and Oak Ridge during World War II. An able administrator, he quickly rose through company ranks to become president and later chairman of the board at Du Pont. In the early 1950s Greenewalt became interested in the mechanics of bird flight, and in his spare time he worked closely with Du Pont engineers and MIT's Harold E. Egerton to develop high-speed photographic equipment capable of capturing the rapid wing movements of hummingbirds. His remarkable photographs eventually appeared in a widely acclaimed book, *The Hummingbirds* (1960).[19] Later Greenewalt explored the physiology of bird song in a series of publications that culminated in *Bird Song: Acoustics and Physiology* (1969).[20]

Though better known than most serious amateur ornithologists, Bent, Broley, and Greenewalt were by no means isolated examples. Well into the twentieth century they and their committed colleagues continued to publish a significant portion of the articles appearing in major American ornithological journals. According to historian Marianne G. Ainley, as late as 1925, 63 percent of the articles in the *Auk*, 91 percent in the *Wilson Bulletin*, and 67 percent in the *Condor* still came from individuals who lacked institutional affiliation and received no compensation for their ornithological research. By 1950 amateur contributions to these three major publications had declined sharply but were still a solid 47, 46, and 34 percent.[21]

While many scientific ornithologists seemed comfortable with the growth of popular interest in birds and the continued amateur presence in their field, others—particularly those fresh from newly established graduate programs— were concerned. Among other things, they feared that recreational birdwatchers, armchair ornithologists, and sentimental conservationists exerted far too much influence on the nation's most prestigious ornithological society, the AOU, and its journal, the *Auk*. Beginning in the 1930s, the younger generation of graduate-trained ornithologists struggled to instill the AOU with a more robust professional consciousness—to reorient it toward modern trends in avian research, to make its elections more meritocratic, and to free its periodical from the influence of subscribers who failed to appreciate the need for new approaches to avian research and for greater rigor in how that research was conducted.

Yet even the most strident reformers generally did not aim to expel all the avocational ornithologists from their midst. Nearly everyone agreed there was still room for the thousands of Americans who regularly enjoyed the Christmas Bird Count or banding migrating birds, as long as participants pursued these activities with a modicum of competence and dutifully submitted their raw data to experts for analysis. Many professionally minded ornithologists believed that serious, dedicated amateurs could also make higher-level contributions to ornithology. Certainly that had been Ernst Mayr's experience with the Bronx County Bird Club in the 1930s, when he channeled the energy and enthusiasm of several talented young birdwatchers into projects with real scientific merit. And even as he led the struggle to establish and maintain rigorous standards for ornithological research over the next several decades, Mayr remained firmly committed to the idea that amateurs could do "splendid work":

> The precision of their observations, the imaginative and highly original posing of prob-
> lems, and the lucid and informative recording of their researches, which characterize the
> work of many nonprofessional ornithologists, would dispel any notion of their work
> being that of dilettantes. . . . They differ or differed from professionals only in one
> respect, by earning their living as doctors, lawyers, or businessman and receiving no pay
> for their ornithological labors. Large areas of ornithology owe their major progress to
> the devotion of such nonprofessionals.[22]

As long as amateurs conformed to the scientists' expectations about what constituted the appropriate questions, methods, and results of research, university-
trained ornithologists have generally continued to welcome them into the fold.

A half-century after Stone delivered his Nuttall Club address, ornithologists in
the United States and Canada were still grappling with the issue of how best to
deal with the significant number of serious amateurs that remained a part of their
field. In 1974 the AOU received a National Science Foundation grant to develop
a plan for American ornithology. The first of the six panels appointed by the
workshop leaders charged with formulating that plan dealt with the role of amateurs in ornithological research. The final report, issued in 1978, stressed the need
for fostering a stronger "professional identity" within the American ornithological community.[23] But it also concluded that ornithology was "blessed with a large
component of participating amateurs, whose numeric strength and qualitative
contribution is perhaps unequaled in any other major biological discipline."[24]
Amateurs not only provided crucial financial support for the major American bird
journals, they also represented an important "army of manpower" for individual
and coordinated field research projects. Dedicated amateurs even continued to
produce a small but significant portion of the technical literature in the field (10–
15 percent).[25]

Over the last two centuries, Western science has experienced a series of profound transformations in structure, practice, and content. In one field after another, formally educated, full-time, paid specialists have pushed aside the largely
self-trained gentlemanly practitioners who once dominated the pursuit of science.
At the same time, prolonged training periods, increased specialization, improved
funding, and access to sophisticated equipment have fueled a long series of break-
throughs. Modern science has fundamentally reshaped our understanding of the
natural world while granting us unprecedented power to manipulate and control
that world for human ends. During the twentieth century scientific knowledge has
become so vast, complex, and expensive to produce that it seems far beyond the
grasp of the average citizen. Yet even in the brave new world of contemporary
science, some specialities continue to attract a significant number of serious amateurs, dedicated individuals who donate funds, gather data, and sometimes even
conduct their own research. Perhaps more than any other field with an enduring
amateur presence, ornithology seems to conform to Jacob Bronowski's inclusive
vision for the scientific endeavor: "Let no one tell you again that science is only

for specialists; it is not. It is no different from history or good talk or reading a novel; some people do it better and some worse; some make a life's work of it; but it is within the reach of everybody."[26]

No doubt much of the continuing attraction of ornithology—what Mayr has called the "*scientia amabilis*"—is the object of study itself.[27] Birds are ubiquitous, vocal, and colorful creatures. Because they are generally conspicuous, they are relatively simple to locate and observe without elaborate equipment. They engage in courtship and nurturing behavior that is easy to perceive in anthropomorphic terms. Their flight suggests a freedom and power that resonates with the most fundamental human desires. Their cyclical migrations have long been used to mark the annual changes of the seasons. No wonder birds occupy such a prominent place in mythology, art, religion, and folklore around the world.[28] And no wonder that over the last century so many Americans have tried to possess, observe, and occasionally even further our understanding of these fascinating creatures.

N O T E S

ABBREVIATIONS

The following abbreviations have been used for organizations cited frequently in the notes and text.

AMNH   American Museum of Natural History, New York
AOU   American Ornithologists' Union
B-W   Blacker-Wood Library, McGill University, Montreal, Quebec
ECC   Emergency Conservation Committee
HUA   Harvard University Archives, Cambridge, Mass.
MCZ   Museum of Comparative Zoology, Cambridge, Mass.
NAAS   National Association of Audubon Societies
NAS   National Audubon Society
NYPL   New York Public Library, New York
NOC   Nuttall Ornithological Club
SIA   Smithsonian Institution Archives, Washington, D.C.
MVZ   Museum of Vertebrate Zoology, University of California, Berkeley

INTRODUCTION

1. Robert Ridgway to Anne Taylor, 26 June 1887, Division of Birds Records, RU 105, Box 1, vol. 3, pp. 406–407, Smithsonian Institution Archives, Washington, D.C. (hereafter cited as SIA).

2. For a brief biographical sketch of Taylor, see T. S. Palmer, "Henry Reed Taylor," *Auk* 35 (1918): 382.

3. On the turn-of-the-century debate about animal thinking, see Ralph H. Lutts, *The Nature Fakers: Wildlife, Science and Sentiment* (Golden, Colo.: Fulcrum, 1990). On the later dispute about adaptive coloration in animals, see Sharon Kingsland, "Abbott Thayer and the Protective Coloration Debate," *Journal of the History of Biology* 11 (1978): 223–244.

4. As Paul Farber has convincingly argued in his book *The Emergence of Ornithology as a Scientific Discipline* (Dordrecht, Holland; D. Reidel, 1982), discipline formation and professionalization are two distinct processes. The former involves establishing a group of "experts, working on a set of fruitful questions, using an accepted rigorous method, and holding a common goal" (p. 100) without necessarily suggesting success in establishing an occupation niche. On scientific disciplines, see also Gerard Lemaine et al., eds., *Perspectives on the Emergence of Scientific Disciplines* (The Hague: Mouton; Chicago: Aldine, 1976).

5. On scientists as gentlemanly practitioners, see Martin J. S. Rudwick, *The Great Devonian Controversy: The Shaping of Scientific Knowledge among Gentlemanly Specialists* (Chicago: University of Chicago Press, 1985); and Steven Shapin, *A Social History of Truth: Civility and Science in Seventeenth-Century England* (Chicago: University of Chicago Press, 1994).

6. Everett Mendelsohn, "The Emergence of Science as a Profession in Nineteenth Century Europe," in *The Management of Scientists*, ed. Karl B. Hill (Boston: Beacon Press, 1964), 3–48.

7. Nathan Reingold, "Definitions and Speculations: The Professionalization of Science in America in the Nineteenth Century," in *The Pursuit of Knowledge in the Early American Republic: American Scientific and Learned Societies from the Colonial Times to the Civil War*, ed. Alexandra Oleson and Sanborn C. Brown (Baltimore: Johns Hopkins University Press, 1976), 33–69, on 34. The following review articles provide useful introductions to the vast literature on the history and sociology of professions and have been relied upon heavily for the account that follows: J. B. Morrell, "Professionalisation," in *Companion to the History of Modern Science*, ed. R. C. Olby et al. (London: Routledge, 1990), 980–989; Patricia A. Roos, "Professions," in *Encyclopedia of Sociology*, ed. Edgar F. Borgatta and Marie L. Borgatta (New York: Macmillan, 1992), 3:1552–1557; and Ivan Waddington, "Professions," in *The Social Science Encyclopedia*, ed. Adam Kuper and Jessica Kuper, 2d ed.

(London: Routledge & Kegan, 1996), 677–678. See also Gerald L. Geison, ed., *Professions and Professional Ideologies in America* (Chapel Hill: University of North Carolina Press, 1983); Robert Dingwall and Philip Lewis, eds., *The Sociology of Professions: Lawyers, Doctors and Others* (London: Macmillan, 1983); and Thomas L. Haskell, *The Authority of Experts: Studies in History and Theory* (Bloomington: Indiana University Press, 1984). Although dated, A. M. Carr-Saunders and P. A. Wilson, *The Professions* (Oxford: Oxford University Press, 1933), also remains useful.

8. See, for example, Samuel Haber, *The Quest for Authority and Honor in the American Professions, 1750–1900* (Chicago: University of Chicago Press, 1991).

9. While those pursuing this approach have failed to agree on a single set of characteristics that adequately captures all professions, these criteria reappear with frequency in the literature. Geoffrey Millerson identified twenty-three attributes included in twenty-one authors' attempts to define a profession. See his *The Qualifying Associations: A Study in Professionalization* (London: Routledge & Kegan, 1964).

10. For the more extreme proponents of this second approach, professional autonomy—the ability to define and control the terms of work—became the single most important attribute of modern professions. For examples of this approach, see Terrence Johnson, *Professions and Power* (London: Macmillan, 1972); Eliot Freidson, *Professional Powers: A Study of the Institutionalization of Formal Knowledge* (Chicago: University of Chicago Press, 1986); Magali S. Larson, *The Rise of Professionalism: A Sociological Analysis* (Berkeley: University of California Press, 1977); Burton J. Bledstein, *The Culture of Professionalism: The Middle Class and the Development of Higher Education in America* (New York: W. W. Norton, 1976); and JoAnne Brown, "Professional Language: Words That Succeed," *Radical History Review* 34 (1986): 33–51.

11. Examples of studies operating within these two frameworks include George H. Daniels, "The Process of Professionalization in American Science: The Emergent Period, 1820–1860," *Isis* 58 (1967): 151–166; Joseph Ben-David, "Science as a Profession and Scientific Professionalism," in *Explorations in General Theory in Social Science: Essays in Honor of Talcott Parsons*, ed. Jan J. Loubser et al. (New York: Free Press, 1976), 871–888; and Edward Shils, "The Profession of Science," *The Advancement of Science* 24 (1968): 469–490.

12. Reingold, "Definitions and Speculations," 33–69.

13. Howard S. Miller, *Dollars for Research:*

Science and Its Patrons in Nineteenth-Century America (Seattle: University of Washington Press, 1970), vii.

14. Based on these two closely related characteristics, he suggested a tripartite classification of nineteenth-century scientific communities: (1) "researchers," characterized by "single-minded devotion to research," which generally translated into significant publications, but not necessarily into an occupation; (2) "practitioners," who were employed in science, but whose research accomplishment was qualitatively and quantitatively less than researchers; and (3) "cultivators," individuals who were often willing to support more advanced practitioners of science (with specimens, money, and time) but who were primarily concerned with "their own self-education, rather than increase or dissemination of new knowledge." Reingold indicated that his third category was roughly analogous to, but lacking the pejorative connotations now associated with, amateurs.

15. Convenient summaries of his arguments and a bibliography of his numerous periodical publications may be found in Robert A. Stebbins, *Amateurs: On the Margin between Work and Leisure* (Beverly Hills: Sage Publications, 1979), and *Amateurs, Professionals, and Serious Leisure* (Montreal: McGill-Queen's University Press, 1992).

16. See, for example, John Lankford, "Amateurs versus Professionals: The Controversy over Telescope Size in Late Victorian Science," *Isis* 72 (1981): 11–28; Marc Rothenberg, "Organization and Control: Professionals and Amateurs in American Astronomy," *Social Studies of Science* 11 (1981): 305–325; Robert A. Stebbins, "Amateur and Professional Astronomers: A Study of Their Interrelationships," *Urban Life* 10 (1982): 433–454, and "Avocational Science: The Avocational Routine in Archeology and Astronomy," *International Journal of Comparative Sociology* 21 (1980): 34–48; Elizabeth B. Keeney, *The Botanizers: Amateur Scientists in Nineteenth-Century America* (Chapel Hill: University of North Carolina Press, 1992); W. Conner Sorensen, *Brethren of the Net: American Entomology, 1840–1880* (Tuscaloosa: University of Alabama Press, 1995); James Roger Fleming, *Meteorology in America, 1800–1870* (Baltimore: Johns Hopkins University Press, 1990).

17. Marianne G. Ainley made the point emphatically several years ago in her pioneering studies, "The Contribution of the Amateur to North American Ornithology: A Historical Perspective," *The Living Bird* 18 (1979): 161–177, and "La professionalisation de l'ornithologie Américaine, 1870–1979" (master's thesis, Université de Montréal, 1980).

18. [Frank M. Chapman,] "An Opportunity

for the Local Ornithologist," *Bird-Lore* 7 (1905): 286.

19. From a letter by Leonhard J. Stejneger, quoted in "The Future Problems and Aims of Ornithology," *Condor* 7 (1905): 66.

20. Ernst Mayr, "Epilogue: Materials for a History," 376.

21. The History of Science and Technology On-Line Catalog cites 245 articles and books published over the last twenty years with the word "community" in the title. In most instances the term is apparently used without formal definition, and it is often restricted to scientists in the narrowest sense of the word. For two suggestive exceptions, see Struan Jacobs, "Scientific Community: Formulations and Critique of a Sociological Motif," *British Journal of Sociology* 38 (1987): 266–267; and Daniel Goldstein, "'Yours for Science': The Smithsonian Institution's Correspondents and the Shape of the Scientific Community in Nineteenth-Century America," *Isis* 85 (1994): 573–599. On ideas about communities within the social sciences, see Sandria B. Freitag, "Community," in *Encyclopedia of Social History*, ed. Peter N. Stear (New York: Garland, 1994), 160–162; and Victor Azarya, "Community," in *The Social Science Encyclopedia*, ed. Adam Kuper and Jessica Kuper, 2d ed. (London: Routledge, 1996), 114–115.

The theory of "social worlds" is part of symbolic-interactionist sociology and pragmatist philosophy. For theoretical statements concerning science as a social world, see Elihu M. Gerson, "Scientific Work and Social Worlds," *Knowledge: Creation, Diffusion, Utilization* 4 (1983): 357–377; Adele E. Clarke and Elihu Gerson, "Symbolic Interactionism in Social Studies of Science," in *Symbolic Interaction and Cultural Studies*, ed. Howard S. Becker and Michal M. McCall (Chicago: University of Chicago Press, 1990), 179–214; and Thomas Gieryn, "Boundaries of Science," in *Handbook of Science and Technology Studies*, ed. Sheila Jasanoff et al. (Thousand Oaks, Calif.: Sage Publications, 1995), 393–443. For case studies applying this theory, see, for example, Adele Clarke, "A Social Worlds Research Adventure: The Case of Reproductive Science," *Theories of Science in Society*, ed. Susan E. Cozzens and Thomas F. Gieryn (Bloomington: University of Indiana Press, 1990), 15–42; and Susan Leigh Star and James Griesemer, "Institutional Ecology, 'Translations,' and Boundary Objects: Amateurs and Professionals in Berkeley's Museum of Vertebrate Zoology, 1907–1939," *Social Studies of Science* 19 (1989): 387–420.

More traditional historical accounts of "networks" in science include A. Hunter Dupree, "The National Pattern of American Learned Societies, 1769–1863," in *The Pursuit of Knowl-*

edge in the Early American Republic: American Scientific and Learned Societies from the Colonial Times to the Civil War, ed. Alexandra Oleson and Sanborn C. Brown (Baltimore: Johns Hopkins University Press, 1976), 21–32; Arnold Thackray, "Scientific Networks in the Age of Revolution," *Nature* 262 (1976): 20–24; William A. Deiss, "Spencer F. Baird and His Collectors," *Journal of the Society for the Bibliography of Natural History* 9 (1980): 635–645; and Keeney, *Botanizers*. Recently sociologists of science have developed an even more inclusive "actor-network" approach that incorporates human and nonhuman participants. See, for example, Bruno Latour, *Science in Action: How to Follow Scientists and Engineers through Society* (Cambridge: Harvard University Press, 1987).

22. Previous studies of American ornithology during this period have treated various other aspects of its development. Frank M. Chapman and T. S. Palmer, eds., *Fifty Years' Progress of American Ornithology, 1883–1933* (Lancaster, Pa.: American Ornithologists' Union, 1933), produced for the fiftieth anniversary of the AOU, was one of the first retrospective views of the field and remains a useful starting point. Robert Henry Welker, *Birds and Men: American Birds in Science, Art, Literature, and Conservation, 1800–1900* (Cambridge: Harvard University Press, 1955), was the first book to highlight the rich cultural implications of bird study in the American context. More recently, Felton Gibbons and Deborah Strom, *Neighbors to the Birds: A History of Birdwatching in America* (New York: W. W. Norton, 1988); and Joseph Kastner, *A World of Watchers* (New York: Alfred A. Knopf, 1986), have focused on the rise of birdwatching, but neither makes sufficient distinction between scientists and recreational observers. See also Charles G. Sibley, "Ornithology," in *A Century of Progress in the Natural Sciences*, ed. Edward L. Kessel (San Francisco: California Academy of Sciences, 1955), 629–659; Erwin Stresemann, *Ornithology from Aristotle to the Present*, trans. Hans J. and Cathleen Epstein, ed. G. William Cottrell (Cambridge: Harvard University Press, 1975), especially Ernst Mayr's epilogue, "Materials for a History of American Ornithology," 365–396; and William E. Davis and Jerome A. Jackson, eds., *Contributions to the History of North American Ornithology* (Cambridge, Mass.: Nuttall Ornithological Club, 1995). All provide convenient overviews, but (with the exception of a couple of contributions in the Davis and Jackson volume) all share the benefits and drawbacks of being written by sympathetic insiders. Developments in Canada, mentioned only in passing in this book, are treated in much more detail in Marianne G. Ainley, "From Natural History to Avian

Biology: Canadian Ornithology, 1860–1950" (Ph.D. diss., McGill University, 1985), and "The Emergence of Canadian Ornithology—An Historical Overview to 1950," in Davis and Jackson, *Contributions*, 283–301.

23. Harold F. Mayfield, "The Amateur in Ornithology," *Auk* 96 (1979): 168–171.

CHAPTER ONE

1. On Roosevelt's interest in natural history, see Paul Russell Cutright, *Theodore Roosevelt: The Making of a Conservationist* (Urbana: University of Illinois Press, 1985). The discussion of the Roosevelt Museum of Natural History is found on pp. 1–2, 8, 26, 29–31, and 70–72.

2. David E. Allen, *The Naturalist in Britain: A Social History*, 2d ed. (Princeton: Princeton University Press, 1994), 89.

3. On the psychological, historical, and theoretical dimensions of collecting, see Susan Stewart, *On Longing: Narratives of the Miniature, the Gigantic, the Souvenir, and the Collection* (Baltimore: Johns Hopkins University Press, 1984); Werner Muensterberger, *Collecting: An Unruly Passion* (Princeton: Princeton University Press, 1994); and John Elsner and Roger Cardinal, eds., *The Cultures of Collecting* (Cambridge: Harvard University Press, 1994). For informative case studies of collecting within two American scientific communities, see Keeney, *Botanizers*; and Sorensen, *Brethren of the Net*.

4. On collecting natural history objects as a means of cultivating self-improvement and gentility, see Keeney, *Botanizers*, 38–50. On displaying natural history objects as a symbol of gentility, see Joseph H. Batty, *Practical Taxidermy and Home Decoration* (New York: Orange Judd Co., 1880), 177–178; Katherine C. Grier, "The Decline of the Memory Palace: The Parlor after 1890," in *American Home Life, 1880–1930: A Social History of Spaces and Services*, ed. Jessica H. Foy and Thomas J. Schlereth (Knoxville: University of Tennessee Press, 1992), 49–74, and *Culture and Comfort: People, Parlors, and Upholstery, 1850–1930* (Rochester, N.Y.: Strong Museum, 1988).

5. Natural theology was the belief that God's attributes could be inferred from an examination of the natural world. The idea has an extensive genealogy that traces backs to the Greeks and Romans, and beginning in the late seventeenth century it became an important impetus for pursuing natural history. See Harold Fruchtbaum, "Natural Theology and the Rise of Science" (Ph.D. diss., Harvard University, 1964); Neal C. Gillespie, "Preparing for Darwin: Conchology and Natural Theology in Anglo-American Natural History," *Studies in the History of Biology* 7 (1984): 93–145, and "Natural History, Natural

Theology, and Social Order: John Ray and the 'Newtonian Ideology,'" *Journal of the History of Biology* 20 (1987): 1–49. On natural theology in the American context, specifically as it relates to collecting, see Keeney, *Botanizers*, 99–111.

6. Oliver Impey and Arthur McGregor, eds., *The Origins of Museums: The Cabinet of Curiosities in Sixteenth- and Seventeenth-Century Europe* (New York: Oxford University Press, 1985).

7. Joel J. Orosz, *Curators and Culture: The Museum Movement in America, 1740–1870* (Tuscaloosa: University of Alabama Press, 1990), 11–25; Raymond Phineas Stearns, *Science in the British Colonies of America* (Urbana: University of Illinois Press, 1970); Brooke Hindle, *The Pursuit of Science in Revolutionary America, 1735–1789* (Chapel Hill: Published for the Institute of Early American History and Culture, Williamsburg, Va., by University of North Carolina, 1956); and John C. Greene, *American Science in the Age of Jefferson* (Ames: Iowa State University Press, 1984).

8. On the growth of the middle class, see Stuart M. Blumin, *The Emergence of the Middle Class: Social Experience in the American City, 1760–1900* (Cambridge: Cambridge University Press, 1989), 13, 258–297.

9. Daniel Goldstein and Elizabeth Keeney make a similar argument about the inclusive nature of the nineteenth-century natural history community. See Goldstein, "'Yours for Science,'" 573–599; and Keeney, *Botanizers*, 22–37. One prominent exception to this generalization (discussed in the next chapter) is that few women collected birds.

10. On the transformation of American society in the second half of the nineteenth century, see Thomas Schlereth, *Victorian America: Transformations in Everyday Life, 1876–1915* (New York: HarperCollins, 1991); Robert Higgs, *The Transformation of the American Economy, 1864–1914: An Essay in Interpretation* (New York: John Wiley and Sons, 1971); and Stephan Thernstrom, *A History of the American People*, vol. 2, 2d ed. (San Diego: Harcourt Brace Jovanovich, 1989). The statistics that follow are drawn from these three works.

11. On the growth of the railroad and its impact on American life, see John F. Stover, *American Railroads* (Chicago: University of Chicago Press, 1978); and Albro Martin, *Railroads Triumphant: The Growth, Rejection, and Rebirth of a Vital American Force* (New York: Oxford University Press, 1992). On the importance of the telegraph, see Menahem Blondheim, *News Over the Wires: The Telegraph and the Flow of Public Information in America, 1844–1897* (Cambridge: Harvard University Press, 1994).

12. Alfred Chandler, *The Visible Hand: The Managerial Revolution in American Business*

(Cambridge: Belknap Press of Harvard University Press, 1977).

13. These and other technological innovations in the publishing industry are briefly surveyed in John Tebbel, *The Expansion of an Industry, 1865–1919*, vol. 2 of *A History of Book Publishing in the United States* (New York: R. R. Bowker, 1975), 654–660. For a suggestive discussion of changes in how publications were illustrated, see Ann Shelby Blum, *Picturing Nature: American Nineteenth-Century Zoological Illustration* (Princeton: Princeton University Press, 1993).

14. Wayne Fuller, *The American Mail: Enlarger of the Common Life* (Chicago: University of Chicago Press, 1972).

15. Lawrence A. Cremin, *American Education: The Metropolitan Experience, 1876–1980* (New York: Harper and Row, 1988).

16. The quotation and the figures are from Frank Luther Mott, *A History of American Magazines, 1865–1885* (Cambridge: Harvard University Press, 1938), 5. For a more recent interpretive history of American periodicals, see John W. Tebbel and Mary E. Zuckerman, *The Magazine in America, 1741–1990* (New York: Oxford University Press, 1991).

17. On the attitude of European settlers toward the North American landscape, see Roderick Nash, *Wilderness and the American Mind*, 3d ed. (New Haven: Yale University Press, 1982), 8–43; William J. Cronon, *Changes in the Land: Indians, Colonists, and the Ecology of New England* (New York: Hill and Wang, 1983); and Carolyn Merchant, *Ecological Revolutions: Nature, Gender, and Science in New England* (Chapel Hill: University of North Carolina Press, 1989).

18. The account of Romanticism that follows is drawn largely from Nash, *Wilderness and the American Mind*, 44–83. See also Hans Huth, *Nature and the American: Three Centuries of Changing Attitudes* (Lincoln: University of Nebraska Press, 1957); Barbara Novak, *Nature and Culture: American Landscape Painting, 1825–1875* (New York: Oxford University Press, 1980); and Franklin L. Baumer, "Romanticism," in *Dictionary of the History of Ideas*, ed. Philip Wiener (New York: Scribner, 1974), 4:198–204.

19. The contribution of Transcendentalism to nature appreciation is discussed in Donald Fleming, "Roots of the New Conservation Movement," *Perspectives in American History* 6 (1972): 8–10; Huth, *Nature and the American*, 57–104; and Nash, *Wilderness and the American Mind*, 84–95.

20. On the various roots and branches of Thoreau's ideas, see Robert D. Richardson, Jr., *Henry David Thoreau: A Life of the Mind* (Berkeley: University of California Press, 1986);

and Lawrence Buell, *The Environmental Imagination: Thoreau, Nature Writing, and the Formation of American Culture* (Cambridge: Belknap Press of Harvard University Press, 1995).

21. Among the most prominent late-nineteenth-century bearers of the Transcendentalist torch was John Muir, philosopher, nature worshiper, and founder of the Sierra Club. See Fleming, "Origins of the New Conservation Movement," 9–10; and Stephen Fox, *The American Conservation Movement: John Muir and His Legacy* (Madison: University of Wisconsin Press, 1985).

22. The most comprehensive account of the turn-of-the-century "back to nature" movement, which discusses everything from school gardens to nature writing, is Peter J. Schmitt, *Back to Nature: The Arcadian Myth in Urban America* (New York: Oxford University Press, 1969). See also Lutts, *Nature Fakers*, 1–36.

23. The first state park was created in 1864 when the federal government turned over Yosemite Valley to the state of California. The first national park was Yellowstone, created by Congress in 1872. For an interpretive history of American national parks, see Alfred Runte, *National Parks: The American Experience*, 2d ed. (Lincoln: University of Nebraska Press, 1987).

24. Schmitt's *Back to Nature* discusses these and other developments. His portrayal of the search for an arcadian middle ground between nature and civilization is informed by Leo Marx's classic study, *The Machine in the Garden: Technology and the Pastoral Idea in America* (New York: Oxford University Press, 1964). For a detailed analysis of the rise of suburbs, see John Stilgoe, *Borderlands: Origins of the American Suburb, 1820–1939* (New Haven: Yale University Press, 1988); and Kenneth T. Jackson, *Crabgrass Frontier: The Suburbanization of the United States* (New York: Oxford University Press, 1985).

25. Thoreau pioneered a new literary genre, the nature essay, to bring his ideas before the American public. See Paul Brooks, *Speaking for Nature: How Literary Naturalists from Henry Thoreau to Rachel Carson Have Shaped America* (Boston: Houghton Mifflin, 1980); Thomas J. Lyon, ed., *This Incomperable Lande: A Book of American Nature Writing* (Boston: Houghton Mifflin, 1989); and Buell, *Environmental Imagination*.

26. This fundamental insight belongs to Nash, *Wilderness and the American Mind*, 44.

27. Daniel T. Rodgers, *The Work Ethic in Industrial America, 1850–1920* (Chicago: University of Chicago Press, 1978), is among the most useful studies on the history of the idea of leisure in America, and I have relied heavily upon it for the interpretation that follows. See also Foster R.

Dulles, *A History of Recreation: America Learns to Play*, 2d ed. (New York: Appleton-Century-Crofts, 1965); and Donna R. Braden, *Leisure and Entertainment in America* (Dearborn, Mich.: Henry Ford Museum and Greenfield Village, 1988).

28. Rodgers, *Work Ethic*, 6.

29. Between 1856 to 1896 the average workweek for full-time employees in twenty selected industries declined from 66 to about 59.4 hours, but six-day workweeks remained a norm. By 1924 the figure for all manufacturing industries had reached 50.4 hours. From David R. Roediger and Philip S. Foner, *Our Own Time: A History of American Labor and the Working Day* (New York: Greenwood Press, 1989), x. I have been unable to locate data on work hours for the middle class alone.

The literature on the history of sports during this period is large, but generally disappointing. Some important exceptions include Donald J. Mrozek, *Sport and American Mentality, 1880–1910* (Knoxville: University of Tennessee Press, 1983); Stephen Hardy, *How Boston Played: Sport, Recreation, and Community* (Boston: Northeastern University Press, 1982); and John R. Betts, *America's Sporting Heritage: 1850–1950* (Reading, Mass.: Addison-Wesley, 1974).

30. Rodgers, *Work Ethic*, 108.

31. One of the few historical studies to take a broader look at the Victorian fascination with collecting is Asa Briggs, *Victorian Things* (London: B. T. Batsford, 1988).

32. Harvey Green, *The Light of the Home: An Intimate View of the Lives of Women in Victorian America* (New York: Pantheon, 1983), 96–97, describes the typical American parlor, complete with prints, figurines, plants, flowers, mementos, and natural history objects. See also Grier, "Decline of the Memory Palace" and *Culture and Comfort*. On the history of stamp collecting, see Briggs, *Victorian Things*, 327–368; and Stephen M. Gelber, "Free Market Metaphor: The Historical Dynamics of Stamp Collecting," *Comparative Studies in Society and History* 34 (1992): 742–769. On Anglo-American interest in amassing natural history objects in particular, see Allen, *The Naturalist in Britain*, and his earlier book, *The Victorian Fern Craze: A History of Pteridomania* (London: Hutchinson, 1969); Lynn L. Merrill, *The Romance of Victorian Natural History* (New York: Oxford University Press, 1989); Keeney, *Botanizers*; Lynn Barber, *The Heyday of Natural History, 1820–1870* (Garden City, N.Y.: Doubleday, 1890); S. Peter Dance, *Shell Collecting: An Illustrated History* (London: Faber and Faber, 1966); and J. M. Chalmers-Hunt, comp., *Natural History Auctions,*

1700–1972: A Register of Sales in the British Isles (London: Sotheby Park Bernet, 1976).

33. Briggs, *Victorian Things*, 225.

34. Quoted in ibid., 353.

35. E. C. Mitchell, "The Collecting Habit," *Oologist* 21 (1904): 25–26.

Oology, the study of eggs (especially birds' eggs), was once spelled with a diaeresis over the second "o" (i.e., oölogy) to indicate that the two adjacent vowels were pronounced separately. In the late nineteenth century, however, authors and publishers used this mark inconsistently, and their twentiety-century counterparts have all but abandoned the practice. Therefore, I have used the modern spelling of oology and its variants throughout the text and citations.

36. John H. Jackson, "Oology vs. Philately," *Oologist* 11 (1894): 280. On the American enthusiasm for exercise, see James C. Whorton, *Crusaders for Fitness: The History of American Health Reformers* (Princeton: Princeton University Press, 1982); and Harvey Green, *Fit for America: Health, Fitness, Sport and American Society* (New York: Pantheon Books, 1986).

37. Jackson, "Oology vs. Philately," 279.

38. Ross H. and Mary E. Arnett have resolved the confusion surrounding the various editions of this invaluable reference work in "The 44 Editions of the Naturalists' Directory," published in the recent edition of the directory that they compiled, *The Naturalists' Directory and Almanac (International)* (Gainesville, Fla.: Flora and Fauna Publications, 1985), 10–21.

39. Frederic Ward Putnam, ed., *The Naturalists' Directory: North America and the West Indies*, 2 parts (Salem, Mass.: Essex Institute, 1865).

40. Frederic Ward Putnam, ed., *The Naturalists' Directory: North America and the West Indies* (Salem, Mass.: Essex Institute, 1866).

41. From 1877 to 1936, Samuel E. Cassino published thirty editions of the *Naturalists' Directory* under a variety of titles. See the bibliographic information and the estimates for the number of entries in each edition in Arnett and Arnett, "44 Editions."

42. Ralph Bates, *Scientific Societies in the United States*, 2d ed. (Cambridge: MIT Press, 1958).

43. These figures come from lists of scientific societies in Samuel Cassino, ed., *Naturalists' Directory for 1878* (Salem, Mass.: Naturalists' Agency, 1878), and *Naturalists' Directory, 1884* (Boston: S. E. Cassino, 1884). On local natural history societies in the Midwest, see Daniel Goldstein, "Midwestern Naturalists: Academies of Science in the Mississippi Valley, 1850–1900" (Ph.D. diss., Yale University, 1989).

44. The Agassiz Association is discussed

briefly in Keeney, *Botanizers*, 140–145; and Lutts, *Nature Fakers*, 28–29.

45. The quotation is from the Constitution of the Agassiz Association, reproduced in Harlan H. Ballard, *Hand-Book of the St. Nicholas Agassiz Association* (Pittsfield, Mass.: Axtell and Pomeroy, 1882), 6. The biographical information on Ballard that follows is from his entry, "Harlan Hoge Ballard," in *National Cyclopedia of American Biography* (New York: James T. White, 1907), 9:488–489.

46. Harlan H. Ballard, *Hand-Book of the St. Nicholas Agassiz Association*, 2d ed. (Lenox, Mass.: Published by the Author, 1884), 10. A full list of the local chapters is found on pp. 91–109.

47. The quotation is from "Harlan Hoge Ballard," 489. The figures are from Harlan H. Ballard, *Three Kingdoms: A Hand-Book of the Agassiz Association*, 4th ed. (St. Louis: I. A. Mekeel, 1897), 17.

48. According to Keeney, *Botanizers*, 141, the association also published proceedings in the *Observer*, *Santa Claus*, and *Popular Science News*. In addition, several local Agassiz Association chapters published their own periodicals.

49. On the history of the nature study movement, see Schmitt, *Back to Nature*, 77–95; Keeney, *Botanizers*, 135–145; Lutts, *Nature Fakers*, 25–30; and E. Laurence Palmer, "Fifty Years of Nature Study and the American Nature Study Society," *Nature Magazine* 50 (November 1957): 473–480.

50. Quoted in Schmidt, *Back to Nature*, 84. Clifton F. Hodge, *Nature Study and Life* (Boston: Ginn, 1902); Liberty H. Bailey, *The Nature-Study Idea* (New York: Doubleday, Page, 1903).

51. At least two earlier periodicals with "Nature Study" in their title predated this one, but both were short-lived: *Nature Study* (1900–1904), published by the Manchester Institute of Arts and Sciences, and *Nature Study in Schools* (1900), published by C. J. Maynard.

52. Anna Botsford Comstock, *Handbook of Nature Study* (Ithaca: Cornell University Press, 1911).

53. The only study of minor natural history periodicals of which I am aware is Jerome A. Jackson's brief article, "Extinct Bird Journals: Forgotten Treasures?" *AB Bookman's Weekly* 77 (1986): 2566–2569.

54. Frank L. Burns, "A Bibliography of Scarce or Out of Print North American Amateur and Trade Periodicals Devoted More or Less to Ornithology," Supplement to the *Oologist* 32 (1915): 1–32; William J. Fox, "A List of American Journals Omitted from Boulton's 'Catalogue of Scientific and Technical Periodicals, 1865–1895,'" *Bulletin of Bibliography* 5 (1908): 82–85; and Margaret Underwood, comp., *Bibli-*

ography of North American Natural History Serials in the University of Michigan Libraries (Ann Arbor: University of Michigan Press, 1954).

55. Quoted in Fuller, *American Mail*, 133.

56. The incident is recorded in a letter, Charles H. Prince to Jonathan Dwight, Jr., 17 October 1896, bound with the copy of the *Oologist's Advertiser* in the Bird Library of the National Museum of Natural History, Smithsonian Institution, Washington, D.C. Among the other periodicals denied second-class rates were *The Collectors' Illustrated Magazine*, published in 1888 by the California dealer Edward M. Haight, and *Our Birds*, published by Frank H. Metcalf in 1880. See Burns, "Bibliography," 8, 25.

57. Fuller, *American Mail*, 138–139.

58. The copy of *American Ornithology* 6 (1906) in the Museum of Comparative Library, Cambridge, Mass., contains a postcard dated 29 September 1906 in which the editor Chester A. Reed announces he had suspended publication because he was denied second-class rates. See also Burns, "Bibliography," 4.

59. As historian Frank L. Mott has observed (*American Magazines, 1865–1885*, 6), obtaining accurate circulation information on periodicals in the age before independent audits is nearly impossible.

60. The circulation figures that follow are from Burns, "Bibliography," 2–3, 5, 17, 25, 27, 31.

61. "Editorial Notes," *Ward's Natural Science Bulletin* 2 (1883): 2.

62. "Editorial," *Ornithologist and Oologist* 11 (1886): 168.

63. [Frank H. Lattin], "20,000 March Oologists," *Oologist* 11 (1894): 37.

64. See the list compiled in the appendix of Mark V. Barrow, Jr., "Birds and Boundaries: Community, Practice, and Conservation in North American Ornithology, 1865–1935" (Ph.D. diss., Harvard University, 1992), 579–590, and the discussion of various entrepreneurial naturalists on 76–101. For a fascinating glimpse of one of the most famous American natural history dealers, see Sally G. Kohlstedt, "Henry A. Ward: The Merchant Naturalist and American Museum Development," *Journal of the Society for the Bibliography of Natural History* 9 (1980): 647–661.

65. This is not unlike the basic distinction between Arcadian and imperialistic science that Donald Worster makes in *Nature's Economy: A History of Ecological Ideas* (Cambridge: Cambridge University Press, 1985).

66. First emphasis is in the original, while the second is mine. Elliott Coues, *Field Ornithology* (Salem, Mass.: Naturalists' Agency, 1874), 12.

67. A similar point is made in Stewart, *On Longing*, 152–166. On collecting as an expression of the need to control, see Muensterberger, *Collecting*, 39 and passim.

CHAPTER TWO

1. Biographical information on Ridgway may be found in Harry Harris, "Robert Ridgway, with a Bibliography of His Published Writings," *Condor* 30 (1928): 5–118; Alexander Wetmore, "Biographical Memoir of Robert Ridgway, 1850–1929," *Biographical Memoirs of the National Academy of Sciences* 15 (1931): 57–101; Frank M. Chapman, "Robert Ridgway, 1850–1929," *Bird-Lore* 31 (1929): 173–178; Harry C. Oberholser, "Robert Ridgeway: A Memorial Appreciation," *Auk* 50 (1933): 159–169; and F. Gavin Davenport, "Robert Ridgway: Illinois Naturalist," *Journal of the Illinois State Historical Society* 63 (1970): 271–289.

2. The letter, Spencer F. Baird to Robert Ridgway, 23 June 1864, is reproduced in Ridgway's memorial address, "Spencer Fullerton Baird," *Auk* 5 (1888): 12.

3. Robert Ridgway to Spencer Fullerton Baird, 13 November 1865, Robert Ridgway Papers, RU 7167, Box 1, SIA.

4. See the series of letters written from Ridgway to Baird in the years 1864 to 1866 in ibid.

5. The details of Ridgway's itinerary are contained in his published report, Robert Ridgway, *Ornithology,* in *United States Geological Exploration of the Fortieth Parallel*, part III, 303–669 (Washington, D.C.: Government Printing Office, 1877). Specific incidents relating to the expedition are also recorded in Harris, "Ridgway," 21–27. The full citation for the book Ridgway helped to complete is Spencer F. Baird, Thomas M. Brewer, and Robert Ridgway, *A History of North American Birds: Land Birds*, 3 vols. (Boston: Little, Brown, 1874).

6. Harris, "Ridgway," 31.

7. The term comes from a chapter title in E. F. Rivinus and E. M. Youseff, *Spencer Baird of the Smithsonian* (Washington, D.C.: Smithsonian Institution Press, 1992).

8. Spencer Trotter, "The Background of Ornithology," *Bird-Lore* 10 (1908): 71.

9. Paul Lawrence Farber, "The Development of Taxidermy and the History of Ornithology," *Isis* 68 (1977): 550–566.

10. H. O. Green, "The Beginning of Oology," *Oologist* 52 (1935): 2–3, argues that Étienne François Turgot, *Mémoire instructif sur la maniere de rassembler, de preparer, de conserver, et d'envoyer les diverses curiositiés d'histoire naturelle* (Lyon: J. M. Bruyset, 1758), was one of the earliest published accounts to explain how to preserve birds' eggs. One of the early major egg collectors appears to have been Denis Joseph Manesse, taxidermist and author of *Traité sur la manière d'empailler et de conserver les animaux, les pelléteries et les laines* (Paris: Guillot, 1787). See H. O. Green, "An Early Oologist," *Oologist* 52 (1935): 42–43.

11. Farber, "Taxidermy and Ornithology," 562–563. Hugh Strickland, "Report of the Recent Progress and Present State of Ornithology," *Report of the Fourteenth Meeting of the British Association for the Advancement of Science* (1844): 216–217, lists most of the major collections of his day.

12. Peale's Philadelphia Museum was the most important American natural history museum in the late eighteenth and early nineteenth centuries and has attracted a great deal of scholarly attention. See, for example, Charles Coleman Sellers, *Mr. Peale's Museum: Charles Willson Peale and the First Popular Museum of Natural Science and Art* (New York: W. W. Norton, 1980); Orosz, *Curators and Culture*; and Tobey Appel, "Science, Popular Culture and Profit: Peale's Philadelphia Museum," *Journal of the Society for the Bibliography of Natural History* 9 (1980): 619–634.

13. Quoted in Witmer Stone, "Some Philadelphia Ornithological Collections and Collectors, 1784–1850," *Auk* 16 (1899): 168.

14. Porter, *Eagle's Nest*, 30; Clark Hunter, *The Life and Letters of Alexander Wilson* (Philadelphia: American Philosophical Society, 1983), 4; Sellers, *Mr. Peale's Museum*, 203, 205–206. Wilson's *American Ornithology* includes the specimen numbers in Peale's museum upon which the descriptions were based.

15. Porter, *Eagle's Nest*, 27. For a broad historical review of the development of habitat exhibits, see Karen E. Wonders, "Bird Taxidermy and the Origin of the Habitat Diorama," in *Non-Verbal Communication in Science Prior to 1900*, ed. Renato G. Mazzolini (Firenze: Leo S. Olschki, 1993), 411–447.

16. Walter Faxon, "Relics of Peale's Museum," *Bulletin of the Museum of Comparative Zoology* 59 (1915): 119–133.

17. The academy has been the subject of several historical studies: Patsy A. Gerstner, "The Academy of Natural Sciences of Philadelphia, 1812–1850," in *The Pursuit of Knowledge in the Early American Republic: American Scientific and Learned Societies from the Colonial Times to the Civil War*, ed. Alexandra Oleson and Sanborn C. Brown (Baltimore: Johns Hopkins University Press, 1976), 174–193; Porter, *Eagle's Nest*, and Orosz, *Curators and Culture*. See also Frank B. Gill, "Philadelphia: 180 Years of Ornithology at the Academy of Natural Sciences," in *Contributions to the History of North American Ornithology*, ed. William E. Davis, Jr., and Je-

rome A. Jackson (Cambridge, Mass.: Nuttall Ornithological Club, 1995), 1–31.

18. Gerstner, "Academy," 179.

19. Witmer Stone, "Thomas B. Wilson, M.D.," *Cassinia* 13 (1909): 5–6.

20. Philip Lutley Sclater, "Notes on the Birds in the Museum of the Academy of Natural Sciences of Philadelphia, and Other Collections in the United States of America," *Proceedings of the Zoological Society of London* 25 (1857): 1–9, on 1.

21. Elliott Coues, *Key to North American Birds*, 5th ed. (Boston: Dana Estes, 1903), xxiv. For biographical sketches of Cassin, see Witmer Stone, "John Cassin," *Cassinia* 5 (1901): 1–7; and Theodore Gill, "Biographical Notice of John Cassin," *Osprey* n.s. 1 (1902): 50–53.

22. See Deborah Jean Warner, *Graceanna Lewis: Scientist and Humanitarian* (Washington, D.C.: Smithsonian Institution Press, 1979), 54.

23. The history of the Boston Society of the History of Natural History has been examined in Thomas Bouvé, *Historical Sketch of the Boston Society of Natural History* (Boston: The Society, 1880), and more recently in two articles by Sally G. Kohlstedt, "The Nineteenth-Century Amateur Tradition: The Case of the Boston Society of the History of Natural History," in *Science and Its Public*, ed. Gerald Holton and W. A. Blanpied (Dordrecht, Holland: D. Reidel, 1976), 173–190, and "From Learned Society to Public Museum: The Boston Society of Natural History," in *The Organization of Knowledge in Modern America, 1860–1920*, ed. Alexandra Oleson and John Voss (Baltimore: Johns Hopkins University Press, 1979), 386–406.

24. The figures are from Bouvé, *Historical Sketch*, 34, 53.

25. Ibid., 108–110.

26. Orosz, *Curators and Culture*; Sally Kohlstedt, "Curiosities and Cabinets: Natural History Museums and Education on the Ante-Bellum Campus," *Isis* 79 (1988): 405–426; Bates, *Scientific Societies in the United States*; Charlotte Porter, "The Natural History Museum," in *The Museum: A Reference Guide*, ed. Michael S. Shapiro (New York: Greenwood Press, 1990), 1–29.

27. The collections of Cassin, Lawrence, Brewer, Samuel Cabot, and Baird are singled out for praise in 1857 by P. L. Sclater, "Notes on the Birds," 1–3. For biographical information on these ornithologists, see Francis H. Herrick, *Audubon the Naturalist*, 2d ed. (New York: D. Appleton-Century, 1938); Alice Ford, *John James Audubon: A Biography* (New York: Abbeville Press, 1988); D. G. Elliot, "In Memoriam: George Newbold Lawrence," *Auk* 13 (1896): 1–10; J. A. Allen, "Dr. Samuel Cabot," *Auk* 3 (1886): 144, and "Thomas Mayo Brewer," *Bulletin of the Nuttall Ornithological Club*

5 (1880): 102–104; George E. Gifford, Jr., "Thomas Mayo Brewer, M.D. . . . A Blackbird and Duck, Sparrow and Mole," *Harvard Medical Alumni Bulletin* 37, no. 1 (1962): 32–35; Witmer Stone, "John Kirk Townsend," *Dictionary of American Biography* 18: 617–618; and Clark A. Elliott, *Biographical Dictionary of American Science: The Seventeenth through the Nineteenth Centuries* (Westport, Conn: Greenwood Press, 1979).

28. Edward Lurie, *Louis Agassiz: A Life in Science* (Chicago: University of Chicago Press, 1960); Mary P. Winsor, *Reading the Shape of Nature: Comparative Zoology at the Agassiz Museum* (Chicago: University of Chicago Press, 1991); Miller, *Dollars for Research*, 48–97.

29. For example, in preparation for a proposed (but never published) *Natural History of the Fishes of the United States*, in 1853 Agassiz distributed six thousand copies of a circular request for specimens to "amateur naturalists, sportsmen, fishermen, government officials, and professional scientists." Lurie, *Louis Agassiz*, 186–189. A copy of one version of this circular survives in the MCZ Archives: Louis Agassiz, "Directions for Collecting Fishes and Other Objects of Natural History," new ed. (Cambridge, Mass., 1853).

30. Lurie, *Louis Agassiz*, 246.

31. *Annual Report of the Trustees of the Museum of Comparative Zoology, at Harvard College, in Cambridge, together with the Report of the Director, 1866* (Boston: Wright and Potter, State Printers, 1867), 17.

32. This policy is discussed in ibid., 10.

33. Biographical information on Allen, one of the most important American ornithologists in the second half of the nineteenth century, may be found in J. A. Allen, *Autobiographical Notes and a Bibliography of the Scientific Publications* (New York: American Museum of Natural History, 1916); Frank Sulloway, "Joel Asaph Allen," *Dictionary of Scientific Biography* 17:20–23; Frank M. Chapman, "Joel Asaph Allen," *Memoirs of the National Academy of Sciences* 21 (1927): 1–20, and "In Memoriam: Joel Asaph Allen," *Auk* 39 (1922): 1–14.

34. The sale of collections often provided naturalists with income. See, for example, Henry W. Henshaw, "Autobiographical Notes," *Condor* 22 (1920): 56–57; and T. Gilbert Pearson, *Adventures in Bird Protection: An Autobiography* (New York: D. Appleton-Century, 1937), 15–23.

35. Allen, *Autobiographical Notes*, 10.

36. In the mid-to-late 1860s, Allen frequently purchased specimens from C. J. Maynard, a dealer from Newtonville, Massachusetts, who is discussed in more detail below. See, for example, "Catalog of Birds," MCZ Department of Birds, vol. 2, beginning at specimen no. 4326.

37. *Annual Report of the Trustees of the Museum of Comparative Zoology, at Harvard College, in Cambridge, together with the Report of the Director for 1869* (Boston: Wright and Potter, 1870), 15.

38. "Catalog of Birds," Department of Ornithology, MCZ, Cambridge, Mass.

39. Baird's life and extensive contributions to the development of North American natural history are discussed in three biographies: Dean C. Allard, *Spencer Fullerton Baird and the U.S. Fish Commission* (New York: Arno Press, 1978); William Healey Dall, *Spencer Fullerton Baird: A Biography* (Philadelphia: J. P. Lippincott, 1915); and Rivinus and Youssef, *Baird of the Smithsonian*. One of the most useful articles on the development of Baird's extensive collecting network is William Deiss, "Spencer F. Baird and His Collectors," *Journal of the Society for the Bibliography of Natural History* 9 (1980): 635–645, from which the following account is largely based. On the Baird/Agassiz relationship, see Elmer Charles Herber, ed., *Correspondence between Spencer Fullerton Baird and Louis Agassiz: Two Pioneer Naturalists* (Washington, D.C.: Smithsonian Institution Press, 1963).

40. No doubt family connections played a role in Baird's success at recruiting military personnel to collect for him; his father-in-law was Brigadier General Sylvester Churchill, inspector general of the army. Most of the army surgeons discussed in Edgar E. Hume, *Ornithologists of the United States Army Medical Corps: Thirty-Six Biographies* (Baltimore: John Hopkins University Press, 1942), collected for Baird. One Baird collector in particular, the Hungarian John Xantus, has attracted the attention of scholars. See Ann Zwinger, ed., *John Xantus: The Fort Tejon Letters, 1857–1859* (Tucson: University of Arizona Press, 1986), and *Xantus: The Letters of John Xantus to Spencer Fullerton Baird, from San Francisco and Cabo San Lucas, 1859–1861* (Los Angeles: The Castle Press for Dawson's Bookshop, 1986); John Xantus, *Travels in Southern California*, trans. and ed. Theodore Shoenman and Helen Bendele (Detroit: Wayne State University Press, 1976); and, *Letters from North America*, trans. and ed. Theodore Shoenman and Helen Bendele (Detroit: Wayne State University Press, 1975); and Henry Miller Madden, *Xantus, Hungarian Naturalist in the Pioneer West* (Linz, Austria: Oberosterreichischer Landesverlag, 1949).

41. This list is largely derived from Deiss, "Spencer Fullerton Baird," 639. On the relationship between naturalists in collecting networks, see also Keeney, *Botanizers*.

42. Deiss, "Spencer F. Baird," 635.

43. The chronicle of the Division of Birds that follows comes from a manuscript history prepared by Charles W. Richmond in 1906 and now deposited in the Division of Birds, National Museum of Natural History, Records, RU 105, Box 36, SIA. See also Richard C. Banks, "Ornithology at the U.S. National Museum," in *Contributions to the History of North American Ornithology*, ed. William E. Davis, Jr., and Jerome A. Jackson (Cambridge, Mass.: Nuttall Ornithological Club, 1995), 33–54.

44. On the relationship between the Wilkes Expedition collections and the Smithsonian, see Nathan Reingold and Marc Rothenberg, "The Exploring Expedition and the Smithsonian Institution," in *Magnificent Voyagers: The U.S. Exploring Expedition, 1838–1842*, ed. Herman J. Viola and Carolyn Margolis (Washington, D.C.: Smithsonian Institution Press, 1985), 242–253. The western surveys that stocked the National Museum are discussed in William Goetzmann's two major studies, *Army Exploration in the American West, 1803–1863* (New Haven: Yale University Press, 1959), and *Exploration and Empire: The Explorer and the Scientist in the Winning of the American West* (New York: Alfred A. Knopf, 1966).

45. The actual number of specimens in the collection cannot be directly inferred from the catalog. From the beginning the Smithsonian had a policy of distributing duplicate material to other institutions.

46. Boardman has been the subject of an uncritical but useful biography written by his son: Samuel Lane Boardman, *The Naturalist of the Saint Croix: Memoir of George A. Boardman* (Bangor, Maine: Privately printed, 1903). Some of the correspondence used in the construction of that biography survives in the George A. Boardman Papers, RU 7071, SIA.

47. For example, in 1871 George Boardman found a strange duck in a New York game market that he regularly frequented and took it to Washington for identification. Baird identified the specimen as a European crested duck. Boardman, *Naturalist*, 114–115.

48. William Wood to George A. Boardman, 20 September 1864, quoted in ibid., 217.

49. These developments are discussed in much greater detail in chapter 4.

50. Coues, *Field Ornithology*, 27–28. Essentially the same advice appeared in the later editions of Coues's popular guide: *Key to North America Birds*, 5th ed., 12–13.

51. By 1933 J. H. Fleming's collection numbered thirty-three thousand skins. James Peters, "Collections of Birds in the United States and Canada: Study Collections," in *Fifty Years' Progress of American Ornithology, 1883–1933*, ed. Frank M. Chapman and T. S. Palmer (Lancaster, Pa.: American Ornithologists' Union, 1933), 137. Edgar A. Kahn, "Max Minor Peet,

1885–1949," *Surgical Neurology* 5 (1976): 63. At the time John Thayer donated his collection to the Museum of Comparative Zoology at Harvard, it numbered thirty thousand skins and "several thousand" nests and eggs. R[ichard] M. B[arnes], "A Wonderful Gift," *Oologist* 48 (1931): 170–171.

52. The completed returns from this survey of over a thousand Smithsonian correspondents survive in the Spencer F. Baird Papers, RU 7002, Box 64, SIA. Daniel Goldstein provides a fascinating analysis of this community in his article, " 'Yours for Science.' "

53. James L. Peters, "The Bird Collection," in *Notes Concerning the History and Contents of the Museum of Comparative Zoology* (n.p., 1936), 50–52.

54. William Brewster Papers, Museum of Comparative Zoology Archives, Harvard University, Cambridge, Mass (hereafter cited as MCZ Archives). Besides a large body of incoming correspondence, the collection also includes his extensive journals, photographs, and copies of some outgoing letters.

55. The biographical sketch of Bishop that follows comes from Hildegard Howard, "Louis Bennett Bishop, 1865–1950," *Auk* 68 (1951): 440–446; and L. C. Sanford, "Louis B. Bishop: A Reminiscence," manuscript in Louis B. Bishop folder, Archives, Department of Ornithology, American Museum of Natural History, New York (hereafter cited as AMNH).

56. Like Bishop, Sanford became a physician and continued to collect birds. In 1903 the two joined with T. S. Van Dyke to publish *The Water-Fowl Family* (New York: Macmillan, 1903). Sanford was later an important patron of the AMNH bird department. See chapter 8.

57. See, for example, Jonathan Dwight, Jr., "Sequence of Plumage and Moults of the Passerine Birds of New York," *Annals of the New York Academy of Sciences* 13 (1900): 73–360.

58. J. C. Merrill, "In Memoriam: Charles Emil Bendire," *Auk* 15 (1898): 1–6; F. H. Knowlton, "Major Charles E. Bendire," *Osprey* 1 (1897): 87–90; and Hume, *Ornithologists*, 22–37.

59. *A Catalogue of the Oological Collection of J. Parker Norris and J. Parker Norris, Jr.* (Philadelphia: Privately printed, 1894), [i].

60. The collection belonged to Jean Bell of Pennsylvania, who spent over $25,000 amassing it. [Frank H. Lattin,] [Announcement,] *Oologist* 19 (1901): 117. In 1906 Childs published a catalog of his collection, "The Ornithological Collections of John Lewis Childs, Floral Park, N.Y.," *The Warbler*, 2d series, 2 (1906): 66–106.

61. Biographical information on Barnes and his connection with the *Oologist*, which he owned and edited for over thirty years, is found in the last issue of that periodical issued in December 1941: *Oologist* 58 (1941): 148–162.

62. Charles F. Batchelder, *An Account of the Nuttall Ornithological Club, 1873 to 1919* (Cambridge, Mass.: The Club, 1937), 13.

63. Quoted in Stone, "John Cassin," 5, 7.

64. See, for example, Dulles, *A History of Recreation*, 24–26, 43, 70–71. The distinction between utilitarian and ritualistic sport hunting comes from John M. MacKenzie, *The Empire of Nature: Hunting, Conservation, and British Imperialism* (Manchester: Manchester University Press, 1988), 2–3. See also Stuart A. Marks, *Southern Hunting in Black and White: Nature, History, and Ritual in a Carolina Community* (Princeton: Princeton University Press, 1991); and Matt Cartmill, *A View to Death in the Morning: Hunting and Nature through History* (Cambridge: Harvard University Press, 1993).

65. John F. Reiger, *American Sportsmen and the Origins of Conservation* (New York: Winchester Press, 1976), 26.

66. The full title provides more of an indication of the contents: *The Sportsman's Companion; or, An Essay on Shooting: Illustriously Shewing in What Manner to Fire at Birds of Game, in Various Directions and Situations—and Directions to Gentlemen for the Treatment and Breaking Their Own Pointers and Spaniels* (New York: Robertson, Mills and Hicks, 1783).

67. E[lisha] J[arett] Lewis, *Hints to Sportsmen* (Philadelphia: Lea & Blanchard, 1851); and Frank Forester [Henry William Herbert], *The Complete Manual for Young Sportsmen* (New York: Stringer & Townsend, 1856). For a list of similar works, see John C. Phillips, *American Game Birds and Mammals: A Catalogue of Books, 1582 to 1925: Sport, Natural History, and Conservation* (New York: Houghton Mifflin, 1930); and Robert W. Henderson, *Early American Sport: A Checklist of Books by American and Foreign Authors Published in America Prior to 1860, including Sporting Songs*, 3d ed. (London: Associated University Press, 1977).

68. Reiger, *American Sportsmen*, 39–40.

69. For example, for several years the Nuttall Ornithological Club, the first society in North America devoted exclusively to ornithology, published its papers in the *American Sportsman*. See chapter 4, below.

70. Harry B. Bailey indexed the extensive series of bird notes in *Field and Stream*. See his *"Forest and Stream" Bird Notes: An Index and Summary of all the Ornithological Matter Contained in "Forest and Stream," Vols. I–XII* (New York: Forest and Stream, 1881). Frank Chapman recalled that "*Forest and Stream* was not only the leading journal for sportsmen but its high standing made it a recognized means of communication between naturalists. I read it from cover to

cover." *Autobiography of a Bird Lover* (New York: D. Appleton-Century, 1933), 32.

71. Charles Hallock to George A. Boardman, 20 May 1873, George A. Boardman Papers, RU 7071, Box 1, Folder 18, SIA.

72. William Bullock, *A Concise and Easy Method of Preserving Objects of Natural History, Intended for the Use of Sportsmen, Travellers, and Others* (New York: Printed for the Publisher, 1829).

73. Frank M. Chapman, "John G. Bell," *Auk* 7 (1890): 98–99. Chapman described a visit to Bell's establishment in his *Autobiography*, 30–31.

74. On the use of stuffed specimens for decorations, see Batty, *Practical Taxidermy*.

75. Quoted in Chapman, "Bell," 31.

76. William Dutcher, "Notes on Some Rare Birds in the Collection of the Long Island Historical Society," *Auk* 10 (1893): 268–269.

77. What we know about nineteenth-century commercial game hunting comes largely from the literature produced by the turn-of-the-century movement to suppress the practice. See, for example, Frank Graham, Jr., *The Audubon Ark: A History of the National Audubon Society* (New York: Alfred A. Knopf, 1990), 8, 17, 63–65; Reiger, *American Sportsmen*, 26–28, 38, 63, 70–72; and chapters 5 and 6, below. For a contemporary discussion of the many ways birds were used in the nineteenth century, see T. S. Palmer, "A Review of Economic Ornithology in the United States," *Yearbook of Department of Agriculture for 1899* (Washington, D.C.: Government Printing Office, 1900), 267–278. Alan Devoe, "Robins for Sale: Five Cents," *Audubon Magazine* 49 (1947): 108–112, calls attention to a fascinating account of the offerings in New York and Boston game markets: Thomas F. De Voe, *The Market Assistant* (New York: Hurd and Houghton, 1867).

78. The description is from W. E. D. Scott, *The Story of a Bird-Lover* (New York: Macmillan, 1904), 71.

79. E. P. Bicknell, "The Status of the Black Gyrfalcon as a Long Island Bird," *Auk* 41 (1924): 65.

80. Keir B. Sterling, *The Last of the Naturalists: The Career of C. Hart Merriam* (New York: Arno Press, 1974), 14.

81. See chapters 5 and 6.

82. The episode is recounted in great detail in Scott, *Story of a Bird Lover*, 70–77.

83. Spencer Trotter, "Some Old Philadelphia Bird Collectors and Taxidermists," *Cassinia* 18 (1914): 2–3.

84. Frank L. Burns, "John Krider, a Typical Professional Collector, 1838–1878," *Oologist* 50 (1933): 74; and Trotter, "Old Philadelphia Collectors," 5–6. In his later advertisements,

Krider claims to have established his business in 1836. See *Forest and Stream* 20 (8 March 1883): iii.

85. John Krider, *Krider's Sporting Anecdotes, Illustrative of the Habits of Certain Varieties of American Game*, ed. H. Milnor Klapp (Philadelphia: A. Hart, 1853), and *Forty Years Notes of a Field Ornithologist* (Philadelphia: Joseph H. Weston, 1879).

86. See the list in Reiger, *American Sportsmen*, 46–47.

87. One of the earliest examples is Spencer F. Baird's twelve-page pamphlet, *Hints for Preserving Objects of Natural History* (Carlisle, Pa.: Gitt and Hinkley, 1846).

88. The most complete guide to this early literature is Stephen P. Rogers, Mary Ann Schmidt, and Thomas Gütebier, *An Annotated Bibliography on Preparation, Taxidermy, and Collection Management of Vertebrates with Emphasis on Birds*, Carnegie Museum of Natural History, special publication no. 15 (Pittsburgh: Carnegie Museum of Natural History, 1989).

89. Although Maynard's book treated mammals, insects, fishes, reptiles, and a number of invertebrate organisms, its primary emphasis was on birds. C. J. Maynard, *The Naturalist's Guide in Collecting and Preserving Objects of Natural History, with a Complete Catalogue of the Birds of Eastern Massachusetts* (Boston: Fields, Osgood, 1870). Maynard's popular book was subsequently issued in many reprinted and new editions. For a complete list of these and Maynard's numerous other publications, see Charles Foster Batchelder, "Bibliography of the Published Writings of Charles Johnson Maynard (1845–1929)" *Journal of the Society for the Bibliography of Natural History* 2 (1951): 227–251.

90. The sources of biographical information on Maynard are Charles W. Townsend, "Charles Johnson Maynard," *Bulletin of the Boston Society of Natural History* 54 (1939): 3–7; Batchelder, "Bibliography of Charles Johnson Maynard"; Witmer Stone, "Charles Johnson Maynard," *Dictionary of American Biography* 2:457; and Ruth D. Turner, "Charles Johnson Maynard and His Work in Malacology," *Occasional Papers on Mollusks* 2 (1957): 137–152.

91. The precise date that Maynard opened his business is unclear. It is listed in the 1865 edition of *The Naturalists' Directory*.

92. For example, in the mid-1860s Maynard sold many specimens to the MCZ. See, "Catalogue of the Bird Collection," vol. 2, Department of Ornithology, MCZ.

93. Maynard, *Guide*, 12.

94. The only way to achieve lifelike mounts, he argued, was extensive study of the attitudes and activities of birds in nature. Ibid., 36.

95. Ibid., 81–159.

96. Elliott Coues, *Key to North American Birds* (Salem, Mass.: Naturalists' Agency, 1872).

97. The standard biography of Coues is Paul Russell Cutright and Michael J. Brodhead, *Elliott Coues: Naturalist and Frontier Historian* (Urbana: University of Illinois Press, 1981). See also [Frank M. Chapman,] "Elliott Coues," *Bird-Lore* (1900): 3–4; D. G. Elliot, "In Memoriam: Elliott Coues," *Auk* 18 (1901): 1–11; and J. A. Allen, "Biographical Memoir of Elliott Coues," *Biographical Memoirs of National Academy of Sciences* 6 (1909): 397–446.

98. Cutright and Brodhead, *Elliott Coues*, 30.

99. Elliott Coues to Frederic Ward Putnam, 30 April 1868, Frederic Ward Putnam Papers, Harvard University Archives, Cambridge, Mass.

100. Elliott Coues to Spencer Fullerton Baird, 12 July 1869, quoted in Cutright and Brodhead, *Coues*, 127.

101. J. A. A[llen], "Coues's Key to North American Birds, Second Edition," *Auk* 1 (1884): 282.

102. Elliott Coues, *A Check List of North American Birds* (Salem, Mass.: The Naturalists' Agency, 1873).

103. Spencer F. Baird, *Catalogue of North American Birds, Chiefly in the Museum of the Smithsonian Institution* (Washington, D.C.: Smithsonian Institution, 1859). Baird's *Catalogue* was largely based on his Pacific Railroad Survey Report, completed a year previously with the aid of John Cassin and Thomas M. Brewer.

104. Coues, *Field Ornithology*.

105. Ibid., 3.

106. Walter Hoxie to William Brewster, 4 December 1885, William Brewster Papers, MCZ Archives. On the decline of the Bachman's warbler, which is probably now extinct, see Paul B. Hamel, *Bachman's Warbler: A Species in Peril* (Washington, D.C.: Smithsonian Institution Press, 1986).

107. Coues, *Field Ornithology*, 28–30.

108. Elliott Coues, *Key to North American Birds*, 2d ed. (Boston: Estes and Lauriat, 1884).

109. Chapman, *Autobiography*, 31–32.

110. Cutright and Brodhead, *Elliott Coues*, 258.

111. In the early 1870s, Baird and Ridgway had begun printing an identification guide, *Outlines of American Ornithology*, from the stereotype plates of the keys found in their three-volume *History of North American Birds: Land Birds* (1874). Apparently the success of Coues's *Key* and the long delay in publishing the two companion volumes on water birds (which did not appear until 1884) undermined their efforts. Only two copies, made from bound proofs, appear to have survived: one in the Bird Library of the Smithsonian Institution and the other in the

MCZ Archives. The publication is discussed in Harris, "Ridgway," 38–39.

112. My emphasis. Robert Ridgway to Spencer Fullerton Baird, 30 January 1886, Division of Birds, National Museum of Natural History, Records, RU 105, Box 1, vol. 1, 356–359, SIA.

113. Robert Ridgway, *A Manual of North American Birds* (Philadelphia: J. B. Lippincott, 1887). A second revised edition, incorporating the latest additions and changes in nomenclature, appeared in 1896. The two subsequent editions were merely reprints of the second edition. Harris, "Ridgway," 94–95.

114. Robert Ridgway, "Directions for Collecting Birds," United States National Museum, Bulletin no. 39, Part A (Washington, D.C.: Government Printing Office, 1891).

115. William T. Hornaday, *Taxidermy and Zoological Collecting: A Complete Handbook for the Amateur Taxidermist, Collector, Osteologist, Museum-Builder, Sportsman, and Traveller* (New York: Charles Scribner's Sons, 1891).

116. Ibid., i, 2.

117. See chapters 5 and 6.

118. The first and second editions of Oliver Davie's popular book were misleadingly titled *An Egg Check List of North American Birds* (Columbus: Hann & Adair, 1885) and *Egg Check List and Key to the Nests and Eggs of North American Birds* (Columbus: Hann & Adair, 1886). By the time of the greatly enlarged third edition, Davie had settled on the more appropriate *Nest and Eggs of North American Birds* (Columbus: Hann & Adair, 1889), which was published in two subsequent editions.

Lattin's *The Oologists' Hand-Book* (Rochester, N.Y.: John P. Smith, 1885) was largely a listing of the values of North American eggs, but it also contained instructions for collecting, preparing, displaying, and exchanging eggs.

119. His letterhead in 1881 listed him as a dealer in "stuffed birds, minerals, shells, grasses, artificial eyes for birds and animals, glass shades, naturalists' and taxidermists' supplies, and standard books on natural history." Oliver Davie to William Brewster, 19 May 1881, Brewster Papers, MCZ Archives. In addition to the several editions of his *Nests and Eggs of North American Birds*, Davie also published an illustrated guide to collecting and preserving animals, *Methods in the Art of Taxidermy* (Columbus: Hann & Adair, 1894). A biographical sketch in William Coyle, ed., *Ohio Authors and Their Books* (Cleveland: World Publishing Co., 1962), 158, mentions that as a boy Oliver Davie opened a shop dealing in "Indian relics, mineral specimens, and curios" above his father's store in Columbus, Ohio.

120. Oliver Davie to William Brewster, 26 August 1889, William Brewster Papers, MCZ Archives.

121. On Lattin and his business, see Barrow, "Birds and Boundaries," 94–101.

122. In the 1880s Lattin sold these for two cents each and $1.50 per hundred.

123. These periodicals are discussed in more detail in chapter 1.

124. *Young Oologist* 1 (1884): 3–5, 19–20.

125. Fred J. Davis, "Methods of Climbing for Nests," *Oologist* 3 (1878): 93–94; G. Sirrom [i.e., Morris Gibbs], "Courtesy and Business in Exchanging," *Oologist* 10 (1893): 136–138; W. G. F., "Auxiliary Gun Barrels for Collecting Bird Specimens," *Wilson Bulletin* 39 (1927): 219–222; J. A. Singley, "Instructions for Collecting and Preserving Eggs," *Ornithologists' and Oologists' Semi-Annual* 1 (1889): 1–12, an expanded version of an earlier article of the same title first printed in *Bay State Oologist* 1 (1880): 20–21, 28–29, 36–37; Herbert Massey, "Arrangement of an Oological Collection," *Condor* 10 (1908): 223–225; Frank Stephens, "About Collecting Chests," *Condor* 8 (1906): 112–114; and Loye Holmes Miller, "A Convenient Collecting Gun," *Condor* 17 (1915): 226–228.

126. Frank B. Webster, "Practical Taxidermy," *Ornithologist and Oologist* 10 (1885): 137.

127. C. A. H., "Notes for Collectors," *Oologist* 5 (1888): 126.

128. "The Object of Collecting," *Oologist* 2 (1876–1877): 52. See also Louis A. Zerega, "The Great American Egg-Hog," *Ornithologist and Oologist* 7 (1882): 183, in which the author asserts that "nine men out of ten prefer to collect their own specimens when possible."

129. For example, an anonymous story in the *Young Oologist* 1 (1884): 67, "Egg-Nesting," described the collecting experiences of William C. Flint, a lawyer from San Francisco who found collecting a "pleasing outdoor recreation" and a "means of restoring his shattered health." The argument that collecting skins and eggs was important for the training of ornithologists, even if they did observational studies, is discussed in chapter 6.

130. Henry W. Henshaw to William Brewster, 14 September 1901, William Brewster Papers, MCZ Archives. Robert Stebbins speaks of a similar reaction in a community of amateur archaeologists in *Amateurs*, 131–132.

131. Walter Hoxie, "On Making Exchanges," *Ornithologist and Oologist* 13 (1888): 54–55.

132. Besides the various editions of *The Naturalists' Directory*, mentioned in chapter 1, there were also several more specialized listings of bird and egg collectors: S. L. Willard, comp., *A Directory of the Ornithologists of the United States* (Utica, N.Y.: Office of the Oologist, 1877); H. W. Davis and Geo. C. Baker, comps., *The Oologist Directory* (Columbus: Hann &

Adair, 1885); Letson Balliet, comp., *American Naturalist's Directory* (Garland, Maine: H. Stanton Sawyer, 1890).

133. See, for example, Ora Knight to J. A. Allen, 1 October and 12 October 1908, American Ornithologists' Union, Records, RU 7440, SIA, and William Brewster, "An Ornithological Swindler," *Auk* 1 (1884): 295–297.

134. Manly Hardy charged Charles K. Worthen, a dealer from Warsaw, Illinois, with this practice in a letter to William Brewster, 7 September 1885, William Brewster Papers, MCZ Archives.

135. See chapter 4, below.

136. See, for example, J. P. Norris, "Instructions for Collecting Birds' Eggs," *Young Oologist* 1 (1884): 3–4.

137. This was the accusation against A. H. Verrill, the son of Addison E. Verrill, in [Henry R. Taylor,] [Announcement,] *Nidiologist* 3 (1896): 80.

138. See, for example, *Oologist* 9 (1892): 16; R. W. Shufeldt, "Raineism," *Nidologist* 3 (1896): 146–148; and W. H. Winkley, "Correspondence," *The Hawkeye Ornithologist and Oologist* 2 (1889): 58–60.

139. The standard biographies of this important figure in American ornithological circles and author of two volumes on the *Life Histories of North America Birds* are James C. Merrill, "In Memoriam: Charles Emil Bendire," *Auk* 15 (1898): 1–6; F. H. Knowlton, "Major Charles E. Bendire," *Osprey* 1 (1897): 87–90; and Edgar E. Hume, "Charles E. Bendire (1836–1897): 22–37.

140. The episode is told in Bendire, *Life Histories*, 231–232. I thank John Hendrickson for bringing the story to my attention.

141. For example, in his frequently reprinted collecting guide, Maynard warned that "Too much caution cannot be used in handling a loaded gun, especially by a professional collector, who may spend up to two thirds of his time with a gun in his hand." Maynard, *Naturalists' Guide*, 8. See also a similar warning in Coues, *Field Ornithology*, 12–13.

142. Cairns, who was an associate member of the AOU, was the subject of a brief obituary published as J. A. Allen, "John S. Cairns," *Auk* 12 (1895): 315. Additional information on Cairns may be found in his correspondence with William Brewster in the William Brewster Papers, MCZ Archives.

143. See J. A. Allen, "J. H. Batty," *Auk* 23 (1906): 356–357. More details on the life and career of Batty are provided in chapter 5, below.

144. Batty's difficulties in the field collecting for the AMNH are detailed in a series of letters to J. A. Allen in the Joseph Batty Folder, Archives, Department of Ornithology, AMNH.

145. Allen, "Batty," 357.

146. The episode is recounted in R[ichard] M. B[arnes], "Richard C. Harlow," *Oologist* 38 (1921): 42.

147. Details surrounding Crispin's death are found in "William B. Crispin," *Oologist* 30 (1913): 90; R. P. Sharples, "Wm. B. Crispin Killed by a Fall," *Oologist* 30 (1913): 90–91.

148. The story of Birtwell's demise is provided in Olivia Birtwell, "Francis J. Birtwell," *Auk* 27 (1910): 413–414; "Death of Francis Joseph Birtwell," *Osprey* 5 (1901): 104; and "General Notes and News," *Condor* 3 (1901): 107.

149. Biographical information on Cahoon may be found in F[rank] B[lake] W[ebster], "Horrible Fate," *Ornithologist and Oologist* 16 (1891): 73–75; and J. A. Allen, "John C. Cahoon," *Auk* 8 (1891): 320–321.

150. Article from *St. John's Evening Telegraph*, July 1889, reproduced in *Ornithologist and Oologist* 15 (1890): 120–121.

151. W[ebster], "Horrible Fate," 75.

152. The important role of women in botany is discussed in Emanuel D. Rudolph, "Women in Nineteenth-Century American Botany: A Generally Unrecognized Constituency," *American Journal of Botany* 69 (1982): 1346–1355, and "Women Who Studied Plants in the Pre-Twentieth Century United States and Canada," *Taxon* 39 (1990): 151–205; and Keeney, *Botanizers*. On women in entomology, see Sorensen, *Brethren of the Net*, 188–193, 257–258. On women naturalists more generally, see Marcia Myers Bonta, *Women in the Field: America's Pioneering Women Naturalists* (College Station: Texas A & M University Press, 1991). On women as marginalized scientists, see Margaret Rossiter, *Women Scientists in America: Struggles and Strategies* (Baltimore: Johns Hopkins University Press, 1982); and Sally G. Kohlstedt, "In from the Periphery: American Women in Science, 1830–1880," *Signs: Journal of Women and Culture and Society* 4 (1978): 81–96.

153. Bonta, *Women in the Field*, 181. Bonta's book also includes a biographical sketch of Maxwell (pp. 30–41) based on Maxine Benson, *Martha Maxwell, Rocky Mountain Naturalist* (Lincoln: University of Nebraska Press, 1986).

154. Elizabeth Keeney addresses the many challenges women botanists faced in *Botanizers*, 69–82.

155. Nell Harrison, "From a Woman's Standpoint," *Proceedings of the Nebraska Ornithologist' Union* 3 (Dec. 1902): 41. Thirty years earlier the nature writer Wilson Flagg also noted this difficulty: "Women cannot conveniently become hunters or anglers, nor can they without some eccentricity of conduct follow birds and quadrupeds to the woods." Quoted in Keeney, *Botanizers*, 72.

156. At about the same time Harrison was writing, Margaret Morse Nice's parents were strongly discouraging her from tramping in the woods with a rifle for fear that it was dangerous and that she would be branded "an eccentric." Margaret Morse Nice, *Research Is a Passion with Me: The Autobiography of Margaret Morse Nice*, ed. Doris H. Speirs (Toronto: Consolidated Amethyst Communications, 1979), 19–20.

157. Deborah Jean Warner, *Graceanna Lewis: Scientist and Humanitarian* (Washington, D.C.: Smithsonian Institution Press, 1979). See also Marcia Bonta's biographical sketch, which is largely based on Warner, in *Women in the Field*, 18–29.

158. Bonta, *Women in the Field*, 21.

159. See Elliott Coues's variously titled reviews of Jones and Schulze, *Nests and Eggs of the Birds of Ohio*, *Bulletin of the Nuttall Ornithological Club* 4 (1879): 52, 228; 5 (1880): 39; 7 (1882): 45, 112; 8 (1883): 112, 166; *Auk* 2 (1885): 289; 3 (1886): 406. See also J. A. Allen's review of the finished production: "Conclusion of the Great Work on the Nests and Eggs of the Birds of Ohio," *Auk* 4 (1887): 150–152. On the history of this project, see Edward Wessen, "Jones' Nests and Eggs of the Birds of Ohio," *Papers of the Bibliographical Society of America* 47 (1953): 218–230.

160. Her death was lamented by Elliott Coues in "Genevieve E. Jones," *Bulletin of the Nuttall Ornithological Club* 4 (1879): 228.

161. The title page issued with the final part of the work read: *Illustrations of the Nests and Eggs of the Birds of Ohio. Illustrations by Mrs. N. E. Jones, with Text by Howard Jones, A.M., M.D.* (Circleville, Ohio, 1886). On page vii of the preface, Howard Jones indicated that the plates were "in nearly every instance" based on nests collected for the purpose by himself.

162. The incident is related in Chapman, *Autobiography* 160–163.

CHAPTER THREE

1. On the history of the AOU, see Cutright and Brodhead, *Elliott Coues*; and Keir Sterling and Marianne G. Ainley, "A Centennial History of the American Ornithologists' Union, 1883–1983," ms. Both works have been crucial to the chapter that follows. See also J. A. Allen, *The American Ornithologists' Union: A Seven Years' Retrospective* (New York: AOU, 1891); T. S. Palmer, "A Brief History of the American Ornithologists' Union," in *Fifty Years' Progress of American Ornithology, 1883–1933*, ed. Frank M. Chapman and T. S. Palmer (Lancaster, Pa.: American Ornithologists' Union, 1933), 7–27; and Peter F. Cannell, "An Annotated Bibliography of the Founding of the American Ornitholo-

gists' Union," *American Birds* 37 (July–August 1983): 355–357.

2. "The American Ornithologists' Union," *Bulletin of the Nuttall Ornithological Club* 8 (1883): 225.

3. Although dated, Bates, *Scientific Societies in the United States*, remains useful. More focused are two recent papers: Toby A. Appel, "The Mapping of Biology: Disciplinary Societies in the Biological Sciences," paper delivered to the annual meeting of the History of Science Society, October 1987, and "Organizing Biology: The American Society of Naturalists and Its 'Affiliated Societies,' 1883–1923," in *The American Development of Biology*, ed. Ronald Rainger, et al. (Philadelphia: University of Pennsylvania Press, 1988), 87–120.

4. Appel, "Organizing Biology," 103–106; and Keith R. Benson and C. Edward Quinn, "The American Society of Zoologists, 1889–1989: A Century of Integrating the Biological Sciences," *American Zoologist* 30 (1990): 353–396.

5. Herman K. Skolnick and Kenneth M. Reese, eds., *A Century of Chemistry: The Role of Chemists and the American Chemical Society* (Washington, D.C.: American Chemical Society, 1976).

6. The AOU campaign for nomenclatural reform is discussed in the next chapter.

7. Frank M. Chapman to Lynds Jones, 18 December 1914, Archives, Department of Ornithology, AMNH.

8. On the history of the Nuttall Ornithological Club, see Batchelder, *Account*; and William E. Davis, Jr., *History of the Nuttall Ornithological Club, 1873–1986* (Cambridge, Mass.: The Club, 1987). The archives of the Nuttall Ornithological Club are located in the Bird Department, MCZ).

9. Jeannette E. Graustein, *Thomas Nuttall, Naturalist: Explorations in America, 1808–1841* (Cambridge: Harvard University Press, 1967).

10. Quoted from the copy of the Nuttall Ornithological Club Constitution, adopted 14 December 1873, bound with the "Nuttall Ornithological Club, Records of Meetings, Vol. 1," Nuttall Ornithological Club Archives (hereafter cited as NOC Archives), Bird Department, MCZ.

11. Davis, *History*, 5, 89–92.

12. Charles J. Maynard to J. A. Allen, 30 July 1876, Archives, Department of Ornithology, AMNH.

13. Several years earlier, Maynard and another Nuttall Club member, Ruthven Deane, had tried to launch their own periodical, the *American Ornithologist*. They got as far as issuing a prospectus in the *American Sportsman*, but the periodical was never published. C. J. Maynard to J. A. Allen, 30 July 1876, Archives, Department of Ornithology, AMNH.

14. See the accounts in Batchelder, *Account*,

28–30, and Davis, *History*, 13. Both authors rely almost entirely on the cryptic minutes kept of the meetings of 6, 13, 20, 23, and 27 May 1876; 8, 15, and 22, July 1876; and 5 August 1876 in "Records of Meetings," vol. 1, NOC Archives, Bird Department, MCZ.

15. The position was largely honorary and intended to bring prestige to the new venture. On Baird's acceptance of the position, see Spencer F. Baird to J. A. Allen, 23 May 1876, Archives, Department of Ornithology, AMNH.

16. Maynard's position is detailed in a lengthy letter written to J. A. Allen, 30 July 1876, Archives, Department of Ornithology, AMNH.

17. Batchelder, *Account*, 45.

18. The best treatment of the social and ecological consequences the English sparrow's introduction into North America is Robin Doughty, "The English Sparrow in the American Landscape: A Paradox in Nineteenth Century Wildlife Conservation," Oxford University, School of Geography, Research Papers 19 (Oxford: Oxford Publishing Co., 1978). See also Michael J. Brodhead, "Elliott Coues and the Sparrow War," *New England Quarterly* 44 (1971): 420–432.

19. Doughty, "English Sparrow," 12.

20. Quoted in Thomas Gentry, *The House Sparrow at Home and Abroad* (Philadelphia: Claxton, Remsen, and Haffelfinger, 1878), 83.

21. Coues's claim appears on p. 190 of his extensive annotated bibliography of the sparrow question: "On the Present Status of Passer Domesticus in America, with Special Reference to the Western States and Territories," Department of the Interior, United States Geological and Geographical Survey, *Bulletin* 5, no. 2 (1879): 175–193.

22. Roosevelt had entered Harvard with the hope of becoming a professional naturalist. After discovering that the biological curriculum at Harvard was devoid of the field studies he so loved, he abandoned his plans. See Paul Cutright, *Theodore Roosevelt: The Making of a Conservationist* (Urbana: University of Illinois Press, 1985), 97–133.

23. Batchelder, *Account*, 38.

24. See, for example, "Sparrows—The Nuttall Ornithological Club Decides against Them," *Boston Daily Advertiser*, 23 February 1878; C. E. H[amlin], "The English Sparrows," *The [Bath, Maine] Times*, 26 February 1878; and "Sparrows Brought to Judgment—Discussion of the Nuttall Ornithological Club upon the Merits and Demerits of the English Sparrow in the United States," *The Country* 1 (23 February 1878): 245–246.

25. Munchausen, "The Sparrows," *Boston Evening Transcript*, 27 February 1878, which states, "There seems to be a growing impression that one or two of the boys of the Nuttall Club

rather overloaded their fowling pieces in their war on the sparrow."

26. J. A. Allen to Thomas M. Brewer, 19 March 1878, Archives, Department of Ornithology, AMNH.

27. "History Repeating Itself," *Boston Journal*, 14 March 1878, reproduced in Batchelder, *Account*, 39–40.

28. J. A. Allen to William Brewster, 17 March 1878, William Brewster Papers, MCZ Archives.

29. J. A. Allen, "The Nuttall Ornithological Club," letter to the editor of *Boston Evening Transcript*, 21 March 1878, 4. See also a similar letter in the *Boston Journal*, 19 March 1878.

30. William Brewster, "The Nuttall Ornithological Club of Cambridge," *Boston Daily Advertiser*, 20 March 1878.

31. Davis, *History*, 15.

32. William Brewster to Charles F. Batchelder, 10 February 1883, quoted in Batchelder, *Account*, 46.

33. The issue of the AOU and nomenclatural reform is discussed in detail in chapter 4.

34. Elliott Coues, "Compliments of the Season," *Bulletin of the Nuttall Ornithological Club* 8 (1883): 1–6, on 5–6.

35. Elliott Coues to J. A. Allen, 19 and 30 March 1883, manuscript copies of original from the Blacker-Wood Library, McGill University (hereafter cited as B-W), American Ornithologists' Union, Records (hereafter cited as AOU Records), RU 7150, Box 1, Folder 1, SIA.

36. See Elliott Coues to J. A. Allen, 3 May 1883 and 24 May 1884, manuscript copy of originals in B-W, ibid. Elliott Coues to J. A. Allen, 29 April 1883, Brewster Papers, MCZ Archives.

37. Elliott Coues to William Brewster, 1 and 12 June 1883, William Brewster Papers, MCZ Archives.

38. Elliott Coues to J. A. Allen, 8 June 1883, manuscript copy of original in B-W, AOU Records, RU 7150, Box 1, Folder 1, SIA.

39. Early in the series of extensive deliberations that led to the creation of the AOU, Coues had suggested that they might want to invite Henry A. Ward, of Ward's Natural Science Establishment, and "Webster, Halliday and Lucas," three of the taxidermists who had trained under Ward. However, the final invitation list included neither these nor any other commercial naturalists. Elliott Coues to J. A. Allen, 4 and 13 June 1883, manuscript copies of originals in ibid.

40. Ibid.

41. Elliott Coues to J. A. Allen, 5 June 1883, manuscript copy of original in B-W, ibid.

42. J. A. Allen, Elliott Coues, and William Brewster to———(printed invitation), 1 August 1883, reproduced in Cutright and Brodhead, *Elliott Coues*, 267; *Bulletin of the Nuttall Ornitho-*

logical Club 8 (1883): 221; and *Forest and Stream* 21 (1883): 45.

43. Several responses to the invitation are found in the Joel Asaph Allen Papers, 67/125z, Bancroft Library, University of California, Berkeley (hereafter cited as J. A. Allen Papers, Bancroft).

44. AOU Meeting Minutes, 26 September 1883, AOU Records, RU 7150, Box 5, vol. 1, p. 28, SIA. Baird's formal letter accepting membership is also in the AOU Records: Spencer F. Baird to Clinton Hart Merriam, 7 November 1883, Box 1, Folder 7. Brewster reported to Allen on the success of the meeting in William Brewster to J. A. Allen, 27 September 1883, J. A. Allen Papers, Bancroft.

45. Apparently Brewster expected to be elected chair of the meeting. Brewster's proposed agenda survives in the AOU archives with the notation "Moved, seconded, & put to vote. Exit W.B." AOU Records, RU 7150, Box 1, Folder 12, SIA.

46. See the announcement in *Bulletin of the Nuttall Ornithological Club* 8 (1883): 223. Corresponding membership was quickly restricted to individuals living outside the United States and Canada, leaving, in effect, two membership categories for North Americans. Honorary memberships were established in 1887, when the foreign membership category was dropped.

47. AOU Meeting Minutes, 27 September 1883, AOU Records, RU 7150, Box 5, vol. 1, SIA.

48. J. B. Holder of the AMNH chaired the committee, which gathered information on the sparrow through a widely circulated letter. The final report of the Sparrow Committee is in AOU Records, ibid. The committee's findings were also published in *Forest and Stream* 25 (1885): 24–25.

49. See, Elliott Coues to J. A. Allen, 30 March 1883, manuscript copy of original in B-W, AOU Records, RU 7150, Box 1, Folder 1, SIA.

50. AOU Council Minutes, 28 September 1883, AOU Records, RU 7150, Box 3, vol. 1, SIA. The offer became "official" at the 1 October 1883 meeting of the Nuttall Ornithological Club in which members offered their "goodwill and subscription list" to the AOU. See "Records of Meetings," vol. 2, NOC Archives, Bird Department, MCZ.

51. The other contenders were *American Ornithologist* and *Bulletin of the American Ornithologists' Union*.

52. On the history of the British Ornithologists' Union, see Allen, *Naturalist in Britain*; and P. L. Sclater, "A Short History of the British Ornithologists' Union," *Ibis*, series 9, vol. 2 (1908): Jubilee Supplement, 19–69.

53. AOU Council Minutes, 13 December 1883, AOU Records, RU 7150, Box 3, vol. 1, SIA. Several weeks earlier Chamberlain had agreed to serve as associate editor. He made it clear that he considered himself an "amateur" and intended to represent the interests of amateurs both on the council and as an associate editor. See J. A. Allen to Montague Chamberlain, 18 and 23 November, 3 and 5 December, 1883, J. A. Allen Papers, Bancroft.

54. The announcement that invitations had been mailed appeared in *Forest and Stream, Nation,* and *Canadian Naturalist.* On complaints about the private invitations, see, for example, W. A. Stearns to J. A. Allen, 21 September 1883, J. A. Allen Papers, Bancroft; and C. J. Maynard to C. Hart Merriam, 20 September 1883, Clinton Hart Merriam Papers, 83/129c, Bancroft Library, University of California, Berkeley (hereafter cited as C. Hart Merriam Papers, Bancroft).

55. An appreciative biographical sketch of Wade is W. Otto Emerson, "Joseph Marshall Wade: An Appreciation," *Oologist* 28 (1911): 158–161. On his connection to the *Ornithologist and Oologist* and its predecessor, the *Oologist,* see Frank A. Bates, "Reminiscences," *Ornithologist and Oologist* 16 (1891): 177–179; and [Samuel L. Willard], "The Oologist: Its History from the Commencement," *Ornithologist and Oologist* 6 (1881): 1–3.

56. C. Hart Merriam to J. M. Wade, 13 September 1883, William Brewster Papers, MCZ Archives.

57. C. Hart Merriam to William Brewster, 20 September 1883, ibid.

58. J[oseph] M. Wade, "Plain English," *Ornithologist and Oologist* 8 (1883): 85, suppressed editorial appended to William Brewster's copy of *Ornithologist and Oologist* now in the MCZ library.

59. Ibid.

60. Witmer Stone, "In Memoriam—John Hall Sage," *Auk* 43 (1926): 9.

61. Montague Chamberlain to William Brewster, 11 October 1883, William Brewster Papers, MCZ Archives.

62. William Brewster to [J. A.] A[llen], note on letter from Montague Chamberlain to William Brewster, ibid.

63. Montague Chamberlain to William Brewster, 22 October 1883, ibid. On Chamberlain's attempts to buy the *Ornithologist and Oologist,* see also Montague Chamberlain to C. Hart Merriam, 25 October and 8 November 1883, C. Hart Merriam Papers, Bancroft.

64. Montague Chamberlain to William Brewster, 12 November 1883, William Brewster Papers, MCZ Archives.

65. My italics. AOU Meeting Minutes, 28

September 1883, AOU Records, RU 7150, Box 5, vol. 1, p. 49, SIA.

66. Wade declined the invitation to join the organization he had criticized. Joseph M. Wade to C. Hart Merriam, 9 December 1883, AOU Records, RU 7150, Box 7, Folder 8, SIA.

67. AOU Council Minutes, 28 September 1883, AOU Records, RU 7150, Box 3, vol. 1, pp. 13–15, SIA.

68. See, for example, Montague Chamberlain to William Brewster, 29 July 1884, William Brewster Papers, MCZ Archives, in which Chamberlain claims that "All the amateurs that I have heard from, who have seen the magazine [the *Auk*], think it is too scientific tho' some have subscribed to it." See also, J. C. Know, "Some Suggestions," *Auk* 20 (1903): 234, which complains that too much of *Auk* was taken up with "technical and local faunal articles." See also the last section of this chapter.

69. Montague Chamberlain to C. Hart Merriam, 22 July 1884, C. Hart Merriam Papers, Bancroft.

70. Ainley, "Contribution of the Amateur," 66. Earlier Frank Chapman pointed out that in 1883 the ornithologists W. E. D. Scott and Ernest F. Lorquin also had paid curatorships (at Princeton University and the California Academy of Sciences, respectively), though neither was an active AOU member during this period. See Chapman, "Collections of Birds," 143.

71. Merriam's life has been the subject of a full-length biographical study that stresses his contribution to field of mammalogy and to the work of what became the Bureau of the Biological Survey: Sterling, *Last of the Naturalists,* which was also published in a revised edition in 1977. The biographical information that follows comes largely from pp. 6–77 of that book. See also Elizabeth Noble Shor, "Clinton Hart Merriam," *Dictionary of Scientific Biography* 9:313–314; Wilfred H. Osgood, "Biographical Memoir of Clinton Hart Merriam," *Biographical Memoirs of the National Academy of Sciences* 24 (1944): 1–57; and T. S. Palmer, "In Memoriam: Clinton Hart Merriam," *Auk* 71 (1954): 130–136.

72. On John Wallace and his role in ornithology, see chapter 2, above.

73. A. K. Fisher describes the exploits of the young medical students in an unpublished biographical fragment in A. K. Fisher Papers, Box 40, Library of Congress, Washington, D.C.

74. On physicians as naturalists, see the testimony of Dr. W. S. Strode, "A Difficult Climb after a Red-Tailed Hawk's Nest," *Oologist* 3 (1886): 34–35. See also William Wood to George Boardman, 29 November 1872, George A. Boardman Papers, RU 7071, Box 1, Folder 37, SIA.

75. The two offices were divided in 1885,

after Merriam resigned as treasurer. He held the post of secretary until 1889.

76. In establishing his extensive migration monitoring network, Merriam was following several precedents. The most notable of these were the networks organized by the Allgemeine Deutsche Ornithologische Gesellschaft, Brunswick, in 1875, by J. A. Harvie-Brown and John Cordeaux in Great Britain in 1879, and by W. W. Cooke in the United States in 1881. See Allen, *Naturalist in Britain*, 196–201; Stresemann, *Ornithology from Aristotle to the Present*, 334–335; and T. S. Palmer, "In Memoriam: Wells Woodbridge Cooke," *Auk* 39 (1917): 122–123.

77. C. Hart Merriam, "American Ornithologists' Union: Bird Migration," circular issued in 1884, p. 1, from copy bound with AOU Meeting Minutes, 2 October 1884, AOU Records, RU 7150, Box 5, vol. 1, following p. 101, SIA Archives. A copy of the circular was also published in the *Auk* 1 (1884): 71–76.

78. Ibid.

79. "Second Annual Report of the American Ornithologists' Union," *Auk* 1 (1884): 377–378. See also the more extensive manuscript version of that report in the AOU Meeting Minutes, 2 October 1884, AOU Records, RU 7150, Box 5, vol. 1, pp. 101–111, SIA.

80. Sterling, *Last of the Naturalists*, 56, 61.

81. Ibid., 109.

82. AOU Meeting Minutes, 2 October 1884, AOU Records, RU 7150, Box 5, vol. 1, p. 109, SIA.

83. Sterling, *Last of the Naturalists*, 110–111.

84. AOU Meeting Minutes, 17 November 1885, AOU Records, RU 7150, Box 5, vol. 1, p. 159, SIA.

85. Palmer, "A Review of Economic Ornithology," 259–292; W. L. McAtee, "Economic Ornithology," in *Fifty Years' Progress in American Ornithology, 1833–1933*, ed. Frank M. Chapman and T. S. Palmer (Lancaster, Pa.: American Ornithologists' Union, 1933), 111–129; and Matthew D. Evenden, "The Laborers of Nature: Economic Ornithology and the Role of Birds as Agents of Biological Control in North American Agriculture, ca. 1880–1930," *Forest and Conservation History* 39 (1995): 172–183.

86. A copy of the memorial was published as [C. Hart Merriam], "Memorial to Congress," *Ornis* 1 (1885): 60–67.

87. Merriam indicated that, if properly funded, analysis of migration data would be the first in a long line of research on the "interrelation of birds and agriculture" that he hoped to complete. Ibid., 63.

88. Ibid., 66.

89. *Congressional Record*, vol. 16, part 1, 48th Congress, 2d session (1884–1885), 539, 540.

90. AOU Council Minutes, 21 April 1885,

AOU Records, RU 7150, Box 3, vol. 1, pp. 71–77, SIA.

91. A portion of the letter is reproduced in *Congressional Record*, vol. 16, part 3, 48th Congress, 2d session (1885), 1939.

92. Sterling, *Last of the Naturalists*, 100.

93. C. Hart Merriam to J. A. Allen, 8 January 1884 [i.e., 1885], Archives, Department of Ornithology, AMNH. He repeated his claim in C. Hart Merriam to C. V. Riley, 2 April 1885, C. Hart Merriam Papers, Bancroft.

94. C. V. Riley to B[i.e., J]. A. Allen, 10 March 1885, AOU Records, RU 7440, SIA.

95. Sterling, *Last of the Naturalists*, 101. On the terms of Merriam's acceptance and his difficult negotiations with his new boss, see C. Hart Merriam to C. V. Riley, 4, 12, and 18 June 1885, C. Hart Merriam Papers, Bancroft.

96. AOU Council Minutes, 21 April 1885, AOU Records, RU 7150, Box 3, vol. 1, pp. 71–77, SIA.

97. Jenks Cameron, *Bureau of the Biological Survey: Its History, Activities and Organization* (Baltimore: Johns Hopkins University Press, 1929), 22–23. On the early history of the Bureau of the Biological Survey, see Keir B. Sterling, "Builders of the U.S. Biological Survey, 1885–1930," *Journal of Forest History* 33 (1989): 180–187; Henry Wetherbee Henshaw, "The Policemen of the Air: An Account of the Biological Survey of the Department of Agriculture," *National Geographic Magazine* 19 (1908): 79–118; and the annual *Reports of the Chief of the Biological Survey*.

98. Cameron, *Biological Survey*, 24. This material was published as Walter B. Barrows, *The English Sparrow (Passer Domesticus) in North America, Especially in Its Relations to Agriculture*, U.S. Department of Agriculture, Division of Economic Ornithology and Mammalogy, Bulletin no. 1 (Washington, D.C: Government Printing Office, 1889).

99. Cameron, *Biological Survey*, 24–32.

100. Sclater, "Notes on the Birds."

101. On Coues's European trip, see Cutright and Brodhead, *Elliott Coues*, 277–291.

102. Elliott Coues to J. A. Allen, date illegible, AOU Records, RU 440, Box 1, SIA.

103. On the development of ideas about type specimens, see Paul Farber, "The Type-Concept during the First Half of the Nineteenth Century," *Journal of the History of Biology* 9 (1976): 93–119. Sclater's remarks and the resulting discussion are in the AOU Meeting Minutes, 1 October 1884, AOU Records, RU 7150, Box 5, vol. 1, pp. 91–99, SIA.

104. Sclater's remarks were also incorporated into a letter written to Merriam at his request after the British ornithologist had returned to England: Philip Lutley Sclater to the Secretary of

the American Ornithologists' Union, 18 December 1884, AOU Records, RU 7150, Box 1, Folder 33, SIA.

105. AOU Council Minutes, 2 October 1884, AOU Records, RU 7150, Box 3, vol. 1, pp. 61–63, SIA.

106. On Alexander Agassiz's role in financing and running the MCZ, see G. R. Agassiz, *Letters and Recollections of Alexander Agassiz, with a Sketch of His Life and Work* (Boston: Houghton Mifflin, 1913); and Winsor, *Reading the Shape of Nature,* 134–163 and passim.

107. See Henry W. Henshaw to J. A. Allen, 24 May 1884 and 12 January 1885, Archives, Department of Ornithology, AMNH.

108. Ronald Rainger, *An Agenda for Antiquity: Henry Fairfield Osborn and Vertebrate Paleontology at the American Museum of Natural History, 1890–1935* (Tuscaloosa: University of Alabama Press, 1991), 57–61.

109. On the history of the bird and mammal department, see Allen, *Autobiographical Notes,* 33–39; Frank M. Chapman, "The Department of Birds, American Museum: Its History and Aims," *Natural History* 22 (1922): 307–318; and Wesley E. Lanyon, "Ornithology at the American Museum of Natural History," in *Contributions to the History of North American Ornithology,* ed. William E. Davis, Jr., and Jerome A. Jackson (Cambridge, Mass.: Nuttall Ornithological Club, 1995), 113–144.

110. See, for example, his first report as curator of the department of ornithology and mammalogy at the AMNH: *Annual Report of the Trustees for the Year 1885* (New York: American Museum of Natural History, 1886), 9–12.

111. Allen, *Autobiographical Notes,* 35.

112. On scientific societies as gentlemen's organizations, see Jack Morrell and Arnold Thackray, *Gentlemen of Science: Early Years of the British Association for the Advancement of Science* (Oxford: Clarendon Press, 1981).

113. Elliott Coues to William Brewster, 28 September and 31 October 1897, William Brewster Papers, MCZ Archives.

114. Biographical information on Shufeldt may be found in Hume, *Ornithologists,* 390–412; Kahman Lambrecht, "In Memoriam: Robert Wilson Shufeldt, 1850–1934," *Auk* 52 (1935): 359–361; R. W. Shufeldt, "Complete List of My Published Writings, with Brief Biographical Notes," *Medical Review of Reviews* 26 (1920): 17–24, 70–75, 123–130, 200–206, 251–257, 314–320, 368–377, 437–447, and 495–498; and "Robert Wilson Shufeldt," *National Cyclopedia of American Biography* 6:242–244 (New York: James T. White, 1896).

115. The account of the meeting of Shufeldt and the Audubons is from Shufeldt, "Complete List," 124.

116. Robert W. Shufeldt, "Audubon the Naturalist," *The Great Divide* 10 (1893): 8–9.

117. R. W. Shufeldt and M. R. Audubon, "The Last Portrait of Audubon, Together with a Letter to His Son," *Auk* 11 (1894): 309–313.

118. She returned briefly to Takoma Park for two days in November, only to leave again permanently. "Shufeldt *v.* Shufeldt," *Atlantic Reporter* 39 (1898): 417.

119. The claim of blackmail was first raised in a letter from Elliott Coues to William Brewster, 7 February 1897, which is included in the documents gathered on the incident by John Sage, secretary of the AOU: "AOU, Dr. Robert Shufeldt Matter" (hereafter referred to as "Shufeldt Matter"). This collection is now in the Alexander Wetmore Papers, RU 7006, Box 61, SIA, Washington, D.C.

120. Shufeldt first circulated his charges as a self-published pamphlet in 1896, "On a Case of Female Impotency." This was later incorporated into "On the Medico-Legal Aspect of Impotency in Women," *The Medico-Legal Journal* 14 (December 1896): 289–296. A manuscript copy of this article is found in "Shufeldt Matter."

121. Shufeldt, "Impotency in Women," 294–295.

122. "Shufeldt *v.* Shufeldt," *Atlantic Reporter* 39 (1898): 416–421. In 1898, the same year that his divorce from Audubon was finalized, Shufeldt married his former housekeeper.

123. S. P. Langley to R. W. Shufeldt, 8 February 1897, Assistant Secretary in Charge of the U.S. National Museum, 1879–1907, Outgoing Correspondence, RU 112, vol. L125, SIA.

124. R. W. Shufeldt to S. P. Langley, 18 February 1897, Assistant Secretary in Charge of the U.S. National Museum, 1860–1908, Incoming Correspondence, RU 189, Box 117, Folder 1, SIA.

125. The move prompted Shufeldt to ask in feigned innocence if some mistake had been made, to which Acting Assistant Secretary Walcott replied (with obvious relish), "I have the honor to state that the omission of your name from the revised list of Associates of the U.S. National Museum, was fully considered by the Secretary before receiving his approval." R. W. Shufeldt to Charles D. Walcott, 18 November 1897, Assistant Secretary in Charge of the U.S. National Museum, 1860–1908, Incoming Correspondence, RU 189, Box 117, Folder 1; and Charles Walcott to R. W. Shufeldt, Assistant Secretary in Charge of the U.S. National Museum, 1879–1907, Outgoing Correspondence, RU 112, vol. L134, p. 356, SIA. In retaliation, Shufeldt demanded that the Smithsonian pay for a collection of birds he had previously "donated" to the museum. Anxious to avoid tarnishing the reputation of the Smithsonian, officials reluc-

tantly agreed to Shufeldt's demands. See the various documents, especially Charles D. Walcott to R. W. Shufeldt, 14 January 1898, in Assistant Secretary in Charge of the U.S. National Museum, 1860–1908, Incoming Correspondence, RU 189, Box 117, Folder 1, SIA.

126. Elliott Coues to William Brewster, 29 January 1897, in "Shufeldt Matter."

127. William Brewster to Elliott Coues, 4 February 1897, in "Shufeldt Matter."

128. American Ornithologists' Union, *By-Laws and Rules and List of Members* (New York: L. S. Foster, 1887), 4.

129. Elliott Coues to J. A. Allen, 7 February 1897; Elliott Coues to D. G. Elliott, 12 February 1897; Elliott Coues to C. Hart Merriam, 17 February 1897; Elliott Coues to William Dutcher, 8 March 1897, all in "Shufeldt Matter."

130. J. A. Allen to Elliott Coues, 11 February 1897; D. G. Elliot to Elliott Coues, 15 February 1897; Frank Chapman to Elliott Coues, 15 February 1897; Ruthven Deane to Elliott Coues, 15 February 1897; William Dutcher to Elliott Coues, 12 March 1897, all in "Shufeldt Matter." Deane, Elliott, and Dutcher favored pressuring Shufeldt to resign, which he refused to do.

131. D. G. Elliot to Elliott Coues, 15 February 1897, in "Shufeldt Matter."

132. C. Hart Merriam to Elliott Coues, 5 March 1897; H. Randall Webb, Esquire, to Elliott Coues, 11 and 17 March 1897, in "Shufeldt Matter." On the discussions between Coues and Merriam regarding the episode, see Elliott Coues to C. Hart Merriam, 8 and 14 March, 4 May, 21, 22, and 29 June, 1 and 5 November, 1897, C. Hart Merriam Papers, Bancroft. I have been unable to locate a copy of the formal printed charges in the AOU Archives.

133. Elliott Coues to William Brewster, 30 July 1897, William Brewster Papers, MCZ Archives.

134. Ibid.

135. Robert Ridgway relayed the counter-charges to AOU Secretary Sage in early August with the recommendation that the union drop the matter. See Robert Ridgway to John H. Sage, 6, 14, and 18 August, 1897; and Robert Ridgway to William Dutcher, 16 September 1897, Division of Birds, National Museum of Natural History, Records, RU 105, Box 10, Letterbook vol. 1887–1900, SIA.

136. Shufeldt's fourteen-page document, "Charges and Specifications Preferred against Dr. Elliott Coues, of Washington, D.C.," survives in the Alexander Wetmore Papers, RU 7006, Box 61, SIA. I have been unable to locate Shufeldt's specific charges against Merriam, which had originally accompanied this document. Shufeldt also threatened to file charges against Merriam at the Department of Agricul-

ture, but I do not know if he followed through on this threat. John Sage to J. A. Allen, 3 August 1897, AOU Records, RU 7440, Box 1, Folder 10, SIA.

137. Elliott Coues to William Brewster, 26 August 1897, William Brewster Papers, MCZ Archives. See also Elliott Coues to William Brewster, 2 September 1897 and 31 October 1897, from the same collection.

138. J. A. Allen to William Brewster, 20 October 1897, William Brewster Papers, MCZ Archives. See also Allen's letters of 1 and 7 December 1897 in the same collection.

139. Elliott Coues to William Brewster, 14 November 1897, William Brewster Papers, MCZ Archives. Coues argued that the council was evenly split (five to five) on whether or not to recommend expulsion. Allen, on the other hand, said that only three council members favored expulsion and eight were against it. Moreover, Allen claimed that of the eighteen active members present at the meeting, "*two thirds* were *against* expulsion." J. A. Allen to William Brewster, 1 December 1897, William Brewster Papers, MCZ Archives.

140. AOU Council Minutes, 10 November 1897, AOU Records, RU 7150, Box 3, vol. 2, pp. 129–131, SIA.

141. According to Toby A. Appel, the inclusive membership policy of the AOU was more the exception than the rule among the disciplinary societies created in the biological sciences in the late nineteenth and early twentieth centuries. It was similar, however, to other national societies devoted to natural history. See Appel, "The Mapping of Biology" and "Organizing Biology."

142. Eds. [of *Auk*], [Reply to letter of J. C. Knox,] *Auk* 20 (1903): 234–235.

143. See, for example, L. S. Foster to the Members of the A.O.U., 1 July 1886, circular letter, copy in Division of Birds, National Museum of Natural History, Records, RU 105, Box 17, Folder 6, SIA. See also notice in *Auk* 5 (1888): 222. Although several active members followed Foster's advice or simply donated the funds to meet the annual budget shortfalls during this period, AOU leaders were anxious to make the *Auk* financially self-sufficient. See, for example, the copy of printed circular dated 16 November 1886 requesting donations to place the "Union upon a substantial financial footing," in AOU Records, RU 7440, SIA.

144. William Dutcher, circular letter, 5 October 1898, copy in AOU Records, RU 7440, SIA.

145. During this same period (1900–1930), the total population of the United States increased approximately 50 percent, from 76 million to 123 million.

146. Mayr, "Epilogue: Materials for a History of American Ornithology," 380. The following organizations should be added to Mayr's list: Maine Ornithological Society (1893); Iowa Ornithological Association (1894); Michigan Ornithological Club (1894); Colorado Ornithological Association (1900); Nebraska Ornithologists' Union (1894). See I. S. Trostler, "President's Address—History of Ornithology in Nebraska, and of State Ornithological Societies in General," *Proceedings of the Nebraska Ornithologists' Union* 2 (1901): 13–18.

147. Information on the creation of the society comes from the *Transactions of the Linnaean Society of New York* 1 (1882); and Eugene Eisenmann, "Seventy-Five Years of the Linnaean Society of New York," *Proceedings of the Linnaean Society of New York*, nos. 63–65 (1951–1953): 1–9. On the founding and the subsequent development of the DVOC, see Witmer Stone, "The Delaware Valley Ornithological Club," *Auk* 7 (1890): 298–299; and Samuel N. Rhoads, "Bird Clubs in America: II. The Delaware Valley Club," *Bird-Lore* 4 (1902): 57–61.

148. On the history of the Wilson Ornithological Society, see chapter 7, below. Much less has been written about the history of Cooper Club. See H. S. Swarth, *A Systematic Study of the Cooper Ornithological Club* (San Francisco: n.p., 1929); Harold C. Bryant, "The Cooper Club and Scientific Work," *Condor* 16 (1914): 101–107; and Henry B. Keading, "Retrospective," *Condor* 10 (1908): 215–218. Much of the early correspondence of the Cooper Ornithological Club is in the Joseph Grinnell Papers, BANC MSS C-B 995, Bancroft Library, Berkeley, California.

149. See for example, Lynds Jones to Frank M. Chapman, 16 June 1915, Archives, Department of Ornithology, AMNH, in which Jones stated that most of the members of the Wilson Ornithological Club viewed the AOU as a "strictly eastern organization." Of the AOU's first forty annual meetings, thirty-eight were held in four eastern cities: New York, (thirteen), Washington (eleven), Cambridge (eight), and Philadelphia (six). From the appendix to Frank Chapman and T. S. Palmer, eds., *Fifty Years' Progress of American Ornithology, 1883–1933* (Lancaster, Pa.: American Ornithologists' Union, 1933), 241–242.

150. See chapters 5 and 6.

151. "Brief Notes," *Ornithologist and Oologist* 16 (1891): 30.

152. A. B. Farnham, "Association of American Ornithologists," *Ornithologist and Oologist* 16 (1891): 76. Notice of the meeting also appeared in the *Oologist* 8 (1891): 103. See also J. H. Langille, "The New Era of Ornithology," *Oologist* 8 (1891): 136–137.

153. P. B. Peabody, "Correspondence," *Ornithologist and Oologist* 16 (1891): 175.

154. Frank S. Daggett, "Concerning the Active Membership of the A.O.U.," *Condor* 2 (1900): 68. Although Daggett was correct in his assertion that the AOU was primarily an eastern society, there were three California members at the time he penned his complaint. See the membership list in *Auk* 17 (1900): x–xi.

155. The bird protection activities of the AOU and the tensions they engendered are discussed in much greater detail in chapters 5 and 6, below.

156. Frank Chapman, "The A.O.U. and Audubon Societies," *Bird-Lore* 2 (1900): 161–162.

157. The proposed changes were announced in "Notes and News," *Auk* 18 (1901): 128.

158. "Editorial Notes," *Condor* 3 (1901): 24.

159. Harriet Kofalk, *No Woman Tenderfoot: Florence Merriam Bailey, Pioneer Naturalist* (College Station: Texas A & M Press, 1989), 29.

160. The term comes from the standard authority on American women in science in the pre–World War II era, Rossiter, *Women Scientists in America*, 78.

161. The figures on female membership in the AOU are from Sterling and Ainley, "Centennial History," chap. 16, p. 20.

162. Biographical information on Childs may be found in T. S. Palmer, "John Lewis Childs," *Auk* 38 (1921): 494–495; H. H. Bailey, "John Lewis Childs—As I Knew Him," *Oologist* 38 (1921): 102–104; "John Lewis Childs," ibid., 104–106; R. M. B[arnes], "John Lewis Childs," ibid., 44–45. The limit on the number of elective members had been gradually increased over the years from the original 75 to 100 (1906) to 125 (1925).

163. John Lewis Childs, "Membership Condition in the A.O.U.," *Auk* 25 (1908): 494.

164. Ibid.

165. H. H. Bailey, "Proposed Revision of the By-Laws of the American Ornithologists' Union," *Auk* 22 (1915): 134–136. Besides the *Auk*, Bailey sent identical letters to the editors of the *Condor*, the *Bulletin of the Wilson Ornithological Club*, and the *Oologist*. Only the *Auk* and the *Oologist* 32 (1915): 169–171, published the letter. See his biographical sketch in *Who Was Who in America, with World Notables* 6 (1974–1976): 17 (Chicago: Marquis Who's Who, 1976).

166. Bailey, "Proposed Revision," 135.

167. Witmer Stone, [Reply to H. H. Bailey], *Auk* 22 (1915): 138.

168. Ibid. The same argument appeared in Frank M. Chapman to Lynds Jones, 18 December 1914, Archives, Department of Ornithology, AMNH.

169. In May 1903 the AOU held a special meeting in San Francisco in celebration of the

tenth anniversary of the Cooper Ornithological Club. Later that year the organization also held its regular annual meeting in Philadelphia.

170. John Hall Sage, "Thirty-Third Stated Meeting of the American Ornithologists' Union," *Auk* 32 (1915): 491.

171. Harold H. Bailey, "Membership in the A.O.U.," *Auk* 33 (1916): 227.

172. Witmer Stone to Alexander Wetmore, 18 August 1935, Alexander Wetmore Papers, RU 7006, Box 66, SIA.

173. T. S. Palmer, "The Fifty-Fourth Stated Meeting of the American Ornithologists' Union," *Auk* 54 (1937): 117.

CHAPTER FOUR

1. The terms "systematics" and "taxonomy" are used interchangeably in this chapter. Nineteenth- and early-twentieth-century American ornithologists were primarily interested in microtaxonomy, the study of natural relationships of organisms at the level of species and below. The study of geographical distribution was central to this research. Very few Americans pursued research in macrotaxonomy, the study of the natural relationships of organisms at the higher taxonomic levels. On the distinction between micro- and macrotaxonomy, see Ernst Mayr and Peter D. Ashlock, *Principles of Systematic Zoology*, 2d ed. (New York: McGraw-Hill, 1991); and Ernst Mayr, *The Growth of Biological Thought: Diversity, Evolution, and Inheritance* (Cambridge: The Belknap Press of Harvard University Press, 1982).

2. Ridgway began collecting notes for his magnum opus in the 1880s and completed eight volumes before his death in 1929.

3. Robert Ridgway, *The Birds of North and Middle America*, Bulletin no. 50, United States National Museum (Washington, D.C.: Government Printing Office, 1901), 1:1–2.

4. For a contemporary critique of Ridgway's characterization, see Joseph Grinnell, Review of *Birds of North and Middle America* by Robert Ridgway, *Condor* 4 (1902): 22–23.

5. A synonymy is a "chronological list of the scientific names which have been applied correctly or incorrectly to a given taxonomic unit, including dates of publication and the authors applying the names." Mayr and Ashlock, *Principles*, 431.

6. Frank Chapman, *Handbook of Birds of Eastern North America* (New York: D. Appleton, 1895), 3.

7. Farber, *Emergence of Ornithology*, 100.

8. Ibid., 115.

9. The development of biological nomenclature is only beginning to gain the serious historical scrutiny it deserves. The best treatment of the subject is Antonella La Vergata, "Au nom de l'espèce: Classification et nomenclature au XIXe siècle," in *Histoire du concept d'espèce dans les sciences de la vie* (Paris: Fondation Singer-Polignac, 1987), 191–225. Earlier discussions also remain useful: David Heppell, "The Evolution of the Code of Zoological Nomenclature," in *History in the Service of Systematics*, ed. Alwyne Wheeler and James H. Price (London: Society for the Bibliography of Natural History, 1981), 135–141; and E. G. Linsley and R. L. Usinger, "Linnaeus and the Development of the International Code of Zoological Nomenclature," *Systematic Zoology* 8 (1958): 39–47. For accounts from some of the participants mentioned in this chapter, see Leonhard J. Stejneger, "A Chapter in the History of Zoological Nomenclature," *Smithsonian Miscellaneous Collections* 8 (1924): 1–21; and the introduction of *The Code of Nomenclature and Check-List of North American Birds Adopted by the American Ornithologists' Union* (New York: American Ornithologists' Union, 1886) (hereafter cited as AOU Code and Check-list).

Nomenclatural issues often loomed large in the early years of disciplinary societies in biology. See, for example, Richard A. Overfield, *Science with Practice: Charles E. Bessey and the Maturing of American Botany* (Ames: Iowa State University Press, 1993), 100–120; and Sorensen, *Brethren of the Net*, 242–252.

10. See, for example, the extensive discussion in Jürgen Haffer, "The History of Species Concepts and Species Limits in Ornithology," *Bulletin of the British Ornithologists' Club*, Centenary Supplement 112A (1992): 107–158.

11. Elliott Coues, "On the Application of Trinomial Nomenclature to Zoology," *Zoologist*, 3d series, 8 (1884): 244.

12. Janet Browne's excellent study, *The Secular Ark: Studies in the History of Biogeography* (New Haven: Yale University Press, 1983), examines pre-Darwinian work in geographical distribution. See also Ronald C. Tobey, *Saving the Prairies: The Life Cycle of the Founding School of American Plant Ecology, 1895–1955* (Berkeley: University of California Press, 1981); G. Nelson, "From Candolle to Croizat: Comments on the History of Biogeography," *Journal of the History of Biology* 11 (1978): 269–305; Philip F. Rehbock, *The Philosophical Naturalists: Themes in Early Nineteenth-Century British Biology* (Madison: University of Wisconsin Press, 1983); Robert P. McIntosh, *The Background of Ecology: Concept and Theory* (Cambridge: Cambridge University Press, 1985), 107–110; François Vuilleumier and Allison V. Andors, "Origins and Development of North American Avian Biogeography," in *Contributions to the History of North American Ornithology*, ed.

William E. Davis, Jr., and Jerome A. Jackson (Cambridge, Mass.: Nuttall Ornithological Club, 1995), 387–428; Jane R. Camerini, "Evolution, Biogeography, and Maps: An Early History of Wallace's Line," *Isis* 84 (1993): 700–727.

13. Agassiz's notion of biological provinces is discussed in a series of articles: "Notice sur la géographie des animaux," *Revue Suisse et chronique littéraire* 8 (1845): 441–452, 538–585; "Sur la distribution géographique des animaux et de l'homme," *Bulletin de la Société Neuchâteloise des sciences naturelles* 1 (1845): 162–166; "Observations sur las distribution géographique des être organisés," *Bulletin de la Société Neuchâteloise des sciences naturelles* 1 (1846): 357–361, "Observations sur . . . las distribution géographique des différents types actuels d'animaux," *Bulletin de la Société Neuchâteloise des sciences naturelles,* 1 (1846): 366–369; and "Geographical Distribution of Animals," *The Edinburgh New Philosophical Journal* 49 (1850): 1–23; and "Sketch of the Natural Provinces of the Animal World and Their Relation to the Different Types of Mankind," in *Types of Mankind,* J. C. Nott and George R. Gliddon (Philadelphia: J. B. Lippincott, Grambo, 1854), lviii.

14. Agassiz's early and somewhat crude geographical groupings of the animals that inhabited the globe were subsequently revised by the British naturalists Philip L. Sclater and Alfred R. Wallace and the Americans Spencer F. Baird and Joseph LeConte. See, for example, Philip L. Sclater, "On the General Geographical Distribution of the Members of the Class Aves," *Journal of the Linnaean Society (Zoology)* 2 (1858): 130–145; and Spencer F. Baird, "The Distribution and Migrations of North American Birds," *American Journal of Science,* n.s. 41 (1866): 73–91.

15. Louis Agassiz, *Essay on Classification,* ed. Edward Lurie (1857; Cambridge: Harvard University Press, 1962), 138–191.

16. Ibid., 177–178.

17. Ibid., 38.

18. Louis Agassiz, "Directions for Collecting Objects of Natural History" [Cambridge, Mass., 1863]. Copy in MCZ Archives.

19. [Spencer F. Baird,] "Directions for Collecting, Preserving, and Transporting Specimens of Natural History. Prepared for the Use of the Smithsonian Institution," 3d ed. (Washington, D.C.: Smithsonian Institution, 1859), 5. Reproduced in *Smithsonian Miscellaneous Collections* 2 (1862): article 7.

20. See, for example, George Boardman's statement about aiming to get a "pair of each species" for his collection in William Dutcher, "The Labrador Duck:—A Revised List of Extant Specimens in North America, with Some Historical Data," *Auk* 8 (1891): 201–216, on 216.

21. See Witmer Stone, "Problems in Modernizing an Old Museum," *Proceedings of the American Association of Museums* 3 (1909): 122–127.

22. Spencer F. Baird, John Cassin, and G. N. Lawrence, *Reports of the Explorations and Surveys to Ascertain the Most Practical and Economical Route for a Railroad from the Mississippi River to the Pacific Ocean . . . 1853–1856 . . . Volume IX . . . Birds* (Washington, D.C.: Beverly Tucker, 1858) (hereafter cited as Pacific Railroad Survey Report).

23. William H. Goetzmann has written extensively on these and other western surveys in *Army Exploration and the American West* and *Exploration and Empire.* On the scientific results of these expeditions, see John A. Moore, "Zoology of the Pacific Railroad Surveys," *American Zoologist* 26 (1986): 331–341.

24. For a general survey of the development of North American ornithology in the eighteenth and early nineteenth centuries, see Elsa G. Allen, *The History of American Ornithology before Audubon,* Transactions of the American Philosophical Society, n.s. 41, no. 3 (Philadelphia: American Philosophical Society, 1951). The best biographical treatments of Bonaparte are Farber, *Emergence of Ornithology,* 116–122; and Stresemann, *Ornithology,* 153–169. Audubon has been the subject of several biographies, but Francis Herrick's study, *Audubon the Naturalist,* is still one of the most useful. See also Ford, *John James Audubon.*

25. See, for example, the praise in J. A. Allen, "Progress of Ornithology in the United States during the Last Century," *American Naturalist* 10 (1876): 541; Coues, *Key to North American Birds,* 5th ed., xxv; and Leonhard Stejneger, "On the Use of Trinomials in American Ornithology," *Proceedings of the U.S. National Museum* 7 (1884): 70–89. The publication of tables providing detailed measurements of individual specimens was not entirely without precedent. See, for example, J. H. Blasius, "Beilage zum Protokoll der Zehnten Versammlung der deutschen Ornithologen-Gesellschaft," *Naumannia* 6 (1856): 433–474. I thank Jürgen Haffer for this reference.

26. Mary P. Winsor, "Louis Agassiz and the Species Question," *Studies in the History of Biology* 3 (1979): 98–102.

27. Louis Agassiz, *Contributions to the Natural History of the United States of America* (Boston: Little Brown, 1857), 1:445, quoted in Winsor, "Louis Agassiz," 100. One example of Agassiz's later denial of the existence of constant variation within a species occurs during a justification of the practice of serial collecting: Louis Agassiz, *Annual Report to the Trustees of the Museum of Comparative Zoology, Together with the Report of the Director, 1863* (Boston: Wright and Potter, 1864), 11.

28. Louis Agassiz, "Circular in Reference to Obtaining Data Concerning the Distribution of North American Birds in the Breeding Season," 4 June 1868. A copy of this circular is in the George A. Boardman Papers, RU 7071, SIA.

29. Agassiz's well-known opposition to the theory of evolution by natural selection is discussed in Edward J. Pfeifer, "United States," in *The Comparative Reception of Darwinism*, ed. Thomas F. Glick (Austin: University of Texas Press, 1974), 168–206; Lurie, *Louis Agassiz*, 252–302; and Winsor, *Reading the Shape of Nature*, 104–113.

30. By 1863 Agassiz was arguing that his examination of the series collections at the MCZ had demonstrated that varieties did not exist in nature. See Louis Agassiz, *Annual Report to the Trustees of the Museum of Comparative Zoology, Together with the Report of the Director, 1863* (Boston: Wright and Potter, 1864), 11.

31. See, for example, Baird, Cassin, and Lawrence, Pacific Railroad Survey Report, 526–527.

32. S. F. Baird, "Notes on a Collection of Birds Made by Mr. John Xantus, at Cape St. Lucas, Lower California," *Proceedings of the Philadelphia Academy of Natural Sciences* 11 (1859): 300. Baird's correlation between altitude and latitude had deep roots in the biogeographical tradition, beginning with Linnaeus's notion (borrowed from Tournefort) that the Paradise described in the Bible was a mountain of various ecological conditions, arranged as belts from tropical through temperate to polar zones. The close identification between altitude and latitude was later more fully elaborated by Humboldt. See Browne, *Secular Ark*, 16–23, 44–46.

33. Spencer F. Baird, "The Distribution and Migrations of North American Birds," *American Journal of Science*, 2d series, 41 (1866): 78–90, 184–192. He discusses the laws of geographic variation on pp. 189–192.

34. Constantin Lambert Gloger, *Das Abändern der Vögel durch Einfluss des Klima's* (Breslau: A. Schulz, 1833). When J. A. Allen repeated many of Baird's geographic variation laws in his "On the Mammals and Winter Birds of East Florida, with an Examination of Certain Assumed Specific Characters in Birds, and a Sketch of the Bird Faunae of Eastern North America," *Bulletin of the Museum of Comparative Zoology* 2, no. 3 (1871): 161–450, discussed below, he failed to cite Gloger in the lengthy bibliography appended to his work. In addition, both Allen and Baird were apparently unaware that they had also been anticipated by Carl Bergmann, *Über die Verhältnisse der Wärmeökonomie der Thiere zu ihrer Grösse* (Göttingen: Vandenhoeck and Ruprecht, 1847). On Bergmann, see William Coleman, "Bergmann's Rule: Animal Heat as a Biological Phenomena," *Studies in History of Biology* 3 (1979): 67–88. According to Haffer, "History of the Species Concept," 123, Peter Simon Pallas, Frederik Faber, and others also noted the phenomenon of geographical variation in the early nineteenth century.

35. Allen, "Mammals and Winter Birds," 228.

36. Although the point was only implicit in "Mammals and Winter Birds," Allen was later to argue explicitly that the characteristics exhibited by different geographical forms of a species were directly induced by environmental conditions. J. A. Allen, "The Influence of Physical Conditions in the Genesis of Species," *Radical Review* 1 (1877): 108–140. Allen's views on the influence of the environment on the formation of species have been lumped together with the ideas of many other Americans—the so-called Neo-Lamarckians—who accepted evolution but rejected the mechanism of natural selection in causing the transmutation of species. See Pfeifer, "United States," 168–206. See also Peter Bowler, *The Eclipse of Darwinism: Anti-Darwinian Evolutionary Theories in the Decades around 1900* (Baltimore: Johns Hopkins University Press, 1983).

Allen's arguments for the direct influence of the environment on organisms (unmediated by natural selection) seem to have found a sympathetic audience among naturalists in this country. Even Darwin was impressed. See Charles Darwin to E. S. Morse, 23 April 1877, reproduced in Francis Darwin, ed. *The Life and Letters of Charles Darwin* (New York: Basic Books, 1959), 2:409.

37. Allen, "Mammals and Winter Birds," 246. In his entry on "Geographical Distribution" for the *Dictionary of Birds* (London: Adam and Charles Black, 1893–1896), 344, Alfred Newton noted the importance of serial collecting practices in North America to the discovery of laws of geographical distribution and the general absence of such collections in Europe.

38. Stejneger, "Use of Trinomials," 75.

39. Stejneger provided several examples of the use of trinomialism before the adoption of the AOU Code in 1886. Ibid., 70–81. Haffer's recent "History of Species Concepts" is even more detailed. According to Haffer, the Gloger-Middendorff school deserves credit for developing the concept of the subspecies and the establishment of modern trinomialism but gained few contemporary followers. Even British ornithologists, who were generally unsympathetic to the later nomenclatural innovations associated with geographical variation, were unstinting in their praise of Allen's 1871 paper, especially the tables of measurements. See, for example, R. B. Sharpe's review in *Zoological Record for 1871*, ed. Alfred Newton (London: John Van Voorst, 1873), 24–25.

40. Elliott Coues, "Progress of American Ornithology," *American Naturalist* 5 (1871): 371–372.

41. Ibid., 373; J. A. Allen, "Recent Literature," *Bulletin of the Nuttall Ornithological Club* 4 (1879): 168.

42. For a contemporary account of American contributions to evolutionary thought, see E. S. Morse, "Address," *Proceedings of the American Association for the Advancement of Science* 25 (1876): 137–176.

43. Coues, *Key to North American Birds.*

44. Soon Coues would be among those who would call for the elimination of this abbreviation.

45. Coues also issued revised checklists of North American birds based on the catalogues in his *Key*: Coues, *A Check List of North American Birds*, and *The Coues Check List of North American Birds*, 2d ed. (Boston: Estes and Lauriat, 1882).

46. Allen, "Notes of an Ornithological Reconnaissance of Portions of Kansas, Colorado, Wyoming, and Utah," *Bulletin of the Museum of Comparative Zoology* 3 (July 1872): 113–183. On earlier uses of trinomial nomenclature, see Stegneger, "Use of Trinomials," and Haffer, "History of Species Concepts."

47. Allen, "Progress of Ornithology," 549.

48. Ibid., 549–550.

49. Ibid., 550.

50. Ridgway, "On the Use of Trinomials in Zoological Nomenclature," *Bulletin of the Nuttall Ornithological Club* 4 (1879): 132. A series of statements in support of trinomialism and nomenclatural reform followed in the *Bulletin*: J. A. Allen, "Recent Literature," ibid., 168; Elliott Coues, ibid., 171; Henry Henshaw, "The Use of Trinomials," ibid., 232–233.

51. Opposition to the American use of trinomial nomenclature was particularly strong in Britain. See, for example, R. Bowlder Sharpe, "The AOU Code and Checklist of American Birds," *Nature* 34 (1886): 168–170; "Zoological Nomenclature," *Nature* 30 (1884): 256–259, 277–279; J. A. Allen, "Zoological Nomenclature," *Auk* 1 (1884): 338–353; and Alfred Newton, *Dictionary of Birds*, 343.

52. Robert Ridgway, "A Catalogue of the Birds of North America," *Proceedings of the U.S. National Museum* 3 (1880): 163–246.

53. The ongoing feud between the two is documented in Cutright and Brodhead, *Elliott Coues*, 151–155, 157, 289, 316, and passim.

54. Robert Ridgway, *Nomenclature of North American Birds, Chiefly Contained in the United States National Museum*, United States National Museum, Bulletin no. 21 (Washington, D.C.: Government Printing Office, 1881).

55. Charles B. Cory to J. A. Allen, 14 June 1881, Charles B. Cory Folder, Archives, Department of Ornithology, AMNH.

56. One collector, Montague Chamberlain, commented in 1883 that he, like many other naturalists, dealers, and collectors, preferred the "Smithsonian system" to arrange his specimens. Montague Chamberlain to William Brewster, 15 August 1883, William Brewster Papers, MCZ Archives. See also the favorable notice of Ridgway's list in "Nomenclature of North American Birds," *Ornithologist and Oologist* 6 (1881): 28.

57. Coues, *The Coues Check List of North American Birds*. A rough idea of the differences in the two lists can be gained by comparing the number of bird forms contained in each. Ridgway's 1880 "Catalogue" contained 924 forms (species and subspecies), while Coues's 1882 *Check List* contained 888.

58. C. Hart Merriam to Joel A. Allen, 7 August 1881, Archives, Department of Ornithology, AMNH.

59. "The Coues Checklist," *Ornithologist and Oologist* 6 (1882): 93. Starting from Baird's 1859 list, American checklists invariably contained separate numbers attached to each entry. Collectors used these numbers as a shorthand for the species name to ease labeling and exchanging specimens.

60. Coues, "Compliments of the Season."

61. J. A. Allen, Elliott Coues, and William Brewster to ——— (printed invitation), 1 August 1883, AOU Records, RU 7150, SIA. A published version of the invitation later appeared in the *Bulletin of the Nuttall Ornithological Club* 8 (1883): 221.

62. Robert Ridgway to Elliott Coues, 11 August 1883, Division of Birds, National Museum of Natural History, Records, RU 105, Box 15, Folder 3, SIA.

63. Robert Ridgway to J. A. Allen, 18 August 1883, copies in Division of Birds, National Museum of Natural History, Records, RU 105, Box 12, Folder 2, SIA; and Joel Asaph Allen Papers, 67/125z, Bancroft Library, University of California, Berkeley.

64. AOU Meeting Minutes, 27 September 1883, AOU Records, RU 7150, Box 5, vol. 1, SIA.

65. The minutes of the committee still survive as "Proceedings of the Committee on Classification and Nomenclature, 1883–1885," AOU Records, RU 7150, Box 38, SIA. The story of the committee and its meetings is told in great detail in Sterling and Ainley, "Centennial History."

66. AOU Council Minutes, 21 April 1885, AOU Records, RU 7150, Box 3, vol. 1, SIA.

67. AOU Code and Checklist, 11.

68. Ibid., 30.

69. Ibid., 31.

70. Ibid.

71. Ibid., 31–32.

72. David S. Jordan, "The A.O.U. Code and Check-List of North American Birds," *Auk* 3 (1886): 393–397. The correspondence between Allen and Jordan leading up to the review is in the Archives, Department of Ornithology, AMNH. On Jordan's role in the development of evolutionary theory, see David C. Magnus, "In Defense of Natural History: David Starr Jordan and the Role of Isolation in Evolution," Ph.D. diss., Stanford University, 1993.

73. Jordan, "AOU Code," 397.

74. Even before the official publication of the AOU Code and Checklist in 1886, Allen began editing *Auk* papers to conform to it. See William Brewster to J. A. Allen, 15 December 1885, AOU Records, RU 7440, Box 1, Folder 8, SIA.

75. "Notes and News," *Auk* 4 (1889): 82.

76. A manuscript copy of this committee's report, dated 18 November 1890, is in the AOU Records, RU 7150, Box 39, SIA.

77. S. Prentiss Baldwin, Harry C. Oberholser, and Leonard G. Worley, *The Measurement of Birds*, Scientific Publications of the Cleveland Museum of Natural History, no. 2 (Cleveland: Cleveland Museum of Natural History, 1931). This work attempted to standardize methods for measuring 176 different external parameters.

78. C. Hart Merriam, "A Plea for the Metric System in Ornithology," *Auk* 1 (1884): 203–205.

79. AOU Council Minutes, 12 November 1888, AOU Records, RU 7150, Box 3, vol. 1, p. 143, SIA.

80. Robert Ridgway, *A Nomenclature of Colors for Naturalists and Compendium of Useful Knowledge for Ornithologists* (Boston: Little, Brown, 1886).

81. Robert Ridgway, *Color Standards and Color Nomenclature* (Washington, D.C.: The author, 1912).

82. See, for example, William T. Hornaday's "A Demand for English," *Auk* 12 (1895): 90–92, in which he decried the tendency to give new species only Latin names. Hornaday reminded scientists that they depended on the "money and the friendly interest of the unscientific public" to support their studies and lamented the fact that the gap between the two was "growing wider and wider, day by day." Hornaday also complained about the growing use of the metric system. For a reply, see F. E. L. Beal, "A Demand for English Names," *Auk* 12 (1895): 192–194, in which the author defended the use of scientific names and the public's ability to learn and use them. Others complained about the particular common names chosen for the AOU Checklist. See, for example, Ernest E. T. Seton, "The Popular Names of Birds," *Auk* 2 (1885): 316–317, and his plea that appeared almost thirty-five years later, "On the Popular Names of Birds," *Auk* 36 (1919): 229–

233, to allow the people, not scientists, to decide on common names.

83. See chapter 3.

84. Montague Chamberlain, "Plain English," *Ornithologist and Oologist* 8 (1883): 53–54, on 53.

85. Montague Chamberlain, "A Reply to Dr. Coues," *Ornithologist and Oologist* 8 (1883): 57–59. Chamberlain, who for reasons discussed in the previous chapter was soon elected to the AOU Council, later diminished, but did not entirely recant, his criticism of the use of scientific nomenclature. See his "More 'Plain English,' " *Ornithologist and Oologist* 10 (1885): 9. As Haffer, "History of the Species Concept," has made clear, not all European naturalists rejected trinomialism.

86. Besides the AOU (1886), Coues (1882), and Ridgway (1881) lists, the author is probably referring to the Baird (1859) and the earlier Coues (1873) checklists.

87. "Editorial," *Ornithologist and Oologist* 11 (1886): 72.

88. "Brief Notes," *Ornithologist and Oologist* 13 (1888): 144; and "Editorial," *Ornithologist and Oologist* 14 (1889): 60–62, on 62.

89. XX, "A New Sub-Species," *Ornithologist and Oologist* 14 (1889): 80.

90. " 'H' A.O.U." refers to honorary membership in the AOU.

91. Another, "The Mystery Solved," *Ornithologist and Oologist* 14 (1889): 144.

92. This refers to the common practice of indicating membership in a learned society by appending an abbreviation of the society's name to an individual's name.

93. The *L. b.* portion of the name is an abbreviation of the binomial designation of the Northern shrike, *Lanius borealis*.

94. "Jottings," *Young Oologist* 1 (1884): 139.

95. Harry G. Parker, "A Review of the Check Lists of North American Birds, with Special Reference to the New A.O.U. List," *Oologist* 3 (1886): 37–39. See also the explanation of scientific nomenclature in the article by S, "Trinomial Nomenclature," *Oologist* 10 (1893): 155–156.

96. "The Editor [R. M. Barnes]," "Widening," *Oologist* 39 (1922): 136.

97. R. M. B[arnes], "Scientific Snobbery," *Oologist* 40 (1923): 81. See also [R. M. Barnes,] "Technical Names," *Oologist* 35 (1918): 165–166, in which the editor attacks the tendency to overuse scientific nomenclature in the *Auk* when the publication is almost exclusively supported by associate members, most of whom "are compelled to make a living in the business world and have no time to delve into the intricacies and mysteries of super-scientific ornithology and latinized bird names." Similar critiques appeared regularly in Barnes's publication. See, for

example, the following authored by Barnes in *Oologist*: "Business is Dull," 34 (1917): 217; "More Chaos," 35 (1918): 82; "The Result of Being Too Scientifically Scientific," 40 (1923): 167–168; "More About Names," 41 (1924): 91; "Ad Nauseate," 47 (1930): 139–140; "Some Books," 48 (1931): 135–137; "The 1931 A.O.U. Checklist," 28 (1931): 171; "More Millimeter Races," 50 (1933): 27–28. See also P. B. Peabody, "Amenities of Nomenclature," 36 (1919): 25–27, and "Millimeter Races," 39 (1922): 52; and Fred M. Dille, "The Fourth Edition: The New A.O.U. Checklist," 49 (1932): 2–8.

98. See, for example, the series of letters from Montague Chamberlain to J. A. Allen, beginning in November 1883, Joel Asaph Allen Papers, 67/125z, Bancroft Library, University of California, Berkeley, and the series of letters between Chamberlain and C. Hart Merriam, Clinton Hart Merriam Papers, BANC MSS C-B 995, Bancroft Library, University of California, Berkeley.

99. Montague Chamberlain, "Are Trinomials Necessary?" *Auk* 1 (1884): 101–102.

100. Chamberlain mentioned in particular the opposition of Mr. Harting, the editor of the *Zoologist*, and the complete lack of trinomials in the catalog of British birds published by the British Ornithologists' Union. As I have already suggested, Chamberlain's claim about the opposition to trinomialism abroad ignores the proponents of trinomialism in the Gloger-Middendorff school (described by Haffer, "History of the Species Concept"). It was more accurate in describing the British response to the idea until the end of the nineteenth century.

101. J. A. A[llen], [Reply to Chamberlain,] *Auk* 1 (1884): 102–104.

102. Montague Chamberlain, "Are Trinomials Necessary?" *Auk* 1 (1884): 198–200, on 199.

103. J. A. A[llen], [Reply to Chamberlain II,] *Auk* 1 (1884): 200–202.

104. Walter B. Hull to J. A. Allen, 8 November 1897, AOU Records, RU 7440, SIA.

105. There were some notable exceptions. For example, throughout his five-volume handlist of the genera and species of birds, the British ornithologist R. Bowdler Sharpe refused to provide formal designation to subspecies, although he believed they existed in nature. See his *A Hand-List of the Genera and Species of Birds* (London: British Museum [Natural History], 1909), 5:vi.

106. These included the Dall Code, authorized by the American Association for the Advancement of Science (1877), the Chaper Code, published by the Société Zoologique de France (1881), the Douvillé Code, passed at the International Geological Congress (1893), the code passed by the Deutsche Zoologische Gesellschaft (1893), and the Blanchard Code, adopted

by the First International Zoological Congress (1889, published 1890). Linsley and Usinger, "Development of the International Code," 41–42; Heppell, "Code of Zoological Nomenclature," 136–137.

107. J. A. Allen (*Autobiographical Notes*, 40) claimed that the "A.O.U. Code later became the basis of the International Code of Zoological Nomenclature, framed on essentially the same lines and departing from it in no essential respect, except in point of brevity." The claim is repeated in Stejneger, "Chapter," 11–12; and Linsley and Usinger, "International Code," 44.

108. Heppell, "Evolution of the Code," 137; Linsley and Usinger, "International Code," 42.

109. American Ornithologists' Union, *Check-List*, 2d and rev. ed. (New York: AOU, 1895); 3d ed. (New York: AOU, 1910); 4th ed. (New York: AOU, 1931). Supplements were published in 1889, 1890, 1891, 1892, 1893, 1894 (2), 1897, 1899, 1901, 1902, 1903, 1904, 1908, 1909, 1912, 1920, and 1923.

110. In an attempt to achieve nomenclatural stability, naturalists suggested several alternatives to the law of priority. One proposal that gained a wide following was the establishment of a list of *nomina conservanda*, which would remain in effect even if earlier names for a given species were discovered. Although the International Code of Nomenclature was largely based on the law of priority, it also allowed deviations from that law in certain cases. See Usinger and Linsley, "International Code," 43–44; and Heppell, "Evolution," 137–138.

111. Christopher Leahy, *The Birdwatcher's Companion: An Encyclopedic Handbook of North American Birdlife* (London: Robert Hale, 1982), 617.

112. AOU, *Check-List*, 1st ed. (1886), 344; 2d ed. (1895), 320; 3d ed. (1910), 363; 4th ed. (1931), 255.

113. [Frank M. Chapman,] [Editorial,] *Bird-Lore* 27 (1925): 276; and J. D. Dwight, "The Auk," *Bird-Lore* 10 (1908): 218.

114. William Leon Dawson, "A Plea for Ten Years of Stability in Nomenclature: An Open Letter to the A.O.U. Committee," enclosed with his letter to J. A. Allen, 5 October 1905, AOU Records, RU 7440, SIA.

115. William Brewster, "Something More about Black Ducks," *Auk* 26 (1909): 179. Similar sentiments are expressed in a letter from Louis B. Bishop to Alexander Wetmore, 30 November 1926, Alexander Wetmore Papers, RU 7006, Box 6, SIA. For an opposing view, see Witmer Stone's review of W. L. McAtee's "Local Names of Migratory Game Birds," *Auk* 41 (1924): 187.

116. I have not discovered the origin of the terms "splitting" and "lumping" as applied to taxonomic practice, but they were in wide

enough usage by the second half of the nineteenth century not to require special explanation. See, for example, J. A. Allen, "To What Extent Is It Profitable to Recognize Geographical Forms among North American Birds?," *Auk* 7 (1890): 1–9.

117. Joseph Grinnell, "Some Inferences from the New Check-list," *Auk* 49 (1932): 9–13, on 10.

118. A. K. Fisher attributes the term "north light subspecies" to Elliott Coues in his brief biographical sketch of William Brewster, A. K. Fisher Papers, Box 40, Library of Congress, Washington, D.C. See also Jonathan D. Dwight, Jr., Review of *The Auk*, *Bird-Lore* 3 (1901): 112.

119. Quoted in A. K. Fisher's short, unpublished biographical sketch of Brewster found in the A. K. Fisher Papers, Box 40, Library of Congress, Washington, D.C.

120. *Auk* 7 (1890): 1–9.

121. Ibid., 2.

122. Robert Ridgway, "A Plea for Caution in Use of Trinomials," *Auk* 40 (1923): 375–376.

123. Allen, "To What Extent," 5.

124. Ibid., 8–9.

125. J. A. Allen, "The A.O.U. Check-List—Its History and Its Future," *Auk* 20 (1903): 1–9, on 9.

126. Theodore Gill, "A Great Work," *Osprey* 3 (1899): 88–94, on 92.

127. Leverett M. Loomis, "Recognition of Geographic Variation in Nomenclature," *Auk* 20 (1903): 294–299.

128. Harry S. Swarth, "The Tyranny of the Trinomial," *Condor* 33 (1931): 160–162; Jonathan Dwight, Jr., "The Exaltation of the Subspecies," *Auk* 21 (1904): 64–66; and J. D. Figgins, "The Fallacy of the Tendency towards Ultraminute Distinctions," *Auk* 21 (1904): 62–69.

129. Jonathan Dwight, Jr., "A Method of Obtaining a Temporary Stability of Names," *Auk* 21 (1904): 406; William L. Dawson, "A Plea for Ten Years of Stability in Nomenclature," enclosed with William L. Dawson to J. A. Allen, 5 October 1905, AOU Records, RU 7440, SIA.

130. Wilfred H. Osgood, "Questions of the Day," *Condor* 3 (1901): 50–51. Osgood's sentiments are echoed in Witmer Stone, [Reply to Bergtold,] *Auk* 44 (1927): 28–34. See also P. A. Taverner, "Subspecific Designations," *Auk* 34 (1917): 370–372, which argues that subspecies can safely be ignored by nontechnically oriented students of birds.

CHAPTER FIVE

1. The account of the decline of the parakeet that follows is from Daniel McKinley, *The Carolina Parakeet in Florida*, Special Publication no. 2 (Gainesville: Florida Ornithological Society, 1985), 27–30; James Greenway, *Extinct and Vanishing Birds of the World*, 2d ed. (New York: Dover Publications, 1967); and Maikku Saikku, "The Extinction of the Carolina Parakeet," *Environmental History Review* 14 (1990): 1–18.

2. Charles E. Bendire, *Life Histories of North American Birds*, U.S. National Museum, Special Bulletin no. 3 (Washington, D.C.: Government Printing Office, 1895), 4.

3. On the role of aesthetics in natural history, see, for example, Merrill, *Romance of Victorian Natural History*; and Dance, *Shell Collecting*.

4. Hornaday, *Taxidermy and Zoological Collecting*, 2.

5. For a comprehensive account of the various attempts to secure the parakeet in Florida, see McKinley, *Carolina Parakeet*.

6. Ibid., 27, calls the specimens secured on Chapman's 1889 expedition "the most widely advertised collection of parakeets ever made." The publicity surrounding this particular set of parakeets is in part due to the various accounts of the trip provided over the years. Chapman published two contemporary descriptions of his trip in "[Notes on Collecting Trip to Brevard County, Florida, Spring 1889,]" *Abstract of the Proceedings of the Linnaean Society, for the Year Ending March 7, 1890*, 2, and "Notes on the Carolina Parakeet," ibid, 4–6. Chapman's letters to J. A. Allen relating to the expedition have also survived: Frank M. Chapman to J. A. Allen, 18 March 1889 and 20 March 1889, Archives, Department of Ornithology, AMNH. Elizabeth S. Austin, ed., *Frank M. Chapman in Florida: His Journals and Letters* (Gainesville: University of Florida Press, 1967), reproduces these and other documents from the period. The account that follows is largely from Chapman's previously lost manuscript journal from the expedition found among his papers at the AMNH (hereafter cited as "Parakeet Journal").

7. The large number of biographical sketches of Chapman in part reflect his influential role in the scientific and popular ornithology of his day. See Austin, *Chapman in Florida*; Chapman, *Autobiography*; William K. Gregory, "Biographical Memoir of Frank Michler Chapman, 1864–1945," National Academy of Sciences, *Biographical Memoirs* 35 (1949): 111–145; Robert H. Welker, "Frank Michler Chapman," *Dictionary of American Biography*, Supplement 3 (1941–1945): 61–62; Robert C. Murphy, "Frank M. Chapman, 1864–1945," *Auk* 67 (1950): 307–315; Ludlow Griscom, "Frank M. Chapman," *Audubon Magazine* 48 (1946): 49–52; and Ernst Mayr, "Frank Michler Chapman," *Dictionary of Scientific Biography* 17:152–153.

8. Chapman, *Autobiography*, 25–26; Frank M. Chapman, "Frederick J. Dixon," *Auk* 40 (1933): 153.

9. Chapman, *Autobiography*, 26–27; T. S. Palmer, "Clarence Bayley Riker," *Auk* 67 (1950): 550.

10. Chapman, *Autobiography*, 32–35.

11. Ibid., 42.

12. C. Hart Merriam to Frank M. Chapman, 5 March 1888, Archives, Department of Ornithology, AMNH.

13. Chapman, *Autobiography*, 62.

14. Parakeet Journal, 6–7.

15. Ibid., 13.

16. Ibid., 29–30.

17. Ibid., 31.

18. McKinley (*Carolina Parakeet*, 4) has located 806 specimens in museums throughout the world. The locations and information on when, where, and by whom they were collected are given for most in Paul Hahn, *Where Is That Vanished Bird?: An Index to the Known Specimens of the Extinct North American Species* (Toronto: Royal Ontario Museum, University of Toronto, 1963), 291–339.

On the last known parakeet, who died in the Cincinnati Zoo only four years after the last passenger pigeon, see George Laycock, "The Last Parakeet," *Audubon Magazine* 71 (March 1969): 21–25; and Daniel McKinley, "The Last Days of the Carolina Parrakeet: Life in the Zoos," *Avicultural Magazine* 83 (1977): 42–49.

19. Peter J. Kuznick, *Beyond the Laboratory: Scientists as Political Activists in 1930s America* (Chicago: University of Chicago Press, 1987), is one of the few studies to examine scientists' attempts to grapple with the issues of social responsibility and political activism in the prewar period.

20. Welker, *Birds and Men*, 158.

21. Lee Clark Mitchell has gathered many of these early expressions of concern for the destruction of the environment in *Witnesses to a Vanishing America: The Nineteenth-Century Response* (Princeton: Princeton University Press, 1981).

22. The best accounts of the decline and rescue of the North American buffalo are Larry Barsness, *Heads, Hides and Horns: The Compleat Buffalo Book* (Fort Worth: Texas Christian University, 1985); and David Dary, *The Buffalo Book: The Full Saga of the American Animal* (Chicago: Swallow Press, 1974). See also James A. Tober, *Who Owns Wildlife: The Political Economy of Conservation in Nineteenth-Century America* (Westport, Conn.: Greenwood Press, 1981). A. W. Schorger's *The Passenger Pigeon: Its Natural History and Extinction* (Madison: University of Wisconsin Press, 1955) is an exhaustive compilation of virtually everything written on that species up to the time of its publication. See also Enrique H. Bucher, "The

Causes of Extinction of the Passenger Pigeon," in *Current Ornithology*, ed. Dennis M. Power (New York: Plenum Press, 1992), 9:1–36.

23. Schorger, *Passenger Pigeon*, 199.

24. Wilson, *American Ornithology*, 5:106.

25. Schorger, *Passenger Pigeon*, 222.

26. William C. Herman, "The Last Passenger Pigeon," *Auk* 65 (1948): 77–79; and McKinley, "Last Days."

27. Dary, *Buffalo Book*, 286–287.

28. Ibid., 84–120. Dan Flores argues that native Americans trading with white settlers had already begun to deplete the bison herds by the 1850s. See his "Bison Ecology and Bison Diplomacy: The Southern Plains from 1800 to 1850," *Journal of American History* 78 (1991): 465–485.

29. The best summary of the evidence for federal promotion of bison extermination is David Smits, "The Frontier Army and the Destruction of the Buffalo, 1865–1883," *Western Historical Quarterly* 25 (1994): 313–338.

30. For example, as early as 1832 the artist George Catlin predicted that the extinction of the species was "near at hand" and proposed the creation of a national park to protect both the buffalo and the American Indians. Roderick Nash, *American Environmentalism: Readings in Conservation History*, 3d ed. (New York: McGraw-Hill, 1990), 31–35. For this and other early discussions about the decline of the buffalo, see Dary, *Buffalo Book*, 121–130.

31. Allen's collecting exploits are more fully described in his *Autobiographical Notes*, 20–27.

32. J. A. Allen, *The American Bisons, Living and Extinct*, Memoirs of the Museum of Comparative Zoology, vol. 4, no. 10 (Cambridge, Mass.: Welch, Bigelow, 1876), 180, my italics. Similar statements abound in the work (e.g., 55, 70).

33. J. A. Allen, "The North American Bison and Its Extermination," *The Penn Monthly* 7 (1876): 216.

34. J. A. Allen, "The Extirpation of the Larger Indigenous Mammals of the United States," *The Penn Monthly* 7 (1876): 794.

35. Ibid., 798.

36. J. A. Allen, "The Extinction of the Great Auk at the Funk Islands," *American Naturalist* 10 (1876): 48. The account of the auk that follows is from Allen's notice; Greenway, *Extinct and Vanishing Birds*, 271–291; and David N. Nettleship and Peter G. H. Evans, "Distribution and Status of Atlantic Alcidae," in *The Atlantic Alcidae: The Evolution, Distribution and Biology of the Auks Inhabiting the Atlantic Ocean and Adjacent Water Areas*, ed. David N. Nettleship and Tim R. Birkhead (London: Academic Press, 1985), 61–69.

37. J. A. Allen, "Decrease of Birds in Massachusetts," *Bulletin of the Nuttall Ornithological Club* 1 (1876): 53–60.

38. J. A. Allen, "On the Decrease of Birds in the United States," *The Penn Monthly* 7 (1876): 931–945.

39. Ibid., 944.

40. Reiger, *American Sportsmen*; and James B. Trefethen, *An American Crusade for Wildlife* (New York: Winchester Press and the Boone and Crockett Club, 1975). For a critique of these claims, see Thomas R. Dunlap, "Sport Hunting and Conservation, 1880–1920," *Environmental Review* 12 (1988): 51–59; and for John Reiger's reply, see ibid., 94–96.

41. T. S. Palmer, "Chronology and Index of the More Important Events in American Game Protection, 1776–1911," United States Department of Agriculture, Biological Survey Bulletin no. 41 (Washington, D.C.: Government Printing Office, 1912).

42. See Reiger, *American Sportsmen*, 25–49.

43. Allen, "Decrease of Birds," 944.

44. The best history of the Anglo-American humane movement is James Turner, *Reckoning with the Beast: Animals, Pain, and Humanity in the Victorian Mind* (Baltimore: Johns Hopkins University Press, 1980). For an assessment of the role of the humanitarians in wildlife protection, see Lisa Mighetto, "Wildife Protection and the New Humanitarianism," *Environmental Review* 12 (1988): 37–49, and *Wild Animals and American Environmental Ethics* (Tucson: University of Arizona Press, 1991). On changing conceptions of the human-nature boundary, see James J. Sheehan and Morta Sosna, eds., *The Boundaries of Humanity: Humans, Animals, Machines* (Berkeley: University of California Press, 1991).

45. The contributions of Romanticism and Transcendentalism to nature appreciation are discussed in Fleming, "Roots of the New Conservation Movement," 8–10; Huth, *Nature and the American Mind*, 57–104; and Nash, *Wilderness and the American Mind*, 84–95.

46. The most comprehensive account of the turn-of-the-century "back to nature" movement, which discusses everything from school gardens and Boy Scouts to literary genres, is Schmitt, *Back to Nature*. See also Lutts, *Nature Fakers*, 1–36.

47. Allen, "Decrease of Birds," 944.

48. "Second Meeting of the American Ornithologists' Union," *Auk* 1 (1884): 376. The other members of the original AOU bird protection committee were H. A. Purdie, George B. Grinnell, Eugene P. Bicknell, William Dutcher, and Frederic A. Ober.

49. William Brewster to J. A. Allen, 18 January 1885, AOU Records, RU 7440, Box 1, Folder 8, SIA. See also J. A. Allen to William Brewster, 16 January 1885, William Brewster Papers, MCZ Archives.

50. George B. Grinnell to J. A. Allen, 24 February 1885, Archives, Department of Ornithology, AMNH.

51. "Third Meeting of the American Ornithologists' Union," *Auk* 3 (1886): 120.

52. J. A. Allen was apparently working behind the scenes to assure the success of the new committee. See J. A. Allen to William Brewster, 29 November 1885, William Brewster Papers, MCZ Archives.

53. The description of the vitality of the new committee is from J. A. Allen to William Brewster, 13 December 1885, William Brewster Papers, MCZ Archives. Details of Sennett's life are treated in J. A. Allen, "In Memoriam: George Burritt Sennett," *Auk* 18 (1901): 11–23.

54. "Fourth Meeting of the American Ornithologists' Union," *Auk* 4 (1887): 58. The minutes of those meetings survive in the National Audubon Society Records, Box A-188, Rare Books and Manuscripts Division, New York Public Library, New York (hereafter cited as NAS Records, NYPL).

55. "Notes and News," *Auk* 3 (1886): 143.

56. N. D. C. Hodges to J. A. Allen, 1 December 1885, Archives, Department of Ornithology, AMNH. Hodges's offer was read at the 12 December meeting of the bird protection committee and may have been one of the factors prompting the meeting. George B. Sennett, "Report of the Committee on the Protection of North American Birds, November 1886," AOU Records, RU 7150, Box 1, Folder 15, SIA.

57. AOU Committee on Bird Protection, "Supplement," *Science* 7 (1886): 191–205, reprinted with limited revisions as the first AOU Bird Protection Bulletin. Figures for the circulation of this pamphlet are from *Auk* 3 (1886): 191.

58. J. A. Allen, "The Present Wholesale Destruction of Bird-Life in the United States," *Science* 7 (1886): 191–193.

59. The rise of the millinery trade in America and Europe is thoroughly examined in Robin Doughty's *Feather Fashions and Bird Preservation: A Study in Nature Protection* (Berkeley: University of California Press, 1975).

60. [J. A. Allen], "Destruction of Birds for Millinery Purposes," *Science* 7 (1886): 196–197. In 1884 Frank Chapman took a late afternoon stroll through the uptown shopping district of New York and counted 700 women wearing hats, of which 542 were decorated with feathers from over 40 North American species. See his "Birds and Bonnets," *Forest and Stream* 26 (1886): 84, which was incorporated into the pamphlet version of the first AOU Bird Protection Bulletin.

61. Allen, "Present Wholesale Destruction," 194.

62. John Burroughs, "Bird Enemies," *Century Magazine* 31 (1885–1886): 273.

63. Ibid., 274.

64. *Wake-Robin* (New York: Hurd and Houghton, 1871). Quoted from 14th ed. (Houghton, Mifflin, 1877), 231.

65. The quote is from an expanded version of the "Bird Enemies" essay in *Signs and Seasons* (Boston: Houghton, Mifflin, 1886), 213.

66. Ibid.

67. See William Brewster to J. A. Allen, 29 December 1885, AOU Records, RU 7440, Box 1, Folder 8, SIA.

68. [J. A. Allen], "Notes and News," *Auk* 3 (1886): 142.

69. Ibid., 142–143.

70. This argument continues to appear. See, for example, "Report of the Ad Hoc Committee on Scientific and Educational Uses of Wild Birds," *Auk* 92 (1975): 1A–27A; and American Ornithologists' Union, *Checklist of North American Birds*, 6th ed. (Lawrence, Kans: American Ornithologists' Union, 1983), xxviii–xxix.

71. Allen, "Present Wholesale Destruction," 194.

72. Numerous ornithologists have concluded that collecting could greatly affect local populations of already endangered species. See, for example, Carl B. Koford, *The California Condor*, National Audubon Society, Research Report no. 4 (New York: National Audubon Society, 1953), 130; William Brewster, "Nesting Habits of the Parrakeet," *Auk* 6 (1889): 336–337; Frank Chapman, Review of "An Attempt to List Extinct and Vanishing Birds," by J. C. Phillips, *Bird-Lore* 31 (1929): 352–353; and Hamel, *Bachman's Warbler*, 26.

73. W. E. D. Scott, "The Present Condition of Some of the Bird Rookeries of the Gulf Coast of Florida," *Auk* 4 (1887): 135–144, 213–222, 273–284. Biographical information on Scott may be found in J. A. Allen, "William Earl Dodge Scott," *Auk* (1910): 486–488, and in Scott's fascinating autobiography, *Story of a Bird Lover*.

74. Scott, "Present Condition," 277. On Lechevalier, see Walter P. Fuller, "Who Was the Frenchmen of Frenchman's Creek?" *Tequesta* 29 (1969): 45–59.

75. W. E. D. Scott to J. A. Allen, 17 June 1886, Archives, Department of Ornithology, AMNH; and W. E. D. Scott to J. A. Allen, 30 June 1886, AOU Records, RU 7440, SIA. By October 1886 Scott had sold 114 terns to the AMNH, and one year later he was offering a thousand more Florida specimens. See W. E. D. Scott to J. A. Allen, 25 October 1886 and 14 December 1887, Archives, Department of Ornithology, AMNH.

76. Charles E. Bendire to Robert Ridgway, 9 September 1888, Division of Birds, National Museum of Natural History, Records, RU 105, Box 13, Folder 3, SIA. Christopher Leahy, who is skeptical about the ability of collectors to affect bird populations, called the Bachman's warbler "the exceptional case in which overcollecting contributed to extinction." *The Bird-watcher's Companion: An Encyclopedic Handbook of North American Birdlife* (London: Robert Hale, 1982), 232. On the demise of the species, see Hamel, *Bachman's Warbler*.

77. J. A. Allen, "J. H. Batty," *Auk* 23 (1906): 356–357.

78. See, for example, the complaints of Leander S. Keyser and Reginald C. Robbins in chapter 6, below.

79. Allen, "Present Wholesale Destruction," 193.

80. Ibid.

81. Ibid., 195. Allen also contributed a separate short essay on the subject for the first AOU Bird Protection Bulletin, [J. A. Allen,] "The Relation of Birds to Agriculture," *Science* 7 (1886): 201–202.

82. The notion that nature remains in balance has a history stretching back to the Greeks. See Clarence Glacken, *Traces on the Rhodian Shore: Nature and Culture in Western Thought from Ancient Times to the End of the Eighteenth Century* (Berkeley: University of California Press, 1967); and Frank N. Egerton, "Changing Concepts in the Balance of Nature," *Quarterly Review of Biology* 48 (1973): 322–350.

83. The story of the creation of the USDA's Division of Economic Ornithology and Mammalogy is told in greater detail in chapter 3, above.

84. [J. A. Allen], "Bird Laws," *Science* 7 (1886): 202–204.

85. Following protests from several ornithologists who feared that the age limit in the AOU model law would discourage aspiring young ornithologists, the bird protection committee soon dropped the age requirement from its model law. See American Ornithologists' Union, "Bulletin No. 2 of the Committee on Protection of Birds," *Forest and Stream* 27 (1886): 304–305.

86. The biographical sketch that follows comes from John G. Mitchell, "A Man Called Bird," *Audubon Magazine* 89 (March 1987): 81–104; and A. K. Fisher, "In Memoriam: George Bird Grinnell," *Auk* 56 (1939): 1–12. As editor of *Forest and Stream*, founder of the first Audubon Society (1886), and cofounder of the Boone and Crockett Club (1887), Grinnell looms large in the histories of turn-of-the-century conservation that stress the contribution of recreational hunters. See Trefethen, *American Crusade for Wildlife*; and Reiger, *American Sportsmen*.

87. Quoted in Mitchell, "A Man Called Bird," 91.

88. Grinnell was among the forty-eight naturalists invited to the founding meeting of the AOU (AOU Minutes, 26 September 1883, AOU Records, RU 7150, Box 5, vol. 1, pp. 27–28, SIA) but apparently did not attend and was therefore not listed as one of the twenty-five "founding members."

89. Dutcher, "History of the Audubon Movement," 45. See, for example, [George Bird Grinnell,] "Spare the Swallows," *Forest and Stream* 21 (1883): 121.

90. George B. Grinnell to J. A. Allen, 24 February 1885, Archives, Department of Ornithology, AMNH.

91. [George Bird Grinnell], "The Audubon Society," *Forest and Stream* 26 (1886): 41.

92. Ibid.

93. Ibid. As chair of the bird protection committee, Sennett sent a letter to Grinnell granting the "sanction of our authority" to the new Audubon Society. Reproduced in an early (undated) pamphlet from the society, "The Audubon Society for the Protection of Birds," located in the AOU Records, RU 7150, Box 1, Folder 15, SIA.

94. The creation of the society is discussed in Merriam's article "Our Smith College Audubon Society," *Audubon Magazine* 1 (1887): 175–178. The episode is also treated in Kofalk, *No Woman Tenderfoot*, 32–38, which is largely based on Merriam's article.

95. Fanny Hardy [Eckstrom] to William Brewster, 24 March 1886, William Brewster Papers, MCZ Archives.

96. "Membership of the Audubon Society," *Audubon Magazine* 1 (1887): 19.

97. "The Audubon Magazine," *Audubon Magazine* 1 (1887): 5.

98. Celia Thaxter, "Woman's Heartlessness," *Audubon Magazine* 1 (1887): 13–14.

99. AOU Minutes, 26 September 1883, AOU Records, RU 7150, Box 5, vol. 1, pp. 27–28, SIA. Biographical information on Langdon is from T. S. Palmer, "Frank Warren Langdon," *Auk* 51 (1934): 132.

100. Langdon's remarks were originally published in his local paper, the Cincinnati *Commercial-Gazette*, and then as "Fourth Paper" in a series of "Papers on the Destruction of Native Birds," *Journal of the Cincinnati Society of Natural History* 9 (1886): 181–191. As J. A. Allen pointed out in his reply to the critique ("Bird-Destruction," *Science* 8 (1886): 118), Langdon's ideas were "eagerly seized upon by newspaper editors" and widely reprinted. They were also picked up by natural history periodicals. See, for example, *Science* 8 (1886): 2; "Facts about the Birds: Misleading Statistics Respecting Fashion's Demands," *The Hawkeye Ornithologist*

and Oologist 1 (1888): 29–33; and "The Destruction of Our Native Birds," *Oologist* 5 (1888): 54–58. The collecting press saw Langdon as an ally in their challenge to the AOU bird protection committee (see below).

101. Allen, "Bird-Destruction," 118.

102. Langdon, "Fourth Paper," 191.

103. The letter and the ensuing exchange are recorded in the AOU Minutes, 17 November 1886, AOU Records, RU 7150, Box 5, vol. 1, pp. 251–253, SIA. Another account is in "News and Notes," *Auk* (1887): 82–83.

104. On the short-lived Society of American Taxidermists, see Susan Leigh Star, "Craft vs. Commodity, Mess vs. Transcendence: How the Right Tool Became the Wrong One in the Case of Taxidermy and Natural History," in *The Right Tools for the Job: At Work in Twentieth-Century Life Sciences*, ed. Adele E. Clarke and Joan H. Fujimura (Princeton: Princeton University Press, 1992), 257–286.

105. For example, M. Abbott Frazar and John C. Cahoon, both professional collectors, taxidermists, and natural history dealers, had done extensive collecting for Brewster.

106. William Brewster to G. B. Sennett, 2 February 1886, William Brewster Papers, MCZ Archives.

107. "Notes and News," *Auk* 4 (1887): 82.

108. Ibid., 83.

109. "Editorial," *Ornithologist and Oologist* 9 (1884): 70.

110. F. A. Lucas, "The Destruction of Birds for Millinery Purposes," *Ornithologist and Oologist* 9 (1884): 98.

111. W. W. C[astle], "The Destruction of Birds for Millinery Purposes: A Request for Facts," *Ornithologist and Oologist* 9 (1884): 116.

112. F. A. Lucas, "The Destruction of Birds for Millinery Purposes," *Ornithologist and Oologist* 9 (1884): 128; L. M. McCormick, "The Destruction of Birds for Millinery Purposes," *Ornithologist and Oologist* 9 (1884): 138–140. Castle tried to draw Lucas back into the argument by accusing him of withdrawing because he could not produce the facts Castle had earlier demanded. W. W. C[astle], "Editor O. and O," *Ornithologist and Oologist* 9 (1884): 140.

113. W. W. C[astle], "The Destruction of Birds for Millinery Purposes," *Ornithologist and Oologist* 10 (1885): 15–16. In the interim, a letter in the same periodical blamed the decrease in the number of birds on the large number of cats roaming freely throughout the countryside. A. T. G., "The Destruction of Birds for Millinery Purposes," *Ornithologist and Oologist* 9 (1885): 152.

114. F. A. Lucas, "The Destruction of Birds for Millinery Purposes," *Ornithologist and*

Oologist 10 (1885): 31–32; and L. M. Mc-Cormick, "The Destruction of Birds for Millinery Purposes," *Ornithologist and Oologist* 10 (1885): 48.

115. The exception to this general trend is a letter from C. S. Brimley, a dealer from North Carolina who argued that "it is not so wicked to kill a bird to adorn a hat as many seem to think." "The Destruction of Birds for Millinery Purposes," *Ornithologist and Oologist* 11 (1886): 160.

116. C. F. Freeman, "The Medium of 'Bird Protection,'" *Ornithologist and Oologist* 11 (1886): 48.

117. "Bird Protection," *Ornithologist and Oologist* 11 (1884): 56–57.

118. "Editorial," *Ornithologist and Oologist* 11 (1886): 72–73. The response was at least partially informed by recent hearings in the Massachusetts state house on the reform of game laws, in which the new inland fish commissioner declared "a war on taxidermists." Massachusetts Taxidermist, "War Against Taxidermists," *Ornithologist and Oologist* 11 (1886): 63–64.

119. W. DeForrest Northrup, "The Study of Ornithology and its Relation to the Decrease of Our Birds," *Ornithologist and Oologist* 11 (1886): 112.

120. J. A. Allen to William Brewster, 11 August 1886, William Brewster Papers, MCZ Archives.

121. Montague Chamberlain, "The A.O.U. and Amateurs," *Ornithologist and Oologist* 11 (1886): 160.

122. "That the pursuits of amateur naturalists have come under a ban to a considerable extent (in the east) from the results of the action of the A.O.U., I believe to be true; perhaps not intentionally." Massachusetts Taxidermist, "Amateur and A.O.U.," *Ornithologist and Oologist* 11 (1886): 176.

123. W. DeForrest Northrup, "The A.O.U. and Amateurs," *Ornithologist and Oologist* 11 (1887): 192.

124. Montague Chamberlain, "The A.O.U. and the Amateurs," *Ornithologist and Oologist* 12 (1887): 32.

125. J. A. Allen, "The A.O.U. and the Amateurs," *Ornithologist and Oologist* 12 (1887): 47–48.

126. Batchelder, *Account of the Nuttall Ornithological Club*, 49.

127. As has already been mentioned, "Bulletin No. 2. Protection of Birds by Legislation" was first published in *Forest and Stream* 27 (1886): 304–305, and was largely devoted to a discussion of the bird protection law recently enacted in New York. It also contained a slightly revised version of the AOU model law.

128. Sennett published his 1889 testimony to the Pennsylvania Board of Agriculture as B. G. [i.e., G. B.] Sennett, *Bird Legislation* (Harrisburg, Pa.: State Printer, 1890).

129. "Notes and News," *Auk* 11 (1894): 87. See also AOU Minutes, 20 November 1893, AOU Records, RU 7150, Box 5, vol. 3, pp. 81–83, SIA. The claim that "most" states had enacted excellent bird protection laws is false.

130. In a letter to Frank M. Chapman, who was then contemplating initiating *Bird-Lore* magazine, George B. Grinnell wrote, "Of the 50,000 members of the [Audubon] society which we had at the time on our books, not more than 5% were subscribers [to *Audubon Magazine*]. The venture was a losing one from the start, as we expected, but after running for two years it gave no prospect of doing much better." 10 November 1898, Archives, Department of Ornithology, AMNH.

CHAPTER SIX

1. Hemenway's role in the creation of the Massachusetts Audubon Society is detailed in several recent publications: Graham, *Audubon Ark*, 14–18; Joseph Kastner, "Long before Furs, It Was Feathers That Stirred Reformist Ire," *Smithsonian* 25 (July 1994): 96–104; Richard K. Walton, "A History of the Massachusetts Audubon Society from 1896 into the 1950s" (ms. available from Massachusetts Audubon Society); and John H. Mitchell, "The Mothers of Conservation," *Sanctuary* (January–February 1996): 1–20.

2. Quoted in William Dutcher, "Report of the A.O.U. Committee on Protection of North American Birds [for 1896]," *Auk* 14 (1897): 31.

3. A list of the early publications of the Massachusetts Audubon Society is reproduced in William Dutcher, "Report of the Committee of the A.O.U. Committee on Protection of North American Birds [for 1897]," *Auk* 15 (1898): 83–84.

4. This was the primary reason given for the failure of the first Audubon movement by William Dutcher in "History of the Audubon Movement," *Bird-Lore* 7 (1905): 55–56.

5. On the historiography of the progressive movement, see Arthur Link and Richard McCormick, *Progressivism* (Arlington Heights, Ill.: Harlan Davidson, 1983). For a discussion of the various manifestations of the pervasive turn-of-the-century desire to reconnect with nature, see Schmitt, *Back to Nature*.

6. Among the original participants who have written histories of the second Audubon movement are William Dutcher, "History of the Audubon Movement," *Bird-Lore* 7 (1905): 45–57; T. Gilbert Pearson, "Fifty Years of Bird Protection," in *Fifty Years' Progress of American Orni-*

thology, 1883–1933, ed. Frank M. Chapman and T. S. Palmer (Lancaster, Pa.: AOU, 1933), 199–213, and *Adventures in Bird Protection*. More recent histories of the movement are Frank Graham, Jr., and Carl Buchheister, "From the Swamps and Back: A Concise and Candid History of the Audubon Movement," *Audubon* 75 (1973): 4–45; Doughty, *Feather Fashions and Bird Preservation*; Fox, *American Conservation Movement*, 151–159; Graham, *Audubon Ark*; and Oliver H. Orr, Jr., *Saving American Birds: T. Gilbert Pearson and the Founding of the Audubon Movement* (Gainesville: University Press of Florida, 1992).

7. AOU Minutes, 11 November 1895, AOU Records, RU 7150, Box 5, vol. 3, p. 149, SIA. Following Sennett's resignation in 1893, the committee remained inactive under the leadership of its two subsequent chairs, Frank M. Chapman and Gordon Trumbull.

8. The biographical sketch that follows is largely from T. S. Palmer, "In Memoriam: William Dutcher," *Auk* 38 (1921): 501–513. For additional biographical information on Dutcher, see Graham, *Audubon Ark*, 19–22, 26–33, 42–47, and 68–73.

9. William Dutcher, "Wilson's Plover on Long Island, N.Y.," *Bulletin of the Nuttall Ornithological Club* 4 (1879): 242.

10. For example, in an untitled announcement in 1897, Dutcher reported on the recent organization of the Audubon Society of New York and "earnestly" urged the formation of additional state societies. William Dutcher, "Notes and News," *Auk* 14 (1897): 257–258. See also the long series of letters between Dutcher and T. Gilbert Pearson in National Audubon Society Records, Box A-6, Rare Books and Manuscripts Division, New York Public Library (hereafter cited as NAS Records, NYPL), which led to the creation of the North Carolina Audubon Society.

11. The early records of the Audubon Society of the District of Columbia are found in Audubon Naturalist Society of the Central Atlantic States Archives, RU 7294, SIA.

12. See the list of states in Dutcher, "History of the Audubon Movement," 47. In several instances members of existing humane societies were the primary force behind the new bird protection societies. For example, see William Dutcher, "Report [for 1897]," 100, 107.

13. A list of pamphlets and circulars issued during the early years of the New York Audubon Society is found in Dutcher, "Report [for 1897]," 91. Copies of these publications are located in the Audubon Society Records, Archives, Department of Ornithology, AMNH.

14. Frank M. Chapman to William Brewster, 13 November 1897, William Brewster Papers, MCZ Archives.

15. Dutcher, "Report [for 1896]," 32.

16. On the origins and early celebration of Arbor Day, see Robert H. Schauffler, ed., *Arbor Day: Its History, Observance, Spirit and Significance* (New York: Moffat, Yard 1909). The quotation is from T. S. Palmer, *Bird Day in the Schools*, U.S. Department of Agriculture, Division of the Biological Survey, circular no. 17, 2 July 1896, p. 1.

17. The letter from Florence Merriam outlining this proposal is reproduced in Dutcher, "Report [for 1897]," 111–112.

18. See "Notes and News," *Auk* 18 (1901): 127.

19. B. L. Bowdish, "Nature Study," *Oologist* 14 (1897): 99.

20. Chapman said as much when he pronounced that "the Union's Committee on the Protection of North American Birds is, in effect, an Audubon Society." [Frank M. Chapman,] "The A.O.U. and Audubon Societies," *Bird-Lore* 2 (1900): 161–162.

21. The announcement that the committee had been enlarged came in "Notes and News," *Auk* 14 (1897): 116. By 1901 the committee included twenty-two members. See William Dutcher, "Report of the Committee on the Protection of North American Birds for the Year 1900," *Auk* 18 (1901): 103–104.

22. William Dutcher to William Brewster, 4 October 1898, William Brewster Papers, MCZ Archives. See also the complaint in William Dutcher, "Report [for 1897]," 82.

23. Dutcher resigned in December 1897. Within a few years Stone began lobbying for someone to take over the burdensome work. See, for example, Witmer Stone to William Dutcher, 16 March and 1 October 1900, 2 April 1901, 15 November 1901 (filed under 1902); William Dutcher to Witmer Stone, 1 December 1900, NAS Records, Box A-6, NYPL. Dutcher finally agreed to resume chairing the committee in 1901.

24. James A. G. Rehn, "In Memoriam: Witmer Stone," *Auk* 58 (1941): 299–313.

25. Witmer Stone, "Report of the A.O.U. Committee on Protection of North American Birds [for 1899]," *Auk* 16 (1900): 60.

26. Frank M. Chapman to William Brewster, 22 and 29 October 1898, William Brewster Papers, MCZ Archives.

27. Frank M. Chapman to J. A. Allen, 25 April 1899, Archives, Department of Ornithology, AMNH.

28. He began approaching the various Audubon societies about the idea as early as one year previously. See Frank M. Chapman to Mrs. J. D. Patton [i.e., Patten], 26 October 1897, Audubon Naturalist Society of the Central Atlantic States Archives, RU 7294, Box 1, SIA.

29. Witmer Stone, "Report [for 1899]," *Auk* 17 (1900): 52. Chapman continued to own and edit the magazine until 1934, when he sold it to the National Association of Audubon Societies.

30. James B. Trefethen, "John Fletcher Lacey," in *National Leaders of American Conservation*, ed. Richard H. Stroud (Washington, D.C.: Smithsonian Institution Press, 1985), 236–237; and Annette Gallagher, "Citizen of a Nation: John Fletcher Lacey, Conservationist," *Annals of Iowa* 46 (1981): 9–24.

31. The best study of the Lacey Act is Theodore Whaley Cart, "The Lacey Act: America's First Nationwide Wildlife Statute," *Forest History* (October 1973): 4–13, which is based on his earlier dissertation, "The Struggle for Wildlife Protection in the United States, 1870–1900: Attitudes and Events Leading Up to the Lacey Act" (Ph.D. diss., University of North Carolina at Chapel Hill, 1971).

32. On the AOU's role in passing the Lacey Act, see Witmer Stone to William Dutcher, 16 March and 4 May 1900, NAS Records, Box A-6, NYPL.

33. Cart, "Lacey Act," 6.

34. For example, in 1895 a notice in the *Auk* reported that several "scientific and other societies" had secured a "special game protector" during the 1894 breeding season to police a colony of terns on Great Gull Island, N.Y. "Notes and News," *Auk* 12 (1895): 97.

35. Witmer Stone, "Report of the Committee on the Protection of North American Birds for the Year 1900," *Auk* 28 (1901): 69. See also Graham, *Audubon Ark*, 20–22; and the extensive correspondence between Dutcher and Thayer in NAS Records, NYPL.

36. Stone, "Report for 1900," 76–77. Details of the particular areas protected are given in the report on pp. 77–103.

37. The states and dates of passage of their laws were Indiana (1891), Vermont (1892), Arkansas (1897), Illinois (1899), and Rhode Island (1900). From Witmer Stone, "Report of the Committee on the Protection of North American Birds [for 1901]," *Auk* 19 (1902): 36.

38. Between February and August 1901, the District of Columbia and the following states passed bird protection legislation: Wyoming, Massachusetts, Maine, New Hampshire, Wisconsin, Delaware, Florida, New York, Connecticut, and New Jersey. On the lobbying campaigns in each state, see Stone, "Report [for 1901]," 36–44. On Dutcher's role in the passage of this and subsequent state legislation, see "How One Man Secured a Law in Thirty-Two States," *World's Work* 12 (1906): 8137–8138. See also the extensive correspondence between Palmer and Dutcher in NAS Archives, Box A-6, NYPL.

39. Dutcher, "History of the Audubon Movement," 47.

40. Quoted in Graham, *Audubon Ark*, 44. Other published accounts of the events leading up to the creation of Pelican Island include Pearson, *Adventures*, 236–237; and Chapman, *Autobiography*, 181–182.

41. See William Dutcher to Mrs. F. E. B. Latham, 18 March 1902 and 28 April 1902; William Dutcher to T. S. Palmer, 6 June, 24 July, and 1 August 1902, 16 February 1903; T. S. Palmer to William Dutcher, 30 July 1902, 21 and 25 February 1903; NAS Records, Box A-6, NYPL.

42. Palmer, *Adventures*, 236, credits C. L. DuBois with the idea.

43. On Bond's critical role in this process, see T. Gilbert Pearson, "Frank Bond," *Bird-Lore* 13 (1911): 175–177.

44. See the list of reservations established by Roosevelt in "Fifth Annual Report of the National Association of Audubon Societies, 1909," *Bird-Lore* 11 (1909): 291–294.

45. "Notes and News," *Auk* 27 (1900): 404.

46. "Notes and News," *Auk* 28 (1901): 127.

47. Dutcher, "History of the Audubon Movement," 57.

48. William Dutcher, "Report of the A.O.U. Committee on the Protection of North American Birds [for 1902]," *Auk* 20 (1903): 101–159.

49. The specific circumstances surrounding his resignation are discussed below.

50. See chapter 5.

51. For an opposing view, see Charles L. Phillips, "Are Ornithologists Cruel?" *Oologist* 15 (1898): 13–14.

52. Leander Keyser, "The Art of Kicking Gently," *Osprey* 3 (1898–1899): 109–110.

53. Biographical information on Robbins may be found in his entry for *Who Was Who in America* (Chicago: A. N. Marquis, 1966), 3:731.

54. The pamphlet was printed by E. W. Wheeler of Cambridge, Mass. The information on the circulation of the pamphlet comes from B. S. Bowdish, "A Further Consideration," *Oologist* 19 (1902): 87.

55. Biographical information on Hornaday, a central figure in conservation circles during the early twentieth century, may be found in J. A. Dolph, "Bringing Wildlife to the Millions: William Temple Hornaday, The Early Years: 1854–1896" (Ph.D. diss., University of Massachusetts, 1975); Fox, *American Conservation Movement*; and John G. Mitchell, "The Way We Shuffled Off the Buffalo," *Wildlife Conservation* 96 (January–February 1993): 44–51. Hornaday is clearly deserving of a full-length biography.

56. William T. Hornaday, *The Extermination of the American Bison* (Washington, D.C.: Government Printing Office, 1889). The text was

originally prepared for the *Report of the National Museum, 1886–1887.*

57. William T. Hornaday, "The Destruction of Our Birds and Mammals: A Report on the Results of an Inquiry," *Annual Report of the New York Zoological Society* 2 (1898): 77.

58. Dutcher, "Report [for 1897]," *Auk* 15 (1898): 114.

59. Stone, "Report of the A.O.U. Committee on the Protection of North American Birds [for 1898]," *Auk* 16 (1899): 59.

60. An exception is John Lewis Childs to William Dutcher, 8 December 1899, NAS Records, Box A-6, NYPL, in which Childs complains that a proposed bird protection law in New York would put taxidermists out of business.

61. Stone, "Report [for 1898]," 61.

62. Hornaday's protest came in his "Destruction of Our Birds," 88–91, where he pointed to an article in the *Oologist* that included a list of the eggs of warblers in the collection of J. P. Norris of Philadelphia. Among the items in his cabinet were 210 sets of Kentucky warblers numbering some 917 eggs!

63. Stone, "Report [for 1898]," 61.

64. "Editorial Notes," *Condor* 5 (1903): 136.

65. Stone, "Report [for 1898]," 62.

66. Frank T. Antes to William Brewster, 5 February 1904, William Brewster Papers, MCZ Archives. Brewster's reply has not survived.

67. In addition to Stone, its principal author, the pamphlet was signed by J. A. Allen, Frank M. Chapman, Robert Ridgway, Charles W. Richmond, C. Hart Merriam, T. S. Palmer, A. K. Fisher, William Brewster, William Dutcher, and John H. Sage.

68. [Witmer Stone], "Hints to Young Bird Students," reproduced in *Bird-Lore* 1 (1899): 126.

69. Ibid. The New York and Massachusetts Audubon societies refused to distribute the pamphlet because they felt Stone had not gone far enough in denouncing collecting by youngsters. Witmer Stone to William Dutcher, 7 May 1900, NAS Records, Box A-6, NYPL.

70. Five years before the exchange, Norris and his father had already amassed a large collection consisting of 573 species, 5,002 sets, and a total of 20,388 eggs. See *A Catalogue of the Oological Collection of J. Parker Norris and J. Parker Norris Jr.* (Philadelphia: Privately printed, 1894).

71. J. Parker Norris, Jr., *Some Facts about the Consistency of the Chairman of the A.O.U. Committee on Bird Protection and an Answer to His "Hints to Young Students"* (Philadelphia: Privately printed, 1899), 3–5. Norris's "monograph" never materialized.

72. Ibid., 5.

73. Ibid., 6.

74. Ibid.

75. Virtually every issue of volumes 3 and 4 of the *Osprey* contain letters to the editor regarding egg collecting. See the list in Barrow, "Birds and Boundaries," 481, n. 77. See also "Bird Protection Versus Sentiment," *Bulletin of the Cooper Ornithological Club* 11 (1899): 36–37; and Richard McGregor, "Circumstances Alter Cases," ibid., 69–70.

76. Coues, "Editorial Eyrie," *Osprey* 3 (1898–1899): 124.

77. Pearson, *Adventures*, 71.

78. Garrett Newkirk, "Editor of 'The Condor,'" *Condor* 4 (1902): 147.

79. Ibid. The curious reference to Filipinos related to the bloody resistance that American troops had encountered in the colony they had recently acquired following the Spanish-American War.

80. See, for example, William Brewster to "Fiend" [Frank M. Chapman], 23 October 1906, William Brewster Papers, MCZ Archives.

81. William Dutcher, "A Protest," *Condor* 5 (1903): 53–54. The article prompting Dutcher's letter was P. M. Silloway, "The Holboell Grebe in Montana," *Condor* 4 (1902): 128–131.

82. Ibid. In his reply, P. M. Silloway resorted to the prevailing view that God had created nature to serve human purposes. As long as collectors used this material for "the advancement of human pleasure and knowledge," then collecting, on whatever scale, was legitimate. P. M. Silloway, "An Answer," *Condor* 5 (1903): 54–55.

83. A. K. Fisher to William Dutcher, 22 April 1903, A. K. Fisher Papers, Box 39, Library of Congress, Washington, D.C.; and NAS Records, Box A-6, NYPL. Not all scientists agreed with Fisher. See T. S. P[almer], "The Condor," *Bird-Lore* 5 (1903): 33–34.

84. For another example of this trend, see F. R. Stearns, "An Ornithological Sermon," *Osprey* 3 (1898–1899): 43.

85. William Dutcher, "Report of the A.O.U. Committee on the Protection of North American Birds for the Year 1903," *Auk* 21 (1904): 97.

86. Ibid., 103.

87. Ibid., 104.

88. A list of the permits issued through the AMNH survives: "Record of Permits Granted for Collecting Birds," Archives, Department of Ornithology, AMNH.

89. *Annual Reports of the Forest, Fish, and Game Commissioner of the State of New York for 1904, 1905, 1906* (Albany: State Printers, 1907): 232–233. Five years previously, the Massachusetts Department of Fisheries and Game had decided to stop issuing permits for "merely private

collections." See Edward A. Brackett to William Brewster, 13 April 1898, and printed circular enclosed with letter, William Brewster Papers, MCZ Archives. The president of the New Jersey Fish and Game Commission was even more restrictive. See Howard P. Frothingham to William Dutcher, 30 January 1901, NAS Records, Box A-6, NYPL.

90. Fisher failed to mention an Iowa State Supreme Court case that cut off the privilege of collecting game birds for scientific purposes. T. S. Palmer, "Collecting Permits: Their History, Objects, and Restrictions," unpublished speech delivered before the AOU in 1904, p. 1, in T. S. Palmer Papers, Library of Congress, Washington, D.C.

91. [Walter K. Fisher,] "Editorial Notes," *Condor* 5 (1903): 136. In a characteristically caustic reply, J. A. Allen vigorously defended the law: J. A. Allen, "The A.O.U. Model Law," *Condor* 5 (1903): 157–158. Walter K. Fisher's untitled reply follows on 158–159. See also E. W. Nelson's call to eliminate the bonding clause, "On the 'Bonding Clause' of the A.O.U. Model Law," ibid., 159.

92. A. K. Fisher to William Brewster, 23 October 1903, A. K. Fisher Papers, Box 39, Library of Congress, Washington, D.C. See also Fisher's letters to George B. Grinnell (23 October 1903), Charles Batchelder (23 October 1903), and Lynds Jones (22 October 1903) in the same collection.

93. AOU Meeting Minutes, AOU Records, 16 November 1903, RU 7150, Box 5, vol. 3, pp. 114–116, SIA.

94. AOU Council Minutes, 12 November 1906, AOU Records, RU 7150, Box 3, vol. 3, p. 88, SIA.

95. Fisher outlived many of his contemporaries, so published information on his life is sketchy. See Francis M. Uhler, "In Memoriam: Albert Kendrick Fisher," *Auk* 68 (1951): 210–213. A bibliography of his publications until 1926 may be found in T. S. Palmer and W. L. McAtee, "A List of the Publications of A. K. Fisher," *Proceedings of the Biological Society of Washington* 39 (1926): 21–28. Fisher's extensive collection of papers in the Library of Congress, Washington D.C., includes manuscript fragments for an unfinished autobiography (Box 40).

96. A. K. Fisher, *The Hawks and Owls of the United States in Their Relation to Agriculture*, Biological Survey Bulletin Series, no. 3 (Washington, D.C.: Government Printing Office, 1893). Cameron, *Biological Survey*, 217–251, contains a complete bibliography of survey publications until the year 1929.

97. Fisher's statements to the council for 1906 are typical: AOU Council Minutes, 12 Novem-

ber 1906, AOU Records, RU 7150, Box 3, vol. 3, p. 88, SIA.

98. Ibid., 16 November 1908, 130–131.

99. Ibid., 6 December 1909, 147.

100. Ibid., 146–151.

101. "Notes and News," *Auk* 29 (1912): 136.

102. Ibid., 136–137.

103. Ibid., 137.

104. For more on Grinnell, see chapter 8.

105. Joseph Grinnell, "Conserve the Collector," *Science* 41 (1915): 229–232.

106. Ibid., 229.

107. Ibid. Even some ornithologists who were themselves primarily bird observers appreciated the detailed knowledge of birds gained by collectors. See, for example, A. A. Allen, "Studying Birds' Eggs," *Bird-Lore* 22 (1920): 238.

108. Grinnell, "Conserve the Collector," 230.

109. Ibid., 231–232.

110. Ibid., 232.

111. The AOU bird protection committee's continued lack of activity is well documented in the AOU Council Minutes, 8 October 1923, 10 November 1924, 9 November 1925, 10 October 1926, 14 November 1927, 19 November 1928, and 21 October 1929, Box 3, vol. 4, AOU Records, RU 7150, SIA.

112. There are several useful histories of ecology: Sharon E. Kingsland, *Modeling Nature: Episodes in the History of Population Ecology* (Chicago: University of Chicago Press, 1985); McIntosh, *Background of Ecology*; Tobey, *Saving the Prairies*; Worster, *Nature's Economy*; and Gregg Mitman, *The State of Nature: Ecology, Community, and American Social Thought, 1900–1950* (Chicago: University of Chicago Press, 1992). See also Leslie A. Real and James H. Brown, eds., *Foundations of Ecology: Classic Papers with Commentaries* (Chicago: University of Chicago Press, 1991). Tobey and Worster both discuss how ecological notions found their way into conservation discourse, but the most useful study of this development is Thomas R. Dunlap, *Saving America's Wildlife* (Princeton: Princeton University Press, 1988). For an examination of the Ecological Society of America's involvement in conservation issues, see Robert A. Croker, *Pioneer Ecologist: The Life and Work of Victor Ernest Shelford, 1877–1968* (Washington, D.C.: Smithsonian Institution Press, 1991), 120–146; and Sara F. Tjossem, "Preservation of Nature and Academic Respectability: Tensions in the Ecological Society of America, 1915–1979" (Ph.D. diss., Cornell University, 1994).

113. This is a major argument of Dunlap's *Saving America's Wildlife*.

114. The paradigmatic example of the shift from a strictly utilitarian to a more ecologically informed conservation framework is Aldo Leo-

pold. See his highly autobiographical *A Sand County Almanac and Sketches Here and There* (New York: Oxford University Press, 1949); J. Baird Callicott, *Companion to A Sand County Almanac: Interpretive and Critical Essays* (Madison: University of Wisconsin Press, 1987); and Curt Meine, *Aldo Leopold: His Life and Work* (Madison: University of Wisconsin Press, 1988).

115. F. A. Lucas, J. A. Allen, Willard G. Van Name, W. DeW. Miller, G. K. Noble, Roy Chapman Andrews, [name ill.], Ludlow Griscom, Walter Granger, John Treadwell Nichols, James P. Chapin, Jonathan Dwight, Charles H. Rogers, and G. Clyde Fisher to "Members of the Committee on Bird Protection of the American Ornithologists' Union," 9 March 1920, A. K. Fisher Papers, Box 23, Library of Congress, Washington, D.C.

116. A. K. Fisher to F. A. Lucas et al., 15 March 1920, Fisher Papers, Box 23, Library of Congress, Washington, D.C.

117. F. A. Lucas et al. to A. K. Fisher, 31 March 1930; A. K. Fisher to F. A. Lucas, 20 July 1920; F. A. Lucas to A. K. Fisher, 21 July 1920; Willard G. Van Name to A. K. Fisher, 8 October 1920; Willard G. Van Name to John H. Sage, 4 November 1920; A. K. Fisher to Willard G. Van Name, 23 November 1920; A. K. Fisher to F. A. Lucas, 23 November 1923; all in the A. K. Fisher Papers, Library of Congress, Washington, D.C.

118. Henry P. Carey, "Hawk Extermination," *Auk* 43 (1926): 275.

119. Ibid., 276.

120. See, for example, Ernest G. Holt, "Nature-Wasters and Sentimentalists," *Auk* 43 (1926): 409–410; W. L. McAtee, "Hawk Abundance and Hawk Campaigns," *Auk* 43 (1926): 542–544; and G. M. Sutton, "How Can the Bird-Lover Help Save the Hawks and Owls?" *Auk* 46 (1929): 190–195.

121. The Biological Survey's increasing involvement in predator-control activities is detailed in Dunlap, *Saving America's Wildlife*, 38–40, 48–51, 55–59, 66, 77–82, 127–132, 137–141, 160–164; and Jenks, *Biological Survey*, 42–65.

122. Dunlap, *Saving America's Wildlife*, 58.

123. The sixteen-page pamphlet was first privately published in New York and later reissued by the Emergency Conservation Committee, discussed below.

124. The biographical information that follows is from James Chapin, "In Memoriam: Waldron DeWitt Miller, 1879–1929," *Auk* 49 (1932): 1–8.

125. The new classification was announced in Alexander Wetmore and Waldron DeW. Miller, "The Revised Classification for the Fourth Edition of the A.O.U. Check-list," *Auk* 43 (1926): 337–346.

126. Waldron DeW. Miller to *New York Times*, 1 July 1923, Archives, Department of Ornithology, AMNH. The lengthy exchange between Miller and officials at Du Pont survives in the Waldron DeW. Miller Papers, Archives, Department of Ornithology, AMNH.

127. Willard G. Van Name, "Bird Collecting and Ornithology," *Science* 41 (1915): 823–825.

128. A series of Van Name's pamphlets on the subject culminated in a book, *Vanishing Forest Reserves: Problems of the National Forests and National Parks* (Boston: Richard D. Badger, Gorham Press, 1929).

129. Miller, Van Name, and Quinn, "Crisis in Conservation," 2.

130. Ibid., 2–4.

131. Ibid., 15.

132. Ibid.

133. See, for example, Frank M. Chapman to P. B. Phillip, 10 August 1929, Archives, Department of Ornithology, AMNH, in which Chapman urged Phillip to use his influence as an officer of the New Jersey Audubon Society to "prohibit the distribution" of the "unfortunate pamphlet."

134. Irving Brant, *Adventures in Conservation with Franklin D. Roosevelt* (Flagstaff, Ariz: Northland, 1988), 15.

135. The episode is described in Graham, *Audubon Ark*, 112–117, which also includes a biographical sketch of Edge. See also Fox, *American Conservation Movement*, 173–182; and Brant, *Adventures in Conservation*, 15–22.

136. See copy of letter from T. Gilbert Pearson to Rosalie Edge, 11 November 1929, Box 17, Irving Newton Brant Papers, Library of Congress, Washington, D.C.

137. The standard histories of the ECC stress the large role of Rosalie Edge in the organization: Graham, *Audubon Ark*, 112–117; and Fox, *American Conservation Movement*, 175–181, 193–194, 202–203, 212, 215–217, 265, 282, 384. Brant, *Adventures in Conservation*, 13–30, provides a more balanced picture from someone intimately involved in the organization for several years.

138. The titles from some of the early ECC pamphlets are typical: *U.S. Bureau of Destruction and Extermination* and *Compromised Conservation: Can the Audubon Society Explain?*

139. By 1924 Fisher had been replaced as chair of the bird protection committee, but for the next several years the new committee remained inactive and published no reports. As the following account suggests, *A Crisis in Conservation* was one of a series of factors that led to the resurrection of the committee in 1930. Also important were Grinnell's leadership, the controversy surrounding the Biological Survey's predator

control program, pressure from the ECC, and the widespread concern about the drought-induced decline of waterfowl during this period. On the latter problem and its impact on wildlife conservation more generally, see Theodore Cart, "New Deal for Wildlife: A Perspective on Federal Conservation Policy, 1933–40," *Pacific Northwest Quarterly* 63 (July 1972): 113–120.

140. AOU Council Minutes, 21 November 1929, AOU Records, RU 7150, Box 3, vol. 4, p. 188, SIA.

141. Grinnell first approached Bryant about the position in December 1929 and for the first year or so played an important role in spurring on the work of the bird protection committee. See the extensive correspondence between Grinnell and Bryant in MVZ Archives. For biographical information on Bryant, see Ann and Myron Sutton, "The Man from Yosemite," *National Parks Magazine* 28 (July–September 1954): 102–105, 130–132, 140; and William H. Behle, "Henry Child Bryant," *Auk* 87 (1970): 631–632.

142. Harold C. Bryant to Members of the A.O.U. Committee on Bird Protection, 24 March 1930, AOU Records, Box 73, SIA. The letter is part of the Hoyes Lloyd Correspondence file contained in the AOU Records, an invaluable source of the behind-the-scenes activities of the bird protection committee throughout the 1930s. Copies of much of this correspondence are also in the Henry Childs Bryant file, MVZ Archives.

143. The proposals are contained in a H. C. Bryant to Members of the Bird Protection Committee, 4 June 1930, AOU Records, RU 7159, Box 73, SIA.

144. H. C. Bryant to Members of the Bird Protection Committee, 30 September 1930, AOU Records, RU 7150, Box 73, SIA.

145. H. C. Bryant, "Report of the Committee on Bird Protection [for 1930]," *Auk* 39 (1931): 74–76.

146. AOU Council Minutes, 20 October 1930, AOU Records, RU 7150, Box 3, vol. 4, p. 218, SIA.

147. H. C. Bryant to Members of the Bird Protection Committee, 1 November 1930, AOU Records, RU 7150, Box 73, SIA.

148. H. C. Bryant, "Report [for 1930]," 93.

149. Paul G. Redington, "The Bird Work of the Biological Survey," *Auk* 48 (1931): 229–234.

150. "Notes and News," *Auk* 48 (1931): 478. The ornithologists were not entirely opposed to states undertaking limited predator-control programs, only to the Biological Survey's participation in such programs. See also "Notes and News," *Auk* 49 (1932): 275–277.

151. My emphasis. H. C. Bryant, "Report of the Committee on Bird Protection of the American Ornithologists' Union [for 1932]," *Auk* 50 (1933): 89–90.

152. The precise wording of Baldwin's resolution is found in T. S. Palmer to H. C. Bryant, 13 November 1935, AOU Records, RU 7150, Box 73, SIA.

153. These are detailed in excruciating detail in Harrison F. Lewis to S. Prentiss Baldwin, 7 November 1935, AOU Records, RU 7150, Box 70, SIA.

154. The draft resolution is contained in H. C. Bryant to Committee on Bird Protection, 25 May 1936, AOU Records, RU 7150, Box 73, SIA. The American Committee for International Wild Life Protection, organized in 1930, was an offshoot of a Belgian organization begun in the early 1920s. See John C. Phillips and Harold J. Coolidge, Jr., *The First Five Years: The American Committee for International Wild Life Protection* (n.p., 1934), and *Brief History of the Formation of the American Committee for International Wild Life Protection* (n.p., n.d.), both in the Alexander Wetmore Papers, RU 7006, Box 79, SIA.

155. The ECC proposal also included numerous other statements of a similar nature, including a call for the creation of a second list of birds not "holding their own," which could be collected only with special permission; authorities to grant scientific collecting permits only to representatives of public museums and educational institutions; and an end to the practice of collecting rare birds in large series. The full proposal, "Recommendations Concerning Ornithological Collecting Permits," is included in a letter, H. C. Bryant to Committee on Bird Protection, 25 May 1936, AOU Records, RU 7150, Box 73, Folder 6, SIA. P. A. Taverner of the National Museum of Canada responded in detail to the ECC recommendations, calling its authors "sentimental fanatics" who were prone to "exaggeration and absolute misstatements." In Hoyes Lloyd to H. C. Bryant, 3 June 1936, ibid.

156. "Resolution Adopted by the Board of Directors of the National Association of Audubon Societies as a meeting held June 23, 1936," copy contained in John H. Baker to H. C. Bryant, 10 November 1937, ibid. Also published in *Bird-Lore* as "Collecting Resolution Adopted by the Board," *Bird-Lore* 39 (1937): 151–152.

157. The proposed resolution is in a letter, H. C. Bryant to Members of the Bird Protection Committee, 23 October 1937, AOU Records, RU 7150, Box 73, Folder 6, SIA.

158. AOU Council Minutes, 19 October 1936, AOU Records, RU 7150, Box 4, p. 21, SIA.

159. John Baker to H. C. Bryant, 28 November 1936, AOU Records, RU 7150, Box 73, Folder 6, SIA.

160. H. C. Bryant to A. C. Bent, 12 June 1937, ibid.

161. A. C. Bent to H. C. Bryant, 16 June 1937, ibid.

162. The full resolution is printed in H. C. Bryant, "Report of the Committee on Bird Protection, 1938," *Auk* 55 (1938): 328–329.

CHAPTER SEVEN

1. Biographical information on Huxley may be found in C. Kenneth Waters and Albert Van Helden, eds., *Julian Huxley: Biologist and Statesman* (Houston: Rice University Press, 1992).

2. Julian Huxley, "Bird-watching and Biological Science: Some Observations on the Study of Courtship in Birds," *Auk* 33 (1916): 142–161, 256–269, on 142.

3. The term "birdwatching" (initially written as two words) was apparently coined by the British naturalist Edmund Selous in the title of his 1901 book, *Bird Watching* (London: J. M. Dent, 1901). His term was quickly embraced in Britain (see, e.g., E. W. Hendy, "The Aesthetic Appeal of Bird-Watching," *The Contemporary Review* 127 [April 1925]: 482–492) but slow to catch on in the United States. When the British ornithologist E. M. Nicholson published *The Art of Bird-Watching* in 1931, Frank Chapman complained that the author's choice of "major title does not convey a very clear conception of the contents of his book." Chapman preferred the term bird "observer" (see Frank M. Chapman, Review of *The Art of Bird-Watching*, by E. M. Nicholson, *Bird-Lore* 34 [1932]: 81), though at least one American publication appearing in the previous year contained the term in its title: Frances S. Twining, *Birdwatching in the West* (Portland, Ore.: Metropolitan Press, 1931). By the late 1930s, "bird students, bird observers, or ornithologists" were the terms normally used to describe individuals who would later be called birdwatchers. See Leighman Hawkins, "Our Need to Dignify Bird Study," *Audubon Magazine* 60 (March–April 1958): 55–56. The term "birdwatching" finally began to catch on in this country in the 1940s and 1950s, particularly following the publication of Joseph Hickey's *A Guide to Bird Watching* (New York: Oxford University Press, 1943). However, debate continued about whether the term was appropriate. See the responses to Hawkins's 1958 letter to the editor: R. M. Schramm, "A Bird Watcher by Any Other Name," *Audubon Magazine* 60 (May–June 1958): 99; Mrs. Russell Wilson, "Birders and Birding," ibid., 99–100; Earle E. Greene, "Another Dissenter Writes," ibid., 100.

4. On the history of birdwatching in the United States, see Kastner, *World of Watchers*; Gibbons and Strom, *Neighbors to the Birds*. On birdwatching in Great Britain, see Allen, *Naturalist in Britain*, 202–219. For a fascinating sociological analysis of contemporary birdwatching practices, see John Law and Michael Lynch, "Lists, Field Guides, and the Descriptive Organization of Seeing: Birdwatching as an Exemplary Observational Activity," in *Representation in Scientific Practice*, ed. Michael Lynch and Steve Woolgar (Cambridge: MIT Press, 1990), 267–299.

5. Jonathan Dwight, "Editor of 'The Auk,'" *Auk* 35 (1918): 262.

6. J. H. Fleming, "In Memoriam: Jonathan Dwight," *Auk* 47 (1930): 1–6.

7. See the discussion of Dwight in chapter 3.

8. Dwight, "Editor," 262.

9. On the aesthetic attraction of birds, see J. A. Allen, "The Present Wholesale Destruction of Bird-Life in the United States," *Science* 7 (1886): 195; and Hendy, "Aesthetic Appeal."

10. The multitude of activities that Audubon leaders employed to promote birdwatching can be traced in its two official organs: *Audubon Magazine* (1887–1889) and *Bird-Lore*, begun in 1899.

11. See chapter 2 above.

12. Biographical information on Merriam is contained in Kofalk, *No Woman Tenderfoot*; and Bonta, *Women in the Field*, 186–196.

13. On the Smith College Audubon Society, see chapter 6.

14. Florence Merriam, "Hints to Audubon Workers: Fifty Common Birds and How to Know Them," *Audubon Magazine* 1 (1887–1888): 108–113, 132–136, 155–159, 181–185, 200–204, 224–226, 256–259, 271–277; 2 (1888–1889): 6–12, 34–40, 49–53.

15. Florence Merriam, *Birds through an Opera Glass* (Boston: Houghton, Mifflin, 1889).

16. Mabel O. Wright, *Birdcraft: A Field Guide of Two Hundred Song, Game, and Water Birds* (New York: Macmillan, 1895), and Mabel O. Wright and Elliott Coues, *Citizen Bird: Scenes from Bird-Life in Plain English for Beginners* (New York: Macmillan, 1897), both of which went through several printings and editions. Biographical information on Wright, who was a leading light in the turn-of-the-century Audubon movement, may be found in F[rank] M. C[hapman,] "Mabel Osgood Wright, 1859–1934," *Bird-Lore* 36 (1934): 280; Robert H. Welker, "Mabel Osgood Wright," in *Notable American Women, 1607–1950*, ed. Edward T. James (Cambridge: Harvard University Press, 1971), 3:682–684; and Brooks, *Speaking for Nature*, 168–171 and passim.

Neltje Blanchan, *Bird Neighbors* (New York: Doubleday and MacClure, 1897), was the first field guide to rely on color illustration and also went through multiple editions. The scanty biographical information on Blanchan is found in

Gladys Graham, "Neltje De Graff Doubleday," *Dictionary of American Biography* 5 (1930): 392; Robert H. Welker, "Neltje Blanchan De Graff Doubleday," in *Notable American Women, 1607–1950: A Biographical Dictionary*, ed. Edward T. James (Cambridge: Harvard University Press, 1971), 1:508–509; and Gibbons and Strom, *Neighbors*, 291, 331, 333.

17. More details surrounding Chapman's life and early career are contained in chapter 5.

18. [Frank M. Chapman,] [Editorial,] *Bird-Lore* 1 (1899): 28. The motto began appearing on the mast-head beginning with vol. 1, no. 3 (June 1899).

19. Chapman, *Handbook of Birds of Eastern North America*. He issued revised editions in 1912 and 1932. The quotation comes from E[dward] P. B[icknell], "Chapman's 'Handbook of Birds of Eastern North America,'" *Auk* 12 (1895): 282–284, on 283.

20. Frank M. Chapman, *Bird-Life: A Guide to the Study of Our Common Birds* (New York: D. Appleton, 1897).

21. On Seton, who later became a best-selling nature writer, see Betty Keller, *Black Wolf: The Life of Ernest Thompson Seton* (Vancouver: Douglas and McIntyre, 1984); and Lutts, *Nature Fakers*, passim.

22. The quotation comes from a letter from Frank Chapman to William Brewster, 1 October 1903, William Brewster Papers, MCZ Archives. Frank Chapman, *Color Key to North American Birds* (New York: Doubleday, Page, 1903).

23. Chapman, *Color Key*, iv.

24. Biographical information on Reed may be found in Witmer Stone, "Chester A. Reed," *Auk* 30 (1913): 319.

25. *American Ornithology* was published until 1906. Publication information and the quotation are from Frank Burns, "A Bibliography of Scarce and Out of Print North American Amateur and Trade Periodicals Devoted More or Less to Ornithology," supplement to *Oologist* 32 (1915): 3.

26. Chester A. Reed, *Bird Guide*, 2 vols. (Worster, Mass.: C. K. Reed, 1906). The book, which was copyrighted in 1905, was also published by W. B. Clark and Co. of Boston in 1906. The publication dates listed in Gibbons and Strom, *Neighbors to the Birds*, 292, are incorrect.

27. The book was apparently completed by and issued under the name of his father, Charles K. Reed, *Western Bird Guide: Birds of the Rockies and West to the Pacific* (Garden City, N.Y.: Doubleday, Page, 1913).

28. See, for example, the testimony from Olin S. Pettingill, Jr., *My Way to Ornithology* (Norman: University of Oklahoma Press, 1992), 35. On the influence of Reed's guides on

Roger T. Peterson, see Richard L. Zusi, *Roger T. Peterson at the Smithsonian* (Washington, D.C.: Smithsonian Institution, 1984), 14; and John Devlin and Grace Naismith, *The World of Roger Tory Peterson* (New York: New York Times Books, 1977), 6.

29. Gibbons and Strom, *Neighbors to the Birds*, 325.

30. A brief but useful history of binoculars is found in "Binocular Instrument," *Encyclopedia Britannica* 13th ed. (1926), 3:949–951. See also M[oritz] von Rohr, *Die binokularen Instrumente: nach Quellen* (Berlin: J. Springer, 1907).

31. Felix Auerbach, *The Zeiss Works and the Carl Zeiss Foundation in Jena: Their Scientific, Technical and Sociological Development and Importance Popularly Described*, trans. from 5th German ed. by R. Kanthack (London: W & G Foyle, 1927), 85–92.

32. See, for example, the strong endorsement of Lynds Jones, "All Day with the Birds," *Wilson Bulletin* 11 (1899): 43.

33. Alfred A. Gross, "History and Progress of Bird Photography in America," in *Fifty Years' Progress of American Ornithology, 1883–1933*, ed. Frank M. Chapman and T. S. Palmer (Lancaster, Pa.: American Ornithologists' Union, 1933), 159–180.

34. Frank Chapman, *Bird Studies with a Camera* (New York: D. Appleton, 1900); Francis H. Herrick, *The Home Life of Wild Birds* (New York: Putnam, 1901); A. Radclyffe Dugmore, *Nature and the Camera* (New York: Doubleday, Page, 1902); William L. Finley, *American Birds, Studied and Photographed from Life* (New York: C. Scribner's and Sons, 1907); Herbert K. Job, *Among the Waterfowl* (New York: Doubleday, Page, 1903). Finley and Job both became field agents for the National Association of Audubon Societies. On Finley and his career, see Worth Mathewson, *William L. Finley: Pioneer Wildlife Photographer* (Corvallis: Oregon State University Press, 1986).

35. Chapman (*Bird Studies*, 3) argued that "hunting with a camera is the highest development of man's inherent love of the chase."

36. David V. Herlihy, "The Bicycle Story," *American Heritage of Invention and Technology* 7 (Spring 1992): 48–49.

37. Neil F. Posson, "Ornithology and Bicycling," *Oologist* 7 (1890): 9–10.

38. See David L. Lewis and Laurence Goldstein, eds., *The Automobile and American Culture* (Ann Arbor: University of Michigan Press, 1983); James J. Flink, *The Automobile Age* (Cambridge: MIT Press, 1988).

39. David Allen makes a similar argument in *Naturalist in Britain*, 207–208. The quotation comes in a letter from Robert Porter Allen to

Frank M. Chapman, 2 June 1932, Archives, Department of Ornithology, AMNH.

40. The distinction was suggested to me by Carol J. Adams, *The Sexual Politics of Meat: A Feminist-Vegetarian Critical Theory* (New York: Continuum, 1995).

41. Frank M. Chapman, "Bird Clubs in America," *Bird-Lore* 17 (1915): 348.

42. The history of Church and Co. and its bird cards are discussed briefly in Robert Jay, *The Trade Card in Nineteenth-Century America* (Columbia: University of Missouri Press, 1987), 56 and 103; and Elizabeth Pullar, "Baking Soda Bonus Cards: Arm and Hammer Trade Cards Designed by L. A. Fuertes," *Antiques Journal* 35 (January 1980): 36–38.

43. [Frank M. Chapman,] [Editorial,] *Bird-Lore* 14 (1912): 237.

44. The original edition was Robert W. Wood, *How to Tell the Birds from the Flowers: A Manual of Flornithology for Beginners* (San Francisco: P. Elder, 1907). Biographical information on Wood comes from R. B. Lindsay, "Robert Williams Wood," *Dictionary of Scientific Biography* 14 (1976): 497–499; and G. H. Dieke, "Robert Williams Wood, May 2, 1868–August 11, 1955," *Biographical Memoirs of the National Academy of Sciences* 62 (1993): 441–464.

45. In 1908 Wood published a second volume, *Animal Analogues: Verses and Illustrations* (San Francisco: P. Elder, 1908). He subsequently merged the illustrations and text from his two previous volumes in *How to Tell the Birds from the Flowers and Other Woodcuts: A Revised Manual of Flornithology for Beginners* (New York: Dodd, Mead, 1917). According to information gleaned from the OCLC catalog, Wood's popular book was repeatedly reprinted until 1959.

46. The cartoon appeared in the *New Yorker* 11, no. 12 (4 May 1935): 14.

47. On the activities of several early bird clubs, see the series of articles from *Bird-Lore* 17 (1915): 347–372.

48. Chapman, "Bird Clubs," 347.

49. See the list of "Ornithological Societies," *Bird-Lore* 37 (September 1935): 367–372. One of the most active bird club promoters was the nature writer Ernst Harold Baynes, who founded the Meriden (N.H.) Bird Club in 1910 and later helped establish more than two hundred similar institutions during his popular national lecture tours. See the obituary, T. S. Palmer, "Ernest Harold Baynes," *Auk* 42 (1925): 480–481, and the longer (uncritical) biography by Raymond Gorges, *Ernest Harold Baynes: Naturalist and Crusader* (Boston: Houghton Mifflin, 1928).

50. Joseph Hickey, "The Amateur Ornitholo-

gist and His Bird Club," *Bird-Lore* 39 (1937): 425–429, encouraged bird club members to become more active in cooperative studies.

51. [Frank Chapman,] [Editorial,] *Bird-Lore* 1 (1899): 28.

52. The sales figures are from Pearson, "Fifty Years," 203.

53. Though not really a field guide, Rev. J[ames] Hibbert Langille, M.A., *Our Birds in Their Haunts: A Popular Treatise on the Birds of Eastern North America* (Boston: S. E. Cassino, 1884) was among the earliest bird books clearly aimed at a broad audience of noncollectors. In addition to works by Merriam, Wright, Blanchan, Chapman, and Reed, some of the field guides available before Peterson include Austin C. Apgar, *Pocket Key of the Birds of the Northern United States, East of the Rocky Mountains* (Trenton, N.J.: John L. Murphy, 1893); H. E. Parkhurst, *The Birds' Calendar* (New York: Charles Scribner's Sons, 1894); Herbert Eugene Walter and Alice Hall Walter, *Wild Birds in City Parks*, rev. ed. (Chicago, 1902); H. E. Parkhurst, *How to Name All the Birds* (New York: Charles Scribner's Sons, 1903); Ralph Hoffmann, *A Guide to the Birds of New England and Eastern New York* (Boston: Houghton, Mifflin, 1904); John D. Kuser, *The Way to Study Birds* (New York: G. P. Putnam's Sons, 1917); Luther E. Wyman and Elizabeth F. Burnell, *Field Book of Birds of the Southwestern United States* (Boston: Houghton Mifflin, 1925); Ralph Hoffmann, *Birds of the Pacific States* (Boston: Houghton Mifflin, 1927).

54. See chapter 6.

55. See chapter 4.

56. Histories of the Wilson Ornithological Society and its early publication outlets are found in Jerome Jackson, Harold Mayfield, and George A. Hall, "A History of the First One Hundred Years of the Wilson Ornithological Society," *Wilson Bulletin* 100 (1988): 617–618; Harold Mayfield, "The Early Years of the Wilson Ornithological Society: 1885–1921," ibid.: 619–624; George A. Hall, "The Middle Years of the Wilson Ornithological Society: 1922–1955," ibid.: 625–631; Jerome A. Jackson, "The Wilson Ornithological Society in the Last Third of Its First Century: 1956–1988," ibid.: 632–649; and Kastner, *World of Watchers*, 132–138.

57. See, for example, [Lynds Jones?,] "Notes," *Wilson Quarterly* 4, no. 1 (1892): 42, who argued that the Wilson Chapter was unique because "its method is simply co-operation in study."

58. In 1950 the organization changed its name to the Wilson Ornithological Society.

59. The biographical information that follows is from S. Charles Kendeigh, "In Memoriam:

Lynds Jones," *Auk* 69 (1952): 258–265; Mrs.
H. J. Taylor, "Lynds Jones," *Wilson Bulletin* 50
(1938): 225–238; and Keir Sterling, "Lynds
Jones," *Dictionary of American Biography* supplement 5 (1977): 373–375.

60. By 1900 Jones was offering beginning,
advanced, and summer school courses in ornithology. All three were heavily field oriented.
See Lynds Jones, "On Methods in Teaching Ornithology at Oberlin College," *Bird-Lore* 2
(1900): 14–18.

61. See, for example, the description of the
goals of the organization in [Lynds Jones?,]
"Notes," *Wilson Quarterly* 4, no. 1 (1892): 42.
See also Lynds Jones, "A Criticism," *Wilson
Bulletin* 13 (1901): 75.

62. [Lynds Jones,] "Editorial," *Wilson Bulletin* 9 (1897): 10.

63. William L. Dawson, "Editorial," *Wilson
Bulletin* 9 (1897): 32, and "Committee on Geographical Distribution: Further Mechanical
Helps to Observation," *Wilson Bulletin* 10
(1898): 28–29. For a biographical sketch of Dawson, see Witmer Stone, "William Leon Dawson,"
Auk 45 (1928): 417.

64. See, for example, [Lynds Jones,] "All Day
with the Birds: May 7, 1902," *Wilson Bulletin* 14
(1902): 125, in which the author argues: "There
is a fascination about the quest for the largest list
of birds in a day which is not equalled even by
the search for new species in a region which one
has worked for years." See also Lynds Jones, "A
March Horizon," *Wilson Bulletin* 11 (1899):
22–24.

65. On the competitive aspects of listing, see
Bartlett Hendricks, "Birding Is a Sport," *Audubon Magazine* 48 (1946): 246–248, 304–306;
Richard B. Fischer, "That Big Day," *Audubon
Magazine* (May–June 1953): 114–117, 142; and
Roger Tory Peterson, *Birds over America* (New
York: Dodd, Mead, 1948), 13–35. For a defense
of the activity of listing, see Guy Emerson, "The
Lure of the List," *Audubon Magazine* 42 (1940):
36–39. Competitions to find the largest number
of birds in a single day seem to have been particularly popular.

66. See the series of editorials from [Lynds
Jones]: *Wilson Bulletin* 10 (1898): 30–31, 77–78;
and 19 (1907): 161.

67. See, for example, the series of reports and
pleas from Lynds Jones: "A March Horizon,"
Wilson Bulletin 11 (1899): 22–24; "Editorial,"
Wilson Bulletin 11 (1899): 46–47; "A New Year
Horizon for All," *Wilson Bulletin* 14 (1902): 133;
"A May-Day Horizon," *Wilson Bulletin* 15
(1903): 31; "Editorial," *Wilson Bulletin* 16
(1904): 60–61; "Editorial," *Wilson Bulletin*
27 (1915): 287.

68. Lynds Jones, "With the Birds in Fourteen
States," *Wilson Bulletin* 12 (1900): 1; Lynds

Jones, "The Horizons," *Wilson Bulletin* 12
(1900): 10–38. For a criticism of the effort, see
the review by F.S.D., "The Wilson Bulletin,"
Condor 4 (1901): 53–54. For Jones's reply see
"A Criticism," *Wilson Bulletin* 13 (1901): 76–78;
and for Dawson's reply, see "A Defense of Bird
Horizons," *Condor* 4 (1901): 132–133.

69. In the early issues of the *Wilson Bulletin*,
Jones frequently mentioned the need for more articles. See, for example, [Lynds Jones,] "Editorial," *Wilson Bulletin* 9 (1897): 64, and "Editorial," *Wilson Bulletin* 11 (1899): 62.

70. [Lynds Jones,] "Editorial," *Wilson Bulletin* 36 (1924): 93.

71. [Frank M. Chapman,] "A Christmas Bird-Census," *Bird-Lore* 2 (1900): 192.

72. See, for example, Peterson, *Birds over
America*, 37–47; Gibbons and Strom, *Neighbors
to the Birds*, 312–313; and Chandler S. Robbins,
"The Christmas Count," in *Birds in Our Lives*,
ed. Alfred Stefferud (Washington, D.C.: U.S.
Department of the Interior, 1966), 154–163.

73. Chapman once wrote that the AOU migration network signaled the "beginning of the
Epoch of Popular Bird Study." [Frank M. Chapman,] [Editorial,] *Bird-Lore* 17 (1915): 216.

74. William Leon Dawson, "Committee on
Geographical Distribution," *Wilson Bulletin* 9
(1897): 76. Dawson promised that the reports
would be published in the next issue of the *Bulletin*. In January 1898 Jones reported on two
"censo-horizons" that he had undertaken on
31 December 1897 and 4 January 1898 (the latter
in the company of Dawson). At the end of his
report, Jones urged "all who can do so to try this
sort of winter work." Lynds Jones, "The Bird
Census," *Wilson Bulletin*, 10 (1898): 5–9. The
next year Jones printed a series of "December
Horizons," before his efforts were overshadowed
by Chapman's Christmas Census.

75. [Frank M. Chapman,] "The Christmas
Bird Census," *Bird-Lore* 3 (1901): 28–33.

76. These are reported in [Frank M. Chapman,] "Bird-Lore's Tenth Christmas Census,"
Bird-Lore 12 (1910): 19–36. The total count
comes from "Fiftieth Christmas Bird Count,"
Audubon Field Notes 4, no. 2 (April 1950): 45.

77. [Frank M. Chapman,] "Bird-Lore's Thirteenth Christmas Census," *Bird-Lore* 15 (1913):
20–45. As was often the case, Chapman highlighted the record (106 species). On the career of
Allan Brooks, see Hamilton M. Laing, *Allen
Brooks: Artist Naturalist* (Victoria, B.C.: British
Columbia Provincial Museum, 1979).

78. "Bird-Lore's Thirty-fifth Christmas Census," *Bird-Lore* 37 (1935): 31–85. The list of
species located is found on pp. 84–85.

79. "Fiftieth Christmas Count," 45.

80. As early as 1903 Lynds Jones suggested
that observers prepare for a count by first scout-

ing out areas in which birds might be found. See his "New Year Horizon," *Wilson Bulletin* 15 (1903): 113–114.

81. C[harles] H. R[ogers], "Bird-Lore's Fifteenth Christmas Census," *Bird-Lore* 17 (1915): 22.

82. C[harles] H. R[ogers], "Bird-Lore's Eighteenth Christmas Bird Count," *Bird-Lore* 19 (1917): 317–318.

83. See, for example, [Frank M. Chapman,] [Editorial,] *Bird-Lore* 13 (1911): 48.

84. [Frank M. Chapman,] [Editorial,] *Bird-Lore* 24 (1922): 54.

85. The first comment is from "Fiftieth Christmas Bird Count," 43. The second is from Leonard Wing and Millard Jenks, "Christmas Censuses: The Amateurs' Contribution to Science," *Bird-Lore* 41 (1939): 343–350, on 343.

86. "Preliminary Bibliography of Articles Based on Christmas Bird Counts," *Audubon Field Notes* 4, no. 2 (April 1950): 187. By 1950 the number had increased to eighteen, thanks primarily to the work of Leonard Wing, a biologist at the University of Wisconsin who recruited WPA workers to process the mounds of Christmas Census data. On the development of census techniques, see S. Charles Kendeigh, "Measurement of Bird Populations," *Ecological Monographs* 14, no. 1 (1944): 67–106. For a more recent discussion and critique of data gathered by Christmas Census and other cooperative observational projects, see John Terbough, *Where Have All the Birds Gone?: Essays on the Biology and Conservation of Birds that Migrate to the American Tropics* (Princeton: Princeton University Press, 1989), 11–18.

87. Figures for the total number of migration report contributors are mentioned regularly in the annual *Report of the Chief of the Biological Survey.*

88. Wells W. Cooke, *Report on the Bird Migration in the Mississippi Valley in the Years 1884 and 1885,* ed. and rev. by C. Hart Merriam, U.S. Department of Agriculture. Division of Economic Agriculture, Bulletin no. 2 (Washington, D.C.: Government Printing Office, 1888).

89. The quotation comes from T. S. Palmer, "In Memoriam: Wells Woodridge Cooke," *Auk* 34 (1917): 132.

90. Biographical information on Cooke comes from Witmer Stone, "Prof. Wells W. Cooke," *Auk* 33 (1916): 354–355; and Palmer, "In Memoriam," 119–132.

91. See William Rowan's praise in "Fifty Years of Bird Migration," in *Fifty Years' Progress of American Ornithology, 1883–1933,* ed. Frank M. Chapman and T. S. Palmer (Lancaster, Pa.: American Ornithologists' Union, 1933), 51–63, on 54.

92. Wells W. Cooke, "Preliminary Census of the Birds of the United States," U.S. Department of Agriculture, Bulletin no. 187, 11 February 1915.

93. Wells W. Cooke, "Second Annual Report of Bird Counts in the United States, with Discussion of Results," U.S. Department of Agriculture, Bulletin no. 396, 23 October 1916, on 3.

94. The announcement and instructions for volunteers appear in "Bird-Lore's First Breeding-Bird Census," *Bird-Lore* 39 (1937): 147–150.

95. Accounts of the development of bird banding are numerous. See, for example, Frederick C. Lincoln, "Bird Banding," in *Fifty Years' Progress of American Ornithology, 1883–1933,* ed. Frank M. Chapman and T. S. Palmer (Lancaster, Pa.: American Ornithologists' Union, 1933), 65–88; Leon J. Cole, "Early History of Bird Banding in America," *Wilson Bulletin* 34 (1922): 108–114; and Harold B. Wood, "The History of Bird Banding," *Auk* 62 (1945): 256–265.

96. Cole, who is primarily remembered for his work as a geneticist, obtained a Ph.D. degree at Harvard in 1906. See R. A. McCabe, "Wisconsin's Forgotten Ornithologist," *Passenger Pigeon* 41 (1979): 129–131; and A. B. Chapman, "Leon Jacob Cole," *Dictionary of Scientific Biography* 17:173–175.

97. Leon J. Cole, "Suggestions for a Method of Studying the Migration of Birds," *Third Report of the Michigan Academy of Sciences* (1901): 67–70.

98. Among the earliest published results of bird banding studies were Paul Bartsch, "Notes on the Herons of the District of Columbia," *Smithsonian Miscellaneous Collection* 45 (1904): 104–111; and P. A. Taverner, "The Tagging of Birds," *Bulletin of the Michigan Ornithological Club* 5 (1904): 50–51.

99. Cole, "Early History," 109–110.

100. Wood, "History of Bird Banding," 262–263.

101. S. Charles Kendeigh, "In Memoriam: Samuel Prentiss Baldwin," *Auk* 57 (1940): 1–13.

102. S. Prentiss Baldwin, "Bird Banding by Means of Systematic Trapping," *Abstracts of the Proceedings of the Linnaean Society of New York,* no. 31 (1919): 23–56.

103. Lincoln, "Bird Banding," 71. Biographical information on Lincoln, who developed the concept of migratory flyways from the Biological Survey files, is in John K. Terres, "Big Brother to the Waterfowl," *Audubon Magazine* 49 (1947): 150–158; and Ira N. Gabrielson, "Obituary," *Auk* 79 (1962): 495–499.

104. Wood, "History of Bird Banding," 264.

105. Montague Chamberlain, *A Popular Handbook of the Ornithology of the United States Based on Nuttall's Manual* (Boston:

Little, Brown, 1891), 1:vi–vii. Chamberlain repeated the gist of this statement in a revised edition of Nuttall's manual published five years later: *Popular Handbook of the Ornithology of Eastern North America, By Thomas Nuttall*, 2d rev. ed. (Boston: Little, Brown, 1896), 1:viii–ix.

106. Frank M. Chapman to William Brewster, 15 June 1890, William Brewster Papers, MCZ Archives.

107. Thomas Mayo Brewer, *North American Oology*, Smithsonian Contributions to Knowledge, no. 11 (Washington, D.C.: Smithsonian Institution, 1857). Biographical information on Brewer may be found in George E. Gifford, "Thomas Mayo Brewer, M.D. . . . A Blackbird and Duck, Sparrow and Mole," *Harvard Medical Bulletin* 37, no. 1 (Fall 1962): 32–34; and "Thomas Mayo Brewer," *Bulletin of the Nuttall Ornithological Club* 5 (1880): 102–104.

108. In 1840 Brewer published an inexpensive edition of Wilson's *American Ornithology*. He was also a correspondent and friend of Audubon, who named two bird species after him. See Gifford, "Brewer," 33–34.

109. [Thomas Mayo Brewer,] "Instructions in Reference to Collecting Nests and Eggs of North American Birds," Smithsonian Miscellaneous Collections, 2, no. 9 (1860): 1–22. The reference to the high cost of illustrations is from "Thomas Mayo Brewer," 104.

110. Charles Bendire, *Life Histories of North America Birds, with Special Reference to Their Breeding Habits and Eggs*, U.S. National Museum, Special Bulletin no. 1 (Washington, D.C.: Government Printing Office, 1892). Biographical information on Bendire may be found in James C. Merrill, "In Memoriam: Charles Emil Bendire," *Auk* 15 (1898): 1–6; F. H. Knowlton, "Major Charles E. Bendire," *Osprey* 1 (1897): 87–90; and Hume, *Ornithologists of the United States Army Medical Corps*, 22–37.

111. According to the index of Bendire, *Life Histories*, 1: 439–446, over 100 individuals contributed observations for the first volume alone.

112. Ridgway's experiences are described in John Ridgway, "Ridgway's Drawing for Bendire Plates," *Condor* 29 (1927): 177–181.

113. Charles Bendire, *Life Histories of North American Birds, with Special Reference to Their Breeding Habits*, vol. 2, Special Bulletin no. 3 (Washington, D.C.: Government Printing Office, 1895).

114. For biographical information on Ralph, see A. K. Fisher, "Dr. William LaGrange Ralph," *Auk* 24 (1907): 461–462.

115. Arthur Cleveland Bent to Charles D. Walcott, 2 March 1910, Office of the Secretary, 1890–1929, RU 45, Box 7, SIA. This collection contains extensive documentation of Bent's relationship with the Smithsonian and his negotia-

tions over the right to complete the *Life Histories* series. Biographical sketches of Bent are found in Wendell Taber, "In Memoriam: Arthur Cleveland Bent," *Auk* 72 (1955): 332–339; and Edwin Way Teale, "A. C. Bent: Plutarch of Birds," *Audubon Magazine* 48 (1946): 14–20. By the time of his death, Bent's egg collection numbered over thirty thousand specimens.

116. Frank L. Burns, "The American Crow (*Corvus americanus*)," *Wilson Bulletin* 7 (1895): 2–41, and "The Flicker," *Wilson Bulletin* 12 (1900): 1–83. For biographical information on Burns, see Frank L. Burns, "The Autobiography of Franklin Lorenzo Burns," *Wilson Bulletin* 38 (1926): 132–139; and T. S. Palmer, "Franklin L. Burns," *Auk* 65 (1948): 646–647.

117. Frank M. Chapman, "The Warbler Book," *Bird Lore* 6 (1904): 61–63.

118. Frank M. Chapman, *The Warblers of North America* (New York: D. Appleton, 1907). The list of contributors is found on pp. 5–6.

119. Arthur Cleveland Bent to Charles D. Walcott, 29 April 1921, Office of the Secretary, 1890–1929, RU 45, Box 7, SIA.

120. A short history of the series, including titles and dates of each volume and the arrangements made to complete it after Bent's death in 1954, is found in Oliver L. Austin, Jr., comp. and ed., *Life Histories of North American Cardinals, Grosbeaks, Buntings, Towhees, Finches, Sparrows, and Allies; Order Passiformes: Family Fringillidae. Part One: Genera Richmondena through Piplio (Part)* (Washington, D.C: Smithsonian Institution Press, 1968), xxiii–xxvii. See also the review of the series by Richard C. Banks, Review of *Life Histories of North American Cardinals*, by A. C. Bent, *Auk* 86 (1969): 768–770.

121. A list of Bent's travels is contained in Taber, "Arthur Cleveland Bent," 336.

122. A. C. Bent to Charles D. Walcott, 21 March 1910, RU 45, Office of the Secretary, 1907–1924 (Charles D. Walcott), Records, Box 7, SIA.

123. See, for example, Arthur C. Bent, "Smithsonian Institution: Circular Letter Regarding the Work Entitled 'Life Histories of North American Birds,'" Office of the Secretary (Charles D. Walcott), 1903–1924, RU 45, Box 10, last folder, SIA, and his "Life Histories of North American Birds," *Auk* 39 (1922): 590–591.

124. Arthur Cleveland Bent, *Life Histories of North American Diving Birds: Order Pygopodes*, Smithsonian Institution, U.S. National Museum, Bulletin no. 107 (Washington, D.C: Government Printing Office, 1919).

125. Oliver L. Austin, Jr., comp. and ed., *Life Histories of North American Cardinals, Grosbeaks, Buntings, Towhees, Finches, Sparrows,*

and Allies (Washington, D.C.: Smithsonian Institution Press, 1968), xxiv.

126. See chapter 4.

127. See, for example, [T. C. Stephens?,] "Editorial," *Wilson Bulletin* 34 (1927): 231.

128. The original article was by G.R.C., "Field Glass," *Ornithologist and Oologist* 7 (1882): 150–151; 8 (1883): 5–6. The anonymous review is in *Bulletin of the Nuttall Ornithological Club* 8 (1883): 236.

129. For biographical information on Brewster, see chapter 2.

130. William Brewster and Ralph Hoffmann, "Unsatisfactory Records," *Auk* 19 (1902): 420.

131. Or so Ludlow Griscom claimed in his article, "Historical Development of Sight Recognition," *Proceedings of the Linnaean Society of New York*, nos. 63–65 (1954): 16–20, on 19–20. The term "personal equation" appears regularly in discussions about the problem of sight records and was borrowed from the fields of astronomy and psychology. See Simon Schaffer, "Astronomers Mark Time: Discipline and the Personal Equation," *Science in Context* 2 (1988): 115–145.

132. J. A. A[llen], Review of *Birds of the Cambridge Region of Massachusetts*, by William Brewster, *Auk* 23 (1906): 466–470.

133. William Brewster, *The Birds of the Cambridge Region of Massachusetts*, Memoirs of the Nuttall Ornithological Club, no. 4 (Cambridge, Mass.: The Club, 1906), 5.

134. See Walter Faxon, "Brewster's Warbler (*Helminthophila leucobronchialis*) a Hybrid between the Golden-winged Warbler (*Helminthophila chrysoptera*) and the Blue-Winged Warbler (*Helminthophila pinus*)," *Memoirs of the Museum of Comparative Zoology* 40 (August 1913): 311–316. See also F[rank] M. C[hapman], Review of "Brewster's Warbler," by Walter Faxon, *Bird-Lore* 15 (1913): 312.

135. [Frank M. Chapman,] "A Question of Identity," *Bird-Lore* 4 (1902): 166–167.

136. [Frank M. Chapman,] [Editorial,] *Bird-Lore* 11 (1909): 37.

137. Griscom is the subject of a recent biography, William E. Davis, Jr., *Dean of the Birdwatchers: A Biography of Ludlow Griscom* (Washington, D.C.: Smithsonian Institution Press, 1994). Also useful are Roger Tory Peterson, "In Memoriam: Ludlow Griscom," *Auk* 82 (1965): 598–605; Edwin Way Teale, "Ludlow Griscom: Virtuoso of Field Identification," *Audubon Magazine* 47 (1945): 349–358; and John H. Baker, "Ludlow Griscom: The Man," *Audubon Magazine* 61 (1959): 200–201, 213, 238–239.

138. Ludlow Griscom, "The Identification of the Commoner Anatidae of Eastern United States" (master's thesis, Cornell University,

1915), published as "Field Studies of the Anatidae of the Atlantic Coast," *Auk* 39 (1922): 517–530; 40 (1923): 69–80.

139. Ludlow Griscom, "Problems of Field Identification," *Auk* 39 (1922): 31–41, on 33.

140. Ibid., 40.

141. Ludlow Griscom, *Birds of New York City Region* (New York: American Museum of Natural History, 1923).

142. Witmer Stone, Review of *Birds of the New York City Region*, by Ludlow Griscom, *Auk* 41 (1924): 173.

143. On the importance of the Bronx Country Bird Club, see the discussion in John Farrand, Jr., "The Bronx County Bird Club: Memories of Ten Boys and an Era That Shaped American Birding," *American Birds* 45 (1991): 372–381; Davis, *Dean of the Birdwatchers*, 107–109; Peterson, "Ludlow Griscom," 600–601; and Kastner, *World of Watchers*, 185–194.

144. Roger Tory Peterson, "The Era of Ludlow Griscom," *Audubon Magazine* 62 (1960): 102–103, 131, 146. Quoted in Davis, *Dean of the Birdwatchers*, 107.

145. The appearance of Peterson's field guide is generally considered to have contributed greatly to the post–World War II birding boom, a subject beyond the scope of the present book. See the discussions in Gibbons and Strom, *Neighbors to the Birds*, 287–288, 295–305; and Kastner, *World of Watchers*, 195–208.

146. See for example, Joseph Grinnell's argument that photographs of birds could replace study skins in documenting the existence of rare species: J. G., "Notes and News," *Condor* 39 (1937): 133.

147. On the importance of these early centers of graduate study for the development of ornithology, see the next chapter.

148. Frederick C. Lincoln, "What Constitutes a Record?," *Bulletin of the Audubon Society of New Hampshire* 8, no. 2 (Dec. 1928): 17–20.

149. [Witmer Stone], Review of "What Constitutes a Record?" by F. C. Lincoln, *Auk* 47 (1929): 413–414; and T. C. S[tephens], Review of "What Constitutes a Record?" by F. C. Lincoln, *Wilson Bulletin* 41 (1929): 113.

150. W. L. McAtee, "The Specimen Fetish," *Scientific Monthly* 54 (1942): 565–566.

151. T. S. P[almer], "The Condor," *Bird-Lore* 15 (1913): 314.

152. The first mention I have found of this issue is a comment on the Massachusetts Audubon Society's Bird Lists published in *Bird-Lore*: "Competitive lists of any kind are always in danger of encouraging careless identification." [Witmer Stone,] Review of *Bird-Lore*, *Auk* 30 (1913): 605. See also [Witmer Stone,] Review of *Bird-Lore*, *Auk* 37 (1920): 485–486, and Review of "What Constitutes a Record?," 414.

Chapter Eight

1. Joseph Grinnell to Frank M. Chapman, 12 May 1930, Archives, Department of Ornithology, AMNH.

2. On the growth of the AOU, see chapter 3. On AOU Secretary T. S. Palmer's recruiting efforts, see P. A. Taverner to Ernst Mayr, 26 November 1935, Ernst Mayr Papers, HUG(FP) 14.7, Professional Correspondence, Harvard University Archives, Cambridge, Massachusetts (hereafter cited as Ernst Mayr Papers, HUA).

3. During its first decade of publication, the average number of pages per year in the *Auk* was 427. From 1901 to 1910, the average was nearly 500. By the 1910s, the average had increased to nearly 600 pages per year, and by the 1920s, to nearly 650 pages. However, the AOU was forced to reduce the size of the publication when many members stopped paying their dues during the Depression. During the 1930s, the average number of pages per year declined to 581.

4. T. S. Palmer, "The Forty-seventh Stated Meeting of the American Ornithologists' Union," *Auk* 47 (1930): 218–230.

5. Joseph Grinnell, "An Analysis of Trends in the A.O.U.," ms. speech, Joseph Grinnell Papers, 73/25, Bancroft Library, Berkeley, California. I located twenty-five of the twenty-seven replies in the archives of the MVZ.

6. Ibid., 2.

7. Herbert Friedmann to Joseph Grinnell, 19 June 1930, MVZ Archives; and Division of Birds, National Museum of Natural History, Records, RU 105, Box 18, Folder 6, SIA.

8. On the favorable impression of Stresemann's journal among other American reformers, see also J. H. Fleming to Ernst Mayr, undated letter (ca. early 1930s), Ernst Mayr Papers, HUA.

9. After Grinnell's death in 1939, Ernst Mayr wrote that "He was closer to the ideas of the younger set of American ornithologists than anybody else of his generation." Ernst Mayr to Alden Miller, 6 June 1939, MVZ Archives.

10. Grinnell, "Analysis of Trends," 4. In the corrected copy of the manuscript, Grinnell crossed out the words "real scientists" and inserted "professionals."

11. Ibid., 5–7. As the previous chapter reveals, by the time he presented his address, Grinnell had already taken significant steps to revitalize the bird protection committee.

12. Ibid., 10.

13. Joseph Grinnell to Herbert Friedmann, 17 July 1930, Division of Birds, Records, RU 105, National Museum of Natural History, Box 18, Folder 6, SIA.

14. Witmer Stone to Joseph Grinnell, 1 June 1930, MVZ Archives.

15. See Joseph Grinnell to Witmer Stone, 24 October 1930, appended to the ms. copy of "Analysis of Trends," Joseph Grinnell Papers, Bancroft Library, Berkeley, Calif.

16. Witmer Stone to Joseph Grinnell, 20 March 1931, MVZ Archives. The address was never published.

17. See Ernst Mayr to Joseph Grinnell, 14 October 1937, 16 December 1937, 17 March 1938, MVZ Archives. See also Ernst Mayr to Lawrence Hicks, 28 December 1937, and Ernst Mayr to Arthur C. Bent, 18 October 1937, AOU Records, RU 7440, Box 40, Folder 4, SIA.

18. See, Laurence R. Vesey, *The Emergence of the American University* (Chicago: University of Chicago Press, 1965); Roger L. Geiger, *To Advance Knowledge: The Growth of American Research Universities, 1900–1940* (New York: Oxford University Press, 1986), 1–57; and Robert Kohler, "The Ph.D. Machine: Building on the Collegiate Base," *Isis* 81 (1990): 638–662. The first American Ph.D. degree was awarded in 1861 at Yale, but it was not until a decade later that other institutions followed this lead.

19. Kohler, "Ph.D. Machine," 643.

20. Determining who earned the first Ph.D. degree in "ornithology" is difficult. One candidate for this honor, Reuben M. Strong, completed his doctoral degree at Harvard in 1901. However, his dissertation, "The Development of Color in the Definitive Feather," failed to gain much attention in ornithological circles. A decade later, Arthur A. Allen finished his landmark study, "The Red-Winged Blackbird: A Study in the Ecology of a Cattail Marsh," at Cornell, a dissertation that was widely commented upon by ornithologists and subsequently published.

21. Arthur A. Allen, "Ornithological Education in America," in *Fifty Years' Progress of American Ornithology*, ed. Frank M. Chapman and T. S. Palmer (Lancaster, Pa.: American Ornithologists' Union, 1933), 215–229, on 225. Allen's survey did not attempt to count the number of Ph.D.s in other biological fields who did research on birds and joined the AOU, though my sense is that the number was still small in 1933.

22. Jane Maienschein, *Transforming Traditions in American Biology, 1880–1915* (Baltimore: Johns Hopkins University Press, 1991), 3. Although most who have written on the subject agree that biology changed significantly around the turn of the century, there remains significant disagreement about exactly what changed and why. See William Coleman, *Biology in the Nineteenth Century* (Cambridge: Cambridge University Press, 1977); Garland E. Allen, *Life Science in the Twentieth Century* (Cambridge: Cambridge University Press, 1978), and "Naturalists and Experimentalists: The Genotype and the

Phenotype," *Studies in History of Biology* 3 (1979): 179–209; the series of papers in the "Special Section on American Morphology at the Turn of the Century," in *Journal of the History of Biology* 14 (1981); Philip Pauly, "The Appearance of Academic Biology in Late Nineteenth-Century America," *Journal of the History of Biology* 17 (1984): 369–397; Keith R. Benson, "From Museum Research to Laboratory Biology: The Transformation of Natural History into Academic Biology," in *The American Development of Biology*, ed. Ronald Rainger, Keith R. Benson, and Jane Maienschein (Philadelphia: University of Pennsylvania Press, 1988), 49–83, as well as the other papers in that volume; and Merriley Borell, *Album of Science: The Biological Sciences in the Twentieth Century* (New York: Scribner, 1989).

23. On the history of ecology before World War II, see the references in chapter 6, n. 112. On the history of animal behavior studies in the United States, see Richard W. Burkhardt, Jr., "Charles Otis Whitman, Wallace Craig, and the Biological Study of Animal Behavior in the United States, 1898–1925," in *The American Development of Biology*, ed. Ronald Rainger, Keith R. Benson, and Jane Maienschein (Philadelphia: University of Pennsylvania Press, 1988), 185–218; Donald A. Dewsbury, "A Brief History of the Study of Animal Behavior in North America," *Perspectives in Ethology* 8 (1989): 85–122; and Gregg Mitman and Richard W. Burkhardt, Jr., "Struggling for Identity: The Study of Animal Behavior in America, 1930–1945," in *The Expansion of American Biology*, ed. Keith E. Benson, Jane Maienschein, and Ronald Rainger (New Brunswick, N.J.: Rutgers University Press, 1981), 164–194.

In the 1930s and 1940s, one brand of animal behavior studies coalesced into the scientific discipline of ethology. See W. H. Thorpe, *The Origins and Rise of Ethology* (London: Heinemann, 1979); Richard W. Burkhardt, Jr., "On the Emergence of Ethology as a Scientific Discipline," *Conspectus of History* 1 (1981): 62–81, and "The Development of Evolutionary Ethology," in *Evolution from Molecules to Man*, ed. D. S. Bendall (Cambridge: Cambridge University Press, 1983), 429–444; and John R. Durant, "Innate Character in Animals and Man: A Perspective on the Origins of Ethology," in *Biology, Medicine, and Society*, ed. Charles Webster (Cambridge: Cambridge University Press, 1981), 157–192.

24. The standard history of the MCZ is Winsor, *Reading the Shape of Nature*, but Lurie, *Louis Agassiz*, remains useful for the early years of the institution. On the development of biology at Harvard, see the above volumes as well as Pauly, "Academic Biology," and Alfred Romer, "Zoology at Harvard," *Bios* 19 (1948): 7–20.

25. Mark V. Barrow, Jr., "Gentlemanly Specialists in the Age of Professionalization: The First Century of Ornithology at Harvard's Museum of Comparative Zoology," in *Contributions to the History of North American Ornithology*, ed. William E. Davis, Jr., and Jerome A. Jackson (Cambridge, Mass.: Nuttall Ornithological Club, 1995), 55–94.

26. Peters, "Collections of Birds in the United States," 131–141.

27. The history of this project—which eventually encompassed sixteen volumes and took over six decades to complete—is detailed in Walter J. Bock, "A Special Review: Peters' Check-list of the Birds of the World," *Auk* 107 (1990): 629–648.

28. In 1953 the MCZ hired Raymond Paynter, Jr., its first ornithological curator with a Ph.D. degree. That same year Ernst Mayr accepted an Alexander Agassiz Professorship at the MCZ. Until his retirement in 1975, Mayr chaired the dissertation committees of all the ornithologists who earned Ph.D. degrees at Harvard.

29. On the history of biology at Berkeley, see Richard M. Eakin, "History of Zoology at the University of California, Berkeley," *Bios* 27 (1956): 67–60, and *History of Zoology at Berkeley* (Berkeley: University of California Printing Department, 1988).

30. Eakin, "History of Zoology," 69–73. Although most of his research was done on invertebrates, Ritter was also interested in ornithology. See T. S. Palmer, "William Emerson Ritter," *Auk* 64 (1947): 665–666.

31. Eakin, "History of Zoology," 73–76.

32. Grinnell's life and work are memorialized in three uncritical biographical sketches: Jean M. Linsdale, "In Memoriam: Joseph Grinnell," *Auk* 59 (1942): 285; Hilda Wood Grinnell, "Joseph Grinnell, 1877–1939," *Condor* 42 (1940): 3–34 (which also contains an extensive bibliography); and Alden Miller, "Joseph Grinnell," *Systematic Zoology* 3 (1964): 195–249. Grinnell's contribution to ornithological training is mentioned prominently in Ned K. Johnson, "Ornithology at the Museum of Vertebrate Zoology," in *Contributions to the History of North American Ornithology*, ed. William E. Davis, Jr., and Jerome A. Jackson (Cambridge, Mass.: Nuttall Ornithological Club, 1995), 183–221.

33. Completed in May 1913 and published as Joseph Grinnell and H. S. Swarth, "An Account of the Birds and Mammals of the San Jacinto Area of Southern California with Remarks upon the Behavior of Geographic Races on the Margins of Their Habitat," *University of California Publications in Zoology* 10 (1913): 197–406.

34. On the history of the Museum of Vertebrate Zoology, see the Grinnell obituaries cited above; Susan Leigh Star and James R. Griese-

mer, "Institutional Ecology, 'Translations,' and Boundary Objects: Amateurs and Professionals in Berkeley's Museum of Vertebrate Zoology, 1907–39," *Social Studies of Science* 19 (1989): 387–420; and James R. Griesemer and Elihu Gerson, "Collaboration in the Museum of Vertebrate Zoology," *Journal of the History of Biology* 26 (1993): 185–203. On the differences between Grinnell's and Alexander's visions for the proposed museum, see ibid., 188–189.

35. Alexander shared Grinnell's concern about the decline of California's native wildlife. For a discussion of Grinnell's extensive conservation activities and their relationship to his scientific program, see Alfred Runte, *Yosemite: The Embattled Wilderness*, 2nd ed. (Lincoln: University of Nebraska Press, 1990); and Dunlap, *Saving America's Wildlife.*

36. Grinnell's system is discussed in his "Uses and Methods of a Research Museum," *Popular Science Monthly* 77 (1910): 163–169, and "The Museum Conscience," *Museum Work* 4 (1922): 62–63.

37. Ernst Mayr, "Alden Holmes Miller," *Biographical Memoirs of the National Academy of Sciences* 43 (1973): 177–214, on 179–180. Further discussion of Grinnell's research program is found in Griesemer and Gerson, "Collaboration," 193–201; and James Griesemer, "Modeling in the Museum: On the Role of Remnant Models in the Work of Joseph Grinnell," *Biology and Philosophy* 5 (1990): 3–36.

38. During his long and productive career, Miller advised more than two dozen doctoral students, including several who subsequently joined the faculty at Berkeley. For a complete list, see Johnson, "Ornithology," 187; and Frank A. Pitelka, "Academic Family Tree for Loye and Alden Miller," *Condor* 95 (1995): 1065–1067. On Miller's life and career, see Richard M. Eakin, A. Starker Leopold, and R. A. Stirton, "Alden Holmes Miller," in *In Memoriam* (Berkeley: University of California, 1967), 68–71; John Davis, "In Memoriam: Alden Holmes Miller," *Auk* 84 (1967): 192–202; and Mayr, "Miller."

39. Allen, "Ornithological Education," 225.

40. On Herrick's life and career, see Winfred G. Leutner, "Francis Hobart Herrick," *Science* 92 (1940): 371–372; and "Francis Hobart Herrick," *National Cyclopedia of American Biography* 31 (1944): 276–277. On the history of the Department of Biology that Herrick headed, see Frederick C. Waite, "Natural History and Biology in the Undergraduate Colleges of Western Reserve University," *Western Reserve University Bulletin* 7 (1929): 21–41. Among Herrick's many publications are *The Home Life of Wild Birds* (New York: G. P. Putnam's Sons, 1902); *The American Eagle: A Study in Natural and Civil History* (New York: D. Appleton-Century, 1934); and

Wild Birds at Home (New York: D. Appleton-Century, 1935).

41. See S. Charles Kendeigh, "In Memoriam: Samuel Prentiss Baldwin," *Auk* 57 (1940): 1–12; and Francis H. Herrick, "Samuel Prentiss Baldwin," *Science* 89 (1939): 212–213.

42. On the history of the Department of Zoology and its relationship to the Museum of Zoology, see A. Franklin Shull, "The Department of Zoology," in *The University of Michigan: An Encyclopedic Survey*, ed. Wilfred B. Shaw (Ann Arbor: University of Michigan Press, 1951), 2:738–750; J. Speed Rogers, "The University Museums" and "The Museum of Zoology," in *The University of Michigan: An Encyclopedic Survey*, ed. Walter A. Donnelly (Ann Arbor: University of Michigan Press, 1956), 4:1431–1442, 1502–1519. Ruthven's career is discussed in his autobiography, *Naturalist in Two Worlds: Random Recollections of a University President* (Ann Arbor: University of Michigan Press, 1963). On Van Tyne, see Harold Mayfield, "In Memoriam: Josselyn Van Tyne," *Auk* 74 (1957): 322–332.

43. For an up-to-date list of all those who have earned doctoral degrees with an emphasis on ornithology at Michigan, see the homepage for University of Michigan Museum of Zoology Bird Division, http://www.ummz.lsa.umich.edu/birds/birdweb.html.

44. The glowing assessment of Wilder and the Department of Zoology comes from Morris Bishop, *A History of Cornell* (Ithaca: Cornell University Press, 1962), 172–173. On the history of biology at Cornell, see Albert H. Wright's disjointed chronicle, "Biology at Cornell University," *Bios* 24 (1953): 122–145; and Waterman T. Hewitt, *Cornell University: A History*, 4 vols. (New York: University Publishing Society, 1905), 2:173–228.

45. J. H. Comstock, "Burt Green Wilder," *Science* 61 (1925): 531–533; "Burt Green Wilder," *Who Was Who in America* (Chicago: A. N. Marquis, 1942), 1:1345; and "Burt Green Wilder," *National Cyclopaedia of American Biography* 4 (1897): 481. On Wilder's social views, see Edward H. Beardsley, "The American Scientist as Social Activist," *Isis* 64 (1973): 51–66. The other Agassiz student who came to Cornell was the geologist Charles Frederic Hartt.

46. Burt Green Wilder and Simon H. Gage, *Anatomical Technology as Applied to the Domestic Cat: An Introduction to Human, Veterinary, and Comparative Anatomy* (New York: A.S. Barnes, 1882), which went through several editions.

47. Although biological instruction was initially concentrated in the College of Natural Science, over the years Cornell administrators scattered it across several departments and colleges.

48. The major biographical sketches of Allen's life and career include Olin Sewell Pettingill, Jr., "In Memoriam: Arthur A. Allen," *Auk* 85 (1968): 193–202; Edwin W. Teale, "Arthur A. Allen," *Audubon Magazine* 45 (1943): 85–89; and Richard B. Fischer, "Ambassador of Birdlife," *Audubon Magazine* 67 (January–February 1965): 26–31, and "Arthur Augustus Allen," in *Current Biography Yearbook: 1961*, ed. Charles Moritz (New York: H. W. Wilson, 1962), 5–7.

49. Arthur A. Allen, "The Red-winged Blackbird: Study in the Ecology of a Cat-tail Marsh," *Abstract of the Proceedings of the Linnaean Society of New York*, no. 24 (1914): 43–138.

50. W[itmer] S[tone], Review of "Redwinged Blackbird," by Arthur A. Allen, *Auk* 31 (1914): 414–415. F[rank] M. C[hapman], Review of "Red-winged Blackbird," by Arthur A. Allen, *Bird-Lore* 16 (1914): 284–285.

51. Allen had begun serving as an instructor at Cornell in 1910.

52. The history of graduate education in ornithology at Cornell is discussed in Arthur A. Allen, "Ornithological Education in America," and "Cornell's Laboratory of Ornithology," *The Living Bird* 1 (1962): 7–36; Michael Harwood, "The Lab: From Hatching to Fledging," *Cornell University Laboratory of Ornithology Annual Report* (1986–1987): 4–13; and Gregory S. Butcher and Kevin McGowan, "History of Ornithology at Cornell University," in *Contributions to the History of North American Ornithology*, ed. William E. Davis, Jr., and Jerome A. Jackson (Cambridge, Mass.: Nuttall Ornithological Club, 1995), 223–260.

53. Curiously, for several years Cornell's Laboratory of Ornithology was housed in the Department of Entomology (within the College of Agriculture) before its transfer to the Department of Zoology in the 1939 and the Department of Conservation in the 1948. See the announcement, "Reorganization of the Work in Zoology at Cornell," *Science* 90 (1939): 76–77.

54. Allen, "Ornithological Education," 225–226.

55. For a list of Cornell graduate students in ornithology and the titles of their theses and dissertations, see Butcher and McGowan, "History of Ornithology at Cornell," 246–260.

56. While many of Allen's students seem to have nothing but praise for their mentor and his program, critics charge that his classes were superficial, he failed to supervise theses and dissertations adequately, and he seemed more dedicated to popularization than fundamental research. Expressions of support for Allen and the Cornell ornithology program appear in Harlan Brumsted et al., *Voices from Connecticut Hill: Recollections of Cornell Wildlife Students, 1930–1942* (Ithaca: College of Agriculture and Life Science, Cornell University, 1994), 88–90; Olin S. Pettingill, Jr., *My Way to Ornithology* (Norman: University of Oklahoma Press), 129–192, and "In Memoriam," 193, 195–197; and George M. Sutton, *Bird Student: An Autobiography* (Austin: University of Texas Press, 1980), 210–216. Conflicting assessments come from Walter Bock (personal communication to author, 17 July 1996), an undergraduate at Cornell from 1951 to 1955, and Ernst Mayr (personal communication to author, 6 August 1996).

Additional evidence suggesting that the impressive numbers of Cornell graduate students do not tell the whole story comes from a listing of "Unpublished Theses in Ornithology" issued by the AOU Committee on Research (*Auk* 71 [1954]: 191–197). That bibliography reveals that twenty-five of the sixty individuals (over 40 percent) who earned Ph.D. degrees at Cornell by 1951 had still not published any portion of their dissertation by 1954. On the other hand, not one of the two dozen or so doctoral dissertations completed at Berkeley by 1951 appears on the list (though several master's theses do).

57. For example, within a decade after Arthur Allen's retirement in 1953, fifty-six of his students were teaching in universities, ten were curators in museums, ten worked for state and federal conservation agencies, twelve were independent scholars, and nine were deceased. Figures are from Allen, "Cornell's Laboratory of Ornithology," 7.

58. On Mayr's role in the modern synthesis, see the articles in Ernst Mayr and William B. Provine, eds., *The Evolutionary Synthesis: Perspectives on the Unification of Biology* (Cambridge: Harvard University Press, 1980); Joseph Cain, "Common Problems and Cooperative Solutions: Organizational Activities in Evolutionary Studies, 1937–1946," *Isis* 84 (1993): 1–25, and "Ernst Mayr as Community Architect: Launching the Society for the Study of Evolution and the Journal *Evolution*," *Biology and Philosophy* 9 (1994): 387–427; Vassiliki Betty Smocovitis, "Organizing Evolution: Founding the Society for the Study of Evolution (1939–1950)," *Journal of the History of Biology* 27 (1994): 241–309; Jürgen Haffer, "Ernst Mayr als Ornithologe, Systematiker, und Zoogeograph," *Biologisches Zentralblatt* 114 (1995): 133–142, and "'Es wäre Zeit, einen "allgemeinen Hartert" zu schreiben': Die historischen Wurzeln von Ernst Mayrs Beiträgen zur Evolutionssythese," *Bonner Zoologische Beiträge* 45 (1994): 113–123.

59. The best source of biographical information on Mayr, especially his early years in the United States, is Walter J. Bock, "Ernst Mayr, Naturalist: His Contributions to Systematics and Evolution," *Biology and Philosophy* 9 (1994): 267–327. Bock's article, which I have relied

upon heavily in the account that follows, is one of a series of insightful contributions in a "Special Issue on Ernst Mayr at Ninety," edited by John Greene and Michael Ruse for *Biology and Philosophy*. See also Ernst Mayr, "How I Became a Darwinian," 413–423, and "The Role of Systematics in the Evolutionary Synthesis," in *The Evolutionary Synthesis: Perspectives on the Unification of Biology*, ed. Ernst Mayer and William B. Provine (Cambridge: Harvard University Press, 1980) 123–136; Stephen Jay Gould, "Balzan Prize to Ernst Mayr," *Science* 223 (1984): 255–257; and "Ernst Mayr," in *Current Biography Yearbook 1984*, ed. Charles Moritz (New York: H. W. Wilson, 1985), 258–262.

60. The reason for his decision to attend Greifswald is reported in Mayr, "How I Became a Darwinian," 413.

61. Stresemann's significance for the history of evolutionary biology is discussed in Ernst Mayr, "Erwin Stresemann," *Dictionary of Scientific Biography* 18 (1990): 888–890; and Jürgen Haffer, "The Genesis of Erwin Stresemann's *Aves* (1927–1934) in the *Handbuch der Zoologie*, and His Contribution to the Evolutionary Synthesis," *Archives of Natural History* 21 (1994): 201–216.

62. Quoted in "Ernst Mayr," 259.

63. His dissertation was published as "Die Ausbreitung des Girlitz (*Serinus canaria serinus* L.)," *Journal für Ornithologie* 74 (1926): 571–671.

64. Beyond several technical publications, Mayr also published three popular accounts of his South Pacific expeditions: Ernst Mayr, "My Dutch New Guinea Expedition, 1928," *Novitates Zoologicae* 36 (1930): 20–26; "A Tenderfoot Explorer in New Guinea," *Natural History* 32 (1932): 83–97; and "A Journey to the Solomons," *Natural History* 52 (1943): 30–37, 48.

65. The history of the department is treated in Wesley Lanyon, "Ornithology at the American Museum of Natural History," in *Contributions to the History of North American Ornithology*, ed. William E. Davis, Jr., and Jerome A. Jackson (Cambridge, Mass.: Nuttall Ornithological Club, 1995), 113–144.

66. Chapman's life and career are discussed in chapters 5 and 7. On the accomplishments of the other bird curators associated with the American Museum of Natural History during this period, see the following appreciative biographical sketches: Dean Amadon, "In Memoriam: Robert Cushman Murphy, April 29, 1887–March 20, 1973," *Auk* 91 (1974): 1–9; Herbert Friedmann, "In Memoriam: James Paul Chapin," *Auk* 83 (1966): 240–252; and Robert Cushman Murphy and Dean Amadon, "In Memoriam: John Todd Zimmer," *Auk* 76 (1959): 418–423. On Mayr's

glowing assessment of his colleagues, see Mayr, "Epilogue," 369–372.

67. Part of the reason Mayr was so productive is that he routinely spent long hours in the evenings and on weekends pursuing his research.

68. Bock, "Ernst Mayr," 276.

69. On Sanford's life and his many contributions to the American Museum, especially its Bird Department, see Robert C. Murphy, "Leonard Cutler Sanford," *Auk* 68 (1951): 409–410; and Bock, "Ernst Mayr," 273–278. A glimpse of Sanford's personality is revealed in "Talk of the Town," *New Yorker* 26 (3 June 1950): 17–19.

70. For a fascinating portrait of the financier and polo enthusiast Henry Payne Whitney, see Jack Frost, "Profiles: Up from Fifth Avenue," *New Yorker* 1 (25 July 1925): 8–9. See also Alvin F. Harlow, "Henry Payne Whitney," *Dictionary of American Biography* 20 (1936): 160–161. On tensions between Chapman and Sanford, see Frank Chapman to Leonard C. Sanford, 24 September 1930, Archives, Department of Ornithology, AMNH.

71. The story of Walter Rothschild and his museum at Tring is told in exquisite detail in Miriam Rothschild, *Dear Lord Rothschild: Birds, Butterflies, and History* (Glenside, Pa.: Balaban Publishers, 1983).

72. The sale and transfer of the Rothschild collection are discussed in ibid., 302–304; Robert C. Murphy, "Moving a Museum," *Natural History* 39 (1932): 497–511; and D. W. Snow, "Robert Cushman Murphy and his 'Journal of the Tring Trip,'" *Ibis* 115 (1973): 607–611. After the Rothschild collection was acquired, the number of bird skins in the American Museum of Natural History totaled around 685,000 specimens. The next largest collection in the United States, at the U.S. National Museum, contained only about 252,000. The figures are from a survey that James L. Peters did for the fiftieth anniversary of the AOU: "Collections of Birds in the United States and Canada," 131–141.

73. Among the founding members were C. Hart Merriam and John Burroughs. Eugene Eisenmann, "Seventy-Five Years of the Linnaean Society of New York," *Proceedings of the Linnaean Society of New York*, nos. 63–65 (1951–1953): 1–9, provides a convenient summary of the organization's activities from the time of its founding until the 1950s.

74. The society began issuing the first volume of its *Transactions of the Linnaean Society of New York* by 1882 and its *Abstract of the Proceedings of the Linnaean Society of New York* seven years later. In the early 1930s, the name of the latter series was abbreviated to simply *Proceedings of the Linnaean Society of New York*.

75. The best account of the organization is

John Farrand, Jr., "The Bronx County Bird Club: Memories of Ten Boys and an Era That Shaped American Birding," *American Birds* 45 (Fall 1991): 372–381.

76. Ernst Mayr, "Rousing the Society's Interest in Ornithology," in *Reminiscences by Members Collected on the Occasion of the Centennial of the Linnaean Society of New York, March 1978* (New York: Linnaean Society, 1978), 4. From a copy of this brochure in the Department of Ornithology, AMNH.

77. Irving Kassoy to Ernst Mayr, 8 February 1933, Ernst Mayr Papers, HUA.

78. Joseph J. Hickey, "The Linnaean Society," in *Reminiscences by Members Collected on the Occasion of the Centennial of the Linnaean Society of New York, March 1978* (New York: Linnaean Society, 1978), 1.

79. Many of these studies were ultimately published. See, for example, William Vogt, "Preliminary Notes on the Behavior and Ecology of the Eastern Willet," *Proceedings of the Linnaean Society of New York*, no. 49 (1939): 8–42; Richard G. Kuerzi, "Life History Studies of the Tree Swallow," *Proceedings of the Linnaean Society of New York*, no. 53 (1941): 1–52. On Vogt's establishment of the breeding bird census, see William Vogt to Ernst Mayr, 10 February 1937, and Ernst Mayr to William Vogt, 18 February 1937, Ernst Mayr Papers, HUA.

80. Ernst Mayr to F. B. Kirkman, 14 December 1938, Ernst Mayr Papers, HUA.

81. Hickey, "Linnaean Society," 1. See also Stanley A. Temple and John T. Emlen, "In Memoriam: Joseph J. Hickey, 1907–1993," *Auk* 111 (1994): 450–452.

82. Joseph J. Hickey, *A Guide to Bird Watching* (New York: Oxford University Press, 1943). Mayr not only encouraged Hickey to complete the book but also wrote a highly favorable review of it: Ernst Mayr, "Bird Watching: A Hobby and a Science," *Auk* 61 (1944): 151–152.

83. Hickey's mentor at Wisconsin, Aldo Leopold, shared Mayr's conviction that serious amateurs could make important contributions to science. See his *Sand County Almanac*, 174, 185–186.

84. Joseph Hickey to Ernst Mayr, 29 April 1944, Ernst Mayr Papers, HUA.

85. Ernst Mayr, personal communication, 11 July 1995.

86. Mayr, "Rousing the Society's Interest," 4. Charlie Urner was a birdwatcher, publisher, and active member of the Linnaean Society of New York. See J. L. Edwards, "Charles Anderson Urner, 1882–1938," *Proceedings of the Linnaean Society of New York*, no. 49 (1938): 1–7.

87. Ernst Mayr to Irving Kassoy, 8 November 1934, Ernst Mayr Papers, HUA.

88. Hickey, "Linnaean Society," 2.

89. The feat was recorded in "Bird-Lore's Thirty-Sixth Christmas Bird Census," *Bird-Lore* 38 (1936): 49–50.

90. Mayr, "Rousing the Society's Interest," 4.

91. Quoted in Milton B. Trautman, "In Memoriam: Margaret Morse Nice," *Auk* 94 (1977): 438.

92. For biographical information on Nice, see especially Nice, *Research Is a Passion*; and Trautman, "In Memoriam," 430–441. The role of gender in her work and reception is discussed in Bonta, *Women in the Field*, 222–231; and Marianne Gosztonyi Ainley, "Field Work and Family: North American Women Ornithologists, 1900–1950," in *Uneasy Careers and Intimate Lives: Women in Science, 1789–1979*, ed. Pnina Abir-Am and Dorinda Outram (New Brunswick, N.J.: Rutgers University Press, 1987), 60–76. The best assessment of Nice's contribution to science is Gregg Mitman and Richard W. Burkhardt, Jr., "Struggling for Identity: The Study of Animal Behavior in America, 1930–1945," in *The Expansion of American Biology*, ed. Keith R. Benson, Jane Maienschein, and Ronald Rainger (New Brunswick, N.J.: Rutgers University Press, 1991), 164–194, which I have relied upon heavily for the discussion that follows.

93. Nice, *Research Is a Passion*, 5.

94. Ibid., 21.

95. Ibid., 23.

96. She published her research as Margaret Morse Nice, "Food of the Bobwhite," *Journal of Economic Entomology* 3 (1910): 295–313. However, her master's degree (for her studies of speech development in children) was not awarded until 1926. According to Nice (*Research Is a Passion*, 39), the degree was granted retroactively "as of 1915."

97. Nice's reaction to the meeting is discussed in *Research Is a Passion*, 30–32. Her judgment that women were not taken seriously in the AOU came partly because of an experience in which the "gentlemen of the Union" were invited to a reception held in the private museum of William Brewster, while the "ladies" were invited to the home of Mrs. Charles Foster Batchelder.

98. She later regretted her decision not to continue with her graduate studies. Ibid., 33.

99. Mitman and Burkhardt, "Struggling for Identity," 181.

100. Nice, *Research Is a Passion*, 34–35.

101. Margaret Morse Nice and Leonard Blaine Nice, *The Birds of Oklahoma*, University of Oklahoma Bulletin, new series no. 20 (Norman: University of Oklahoma, 1924).

102. The quotation is from Mitman and Burkhardt, "Struggling for Identity," 181. Biographical information on Sherman may be found in

Ainley, "Field Work and Family," 63–67; Bonta, *Women in the Field*, 197–211; and Sharon E. Wood, "Althea Sherman and the Birds of Prairie and Dooryard: A Scientist's Witness to Change," *The Palimpsest* 70 (1989): 165–184. On the Nice/Sherman relationship, see Margaret Morse Nice, "Some Letters of Althea Sherman," *Iowa Bird Life* 22 (1952): 51–55.

103. The quotation comes from Trautman, "In Memoriam," 440.

104. Nice mentions Wilbur Butts as the inspiration for the idea of using colored celluloid bands to mark her birds in *Research Is a Passion*, 104.

105. Beyond the scientific publications that resulted from her sparrow studies (discussed below), at the encouragement of *Audubon Magazine* editor William Vogt, Nice also authored a delightful popular account of her work: *Watcher at the Nest* (New York: Macmillan, 1939).

106. The relationship between Mayr and Nice is copiously documented in the Ernst Mayr Papers, HUA; the Margaret Morse Nice Papers, Division of Manuscripts and University Archives, Cornell University, Ithaca, N.Y. (which I have not used), and *Research Is a Passion*. That same year she was elected a member of the AOU, only the sixth woman in the organization's history to receive that honor. The previous five were Florence Merriam Bailey, Mabel Osgood Wright, Althea Sherman, Elsie Naumburg, and May Thatcher Cooke.

107. Nice, *Research Is a Passion*, 109.

108. Margaret Morse Nice to Ernst Mayr, 9 November 1931, Ernst Mayr Papers, HUA.

109. Because of the large backlog of articles and the need to economize during the Depression, the *Auk* would generally not accept articles over twenty pages long. Nice (*Research Is a Passion*, 116) blamed this policy on editor Witmer Stone's failure to be more selective in choosing papers.

110. The quotation is from Margaret Morse Nice to Ernst Mayr, 2 June 1933, Ernst Mayr Papers, HUA. The paper was published as Margaret Morse Nice, "Zur Naturgeschichte des Singammers," *Journal für Ornithologie* 81 (1933): 552–595; 82 (1934): 1–96.

111. Margaret Morse Nice to Ernst Mayr, 19 October 1932, Ernst Mayr Papers, HUA.

112. She estimated that she completed over 3,000 of these reviews. Nice, *Research Is a Passion*, 257.

113. Margaret Morse Nice to Joseph Grinnell, 21 December 1932, Ernst Mayr Papers, HUA.

114. Margaret Morse Nice to Ernst Mayr, 13 January 1932 [1933] and 16 January 1933, Ernst Mayr Papers, HUA.

115. Konrad Lorenz's original article appeared as "Der Kumpan in der Umwelt des Vogels," *Journal für Ornithologie* 83 (1935): 137–213, 289–413. Herrick eventually convinced Lorenz to prepare an English summary of his paper, "The Companion in the Bird's World," *Auk* 54 (1937): 245–273.

116. Margaret M. Nice, "The Theory of Territorialism and Its Development," in *Fifty Years' Progress of American Ornithology, 1883–1933*, ed. Frank M. Chapman and T. S. Palmer (Lancaster, Pa.: American Ornithologists' Union, 1933), 89–100; Ernst Mayr, "Bernard Altum and the Territory Theory," *Proceedings of the Linnaean Society of New York*, nos. 45 and 46 (1935): 24–38. This was the first in a series of historical publications that Ernst Mayr was to write. On Mayr's development as a historian of biology, see Richard W. Burkhardt, Jr., "Ernst Mayr: Biologist-Historian," *Biology and Philosophy* 9 (1994): 359–371; and Thomas Junker, "Factors Shaping Ernst Mayr's Concepts in the History of Biology," *Journal of the History of Biology* 29 (1996): 29–77.

117. Niko Tinbergen, *The Behavior of the Snow Bunting in Spring*, Transactions of the Linnaean Society of New York, vol. 5 (New York: Linnaean Society of New York, 1939).

118. Mayr, "Rousing the Society's Interest," 4. Mayr had begun serving as secretary to the Linnaean Society one year previously.

119. Quoted in Nice, *Research Is a Passion*, 127.

120. Mayr, "Rousing the Society's Interest," 4.

121. A second volume, Margaret M. Nice, *The Behavior of the Song Sparrow and Other Passerines*, Transactions of the Linnaean Society of New York, vol. 6 (New York: Linnaean Society of New York, 1943), followed six years later.

122. See Joe Cain's insightful study, "Ernst Mayr as *Community* Architect."

123. Aldo Leopold to Ernst Mayr, 5 August 1937, Ernst Mayr Papers, HUA. Apparently Mayr was unable to convince *Science* to publish Leopold's review, which appeared in *Canadian Field-Naturalist* 51 (November 1937): 126.

124. Ernst Mayr to Joseph Grinnell, 27 May 1937, and Joseph Grinnell to Ernst Mayr, 26 June 1937, Archives, MVZ; and Ernst Mayr to Margaret Morse Nice, 30 September 1938, Ernst Mayr Papers, HUA. Jean M. Linsdale wrote a one-paragraph notice of the book for the "Notes and News" section of *Condor* 39 (1937): 180.

125. Quoted in Nice, *Research Is a Passion*, 159–160.

126. Herbert Friedmann to Ernst Mayr, 10 August 1931, Ernst Mayr Papers, HUA.

127. Stephen I. Rothstein, Ralph W. Schreiber, and Thomas R. Howell, "In Memoriam: Herbert Friedmann," *Auk* 105 (1988): 365–368; S. Dillon Ripley, "Herbert Friedmann, April 22,

1900–May 14, 1987," *Biographical Memoirs of the National Academy of Sciences* 62 (1993): 143–165; Herbert Friedmann Oral Interview, 22 April 1975, RU 9506, SIA.

128. Herbert Friedmann, "The Weaving of the Red-billed Weaver Bird in Captivity," *Zoologica* 2 (1922): 257.

129. Herbert Friedmann, *The Cowbirds: A Study in the Biology of Social Parasitism* (Springfield, Ill.: C. C. Thomas, 1929).

130. Both were fellows of the AOU. See Witmer Stone, "In Memoriam: Charles Wallace Richmond, 1868–1932," *Auk* 50 (1933): 1–22; and Alexander Wetmore, "In Memoriam: Joseph Harvey Riley," *Auk* 60 (1943): 1–15.

131. Herbert Friedmann interview, 3.

132. Ibid., 5.

133. Ibid., 57–59, 72. Friedmann did not eschew all taxonomic research. He published several taxonomic monographs, including three parts of *Birds of Middle and North America* finished between 1941 and 1950. However, he felt that Ridgway lacked the imagination and the training to go beyond the obvious.

134. My italics.

135. Herbert Friedmann to Ernst Mayr, 4 February 1932, Ernst Mayr Papers, HUA.

136. In 1935 Mayr complained "The A.O.U. is in danger of becoming, or at least of remaining, an Eastern bird society, while it really should and could be a national organization." Ernst Mayr to P. A. Taverner, 7 December 1935, Ernst Mayr Papers, HUA. See also Joseph Grinnell to Ernst Mayr, 26 June 1937, Ernst Mayr Papers, HUA.

137. Joseph Grinnell to Ernst Mayr, 26 June 1937, MVZ Archives: "Among zoologists in university circles I too frequently get the insinuation that AOU Fellowship merely involves amateurish or recreational interest in birds—not soundly scientific."

138. Joseph Grinnell to Herbert Friedmann, 17 January 1935, MVZ Archives.

139. Herbert Friedmann to Joseph Grinnell, 22 January 1935, MVZ Archives.

140. The account that follows is pieced together from a personal conversation with Mayr, 11 July 1995. See also Ernst Mayr to P. A. Taverner, 7 December 1935, Ernst Mayr Papers, HUA; and Keir Sterling and Marianne G. Ainley's "Changes in the AOU By-Laws, 1883–1983," part of their unpublished history of the AOU.

141. Apparently Friedmann had pushed Nice's candidacy the previous year as well, but without success. See Herbert Friedmann to Ernst Mayr, 1 November 1934, Ernst Mayr Papers, HUA.

142. No doubt the criticism that Grinnell reported strongly influenced Stone's decision not to publish the address.

143. Mayr was also troubled by his belief that too many notes and papers emphasized unusual records rather than describing the "normal range and normal occurrences" of birds. Ernst Mayr to J. H. Fleming, 26 October 1933, Ernst Mayr Papers, HUA. On the complaints about Stone's editorship, see Keir Sterling and Marianne Ainley, "A Quarterly Journal of Ornithology," in their unpublished history of the AOU.

144. Friedmann commented on this trend in his "The Role of the A.O.U. in Ornithology Today," *Auk* 55 (1938): 316.

145. The term comes from a discussion with Ernst Mayr, 11 July 1995.

146. W. L. McAtee, "In Memoriam: Theodore Sherman Palmer," *Auk* 73 (1956): 367–377; J. S. Wade, "Dr. Theodore Sherman Palmers," *Atlantic Naturalist* 12 (1957): 84–88; and E. R. Kalmbach, "In Memoriam: W. L. McAtee," *Auk* 80 (1963): 474–485.

147. Twice Grinnell sent Palmer completed nomination blanks for George Willett that somehow failed to appear on the ballot passed out at the annual AOU meetings. See Joseph Grinnell to Herbert Friedmann, 13 October 1936, MVZ Archives.

148. Stone had earlier pleaded to be allowed to serve for twenty-five years, a period that ended in 1936. Herbert Friedmann to Joseph Grinnell, 15 May 1935, MVZ Archives.

149. Herbert Friedmann to Joseph Grinnell, 13 March 1935, MVZ Archives. Even before his election was official, Mayr sent Allen a long series of suggestions for improving the *Auk*. See Ernst Mayr to Glover A. Allen, 10 September 1936, Ernst Mayr Papers, HUA.

150. Herbert Friedmann to Joseph Grinnell, 27 October 1936, MVZ Archives.

151. The AOU already had a class of membership known as "retired fellow," but over the years only a handful of fellows had volunteered to transfer themselves to it. Friedmann felt there would be less stigma attached to the term "emeritus," which was widely used in academic circles and did not suggest that an individual was no longer active in the field. To clear the fellow's class of excess "deadwood," he believed that transfer should be automatic when a fellow reached the age of seventy. See Herbert Friedmann to Joseph Grinnell, 22 January 1935, MVZ Archives.

152. A carbon copy of the seven original proposals and Mayr's reasons for each, "Proposed Amendments to the Constitution and By-Laws of the American Ornithologists' Union," is included with Ernst Mayr to Joseph Grinnell, 19 August 1937, MVZ Archives.

153. Mayr and Friedmann were not the only ones concerned about the level of papers presented at the annual AOU meetings. See P. A.

Taverner to Ernst Mayr, 26 November 1935, Ernst Mayr Papers, HUA. For a sociological account of the referee system, see Harriet Zuckerman and Robert K. Merton, "Patterns of Evaluation in Science: Institutionalization, Structure and Functions of the Referee System," *Minerva* 9 (1971): 66–100.

154. According to Mayr, the combined salaries of the two positions amounted to more than 20 percent of the annual income of the organization. Ernst Mayr to Joseph Grinnell, 14 October 1937, MVZ Archives. Friedmann and Mayr also felt that the position of editor should be honorary and that much of the work should be shared with an editorial board.

155. After criticism of this proposal, Mayr dropped it from subsequent drafts that he circulated. See the final version of "Proposed Amendments to the Constitution and By-Laws of the American Ornithologists Union," attached to Ernst Mayr to Joseph Grinnell, 14 October 1937, MVZ Archives.

156. Ernst Mayr to Joseph Grinnell, 14 October 1937, MVZ Archives.

157. The AOU Council did vote to eliminate the honoraria paid to the secretary and treasurer and to publish a detailed budget each year in the *Auk*. See Herbert Friedmann to Joseph Grinnell, 2 December 1938, MVZ Archives; and Ernst Mayr to Alden Miller, 24 November 1937, Ernst Mayr Papers, HUA. Mayr continued to push his reform package, and within the next five years all of his proposals were enacted in one form or another. See, for example, Ernst Mayr to Lawrence Hicks, 26 January 1938, AOU Records, RU 7440, Box 40, File 4, SIA, which includes a copy of Mayr's proposals along with a summary of the reaction from several prominent AOU members. In addition, Mayr's proposal to enlarge the class of members from 125 to 200 (mentioned in Ernst Mayr to Alden Miller, 24 November 1937, Ernst Mayr Papers, HUA) was also passed by the council in 1939.

158. Mayr had been warned that it would be "an exceedingly difficult task to bring about any changes with the present group of senior men in charge." Alden Miller to Ernst Mayr, 22 October 1937, MVZ Archives.

159. In the letter accompanying a copy of the proposals sent to Nice, Mayr mentioned he had "been advised against campaigning too much in favor of these proposals because this would arouse more opposition." Ernst Mayr to Margaret Morse Nice, 13 October 1937, Ernst Mayr Papers, HUA.

160. Herbert Friedmann to Joseph Grinnell, 13 March 1935, MVZ Archives.

161. Edward S. Thomas, "In Memoriam: Lawrence Emerson Hicks," *Auk* 75 (1958): 279–281. On Friedmann's promotion of Hicks's candidacy, see Herbert Friedmann to Joseph Grinnell, 27 October 1936, MVZ Archives.

162. On Palmer's refusal to resign as promised, see Ernst Mayr to Alden H. Miller, 24 November 1937, Ernst Mayr Papers, HUA. Hicks was sympathetic to Mayr's reform proposals. See Lawrence E. Hicks to Ernst Mayr, 14 December 1937, Ernst Mayr Papers, HUA.

163. Herbert Friedmann to Joseph Grinnell, 2 December 1937, MVZ Archives. Mayr had also suggested the need for the AOU to play a larger role in "initiating and assisting ornithological research." See Ernst Mayr to Alden Miller, 24 November 1937, Ernst Mayr Papers, HUA.

164. Friedmann remained wary of the strategy of recruiting associate members to shore up AOU finances. See Herbert Friedmann to Lawrence Hicks, 7 January 1938, and Lawrence Hicks to Herbert Friedmann, 12 January 1938, AOU Records, RU 7440, Box 40, Folder 4, SIA. The new AOU president also pursued the idea of establishing an AOU field station on Cape Cod and approaching the National Research Council for a "substantial grant" to support "bird biology," but apparently he got nowhere with either proposal. See Herbert Friedmann to Ernst Mayr, 30 March 1938, Ernst Mayr Papers, HUA.

165. Not surprisingly, the committee included several active reformers and young Ph.D.s who chaired each subcommittee, including Alden H. Miller, anatomy; Leon J. Cole, migration; Ernst Mayr, migration, homing, and related phenomena; P. A. Taverner, North American faunistics; S. C. Kendeigh, physiology; and Margaret M. Nice, psychology, territory, and individual behavior. See Herbert Friedmann, "The Role of the A.O.U. in Ornithology Today," *Auk* 55 (1938): 316. The AOU Council gave its formal approval of the idea at the next annual meeting. See Lawrence E. Hicks, "The Fifty-Sixth Stated Meeting of the American Ornithologists' Union," *Auk* 56 (1939): 113.

166. Ernst Mayr to Josselyn Van Tyne, 2 January 1946, Ernst Mayr Papers, HUA.

167. A copy of the proposal and list of the organizations is included with Herbert Friedmann to Alden Miller, 28 January 1939, MVZ Archives.

168. See Herbert Friedmann to Alden Miller, 1 August 1941, MVZ Archives.

169. Friedmann lost the election to James Chapin. See the minutes of the meeting of 19 June 1939 in AOU Records, RU 7440, Box 40, Folder 5, SIA. Mayr's campaign to reform the AOU continued for several decades. See the Ernst Mayr Papers, HUA, especially his correspondence with Joseph Hickey and Ludlow Griscom, both of whom shared his interest in reforming the organization.

170. Yet some things were slower to change

than others. When the death of Glover Allen in 1942 necessitated the selection of a new editor for the *Auk*, one of the names discussed as a possible replacement was Margaret M. Nice. Clearly her deep knowledge of ornithological literature, extensive contributions to that literature, and experience as associate editor of *Bird-Banding* and the *Wilson Bulletin* qualified her for the position. However, she failed to gain serious consideration, largely because of her gender. As AOU President James Chapin wrote to P. A. Taverner, "we can hardly pick a woman editor for the Auk." Quoted in Keir Sterling and Marianne Ainley, "A Quarterly Journal of Ornithology," in their unpublished history of the AOU, 24.

CONCLUSION

1. Witmer Stone, "The Ornithology of Today and Tomorrow," in *The Fiftieth Anniversary of the Nuttall Ornithological Club* (Cambridge, Mass.: The Club, 1924), 7–25, on 8.

2. Ibid., 10.

3. Witmer Stone, *Bird Studies at Old Cape May: An Ornithology of Coastal New Jersey*, 2 vols. (Philadelphia: Delaware Valley Ornithological Club, 1937).

4. Stone, "Ornithology," 11.

5. Ibid., 8–9.

6. Ibid., 12.

7. Willard estimated that the actual number of collectors was around eight hundred. S. L. Willard, ed., *A Directory of the Ornithologists of the United States* (Utica, NY: The Oologist, 1877).

8. [Frank M. Chapman,] [Editorial,] *Bird-Lore* 27 (1915): 216. Although most birdwatchers pursued the activity primarily for recreation, enough of them also had scientific aspirations to swell the membership rolls of the AOU.

9. Ridgway, *Birds of Middle and North America*, 1:1–2.

10. [T. C. Stephens?,] "Editorial," *Wilson Bulletin* 44 (1932): 231–232.

11. Joseph Grinnell, "Trends in Modern Ornithology," *Wilson Bulletin* 48 (1936): 73–76, talks not only about the shift of interest toward intensive, observational studies of the living bird, but also about changes in taxonomy itself. On Mayr, systematics, and the evolutionary synthesis, see chapter 8.

12. "Fiftieth Christmas Bird Count," *Audubon Field Notes* 4, no. 2 (April 1950): 45.

13. The count of volunteer bird-banders and the total number of birds banded comes from the *Report of the Chief of the Biological Survey* for the year 1939.

14. One particularly active user of the records

was Frederick C. Lincoln, the ornithologist who ran the bird-banding network for the Biological Survey and developed the concept of migratory flyways based on his analysis of the returns. On Lincoln and his contributions, see John K. Terres, "Big Brother to the Waterfowl," *Audubon Magazine* 49 (1947): 150–158; and Ira N. Gabrielson, "Obituary," *Auk* 79 (1962): 495–499.

15. See chapter 7.

16. Broley has been the subject of a series of biographical sketches. See, for example, "Eagle Bander," *New Yorker* 30 (19 June 1954): 18–19; and Myrtle Jeanne Broley, *Eagle Man: Charles Broley's Field Adventures with American Eagles* (New York: Pellegrini and Cudahy, 1952).

17. See the discussion of Charles Broley's work in Rachel Carson, *Silent Spring* (Boston: Houghton Mifflin, 1962), 118–119, 122. On the rise and fall of DDT, see Thomas R. Dunlap, *DDT: Scientists, Citizens, and Public Policy* (Princeton: Princeton University Press, 1981).

18. On Greenewalt's life and career, see Albert Conway, "In Memoriam: Crawford H. Greenewalt, 1902–1993," *Auk* 111 (1994): 188–189; and "Crawford Hallock Greenewalt," in *Current Biography 1949*, ed. Anna Rothe (New York: H. W. Wilson Co., 1950), 234–236.

19. Crawford H. Greenewalt, *Hummingbirds* (Garden City, N.Y.: Doubleday, 1960).

20. Crawford H. Greenewalt, *Bird Song: Acoustics and Physiology* (Washington, D.C.: Smithsonian Institution Press, 1968).

21. Marianne G. Ainley, "The Contribution of the Amateur to North American Ornithology: A Historical Perspective," *The Living Bird* 18 (1979): 161–177, on 169.

22. Mayr, "Epilogue," 376, and "The Role of Ornithological Research in Biology," *Proceedings of the XIIIth International Ornithological Congress* (1963): 27–38, on 27.

23. James R. King and Walter J. Bock, *Workshop on a National Plan for Ornithology: Final Report* (N.p., n.p., 1978), 4.

24. Ibid., 12. See also Donald A. McCrimmon, Jr., and Alexander Sprunt, IV, eds., *Proceedings of a Conference on the Amateur and North American Ornithology* (Ithaca, N.Y., 1978).

25. King and Bock, *Workshop*, 12–13.

26. Jacob Bronowski, *A Sense of the Future* (Cambridge: MIT Press, 1977), 4.

27. Mayr, "Role of Ornithological Research," 27.

28. See, for example, Beryl Rowland, *Birds with Human Souls: A Guide to Bird Symbolism* (Knoxville: University of Tennessee Press, 1978).

BIBLIOGRAPHY

MANUSCRIPT COLLECTIONS

American Museum of Natural History, New York
  Department of Ornithology, Archives
Bancroft Library, University of California, Berkeley
  Joel Asaph Allen Papers
  Joseph Grinnell Papers
  Clinton Hart Merriam Papers
Harvard University Archives, Cambridge, Mass.
  Ernst Mayr Papers
  Frederic Ward Putnam Papers
Library of Congress, Washington, D.C.
  Irving Newton Brant Papers
  Albert Kendrick Fisher Papers
  Waldo Lee McAtee Papers
  Harry Church Oberholser Papers
  Theodore Sherman Palmer Papers
Museum of Comparative Zoology, Harvard University, Cambridge, Mass.
  Department of Birds, Nuttall Ornithological Club Archives
Museum of Comparative Zoology Archives, Harvard University, Cambridge, Mass.
  William Brewster Papers
Museum of Vertebrate Zoology, University of California, Berkeley
  Archives
New York Public Library, New York
  National Audubon Society Records
Smithsonian Institution Archives, Washington, D.C.
  American Ornithologists' Union, Biographical File, RU 7038
  American Ornithologists' Union, Records, 1883–1977, RU 7150
  American Ornithologists' Union, Records, 1871–1994, RU 7440
  Assistant Secretary in Charge of the U.S. National Museum, Card Index to Correspondence, 1881–1904, RU 116; Outgoing Correspondence, 1879–1907, RU 112; Incoming Correspondence, 1860–1908, RU 189
  Assistant Secretary, Acting (Charles D. Walcott), Outgoing Correspondence, 1897–1898, RU 56
  Audubon Naturalist Society of the Central Atlantic States, Records, 1893–1980, RU 7294
  Spencer F. Baird Papers, 1833–1889, RU 7002
  Arthur Cleveland Bent Papers, 1910–1954, RU 7120
  George A. Boardman Papers, 1860–1899, RU 7071
  Division of Birds, National Museum of Natural History, Records, 1854–1959, RU 105
  Herbert Friedmann Interview, 1975, RU 9506
  Office of the Secretary (Charles D. Walcott), Records, 1903–1924, RU 45
  Potomac Valley Ornithological Club Records, 1892–1896, RU 7111

Edward Alexander Preble Papers, 1887–1957, RU 7252
Robert Ridgway Papers, ca. 1850s–1919, RU 7167
Alexander Wetmore Papers, ca. 1848–1979, RU 7006

PERIODICALS CONSULTED

American Osprey 1 (1890)
Annual Report [of the Museum of Comparative Zoology] (1877–1950)
        Published under a variety of titles.
Audubon Magazine 1–2 (1887–1889)
Audubon Magazine 43–72 (1941–1970)
The Auk 1–67 (1884–1950)
Bay State Oologist 1 (1888)
Bird-Lore 1–42 (1899–1940)
Bulletin of the Michigan Ornithological Club 1–6 (1897–1905)
Cassinia 1–35 (1901–1945)
The Condor 1–51 (1899–1949)
Contributions in American Ornithology 1 (1901)
The Country 1–2 (1877–1878)
Forest and Stream 1–28 (1873–1887)
The Hawkeye Ornithologist and Oologist 1–2 (1888–1889)
The Hummer 1 (1899–1900)
The Iowa Ornithologist 1–4 (1895–1896)
Journal of the Maine Ornithological Society 1–13 (1899–1911)
Maine Ornithologist and Oologist 1–2 (1890–1891)
The Museum 1–6 (1894–1900)
The Nidiologist (later *The Nidologist*) 1–4 (1893–1897)
Notes on Rhode Island Ornithology 1–2 (1900–1901)
The Oologist 1–5 (1875–1879)
The Oologist 1–58 (1884–1941)
The Oologist's Advertiser 1 (1890)
The Oologist's Exchange 1–2 (1888–1890)
The Oologist's Journal 1–2 (1891–1892)
The Ornithologist 1 (1885)
The Ornithologist and Botanist 2 (1891)
Ornithologist and Oologist 6–18 (1881–1893)
Osprey 1–5 (1896–1902)
Our Birds 1 (1885)
Our Feathered Friends 1 (1915)
The Owl 1–3 (1885–1888)
The Petrel 1 (1901)
Proceedings of the Nebraska Ornithologists' Union 1–6 (1899–1905)
Random Notes on Natural History 1–3 (1884–1886)
Report of the Chief of the Biological Survey (1900–1940)
        Published under a variety of titles.
Tidings from Nature 1–2 (1884–1886)
Ward's Natural Science Bulletin 1–3 (1881–1886)
Weekly Oologist & Philatelist 1–2 (1891–1892)
Western Ornithologist 1 (1885)

The Wilson Bulletin 1–62 (1893–1950)
The Young Naturalist 1 (1884)

PRIMARY SOURCES

Agassiz, Louis. ". . . Directions for Collecting Fishes and Other Objects of Natural History." New ed. Cambridge, Mass., 1853. [MCZ Archives.]

———. *Essay on Classification.* 1857. Reprinted by Edward Lurie, ed. Cambridge: Harvard University Press, 1962.

———. "Geographical Distribution of Animals." *The Edinburgh New Philosophical Journal* 49 (1850): 1–23.

———. "Notice sur la géographie des animaux." *Revue Suisse et chronique littéraire* 8 (1845): 441–452, 538–585.

———. "Observations sur . . . las distribution géographique des diffèrents types actuels d'animaux." *Bulletin de la Société Neuchâteloise des sciences naturelles* 1 (1846): 366–369.

———. "Observations sur las distribution géographique des êtres organisés." *Bulletin de la Société Neuchâteloise des sciences naturelles* 1 (1846): 357–361.

———. "Sketch of the Natural Provinces of the Animal World and Their Relation to the Different Types of Mankind." In *Types of Mankind*, by J. C. Nott and George R. Gliddon, lviii–lxxvi. Philadelphia: J. B. Lippincott, Grambo, 1854.

———. "Sur la distribution géographique des animaux et de l'homme." *Bulletin de la Société Neuchâteloise des sciences naturelles* 1 (1845): 162–166.

Allen, Arthur A. "The Red-winged Blackbird: A Study in the Ecology of a Cat-tail Marsh." *Abstract of the Proceedings of the Linnaean Society of New York*, no. 24 (1914): 43–128.

———. "Studying Birds' Eggs." *Bird-Lore* 22 (1920): 238–239.

Allen, J. A. *The American Bisons, Living and Extinct.* Memoirs of the Museum of Comparative Zoology, vol. 4, no. 10. Cambridge, Mass.: Welch, Bigelow, 1876.

———. "The A.O.U. and Amateurs." *Ornithologist and Oologist* 12 (1887): 47–48.

———. "The A.O.U. Check-List—Its History and Its Future." *Auk* 20 (1903): 1–9.

———. "The A.O.U. Model Law." *Condor* 5 (1903): 157–158.

———. *The American Ornithologists' Union. A Seven Years' Retrospective.* New York: Published by Order of the Union, 1891.

———. "Bird-Destruction." *Science* 8 (1886): 118–119.

[———]. "Bird Laws." *Science* 7 (1886): 202–204.

———. "Conclusion of the Great Work on the Nests and Eggs of the Birds of Ohio." *Auk* 4 (1887): 150–152.

———. "Decrease of Birds in Massachusetts." *Bulletin of the Nuttall Ornithological Club* 1 (1876): 53–60.

[———]. "Destruction of Birds for Millinery Purposes." *Science* 7 (1886): 196–197.

———. "The Extinction of the Great Auk at the Funk Islands." *American Naturalist* 10 (1876): 48.

———. "The Extirpation of the Larger Indigenous Mammals of the United States." *The Penn Monthly* 7 (1876): 794–806.

———. "The Influence of Physical Conditions in the Genesis of Species." *Radical Review* 1 (1877): 108–140.

———. "The North American Bison and Its Extermination." *The Penn Monthly* 7 (1876): 214–224.

———. "Notes of an Ornithological Reconnaissance of Portions of Kansas, Colorado,

Wyoming, and Utah." *Bulletin of the Museum of Comparative Zoology* 3 (July 1872): 113–183.

[Allen, J. A.]. "Nuttall Ornithological Club." *Bulletin of the Nuttall Ornithological Club* 1 (1876): 29–32.

———. "The Nuttall Ornithological Club." *Boston Evening Transcript*, 21 March 1878, 4.

———. "On the Decrease of Birds in the United States." *The Penn Monthly* 7 (1876): 931–944.

———. "On the Mammals and Winter Birds of East Florida, with an Examination of Certain Assumed Specific Characters in Birds, and a Sketch of the Bird Faunae of Eastern North America." *Bulletin of the Museum of Comparative Zoology* 2, no. 3 (1871): 161–450.

———. "The Present Wholesale Destruction of Bird-Life in the United States." *Science* 7 (1886): 191–195.

———. "Progress of Ornithology in the United States during the Last Century." *American Naturalist* 10 (1876): 536–550.

———. "Recent Literature." *Bulletin of the Nuttall Ornithological Club* 4 (1879): 168.

[———]. "The Relation of Birds to Agriculture." *Science* 7 (1886): 201–202.

[———]. [Reply to Chamberlain]. *Auk* 1 (1884): 102–104.

[———]. [Reply to Chamberlain II]. *Auk* 1 (1884): 200–202.

[———]. Review of *Birds of the Cambridge Region of Massachusetts*, by William Brewster. *Auk* 23 (1906): 466–470.

———. "To What Extent Is It Profitable to Recognize Geographical Forms among North American Birds?" *Auk* 7 (1890): 1–9.

American Ornithologists' Union. *By-Laws and Rules and List of Members*. New York: L. S. Foster, 1887.

———. *The Code of Nomenclature and Check-List of North American Birds Adopted by the American Ornithologists' Union*. New York: American Ornithologists' Union, 1886.

———. *Check-List of North American Birds*. 2d ed. New York: American Ornithologists' Union, 1895.

———. *Check-List of North American Birds*. 3d ed. New York: American Ornithologists' Union, 1910.

———. *Check-List of North American Birds*. 4th ed. New York: American Ornithologists' Union, 1931.

———. *Check-List of North American Birds*. 5th ed. Baltimore: American Ornithologists' Union, 1957.

———. *Checklist of North American Birds*. 6th ed. Lawrence, Kans.: American Ornithologists' Union, 1983.

———. "Report of the Ad Hoc Committee on Scientific and Educational Uses of Wild Birds." *Auk* 92 (1975): 1A–27A.

———. Committee on Bird Protection. "Bulletin No. 2. Protection of Birds by Legislation." *Forest & Stream* 27 (1886): 304–305.

———. "Supplement." *Science* 7 (1886): 191–205. Also printed separately as "A.O.U. Bird Protection Bulletin no. 1."

Annual Reports of the Forest, Fish, and Game Commissioner of the State of New York for 1904, 1905, 1906. Albany, N.Y.: State Printers, 1907.

Apgar, Austin P. *Pocket Key of Birds of the Northern United States, East of the Rocky Mountains*. Trenton: John L. Murphy, 1893.

Audubon, John James. *Birds of America*. 4 vols. London: Published by the Author, 1827–1838.

————. *Ornithological Biography*. 5 vols. Edinburgh: Adam and Charles Black, 1831–1835.

Austin, Oliver L., Jr., ed. *Life Histories of North American Cardinals, Grosbeaks, Buntings, Towhees, Finches, Sparrows, and Allies; Order Passiformes: Family Fringillidae. Part One: Genera Richmondena through Piplio (Part)*. Washington, D.C.: Smithsonian Institution Press, 1968.

Bailey, Harold H. "Proposed Revision of the By-Laws of the American Ornithologists' Union." *Auk* 32 (1915): 134–136, and *Oologist* 32 (1915): 169–171.

————. "Membership in the A.O.U." *Auk* 33 (1916): 227.

Bailey, Liberty H. *The Nature-Study Idea*. New York: Doubleday, Page, 1903.

Baird, Spencer F. *Catalogue of North American Birds, Chiefly in the Museum of the Smithsonian Institution*. Washington, D.C.: Smithsonian Institution, 1859.

————. "Directions for Collecting, Preserving, and Transporting Specimens of Natural History. Prepared for the Use of the Smithsonian Institution." 2d ed. Washington, D.C.: Smithsonian Institution, 1854.

[————]. "Directions for Collecting, Preserving, and Transporting Specimens of Natural History. Prepared for the Use of the Smithsonian Institution." 3d ed. Washington, D.C.: Smithsonian Institution, 1859. Reproduced in *Smithsonian Miscellaneous Collections* 2 (1862): article 7.

————. "The Distribution and Migrations of North American Birds." *American Journal of Science*, n.s. 41 (1866): 73–91.

————. *Hints for Preserving Objects of Natural History*. Carlisle, Pa.: Gitt and Hinkley, 1846.

————. "Notes on a Collection of Birds Made by Mr. John Xantus, at Cape St. Lucas, Lower California." *Proceedings of the Philadelphia Academy of Natural Sciences* 11 (1859): 299–306.

Baird, Spencer F., Thomas M. Brewer, and Robert Ridgway. *A History of North American Birds: Land Birds*. 3 vols. Boston: Little, Brown, 1874.

————. *The Water Birds of North America*. 2 vols. Boston: Little, Brown, 1884.

Baird, Spencer F., John Cassin, and G. N. Lawrence, *Reports of the Explorations and Surveys to Ascertain the Most Practical and Economical Route for a Railroad from the Mississippi River to the Pacific Ocean . . . 1853–1856 . . . Volume IX . . . Birds*. Washington, D.C.: Beverly Tucker, 1858.

Baldwin, S. Prentiss. "Bird Banding by Means of Systematic Trapping." *Abstracts of the Proceedings of the Linnaean Society of New York*, no. 31 (1919): 23–56.

Baldwin, S. Prentiss, Harry C. Oberholser, and Leonard G. Worley. *The Measurement of Birds*. Cleveland: Cleveland Museum of Natural History, 1931.

Ballard, Harlan H. *Hand-Book of the St. Nicholas Agassiz Association*. Pittsfield, Mass.: Axtell & Pomeroy, 1882.

————. *Hand-Book of the St. Nicholas Agassiz Association*. 2d ed. Lenox, Mass.: The Author, 1884.

————. *Three Kingdoms: A Hand-Book of the Agassiz Association*. 4th ed. St. Louis: I. A. Mekeel, 1897.

Balliet, Letson, ed. *American Naturalist's Directory*. Garland, Maine: H. Stanton Sawyer, 1890.

[Barnes, R. M.] "Ad Nauseate." *Oologist* 47 (1930): 139–140.

————. "Business is Dull." *Oologist* 34 (1917): 217.

[————]. "More about Names." *Oologist* 41 (1924): 91.

[————]. "More Chaos." *Oologist* 35 (1918): 82.

[Barnes, R. M.]. "More Millimeter Races." *Oologist* 50 (1933): 27–28.

[————]. "The 1931 A.O.U. Checklist." *Oologist* 48 (1931): 171.

[————]. "The Result of Being Too Scientifically Scientific." *Oologist* 40 (1923): 167–168.

[————]. "Richard C. Harlow." *Oologist* 38 (1921): 42.

————. "Scientific Snobbery." *Oologist* 40 (1923): 81.

[————]. "Some Books." *Oologist* 48 (1931): 135–137.

[————]. "Technical Names." *Oologist* 35 (1918): 165–166.

[————]. "Widening." *Oologist* 39 (1922): 136.

Barrows, Walter B. *The English Sparrow (Passer Domesticus) in North America, Especially in Its Relations to Agriculture*. U.S. Department of Agriculture, Division of Economic Ornithology and Mammalogy, Bulletin no. 1. Washington, D.C.: Government Printing Office, 1889.

Bartsch, Paul. "Notes on the Herons of the District of Columbia." *Smithsonian Miscellaneous Collection* 45 (1904): 104–111.

Batty, Joseph H. *Practical Taxidermy, and Home Decoration; Together with General Information for Sportsmen*. New York: Orange Judd, 1879.

Beal, F. E. L. "A Demand for English Names." *Auk* 12 (1895): 192–194.

Bendire, Charles E. *Life Histories of North America Birds, with Special Reference to Their Breeding Habits and Eggs*. U.S. National Museum, Special Bulletin nos. 1, 3. 2 vols. Washington, D.C.: Government Printing Office, 1892–1895.

Bent, Arthur C. "Life Histories of North American Birds." *Auk* 39 (1922): 590–591.

————. *Life Histories of North American Birds*. Smithsonian Institution, U.S. National Museum, Bulletin nos. 107, 113, 121, 126, 130, 135, 142, 146, 162, 167, 170, 174, 176, 179, 191, 195, 196, 197, 203, 211. 20 parts. Washington, D.C.: Government Printing Office, 1919–1958.

Bergmann, Carl. *Über die Verhältnisse der Wärmeökonomie der Thiere zu ihrer Grösse*. Göttingen: Vandenhoeck and Ruprecht, 1847.

B[icknell], E[dward] P. "Chapman's 'Handbook of Birds of Eastern North America.'" *Auk* 12 (1895): 282–284.

————. "The Status of the Black Gyrfalcon as a Long Island Bird." *Auk* 41 (1924): 64–67.

"Bird-Lore's First Breeding-Bird Census." *Bird-Lore* 39 (1937): 147–150.

"Bird-Lore's Thirty-fifth Christmas Census." *Bird-Lore* 37 (1935): 31–85.

Blanchan, Neltje. *Bird Neighbors: An Introductory Acquaintance with One Hundred and Fifty Birds Commonly Found in the Gardens, Meadows, and Woods about Our Home*. New York: Doubleday and MacClure, 1897.

Blasius, J. H. "Beilage zum Protokoll der Zehnten Versammlung der deutschen Ornithologen-Gesellschaft." *Naumannia* 6 (1856): 433–474.

Bowdish, B. L. "Nature Study." *Oologist* 14 (1897): 99.

Bowdish, B. S. "A Further Consideration." *Oologist* 19 (1902): 87.

[Brewer, Thomas Mayo]. "Instructions in Reference to Collecting Nests and Eggs of North American Birds." Smithsonian Miscellaneous Collections, 2, no. 9 (1860): 1–22.

————. *North American Oology*. Smithsonian Contribution to Knowledge, 11. Washington, D.C.: Smithsonian Institution, 1857.

Brewster, William. *Birds of the Cambridge Region of Massachusetts*. Memoirs of the Nuttall Ornithological Club, no. 4. Cambridge, Mass.: The Club, 1906.

————. "Nesting Habits of the Parrakeet." *Auk* 6 (1889): 336–337.

————. "The Nuttall Ornithological Club of Cambridge." *Boston Daily Advertiser*, 20 March 1878.

————. "Something More about Black Ducks." *Auk* 26 (1909): 175–179.

Brewster, William, and Ralph Hoffmann. "Unsatisfactory Records." *Auk* 19 (1902): 420.

Brimley, C. S. "The Destruction of Birds for Millinery Purposes." *Ornithologist and Oologist* 11 (1886): 160.

Bryant, H. C. "Report of the Committee on Bird Protection [for 1930]." *Auk* 48 (1931): 91–94.

————. "Report of the Committee on Bird Protection [for 1931]." *Auk* 49 (1932): 74–76.

————. "Report of the Committee on Bird Protection, American Ornithologists' Union [for 1932]." *Auk* 50 (1933): 86–90.

————. "Report of the Committee on Bird Protection [for 1933]." *Auk* 51 (1934): 71–73.

————. "Report of the Committee on Bird Protection [for 1934]." *Auk* 52 (1935): 70–73.

————. "Report of the Committee on Bird Protection, American Ornithologists' Union [for 1935]." *Auk* 53 (1936): 70–73.

————. "Report of the Committee on Bird Protection, 1936." *Auk* 54 (1937): 426–428.

————. "Report of the Committee on Bird Protection, 1937." *Auk* 55 (1938): 326–327.

Bullock, William. *A Concise and Easy Method of Preserving Objects of Natural History, Intended for the Use of Sportsmen, Travellers, and Others*. New York: Printed for the Publisher, 1829.

Burns, Frank L. "The American Crow *(Corvus americanus)*." *Wilson Bulletin* 7 (1895): 2–41.

————. "The Flicker." *Wilson Bulletin* 12 (1900): 1–83.

Burroughs, John. "Bird Enemies." *Century Magazine* 31 (1885–1886): 270–274.

————. *Signs and Seasons*. Boston: Houghton, Mifflin, 1886.

————. *Wake-Robin*. New York: Hurd and Houghton, 1871.

Carey, Henry P. "Hawk Extermination." *Auk* 43 (1926): 275–276.

Cassino, Samuel E., ed. *The Naturalists' Directory for 1878*. Salem, Mass.: Naturalists' Agency, 1878.

————. *The Naturalists' Directory, 1884*. Boston: S. E. Cassino, 1884.

————. *The Naturalists' Directory, 1886*. Boston: S. E. Cassino, 1886.

C[astle], W. W. "The Destruction of Birds for Millinery Purposes: A Request for Facts." *Ornithologist and Oologist* 9 (1884): 116.

————. "The Destruction of Birds for Millinery Purposes." *Ornithologist and Oologist* 10 (1885): 15–16.

————. "Editor O. and O." *Ornithologist and Oologist* 9 (1884): 140.

A Catalogue of the Oological Collection of J. Parker Norris and J. Parker Norris, Jr. Philadelphia: Privately printed, 1894.

Chamberlain, Montague. "The A.O.U. and Amateurs." *Ornithologist and Oologist* 11 (1886): 160.

————. "The A.O.U. and Amateurs." *Ornithologist and Oologist* 12 (1887): 32.

————. "Are Trinomials Necessary?" *Auk* 1 (1884): 101–102.

————. "Are Trinomials Necessary?" *Auk* 1 (1884): 198–200.

————. "More 'Plain English.'" *Ornithologist and Oologist* 10 (1885): 9.

————. "Plain English." *Ornithologist and Oologist* 8 (1883): 53–54.

————. *A Popular Handbook of the Ornithology of the United States Based on Nuttall's Manual*. 2 vols. Boston: Little, Brown, 1891.

————. "A Reply to Dr. Coues." *Ornithologist and Oologist* 8 (1883): 57–59.

[Chapman, Frank M.] "The A.O.U. and Audubon Societies." *Bird-Lore* 2 (1900): 161–162.

———. "Bird Clubs in America" *Bird-Lore* 17 (1915): 347–348.

———. *Bird-Life: A Guide to the Study of Our Common Birds.* New York: D. Appleton, 1897.

[———]. "Bird-Lore's Tenth Christmas Census." *Bird-Lore* 12 (1910): 19–36.

[———]. "Bird-Lore's Thirteenth Christmas Census." *Bird-Lore* 15 (1913): 20–45.

———. *Bird Studies with a Camera.* New York: D. Appleton, 1900.

———. "Birds and Bonnets." *Forest and Stream* 26 (1886): 84.

[———]. "A Christmas Bird-Census." *Bird-Lore* 2 (1900): 192.

[———]. "The Christmas Bird Census." *Bird-Lore* 3 (1901): 28–33.

[———]. [Editorial.] *Bird-Lore* 1 (1899): 28; 2 (1900): 161–162; 11 (1909): 37; 13 (1911): 48; 14 (1912): 237; 17 (1915): 216; 24 (1922): 54. Series of unsigned, untitled editorials.

———. *Handbook of Birds of Eastern North America.* New York: D. Appleton, 1895.

———. "Notes on the Carolina Parakeet." *Abstract of the Proceedings of the Linnaean Society, for the Year Ending March 7, 1890,* 4–6.

———. [Notes on a Collecting Trip to Brevard County, Florida, Spring 1889.] *Abstract of the Proceedings of the Linnaean Society, for the Year Ending March 7, 1890,* 2.

[———]. "An Opportunity for the Local Ornithologist." *Bird-Lore* 7 (1905): 286–287.

[———]. "A Question of Identity." *Bird-Lore* 4 (1902): 166–167.

———. Review of *The Art of Bird-Watching,* by E. M. Nicholson. *Bird-Lore* 34 (1932): 81–82.

———. Review of "Brewster's Warbler," by Walter Faxon. *Bird-Lore* 15 (1913): 312.

———. Review of "An Attempt to List Extinct and Vanishing Birds," by J. C. Phillips. *Bird-Lore* 31 (1929): 352–353.

———. Review of "The Red-Winged Blackbird," by Arthur A. Allen. *Bird-Lore* 16 (1914): 284–285.

———. "The Warbler Book," *Bird-Lore* 6 (1904): 61–63.

———. *The Warblers of North America.* New York: D. Appleton, 1907.

Chapman, Frank M., and Chester A. Reed, *Color Key to North American Birds.* New York: Doubleday, Page, 1903.

Childs, John Lewis. "Membership Condition in the A.O.U." *Auk* 25 (1908): 494.

———. "The Ornithological Collections of John Lewis Childs, Floral Park, N.Y." *The Warbler,* 2d series, 2 (1906): 66–106.

Cole, Leon J. "Suggestions for a Method of Studying the Migration of Birds." *Third Report of the Michigan Academy of Sciences* (1901): 67–70.

Comstock, Anna Botsford. *Handbook of Nature Study.* Ithaca: Cornell University Press, 1911.

Congressional Record. Vol. 16, part 1, 48th Congress, 2d session (1884–1885): 539, 540.

———. Vol. 16, part 3, 48th Congress, 2d session (1885): 1937–1939.

Cooke, Wells W. *Preliminary Census of the Birds of the United States.* U.S. Department of Agriculture, Bulletin no. 187, 11 February 1915.

———. *Report on the Bird Migration in the Mississippi Valley in the Years 1884 and 1885,* edited and revised by C. Hart Merriam. U.S. Department of Agriculture, Division of Economic Agriculture, Bulletin no. 2. Washington, D.C.: Government Printing Office, 1888.

———. *Second Annual Report of Bird Counts in the United States, with Discussion of Results.* U.S. Department of Agriculture, Bulletin no. 396, 23 October 1916.

Coues, Elliott. *Birds of the Colorado Valley.* U.S. Geological Survey of the Territories,

Miscellaneous Publications, no. 11. Washington, D.C.: Government Printing Office, 1878.

———. *A Check List of North American Birds.* Salem, Mass.: Naturalists' Agency, 1873.

———. "Compliments of the Season." *Bulletin of the Nuttall Ornithological Club* 8 (1883): 1–6.

———. *The Coues Check List of North American Birds.* 2d ed. Boston: Estes and Lauriat, 1882.

———. "Editorial Eyrie." *Osprey* 3 (1898–1899): 123–125.

———. *Field Ornithology.* Salem, Mass.: Naturalists' Agency, 1874.

———. "Genevieve E. Jones." *Bulletin of the Nuttall Ornithological Club* 4 (1879): 228.

———. *Key to North American Birds.* Salem, Mass.: Naturalists' Agency, 1872.

———. *Key to North American Birds.* 2d ed. Boston: Estes and Lauriat, 1884.

———. *Key to North American Birds.* 5th ed. Boston: Dana Estes, 1903.

———. "On the Application of Trinomial Nomenclature to Zoology." *The Zoologist*, 3d series, 8 (1884): 241–247.

———. "On the Present Status of Passer Domesticus in America, with Special Reference to the Western States and Territories." Department of the Interior, United States Geological and Geographical Survey, Bulletin, 5, no. 2 (1879): 175–193.

———. [On the Use of Trinomials in Zoological Nomenclature.] *Bulletin of the Nuttall Ornithological Club* 4 (1879): 171.

———. "Progress of American Ornithology." *American Naturalist* 5 (1871): 364–373.

———. Review of *Nests and Eggs of the Birds of Ohio,* by Mrs. N. E. Jones and Howard Jones. *Bulletin of the Nuttall Ornithological Club* 4 (1879): 52, 228; 5 (1880): 39; 7 (1882): 45, 112; 8 (1883): 112, 166; *Auk* 2 (1885): 289; 3 (1886): 406.

Daggett, Frank S. "Concerning the Active Membership of the A.O.U." *Condor* 2 (1900): 68–69.

[———]. "The Wilson Bulletin." *Condor* 3 (1901): 53–54.

Darwin, Francis, ed. *The Life and Letters of Charles Darwin.* New York: Basic Books, 1959.

Davie, Oliver. *Egg Check List and Key to the Nests and Eggs of North American Birds.* 2d ed. Columbus, Ohio: Hann & Adair, 1886.

———. *An Egg Check List of North American Birds.* Columbus, Ohio: Hann & Adair, 1885.

———. *Methods in the Art of Taxidermy.* Columbus, Ohio: Hann & Adair, 1894.

———. *Nest and Eggs of North American Birds.* 3d ed. Columbus, Ohio: Hann & Adair, 1889.

———. *Nests and Eggs of North American Birds.* 5th ed. Philadelphia: David McKay, 1898.

Davis, Fred J. "Methods of Climbing for Nests." *Oologist* 3 (1878): 93–94.

Davis, H. W., and Geo. C. Baker, comps. *The Oologist Directory, Containing the Names and Addresses of Over Four Hundred Collectors of Oological, Ornithological, and Taxidermical Specimens.* Columbus, Ohio: Hann & Adair, 1885.

Dawson, William Leon. "The All-Day Test at Santa Barbara." *Condor* 15 (1913): 153–158.

———. "Committee on Geographical Distribution." *Wilson Bulletin* 9 (1897): 76.

———. "Committee on Geographical Distribution: Further Mechanical Helps to Observation." *Wilson Bulletin* 10 (1898): 28–29.

———. "A Defense of Bird Horizons." *Condor* 3 (1901): 132–133.

Dawson, William Leon. "Editorial." *Wilson Bulletin* 9 (1897): 32.

De Voe, Thomas F. *The Market Assistant*. New York: Hurd and Houghton, 1867.

Dille, Fred M. "The Fourth Edition: The New A.O.U. Checklist." *Oologist* 49 (1932): 2–8.

Dugmore, A. Radclyffe. *Nature and the Camera*. New York: Doubleday, Page, 1902.

Dutcher, William. "The Labrador Duck:—A Revised List of Extant Specimens in North America, with Some Historical Data." *Auk* 8 (1891): 201–216.

———. "Notes and News." *Auk* 14 (1897): 257–258.

———. "Notes on Some Rare Birds in the Collection of the Long Island Historical Society." *Auk* 10 (1893): 267–277.

———. "A Protest." *Condor* 5 (1903): 53–54.

———. "Report of the A.O.U. Committee on Protection of North American Birds [for 1896]." *Auk* 14 (1897): 20–32.

———. "Report of the A.O.U. Committee on Protection of North American Birds [for 1897]." *Auk* 15 (1898): 81–114.

———. "Report of the Committee on the Protection of North American Birds for the Year 1900." *Auk* 18 (1901): 68–104.

———. "Report of the Committee on the Protection of North American Birds [for 1901]." *Auk* 19 (1902): 31–64.

———. "Report of the A.O.U. Committee on the Protection of North American Birds [for 1902]." *Auk* 20 (1903): 101–159.

———. "Report of the A.O.U. Committee on the Protection of North American Birds for the Year 1903." *Auk* 21 (1904): 97–208.

———. "Wilson's Plover on Long Island, N.Y." *Bulletin of the Nuttall Ornithological Club* 4 (1879): 242.

Dwight, Jonathan, Jr. "The Auk." *Bird-Lore* 10 (1908): 218.

———. "Editor of *The Auk.*" *Auk* 35 (1918): 262.

———. "The Exaltation of the Subspecies." *Auk* 21 (1904): 64–66.

———. "A Method of Obtaining a Temporary Stability of Names." *Auk* 21 (1904): 406.

———. Review of "The Auk." *Bird-Lore* 3 (1901): 111–112.

———. "Sequence of Plumage and Moults of the Passerine Birds of New York." *Annals of the New York Academy of Sciences* 8 (1900): 73–360.

Emerson, Guy. "The Lure of the List." *Bird-Lore* 42 (1940): 37–39.

"Facts about the Birds: Misleading Statistics Respecting Fashion's Demands." *The Hawkeye Ornithologist and Oologist* 1 (1888): 29–33.

Farnham, A. B. "Association of American Ornithologists." *Ornithologist and Oologist* 16 (1891): 76.

Faxon, Walter. "Brewster's Warbler (*Helminthophilia leucobronchialis*) a Hybrid between the Golden-winged Warbler (*Helminthophilia chrysoptera*) and the Blue-Winged Warbler (*Helminthophilia pinus*)." *Memoirs of the Museum of Comparative Zoology* 40 (August 1913): 311–316.

"Fifth Annual Report of the National Association of Audubon Societies, 1909," *Bird-Lore* 11 (1909): 281–348.

"Fiftieth Christmas Bird Count." *Audubon Field Notes* 4, no. 2 (April 1950): 45.

Figgins, J. D. "The Fallacy of the Tendency Towards Ultraminute Distinctions." *Auk* 21 (1904): 62–69.

Finley, William L. *American Birds, Studied and Photographed from Life*. New York: C. Scribner's and Sons, 1907.

Fischer, Richard B. "That Big Day." *Audubon Magazine* 55 (May–June 1953): 114–117, 142.

Fisher, A. K. *The Hawks and Owls of the United States in Their Relation to Agriculture.* Biological Survey Bulletin Series, no. 3. Washington, D.C.: Government Printing Office, 1893.

[Fisher, Walter K.] "Editorial Notes." *Condor* 5 (1903): 136.

———. [Reply to J. A. Allen, "The A.O.U. Model Law."] *Condor* 5 (1903): 158–159.

Forester, Frank [Henry William Herbert]. *The Complete Manual for Young Sportsmen.* New York: Stringer & Townsend, 1856.

Freeman, C. F. "The Medium of 'Bird Protection.'" *Ornithologist and Oologist* 11 (1886): 48.

Friedmann, Herbert. *The Cowbirds: A Study in the Biology of Social Parasitism.* Springfield, Ill.: C. C. Thomas, 1929.

———. "The Role of the A.O.U. in Ornithology Today." *Auk* 55 (1938): 316.

———. "The Weaving of the Red-billed Weaver Bird in Captivity." *Zoologica* 2 (1922): 257.

G.R.C. "Field Glass." *Ornithologist and Oologist* 7 (1882): 150–151, 8 (1883): 5–6.

Gentry, Thomas. *The House Sparrow at Home and Abroad.* Philadelphia: Claxton, Remsen, and Haffelfinger, 1878.

Gill, Theodore. "A Great Work." *Osprey* 3 (1899): 88–94.

Gloger, Constantin Lambert. *Das Abändern der Vögel durch Einfluss des Klima's.* Breslau: A. Schulz, 1833.

Greene, Earle E. "Another Dissenter Writes." *Audubon Magazine* 60 (May–June 1958): 100.

Greenewalt, Crawford H. *Bird Song: Acoustics and Physiology.* Washington, D.C.: Smithsonian Institution Press, 1968.

———. *Hummingbirds.* Garden City, N.Y.: Doubleday, 1960.

[Grinnell, George Bird]. "The Audubon Society." *Forest and Stream* 26 (1886): 41.

[———]. "Spare the Swallows." *Forest and Stream* 21 (1883): 121.

Grinnell, Joseph. "Conserve the Collector." *Science* 41 (1915): 229–232.

———. "The Museum Conscience." *Museum Work* 4 (1922): 62–63.

[———]. "Notes and News." *Condor* 39 (1937): 133.

[———]. "Record Criteria." *Condor* 8 (1906): 156.

———. Review of *Birds of Middle and North America*, by Robert Ridgway. *Condor* 4 (1902): 22–23.

———. "Some Inferences from the New Check-list." *Auk* 49 (1932): 9–13.

———. "Trends in Modern Ornithology." *Wilson Bulletin* 48 (1936): 73–76

———. "Two Check-Lists of 1931—A Critical Commentary." *Condor* 34 (1932): 87–95.

———. "Uses and Methods of a Research Museum." *Popular Science Monthly* 77 (1910): 163–169.

Grinnell, Joseph, and H. S. Swarth. "An Account of the Birds and Mammals of the San Jacinto Area of Southern California with Remarks upon the Behavior of Geographic Races on the Margins of their Habitat." *University of California Publications in Zoology* 10 (1913): 197–406.

Griscom, Ludlow. *Birds of New York City Region.* New York: American Museum of Natural History, 1923.

———. "Field Studies of the Anatidae of the Atlantic Coast." *Auk* 39 (1922): 517–530; 40 (1923): 69–80.

———. "The Identification of the Commoner Anatidae of the Eastern United States." Master's thesis, Cornell University, 1915.

———. *Modern Bird Study.* Cambridge: Harvard University Press, 1945.

Griscom, Ludlow. "Problems of Field Identification." *Auk* 39 (1922): 31–41.

H[amlin], C. E. "The English Sparrows." *The [Bath, Maine.] Times*, 26 February 1878.

Harrison, Nell. "From a Woman's Standpoint." *Proceedings of the Nebraska Ornithologists' Union* 3 (Dec. 1902): 41–42.

Hawkins, Leighman. "Our Need to Dignify Bird Study." *Audubon Magazine* 60 (March–April 1958): 55–56.

Hendricks, Bartlett. "Birding as a Sport." *Audubon Magazine* 48 (1946): 246–248, 304–306.

Hendy, E. W. "The Aesthetic Appeal of Bird-Watching." *Contemporary Review* 127 (April 1925): 482–492.

Henshaw, Henry Wetherbee. "The Policemen of the Air: An Account of the Biological Survey of the Department of Agriculture." *National Geographic Magazine* 19 (1908): 79–118.

———. "The Use of Trinomials." *Bulletin of the Nuttall Ornithological Club* 4 (1879): 232–233.

Herrick, Francis H. *The American Eagle: A Study in Natural and Civil History*. New York: D. Appleton-Century, 1934.

———. "Biological Laboratory of Western Reserve University." *Journal of Applied Microscopy* 3 (1899): 949–955.

———. *The Home Life of Wild Birds: A New Method of the Study and Photography of Birds*. New York: Putnam, 1901.

———. *Wild Birds at Home*. New York: D. Appleton-Century, 1935.

Hickey, Joseph. "The Amateur Ornithologist and His Bird Club." *Bird-Lore* 39 (1937): 425–429.

———. *A Guide to Bird Watching*. New York: Oxford Univ. Press, 1943.

Hicks, Lawrence E. "The Fifty-Sixth Stated Meeting of the American Ornithologists' Union." *Auk* 56 (1939): 112–123.

"History Repeating Itself." *Boston Journal*, 14 March 1878.

Hodge, Clifton F. *Nature Study and Life*. Boston: Ginn, 1902.

Hoffmann, Ralph. *Birds of the Pacific States*. Boston: Houghton Mifflin, 1927.

———. *A Guide to the Birds of New England and Eastern New York*. Boston: Houghton Mifflin, 1904.

Holt, Ernest G. "Nature-Wasters and Sentimentalists." *Auk* 43 (1926): 409–410.

Hornaday, William T. "A Demand for English." *Auk* 12 (1895): 90–92.

———. "The Destruction of Our Birds and Mammals: A Report on the Results of an Inquiry." *Annual Report of the New York Zoological Society* 2 (1898): 77–107.

———. *The Extermination of the American Bison*. Washington, D.C.: Government Printing Office, 1889.

———. *Taxidermy and Zoological Collecting: A Complete Handbook for the Amateur Taxidermist, Collector, Osteologist, Museum-Builder, Sportsman, and Traveller*. New York: Charles Scribner's Sons, 1891.

Howe, Reginald H. *Every Bird: A Guide to the Identification of the Birds of Woodland, Beach and Ocean*. Boston: Bradlee Whidden, 1896.

Hoxie, Walter. "On Making Exchanges." *Ornithologist and Oologist* 13 (1888): 54–55.

Huxley, Julian. "Bird-watching and Biological Science: Some Observations on the Study of Courtship in Birds." *Auk* 33 (1916): 142–161, 256–270.

Jackson, John H. "Oology vs. Philately." *Oologist* 11 (1894): 279.

Job, Herbert K. *Among the Waterfowl*. New York: Doubleday, Page, 1903.

Jones, Lynds. "All Day with the Birds." *Wilson Bulletin* 11 (1899): 41–45.

[————]. "All Day with the Birds: May 7, 1902," *Wilson Bulletin* 14 (1902): 125–129.

————. "The Bird Census." *Wilson Bulletin*, 10 (1898): 5–9.

————. "A Criticism." *Wilson Bulletin* 13 (1901): 76–78.

[————]. "Editorial." *Wilson Bulletin* 9 (1897): 10; 9 (1897): 64–65; 10 (1898): 30–31; 10 (1898): 77–78; 11 (1899): 46–47; 11 (1899): 62–63; 16 (1904): 60–61; 19 (1907): 161; 27 (1915): 287; 36 (1924): 93. Series of unsigned editorials.

————. "The Horizons." *Wilson Bulletin* 12 (1900): 10–38.

————. "A March Horizon." *Wilson Bulletin* 11 (1899): 22–24.

[————]. "A May-Day Horizon." *Wilson Bulletin* 15 (1903): 31.

[————]. "New Year Horizon." *Wilson Bulletin* 15 (1903): 113–114.

[————]. "A New Year Horizon for All." *Wilson Bulletin* 14 (1902): 133.

[————?]. "Notes." *Wilson Quarterly*, no. 4 (1892): 41–43.

————. "On Methods in Teaching Ornithology at Oberlin College." *Bird-Lore* 2 (1900): 14–18.

————. "With the Birds in Fourteen States." *Wilson Bulletin* 12 (1900): 1.

Jones, Mrs. N. E., and Howard Jones. *Illustrations of the Nests and Eggs of the Birds of Ohio. Illustrations by Mrs. N. E. Jones, with Text by Howard Jones, A.M., M.D.*. Circleville, Ohio, 1886.

Jordan, David S. "The A.O.U. Code and Check-List of North American Birds." *Auk* 3 (1886): 393–397.

Keyser, Leander. "The Art of Kicking Gently." *Osprey* 3 (1898–1899): 109–110.

King, James R. and Walter J. Bock. *Workshop on a National Plan for Ornithology: Final Report*. N.p., 1978.

Knobel, Edward. *Field Key to the Land Birds*. Boston: Brandlee Whidden, 1899.

Know, J. C. "Some Suggestions." *Auk* 20 (1903): 234.

Koford, Carl B. *The California Condor*. Research Report no. 4 of the National Audubon Society. New York: National Audubon Society, 1953.

Krider, John. *Forty Years Notes of a Field Ornithologist*. Philadelphia: Joseph H. Weston, 1879.

————. *Krider's Sporting Anecdotes, Illustrative of the Habits of Certain Varieties of American Game*, edited by H. Milnor Klapp. Philadelphia: A. Hart, 1853.

————. *Ornithological and Oological List of North America*. Philadelphia: W. W. Mayberry, n.d.

Kuerzi, Richard G. "Life History Studies of the Tree Swallow." *Proceedings of the Linnaean Society of New York*, nos. 52–53 (1941): 1–52.

Kumlien, Ludwig. "Value(?) of Ornithological Observations by Amateurs." *Osprey* 1 (1896–1897): 137.

Kuser, John D. *The Way to Study Birds*. New York: G. P. Putnam's Sons, 1917.

Langdon, Frank. "Papers on the Destruction of Native Birds: Fourth Paper." *Journal of the Cincinnati Society of Natural History* 9 (1886): 181–191.

Langille, Rev. J[ames] Hibbert. *Our Birds in Their Haunts: A Popular Treatise on the Birds of Eastern North America*. Boston: S. E. Cassino, 1884.

————. "The New Era of Ornithology." *Oologist* 8 (1891): 136–137.

Lattin, Frank H. *The Oologists' Hand-Book*. Rochester, N.Y.: John P. Smith, 1885.

————. *The Standard Catalogue of North American Birds' Eggs*. 3rd ed. Albion, N.Y.: Frank H. Lattin, 1892.

————. *The Standard Catalogue of North American Birds' Eggs*. 4th ed. Albion, N.Y.: 1896.

[————]. "20,000 March Oologists." *Oologist* 11 (1894): 37.

Leopold, Aldo. Review of *Studies in the Life History of the Song Sparrow*, vol. 1, by Margaret Morse Nice. *The Canadian Field-Naturalist* 51 (November 1937): 126.

———. *A Sand County Almanac and Sketches Here and There*. New York: Oxford University Press, 1949.

Lewis, E[lisha] J[arett]. *Hints to Sportsmen*. Philadelphia: Lea & Blanchard, 1851.

Lincoln, Frederick C. "What Constitutes a Record." *Bulletin of the Audubon Society of New Hampshire* 8, no. 2 (1928): 17–20.

Linsdale, Jean M. "Notes and News." *Condor* 39 (1937): 180.

Loomis, Leverett M. "Recognition of Geographic Variation in Nomenclature." *Auk* 20 (1903): 294–299.

Lorenz, Konrad. "The Companion in the Bird's World." *Auk* 54 (1937): 245–273.

———. "Der Kumpan in der Umwelt des Vogels." *Journal für Ornithologie* 83 (1935): 137–213, 289–413.

Lucas, F. A. "The Destruction of Birds for Millinery Purposes." *Ornithologist and Oologist* 9 (1884): 98–99.

———. "The Destruction of Birds for Millinery Purposes." *Ornithologist and Oologist* 9 (1884): 128.

———. "The Destruction of Birds for Millinery Purposes." *Ornithologist and Oologist* 10 (1885): 31–32.

McAtee, W. L. "Hawk Abundance and Hawk Campaigns." *Auk* 43 (1926): 542–544.

———. "The Specimen Fetish." *Scientific Monthly* 54 (1942): 565–566.

McCormick, L. M. "The Destruction of Birds for Millinery Purposes." *Ornithologist and Oologist* 9 (1884): 138–140.

———. "The Destruction of Birds for Millinery Purposes." *Ornithologist and Oologist* 10 (1885): 48.

McCrimmon, Donald A., Jr. and Alexander Sprunt, IV, eds. *Proceedings of a Conference on the Amateur and North American Ornithology*. Ithaca, N.Y., n.p., 1978.

McGregor, Richard. "Circumstances Alter Cases." *Bulletin of the Cooper Ornithological Club* 1 (1899): 69–70.

Massachusetts Taxidermist. "War Against Taxidermists." *Ornithologist and Oologist* 11 (1886): 63–64.

———. "Amateur and A.O.U." *Ornithologist and Oologist* 11 (1886): 176.

Massey, Herbert. "Arrangement of an Oological Collection." *Condor* 10 (1908): 223–225.

Mayfield, Harold F. "The Amateur in Ornithology." *Auk* 96 (1979): 168–171.

Maynard, C. J. *The Naturalist's Guide in Collecting and Preserving Objects of Natural History, with a Complete Catalogue of the Birds of Eastern Massachusetts*. Boston: Fields, Osgood, 1870.

Mayr, Ernst "Die Ausbreitung des Girlitz (*Serinus canaria serinus* L.)." *Journal für Ornithologie* 74 (1926): 571–671.

———. "A Journey to the Solomons." *Natural History* 52 (1943): 30–37, 48.

———. "Bird Watching: A Hobby and a Science." *Auk* 61 (1944): 151–152.

———. "My Dutch New Guinea Expedition, 1928." *Novitates Zoologicae* 36 (1930): 20–26.

———. "A Tenderfoot Explorer in New Guinea." *Natural History* 32 (1932): 83–97.

[Merriam, C. Hart]. "Memorial to Congress." *Ornis* 1 (1885): 60–67.

———. "A Plea for the Metric System in Ornithology." *Auk* 1 (1884): 203–205.

Merriam, Florence A. *Birds of Village and Field: A Bird Book for Beginners*. Boston: Houghton, Mifflin and Co., 1898.

———. *Birds through an Opera Glass*. Boston: Houghton, Mifflin, 1889.

————. "Hints to Audubon Workers: Fifty Common Birds and How to Know Them." *Audubon Magazine* 1 (1887–1888): 108–113, 132–136, 155–159, 181–185, 200–204, 224–226, 256–259, 271–277; 2 (1888–1889): 6–12, 34–40, 49–53.

————. "Our Smith College Audubon Society." *Audubon Magazine* 1 (1887): 175–178.

Miller, Waldron DeWitt, Willard G. Van Name, and Davis Quinn. *A Crisis in Conservation: Serious Danger of Extinction of Many North American Birds*. New York, n.p., 1929.

Mitchell, E. C. "The Collecting Habit." *Oologist* 21 (1904): 25–26.

Morse, E. S. "Address." *Proceedings of the American Association for the Advancement of Science* 25 (1876): 137–176.

Munchausen. "The Sparrows." *Boston Evening Transcript*, 27 February 1878.

Nelson, E. W. "On the 'Bonding Clause' of the A.O.U. Model Law." *Condor* 5 (1903): 159.

Newkirk, Garrett. "Editor of 'The Condor.'" *Condor* 4 (1902): 146–147.

Newton, Alfred. *Dictionary of Birds*. 4 parts. London: Adam and Charles Black, 1893–1896.

Nice, Margaret M. *The Behavior of the Song Sparrow and Other Passerines*. Transactions of the Linnaean Society of New York, vol. 6. New York: Linnaean Society, 1943.

————. "Food of the Bobwhite." *Journal of Economic Entomology* 3 (1910): 295–313.

————. *A Population Study of the Song Sparrow*. Transactions of the Linnaean Society of New York, vol. 4. New York: Linnaean Society of New York, 1937.

————. "Some Letters of Althea Sherman." *Iowa Bird Life* 22 (1952): 51–55.

————. "Zur Naturgeschichte des Singammers." *Journal für Ornithologie* 81 (1933): 552–595, 82 (1934): 1–96.

Nice, Margaret M., and Leonard Blaine Nice. *The Birds of Oklahoma*. University of Oklahoma, Bulletin, new series no. 20. Norman: University of Oklahoma, 1924.

Nicholson, E. M. *The Art of Bird-Watching: A Practical Guide to Field Observation*. London: H. F. and G. Witherby, 1931.

Norris, J. Parker. "Instructions for Collecting Birds' Eggs." *Young Oologist* 1 (1884): 3–4.

Norris, J. Parker, Jr. *Some Facts about the Consistency of the Chairman of the A.O.U. Committee on Bird Protection and an Answer to His "Hints to Young Students."* Philadelphia: Privately printed, 1899

Northrup, W. DeForrest. "The A.O.U. and Amateurs." *Ornithologist and Oologist* 11 (1886): 192.

————. "The Study of Ornithology and Its Relation to the Decrease of Our Birds." *Ornithologist and Oologist* 11 (1886): 112.

Osgood, Wilfred H. "Questions of the Day." *Condor* 3 (1901): 50–51.

Palmer, T. S. *Bird Day in the Schools*. U.S. Department of Agriculture, Division of the Biological Survey, Circular no. 17. Washington, D.C.: Government Printing Office, 1896.

[————]. "The Condor," *Bird-Lore* 5 (1903): 33–34.

————. "The Condor." *Bird-Lore* 15 (1913): 314.

————. "The Fifty-Fourth Stated Meeting of the American Ornithologists' Union." *Auk* 54 (1937): 117–122.

————. "The Forty-Seventh Stated Meeting of the American Ornithologists' Union." *Auk* 47 (1930): 218–230.

Parker, Harry G. "A Review of the Check Lists of North American Birds, with Special Reference to the New A.O.U. List." *Oologist* 3 (1886): 37–39.

Parkhurst, H. E. *The Birds' Calendar*. New York: Charles Scribner's Sons, 1894.

Parkhurst, H. E. *How to Name the Birds: A Pocket Guide*. New York: Charles Scribner's Sons, 1898.

Peabody, P. B. "Amenities of Nomenclature." *Oologist* 36 (1919): 25–27.

———. "Correspondence." *Ornithologist and Oologist* 16 (1891): 175.

———. "Millimeter Races." *Oologist* 39 (1922): 52.

Peters, James Lee. *Check-List of Birds of the World*. Vol. 1. Cambridge: Harvard University Press, 1931.

Peterson, Roger T. *A Field Guide to the Birds, Giving Field Marks of Species Found in Eastern North America*. Boston: Houghton Mifflin, 1934.

Phillips, Charles L. "Are Ornithologists Cruel?" *Oologist* 15 (1898): 13–14.

Posson, Neil F. "Ornithology and Bicycling." *Oologist* 7 (1890): 9–10.

Putnam, Frederic Ward, ed. *Naturalists' Directory*. Salem, Mass.: Essex Institute Press, 1865.

———. *Naturalists' Directory*. 2d ed. Salem, Mass.: Essex Institute, 1866.

Redington, Paul G. "The Bird Work of the Biological Survey." *Auk* 48 (1931): 229–234.

Reed, Charles K. *Western Bird Guide: Birds of the Rockies and West to the Pacific*. Garden City, N.Y.: Doubleday, Page, 1913.

Reed, Chester A. *Bird Guide*. 2 vols. Worster, Mass.: C. K. Reed, 1906.

"Reorganization of the Work in Zoology at Cornell." *Science* 90 (1939): 76–77.

Review of "Field Glass," by G.R.C. *Bulletin of the Nuttall Ornithological Club* 8 (1883): 236.

Richards, Harriet E., and Emma G. Cummings. *Baby Pathfinder to the Birds: A Pocket Guide to One Hundred and Ten Land Birds of New England*. Boston: W. A. Butterfield, 1904.

Ridgway, Robert. "A Catalogue of the Birds of North America." *Proceedings of the U.S. National Museum* 3 (1880): 163–246.

———. *Color Standards and Color Nomenclature*. Washington, D.C.: The Author, 1912.

———. *Directions for Collecting Birds*. U. S. National Museum, Bulletin no. 39, Part A. Washington, D.C.: Government Printing Office, 1891.

———. *A Manual of North American Birds*. Philadelphia: J. B. Lippincott, 1887.

———. *A Nomenclature of Colors for Naturalists and Compendium of Useful Knowledge for Ornithologists*. Boston: Little, Brown, 1886.

———. *Nomenclature of North American Birds, Chiefly Contained in the United States National Museum*. U.S. National Museum, Bulletin no. 21. Washington, D.C.: Government Printing Office, 1881.

———. "On the Use of Trinomials in Zoological Nomenclature." *Bulletin of the Nuttall Ornithological Club* 4 (1879): 132.

———. *Ornithology*. In *United States Geological Exploration of the Fortieth Parallel*, part III, 303–669. Washington, D.C.: Government Printing Office, 1877.

———. "A Plea for Caution in Use of Trinomials." *Auk* 40 (1923): 375–376.

Ridgway, Robert, and Herbert Friedmann. *The Birds of North and Middle America*. U.S. National Museum, Bulletin no. 50. 11 vols. Washington, D.C.: Government Printing Office, 1901–1950.

Robbins, Reginald C. *Bird-Killing as a Method in Ornithology*. Cambridge, Mass.: E. W. Wheeler, 1901.

R[ogers], C[harles] H. "Bird-Lore's Eighteenth Christmas Bird Count." *Bird-Lore* 19 (1917): 317–318.

R[ogers], C[harles] H. "Bird-Lore's Fifteenth Christmas Census." *Bird-Lore* 17 (1915): 22–48.

Sage, John Hall. "Thirty-Third Stated Meeting of the American Ornithologists' Union." *Auk* 32 (1915): 491.

Schramm, R. M. "A Bird Watcher by Any Other Name." *Audubon Magazine* 60 (May–June 1958): 99.

Sclater, Philip Lutley. "Notes on the Birds in the Museum of the Academy of Natural Sciences of Philadelphia, and Other Collections in the United States of America." *Proceedings of the Zoological Society of London* 25 (1857): 1–9.

———. "On the General Geographical Distribution of the Members of the Class Aves." *Journal of the Linnaean Society (Zoology)* 2 (1858): 130–145.

Scott, W. E. D. *Bird Studies: An Account of the Land Birds of Eastern North America*. New York: G. P. Putnam's Sons, 1898.

———. "The Present Condition of Some of the Bird Rookeries of the Gulf Coast of Florida." *Auk* 4 (1887): 135–144, 213–222, 273–284.

Selous, Edmund. *Bird Watching*. London: J. M. Dent, 1901.

Sennett, B. G. [i.e., G. B.] *Bird Legislation*. Harrisburg, Pa.: State Printer, 1890.

Seton, Ernest T. "The Popular Names of Birds." *Auk* 2 (1885): 316–317.

———. "On the Popular Names of Birds." *Auk* 36 (1919): 229–233.

Sharpe, R. Bowlder, ed. "Aves." In *Zoological Record for 1871*, edited by Alfred Newton, 23–76. London: John Van Voorst, 1873.

———. "The A.O.U. Code and Checklist of American Birds." *Nature* 34 (1886): 168–170.

———. *A Hand-List of the Genera and Species of Birds*. 5 vols. London: British Museum (Natural History), 1909.

Sharples, R. P. "Wm. B. Crispin Killed by a Fall." *Oologist* 30 (1913): 90–91.

Sherman, Althea R. "At the Sign of the Northern Flicker." *Wilson Bulletin* 22 (1910): 135–171.

Shufeldt, Robert W. "Audubon the Naturalist." *The Great Divide* 10 (1893): 8–9.

———. "The Couesian Period." *Forest and Stream* 22 (1884): 323, 343, 362–363.

———. "On the Medico-Legal Aspect of Impotency in Women." *The Medico-Legal Journal* 14 (December 1896): 289–296.

Shufeldt, Robert W., and Maria R. Audubon. "The Last Portrait of Audubon, together with a Letter to His Son." *Auk* 11 (1894): 309–313.

"Shufeldt *v.* Shufeldt." *Atlantic Reporter* 39 (1898): 416–421.

Silloway, P. M. "An Answer." *Condor* 5 (1903): 54–55.

———. "The Holboell Grebe in Montana." *Condor* 4 (1902): 128–131.

Singley, J. A. "Instructions for Collecting and Preserving Eggs." *Ornithologists' and Oologists' Semi-Annual* 1 (1889): 1–12.

———. "Instructions for Collecting and Preserving Eggs." *Bay State Oologist* 1 (1880): 20–21; 28–29; 36–37.

Sirrom, G. [i.e., Morris Gibbs]. "Courtesy and Business in Exchanging." *Oologist* 10 (1893): 136–138.

"Sparrows Brought to Judgment—Discussion of the Nuttall Ornithological Club upon the Merits and Demerits of the English Sparrow in the United States." *The Country*, 23 February 1878.

"Sparrows—The Nuttall Ornithological Club Decides against Them." *Boston Daily Advertiser*, 23 February 1878, 245–246.

The Sportsman's Companion; or, An Essay on Shooting. New York: Robertson, Mills and Hicks, 1783.

Sprunt, Alexander, Jr. "Sight Records." *The Chat: Bulletin of the North Carolina Bird Club* 6 (September 1942): 50–54.

Stearns, F. R. "An Ornithological Sermon." *Osprey* 3 (1898–1899): 43.

[Stejneger, Leonhard J.] "The Couesian Period?" *Forest and Stream* 22 (1884): 384, 423.

————. "The Future Problems and Aims of Ornithology." *Condor* 7 (1905): 63–66.

————. "On the Use of Trinomials in American Ornithology." *Proceedings of the U.S. National Museum* 7 (1884): 70–89.

Stephens, Frank. "About Collecting Chests." *Condor* 8 (1906): 112–114.

[Stephens, T. C.?] "Editorial." *Wilson Bulletin* 39 (1927): 231.

[————?] "Editorial," *Wilson Bulletin* 44 (1932): 231–232.

S[tephens,] T. C. Review of "What Constitutes a Record?" by F. C. Lincoln. *Wilson Bulletin* 41 (1929): 113.

Stone, Witmer. *Bird Studies at Old Cape May: An Ornithology of Coastal New Jersey.* 2 vols. Philadelphia: Delaware Valley Ornithological Club, 1937.

[————]. "Hints to Young Bird Students." *Bird-Lore* 1 (1899): 126.

————. "Ornithology of Today and Tomorrow." *The Fiftieth Anniversary of the Nuttall Ornithological Club*, 7–25. Cambridge, Mass.: The Club, 1924.

————. [Reply to H. H. Bailey]. *Auk* 22 (1915): 136–139.

————. "Problems in Modernizing an Old Museum." *Proceedings of the American Association of Museums* 3 (1909): 122–127.

————. "Report of the A.O.U. Committee on Protection of North American Birds [for 1898]." *Auk* 16 (1899): 55–74.

————. "Report of the A.O.U. Committee on the Protection of North American Birds [for 1899]." *Auk* 17 (1900): 51–58.

————. "Report of the Committee on the Protection of North American Birds for the Year 1900." *Auk* 28 (1901): 68–104.

————. "Report of the Committee on the Protection of North American Birds [for 1901]." *Auk* 19 (1902): 31–64.

[————]. Review of *Bird-Lore. Auk* 30 (1913): 605.

[————]. Review of *Bird-Lore. Auk* 37 (1920): 485–486

[————]. Review of *Birds of the New York City Region*, by Ludlow Griscom. *Auk* 41 (1924): 173.

[————]. Review of "Red-Winged Blackbird," by Arthur A. Allen. *Auk* 31 (1914): 414–415.

[————]. Review of "What Constitutes a Record?" by F. C. Lincoln. *Auk* 47 (1929): 413–414.

Strickland, Hugh. "Report of the Recent Progress and Present State of Ornithology." *Report of the Fourteenth Meeting of the British Association for the Advancement of Science* (1844): 170–221.

Strode, W. S. "A Difficult Climb After a Red-Tailed Hawk's Nest." *Oologist* 3 (1886): 34–35.

Strong, Reuben M. "The Development of Color in the Definitive Feather." Ph.D. dissertation, Harvard University, 1901.

Sutton, G. M. "How Can the Bird-Lover Help Save the Hawks and Owls?" *Auk* 46 (1929): 190–195.

Swarth, Harry S. "The Tyranny of the Trinomial." *Condor* 33 (1931): 160–162.

"Talk of the Town." *New Yorker* 26 (3 June 1950): 17–19.

Taverner, P. A. "The Tagging of Birds." *Bulletin of the Michigan Ornithological Club* 5 (1904): 50–51.

Thaxter, Celia. "Woman's Heartlessness." *Audubon Magazine* 1 (1887): 13–14.

Tinbergen, Niko. *The Behavior of the Snow Bunting in Spring.* Transactions of the Linnaean Society of New York, vol. 5. New York: Linnaean Society of New York, 1939.

Trotter, Spencer. "The Background of Ornithology." *Bird-Lore* 10 (1908): 68–71.

Twining, Frances S. *Birdwatching in the West.* Portland, Ore.: Metropolitan Press, 1931.

Van Name, Willard G. "Bird Collecting and Ornithology." *Science* 41 (1915): 823–825.

———. *Vanishing Forest Reserves: Problems of the National Forests and National Parks.* Boston: Richard D. Badger, Gorham Press, 1929.

Vogt, William. "Preliminary Notes on the Behavior and Ecology of the Eastern Willet." *Proceedings of the Linnaean Society of New York,* no. 49 (1939): 8–42.

[Wade, Joseph M.] "Plain English." *Ornithologist and Oologist* 8 (1883): 85–86. Suppressed editorial appended to William Brewster's copy of *Ornithologist and Oologist,* now in the MCZ Library.

Walter, Herbert Eugene, and Alice Hall Walter. *Wild Birds in City Parks.* Kankakee, Ill.: Joseph H. Dodson, 1901.

Webb, Walter F. *Ornithologists' and Oologists' Manual.* Albion, N.Y.: Webb, 1895.

Webster, Frank B. "Practical Taxidermy." *Ornithologist and Oologist* 10 (1885): 137–139.

Wetmore, Alexander, and Waldron DeW. Miller. "The Revised Classification for the Fourth Edition of the A.O.U. Check-list." *Auk* 43 (1926): 337–346.

Wilder, Burt Green and Simon H. Gage. *Anatomical Technology as Applied to the Domestic Cat: An Introduction to Human, Veterinary, and Comparative Anatomy.* New York, Chicago: A.S. Barnes and Company, 1882.

Willard, S. L., comp. *A Directory of the Ornithologists of the United States.* Utica, N.Y.: Office of the Oologist, 1877.

Wilson, Alexander. *American Ornithology, or the Natural History of Birds of the United States.* 9 vols. Philadelphia: Bradford and Inskeep, 1808–1814.

Wilson, Mrs. Russell. "Birders and Birding." *Audubon Magazine* 60 (May-June 1958): 99–100.

Wing, Leonard, and Millard Jenks. "Christmas Censuses: The Amateurs' Contribution to Science." *Bird-Lore* 41 (1939): 343–350.

Wood, Robert W. *Animal Analogues: Verses and Illustrations.* San Francisco: P. Elder, 1908.

———. *How to Tell the Birds from the Flowers: A Manual of Flornithology for Beginners.* San Francisco: P. Elder, 1907.

———. *How to Tell the Birds from the Flowers and Other Woodcuts: A Revised Manual of Flornithology for Beginners.* New York: Dodd, Mead, 1917.

Wright, Mabel Osgood. *Birdcraft: A Field Book of Two Hundred Common Birds of Eastern United States.* New York: Macmillan, 1895.

Wright, Mabel Osgood, and Elliott Coues. *Citizen Bird: Scenes from Bird-Life in Plain English for Beginners.* New York: Macmillan, 1897.

Wyman, Luther E., and Elizabeth F. Burnell, *Field Book of the Birds of the Southwestern United States.* Boston: Houghton Mifflin, 1925.

Zerega, Louis A. "The Great American Egg-Hog." *Oologist* 7 (1882): 183.

SECONDARY SOURCES

Adams, Carol J. *The Sexual Politics of Meat: A Feminist-Vegetarian Critical Theory.* New York: Continuum, 1995.

Agassiz, G. R., ed. *Letters and Recollections of Alexander Agassiz, with a Sketch of His Life and Work.* Boston: Houghton Mifflin, 1913.

Ainley, Marianne G. "The Contribution of the Amateur to North American Ornithology: A Historical Perspective." *The Living Bird* 18 (1979): 161–177.

———. "The Emergence of Canadian Ornithology—An Historical Overview to 1950." In *Contributions to the History of North American Ornithology*, edited by William E. Davis, Jr., and Jerome A. Jackson, 283–301. Cambridge, Mass.: Nuttall Ornithological Club, 1995.

———. "Field Work and Family: North American Women Ornithologists, 1900–1950." In *Uneasy Careers and Intimate Lives: Women in Science, 1789–1979*, edited by Pnina Abir-Am and Dorinda Outram, 60–76. New Brunswick, N.J.: Rutgers University Press, 1987.

———. "From Natural History to Avian Biology: Canadian Ornithology, 1860–1950." Ph.D. dissertation, McGill University, 1985.

———. "La professionalisation de l'ornithologie Américaine, 1870–1979." Master's thesis, Université de Montréal, 1980.

———. *Restless Energy: A Biography of William Rowan, 1891–1957*. Montreal: Véhicule Press, 1993.

Allard, Dean C. *Spencer Fullerton Baird and the U.S. Fish Commission*. New York: Arno Press, 1978.

Allen, Arthur A. "Cornell's Laboratory of Ornithology." *Living Bird* 1 (1962): 7–36.

———. "Ornithological Education in America." In *Fifty Years' Progress of American Ornithology, 1883–1933*, edited by Frank M. Chapman and T. S. Palmer, 215–229. Lancaster, Pa.: American Ornithologists' Union, 1933.

Allen, David E. *The Naturalist in Britain: A Social History*. 2d ed. Princeton: Princeton University Press, 1994.

———. *The Victorian Fern Craze: A History of Pteridomania*. London: Hutchinson, 1969.

Allen, Elsa G. *The History of American Ornithology before Audubon*. Transactions of the American Philosophical Society, n.s. 41, no. 3. Philadelphia: American Philosophical Society, 1951.

Allen, Garland E. *Life Science in the Twentieth Century*. Cambridge: Cambridge University Press, 1978.

———. "Naturalists and Experimentalists: The Genotype and the Phenotype." *Studies in the History of Biology* 3 (1979): 179–209.

Allen, J. A. *The American Ornithologists' Union: A Seven Years' Retrospective*. New York: AOU, 1891.

———. *Autobiographical Notes and a Bibliography of the Scientific Publications of Joel Asaph Allen*. New York: American Museum of Natural History, 1916.

———. "Biographical Memoir of Elliott Coues." *Biographical Memoirs of the National Academy of Sciences* 6 (1909): 397–446.

———. "Dr. Samuel Cabot." *Auk* 3 (1886): 144.

———. "In Memoriam: George Burritt Sennett." *Auk* 18 (1901): 11–23.

———. "J. H. Batty." *Auk* 23 (1906): 356–357.

———. "John S. Cairns." *Auk* 12 (1895): 315.

———. "Perry O. Simons." *Auk* 20 (1903): 94–96.

———. "Thomas Mayo Brewer." *Bulletin of the Nuttall Ornithological Club* 5 (1880): 102–104.

———. "William Earl Dodge Scott." *Auk* 27 (1910): 486–488.

Amadon, Dean. "In Memoriam: Robert Cushman Murphy, April 29, 1887–March 20, 1973." *Auk* 91 (1974): 1–9.

AOU Committee on Research. "Unpublished Theses in Ornithology." *Auk* 71 (1954): 191–197.

Appel, Tobey A. "The Mapping of Biology: Disciplinary Societies in the Biological Sciences." Paper delivered at the History of Science Society Annual Meeting, October 1987.

———. "Organizing Biology: The American Society of Naturalists and Its 'Affiliated Societies,' 1883–1923." In *The American Development of Biology*, edited by Ronald Rainger, Keith R. Benson, and Jane Maienschein, 87–120. Philadelphia: University of Pennsylvania Press, 1988.

———. "Science, Popular Culture and Profit: Peale's Philadelphia Museum." *Journal of the Society for the Bibliography of Natural History* 9 (1980): 619–634.

Arnett, Ross H., and Mary E. Arnett. "The 44 Editions of the Naturalists' Directory." In *The Naturalists' Directory and Almanac (International)*, edited by Ross H. Arnett and Mary E. Arnett, 1–7. Gainesville, Fla.: Flora and Fauna Publications, 1985.

"Arthur Augustus Allen." *Current Biography Yearbook 1961*, edited by Charles Moritz, 5–7. New York: H. W. Wilson, 1962.

Auerbach, Felix. *The Zeiss Works and the Carl Zeiss Foundation in Jena: Their Scientific, Technical and Sociological Development and Importance Popularly Described.* Translated from 5th German ed. by R. Kanthack. London: W & G Foyle, 1927.

Austin, Elizabeth S., ed. *Frank M. Chapman in Florida: His Journals and Letters.* Gainesville: University of Florida Press, 1967.

Azarya, Victor. "Community." In *The Social Science Encyclopedia*, edited by Adam Kuper and Jessica Kuper, 114–115. London: Routledge, 1996.

Bailey, Harold H. "John Lewis Childs—As I Knew Him." *Oologist* 38 (1921): 102–104.

Bailey, Harry B., ed. *"Forest and Stream" Bird Notes: An Index and Summary of all the Ornithological Matter Contained in "Forest and Stream," Vols. I–XII.* New York: Forest and Stream, 1881.

Baker, John H. "Ludlow Griscom: The Man." *Audubon Magazine* 61 (1959): 200–201, 213, 238–239.

Banks, Richard C. "Ornithology at the U.S. National Museum." In *Contributions to the History of North American Ornithology*, edited by William E. Davis, Jr., and Jerome A. Jackson, 22–54. Cambridge, Mass.: Nuttall Ornithological Club, 1995.

———. Review of *Life Histories of North American Cardinals*, by A. C. Bent. *Auk* 86 (1969): 768–770.

Barber, Lynn. *The Heyday of Natural History, 1820–1870.* Garden City, N.Y.: Doubleday, 1980.

B[arnes], R[ichard] M. "John Lewis Childs." *Oologist* 38 (1921): 44–45.

[———]. "John Lewis Childs." *Oologist* 38 (1921): 104–106.

Barrow, Mark V., Jr. "Birds and Boundaries: Community, Practice, and Conservation in North American Ornithology, 1865–1935." Ph.D. dissertation, Harvard University, 1992.

———. "Gentlemanly Specialists in the Age of Professionalization: The First Century of Ornithology at Harvard's Museum of Comparative Zoology." In *Contributions to the History of North American Ornithology*, edited by William E. Davis, Jr., and Jerome A. Jackson, 55–94. Cambridge, Mass.: Nuttall Ornithological Club, 1995.

Barrus, Clara. *The Life and Letters of John Burroughs.* 2 vols. Boston: Houghton Mifflin, 1925.

Barsness, Larry. *Heads, Hides and Horns: The Compleat Buffalo Book.* Fort Worth: Texas Christian University, 1985.

Batchelder, Charles Foster. *An Account of the Nuttall Ornithological Club, 1873 to 1919.* Cambridge, Mass.: The Club, 1937.

———. "Bibliography of the Published Writings of Charles Johnson Maynard (1845–1929)." *Journal of the Society for the Bibliography of Natural History* 2 (1951): 227–251.

———. *A Bibliography of the Published Writings of William Brewster.* Memoirs of the Nuttall Ornithological Club, no. 10. Cambridge, Mass.: The Club, 1951.

Bates, Frank A. "Reminiscences." *Ornithologist and Oologist* 16 (1891): 177–179.

Bates, Ralph. *Scientific Societies in the United States.* 2d ed. Cambridge: MIT Press, 1958.

Baumer, Franklin L. "Romanticism." In *Dictionary of the History of Ideas*, edited by Philip Wiener, 4:198–205. New York: Scribner, 1974.

Beardsley, Edward H. "The American Scientist as Social Activist." *Isis* 64 (1973): 51–66.

Behle, William H. "Henry Child Bryant." *Auk* 87 (1970): 631–632.

Ben-David, Joseph. "Science as a Profession and Scientific Professionalism." In *Explorations in General Theory in Social Science: Essays in Honor of Talcott Parsons*, edited by Jan J. Loubser, R. Brum, A. Effrat, V. Lidz, 871–888. New York: Free Press, 1976.

Benson, Keith R. "From Museum Research to Laboratory Biology: The Transformation of Natural History into Academic Biology." In *The American Development of Biology*, edited by Ronald Rainger, Keith R. Benson, and Jane Maienschein, 49–83. Philadelphia: University of Pennsylvania Press, 1988.

Benson, Keith R., and C. Edward Quinn. "The American Society of Zoologists, 1889–1989: A Century of Integrating the Biological Sciences." *American Zoologist* 30 (1990): 353–396.

Benson, Maxine. *Martha Maxwell, Rocky Mountain Naturalist.* Lincoln: University of Nebraska Press, 1986.

Betts, John R. *America's Sporting Heritage: 1850–1950.* Reading, Mass.: Addison-Wesley, 1974.

"Binocular Instrument." *Encyclopedia Britannica* 13th ed. (1926), 3:949–951.

Birtwell, Olivia M. "Francis J. Birtwell." *Auk* 27 (1910): 413–414.

Bishop, Morris. *A History of Cornell.* Ithaca, N.Y.: Cornell University Press, 1962.

Bledstein, Burton J. *The Culture of Professionalism: The Middle Class and the Development of Higher Education in America.* New York: W. W. Norton, 1976.

Blondheim, Menahem. *News Over the Wires: The Telegraph and the Flow of Public Information in America, 1844–1897.* Cambridge: Harvard University Press, 1994.

Blum, Ann Shelby. *Picturing Nature: American Nineteenth-Century Zoological Illustration.* Princeton: Princeton University Press, 1993.

Blumin, Stuart M. *The Emergence of the Middle Class: Social Experience in the American City, 1760–1900.* Cambridge: Cambridge University Press, 1989.

Boardman, Samuel Lane. *The Naturalist of the Saint Croix: Memoir of George A. Boardman.* Bangor, Maine: Privately printed, 1903.

Bock, Walter J. "Ernst Mayr, Naturalist: His Contributions to Systematics and Evolution." *Biology and Philosophy* 9 (1994): 267–327.

———. "A Special Review: Peters' *Check-list of the Birds of the World*." *Auk* 107 (1990): 629–648.

Bonta, Marcia Myers. *Women in the Field: America's Pioneering Women Naturalists.* College Station: Texas A & M University Press, 1991.

Bouvé, Thomas. *Historical Sketch of the Boston Society of Natural History.* Boston: The Society, 1880.

Borell, Merriley. *Album of Science: The Biological Sciences in the Twentieth Century.* New York: Scribner, 1989.

Bowler, Peter. *The Eclipse of Darwinism: Anti-Darwinian Evolutionary Theories in the Decades around 1900*. Baltimore: Johns Hopkins University Press, 1983.

Boynton, Mary Fuertes, ed. *Louis Agassiz Fuertes: His Life Briefly Told and His Correspondence*. New York: Oxford University Press, 1956.

Braden, Donna R. *Leisure and Entertainment in America*. Dearborn, Mich.: Henry Ford Museum and Greenfield Village, 1988.

Brant, Irving. *Adventures in Conservation with Franklin D. Roosevelt*. Flagstaff, Ariz.: Northland, 1988.

Briggs, Asa. *Victorian Things*. London: B. T. Batsford, 1988.

Brodhead, Michael J. "Elliott Coues and the Sparrow War." *New England Quarterly* 44 (1971): 420–432.

Broley, Myrtle Jeanne. *Eagle Man: Charles Broley's Field Adventures with American Eagles*. New York: Pellegrini and Cudahy, 1952.

Bronowski, Jacob. *A Sense of the Future*. Cambridge: MIT Press, 1977.

Brooks, Paul. *Speaking for Nature: How Literary Naturalists from Henry Thoreau to Rachel Carson Have Shaped America*. Boston: Houghton Mifflin, 1980.

Brown, JoAnne. "Professional Language: Words That Succeed." *Radical History Review* 34 (1986): 33–51.

Browne, Janet. *The Secular Ark: Studies in the History of Biogeography*. New Haven: Yale University Press, 1983.

Bryant, Harold C. "The Cooper Club and Scientific Work." *Condor* 16 (1914): 101–107.

Bruce, Robert V. *The Launching of Modern American Science, 1846–1876*. New York: Alfred A. Knopf, 1987.

Brumsted, Harlan, et al. *Voices from Connecticut Hill: Recollections of Cornell Wildlife Students, 1930–1942*. Ithaca, N.Y.: College of Agriculture and Life Science, Cornell University, 1994.

Bucher, Enrique H. "The Causes of Extinction of the Passenger Pigeon." In *Current Ornithology*, edited by Dennis M. Power, 9:1–36. New York: Plenum Press, 1992.

Buchheister, Carl, and Frank Graham, Jr. "From the Swamps and Back: A Concise and Candid History of the Audubon Movement." *Audubon* 75 (1973): 4–45.

Buell, Lawrence. *The Environmental Imagination: Thoreau, Nature Writing, and the Formation of American Culture*. Cambridge: Harvard University Press, 1995.

Burkhardt, Richard W., Jr. "Charles Otis Whitman, Wallace Craig, and the Biological Study of Animal Behavior in the United States, 1898–1925." In *The American Development of Biology*, edited by Ronald Rainger, Keith R. Benson, and Jane Maienschein, 185–218. Philadelphia: University of Pennsylvania Press, 1988.

———. "The Development of Evolutionary Ethology." In *Evolution from Molecules to Man*, edited by D. S. Bendall, 429–444. Cambridge: Cambridge University Press, 1983.

———. "Ernst Mayr: Biologist-Historian." *Biology and Philosophy* 9 (1994): 359–371.

———. "On the Emergence of Ethology as a Scientific Discipline." *Conspectus of History* 1 (1981): 62–81.

Burns, Frank L. "The Autobiography of Franklin Lorenzo Burns." *Wilson Bulletin* 38 (1926): 132–139.

———. "A Bibliography of Scarce or Out of Print North American Amateur and Trade Periodicals Devoted More or Less to Ornithology." Supplement to the *Oologist* 32 (1915): 1–32.

———. "John Krider, a Typical Professional Collector, 1838–1878." *Oologist* 50 (1933): 74–80.

"Burt Green Wilder." *National Cyclopaedia of American Biography* 4 (1897): 481.

"Burt Green Wilder." In *Who Was Who in America*, 1:1345. Chicago: A. N. Marquis, 1942.

294   *BIBLIOGRAPHY*

Butcher, Gregory S., and Kevin McGowan. "History of Ornithology at Cornell University." In *Contributions to the History of North American Ornithology*, edited by William E. Davis, Jr., and Jerome A. Jackson, 223–260. Cambridge, Mass.: Nuttall Ornithological Club, 1995.

Cain, Joseph. "Common Problems and Cooperative Solutions: Organizational Activities in Evolutionary Studies, 1937–1946." *Isis* 84 (1993): 1–25.

———. "Ernst Mayr as Community Architect: Launching the Society for the Study of Evolution and the Journal *Evolution*." *Biology and Philosophy* 9 (1994): 387–427.

Callicott, J. Baird, ed. *Companion to A Sand County Almanac: Interpretive and Critical Essays*. Madison: University of Wisconsin Press, 1987.

Camerini, Jane R. "Evolution, Biogeography, and Maps: An Early History of Wallace's Line." *Isis* 84 (1993): 700–727.

Cameron, Jenks. *The Bureau of the Biological Survey: Its History, Activities and Organization*. Baltimore: Johns Hopkins University Press, 1929.

Cannell, Peter F. "An Annotated Bibliography of the Founding of the American Ornithologists' Union." *American Birds* 37 (July–August 1983): 355–357.

Carr-Saunders, A. M., and P. A. Wilson. *The Professions*. Oxford: Oxford University Press, 1933.

Carson, Rachel. *Silent Spring*. Boston: Houghton Mifflin, 1962.

Cart, Theodore Whaley. "The Lacey Act: America's First Nationwide Wildlife Statute." *Forest History* (October 1973): 4–13.

———. "New Deal for Wildlife: A Perspective on Federal Conservation Policy, 1933–40." *Pacific Northwest Quarterly* 63 (July 1972): 113–120.

———. "The Struggle for Wildlife Protection in the United States, 1870–1900: Attitudes and Events Leading Up to the Lacey Act." Ph.D. dissertation, University of North Carolina at Chapel Hill, 1971.

Cartmill, Matt. *A View to Death in the Morning: Hunting and Nature through History*. Cambridge: Harvard University Press, 1993.

Chalmers-Hunt, J. M., comp. *Natural History Auctions, 1700–1972: A Register of Sales in the British Isles*. London: Sotheby Park Bernet, 1976.

Chandler, Alfred. *The Visible Hand: The Managerial Revolution in American Business*. Cambridge: Belknap Press of Harvard University Press, 1977.

Chapin, James. "In Memoriam: Waldron DeWitt Miller, 1879–1929." *Auk* 49 (1932): 1–8.

Chapman, A. B. "Leon Jacob Cole." *Dictionary of Scientific Biography* 17: 173–175.

Chapman, Frank M. *Autobiography of a Bird Lover*. New York: D. Appleton-Century, 1933.

———. "Collections of Birds in the United States and Canada: Exhibition Collections." In *Fifty Years' Progress of American Ornithology, 1883–1933*, edited by Frank M. Chapman and T. S. Palmer, 143–157. Lancaster, Pa.: American Ornithologists' Union, 1933.

———. "The Department of Birds, American Museum: Its History and Aims." *Natural History* 22 (1922): 307–318.

[———]. "Elliott Coues." *Bird-Lore* 2 (1900): 3–4.

———. "Joel Asaph Allen." *Memoirs of the National Academy of Sciences* 21 (1927): 1–20.

———. "John G. Bell." *Auk* 7 (1890): 98–99.

[———]. "Mabel Osgood Wright, 1859–1934." *Bird-Lore* 36 (1934): 280.

Chapman, Frank M., and T. S. Palmer, eds. *Fifty Years' Progress of American Ornithology, 1883–1933*. Lancaster, Pa.: American Ornithologists' Union, 1933.

Cittadino, Eugene. "Ecology and the Professionalization of Botany in America, 1890–1905." *Studies in History of Biology* 4 (1980): 171–198.

Clarke, Adele E. "A Social Worlds Research Adventure: The Case of Reproductive Science." In *Theories of Science in Society*, edited by Susan E. Cozzens and Thomas F. Gieryn, 15–42. Bloomington: University of Indiana Press, 1990.

Clarke, Adele E., and Elihu Gerson. "Symbolic Interactionism in Social Studies of Science." In *Symbolic Interaction and Cultural Studies*, edited by Howard S. Becker and Michal M. McCall, 179–214. Chicago: University of Chicago Press, 1990.

Coan, Eugene V. *James Graham Cooper, Pioneer Western Naturalist.* Moscow, Idaho: University Press of Idaho, 1981.

Cole, Leon J. "Early History of Bird Banding in America." *Wilson Bulletin* 34 (1922): 108–114.

Coleman, William. "Bergmann's Rule: Animal Heat as a Biological Phenomena." *Studies in History of Biology* 3 (1979): 67–88.

———. *Biology in the Nineteenth Century.* Cambridge: Cambridge University Press, 1977.

Comstock, J. H. "Burt Green Wilder." *Science* 61 (1925): 531–533.

Conway, Albert. "In Memoriam: Crawford H. Greenewalt, 1902–1993." *Auk* 111 (1994): 188–189.

Coyle, William, ed. *Ohio Authors and Their Books.* Cleveland: World Publishing Co., 1962.

"Crawford Hallock Greenewalt." In *Current Biography 1949*, edited by Anna Rothe, 234–236. New York: H. W. Wilson, 1950.

Cremin, Lawrence A. *American Education: The Metropolitan Experience, 1876–1980.* New York: Harper and Row, 1988.

Croker, Robert A. *Pioneer Ecologist: The Life and Work of Victor Ernest Shelford, 1877–1968.* Washington, D.C.: Smithsonian Institution Press, 1991.

Cronon, William J. *Changes in the Land: Indians, Colonists, and the Ecology of New England.* New York: Hill and Wang, 1983.

Cutright, Paul. *Theodore Roosevelt: The Making of a Conservationist.* Urbana: University of Illinois Press, 1985.

Cutright, Paul, and Michael J. Brodhead. *Elliott Coues: Naturalist and Frontier Historian.* Urbana: University of Illinois Press, 1981.

Dall, William Healey. *Spencer Fullerton Baird: A Biography.* Philadelphia: J. P. Lippincott, 1915.

Dance, S. Peter. *Shell Collecting: An Illustrated History.* London: Faber and Faber, 1966.

Daniels, George H. "The Process of Professionalization in American Science: The Emergent Period, 1820–1860." *Isis* 58 (1967): 151–166.

Dary, David A. *The Buffalo Book: The Full Saga of the American Animal.* Chicago: Swallow Press, 1974.

Davenport, F. Garvin. "Robert Ridgway: Illinois Naturalist." *Journal of the Illinois State Historical Society* 63 (1970): 271–289.

Davis, John. "In Memoriam: Alden Holmes Miller." *Auk* 84 (1967): 192–202.

Davis, William E., Jr. *History of the Nuttall Ornithological Club, 1873–1986.* Cambridge, Mass.: The Club, 1987.

———. *Dean of the Birdwatchers: A Biography of Ludlow Griscom.* Washington, D.C.: Smithsonian Institution Press, 1994.

Davis, William E., Jr., and Jerome A. Jackson, eds. *Contributions to the History of North American Ornithology.* Cambridge, Mass.: Nuttall Ornithological Club, 1995.

Deiss, William A. "Spencer F. Baird and His Collectors." *Journal of the Society for the Bibliography of Natural History* 9 (1980): 635–645.

Devlin, John C., and Grace Naismith. *The World of Roger Tory Peterson: An Authorized Biography*. New York: New York Times Books, 1977.

Devoe, Alan. "Robins for Sale: Five Cents." *Audubon Magazine* 49 (1947): 108–112.

Dewsbury, Donald A. "A Brief History of the Study of Animal Behavior in North America." *Perspectives in Ethology* 8 (1989): 85–122.

Dieke, G. H. "Robert Williams Wood, May 2, 1868—August 11, 1955." *Biographical Memoirs of the National Academy of Sciences* 62 (1993): 441–464.

Dingwall, Robert, and Philip Lewis, eds. *The Sociology of Professions: Lawyers, Doctors and Others*. London: Macmillan, 1983.

Dolph, James A. "Bringing Wildlife to Millions: William Temple Hornaday, The Early Years: 1854–1896." Ph.D. dissertation, University of Massachusetts, 1975.

Doughty, Robin. "The English Sparrow in the American Landscape: A Paradox in Nineteenth Century Wildlife Conservation." Oxford University, School of Geography, Research Papers no. 19. Oxford: Oxford Publishing Co., 1978.

———. *Feather Fashions and Bird Preservation: A Study in Nature Protection*. Berkeley: University of California Press, 1975.

Dulles, Foster R. *A History of Recreation: America Learns to Play*. 2d ed. New York: Appleton-Century-Crofts, 1965.

Dunlap, Thomas R. *DDT: Scientists, Citizens, and Public Policy*. Princeton: Princeton University Press, 1981.

———. *Saving America's Wildlife*. Princeton: Princeton University Press, 1988.

———. "Sport Hunting and Conservation, 1880–1920." *Environmental Review* 12 (1988): 51–59.

Dupree, A. Hunter. "The National Pattern of American Learned Societies, 1769–1863." In *The Pursuit of Knowledge in the Early American Republic: American Scientific and Learned Societies from the Colonial Times to the Civil War*, edited by Alexandra Oleson and Sanborn C. Brown, 21–32. Baltimore: Johns Hopkins University Press, 1976.

———. *Science in the Federal Government: A History of Policies and Activities*. Cambridge: Belknap Press of Harvard University Press, 1957.

Durant, John R. "Innate Character in Animals and Man: A Perspective on the Origins of Ethology." In *Biology, Medicine, and Society*, edited by Charles Webster, 157–192. Cambridge: Cambridge University Press, 1981.

Dutcher, William. "History of the Audubon Movement." *Bird-Lore* 7 (1905): 45–57.

"Eagle Bander." *New Yorker* 30 (19 June 1954): 18–19.

Eakin, Richard M. *History of Zoology at Berkeley*. Berkeley: University of California Printing Department, 1988.

———. "History of Zoology at the University of California, Berkeley." *Bios* 27 (1956): 67–60.

Eakin, Richard M., A. Starker Leopold, and R. A. Stirton. "Alden Holmes Miller." In *In Memoriam*, 68–71. Berkeley: University of California, 1967.

Edwards, J. L. "Charles Anderson Urner, 1882–1938." *Proceedings of the Linnaean Society of New York*, no. 49 (1938): 1–7.

Egerton, Frank N. "Changing Concepts in the Balance of Nature." *Quarterly Review of Biology* 48 (1973): 322–350.

Eisenmann, Eugene. "Seventy-Five Years of the Linnaean Society of New York." *Proceedings of the Linnaean Society of New York*, nos. 63–65 (1951–1953): 1–9.

Elliot, D. G. "In Memoriam: Elliott Coues." *Auk* 18 (1901): 1–11.

Elliott, Clark A. *Biographical Dictionary of American Science: The Seventeenth through the Nineteenth Centuries.* Westport, Conn.: Greenwood Press, 1979.

Elsner, John, and Roger Cardinal, eds. *The Cultures of Collecting.* Cambridge: Harvard University Press, 1994.

Emerson, W. Otto. "Joseph Marshall Wade: An Appreciation." *Oologist* 28 (1911): 158–161.

"Ernst Mayr." *Current Biography Yearbook 1984*, edited by Charles Moritz, 258–262. New York: H. W. Wilson, 1985.

Evenden, Matthew D. "The Laborers of Nature: Economic Ornithology and the Role of Birds as Agents of Biological Control in North American Agriculture, ca. 1880–1930." *Forest and Conservation History* 39 (1995): 172–183.

Farber, Paul Lawrence. "The Development of Taxidermy and the History of Ornithology." *Isis* 68 (1977): 550–566.

———. *The Emergence of Ornithology as a Scientific Discipline: 1760–1850.* Dordrecht, Holland: D. Reidel, 1982.

———. "The Type-Concept during the First Half of the Nineteenth Century." *Journal of the History of Biology* 9 (1976): 93–119.

Farrand, John, Jr. "The Bronx County Bird Club: Memories of Ten Boys and an Era That Shaped American Birding." *American Birds* 45 (Fall 1991): 372–381.

Faxon, Walter. "Relics of Peale's Museum." *Bulletin of the Museum of Comparative Zoology* 59 (1915): 119–133.

Fischer, Richard B. "Ambassador of Birdlife." *Audubon Magazine* 67 (January–February 1965): 26–31.

Fisher, A. K. "In Memoriam: George Bird Grinnell." *Auk* 56 (1939): 1–12.

———. "Dr. William LaGrange Ralph." *Auk* 24 (1907): 461–462.

Fleming, Donald. "Roots of the New Conservation Movement." *Perspectives in American History* 6 (1972): 7–91.

Fleming, J. H. "In Memoriam: Jonathan Dwight." *Auk* 47 (1930): 1–6.

Fleming, James Roger. *Meteorology in America, 1800–1870.* Baltimore: Johns Hopkins University Press, 1990.

Flink, James J. *The Automobile Age.* Cambridge: MIT Press, 1988.

Flores, Dan. "Bison Ecology and Bison Diplomacy: The Southern Plains from 1800 to 1850." *Journal of American History* 78 (1991): 465–485.

Ford, Alice. *John James Audubon: A Biography.* New York: Abbeville Press, 1988.

Fox, Stephen. *The American Conservation Movement: John Muir and His Legacy.* Madison: University of Wisconsin Press, 1985.

Fox, William J. "A List of American Journals Omitted from Bolton's 'Catalogue of Scientific and Technical Periodicals, 1865–1895.'" *Bulletin of Bibliography* 5 (1908): 82–85.

"Francis Hobart Herrick." *National Cyclopaedia of American Biography* 31 (1944): 276–277.

Freidson, Eliot. *Professional Powers: A Study of the Institutionalization of Formal Knowledge.* Chicago: University of Chicago Press, 1986.

Freitag, Sandria B. "Community." In *Encyclopedia of Social History*, edited by Peter N. Stear, 160–162. New York: Garland, 1994.

Friedmann, Herbert. "Advances in Life History Work." In *Fifty Years' Progress in American Ornithology, 1883–1933*, edited by Frank M. Chapman and T. S. Palmer, 101–109. Lancaster, Pa.: American Ornithologists' Union, 1933.

———. "In Memoriam: James Paul Chapin." *Auk* 83 (1966): 240–252.

Fries, Waldemar H. *The Double Elephant Folio: The Story of Audubon's "Birds of America."* Chicago: American Library Association, 1973.

Frost, Jack. "Profiles: Up From Fifth Avenue." *New Yorker* 1 (25 July 1925): 8–9.

Fruchtbaum, Harold. "Natural Theology and the Rise of Science." Ph.D. dissertation, Harvard University, 1964.

Fuller, Walter P. "Who Was the Frenchmen of Frenchman's Creek?" *Tequesta: Journal of the Historical Association of Southern Florida* 29 (1969): 45–59.

Fuller, Wayne. *The American Mail: Enlarger of the Common Life.* Chicago: University of Chicago Press, 1972.

Gabrielson, Ira N. "Obituary." *Auk* 79 (1962): 495–499.

Gallagher, Annette. "Citizen of a Nation: John Fletcher Lacey, Conservationist." *Annals of Iowa* 46 (1981): 9–24.

Geiger, Roger L. *To Advance Knowledge: The Growth of American Research Universities, 1900–1940.* New York: Oxford University Press, 1986.

Geison, Gerald L., ed. *Professions and Professional Ideologies in America.* Chapel Hill: University of North Carolina Press, 1983.

Gelber, Steven M. "Free Market Metaphor: The Historical Dynamics of Stamp Collecting." *Comparative Studies in Society and History* 34 (1992): 742–769.

Gerson, Elihu M. "Scientific Work and Social Worlds." *Knowledge: Creation, Diffusion, Utilization* 4 (1983): 357–377.

Gerstner, Patsy A. "The Academy of Natural Sciences of Philadelphia, 1812–1850." In *The Pursuit of Knowledge in the Early American Republic: American Scientific and Learned Societies from the Colonial Times to the Civil War*, edited by Alexandra Oleson and Sanborn C. Brown, 174–193. Baltimore: Johns Hopkins University Press, 1976.

Gibbons, Felton, and Deborah Strom. *Neighbors to the Birds: A History of Birdwatching in America.* New York: W. W. Norton, 1988.

Gieryn, Thomas. "Boundaries of Science." In *Handbook of Science and Technology Studies*, edited by Sheila Jasanoff, Gerald E. Markle, James C. Petersen, and Trevor Pinch, 393–443. Thousand Oaks, Calif.: Sage Publications, 1995.

Gifford, George E., Jr. "Thomas Mayo Brewer, M.D. . . . A Blackbird and Duck, Sparrow and Mole." *Harvard Medical Alumni Bulletin* 37, no. 1 (Fall 1962): 32–35.

Gill, Frank B. "Philadelphia: 180 Years of Ornithology at the Academy of Natural Sciences." In *Contributions to the History of North American Ornithology*, edited by William E. Davis, Jr., and Jerome A. Jackson, 1–31. Cambridge, Mass.: Nuttall Ornithological Club, 1995.

Gill, Theodore. "Biographical Notice of John Cassin." *Osprey* n.s. 1 (1902): 50–53.

Gillespie, Neal C. "Natural History, Natural Theology, and Social Order: John Ray and the 'Newtonian Ideology.'" *Journal of the History of Biology* 20 (1987): 1–49.

―――. "Preparing for Darwin: Conchology and Natural Theology in Anglo-American Natural History." *Studies in History of Biology* 7 (1984): 93–145.

Glacken, Clarence. *Traces on the Rhodian Shore: Nature and Culture in Western Thought from Ancient Times to the End of the Eighteenth Century.* Berkeley: University of California Press, 1967.

Glick, Thomas F., ed. *The Comparative Reception of Darwinism.* College Station: University of Texas Press, 1974.

Goetzmann, William. *Army Exploration in the American West, 1803–1863.* New Haven: Yale University Press, 1959.

―――. *Exploration and Empire: The Explorer and the Scientist in the Winning of the American West.* New York: Alfred A. Knopf, 1966.

Goldstein, Daniel. "Midwestern Naturalists: Academies of Science in the Mississippi Valley, 1850–1900." Ph.D. dissertation, Yale University, 1989.

———. "'Yours for Science': The Smithsonian Institution's Correspondents and the Shape of the Scientific Community in Nineteenth-Century America." *Isis* 85 (1994): 573–599.

Gorges, Raymond. *Ernest Harold Baynes: Naturalist and Crusader.* Boston: Houghton Mifflin, 1928.

Gould, Stephen Jay. "Balzan Prize to Ernst Mayr." *Science* 223 (1984): 255–257.

Graham, Frank, Jr. *The Audubon Ark: A History of the National Audubon Society.* New York: Alfred A. Knopf, 1990.

Graham, Gladys. "Neltje De Graff Doubleday." *Dictionary of American Biography* 5 (1930): 392.

Graustein, Jeannette E. *Thomas Nuttall, Naturalist: Explorations in America, 1808–1841.* Cambridge: Harvard University Press, 1967.

Green, H. O. "The Beginning of Oology." *Oologist* 52 (1935): 2–3.

———. "An Early Oologist." *Oologist* 52 (1935): 42–43.

Green, Harvey. *Fit for America: Health, Fitness, Sport, and American Society.* New York: Pantheon Books, 1986.

———. *The Light of the Home: An Intimate View of the Lives of Women in Victorian America.* New York: Pantheon Books, 1983.

Greene, John C. *American Science in the Age of Jefferson.* Ames: Iowa State University Press, 1984.

Greenway, James C. *Extinct and Vanishing Birds of the World.* 2d ed. New York: Dover Publications, 1967.

Gregory, William K. "Biographical Memoir of Frank Michler Chapman, 1864–1945." *Biographical Memoirs of the National Academy of Sciences* 35 (1949): 111–145.

Grier, Katherine C. *Culture and Comfort: People, Parlors, and Upholstery, 1850–1930.* Rochester, N.Y.: Strong Museum, 1988.

———. "The Decline of the Memory Palace: The Parlor after 1890." In *American Home Life, 1880–1930: A Social History of Spaces and Services,* edited by Jessica H. Foy and Thomas J. Schlereth, 49–74. Knoxville: University of Tennessee Press, 1992.

Griesemer, James. "Modeling in the Museum: On the Role of Remnant Models in the Work of Joseph Grinnell." *Biology and Philosophy* 5 (1990): 3–36.

Griesemer, James, and Elihu Gerson. "Collaboration in the Museum of Vertebrate Zoology." *Journal of the History of Biology* 26 (1993): 185–203.

Grinnell, Hilda Wood. "Joseph Grinnell: 1877–1939." *Condor* 42 (1940): 3–34.

Griscom, Ludlow. "Frank M. Chapman." *Audubon Magazine* 48 (1946): 49–52.

———. "Historical Development of Sight Recognition." *Proceedings of the Linnaean Society of New York,* nos. 63–65 (1954): 16–20.

Gross, Alfred O. "History and Progress of Bird Photography in America." In *Fifty Years' Progress of American Ornithology, 1833–1933,* edited by Frank M. Chapman and T. S. Palmer, 159–180. Lancaster, Pa.: American Ornithologists' Union, 1933.

Guide to the Smithsonian Archives: 1983. Archives and Special Collections of the Smithsonian Institution, no. 4. Washington, D.C.: Smithsonian Institution Press, 1983.

Guralnick, Stanley M. *Science and the Ante-Bellum American College.* Philadelphia: American Philosophical Society, 1975.

Guthe, Carl E. "The Museums at Michigan." *Michigan Alumnus* 42 (1937): 469–477.

Haber, Samuel. *The Quest for Authority and Honor in the American Professions, 1750–1900.* Chicago: University of Chicago Press, 1991.

Haffer, Jürgen. "Ernst Mayr als Ornithologe, Systematiker, and Zoogeograph," *Biologisches Zentralblatt* 114 (1995): 133–142.

———. "'Es wäre Zeit, einen "allgemeinen Hartert" zu schreiben': Die historischen Wurzeln von Ernst Mayrs Beiträgen zur Evolutionssythese." *Bonner Zoologische Beiträge* 45 (1994): 113–123.

———. "The Genesis of Erwin Stresemann's *Aves* (1927–1934) in the *Handbuch der Zoologie*, and His Contribution to the Evolutionary Synthesis." *Archives of Natural History* 21 (1994): 201–216.

———. "The History of Species Concepts and Species Limits in Ornithology." *Bulletin of the British Ornithologists' Club*, Centenary Supplement 112A (1992): 107–158.

Hagen, Joel. "Organism and Environment: Frederic Clements's Vision of a Unified Physiological Ecology." In *The American Development of Biology*, edited by Ronald Rainger, Keith Benson, and Jane Maienschein, 257–280. Philadelphia: University of Pennsylvania Press, 1988.

Hahn, Paul. *Where Is That Vanished Bird?: An Index to the Known Specimens of the Extinct North American Species.* Toronto: Royal Ontario Museum, University of Toronto, 1963.

Hall, George A. "The Middle Years of the Wilson Ornithological Society: 1922–1955." *Wilson Bulletin* 100 (1988): 625–631.

Hamel, Paul B. *Bachman's Warbler: A Species in Peril.* Washington, D.C.: Smithsonian Institution Press, 1986.

Hardy, Stephen. *How Boston Played: Sport, Recreation, and Community.* Boston: Northeastern University Press, 1982.

Harford, Henry. "Getting Closer to the Birds." *Audubon Magazine* 51 (1949): 368–373.

"Harlan Hoge Ballard." *National Cyclopedia of American Biography* 9: 488–489. New York: James T. White, 1907.

Harlow, Alvin F. "Henry Payne Whitney." *Dictionary of American Biography* 20 (1936): 160–161.

Harris, Harry. "Robert Ridgway, with a Bibliography of His Published Writings." *Condor* 30 (1928): 5–118.

Harwood, Michael. "The Lab: From Hatching to Fledging." *Cornell University Laboratory of Ornithology Annual Report* (1986–1987): 4–13.

Haskell, Thomas L., ed. *The Authority of Experts: Studies in History and Theory.* Bloomington: Indiana University Press, 1984.

Hellman, Geoffroy Hellman. *Bankers, Bones and Beetles: The First Century of the American Museum of Natural History.* Garden City, N.Y.: The Natural History Press, 1968.

Henderson, Robert W., ed. *Early American Sport: A Checklist of Books by American and Foreign Authors Published in America Prior to 1860, including Sporting Songs.* 3d ed. London: Associated University Press, 1977.

Henshaw, Henry W. "Autobiographical Notes." *Condor* 21 (1919): 102–107, 165–171, 177–181, 217–222; 22 (1920): 55–60, 95–101.

Heppell, David. "The Evolution of the Code of Zoological Nomenclature." In *History in the Service of Systematics*, edited by Alwyne Wheeler and James H. Price, 135–141. London: Society for the Bibliography of Natural History, 1981.

Herber, Elmer Charles, ed. *Correspondence between Spencer Fullerton Baird and Louis Agassiz: Two Pioneer Naturalists.* Washington, D.C.: Smithsonian Institution Press, 1963.

Herlihy, David V. "The Bicycle Story." *American Heritage of Invention and Technology* 7 (Spring 1992): 48–59.

Herrick, Francis H. *Audubon the Naturalist.* 2d ed. New York: D. Appleton-Century, 1938.
———. "Samuel Prentiss Baldwin." *Science* 89 (1939): 212–213.
Hewitt, Waterman T. *Cornell University: A History.* 4 vols. New York: University Publishing Society, 1905.
Hickey, Joseph J. "The Linnaean Society." In *Reminiscences by Members Collected on the Occasion of the Centennial of the Linnaean Society of New York, March 1978,* 1–2. New York: Linnaean Society, 1978.
Higgs, Robert. *The Transformation of the American Economy, 1864–1914: An Essay in Interpretation.* New York: John Wiley and Sons, 1971.
Hindle, Brooke. *The Pursuit of Science in Revolutionary America, 1735–1789.* Chapel Hill: Published for the Institute of Early American History and Culture, Williamsburg, Va., by University of North Carolina Press, 1956.
"How One Man Secured a Law in Thirty-Two States." *World's Work* 12 (1906): 8137–8138.
Howard, Hildegard. "Louis Bennett Bishop, 1865–1950," *Auk* 68 (1951): 440–446.
Hume, Edgar Erskine. *Ornithologists of the United States Army Medical Corps: Thirty-Six Biographies.* Baltimore: John Hopkins University Press, 1942.
Hunter, Clark. *The Life and Letters of Alexander Wilson.* Philadelphia: American Philosophical Society, 1983.
Huth, Hans. *Nature and the American: Three Centuries of Changing Attitudes.* Lincoln: University of Nebraska Press, 1957.
Impey, Oliver, and Arthur McGregor, eds. *The Origins of Museums: The Cabinet of Curiosities in Sixteenth- and Seventeenth-Century Europe.* New York: Oxford University Press, 1985.
Jackson, Jerome A. "Extinct Bird Journals: Forgotten Treasures?" *AB Bookman's Weekly* 77 (1986): 2566–2569.
———. "The Wilson Ornithological Society in the Last Third of Its First Century: 1956–1988." *Wilson Bulletin* 100 (1988): 632–649.
Jackson, Jerome A., Harold Mayfield, and George A. Hall. "A History of the First One Hundred Years of the Wilson Ornithological Society." *Wilson Bulletin* 100 (1988): 617–618.
Jackson, Kenneth T. *Crabgrass Frontier: The Suburbanization of the United States.* New York: Oxford University Press, 1985.
Jacobs, Struan. "Scientific Community: Formulations and Critique of a Sociological Motif." *British Journal of Sociology* 38 (1987): 266–267.
Jardine, N., J. A. Secord, and E. C. Spary, eds. *Cultures of Natural History.* Cambridge: Cambridge University Press, 1996.
Jay, Robert. *The Trade Card in Nineteenth-Century America.* Columbia: University of Missouri Press, 1987.
Johnson, Ned K. "Ornithology at the Museum of Vertebrate Zoology." In *Contributions to the History of North American Ornithology,* edited by William E. Davis, Jr., and Jerome A. Jackson, 183–221. Cambridge, Mass.: Nuttall Ornithological Club, 1995.
Johnson, Terrence. *Professions and Power.* London: Macmillan, 1972.
Junker, Thomas. "Factors Shaping Ernst Mayr's Concepts in the History of Biology." *Journal of the History of Biology* 29 (1996): 29–77.
Kahn, Edgar A. "Max Minor Peet, 1885–1949." *Surgical Neurology* 5 (1976): 63–66.
Kalmbach, E. R. "In Memoriam: W. L. McAtee." *Auk* 80 (1963): 474–485.
Kastner, Joseph. "Long before Furs, It Was Feathers That Stirred Reformist Ire." *Smithsonian* 25 (July 1994): 96–104.

Kastner, Joseph. *A World of Watchers*. New York: Alfred A. Knopf, 1986.

Keading, Henry B. "Retrospective." *Condor* 10 (1908): 215–218.

Keeney, Elizabeth B. *The Botanizers: Amateur Scientists in Nineteenth-Century America.* Chapel Hill: University of North Carolina Press, 1992.

Keller, Betty. *Black Wolf: The Life of Ernest Thompson Seton*. Vancouver: Douglas & McIntyre, 1984.

Kendeigh, S. Charles. "In Memoriam: Lynds Jones." *Auk* 69 (1952): 258–265.

———. "In Memoriam: Samuel Prentiss Baldwin." *Auk* 57 (1940): 1–13.

———. "Measurement of Bird Populations." *Ecological Monographs* 14 (1944): 67–106.

Kingsland, Sharon. "Abbott Thayer and the Protective Coloration Debate." *Journal of the History of Biology* 11 (1978): 223–244.

———. *Modeling Nature: Episodes in the History of Population Ecology*. Chicago: University of Chicago Press, 1985.

Knowlton, F. H. "Major Charles E. Bendire." *Osprey* 1 (1897): 87–90.

Kofalk, Harriet. *No Woman Tenderfoot: Florence Merriam Bailey, Pioneer Naturalist.* College Station: Texas A & M University Press, 1989.

Koford, Carl B. *The California Condor*. National Audubon Society, Research Report no. 4. New York: National Audubon Society, 1953.

Kohler, Robert E. "The Ph.D. Machine: Building on the Collegiate Base." *Isis* 81 (1990): 638–662.

Kohlstedt, Sally G. "Curiosities and Cabinets: Natural History Museums and Education on the Ante-Bellum Campus." *Isis* 79 (1988): 405–426.

———. "From Learned Society to Public Museum: The Boston Society of Natural History." In *The Organization of Knowledge in Modern America, 1869–1920*, edited by Alexandra Oleson and John Voss, 386–406. Baltimore: Johns Hopkins University Press, 1979.

———. "Henry A. Ward: The Merchant Naturalist and American Museum Development." *Journal of the Society for the Bibliography of Natural History* 9 (1980): 647–661.

———. "In from the Periphery: American Women in Science, 1830–1880." *Signs: Journal of Women and Culture and Society* 4 (1978): 81–96.

———. "Museums on Campus: A Tradition of Inquiry and Teaching." In *The American Development of Biology*, edited by Ronald Rainger, Keith Benson, and Jane Maienschein, 15–47. Philadelphia: University of Pennsylvania Press, 1988.

———. "The Nineteenth-Century Amateur Tradition: The Case of the Boston Society of Natural History." In *Science and Its Public*, edited by Gerald Holton and W. A. Blanpied, 173–190. Dordrecht, Holland: D. Reidel, 1976.

Kuznick, Peter J. *Beyond the Laboratory: Scientists as Political Activists in 1930s America*. Chicago: University of Chicago Press, 1987.

La Vergata, Antonella. "Au nom de l'espèce: Classification et nomenclature au XIXe siècle." In *Histoire du concept d'espèce dans les sciences de la vie*, 191–225. Paris: Fondation Singer-Polignac, 1987.

Laing, Hamilton M. *Allen Brooks: Artist Naturalist*. Victoria, B.C.: British Columbia Provincial Museum, 1979.

Lambrecht, Kahman. "In Memoriam: Robert Wilson Shufeldt, 1850–1934." *Auk* 52 (1935): 359–361.

Lankford, John. "Amateurs versus Professionals: The Controversy over Telescope Size in Late Victorian Science." *Isis* 72 (1981): 11–28.

Lanyon, Wesley E. "Ornithology at the American Museum of Natural History." In *Contributions to the History of North American Ornithology*, edited by William E. Davis, Jr., and Jerome A. Jackson, 113–144. Cambridge, Mass.: Nuttall Ornithological Club, 1995.

Larsen, Anne, "Equipment for the Field." In *Cultures of Natural History*, edited by N. Jardine, J. A. Secord, and E. C. Spary, 358–377. Cambridge: Cambridge University Press, 1996.

———. "'Not since Noah': English Scientific Zoologists and the Craft of Collecting, 1800–1840." Ph.D. dissertation, Princeton University, 1993.

Larson, Magali S. *The Rise of Professionalism: A Sociological Analysis*. Berkeley: University of California Press, 1977.

Latour, Bruno. *Science in Action: How to Follow Scientists and Engineers through Society*. Cambridge: Harvard University Press, 1987.

Law, John, and Michael Lynch. "Lists, Field Guides, and the Descriptive Organization of Seeing: Birdwatching as an Exemplary Observational Activity." In *Representation in Scientific Practice*, edited by Michael Lynch and Steve Woolgar, 267–299. Cambridge: MIT Press, 1990.

Laycock, George. "The Last Parakeet." *Audubon Magazine* 71 (March 1969): 21–25.

Leahy, Christopher. *The Birdwatcher's Companion: An Encyclopedic Handbook of North American Birdlife*. London: Robert Hale, 1982.

Lemaine, Gerard, Roy Macleod, Michael Mulkay, and Peter Weingart, eds. *Perspectives on the Emergence of Scientific Disciplines*. The Hague: Mouton; Chicago: Aldine, 1976.

Leutner, Winfred G. "Francis Hobart Herrick." *Science* 92 (1940): 371–372.

Lewis, David L., and Laurence Goldstein, eds. *The Automobile and American Culture*. Ann Arbor: University of Michigan Press, 1983.

Lincoln, Frederick C. "Bird Banding." In *Fifty Years' Progress of American Ornithology, 1883–1933*, edited by Frank M. Chapman and T. S. Palmer, 65–87. Lancaster, Pa.: American Ornithologists' Union, 1933.

Lindsay, R. B. "Robert Williams Wood." *Dictionary of Scientific Biography* 14 (1976): 497–499.

Link, Arthur, and Richard McCormick. *Progressivism*. Arlington Heights, Ill.: Harlan Davidson, 1983.

Linsdale, Jean M. "In Memoriam: Joseph Grinnell." *Auk* 59 (1942): 269–285.

Linsley, E. G., and R. L. Usinger. "Linnaeus and the Development of the International Code of Zoological Nomenclature." *Systematic Zoology* 8 (1958): 39–47.

Lurie, Edward. *Louis Agassiz: A Life in Science*. Chicago: University of Chicago Press, 1960.

Lutts, Ralph H. *The Nature Fakers: Wildlife, Science & Sentiment*. Golden, Colo.: Fulcrum, 1990.

Lyon, Thomas J., ed. *This Incomperable Lande: A Book of American Nature Writing*. Boston: Houghton Mifflin, 1989.

McAtee, W. L. "Economic Ornithology." In *Fifty Years' Progress in American Ornithology, 1883–1933*, edited by Frank M. Chapman and T. S. Palmer, 111–129. Lancaster, Pa.: American Ornithologists' Union, 1933.

———. "In Memoriam: Theodore Sherman Palmer." *Auk* 73 (1956): 367–377.

McCabe, R. A. "Wisconsin's Forgotten Ornithologist." *Passenger Pigeon* 41 (1979): 129–131.

McIntosh, Robert P. *The Background of Ecology: Concept and Theory*. Cambridge: Cambridge University Press, 1985.

MacKenzie, John M. *The Empire of Nature: Hunting, Conservation, and British Imperialism*. Manchester: Manchester University Press, 1988.

McKinley, Daniel. *The Carolina Parakeet in Florida*. Special Publication no. 2. Gainesville: Florida Ornithological Society, 1985.

McKinley, Daniel. "The Last Days of the Carolina Parrakeet: Life in the Zoos." *Avicultural Magazine* 83 (1977): 42–49.

Madden, Henry Miller. *Xantus, Hungarian Naturalist in the Pioneer West*. Linz, Austria: Oberosterreichischer Landesverlag, 1949.

Magnus, David C. "In Defense of Natural History: David Starr Jordan and the Role of Isolation in Evolution." Ph.D. dissertation, Stanford University, 1993.

Maienschein, Jane. *Transforming Traditions in American Biology, 1880–1915*. Baltimore: Johns Hopkins University Press, 1991.

Marks, Stuart A. *Southern Hunting in Black and White: Nature, History, and Ritual in a Carolina Community*. Princeton: Princeton University Press, 1991.

Martin, Albro. *Railroads Triumphant: The Growth, Rejection, and Rebirth of a Vital American Force*. New York: Oxford University Press, 1992.

Marx, Leo. *The Machine in the Garden: Technology and the Pastoral Idea in America*. New York: Oxford University Press, 1964.

Mathewson, Worth. *William L. Finley: Pioneer Wildlife Photographer*. Corvallis: Oregon State University Press, 1986.

Mayfield, Harold. "The Early Years of the Wilson Ornithological Society: 1885–1921." *Wilson Bulletin* 100 (1988): 619–624.

———. "In Memoriam: Josselyn Van Tyne." *Auk* 74 (1957): 322–332.

Mayr, Ernst. "Alden Holmes Miller." *Biographical Memoirs of the National Academy of Sciences* 43 (1973): 177–214.

———. "Bernard Altum and the Territory Theory." *Proceedings of the Linnaean Society of New York*, nos. 45 and 46 (1935): 24–38.

———. "Epilogue: Materials for a History of North American Ornithology." In *Ornithology from Aristotle to the Present*, by Erwin Stresemann, 365–396. Cambridge: Harvard University Press, 1975.

———. "Erwin Stresemann." *Dictionary of Scientific Biography* 18: 888–890.

———. "Frank Michler Chapman." *Dictionary of Scientific Biography*, 17:152–153.

———. *The Growth of Biological Thought: Diversity, Evolution, and Inheritance*. Cambridge: Belknap Press of Harvard University Press, 1982.

———. "How I Became a Darwinian." In *The Evolutionary Synthesis: Perspectives on the Unification of Biology*, edited by Ernst Mayr and William B. Provine, 413–423. Cambridge: Harvard University Press, 1980.

———. "The Role of Ornithological Research in Biology." *Proceedings of the XIIIth International Ornithological Congress*, 1:27–35. Baton Rouge: American Ornithologists' Union, 1963.

———. "The Role of Systematics in the Evolutionary Synthesis." In *The Evolutionary Synthesis: Perspectives on the Unification of Biology*, edited by Ernst Mayr and William B. Provine, 123–136. Cambridge: Harvard University Press, 1980.

———. "Rousing the Society's Interest in Ornithology." In *Reminiscences by Members Collected on the Occasion of the Centennial of the Linnaean Society of New York, March 1978*, 4. New York: Linnaean Society, 1978.

Mayr, Ernst, E. G. Linsley, and R. L. Usinger. *Methods and Principles of Systematic Zoology*. New York: McGraw-Hill, 1953.

Mayr, Ernst, and William B. Provine, eds. *The Evolutionary Synthesis: Perspectives on the Unification of Biology*. Cambridge, Mass.: Harvard University Press, 1980.

Mayr, Ernst, and Peter D. Ashlock. *Principles of Systematic Zoology*. 2d ed. New York: McGraw-Hill, 1991.

Meine, Curt. *Aldo Leopold: His Life and Work*. Madison: University of Wisconsin Press, 1988.

Mendelsohn, Everett. "The Emergence of Science as a Profession in Nineteenth Century Europe." In *The Management of Scientists*, edited by Karl B. Hill, 3–48. Boston: Beacon Press, 1964.

Merchant, Carolyn. *Ecological Revolutions: Nature, Gender, and Science in New England*. Chapel Hill: University of North Carolina Press, 1989.

Merrill, James C. "In Memoriam: Charles Emil Bendire." *Auk* 15 (1898): 1–6.

Merrill, Lynn L. *The Romance of Victorian Natural History*. New York: Oxford University Press, 1989.

Merton, Robert K. *The Sociology of Science: Theoretical and Empirical Investigations*. Chicago: University of Chicago Press, 1973.

Mighetto, Lisa. *Wild Animals and American Environmental Ethics*. Tucson: University of Arizona Press, 1991.

Miller, Alden. "Joseph Grinnell." *Systematic Zoology* 3 (1964): 195–249.

Miller, Howard S. *Dollars for Research: Science and Its Patrons in Nineteenth-Century America*. Seattle: University of Washington Press, 1970.

Millerson, Geoffrey. *The Qualifying Associations: A Study in Professionalization*. London: Routledge & Kegan, 1964.

Mitchell, John G. "A Man Called Bird." *Audubon Magazine* 89 (March 1987): 81–104.

———. "The Way We Shuffled Off the Buffalo." *Wildlife Conservation* 96 (January–February 1993): 44–51.

Mitchell, John H. "The Mothers of Conservation." *Sanctuary* (January–February 1996): 1–20.

Mitchell, Lee Clark. *Witnesses to a Vanishing America: The Nineteenth-Century Response*. Princeton: Princeton University Press, 1981.

Mitman, Gregg. *The State of Nature: Ecology, Community, and American Social Thought, 1900–1950*. Chicago: University of Chicago Press, 1992.

Mitman, Gregg, and Richard W. Burkhardt, Jr. "Struggling for Identity: The Study of Animal Behavior in America, 1930–1945." In *The Expansion of American Biology*, edited by Keith R. Benson, Jane Maienschein, and Ronald Rainger, 164–194. New Brunswick, N.J.: Rutgers University Press, 1991.

Moore, John A. "Zoology of the Pacific Railroad Surveys." *American Zoologist* 26 (1986): 311–341.

Morrell, J. B. "Professionalisation." In *Companion to the History of Modern Science*, edited by R. C. Olby, G. N. Cantor, J. R. R. Christie, and M. J. S. Hodge, 980–989. London: Routledge, 1990.

Morrell, Jack, and Arnold Thackery. *Gentlemen of Science: Early Years of the British Association for the Advancement of Science*. Oxford: Clarendon Press, 1981.

Mott, Frank Luther. *A History of American Magazines*. 5 vols. Cambridge, Mass.: Harvard University Press, 1938–1968.

Mrozek, Donald J. *Sport and American Mentality, 1880–1910*. Knoxville: University of Tennessee Press, 1983.

Muensterberger, Werner. *Collecting: An Unruly Passion*. Princeton: Princeton University Press, 1994.

Murphy, Robert Cushman. "Frank M. Chapman, 1864–1945." *Auk* 67 (1950): 307–315.

———. "Leonard Cutler Sanford." *Auk* 68 (1951): 409–410.

———. "Moving a Museum." *Natural History* 39 (1932): 497–511.

Murphy, Robert Cushman, and Dean Amadon. "In Memoriam: John Todd Zimmer." *Auk* 76 (1959): 418–423.

Nash, Roderick, ed. *American Environmentalism: Readings in Conservation History*. 3d ed. New York: McGraw-Hill, 1990.

Nash, Roderick. *Wilderness and the American Mind.* 3d ed. New Haven: Yale University Press, 1982.

Nelson, Gareth. "From Candolle to Croizat: Comments on the History of Biogeography." *Journal of the History of Biology* 11 (1978): 269–305.

Nettleship, David N., and Peter G. H. Evans. "Distribution and Status of Atlantic Alcidae." In *The Atlantic Alcidae: The Evolution, Distribution and Biology of the Auks Inhabiting the Atlantic Ocean and Adjacent Water Areas,* edited by David N. Nettleship and Tim R. Birkhead, 54–154. London: Academic Press, 1985.

Nice, Margaret Morse. *Research Is a Passion with Me: The Autobiography of Margaret Morse Nice,* edited by Doris Huestis Speirs. Toronto: Consolidated Amethyst Communications, 1979.

———. "The Theory of Territorialism and Its Development." In *Fifty Years' Progress of American Ornithology, 1883–1933,* edited by Frank M. Chapman and T. S. Palmer, 89–100. Lancaster, Pa.: American Ornithologists' Union, 1933.

———. *The Watcher at the Nest.* New York: Macmillan, 1939.

Norwood, Vera. *Made from This Earth: American Women and Nature.* Chapel Hill: University of North Carolina Press, 1993.

Novak, Barbara. *Nature and Culture: American Landscape Painting, 1825–1875.* New York: Oxford University Press, 1980.

Nyhart, Lynn K. "Natural History and the 'New' Biology." In *Cultures of Natural History,* edited by N. Jardine, J. A. Secord, and E. C. Spary, 426–443. Cambridge: Cambridge University Press, 1996.

Oberholser, Harry C. "Robert Ridgway: A Memorial Appreciation." *Auk* 50 (1933): 156–169.

Oleson, Alexandra, and Sanborn C. Brown, eds. *The Pursuit of Knowledge in the Early American Republic: American Scientific and Learned Societies from the Colonial Times to the Civil War.* Baltimore: Johns Hopkins University Press, 1976.

Oleson, Alexandra, and John Voss, eds. *The Organization of Knowledge in Modern America, 1860–1920.* Baltimore: Johns Hopkins University Press, 1979.

Orosz, Joel J. *Curators and Culture: The Museum Movement in America, 1740–1870.* Tuscaloosa: University of Alabama Press, 1990.

Orr, Oliver H., Jr. *Saving American Birds: T. Gilbert Pearson and the Founding of the Audubon Movement.* Gainesville: University Press of Florida, 1992.

Osgood, Wilfred H. "Biographical Memoir of Clinton Hart Merriam." *Biographical Memoirs of the National Academy of Sciences* 24 (1944): 1–57.

Overfield, Richard A. *Science with Practice: Charles E. Bessey and the Maturing of American Botany.* Ames: Iowa State University Press, 1993.

Palmer, E. Laurence. "Fifty Years of Nature Study and the American Nature Study Society." *Nature Magazine* 50 (November 1957): 473–480.

Palmer, T. S. "A Brief History of the American Ornithologists' Union." In *Fifty Years' Progress of American Ornithology, 1883–1933,* edited by Frank M. Chapman and T. S. Palmer, 7–27. Lancaster, Pa.: American Ornithologists' Union, 1933.

———. *Chronology and Index of the More Important Events in American Game Protection, 1776–1911.* U.S.D.A, Biological Survey Bulletin 41. Washington, D.C.: Government Printing Office, 1912.

———. "Ernest Harold Baynes." *Auk* 42 (1925): 480–481.

———. "Frank Slater Daggett." *Auk* 37 (1920): 508–509.

———. "Frank Warren Langdon." *Auk* 51 (1934): 132.

———. "Franklin L. Burns." *Auk* 65 (1948): 646–647.

————. "Henry Reed Taylor." *Auk* 35 (1918): 382.

————. "In Memoriam: Clinton Hart Merriam." *Auk* 71 (1954): 130–136.

————. "In Memoriam: Wells Woodbridge Cooke." *Auk* 34 (1917): 119–133.

————. "In Memoriam: William Dutcher." *Auk* 38 (1921): 501–513.

————. "William Emerson Ritter." *Auk* 64 (1947): 665–666.

————. "John Lewis Childs." *Auk* 38 (1921): 494–495.

————. "A Review of Economic Ornithology in the United States." In *Yearbook of Department of Agriculture for 1899*, 259–292. Washington, D.C.: Government Printing Office, 1900.

Palmer, T. S., and W. L. McAtee. "A List of the Publications of A. K. Fisher." *Proceedings of the Biological Society of Washington* 39 (1926): 21–28.

Palmer, T. S., et al. *Biographies of Members of the American Ornithologists' Union. Reprinted from "The Auk," 1884–1954.* Edited by Paul Oehser. Washington, D.C., 1954.

Pauly, Philip J. "The Appearance of Academic Biology in Late Nineteenth-Century America." *Journal of the History of Biology* 17 (1984): 369–398.

Pearson, T. Gilbert. *Adventures in Bird Protection: An Autobiography.* New York: D. Appleton-Century, 1937.

————. "Fifty Years of Bird Protection." In *Fifty Years' Progress of American Ornithology, 1883–1933*, edited by Frank M. Chapman and T. S. Palmer, 199–213. Lancaster, Pa.: American Ornithologists' Union, 1933.

————. "Frank Bond." *Bird-Lore* 13 (1911): 175–177.

Peck, Robert M. *A Celebration of Birds: The Life and Art of Louis Agassiz Fuertes.* Philadelphia: Academy of Natural Sciences of Philadelphia, 1982.

Peters, James L. "The Bird Collection." *Notes Concerning the History and Contents of the Museum of Comparative Zoology*, 50–52. N.p., 1936.

————. "Collections of Birds in the United States and Canada: Study Collections." In *Fifty Years' Progress of American Ornithology, 1883–1933*, edited by Frank M. Chapman and T. S. Palmer, 131–141. Lancaster, Pa.: American Ornithologists' Union, 1933.

Peterson, Roger Tory. *Birds over America.* New York: Dodd, Mead, 1948.

————. "The Era of Ludlow Griscom." *Audubon Magazine* 62 (1960): 102–103, 131, 146.

————. "In Memoriam: Ludlow Griscom." *Auk* 82 (1965): 598–605.

Pettingill, Olin Sewall, Jr. "In Memoriam: Arthur A. Allen." *Auk* 85 (1968): 192–202.

————. *Ornithology in Field and Laboratory.* 5th ed. New York: Academic Press, 1985.

————. *My Way to Ornithology.* Norman: University of Oklahoma Press, 1992.

Pfeifer, Edward J. "United States." In *The Comparative Reception of Darwinism*, edited by Thomas F. Glick, 168–206. Austin: University of Texas Press, 1974.

Phillips, John C. *American Game Birds and Mammals: A Catalogue of Books, 1582 to 1925: Sport, Natural History, and Conservation.* New York: Houghton Mifflin, 1930.

Phillips, John C., and Harold J. Coolidge, Jr. *The First Five Years: The American Committee for International Wild Life Protection.* N.p., 1934.

————. *Brief History of the Formation of the American Committee for International Wild Life Protection.* N.p., n.d.

Pitelka, Frank A. "Academic Family Tree for Loye and Alden Miller." *Condor* 95 (1993): 1065–1067.

Porter, Charlotte M. *The Eagle's Nest: Natural History and American Ideas, 1812–1842.* University: University of Alabama Press, 1986.

————. "The Natural History Museum." In *The Museum: A Reference Guide*, edited Michael S. Shapiro, 1–29. New York: Greenwood Press, 1990.

"Preliminary Bibliography of Articles Based on Christmas Bird Counts." *Audubon Field Notes* 4, no. 2 (April 1950): 187.

Pullar, Elizabeth. "Baking Soda Bonus Cards: Arm and Hammer Trade Cards Designed by L. A. Fuertes." *Antiques Journal* 35 (January 1980): 36–38.

Rainger, Ronald. *An Agenda for Antiquity: Henry Fairfield Osborn and Vertebrate Paleontology at the American Museum of Natural History, 1890–1935*. Tuscaloosa: University of Alabama Press, 1991.

Rainger, Ronald, Keith R. Benson, and Jane Maienschein, eds. *The American Development of Biology*. Philadelphia: University of Pennsylvania Press, 1988.

Ratner, Sidney, James H. Soltow, and Richard Sylla. *The Evolution of the American Economy: Growth, Welfare, and Decision Making*. New York: Basic Books, 1979.

Real, Leslie A., and James H. Brown, eds. *Foundations of Ecology: Classic Papers with Commentaries*. Chicago: University of Chicago Press, 1991.

"Reginald C. Robbins." In *Who Was Who in America: A Component of Who's Who in American History*, 3:731. Chicago: The A. N. Marquis Co, 1966.

Rehn, James A. G. "In Memoriam: Witmer Stone." *Auk* 58 (1941): 299–313.

Reiger, John F. "Reply to Dunlap's Critique." *Environmental Review* 12 (1988): 94–96.

————. *American Sportsmen and the Origins of Conservation*. New York: Winchester Press, 1976.

Reingold, Nathan. "Definitions and Speculations: The Professionalization of Science in America in the Nineteenth Century." In *The Pursuit of Knowledge in the Early American Republic: American Scientific and Learned Societies from the Colonial Times to the Civil War*, edited by Alexandra Oleson and Sanborn C. Brown, 33–69. Baltimore: Johns Hopkins University Press, 1976.

Reingold, Nathan, and Marc Rothenberg. "The Exploring Expedition and the Smithsonian Institution." In *Magnificent Voyagers: The U.S. Exploring Expedition, 1838–1842*, edited by Herman J. Viola and Carolyn Margolis, 242–253. Washington, D.C.: Smithsonian Institution Press, 1985.

Renehan, Edward J., Jr. *John Burroughs: An American Naturalist*. Post Mills, Vt.: Chelsea Green, 1992.

Rhoads, Samuel N. "Bird Clubs in America: II. The Delaware Valley Club." *Bird-Lore* 4 (1902): 57–61.

Richardson, Robert D., Jr. *Henry David Thoreau: A Life of the Mind*. Berkeley: University of California Press, 1986.

Ridgway, John. "Ridgway's Drawing for Bendire Plates." *Condor* 29 (1927): 177–181.

Ridgway, Robert. "Spencer Fullerton Baird." *Auk* 5 (1888): 1–14.

Ripley, S. Dillon. "Herbert Friedmann, April 22, 1900-May 14, 1987." *Biographical Memoirs of the National Academy of Sciences* 62 (1993): 143–165.

Rivinus, Edward F., and E. M. Youssef. *Spencer Baird of the Smithsonian*. Washington, D.C.: Smithsonian Institution Press, 1992.

Robbins, Chandler S. "The Christmas Count." In *Birds in Our Lives*, edited by Alfred Stefferud, 154–163. Washington, D.C.: U.S. Department of the Interior, 1966.

"Robert Wilson Shufeldt." *National Cyclopedia of American Biography* 6:242–244. New York: James T. White, 1896.

Rodgers, Daniel T. *The Work Ethic in Industrial America, 1850–1920*. Chicago: University of Chicago Press, 1978.

Roediger, David R., and Philip S. Foner. *Our Own Time: A History of American Labor and the Working Day*. New York: Greenwood Press, 1989.

Rogers, J. Speed. "The Museum of Zoology." In *The University of Michigan: An Encyclo-*

pedic Survey, edited by Walter A. Donnelly, 4: 1502–1519. Ann Arbor: University of Michigan Press, 1956.

———. "The University Museums." In *The University of Michigan: An Encyclopedic Survey*, edited by Walter A. Donnelly, 4:1431–1442. Ann Arbor: University of Michigan Press, 1956.

Rogers, Stephen P., Mary Ann Schmidt, and Thomas Gütebier. *An Annotated Bibliography on Preparation, Taxidermy, and Collection Management of Vertebrates with Emphasis on Birds*. Carnegie Museum of Natural History, Special Publication no. 15. Pittsburgh: Carnegie Museum of Natural History, 1989.

Romer, Alfred. "Zoology at Harvard." *Bios* 19 (1948): 7–20.

Roos, Patricia A. "Professions." In *Encyclopedia of Sociology*, edited by Edgar F. Borgatta and Marie L. Borgatta, 3:1552–1557. New York: Macmillan, 1992.

Rossiter, Margaret. *Women Scientists in America: Struggles and Strategies to 1940*. Baltimore: Johns Hopkins University Press, 1982.

Rothenberg, Marc, ed. *The History of Science and Technology in the United States: A Critical and Selective Bibliography*. New York: Garland, 1982.

———. "Organization and Control: Professionals and Amateurs in American Astronomy." *Social Studies of Science* 11 (1981): 305–325.

Rothschild, Miriam. *Dear Lord Rothschild: Birds, Butterflies and History*. Glenside, Pa.: Balaban, 1983.

Rothstein, Stephen I., Ralph W. Schreiber, and Thomas R. Howell. "In Memoriam: Herbert Friedmann." *Auk* 105 (1988): 365–368.

Rowan, William. "Fifty Years of Bird Migration." In *Fifty Years' Progress of American Ornithology, 1883–1933*, edited by Frank M. Chapman and T. S. Palmer, 51–63. Lancaster, Pa.: American Ornithologists' Union, 1933.

Rowland, Beryl. *Birds with Human Souls: A Guide to Bird Symbolism*. Knoxville: University of Tennessee Press, 1978.

Rudolph, Emanual D. "Women in Nineteenth-Century American Botany: A Generally Unrecognized Constituency." *American Journal of Botany* 69 (1982): 1346–1355.

———. "Women Who Studied Plants in the Pre-Twentieth Century United States and Canada." *Taxon* 39 (1990): 151–205.

Rudwick, Martin J. S. *The Great Devonian Controversy: The Shaping of Scientific Knowledge among Gentlemanly Specialists*. Chicago: University of Chicago Press, 1985.

Runte, Alfred. *National Parks: The American Experience*. 2d ed. Lincoln: University of Nebraska Press, 1987.

———. *Yosemite: The Embattled Wilderness*. Lincoln: University of Nebraska Press, 1990.

Ruthven, Alexander G. *Naturalist in Two Worlds: Random Recollections of a University President*. Ann Arbor: University of Michigan Press, 1963.

Saikku, Maikku. "The Extinction of the Carolina Parakeet." *Environmental History Review* 14 (1990): 1–18.

Schaffer, Simon. "Astronomers Mark Time: Discipline and The Personal Equation." *Science in Context* 2 (1988): 115–145.

Schauffler, Robert H., ed. *Arbor Day: Its History, Observance, Spirit and Significance*. New York: Moffat, Yard, 1909.

Schlereth, Thomas. *Victorian America: Transformations in Everyday Life, 1876–1915*. New York: HarperCollins, 1991.

Schmitt, Peter J. *Back to Nature: The Arcadian Myth in Urban America*. New York: Oxford University Press, 1969.

Schorger, A. W. *The Passenger Pigeon: Its Natural History and Extinction*. Madison: University of Wisconsin Press, 1955.

Sclater, P. L. "A Short History of the British Ornithologists' Union." *Ibis*, series 9, vol. 2 (1908): Jubilee Supplement, 19–69.

Scott, W. E. D. *The Story of a Bird-Lover*. New York: Macmillan, 1904.

Sellers, Charles Coleman. *Mr. Peale's Museum: Charles Willson Peale and the First Popular Museum of Natural Science and Art*. New York: W. W. Norton, 1980.

Shapin, Steven. *A Social History of Truth: Civility and Science in Seventeenth-Century England*. Chicago: University of Chicago Press, 1994.

Sharpe, R. Bowlder. "Birds." In *The History of the Collections Contained in the Natural History Departments of the British Museum*, 2:79–515. London: British Museum (Natural History), 1906.

Sheehan, James J. and Morta Sosna, eds. *The Boundaries of Humanity: Humans, Animals, Machines*. Berkeley: University of California Press, 1991.

Shils, Edward. "The Profession of Science." *The Advancement of Science* 24 (1968): 469–490.

Shor, Elizabeth Noble. "Clinton Hart Merriam." *Dictionary of Scientific Biography* 9:313–314.

Shufeldt, Robert W. "Complete List of My Published Writings, with Brief Biographical Notes." *Medical Review of Reviews* 26 (1920): 17–24, 70–75, 123–130, 200–206, 251–257, 314–320, 368–377, 437–447, and 495–498.

Shull, A. Franklin. "The Department of Zoology." In *The University of Michigan: An Encyclopedic Survey*, edited by Wilfred B. Shaw, 2:738–750. Ann Arbor: University of Michigan Press, 1951.

Sibley, Charles G. "Ornithology." In *A Century of Progress in the Natural Sciences*, edited by Edward L. Kessel, 629–659. San Francisco: California Academy of Sciences, 1955.

Skolnick, Herman K., and Kenneth M. Reese, eds. *A Century of Chemistry: The Role of Chemists and the American Chemical Society*. Washington, D.C.: American Chemical Society, 1976.

Smits, David. "The Frontier Army and the Destruction of the Buffalo, 1865–1883." *Western Historical Quarterly* 25 (1994): 313–338.

Smocovitis, Vassiliki Betty. "Organizing Evolution: Founding the Society for the Study of Evolution (1939–1950)." *Journal of the History of Biology* 27 (1994): 241–309.

Snow, D. W. "Robert Cushman Murphy and His 'Journal of the Tring Trip.'" *Ibis* 115 (1973): 607–611.

Sorensen, W. Conner. *Brethren of the Net: American Entomology, 1840–1880*. Tuscaloosa: University of Alabama Press, 1995.

Star, Susan Leigh. "Craft vs. Commodity, Mess vs. Transcendence: How the Right Tool Became the Wrong One in the Case of Taxidermy and Natural History." In *The Right Tools for the Job: At Work in Twentieth-Century Life Sciences*, edited by Adele E. Clarke and Joan H. Fujimura, 257–286. Princeton: Princeton University Press, 1992.

Star, Susan Leigh, and James R. Griesemer. "Institutional Ecology, 'Translations,' and Boundary Objects: Amateurs and Professionals in Berkeley's Museum of Vertebrate Zoology, 1907–1939." *Social Studies of Science* 19 (1989): 387–420.

Stearns, Raymond Phineas. *Science in the British Colonies of America*. Urbana: University of Illinois Press, 1970.

Stebbins, Robert A. "Amateur and Professional Astronomers: A Study of Their Interrelationships." *Urban Life* 10 (1982): 433–454.

———. *Amateurs: On the Margin between Work and Leisure*. Beverly Hills: Sage Publications, 1979.

———. *Amateurs, Professionals, and Serious Leisure*. Montreal: McGill-Queen's University Press, 1992.

———. "Avocational Science: The Avocational Routine in Archeology and Astronomy." *International Journal of Comparative Sociology* 21 (1980): 34–48.

Stejneger, Leonhard. "A Chapter in the History of Zoological Nomenclature." *Smithsonian Miscellaneous Collections* 8 (1924): 1–21.

Sterling, Keir B. "Builders of the U.S. Biological Survey, 1885–1930." *Journal of Forest History* 33 (1989): 180–187.

———. *The Last of the Naturalists: The Career of C. Hart Merriam*. New York: Arno Press, 1974.

———. "Lynds Jones." *Dictionary of American Biography*, Supplement 5 (1977): 373–375.

Sterling, Keir B., and Marianne G. Ainley. "A Centennial History of the American Ornithologists' Union, 1883–1983." Manuscript.

Stewart, Susan. *On Longing: Narratives of the Miniature, the Gigantic, the Souvenir, and the Collection*. Baltimore: Johns Hopkins University Press, 1984.

Stilgoe, John. *Borderlands: Origins of the American Suburb, 1820–1939*. New Haven: Yale University Press, 1988.

Stone, Witmer. "Charles Johnson Maynard." *Dictionary of American Biography* 2:457.

———. "In Memoriam: Charles Wallace Richmond, 1868–1932." *Auk* 50 (1933): 1–22.

———. "Chester A. Reed." *Auk* 30 (1913): 319.

———. "The Delaware Valley Ornithological Club." *Auk* 7 (1890): 298–299.

———. "In Memoriam—John Hall Sage." *Auk* 43 (1926): 1–17.

———. "John Cassin." *Cassinia* 5 (1901): 1–7.

———. "Prof. Wells W. Cooke." *Auk* 33 (1916): 354–355.

———. "Some Philadelphia Ornithological Collections and Collectors, 1784–1850." *Auk* 16 (1899): 166–176.

———. "Thomas B. Wilson, M.D." *Cassinia* 13 (1909): 1–6.

———. "William Leon Dawson." *Auk* 45 (1928): 417.

———. "William Louis Abbott." *Auk* 53 (1936): 369–370.

Stover, John F. *American Railroads*. Chicago: University of Chicago Press, 1978.

Stresemann, Erwin. *Ornithology from Aristotle to the Present*. Translated by Hans J. and Cathleen Epstein. Edited by G. William Cottrell. Cambridge: Harvard University Press, 1975.

Stroud, Richard H., ed. *National Leaders of American Conservation*. Washington, D.C.: Smithsonian Institution Press, 1985.

Sulloway, Frank. "Darwin and His Finches: The Evolution of A Legend," *Journal of the History of Biology* 15 (1982): 1–53.

———. "Joel Asaph Allen." *Dictionary of Scientific Biography* 17:20–23.

Sutton, Ann, and Myron Sutton. "The Man from Yosemite." *National Parks Magazine* 28 (July–September 1954): 102–105, 130–132, 140.

Sutton, George M. *Bird Student: An Autobiography*. Austin: University of Texas Press, 1980.

Swarth, H. S. *A Systematic Study of the Cooper Ornithological Club*. San Francisco: n.p., 1929.

Taber, Wendell. "In Memoriam: Arthur Cleveland Bent." *Auk* 72 (1955): 332–339.

Taylor, Mrs. H. J. "Lynds Jones." *Wilson Bulletin* 50 (1938): 225–238.

Teale, Edwin Way. "A. C. Bent: Plutarch of Birds." *Audubon Magazine* 48 (1946): 14–20.

———. "Arthur A. Allen." *Audubon Magazine* 45 (1943): 85–89.

———. "Ludlow Griscom: Virtuoso of Field Identification." *Audubon Magazine* 47 (1945): 349–358.

Tebbel, John. *A History of Book Publishing in the United States.* 4 vols. New York: R. R. Bowker, 1972–1981.

Tebbel, John, and Mary Ellen Zuckerman. *The Magazine in America, 1741–1990.* New York: Oxford University Press, 1991.

Temple, Stanley A., and John T. Emlen. "In Memoriam: Joseph J. Hickey, 1907–1993." *Auk* 111 (1994): 450–452.

Terbough, John. *Where Have All the Birds Gone?: Essays on the Biology and Conservation of Birds That Migrate to the American Tropics.* Princeton: Princeton University Press, 1989.

Terres, John K. "Big Brother to the Waterfowl." *Audubon Magazine* 49 (1947): 150–158.

Thackray, Arnold. "Scientific Networks in the Age of Revolution." *Nature* 262 (1976): 20–24.

Thernstrom, Stephan. *A History of the American People*, vol. 2. 2d ed. San Diego: Harcourt Brace Jovanovich, 1989.

Thomas, Edward S. "In Memoriam: Lawrence Emerson Hicks." *Auk* 75 (1958): 279–281.

Thorpe, W. H. *The Origins and Rise of Ethology.* London: Heinemann, 1979.

Tjossem, Sara F. "Preservation of Nature and Academic Respectability: Tensions in the Ecological Society of America, 1915–1979." Ph.D. dissertation, Cornell University, 1994.

Tober, James A. *Who Owns Wildlife: The Political Economy of Conservation in Nineteenth-Century America.* Westport, Conn.: Greenwood Press, 1981.

Tobey, Ronald C. *Saving the Prairies: The Life Cycle of the Founding School of American Plant Ecology, 1895–1955.* Berkeley: University of California Press, 1981.

Townsend, Charles W. "Charles Johnson Maynard." *Bulletin of the Boston Society of Natural History* 54 (1939): 3–7.

Trautman, Milton B. "In Memoriam: Margaret Morse Nice." *Auk* 94 (1977): 430–441.

Trefethen, James B. *An American Crusade for Wildlife.* New York: Winchester Press and the Boone and Crockett Club, 1975.

———. "John Fletcher Lacey." In *National Leaders of American Conservation*, edited by Richard H. Stroud, 236–237. Washington, D.C.: Smithsonian Institution Press, 1985.

Trostler, I. S. "President's Address—History of Ornithology in Nebraska, and of State Ornithological Societies in General." *Proceedings of the Nebraska Ornithologists' Union* 2 (1901): 13–18.

Trotter, Spencer. "Some Old Philadelphia Bird Collectors and Taxidermists." *Cassinia* 18 (1914): 1–8.

Turner, James. *Reckoning with the Beast: Animals, Pain, and Humanity in the Victorian Mind.* Baltimore: Johns Hopkins University Press, 1980.

Turner, Ruth D. "Charles Johnson Maynard and His Work in Malacology." *Occasional Papers on Mollusks* 2 (1957): 137–152.

Uhler, Francis M. "In Memoriam: Albert Kendrick Fisher." *Auk* 68 (1951): 210–213.

Underwood, Margaret H., comp. *Bibliography of North American Minor Natural History Serials in the University of Michigan Libraries.* Ann Arbor: University of Michigan Press, 1954.

Veysey, Lawrence R. *The Emergence of the American University.* Chicago: University of Chicago Press, 1965.

von Rohr, M[oritz]. *Die binokularen Instrumente: nach Quellen.* Berlin: J. Springer, 1907.

Vuilleumier, François, and Allison V. Andors. "Origins and Development of North American Avian Biogeography." In *Contributions to the History of North American Ornithology,* edited by William E. Davis, Jr., and Jerome A. Jackson, 387–428. Cambridge, Mass.: Nuttall Ornithological Club, 1995.

Waddington, Ivan. "Professions." In *The Social Science Encyclopedia,* edited by Adam Kuper and Jessica Kuper, 677–678. 2d ed. London: Routledge & Kegan, 1996.

Wade, J. S. "Dr. Theodore Sherman Palmer." *Atlantic Naturalist* 12 (1957): 84–88.

Wadland, John Henry. *Ernest Thompson Seton: Man and Nature and the Progressive Tradition.* New York: Arno Press, 1978.

Waite, Frederick C. "Natural History and Biology in the Undergraduate Colleges of Western Reserve University." *Western Reserve University Bulletin* 7 (1929): 21–41.

Walton, Richard K. "A History of the Massachusetts Audubon Society from 1896 into the 1950s." Manuscript available from Massachusetts Audubon Society.

Warner, Deborah Jean. *Graceanna Lewis: Scientist and Humanitarian.* Washington, D.C.: Smithsonian Institution Press, 1979.

Waters, C. Kenneth, and Albert Van Helden, eds. *Julian Huxley: Biologist and Statesman.* Houston: Rice University Press, 1992.

W[ebster], F[rank] B[lake]. "Horrible Fate." *Ornithologist and Oologist* 16 (1891): 73–75.

Welker, Robert Henry. *Birds and Men: American Birds in Science, Art, Literature, and Conservation, 1800–1900.* Cambridge: Harvard University Press, 1955.

———. "Frank Michler Chapman." *Dictionary of American Biography,* Supplement 3 (1941–1945): 61–62.

———. "Mabel Osgood Wright." In *Notable American Women, 1607–1950, A Biographical Dictionary,* edited by Edward T. James, 3:682–684. Cambridge: Harvard University Press, 1971.

———. "Neltje Blanchan De Graff Doubleday." In *Notable American Women, 1607–1950: A Biographical Dictionary,* edited by Edward T. James, 1:508–509. Cambridge: Harvard University Press, 1971.

Wessen, Ernest J. "Jones' *Nests and Eggs of the Birds of Ohio.*" *Papers of the Bibliographical Society of America* 47 (1953): 218–230.

Wetmore, Alexander. "Biographical Memoir of Robert Ridgway, 1850–1929." *Biographical Memoirs of the National Academy of Sciences* 15 (1931): 57–101.

———. "In Memoriam: James Lee Peters." *Auk* 74 (1957): 166–173.

———. "In Memoriam: Joseph Harvey Riley." *Auk* 60 (1943): 1–15.

Whorton, James C. *Crusaders for Fitness: The History of American Health Reformers.* Princeton: Princeton University Press, 1982.

Wiebe, Robert H. *The Search for Order, 1877–1920.* New York: Hill and Wang, 1967.

[Willard, Samuel L.] "The Oologist: Its History from the Commencement." *Ornithologist and Oologist* 6 (1881): 1–3.

Winsor, Mary P. "Louis Agassiz and the Species Question." *Studies in the History of Biology* 3 (1979): 89–117.

———. *Reading the Shape of Nature: Comparative Zoology at the Agassiz Museum.* Chicago: University of Chicago Press, 1991.

Wonders, Karen E. "Bird Taxidermy and the Origin of the Habitat Diorama." In *Non-Verbal Communication in Science Prior to 1900,* edited by Renato G. Mazzolini, 411–447. Firenze: Leo S. Olschki, 1993.

Wood, Harold B. "The History of Bird Banding." *Auk* 62 (1945): 256–265.

Wood, Sharon E. "Althea Sherman and the Birds of Prairie and Dooryard: A Scientist's Witness to Change." *The Palimpsest* 70 (1989): 165–184.

Worster, Donald. *Nature's Economy: A History of Ecological Ideas.* Cambridge: Cambridge University Press, 1985.

Wright, Albert H. "Biology at Cornell University." *Bios* 24 (1953): 122–145.

XYZ. "Henry R. Taylor!" *Oologist* 12 (1895): 26–27.

Xantus, John. *Letters from North America*, translated and edited by Theodore Shoenman and Helen Bendele. Detroit: Wayne State University Press, 1975.

——. *Travels in Southern California*, translated and edited by Theodore Shoenman and Helen Bendele. Detroit: Wayne State University Press, 1976.

Zuckerman, Harriet and Robert K. Merton. "Patterns of Evaluation in Science: Institutionalization, Structure and Functions of the Referee System." *Minerva* 9 (1971): 66–100.

Zusi, Richard L. *Roger T. Peterson at the Smithsonian.* Washington, D.C.: Smithsonian Institution, 1984.

Zwinger, Ann, ed. *Xantus: The Letters of John Xantus to Spencer Fullerton Baird, from San Francisco and Cabo San Lucas, 1859–1861.* Los Angeles: The Castle Press for Dawson's Bookshop, 1986.

——. *John Xantus: The Fort Tejon Letters, 1857–1859.* Tucson: University of Arizona Press, 1986.

INDEX

A-Birding on a Bronco (Bailey), 157
Abbe, Ernst, 160
Academy of Natural Sciences of Philadelphia, 23–24, 61, 132, 139
advertising, birds in, 162
Agassiz, Louis, 188; and collecting guides, 33, 77; on geographical distribution and variation, 77–78, 79–81; and MCZ, 24
Agassiz Association, 14, 62, 165
Ainley, Marianne G., 57, 209
Alexander, Annie M., 187
Allen, Arthur A., 178, 189, 196, 199
Allen, Glover M., 202–203, 269n.107
Allen, J. A., 50, 62, 142, 193; and AOU Committee on Classification and Nomenclature, 86–88; on AOU model law, 121–122, 124–125; and Audubon movement, 111, 120; background, 25; on Burroughs, John, 114; defends collecting, 114; as editor, 48, 53, 57, 66–67; and founding of AOU, 46, 51–52; on geographical variation, 80–83; and Shufeldt scandal, 66; on subspecies, 98–99; and trinomial nomenclature, 83–84, 93–94; on value of birds, 116; on wildlife decline, 108–110, 112–113
Almy, Charles, 66
amateurs, 146; and AOU, 54–57, 67–68; and AOU model law, 123–125, 182–184; *Auk*'s dependence on, 67; divergence from expert ornithologists, 92, 100–101; and scientific nomenclature, 88–95, 96, 100; in ornithology, 8, 178, 208–211; and professionals, 8, 154; in science, 5, 6. *See also* American Ornithologists' Union—membership: associate members; community; networks
Amazon River, 104
American Bird Banding Association, 171
American Bison, Living and Extinct (Allen), 108–109
American Chemical Society, 46
American Committee for International Wild Life Protection, 152
American Humane Association, 112
American Magazine of Natural Science, 16
American Museum of Natural History, 25, 104, 142, 147, 148, 149, 150, 178, 189; bird collection, 29, 61, 62, 191–193; habitat groups, 45; inspires budding ornithologists, 199; and professional collectors, 41, 115; as site of first AOU meeting, 46, 52
American Nature Study Society, 14
American Ornithologist, 228n.13
American Ornithologists' Union (AOU): and amateurs, 54–57, 182–184, 209; criticism of, 47, 54–57, 69–73, 182–183, 200–201; develops national plan for ornithology, 210; and Division of Economic Ornithology, 59; endowment, 183, 184, 205; first meeting in West, 73; founding of, 4, 7, 46, 50–57; group photograph, 64; meeting sites, 234n.149; and nomenclatural reform, 76, 85–88; and professionalization of ornithology, 57–62, 67; proposal for field station, 268n.164; reform of, 8, 182–184, 198–205; and research standards, 88; rival organizations, 69; salaries of officers of, 203–204; seeks federal aid, 59–60; and Shufeldt scandal, 63–67; as a social organization, 63, 66–67

committees: Committee on Classification and Nomenclature of North American Birds, 53, 86–88 (*see also* AOU Code and Checklist); Committee on Migration of Birds, 57–61, 104, 143, 167; Committee on the Protection of North American Birds, 7, 106–107, 111–117, 118, 120, 121, 124–125, 128–134, 137–139, 141, 143–145, 146, 147–148, 150–153, 183 (*see also* AOU model law); council, 53, 56–57, 59, 60, 61–62, 66–67, 86, 88, 92, 134, 143, 144, 152–153, 203, 205; creation of, 53; nominating committee, 205; program committee, 203; research committee, 204–205

membership: active members, 47, 53, 70; associate members, 47, 56, 67–68, 70, 72, 73, 89, 201, 204, 206; certification function of, 5; educational background of, 185; elections in, 200–201, 202, 203; elective members, 70–71, 72, 73, 203–204; emeritus fellows, 203, 204; fellows, 70, 71–72, 200, 204, 267n.137; figures for, 68, 182; honorary members, 229n.46; policies for, 46–47, 52–53, 57, 67–73, 89, 94, 203, 204, 233n.141; women, 71, 195, 198, 265n.97, 266n.106
American Ornithology (Wilson), 23, 74–75
American Ornithology for the Home and School, 15, 158
American school of ornithology, 7, 76, 83, 90, 93
American Society of Mammalogists, 73, 148, 152
American Society for the Prevention of Cruelty to Animals, 111
American Society of Zoologists, 46
American Splitters' Union, 98
American Sportsman, 30, 223n.69, 228n.13
Angell, George T., 118
animal rights, 141, 148
Antes, Frank, 137–138